Selected Letters of W. D. Howells

Volume 5

1902–1911

For Marie Marguerite Fréchette.

Dear Vevie:

If any one doubts whether this is like me, you must show how much it is like you, and that will prove it. I am just finishing a letter in this picture, and am about to sign myself Your loving uncle

W. D. Howells.

William Dean Howells
ca. March 1907

W. D. HOWELLS

Selected Letters

Volume 5: 1902-1911

Edited and Annotated by
William C. Fischer
with
Christoph K. Lohmann

Textual Editor
Christoph K. Lohmann

TWAYNE PUBLISHERS

Boston

1983

This volume of Selected Letters is also published as
Volume 28 of A Selected Edition of W. D. Howells

Editorial expenses for this volume have been supported by grants from
the National Endowment for the Humanities.

Published in 1983 by Twayne Publishers, A Division of G. K. Hall & Co.,
70 Lincoln Street, Boston, Massachusetts 02111

Printed on permanent/durable acid-free paper and bound in
the United States of America

First Printing

CENTER FOR EDITIONS OF
AMERICAN AUTHORS
AN APPROVED TEXT
MODERN LANGUAGE
ASSOCIATION OF AMERICA

Library of Congress Cataloging in Publication Information

Howells, William Dean, 1837–1920.
Selected letters.

(His A Selected edition of W. D. Howells: v. 4, 9, 19, 24, 28)
Includes index.
CONTENTS: v. 5. 1902–1911.
1. Howells, William Dean, 1837–1920—Correspondence.
2. Novelists, American—19th century—Correspondence.
I. Arms, George Warren, 1912–
II. Title.

ISBN 0-8057-8531-0

Acknowlegdments

We are grateful for permission to print the letters in this volume, as given by William White Howells and the heirs of W. D. Howells. The following individuals and institutions have also permitted the use of letters in their collections: American Academy and Institute of Arts and Letters, New York City; American Antiquarian Society, Worcester, Massachusetts; George Arms, Albuquerque, New Mexico; The Trustees of the Boston Public Library; County Reference Library, Bristol (England); The British Library Board; Brown University Library; University of California (Berkeley) Library; Mrs. Vincent Chapin, Dublin, New Hampshire; University of Chicago Library; Miller Library, Colby College, Waterville, Maine; University of Colorado (Boulder) Libraries; Columbia University Library; Cornell University Libraries; Dartmouth College Library, Hanover, New Hampshire; Duke University Library; The Filson Club, Louisville, Kentucky; Joseph W. P. Frost, Kittery Point, Maine; Harvard College Library; Rutherford B. Hayes Library, Fremont, Ohio; Huntington Library, San Marino, California; University of Illinois (Urbana-Champaign) Library; Indiana University (Bloomington) Library; University of Kentucky Libraries; Longfellow National Historic Site, Cambridge, Massachusetts; Records Office, House of Lords, London; Miami University Libraries, Oxford, Ohio; Pierpont Morgan Library, New York City; New-York Historical Society; Henry W. and Albert A. Berg Collection, New York Public Library, Astor, Lenox and Tilden Foundations; Newberry Library, Chicago; Royal University Library, Oslo; University of Pennsylvania Library; Princeton University Library; University of Rochester Library; Rutgers University Library; The Sophia Smith Collection (Women's History Archive), Smith College, Northampton, Massachusetts; Hamlin Garland Collection, University of Southern California Library; Southern Illinois University Library, Carbondale; Clifton Waller Barrett Library, University of Virginia Library; Western Reserve Historical Society, Cleveland; The Beinecke Rare Book and Manuscript Library, Yale University.

Special thanks go to David J. Nordloh for his experienced counsel, to our textual research assistant William Snyder, to Anthony W. Shipps, Indiana University Library, who thrives on literary conundrums, and to Pamela F. Lohmann for assistance in preparing the index.

Contents

A NOTE ON EDITORIAL PRACTICE   xi

I.   The Season of the Falling Leaf (1902–1905)   1

     Introduction
     Letters and Notes

II.   Friend, Epitapher, and Grandfather (1906–1909)   147

     Introduction
     Letters and Notes

III.   A Deathful Time (1910–1911)   297

     Introduction
     Letters and Notes

TEXTUAL APPARATUS

     Introduction   383
     Textual Record   389
     Word-Division   423

LIST OF HOWELLS' CORRESPONDENTS   427

INDEX   431

A Note on Editorial Practice

Two basic principles inform the treatment of the texts of the Howells correspondence which have been selected for publication in these volumes: one, the contents of the original documents are reproduced as fully and correctly as possible; and, two, all physical details of the manuscripts necessary for accurate reconstruction of the text are reported, though without encumbering the reading text itself. Consistent with these principles, the printed versions of the letters which form the body of these volumes retain the eccentricities of Howells' spelling, punctuation, and occasionally elliptical epistolary style, and are presented without such editorial appurtenances as brackets, arrows, virgules, and *sic*'s. The printed text is, insofar as possible, that of the finished letter, after Howells revised it either locally or generally by writing over, crossing out, and interlining. Howells' errors, except for inadvertent repetitions of words or syllables, are printed as they appear in the holographs, so long as the sense of the text can be discerned.

In accordance with the principle of reporting significant manuscript information, each letter is represented by a full itemization of cancellations, interlineations, the unusual placement of postscripts and marginal comments, and the presence of nonauthorial notes and comments believed to be contemporary with the composition or receipt of the letter, as well as of those editorial revisions necessary to insure comprehension. The reader should be aware, therefore, that some few words, letters, and marks of punctuation printed in this text are not in the original letters (or in transcriptions which have been employed when the originals are no longer extant or accessible). The full record of emendations, editorial comments, textual details, and Howells' revisions is provided in the Textual Apparatus, the introduction to which explains the symbols and abbreviations used to allow for the printing of the maximum of evidence in a minimum of space. Several exceptions, however, should be noted. Howells frequently failed to lift his pen when moving from one word to the next; thus, he often joined words that were not meant to be joined. Occasionally, though not always, he would repair such errors by separating these inadvertently joined words with a vertical line. Conversely, he sometimes lifted his pen while writing a single word, or he disconnected compounds that appear elsewhere as one word. In such cases, no notation of these irregularities has been included in the apparatus, while an attempt has been made, through comparisons among the letters, to render Howells' texts as nearly as possible in the form that he seems likely to have intended.

Given the wealth of references to personal and public events in the letters and the relevance of the letters to the shape and movement of Howells' career, annotation is potentially endless. The policy of these volumes is to present only the basic information which will make the context of the letters understandable and the letters themselves useful to both scholar and general reader. Annotation is thus restricted to explanation and clarification of references to people, places, events, literary works, and other such primary data. Interpretive comment is excluded.

Since the letters in this series represent only a portion of the extant Howells correspondence, it is also important that their relationship to each other and to letters not printed in these volumes be indicated. Cross references to other letters printed in the series simply identify correspondent and date: e.g., "Howells to Comly, 7 July 1868"; references to annotation accompanying letters add to this citation the specific footnote number: e.g., "Howells to Comly, 7 July 1868, n. 4." Manuscript letters not printed in this edition but cited or quoted are identified by correspondent and date, followed by the library location or collector's name in parentheses: e.g., "(MH)" for Harvard University or "(Ray)" for the collection of Gordon N. Ray.[1] Special collections within libraries are not indicated. When manuscripts of texts cited are also available in major printed collections (e.g., *Mark Twain–Howells Letters*), publication information follows the library symbol. Publication information appearing without notation of manuscript location should be assumed to designate texts extant only in published form. Quotations from letters in annotations follow the final, revised forms, and do not include a record of internal revisions. In addition, to avoid the proliferation of annotation, information necessary to the understanding of such quoted letters is provided within brackets at appropriate points within the quotations.

To further reduce the bulk and duplication of annotation, several other conventions have been adopted. People, events, and literary works are identified in footnotes at the points where their first significant mention appears in the whole series of letters. Further annotation of

---

1. Libraries are indicated by the abbreviations detailed in *Symbols of American Libraries*, 10th ed. (Washington: Library of Congress, 1969).

these same details is provided only where the context of a specific letter demands elaboration. The basic information can be located by using the indexes to the individual volumes or the cumulative index in the final volumes of letters, where major references are distinguished by the printing of the appropriate page numbers in italic type. References to books give the year of first publication; however, books reviewed in dated articles should be assumed to have been published in the same year as the review, unless information to the contrary is provided. Whenever possible, references to books by Howells identify volumes published in "A Selected Edition of W. D. Howells," signed by the abbreviation "HE" immediately following the title; references to works not available in this form generally cite the American first edition, which is identified by date of publication.

The editors have followed a consistent policy in the use of ellipses in quotations. If the first period is close up to the word preceding it, it stands for an end-of-sentence period in the original, with the omission following it. Thus, "invention. . . . develop" indicates that there is a period in the original after "invention," with the omitted portion of the text following it. However, "hereafter . . . . Good lord!" indicates that there is more text in the same sentence after "hereafter."

Titles of most secondary sources are given in full, but a number of them are cited so often in this series that the following list of short titles has been adopted.

Cady, *Howells*, I.

Edwin H. Cady, *The Road to Realism: The Early Years, 1837–1885, of William Dean Howells* (Syracuse, N.Y.: Syracuse University Press, 1956)

Cady, *Howells*, II

Edwin H. Cady, *The Realist at War: The Mature Years, 1885–1920, of William Dean Howells* (Syracuse, N.Y.: Syracuse University Press, 1958)

Gibson-Arms, *Bibliography*

William M. Gibson and George Arms, *A Bibliography of William Dean Howells* (New York: New York Public Library, 1948; reprinted, New York Public Library and Arno Press, 1971)

James Letters	*Henry James Letters*, ed. Leon Edel, 3 vols. (Cambridge, Mass.: Harvard University Press, Belknap Press, 1974–)
Life in Letters	*Life in Letters of William Dean Howells,* ed. Mildred Howells, 2 vols. (Garden City, N.Y.: Doubleday, Doran & Co., 1928)
Lynn, *Howells*	Kenneth S. Lynn, *William Dean Howells: An American Life* (New York: Harcourt Brace Jovanovich, 1971)
Norton, *Lowell Letters*	*Letters of James Russell Lowell*, ed. C. E. Norton, 2 vols. (New York: Harper & Brothers, 1894)
Transatlantic Dialogue	*Transatlantic Dialogue: Selected American Correspondence of Edmund Gosse*, ed. Paul T. Mattheisen and Michael Millgate (Austin: University of Texas Press, 1965)
Twain-Howells	*Mark Twain-Howells Letters*, ed. Henry Nash Smith and William M. Gibson, 2 vols. (Cambridge, Mass.: Harvard University Press, Belknap Press, 1960)
Woodress, *Howells & Italy*	James L. Woodress, Jr., *Howells & Italy* (Durham, N.C.: Duke University Press, 1952)

C. K. L.

D. J. N.

I

The Season of the Falling Leaf

1902 – 1905

Introduction

As Howells entered his sixty-fifth year, he could in some respects feel that his personal and professional affairs were well ordered. Having the surety of a generous contract with Harper & Brothers, he would continue to be permanently if not always contentedly settled in New York. Perhaps more important, however, was the emotional haven secured with the purchase in 1902 of a summer home at Kittery Point, Maine, to which he retreated each year between May and November to take care of literary business and to tend his beloved garden—a chance to touch the soil which he had not had since his boyhood. Shortly after taking the cottage he wrote to his sister Aurelia that he would "begin a garden as soon as the spring opens" (30 March 1902), a ritual he would faithfully repeat each year thereafter.

Reassuring as all this might have been, Howells at the same time felt increasingly uncomfortable with the world around him. The recent Spanish-American War along with the assassination of McKinley in September 1901 were to his mind watershed events, moving him to observe at the beginning of 1902 that he found himself writing in the season of "the falling leaf, the falling man." It was a time of convulsive change that had arrived "with a seismic shock, a cyclonic violence," a season of ethical decline and uncertainty: "We have not yet openly owned it, but we all know that the Americans of January 1, 1902, are different from the Americans of September 1, 1901, and that they already face strange problems upon unprecedented conditions."[1] At the worst, as he said in a letter of 27 May 1902 to Charles E. Norton, it was a "rather odious time."

By early 1902, Howells' heavy work schedule had brought about a state of general fatigue with symptoms of recurrent insomnia and indigestion, from which he sought temporary relief with a trip on the Ohio River with his brother Joseph in March. He was also anxious about the tenuous state of his family's health. His two grown children, still living at home, were frequently indisposed, Mildred with a perennial sore throat and John, the architect, with troublesome dyspepsia. Elinor Howells, meanwhile, remained virtually confined to the apartment by her long-standing nervous condition. Also, the lengthening death-roll of

---

1. "Editor's Easy Chair," *Harper's Monthly* 104 (January 1902), 334, 336.

friends and literary acquaintance heightened Howells' sense of earthly insolvency—Frank Stockton, Bret Harte, Frank Norris, Horace E. Scudder, and Edwin L. Godkin all died in 1902. He particularly felt the ineffectualness of proffered consolation at the death of Olivia Clemens in 1904, writing with sorrowful honesty to his old friend who was now a widower: "I will not try to say anything in the stupid notion of trying to help you" (7 June 1904).

As he faced these encroaching reminders of his own fragility, Howells delved more insistently into matters of psychology and immortality. Notable among his literary explorations in this regard are the tentative psychic romances collected in *Questionable Shapes* (1903) and his wrestling with the "question of the life hereafter" in the "Editor's Easy Chair."[2] "I should not mind being old," he revealed to Thomas B. Aldrich in the less guarded confines of a letter of 3 July 1902, if only it were not accompanied by "this dreamy fumbling about my own identity," a confusion that at times threatened to invalidate his accomplishments as a writer; "I think I could deal with the present, bad and bothering as it is, if it were not for visions of the past in which I appear to be mostly running about, full of sound and fury signifying nothing. Once I thought that I meant something by everything I did; but now I don't know."

Howells' self-doubts were stoked by a succession of novels that were, by the standard of his best achievements, anemic and somewhat detached from the turbulence of events in the society at large. Indeed, their poor sales and indifferent reception—except among his friends—led him to question the efficacy of his particular brand of realism. Defending himself against the charge that the characters and themes of *The Kentons* (1902) were too commonplace, Howells, admittedly "disheartened," wrote to Brander Matthews: "I had hoped I was helping my people . . . to find cause for pride in the loveliness of our apparently homely average, but they don't want it" (3 August 1902). He set immediately to work on the epistolary novel *Letters Home* (1903), intending to produce a contemporary study of manners with more sinew and in a more deliberately experimental form than the thin travel adventures of the Kenton family. But he encountered difficulties and, as he wrote Aurelia Howells, lacking both the "time and nerve to carry out my original plan" (24 May 1902), reduced it to a slighter psychological tale. Though disappointed with the novel's failure, Howells could still maintain a humorous equipoise in writing to John St. Loe Strachey, editor of the *Spectator* in England, where his fiction was then being more warmly

---

2. *Harper's Monthly* 107 (June 1903), 147.

greeted than at home. The American readership of the story in letters, Howells said, seems to have rejected "my fidelity to our life" in the same way as the Kentuckian, who, when offered cornbread, replied that "He was r'ared on it; and declined it with thanks" (14 February 1904). By mid-1903 Howells was also well along with *Miss Bellard's Inspiration*, originally conceived as a lengthy short story, which he deprecated even before its publication by wishing it "might amuse other people a tenth as much as it amuses me."[3]

Although completed by early 1904, the publication of *Miss Bellard's Inspiration* was wisely postponed until June 1905, perhaps so as not to reflect, by implication, any sense of inadequacy on Howells' most accomplished work in this otherwise drab creative interval. As if spurred by his recent struggles with fiction, Howells produced, from a plot conceived fifteen years earlier and in a concentrated spurt of writing between late 1902 and mid-1903, what was to be one of his last strong novels, *The Son of Royal Langbrith*. Serialized in the *North American Review*, January–August 1904, and issued in book form in October of the same year, it was praised on almost every side.[4] Unlike the frustrating spasms of writing that went into *Letters Home, Langbrith* evolved from a single momentum, continuing "to walk along on its own legs to the end, and . . . . to bolt from the start," as Howells explained to Thomas S. Perry, to whom he had read a portion of the completed manuscript a month earlier.[5] Avoiding the less resistant psychic lines and loose characterizations of much of his recent fiction, Howells formulated bolder emotional perplexities in blending the thwarted relationship between Mrs. Langbrith and Dr. Anther with the conventional "love story" involving young James Langbrith and Hope Hawberk.[6] At the least, the careful modulation of mental life in that novel was in accord with Howells' assertion that the psychological focus "will be the most enduring as it has been the most constant phase of fiction."[7] Satisfying though the effort was, the ongoing demands of the "Editor's Easy Chair" for *Harper's Monthly* and of numerous topical essays for the *Weekly* had to be met as well. Consequently, *Langbrith* took its toll, as Howells wrote Clemens, by keeping him "writing, with the other things, too hard, so that I'm rather run down nervously" (14 February 1904).

As Howells struggled to sustain his fictional writing, he also tentatively

---

3. Howells to Henry B. Fuller, 20 September 1903.

4. For a comprehensive review of the book's critical reception, see *The Son of Royal Langbrith*, HE, pp. xix–xxii.

5. Howells to Thomas S. Perry, 27 October 1903.

6. Howells to David A. Munro, 9 September 1903.

7. "Will the Novel Disappear?" *North American Review* 175 (September 1902), 293.

renewed an impulse toward autobiographical reminiscence begun over a decade earlier with *A Boy's Town* (1890) and *My Year in a Log Cabin* (1893). The connection between these earlier books and *The Flight of Pony Baker* (1902) is suggested by its subtitle, "A Boy's Town Story." The following year, after sorting through his immense correspondence, he was attracted to the possibility of a mature autobiography. Finding himself wealthy in letters "beyond the dreams of avarice," as he wrote to Aurelia on 4 October 1903, Howells felt that he alone could interpret the record of his life with integrity: "What should you think of my writing my autobiography? My published reminiscences have made a beginning, and it would forestall a biography always a false and mistaken thing." A month later, when Harper & Brothers wanted him to do a book on Clemens, Howells, as if acting on that very scruple, declined. He felt that despite Clemens' tolerance such a biography would be an uneasy breach of friendship. Thanking Thomas S. Perry for supporting the decision not to do Clemens' life, Howells also defined the permissible boundaries, as he saw them, of his own autobiography: "I think I will write my own life, but . . . if I am to make a worth-while book, I must tell of what I have been in the love of literature, rather than of what I have done" (22 November 1903). In effect, he had already made such a beginning with *My Literary Passions* (1895) and, in a more biographical manner, with *Literary Friends and Acquaintance* (1900). When Clemens began dictating the story of his life in 1904, the example of his bewildering "veracity" brought Howells to the realization that the challenge of pure autobiography was perhaps more than he could comfortably manage. Clemens' enthusiasm for the natural effects achieved by spontaneous dictation made Howells feel keenly that his own cautious temperament was by comparison unsuited to the rigors of self-representation. "You are dramatic and unconscious," he wrote his closest friend of thirty-five years, while remarking perceptively if ruefully of himself, "I am cursed with consciousness to the core, and can't say myself out; I am always saying myself *in*, and setting myself above all that I say, as of more worth."[8] The difficult and onerous task of writing a personal memoir would be deferred, and then only offered as an account concluding with his early manhood, until *Years of My Youth* (1916).

Whatever the disappointments on the literary side, the first years of the twentieth century were ones of recognized distinction for Howells, although he always found ceremony and public acclaim distasteful. In 1904 he was academically honored, first in England with a doctor of

---

8. Howells to Samuel L. Clemens, 14 February 1904.

letters bestowed by Oxford University and then in his native state with
a doctor of law from Western Reserve, followed in 1905 by a doctor
of literature from Columbia University. In his culturally visible office
as president of the National Institute of Arts and Letters, he was at
odds with those members who supported a policy of seeking private en-
dowments, causing him to resign the post in early 1904 only to accept
his election to the same office with the more prestigious American
Academy of Arts and Letters after its founding later that year, a position
he retained until his death. His considerable public reputation gave him
entré to more sociable experiences as well. He was several times a guest
at the table of Andrew Carnegie, and he was invited to attend various
social functions in connection with the Portsmouth Peace Conference,
called by Roosevelt in the late summer of 1905, at the Portsmouth Navy
Yard near Kittery Point, to resolve the Russo-Japanese War. After meeting the envoys, Howells took the unpopular position of siding with the
Russians because "they seem more our kind, and I always make the
grandeur of their literature do duty for the whole nation."[9] In the
same year Howells was in direct correspondence with Roosevelt himself,
successfully interceding with the president to obtain a consular appointment at the Turks Islands, British West Indies, for his older brother
Joe. Howells admired Roosevelt as a literary man, if not always as a
politician, characterizing him as "a man who lives and feels poetry,"[10]
while Roosevelt reciprocated by especially appreciating Howells as the
author of two of his favorite novels, *The Lady of the Aroostook* and
Indian Summer.

Seeking both a personal and literary respite after the expenditure of
energy on *The Son of Royal Langbrith*, Howells arranged with Harper &
Brothers to go to England in early 1904, spend the summer there collecting material for a travel book, and then winter at San Remo, near Genoa.
Some of the correspondence of this period is in the form of lengthy
diary letters to Elinor Howells (who did not join her husband abroad
until late June), detailed if somewhat abrupt notes that were gracefully transformed over the next year and a half into *London Films*
(1905), which he envisioned as "a pleasant, harmless book,"[11] and
Certain Delightful English Towns (1906). It was an occasion not only
to write at a more relaxed pace, but also to renew old acquaintance as
well as make new friends. Howells cheerfully reported his busy social
calendar to Elinor while more candidly notifying Clemens, in a letter

---

9. Howells to John St. Loe Strachey, 13 September 1905; quoted in Howells to
David Douglas, 20 August 1905, n. 7.
10. Howells to Madison Cawein, 25 October 1905.
11. Howells to Charles E. Norton, 4 November 1904.

from London of 19 April 1904, that he was suffering the "torments of society." He took genuine delight in visiting at length with Henry James —whom he found "very stout . . . in a sort of *chamfered* squareness"[12]— and forged an affectionate friendship with H. G. Wells, visiting several times with "that fine-eyed little man of intelligence & genius," as James had described him.[13] But even with the relative leisure of half a year in San Remo, where he caught up on his writing and editorial chores, Howells returned home in the spring of 1905 to find himself unexpectedly depleted. "I have been fearfully broken up by my year of travel," he informed his sister Anne Fréchette in a letter of 11 June 1905, "and find a difficulty in putting the pieces together, the greater because at 68 I begin to feel my touch fumbling." By the fall he was distinctly more at home after a summer of frustrating readjustment, so that at the end of the year he could safely extend himself to preside as toastmaster at the lavish seventieth birthday celebration for Mark Twain hosted by the new head of Harper & Brothers, Colonel George Harvey. Howells afterwards described this affair as a "wild burst . . . , which was enough to tear my consciousness in pieces. . . . the strangest mixture of literary celebrity and social notoriety that I have ever seen."[14] Howells was once again feeling self-possessed enough to engage himself with the disordered immediacy of his life in New York.

W. C. F.

---

12. Howells to Elinor Howells, 25 March 1904.
13. Henry James to Howells, 13 May 1904; quoted in Howells to Elinor Howells, 13 May 1904, n. 1.
14. Howells to Charles E. Norton, 6 December 1905.

48 West 59th st.,
Jan. 12, 1902.

Dear Aurelia:

Pilla sailed yesterday morning for Bermuda, and by this time ought to be nearly half way there. It leaves her mother and me rather lonesome, but fortunately John is such a home boy that we have him here to keep us company. Elinor depends upon Pilla for most of her spirits, but she is herself ever so much cheerfuller than she has been that I think she will manage. She is a great hand for people doing things for their health, and is even glad to have Pilla gone in view of the benefit she will get from the climate and the rest.

I have written to William[1] about the books, and he will relieve you of any trouble about boxing them and returning them to me—I mean those I sent you by mistake. His list was excellent—just what I wanted.

I do hope that by this time you have got some sort of girl. I would try for one here, but I know that the wages you can pay would not get one in New York with any amount of love thrown in. By the way I am planning a story in the form of "Letters Home from New York"—this is *very* confidential—written by a dozen different hands,[2] and I wish you could give me a notion of what people, according to your observation, in the country, like to hear of, concerning New York. We are in great trouble about the name of my story which is now being put in type. I had called it "A Family Affair," meaning that a girl's love affair is really the business of the whole family, but none of us quite like the name. Elinor prefers "The Heart of A Girl," and we have thought of "A Daughter's Heart." Have you any ideas or preferences?[3]

I have lately been suffering a great deal from indigestion in the form of gas in the stomach, but I am now trying with much advantage eating the whole meal through, and chewing my food a great deal, without drinking. At the end I take a cup of tea or coffee, or a glass of water. I wonder if Joe has ever tried that. My trouble has been in the form of pretty constant eructation, which is very tiresome.[4]

I hope you and Henry are getting some good walks. The winter here continues almost snowless, though last week, a slight fall painted the Park white.

Your aff'te brother,
Will

1. William Dean Howells II, Howells' nephew, then age forty-five, was working for the Ashtabula *Sentinel* in Jefferson, Ohio.

2. *Letters Home* was first serialized in the *Metropolitan*, April–September 1903, and immediately issued in book form. The "dozen different hands" were, of course, not actually different authors but fictional personae giving their impressions of New York in letters to family members or friends back home.

3. See Howells to Garland, 27 June 1901, n. 2.

4. Howells had also been complaining about his indigestion to Clemens, who had sent him amusingly elaborate instructions for taking Plasmon, a milk-protein mixture Clemens had been using to allay the same discomfort. See *Twain-Howells*, pp. 736–38, and *My Mark Twain* in *Literary Friends and Acquaintance*, HE, 308–9.

19 JANUARY 1902, NEW YORK, TO THOMAS B. ALDRICH

48 West 59th st.,
Jan. 19, 1902.

My dear Aldrich:

I should have written you sooner if I had not sent your letter out to Clemens, and he had not lost it for a couple of weeks. He has now sent it back with this endorsement: "This has been the most prominent object in the study for a week or two, and visible, *aggressively* visible from all points of the compass, and all that time I have been wrecking the whole damn place searching for it. If it had been 30 yards square, b'gosh I never should have found it."[1]

That is great news about the little life, and my wife joins me in congratulating Mrs. Aldrich and you, who naturally come in our thoughts before the young mother and father.[2] I hope it is prophetic of renewed happiness for you all in every way. I always fancied Thomasin for a name; you know Hardy uses it for one of his nicest heroines.[3]

I expected to meet Clemens yesterday at a lunch of a kind that Brander Matthews gives once a year, but he did not come. I hope for him to-night at a dinner to Mrs. Pat Campbell, whom I saw with much convincement the other night as Mrs. Tanqueray. She is a great creature, as good as Duse, I think, and with no more theatre about her.[4] I don't know whether you care for Pinero; I have a great respect for him, though I fancy he aims over the ordinary New York silk hat and seal skin. It is a deplorable level, but I suppose I was spoiled by the Boston of our day for the New York of this. The worst of it is, I am forgetting what that Boston was like in the significant details. I am trying a sort of thing that is so easy I am beginning to find it very hard. I am writing a series of "Letters Home" from New York, by various hands from different parts of the country, and one of these is a belated Bostonian, who writes to his sister-in-law: it is most difficult to recall the tone, and if you were still in Boston, I should ask you to let me come and occupy that upper chamber till I caught it again. The other people in my scheme are a family of new-rich Westerners, trying to get in here, an ardent young literary man, a girl looking for a companion's place, some Southerners, a New England country minister come here to find his daughter who left home with a theatrical combination, and others. A story of common interest is expected to grow up among them, but the letters treat frankly of many actualities unrelated to the story; there are never any answers to them, so that so far the scheme is new. I was very much in love with it at first, and not so much now. But I am going on with it, and I am rather confiding the notion to you. I mean to serialize it anonymously.

An apartment house here has been named "The Henry James." I cut out the advertisement and sent it to him, and I am wondering whether he will abhor it or like it.[5] I think I should rather like such a thing myself, though I should prefer to have it named after one of my books.

Just for the present, I am switched off from my North American Reviewing, to help on the enterprise of rehabilitating the Weekly which Harvey has undertaken himself.[6] It is a curious experience, and I should like it if the things I wrote of were as interesting as they used to be. I wonder if our decay doesn't begin less with failing strength than with failing curiosity. This world used to keep me so full of question that I could never get enough answers, but now I do not care for many answers; do you? I find that I care with difficulty for the answer to the Great Conundrum of all, "If a man die shall he live again?" But perhaps I should if I felt myself in immediate danger.

Have you seen that little new life of Longfellow in the Beacon series? It is by a very nice young Columbia professor,[7] and takes the new view of Longfellow which seems to be composed of his limitations. But what it does not value rightly is the beauty of his art, its refining simplicity within those bounds. I wonder if you think as highly as I do of those laterish sonnets of L.'s, about his three friends,[8] and Chaucer, Milton, etc. They seem to me about as good as things of the kind could be. He must have had a tussle with the Buritanic moral, but he did down it at last, and came out very clear and strong. There is also a beautiful humility—I don't know what else to call it—in those things which I find of a high aesthetic effect. But of course, L. was overrated by the popular love, and it is easy to fault him on that side. I am going to break a lance—a splinter of the Easy Chair—for him.[9] The past obliges.

And poor Scudder is gone.[10] He laughed well, and was a most friendly spirit, with a love for the fine thing in him. I am glad not to be in Cambridge, where I should feel the reality of his death more. As it is he keeps on living, in a way.

Yours ever,
W. D. Howells.

1. The Aldrich letter appears to be no longer extant. Clemens first mentioned it in a letter to Howells, 3 January 1902 (MH), and on 8 January (MH) wrote Howells that he had mislaid it. On 12 January (CU) Howells wrote Clemens not to worry "about Aldrich's lettr [sic]. It will be sure to turn up, unless some one has taken it and is trying to unset the jewels and sell them for the value of the stones." See *Twain-Howells*, pp. 737–40.

2. Lilian Aldrich, the daughter of Charles and Louise Aldrich, was born on 31 December 1901.

3. Thomasin Yeobright is the female protagonist of Thomas Hardy's *The Return of the Native* (1878); however, the Aldriches eventually decided against naming their daughter Thomasin.

4. Mrs. Patrick Campbell, née Beatrice Stella Tanner (1865–1940), was an English actress; her performance in 1893 as Paula in Sir Arthur Wing Pinero's *The Second Mrs. Tanqueray* (1893) established her as one of the leading theatrical figures of the time. She was thought by some to be the equal of Eleonora Duse (1858–1924), the prominent Italian tragedienne. In a letter to Aurelia H. Howells, 19 January 1902 (MH), Howells praised Mrs. Campbell for being "of the very simple, natural school."

5. James, with characteristic wit and condescension, made a lengthy response in his letter of 25 January 1902 (MH): "Your most kind communication, meanwhile, in respect to the miraculously named 'uptown' apartment-house has at once deeply agitated & wildly uplifted me." He suggested facetiously that the advertisement might help bring his books "before the public," but is rather inclined to take the more realistic view that they are "*behind,* irremovably behind, the public, & fixed there for my lifetime at least . . . . The Henry James, I opine, will be a terrifically 'private' hotel . . . . Refined, liveried, 'two-toileted,' it will have been a short-lived, hectic paradox, or will presently have to close in order to reopen as the Mary Johnson [sic] or the K. W. [sic] Wiggin or the James Lane Allen. Best of all as the Edith Wharton. Still, your advertisement gave me an hour of whirling rapture, against which I almost began to draw cheques." James's sardonic allusions are, with the exception of Wharton, to some of the popular sentimentalists and romancers of the time: Mary Johnston authored the best-seller *To Have and to Hold* (1900); Kate Douglas Wiggin had written a children's holiday favorite entitled *The Birds' Christmas Carol* (1888), with her better known *Rebecca of Sunnybrook Farm* (1903) yet to appear; and James Lane Allen wrote the frontier romance *The Choir Invisible* (1899), an unqualified commercial success. James's inclusion of Edith Wharton in this company was no doubt based on his recognition of certain Jamesian qualities clearly evident in some of her early works. She had just written a collection of short stories, *The Greater Inclination* (1899), and a novelette, *The Touchstone* (1900). As James's correspondence with Wharton about this time reveals, he was candidly critical of a short story she had sent him for appraisal. See R. W. B. Lewis, *Edith Wharton: A Biography* (New York: Harper & Row, 1975), p. 125. Howells relished James's irony and wrote to Mildred Howells on 15 February 1902 (MH): "We've had a long delightful letter from H. James, in which he lets himself loose on people most amusingly, so that we can't let it out of our hands."

6. For Colonel George Harvey's role in placing the House of Harper on a sound financial footing, see Howells to James, 10 September 1899, n. 4. Howells' contributions to *Harper's Weekly*, described in Gibson-Arms, *Bibliography*, pp. 133–34, were of a topical nature, embracing a broad range of subjects.

7. George Rice Carpenter's *Henry Wadsworth Longfellow* (1901) was part of the "American Men of Letters" series published by Houghton, Mifflin & Co.

8. Howells' reference is to five sonnet stanzas which make up the poem "Three Friends of Mine" in *A Book of Sonnets*, published as part of *The Masque of Pandora and Other Poems* (1876). Written in 1874, the poem memorializes Cornelius Conway Felton (1807–1862), Eliot Professor of Greek and later president of Harvard College (1860–1862); Jean Louis Rodolphe Agassiz, the famed naturalist; and Charles Sumner, the antislavery senator from Massachusetts.

9. In the "Easy Chair," *Harper's Monthly*, April 1902, Howells praises Carpenter's critical capability, but points out his lack of sensitivity in estimating the worth of some of Longfellow's better poetry, especially that of a later period. See also Howells' "A Little Mistake," *Harper's Weekly*, 2 August 1902, for a further defense of Longfellow against his modern detractors.

10. Horace E. Scudder had been a friend and neighbor during Howells' Cambridge days.

27 JANUARY 1902, NEW YORK, TO JACOB G. SCHURMAN

48 West 59th st.,
January 27, 1902.

Dear President Schurman:[1]

Your speech on the Philippine situation is full of a manly humanity,[2] which is finely supplemented by the courage and good sense of your letter in reply to General Wheaton.[3] You have struck the true note. If we are not in the Philippines to help their people to a safe independence, we are wrongfully there. For one I thank you for the great things you have done in your speech and letter for American civilization.

Yours sincerely
W. D. Howells.

1. Jacob G. Schurman (1854–1942) was the third president of Cornell University (1892–1920). In 1899 President McKinley appointed him president of the first U.S. Commission to the Philippine Islands.

2. Schurman's speech, delivered at Cornell on Founder's Day, 11 January 1902, and before the Massachusetts Reform Club on 20 January, was almost immediately published as *Philippine Affairs: A Retrospect and Outlook*. It is an assessment of the military and political relationships between the United States and the Philippines during and following the Spanish-American War. Schurman took the anti-imperialist position that U.S. policy should be guided by the goals of home rule and ultimate national autonomy.

3. Major General Lloyd Wheaton (1838–1918) was commander of the U.S. occupation forces in Luzon and the North Philippines. Schurman's letter is probably the reply to Wheaton, under the heading "Schurman to Wheaton," appearing on 27 January in the Boston *Globe*, to which Elinor Howells had a subscription. Two days earlier, on 25 January, the New York *Times* reported Wheaton's sharp attack on Schurman's speech: "General Wheaton ... says men have been sent to prison here for remarks such as those of President Schurman of Cornell, and that, if what he advocates were

accomplished, it would mean the expenditure of much treasure and the shedding of blood like water." Schurman, whose public letter was quoted in full by the *Globe*, directly addressed Wheaton's charge: "I do not know what General Wheaton had in mind when he said that my policy 'would mean the expenditure of much treasure and the shedding of blood like water.' For the fact is that the policy I outlined would put an end to both these evils." Supporting Roosevelt's view that it was the responsibility of the United States to fit the Philippines for self-government, Schurman concluded: "I am with President Roosevelt and against Gen Wheaton. And I go further and say that as the American people has not yet passed upon the question of a final Philippines policy, it is as proper for me to advocate eventualities [of self-government] as for Gen Wheaton to recommend colonial servitude like that of Java or India."

14 FEBRUARY 1902, NEW YORK, TO HENRY JAMES

48 West 59th st.,
February 14, 1902.

My dear James:

It will be long before your exemplary letter of Jan'y 27[1] can be fitly answered; a volume of wit and wisdom worth at least $100 a thousand words would be required even to acknowledge it; but now I must write you as enthusiastically as decency will permit of my pleasure in seeing your old, never-before-given Daly comedy done by the pupils of the Dramatic Arts School, yesterday.[2] It had got round to their teacher through Frohman, who has inherited Daly and, it appears, you;[3] and it has ripened into something delightful. It is excellent, and *goes* from first to last; the third act I felt a little *too* densely packed with incident, but that is a good fault, and the only one of the piece. Every point took; the house—most intelligent, almost too intelligent—laughed all through, and gave the company curtain after curtain, staying till 6 o'clock to see the very end, after being delayed from you by the fatuities of two brother-dramatists.[4] It was largely made up of friends and fellow pupils of the players and of the teacher. He, Franklin Sargeant is the son of Mrs. Sargeant who once "opened a saloon" of high literary quality in Boston,[5] and is a good, reluctant critic: he liked your piece as much as anyone, and praised it to me. I will try to find out if he looks for a future to it, and will let you know. If there is anything knowledgeous in the press I will send it; but knowledge is not the forte of the dramatic critic. I have indicated the comparative proficiency of the players on the enclosed programme.[6] Mrs. Jasper was a most beautiful creature—out of Western New York, I should think from the way she broke through into her native *Rs* (from the English accent which the school cultivates) in moments of high excitement. Coverley was altogether and unerringly delightful. As for the piece, to come back to it, I felt as if I had been reading one of your books, and I can't say better than *that*. To be honest, which is also to be disagreeable, I didn't suppose you had it in you. There!

Yours ever
W. D. Howells.

Think of my giving the very marrow of my morning to this letter, and then say there is no longer true friendship in the world!

1. Howells erroneously assigned this date to James's letter of 25 January 1902 (MH).

2. James's comedy, *Mrs. Jasper*, was written in late 1891 or early 1892 for John Augustin Daly and the leading actress in his theater company, Ada Rehan (1860–1916). Although James had made extensive revisions at Daly's request, the play was not produced until the amateur performance attended by Howells on 13 February. For a detailed account of the painful affair, see *The Complete Plays of Henry James*, ed. Leon Edel (Philadelphia: J. B. Lippincott, 1949), pp. 295–99. James's response to Howells' kindly but politely qualified description of the performance was one of feigned surprise mixed with lingering chagrin: "Really, it's most charming, amusing, beguiling, & I hold myself with 10 pair of hands not to say—hum!—Encouraging. It's *better* than that—it's absolute, unsurpassable, ultimissimo. I won't say I wish to goodness I had been there— but I gloat over the possibilities of goodness as I see that *you* couldn't help being! The dear young ingenuous benighted things! I could kiss them all with tears. But the present war to me is that there is so much, so ridiculously much more I could tell you about the poor little old ugly tragic joke of the original *Mrs. J.*, & her squalid Daly-Rehan history (of 10 years ago,) than your very sweetest impression of her, even, could prompt you to tell *me*. But don't be afraid—now. The incident is buried deep; beneath fifty layers of dead nightmares." (James to Howells, 7 March 1902 [MH]).

3. Charles Frohman (1860–1915), son of the famous theater manager Daniel Frohman, was the founder and manager of the Empire Theatre, where *Mrs. Jasper* was performed by the students of the American Academy of Dramatic Arts and the Empire Theatre Dramatic School. In his letter of 7 March, James concurred with Howells that Frohman had inherited Daly's much revised version of the play: "the misguided darlings must have used for their text & study some contraband old type-copy of the play disinterred among Daly's posthumous relics (every rag of whose property in it had ceased long before his death, I receiving back, as I supposed, every syllable of the 3 acts!) and *not* from the fountainhead & classic & authentic last form—the printed play in one of 2 vols. of 'Theatricals' published long since (though after Daly, of course,) by the Harpers...."

4. The theater program Howells enclosed in his letter also lists two one-act plays, *The New Year* by Louisa Meigs Green and *A Gentleman of the Road* by Arthur Ketchum.

5. Franklin Haven Sargent (1856–1923) graduated from Harvard in 1873, studied pantomime privately in Europe, taught elocution at Harvard (1880–1882), and was director of the Madison Square Theatre (1882–1884). In 1884 he founded the Lyceum School of Acting, which later became the American Academy of Dramatic Arts. His mother, Mary Elizabeth Sargent, was married to John Turner Sargent, a prominent Unitarian minister and antislavery reformer. Her salon was the Radical Club, held in her parlor at 13 Chestnut Street (1867–1880) and attended by such notables as Emerson, Whittier, Longfellow, and Wendell Phillips.

6. Howells made brief notations on the program. Of Mrs. Jasper, played by Marian Stone, he penned in "excellent." After Charles Coverley, played by Charles Heidelbach, he noted "admirably done."

5 March 1902, New York, to Thomas B. Aldrich

48 West 59th st.,
March 5, 1902.

My dear Aldrich:

If you ever treat me like that again, I will belt you over the muns, as that unknown friend of yours said long ago in New York when even the tough spoke classic English.[1] As it is, I have half a mind to flourish over your desolate head the cracking good time Clemens and I had at Brander Matthews's.[2] That boy knows how to give a lunch, and get the right people to it, but he does not suppose you would come down from the Adirondacks.[3] Would I could come to you there! But I am going out to Ohio, for a trip on my native river with my brother Joe. Yes, I am tired out, and have lost the trick of sleeping. I expect to start from Pittsburg, and return there from Cincinnati,—1200 miles. It sounds rather nice, I think. But heaven knows how it may turn out.[4] The worst of being run down is that you lose faith in luck.

I am gladder than I can ever tell you that things are going so well with you. Give my love to the young lady, and tell her to keep a coo for me.[5] I used to know her family, on her father's side.

Perhaps I may get a chance for a line to you from my Ohio river steamboat. I suppose the river will be roaring, with these freshets, and I don't envy myself the journey out to Pittsburg. Francis Wilson was at Matthews's, but my! where Clemens is, it is no use for anybody else.[6] I have now given him fair notice that I read no more things of his till he can prove that he has read some of my latest. Do you see Harper's Weekly? You will find some good editorial writing in it—the pieces with the headings.[7]

Yours ever,
W. D. Howells.

1. In his letter to Howells of 2 March 1902 (MH), to which this is a reply, Aldrich had apologized for an earlier "disconnected" letter, probably regarding his son Charles, who had recently contracted tuberculosis, and for imposing on Howells to write back. The "unknown friend" has not been identified.

2. It appears that the Matthews luncheon had originally been planned for 18 January but was postponed until 28 February. Howells, along with Clemens and others, attended the affair, which can be dated from Howells' remark in a letter to Aldrich, 27 February 1902 (MH): "Tomorrow I lunch at Brander Matthews's. Would you did too!" For an erroneous dating of the event and the conclusion that Clemens did not attend, see *Twain-Howells*, p. 740.

3. The Aldriches were staying at Saranac Lake in the hopes that the mountain air would improve the precarious health of their son Charles.

4. The trip, which took place between 6 and 15 March, turned out well on all accounts, as Howells wrote his daughter Mildred on 17 March 1902 (MH): "I had a glorious trip on the Ohio—a thousand miles—and I have come home restored to my sleep, and feeling fine.... My river voyage was a complete rest. I sat on the hurricane deck or in the pilot house every minute I was not eating or sleeping, and purred away with the pilots or uncle Joe, who went with me, and looked after me as if I were sick instead of merely tired out."

5. Aldrich had described his granddaughter, in his letter of 2 March, as being "a marvel of health and amiability. She never cries, and does nothing but smile and coo...." See also Howells to Aldrich, 19 January 1902, n. 2.

6. Francis Wilson (1854–1935) was a successful musical comedy actor and occasional correspondent with Howells.

7. That Howells is here referring to his own contributions to *Harper's Weekly* is indicated by his comment in a letter to Mildred Howells, 2 March 1902 (MH): "My things in the Weekly are mostly always the articles with headings, after the paragraphs of 'Comment.'" See also Howells to Aldrich, 19 January 1902, n. 6.

19 MARCH 1902, NEW YORK, TO CHARLES E. NORTON

48 West 59th st.,
March 19, 1902.

My dear Norton:

I wonder if you could help Mr. Reeves find the helper he wants.[1]

Kenyon College is, you know, an English foundation, of date rather early in the last century, and of churchly influences, at least originally. Some of the best Ohio people, President Hayes among the rest, were graduated from it, and I believe there is a prevailing air of culture in the little town, which I have been told is not out of keeping with the ivied gothicism of the college buildings. Not to paint the lily too gayly, I think $600, though not a tall sum, would go as far there as $1200 in Cambridge. Personally I do not know Mr. Reeves, I believe, though perhaps I have only forgotten him with much other learning.

I am just returned from a voyage on the Ohio River, from Pittsburg to Cincinnati and back—a thousand miles of turbid, Tiber-colored torrent, flowing between the loveliest hills and richest levels in the world. Through veils of coal smoke I saw the little ugly house, in the little ugly town, where I was born, the steamboat not staying for me to visit it.[2] The boat did, however, let me visit a vanished epoch in the life of the shores, where the type of Americanism, for good and for bad, of fifty years ago, still prevails. It is, all, where man could make it so, a scene of hideous industrialism, with topless chimneys belching the fumes of the bottomless pit; but thousands of comfortable farmsteads line the banks which the river is always eating away (to its own hurt,) and the diabolical contrasts of riches and poverty are almost effaced. I should like to write a book about it.[3]—I went because I had pretty much stopped sleeping.

With love to you all,

Yours ever,
W. D. Howells.

1. William P. Reeves was a member of the faculty at Kenyon College and seems to have asked Howells about a possible candidate for a faculty position there. Norton passed on Howells' request to Byron S. Hurlbut, dean of Harvard College, in order to locate, as he says in his reply to Howells of 26 March 1902 (MH), a "young instructor for whom Mr. R[eeves] applied to you." See *Letters of Charles Eliot Norton*, ed. Sara Norton and M. A. De Wolfe Howe (Boston: Houghton Mifflin, 1913), II, 320. Three letters from Howells to Reeves, dated 15, 18, and 20 March 1902 (OOxM), indicate that Howells turned the matter entirely over to Norton. See also George F. Smythe, *Kenyon College, Its First Century* (New Haven: Yale University Press, 1924), pp. 279, 281, 285.

2. Howells was born in Martin's Ferry, Ohio. See also Howells to Aldrich, 5 March 1902, n. 4.

3. Although Howells never wrote "a book about it," he devoted the "Editor's Easy Chair," *Harper's Monthly*, June 1902, to a description of the river trip. It was reprinted as "Floating Down the River on the O-hi-o" in *Literature and Life* (1902).

26 MARCH 1902, NEW YORK, TO JOHN HAY

48 West 59th st.,
March 26, 1902.

My dear Hay:

I wish you would let my friend Mr. Wilcox talk to you about Cuba, where he has just been, and which he has studied with peculiar qualifications from his knowledge of Spanish and Spanish-American character. He has had uncommon facilities for learning the people and the country, and he has no object in seeking you but to serve them most unselfishly.[1] I do not, frankly speaking, share his feeling on all points, especially in relation to the Cuban negroes; but he is a man of such honesty that he could not even wish to misstate the situation, which is what he wants to possess you of, and not his sentiments.

I do not know whether you are acquainted with Mr. Wilcox's literary work; if you were, you would think it delightful, as I do; and I am sure you will not undervalue his observation because he is, in our way, an exquisite artist.[2]

Yours ever
W. D. Howells.

1. Marrion Wilcox (1858–1926), a lawyer, historian, and novelist, was a strong advocate of fair and reciprocal relations between Cuba and the United States. It appears that he had not been candid with Howells about his motives in asking for an introduction to Hay, who was then secretary of state in the Roosevelt cabinet. In his reply of 31 March 1902 (MH) Hay wrote Howells: "I was glad to meet Mr. Wilcox and to talk over with him matters concerning Cuba and the Cosmos. I hope you will not give me away when I tell you that the object of his visit was to be appointed Minister to that country. He is a charming and fascinating personality, and the President likes him very much, but I fear that it will hardly be in his power to meet his wishes." Although Howells apologized to Hay on 2 April 1902 (RPB), he was not unduly upset about the situation: "No, I didn't dream that Wilcox had anything in view but the good of the Cuban Republic. I suppose I should all the same have sent him to you, though with due warning; and I wish he had been open with me, for his own sake if not for mine. Now I feel that I have to excuse him a little to you."

2. Among Wilcox's literary work are *Gray, an Oldhaven Romance* (1888) and *Vengeance of the Female* (1899), which were reviewed by Howells in "Editor's Study," *Harper's Monthly,* April 1888, and in *Literature,* June 1899, respectively.

27 MARCH 1902, NEW YORK, TO JOHN HAY

48 West 59th st.,
March 27, 1902.

My dear Hay:

No sooner have I written you about a man who wants nothing of you, and who will turn up without the extended hat,[1] about the time you get this, than I am entreated to write you again for a man who does want something and wants it badly. It is poor dear old Piatt, whom you have been befriending to your cost any time these fifty years, and who has probably established a claim on your kindness by his enjoyment of it.

You know he was put out of his place by Quincy, under a sort of misunderstanding, and here is his chance, his last chance, to get back into it.[2] He is as meritorious as any other man, (we are all worms) and perfectly qualified for the place by the experience which can alone qualify a human being to draw a consul's salary.

I subjoin his letter and his "character" from the most eminent inhabitants of Dublin,[3] and I entreat you, for SS. Charity and Poetry's sake, to do what you can for him. I know you would do it without being entreated.

He wishes his letter were type-written, and so do I; but you can easily call in a slave, by clapping your hands, and make him read it to you under pain of seeing his head roll at your feet.

Yours sincerely,
W. D. Howells.

I have been told that P. is quite pathetically poor. If you can get him this place he wont be watering any more Hesperian Trees with our tears and sweat.[4]

1. See Howells to Hay, 26 March 1902.

2. In 1893 John J. Piatt had served for a short period as U.S. consul at Dublin, Ireland, after having been consul at Cork (1882–1893). Apparently Josiah Quincy (1859–1919), who later became mayor of Boston (1896–1900) and was assistant secretary of state for six months in 1893, had been instrumental in ousting Piatt from the Dublin consulship, which Piatt now tried to obtain again with Howells' help.

3. Piatt's letter and accompanying endorsements from prominent Dubliners are not extant. Because the Dublin consulship was much sought after, Hay did not think he could be helpful in obtaining it for Piatt, as he wrote Howells on 31 March 1902 (MH): "As to our dear old friend, Piatt, ... I wish he would ask me for something that I could do, but that consulate at Dublin is turning my hair gray by the fight that is on between two or three sets of interests in the Senate . . . . I do not know who will come out first in the fight, but I am sadly sure it will be no friend of mine." A few days later, on 5 April 1902 (MH), Hay wrote again: "today when the President sent me a peremptory order for the nomination of another man to Dublin, my sorrow about Piatt was renewed." Piatt did not get the post.

4. *The Hesperian Tree* was a literary annual edited by Piatt. In the 1903 edition Piatt published three early pieces by Howells. See Gibson-Arms, *Bibliography*, p. 50.

30 MARCH 1902, NEW YORK, TO AURELIA H. HOWELLS

48 West 59th st.,
March 30, 1902.

Dear Aurelia:

I am delighted to hear of the promise of your boy, and if the village does not corrupt him with false ideas of dignity, I don't see why he should not serve your purpose far better than a girl. You can tell him from me that if he stays on with you, and makes himself useful and acceptable, I will give him ten dollars at Christmas, in addition to the wages you pay him.

The idea of tearing down the old hencoop is excellent, and I wish you could tear away that hideous old shed to the left of the barn. But perhaps it will be well to go slow with the improvements.

Yesterday I asked a party of men to meet Col. Harvey, who is going to Europe on the 2d April: Quincy Ward, my old friend the sculptor; Janvier, the story-writer; John La Farge, the painter; Crowninshield, an old friend, painter and poet; Harry Harper, and Rutgers Marshall, a psychologist and architect, all Century Club men.[1] The talk was great, as good almost as I used to hear in Cambridge, without the New England stiffness, and they sat *from half past one till ten minutes past six*! They said that this broke the record. I wish Joe could have been there. (You must not let him say any thing of it in the Sentinel, though.) It is the first entertainment I have given any friends of mine since our early days in the Beacon street house.[2] But Harvey has been so constantly kind to me, so sweet, in fact, that I wanted to do him a pleasure. I should have had Mark Twain, of course, but he is off on a yachting cruise, and it was really better talk without him, for people let him have the talk to himself at such times.

Tell Joe I thank him for the State Journal, with him and me in it, and the old office.[3] I live over our trip daily, and I should like to take it again, with you along. I am doubtful about the plan of a house boat. I'm afraid it would be so close to the water as to get malaria from it.

We have taken our cottage at Kittery Point, and I am going down to begin a garden as soon as the spring opens.

With love to Henry,

Your affectionate brother,
Will.

1. George Harvey, John Quincy Adams Ward, and Joseph Henry Harper have previously been identified. Thomas Allibone Janvier (1849–1913) was a novelist and writer of short fiction. Frederic Crowninshield (1845–1918) was a Boston painter who moved to New York in 1886 to do stained glass and mural work; Howells had recently referred to him as "a mighty good jabber" (*Twain-Howells*, p. 736). Henry Rutgers Marshall (1852–1927) was first trained in architecture but increasingly turned to psychology, philosophy, and aesthetics. Howells had joined the Century Club, composed primarily of artists and writers, in 1897.

2. Howells lived at 302 Beacon Street from August 1884 through February 1887.

3. The morning edition of the *Ohio State Journal* that is available on microfilm does not contain any reference to or picture of the Howells brothers and the *Sentinel* office.

6 APRIL 1902, NEW YORK, TO CHARLES E. NORTON

48 West 59th st.,
April 6, 1902.

My dear Norton:

I am very greatly obliged to you for your Dante,[1] which I have been looking through this afternoon for my favorite passages, and comparing your English with the Italian which I have by heart. It all seems to me mighty well done, with great clarity, grace and conscience. I like your introduction particularly: it is so absolute in its gentle sobriety and refinement. A man is at last what he is at first, and I find in this recent writing of yours the same qualities that I find in your "Notes on Italy,"[2] which I read great part of the other day. You hoped more, then, and thought you believed me, but you were essentially what you are now.

Some things in your recent letter found me of another mood, or outlook, or what you will.[3] Perhaps I was only of the chance which has been most unexpectedly given me to say what I please of current events in Harper's Weekly. The result is that I have fairly given it an anti-imperialistic tone.[4] The present head of the house trusts me so entirely that he said the other day when starting for England to "write what I pleased" for the Weekly. He is young enough to be my son,[5] and my relations with Harper and Brothers have never been so pleasant as now. Perhaps it is the chance of fighting for right things that gives me some hope of them. At any rate you will see that I am trying to say a good word for decency in divers directions. I think my main use is in saying it ironically.

I don't know how long the chance or my will will last. What astounds me in these later years is the rapidity with which I become indifferent to matters that have intensely interested me. Is it that the old soul grows tired sooner, and drops things because it is fagged?

Thank you again for the Dante, which has given me an hour's respite from myself.

Yours affectionately,
W. D. Howells.

1. Norton had sent Howells the recently issued revised edition of his Dante translation, *The Divine Comedy of Dante Alighieri*, the first edition of which had appeared in 1891–1892 and was reviewed by Howells in "Editor's Study," *Harper's Monthly*, February 1892.

2. *Notes of Travel and Study in Italy* (1860).

3. Howells' reference is unclear, since the only extant version of Norton's letter to Howells of 26 March 1902 is an excerpt printed in *Letters of Charles Eliot Norton*, ed. Sara Norton and M. A. De Wolfe Howe (Boston: Houghton Mifflin, 1913), II, 320–21.

4. In "A Fatal Ignorance of Liberty," *Harper's Weekly*, 15 March 1902, Howells had referred to the Philippines as "those . . . prepossessions of ours which have been giving us such an unpleasant foretaste of colonial empire since we had them . . . ."

5. George Harvey, then thirty-eight years old, had granted Howells considerable latitude in his choice of subject matter. See Howells to Aldrich, 19 January 1902, n. 6.

19 APRIL 1902, NEW YORK, TO BRAND WHITLOCK

48 West 59th st.,
April 19, 1902.

My dear friend:

I did not fly to acknowledge your book because I knew you knew how much I liked and honored it.[1] I hope soon to get at in print, somewhere, but I cannot do what your publishers ask.[2] Once I did such a thing, sorely against my conscience; then I vowed to do it no more. It takes all the pleasure out of praising a man's book to him; one seems to be writing at the public, and making one's self part of the commercial enterprise. You are so much of a man in my thinking that I enjoy being frank with you on this point.

It would be a great joy for me to see you. If you come before June, it will be in New York, but if later I should like it even better to be in Kittery Point, Maine, where we shall summer, and whence I can show you the dear old town of Portsmouth, fifteen minutes off by trolley. Do not let this good slip through our fingers.

> Yours cordially,
> W. D. Howells.

1. Whitlock's novel, *The 13th District* (1902).
    Whitlock had with some hesitation relayed a request from his publishers, Bowen-Merrill of Indianapolis, that Howells write a few words of praise for the novel, "some expression which they could use in their advertisements," as Whitlock put it in his letter to Howells of 16 April 1902 (MH). Despite Howells' refusal, the publishers went ahead and used his name. Greatly embarrassed, Whitlock wrote Howells on 28 April 1902 (MH): "I was surprised and pained this morning when I picked up *The Bookman* for May and saw that my publishers had taken what is a most unpardonable liberty and in an advertisement referred to you as an admirer of my book. I am so anxious to have you know that I had absolutely nothing to do with this, that I must write you at once." Howells replied on 29 April 1902 (DLC): "I have not seen the offending advertisement in the Bookman, but probably I shall only rejoice in it as getting my praise into print without my connivance or yours. Don't give the matter another thought except to think that I cannot imagine anything unhandsome of you." Two years later in a letter to Cyrus Townsend Brady of Toledo, 18 February 1906 (PSt), Howells referred to Whitlock as "the author of our greatest political novel...." In "A Political Novelist and More," *North American Review*, July 1910, Howells assessed Whitlock's achievements in literature and politics.

20 APRIL 1902, NEW YORK, TO EDWARD E. HALE

> 48 West 59th st.,
> April 20, 190m.[1]

My dear Hale:

I never knew it was you who sent that wonderful portrait of Dr. Palfrey,[2] and so your shame was unknown to me as well as your crime. But I am glad to have the real thing at last, and will take it to Franklin Square for a new edition.[3] Did it seem to you that in this real portrait there were suggestions of our dear, dear Robert's looks?[4] My wife and I both noticed them.

I am glad you got safely through your commemoration the other day.[5] I should like to have seen it.

John was full of having met you at Hampton.[6]

Yours always and always,
W. D. Howells.

1. Internal evidence indicates that this letter was written in 1902.

2. John G. Palfrey had been one of Howells' Cambridge neighbors. The portrait, that of a purse-lipped, sensitive young man, appears as an illustration in *Literary Friends and Acquaintance* (1900).

3. The 1911 Library Edition of *Literary Friends and Acquaintance,* with many fewer illustrations than the original edition, does not contain a portrait of Palfrey.

4. See Howells to Hale, 23 November 1896.

5. The commemoration was a public celebration of Hale's eightieth birthday, held at Symphony Hall in Boston on 3 April.

6. Hale had a long-standing association with Hampton Institute at Hampton, Virginia, and frequently visited the school. According to a letter from Howells to Aurelia Howells, 16 March 1902 (MH), John Howells had gone on a "health-bat to Hampton" for the last two weeks in March. He must have seen Hale there, although the exact circumstances of their meeting are not known.

7 MAY 1902, NEW YORK, TO THOMAS B. ALDRICH

48 West 59th st.,
May 7, 1902.

My dear Aldrich:

Stockton was bad enough, but Bret Harte![1] He belonged to our youth which was glad, and knew it, and I find that he had a hold upon my heart which I have no logic for. You must be feeling as I do, and words are vain. Do you suppose he knows now what the Bret Harte Mystery is which used to puzzle us all?[2]—That lurid lunch which the divine Keeler gave us out of his poverty at Obers, where the beef-steak with shoe-pegs (your name for the champignons) came on together with the flattened *omelette soufflée,* looms before my dim eyes, and I see Harte putting his hand on Clemens's seal-skin shoulder, and sputtering out, "This is the dream of his life," while Fields pauses from his cursing can-of-peaches story—O me, O my!—[3]

I *thought* you would like Boyne, and I am glad you do, and I thank you for all the kind things you say of the book.[4]

I rejoice more than I could possibly say at the good recovery of your son, which you imply.[5]

With Mrs. Howells's and my love to Mrs. Aldrich,

Yours ever
W. D. Howells

1. Bret Harte died on 5 May 1902, of throat cancer, at the house of his friend Madame Van de Velde, in Camberly, England. Frank R. Stockton (1834–1902) had died on 20 April. Born in Philadelphia, he was a novelist and short-story writer, a fanciful humorist in the genteel tradition. His best known work is *Rudder Grange* (1879).

2. Howells' reference to "the Bret Harte Mystery" is unclear, but possibly alludes to the unfulfilled promise of a great literary career that Howells and others saw in Harte's early works. Howells had written earlier of Harte: "He was indeed a prince, a fairy prince in whom every lover of his novel and enchanting art felt a patriotic property, for his promise and performance in those earliest tales of 'The Luck of Roaring Camp,' and 'Tennessee's Partner,' and 'Miggles,' and 'The Outcasts of Poker Flat,' were the earnests of an American literature to come. If it is still to come, in great measure, that is not Harte's fault, for he kept on writing those stories, in one form or another, as long as he lived." See *Literary Friends and Acquaintance*, HE, p. 243.

3. The luncheon probably took place sometime in 1871; Howells later described it in greater detail in *My Mark Twain*. See *Literary Friends and Acquaintance*, HE, p. 258.

4. Having received a copy of the just published *The Kentons*, Aldrich thanked Howells on 5 May 1902 (MH) and expressed his delight in Boyne, the young boy in the novel, whom he called "a find."

5. See Howells to Aldrich, 5 March 1902, n. 3.

8 MAY 1902, NEW YORK, TO MINNIE M. FISKE

48 West 59th st.,
May 8, 1902.

My dear Mrs. Fiske:

I wish to tell you how very *great* I again thought your Tess, the other night.[1] Your power of *holding down* the passion of the poignant moments of the murder, and in the reproach both of Marian and Angel,[2] is something I have never seen the like of in any hands but yours. I thank you for a tremendous emotion.

Yours sincerely
W. D. Howells.

1. See Howells to Rideing, 3 April 1897, n. 2, for Howells' reaction to Fiske's earlier performance in *Tess of the D'Urbervilles*. The New York *News*, observing Howells' presence at the 1902 performance, assigned him a preeminent role as guardian

of appropriate audience response: "Prominent among those in the audience was William Dean Howells, toward whom many glasses were leveled from time to time when there was any doubt about forgiving certain moral features of the play. [¶] Luckily for the play and for the players, the Dean of American Letters was disposed to be liberal" (quoted in Archie Binns, *Mrs. Fiske and the American Theatre* [New York: Crown Publishers, 1955], p. 126).

2. Present in the scene in which Tess murders Alec D'Urberville are Marian, her long-time friend, and Angel Clare, the husband who had abandoned her.

11 MAY 1902, NEW YORK, TO AURELIA H. HOWELLS

> 48 West 59th st.,
> May 11, 1902.

Dear Aurelia:

Your box of flowers came yesterday morning, and they have got back all their first freshness from being put in water. We all rejoice in them, and they are precious to me from having been sent by you from the familiar trees and grasses. We are quite surprised to find the season a little more advanced with you than it is with us. I expect to go down to Maine to-morrow or next day, and I suppose I shall find the spring fully two weeks behind. But I dare say the apple-blossoms will be out, and our cottage will be in the midst of a sea of flowers.

I enclose one of the sweet letters which Norton always writes me about my books.[1] You can return it when you have read it. *The Kentons* has started off very well: that is, about a week ago they told me at Franklin Square they had sent out 8500. This is not big selling, but for the first three weeks it is not bad, and there is a chance that the book will do well. I try to keep from feeling greedy, and envious of the success of books which I do not respect. I ought to be satisfied with the fortune that has come to me, for it is far beyond my hopes and merits. But I am afraid I am not as patient of being surpassed in any way, as I used to be. This is an old man's vice; it is hard for us to realize that other men have the right to precedence in their time and on their level. What gives me some confidence in the future of the new book is that so many people tell me they have heard it pleasantly spoken of. But I dare say that I am deceiving myself. The fact is that in *my* palmiest days, my novels sold very moderately; A Modern Instance, which was so much talked of, was ten years in reaching ten thousand.

Thursday afternoon I went out with Alden to Metuchen, and passed the night. It is a flat country, much like that about Jefferson, but lovely with the perfect spring. You know he has married again, and his new wife has brought four children into the house; with the three girls there already it is a lively household. But they get on in great apparent harmony, and his wife who is a Virginia woman manages with great tact and patience. She is a poet, and her second daughter writes poetry like Winnie's, and reminded me of her by her gentleness.[2]

You will be glad to hear that our hospital is more in the way of discharging its patients than when I last wrote you. John and Pilla are both much better, and I have slept gloriously the last two nights.

I hope your domestic *modus vivendi* still continues to work, and that your garden as well as your house is prospering. Did you dig up the old chicken house spot for a garden, as you thought of doing? It must be very rich. I shall have to buy fertilizer for my plot at Kittery Point. There are so few horses at the seaside that manure is not to be had.

Give my love to Henry, whose silent image comes so often into my mind, with its strange suggestion of father.

Your affectionate brother,
Will.

1. See Howells to Norton, 27 May 1902, n. 1.
2. Henry Mills Alden's second wife was Ada Foster Murray. She subsequently published a volume of poems entitled *Flowers O' the Grass* (1910). The "second daughter" was probably Aline Murray, who later married Joyce Kilmer and became a poet in her own right, publishing *Selected Poems* (1919).

24 MAY 1902, NEW YORK, TO AURELIA H. HOWELLS

48 West 59th st.,
May 24, 1902.

Dear Aurelia:

I am writing you Saturday instead of Sunday, because tomorrow I want to do an article,[1] so as to have next week clear for finishing my story in letters. I have narrowed the compass of it a good deal, and have made it a bit of psychology instead of the study of manners and contemporary events that I first intended. In some respects it is strengthened by the compression, but I wish I had had time and nerve to carry out my original plan.[2] However!

I enclose two letters that may interest you. The one by the writer who wishes to honor me while I am still above ground has its comic aspect;[3] but I must not recognize it in my answer. Otherwise, it is very appealing, somehow, and genuine.

The weather has suddenly come off very hot, and I am keeping indoors; the asphalt walks in the Park are baking.

You see I really have no news this time; in compensation I enclose the check, so that you may have it before the first of the month.

—I suppose you have your hammock swung between the spruces, and Henry out in it. I always think of father there, sitting with his chair among the money plant—the only money that ever grew about him. Perhaps he *is* there always, when you take his silent Image in Henry to the place. How strange that of all the myriads who have gone not one has sent any whisper back! As soon as I get my breath I am going to write a short story about a young wife who is afraid her husband may not live again because he does not *believe* he shall.[4] I think you will like it.

With love to Henry,

Your aff'te brother
Will.

1. The specific article has not been identified, but it is probably one of four short pieces that appeared in *Harper's Weekly* in June 1902. See Gibson-Arms, *Bibliography*, p. 135.

2. Howells had described the "original plan" for *Letters Home* in his letter to Aldrich, 19 January 1902, but he had misgivings about the project and considerable problems in completing it. Thus he wrote to his sister Aurelia on 20 April 1902 (MH): "I keep working away at the story in letters . . . , but I do not care much for it. I am afraid the form is a mistake." And on 27 July 1902 (MH), having finished the book, he again wrote to Aurelia: "I have had a dreadful bump with my ill-imagined story in letters which, now it is done, seems to me a failure. One great trouble is the unnatural form, and another is that like all old people I have begun to repeat myself."

3. Howells is here referring to a letter from Theodore Dreiser, 14 May 1902 (MH), which was written in response to the April 1902 "Editor's Easy Chair" on Longfellow. Dreiser wanted to convey his "spiritual affection" to Howells, whom he listed with Tolstoy and Hardy as the three writers who had most influenced him. The "comic aspect" Howells will overlook in his answer is the effusive phrasing of Dreiser's final paragraph: "If the common ground is to be credited with the flowering out of such minds as yours I shall not be disturbed to return to the dust. There is enough in the thought to explain the wonder of the night, the sparkle of the waters—the thrill of tender feeling that runs abroad in the odours and murmers [sic] and sighs. Buried Howells and Hardys and Tolstoys shall explain it for me. I shall rejoice and believe that it is they who laugh in the waters—that it is because of such that the hills clap their hands."

4. "Though One Rose from the Dead," *Harper's Monthly*, April 1903; reprinted in *Questionable Shapes* (1903). At the beginning of the story, Mr. Aldering explains his wife's fears to a friend: "'Marion has always had the notion that I should live again if I believed I should, and that as I don't believe I shall, I am not going to.'"

27 MAY 1902, NEW YORK, TO CHARLES E. NORTON

48 West 59th st.,
May 27, 1902.

My dear Norton:

If my books brought me no other reward your letters acknowledging them in their long succession would be enough. I read what you say again and again, and am happier in it than in any other praise; but that is saying little.[1]

The other day came a young man from Houghton, Mifflin & Co., using your kind words about me in reference to a life of Lowell for their Men of Letters series.[2] I have spoken to Harpers, who have a right to my books, and they are willing to arrange for a joint publication. I do not know whether the Boston house would enter into this, and I am not sure whether I could make such a book as should be made. In a sort I have said myself out about Lowell,[3] and I should have to take him up impersonally. But what if I could not? There would be danger of repetition. I have great misgivings; but I am tempted. Scudder's book satisfied me more than when I first spoke of it to you; and it covers the ground I should have to go over.[4] Why, why cannot, will not *you* write Lowell's life? If I ever try it, I shall make you *talk* it for me, first. You have said more luminous things about his New England than any *forastiere*[5] could ever imagine.

An English friend has precipitated on us a terrible question which you alone can answer. Why are the four lions in Nicola Pisano's pulpit gnawing the heads of four horses? In all your delightful account of the Siena cathedral you do not say. Is there no symbolical meaning in the fact, or is it more a caprice of the sculptor? That hardly seems possible.[6]

I hope you are quite well again, and are liking life as well as this rather odious time will let you.—I copied your praise of Mrs. Wharton's book into a note I was writing her, and she was greatly pleased, & told me of your gift of a Doge's letter.[7] I have not read the book yet, dreading somewhat to find Stendhal in it as I find James in her stories. She is a great creature, and I wish she used her own voice solely.

With love to you all,

Yours ever
W. D. Howells.

---

1. Recently confined to his bed, Norton had *The Kentons* read to him and wrote Howells on 2 May 1902: " 'The Kentons' is really, my dear Howells, an admirable study of life, and as it was read to me my chief pleasure in listening was in your

sympathetic, creative imagination, your insight, your humour, and all your other gifts, which make your stories, I believe, the most faithful representations of actual life that were ever written." See *Letters of Charles Eliot Norton*, ed. Sara Norton and M. A. De Wolfe Howe (Boston: Houghton Mifflin, 1913), II, 321–22.

2. The "young man" appears to have been a Mr. Parker, mentioned in Howells' letter to Messrs. Houghton, Mifflin & Co., also dated 27 May 1902 (MH). In that letter Howells indicated that he would "consider writing the book" about Lowell if the Boston firm would agree to Colonel Harvey's stipulation that it would be first published by Harper & Brothers. Later that year, Howells found that he could not go through with such a major project as a Lowell biography (see Howells to Norton, 25 November 1902), and Houghton Mifflin eventually published Ferris Greenslet's *James Russell Lowell: His Life and Work* (1905) in their "American Men of Letters" series.

3. "A Personal Retrospect of James Russell Lowell," *Scribner's*, September 1900; reprinted in *Literary Friends and Acquaintance*, HE, pp. 179–210.

4. Horace E. Scudder, *James Russell Lowell: A Biography* (1901), reviewed by Howells in "Editor's Easy Chair," *Harper's Monthly*, February 1902.

5. Howells' erroneous spelling of *forestiere*, Italian for "foreigner."

6. The "English friend" was R. Harold Paget (1876–1926); born in Leicestershire, England, he had settled in New York, where he founded the Paget Literary Agency, representing such writers as Rudyard Kipling, W. B. Yeats, and Conan Doyle. His question concerned the pulpit of the Siena cathedral done by the sculptor Niccola Pisano (ca. 1215–1281). The four lions stand at the base, supporting on their backs four columns holding up the pulpit proper. Norton's account appears in *Historical Studies of Church-Buildings in the Middle Ages* (1880), pp. 125–33. Apparently still waiting for "Mr. Norton's authoritative interpretation of Pisano's horsehead eating lions," Howells sent Paget on 2 June 1902 (OFH) the following interpretation: "...I send you some interesting passages got together by a friend of mine, which bear upon the question. You will see that they hardly leave the horse a leg to stand on. He represents all mortality, carnality, and banality. The lion you know is one of the Christ symbols, and it is imaginable that Pisano meant the triumph of Christianity over paganism." Paget was editorial director of *An Outline of Christianity* (1926), 5 volumes.

7. The book to which Howells refers was Edith Wharton's historical novel about eighteenth-century Italy, *The Valley of Decision*, published earlier that year. The letter in which Norton praised it is not extant, but elsewhere he expressed strong but qualified approval: "The intellectual element... is stronger than the emotional and the passionate... and her book is to be prized most by those who know Italy best and most love it." See Norton to Samuel G. Ward, *Letters of Charles Eliot Norton*, II, 319. Wharton had recently become friends with Sara Norton, C. E. Norton's younger daughter, and in the course of researching materials for her novel she borrowed Italian phrase books and other items from Sara's father. See R. W. B. Lewis, *Edith Wharton: A Biography* (New York: Harper & Row, 1975), pp. 95, 103. Norton undoubtedly gave Wharton the doge's letter during this period.

9 JUNE 1902, NEW YORK, TO JOHN W. DE FOREST

48 West 59th st.
June 9, 1902.

My dear De Forest:

I do not think the ingenious Nation man could ever have been my old friend Godkin, even when Godkin was alive, for *he* was no prig, whatever else he was.[1] Personally he and I were always on the best terms, and, so far as I know, I had never anything but kindness from him; so that his death was a real grief to me.—This actual critic is very difficult indeed. He will not allow me even to praise novels which he likes; and the other day he would not let me speak pleasantly of the picturesqueness of the house-boats on the Ohio River because I had the "defect" of not saying that they were illicit liqueor shops![2] I have small curiosity as to who he is, and no conjecture, for I rarely see the Post.[3]

I hope you are "keeping your health." It has been one of the misfortunes of my life that I have so seldom met you; and now that we are both "getting on," I do not know that I can repair my bad luck. Withal this, however, I have tried always to keep you in mind of my high regard, and I hope you have been able to forgive to this any harm my zeal may have done your novels.

Yours ever
W. D. Howells.

1. The *Nation* of 29 May 1902 published a brief notice of De Forest's *Poems: Medley and Palestine* (1902), and it appears that De Forest speculated in a letter to Howells which is no longer extant, that the author of the notice may have been Edwin L. Godkin, who died on 20 May 1902 in Brixham, England. The notice reads in part: "The poet is the author of many novels whose success might have been more substantial had not Mr. Howells selected one of them for rather extravagant praise, from which some reaction apparently followed."

2. The critic in the *Nation*, 5 June 1902, commenting on Howells' account of his recent trip on the Ohio as reported in the June "Editor's Easy Chair," (reprinted as "Floating Down the River on the O-hi-o" in *Literature and Life*), had remarked that Howells failed "to recognize the relation of these people [the house-boat dwellers] to illicit liquor traffic...."

3. The New York *Evening Post* and the *Nation* were both published by Henry Villard (1835–1910), financier and journalist. In 1902 the *Nation* was in effect a weekly edition of the *Evening Post*. The notices criticizing Howells may well have been written by Wendell Phillips Garrison, who for many years was the literary editor of the *Nation* until he succeeded Godkin as editor in 1881. For an earlier conflict between Howells and Garrison, see Howells to Garrison, 15 December 1874.

3 July 1902, Kittery Point, to Thomas B. Aldrich

Kittery Point, July 3, 1902.

My dear Aldrich:

I should not mind being old, so much, if I always had the young, sure grip of myself. What I hate is this dreamy fumbling about my own identity, in which I detect myself at odd times. It seems sometimes as if it were somebody else, and I sometimes wish it were. But it will have to go on, and I must get what help I can out of the fact that it always *has* gone on. I think I could deal with the present, bad and bothering as it is, if it were not for visions of the past in which I appear to be mostly running about, full of sound and fury signifying nothing. Once I thought that I meant something by everything I did; but now I don't know.

Clemens has written a very acrid allegory, in the last number of Harper's Weekly, about this subject of old age.[1] How every fellow thinks he has discovered it! And it is not such a great find, either. John's job, by the way, is postponed till next year, a stroke of the coal strike being a blow to Mrs. Clemens's income from her mines.[2] This has not reduced them to want, however, and I am expecting to find Clemens in very tolerable comfort at York Harbor, when I go over to see him, before long. Where *is*, or was, Tenant Harbor, now Nomore in Elmore?[3] I like to dream of visiting you there, though you know I never will, much as I should like it. That it is in Maine says nothing of its neighborhood; Maine is an empire; and Elmore seems to put it in some vulgar Pays du Tendre. We are a wonderfully sloppy people. Do you mind when they changed West Cambridge to Arlington? Arlington!—We are here in the fringe of an apple orchard, with two acres of grass sloping to the Shoals, practically, but bordering Kittery harbor, where six lumber ships have always run in from the wet outside, and a hotel, full of aging admirals and their younging wives, next door. I have a vegetable garden where I hoe, and a table, half as big, where I write. Why can't you drop in on your way to Elmore? You have no idea how your personality peoples Portsmouth for me with the young Aldrich. We are boys together there, and I think you are very gracious to an interloper like me.

I hope your son gets better and better.[4] Our love to his mother, and happiness to you all.—The other night I dreamed of going into partnership with Osgood in the publishing business. It seemed all right.

Yours ever
W. D. Howells.

1. "Five Boons of Life," *Harper's Weekly*, 5 July 1902.

2. John M. Howells' job was to remodel the house purchased by Clemens at Tarrytown, New York. See Howells to Aurelia H. Howells, 27 April 1902 (MH). Later, in 1908, John would design "Stormfield," the Clemenses' house at Redding, Connecticut.

3. Clemens had engaged a cottage at York Harbor, Maine, for the summer. It was located only a few miles from Kittery Point; a trolley line connecting the two places made possible frequent visits. Tenant's Harbor, where the Aldriches summered, is located about 100 miles north of Kittery Point. According to Aldrich's letter to Howells of 29 June 1902 (MH), "its name has been sentimentally changed to 'Elmore', if you ever heard of such a thing!"

4. See Howells to Aldrich, 5 March 1902, n. 1.

3 AUGUST 1902, KITTERY POINT, TO BRANDER MATTHEWS

Kittery Point, Aug. 3, 1902.

My dear Matthews:

At your kind suggestion I am reading Stephens's "George Eliot," but the ground is so familiar that I find a lack of novelty in it, and certainly there is no surprise in the criticism. Perhaps there could be none. I hope to compare it with Brownell's, which I have still to read.[1]

As for the English coming to our position, so loath and so late, I could wish they had the decency to recognize our priority. A series of very earthquaking papers in The Academy seemed merely to be prolonging the seismic disturbances of fifteen years ago in "The Editor's Study."[2] I have not yet got to the point of agreement in Stephens's book.

But I ought to be, and I own I am, feeling kindly towards English book-noticers—I hope that they are also true critics, for once—because of their liking for The Kentons. Here the book has been fairly killed by the stupid and stupefying cry of "commonplace people."[3] I shall not live long enough to live this down, but possibly my books may. I confess that I am disheartened. I had hoped I was helping my people know themselves in the delicate beauty of their everyday lives, and to find cause for pride in the loveliness of our apparently homely average, but they don't want it. They bray at my flowers picked from the fruitful fields of our common life, and turn aside among the thistles with keen appetites for the false and impossible. Pazienza!

Yours ever
W. D. Howells.

1. Sir Leslie Stephen (1832–1904), the British literary critic, had contributed several biographies to the "English Men of Letters" series, among them *George Eliot* (1902). William C. Brownell's *Victorian Prose Masters* (1901) included an essay on George Eliot, and Howells applauded its justness while criticizing Stephen's biography

in "Editor's Easy Chair," *Harper's Monthly*, November 1902. Howells primarily objected to Stephen's inconsistent attitude toward literary realism: "For instance, he constantly exacts, of the author studied, reality, more and more of it; yet he always speaks of 'realism' and the 'realists' as if by those marks he would fence himself from any share in the guilt and ignominy of their devotion to reality."

2. It is unclear what "series of . . . papers" Howells is here referring to; however, they appear to have been published in the British weekly, *The Academy and Literature*, and probably commented on the principles of literary realism that Howells expounded in the 1880s in *Harper's Monthly*.

3. For a summary of the English and American criticism of Howells' most recent novel, see *The Kentons*, HE, pp. xxiv–xxv.

17 AUGUST 1902, KITTERY POINT, TO AURELIA H. HOWELLS

Kittery Point, August 17, 1902.

Dear Aurelia:

We had Pilla at lunch with us on Wednesday, and I am glad to report that she seems to be getting well with a basis of health sounder than ever before. By the end of the month I hope her cure will be complete. It consists of diet, and the habit of rest, with no medicine.

This is a wonderful morning of summer sun and wind, with a sea that sparkles and dances in both. They say we are at the end of our yachting season, but two very handsome big yachts are lying off our shore this morning, and what is somehow pleasanter to the eye a great, black, empty coal barge, high out of the water. I seem very selfish, twitting you with these lovely sights which you cannot share, but I hope that you will yet do so. Meantime, I should like to look across your flat fields to the woods where we gathered the beechnuts with Annie, last fall. There is something in the landscapes we knew when young that no beauty makes up for in those we see later; and though it was mostly a rebellious heartache for me in the scenery about Jefferson, still it is the sense of home.—I want to see you before snowfall, and make up for that short visit in March.[1]—I have lately been reading Crabbe's Tales, in verse, and wondering whether I might not write some like them about the Jefferson we first knew. There were many episodes and characters which could be treated poetically. I must talk the plan over with Joe and you. I find myself inclined, in my autumnal years, to the poetry which I thought would make my fame when I was young, and I am so situated now that I could indulge the taste for it.[2] How it would have pleased father! Love to Henry.

> Your aff'te brother
> Will.

1. Howells had briefly stopped in Jefferson, probably on 7 or 8 March, before setting out on his trip down the Ohio with his brother Joe. See Howells to Aldrich, 5 March 1902, n. 4.

2. Howells' reading of George Crabbe's *Tales* (1812), a series of narrative poems about country life, rekindled his early interest in writing poetry, even to the point of choosing a title, "The Villagers," for his projected work. On 7 September 1902 (MH) he wrote again to Aurelia, expressing similar thoughts: "It is droll how I am taking to verse in my old age. Perhaps I shall turn out yet a greater poet than Shakespear, as I used to expect!—I am mulling over the old Jefferson material, to be called *The Villagers,* if I ever write it out. [¶] *Did we come New Years of 1852? or 1853?* [¶] I wish you would jot down notes of stories that I could use. I want to come out this fall, and talk it over with Joe and you." See also Howells to Norton, 12 October 1902.

7 OCTOBER 1902, KITTERY POINT, TO WILLIAM JAMES

Kittery Point, Oct. 7, 1902.

My dear James:

Your postal card did my very soul good: you praise so gloriously that I could almost wish to deserve your praise,[1] and I cannot wholly believe that I do not. In this case I will own that I like *The Kentons* myself.

No, I have not got your book yet,[2] but it has been flying all round me all summer, and I don't know how it has missed me. I am wanting to read it and I shall get it when we go to New York. I have bought a place here fronting the sea with two acres of shore, and we are holding on till we put it in shape. Just now the stable has rested on its journey from the street corner to the east of the house, where I am going to turn it into a study, and is trying to look into our bay-window; to move a building was about all that remained for me to do; and it is such an American experience!

Yours ever, with love to you all,
W. D. Howells.

I am glad you are so well again.

1. William James had written Howells from Chocorua, New Hampshire, on 28 September 1902 (MH): "I have been squealing over your Kentons, and my eldest son and daughter are now in the act of doing the same. You are 'doing a great work' and long may you live to enlarge it. The perfect veracity and *goodness* of this are beyond all praise. It lightens the burden of existence which sometimes falls heavy."

2. *The Varieties of Religious Experience* (1902).

9 OCTOBER 1902, KITTERY POINT, TO HAMILTON W. MABIE

Kittery Point, Me., Oct. 9, 1902.

My dear Mr. Mabie:

I am very sorry indeed to differ with you and Mr. Johnson in regard to the endowment of the Institute.[1] I think the Institute should remain poor, and free from every tie of gratitude for money benefactions, which as yet it has done nothing to deserve. For us to make a material appearance to the public before we have made any intellectual impression would be a grotesque mistake.

I feel very strongly about the matter, and yet I should be so unwilling to oppose a majority that it is a serious question with me whether I ought not at once to resign from the Institute, and not take any part in a controversy which could not change my feeling.[2]

Yours   sincerely
W. D. Howells.

1. Hamilton W. Mabie was at this time secretary of the National Institute of Arts and Letters, and Robert U. Johnson succeeded him in that position in 1903. Howells, the Institute's president since 1901, opposed the solicitation of private funds to support it.

2. Shortly afterwards, in a letter to Mabie of 27 November 1902 (NNAL), Howells recommended that E. C. Stedman be considered for the presidency. See also Howells to Mabie, 10 February 1903.

12 OCTOBER 1902, KITTERY POINT, TO CHARLES E. NORTON

Kittery Point, Me., Oct. 12, 1902.

My dear Norton:

It has been many times in my mind to write to you, the past summer, because you are so often in my mind, and because I wished to speak to you of correlated things. One day when I was in Boston I found a very pretty little Dante, and night and morning, when my sins woke me, I have been working my way through the Purgatorio, which I had never honestly, or even dishonestly read; and somehow you have been constantly with me in this reading. When I get back to New York where my Norton-Dante is, I am going to follow in your footsteps with my mental translation.[1] Another association with you is the extreme delight I have taken in the metrical tales of George Crabbe, of whom with great difficulty I got a complete edition. I am sure you must like him, and at least that you will be amused to learn that he has shaken into form a vague purpose I have lately had to study in verse the life of the Ohio village where the most wretched years of my later boyhood were passed. I used to hate it, so that for many years after my escape from it I trembled to think my dead body might be brought back prisoner and buried there. But I have long since forgiven it, and I now see it in a tender retrospect which seems friendly to a treatment in heroic couplets,—with the overrun of the Prepopean poets. I should like to show you my beginning, but for the present I spare you.[2]—Mrs. Howells and I are greatly interested in Sir P. Burne-Jones's painting you.[3] That must be a great pleasure to you both, and I hardly know which of you I envy more.—We have bought this little place here at the mouth of the Piscataqua, and are lingering out the fading leaf in order to "make the house some reparations," as my French brother-in-law[4] once phrased it in gentle English; and also to keep out of New York. By the way, I have done a novel about N. Y. in epistolary form, which I call "Letters Home," the letters being all written by sojourners of several types, and the answers not given.—There is a prospect of Harpers, by treaty with Houghtons, doing a library edition of me[5]—it would take a Vatican library to hold me, almost—and I have some hopes that I may find my way, by this means, to doing the life of Lowell. In case I do, will you let me come, and steal everything I can from you? What you said of the optimistic period of New England with respect to him was so luminous, that I have ever since seen him where he really stood in history.[6]—My mainstay for talk, this summer, has been Mark Twain, only forty trolley minutes away.[7] But how sad old men are! We meet, and strike fire and flicker up, and I come away a heap of cold ashes. And in what evil times we are fallen! Now I understand how the Puritans felt after the Restoration. With love to you all,

Yours faithfully
W. D. Howells.

1. See Howells to Norton, 6 April 1902, n. 1.

2. See Howells to Aurelia H. Howells, 17 August 1902, n. 2.

3. Sir Philip Burne-Jones (1861–1926), the only son of Sir Edward Coley Burne-Jones, attended Oxford for two years and then studied painting in London. Two of his portraits, depicting his father and Sir Edward Poynter (his uncle), are in the National Portrait Gallery. The location of his portrait of Norton is not known.

4. Achille Fréchette, Annie Howells' French-Canadian husband.

5. This appears to be the earliest mention of the possibility of issuing a library edition. Harper & Brothers ultimately published only six volumes in 1911. Frederick A. Duneka later stated the Harpers' interest in issuing the edition as early as 1905. See Howells to Duneka, 15 February 1904, n. 3; also Robert W. Walts, "William Dean Howells and His 'Library Edition'," *Publications of the Bibliophile Society of America* 102 (1958), 284–94. For subsequent correspondence regarding the negotiation of terms

under which Houghton Mifflin would grant permission to Harper & Brothers for reissuing Howells' early works, see Howells to George H. Mifflin, 15 May 1905 (MH); Howells to Frederick A. Duneka, 16 May 1905 (NNC); George H. Mifflin *to* Howells, 16 May 1905 (NNC); Howells to George H. Mifflin, 17 May 1905 (MH); Harper & Brothers to Houghton, Mifflin & Co., 19 May 1905 (NNC); Houghton, Mifflin & Co. to Harper & Brothers, 22 May 1905 (NCC).

6. See Howells to Norton, 27 May 1902, n. 2. Norton had published two essays on Lowell nine years earlier: "James Russell Lowell," *Harper's Monthly*, May 1893, and "The Letters of James Russell Lowell," *Harper's Monthly*, September 1893. He had also edited Lowell's correspondence, *The Letters of James Russell Lowell* (1894).

7. See Howells to Aldrich, 3 July 1902, n. 3.

20 OCTOBER 1902, KITTERY POINT, TO SAMUEL L. CLEMENS

Kittery Point, October 20, 1902.

Dear Clemens:

Tell me how Mrs. Clemens is, and how she bore the journey.[1] I hope all has gone well with you.

I have got Huck Finn safe, and will keep it till I come down, or will send it by express, as you say. It is a great layout; what I shall enjoy most will be the return of the old fellows to the scene, and their tall lying. There is a matchless chance there. I suppose you will put plenty of pegs in, in this prefatory part.[2]

On Saturday I went to Boston and got the deed of this place: I ought to have had it twenty-five years ago. But you can't think of everything.

Yesterday I lunched at the Aldis's in York Harbor, and saw your pines as I went by.[3] They looked lovely in a sunshine softer than any this year. The weather is simply glorious, now. I hope you will come back next summer. We are staying till the first of November.

Yours ever
W. D. Howells.

1. Olivia Clemens was taken seriously ill at York Harbor in August, and she suffered a relapse on 20 September. On 12 October Clemens had to make elaborate arrangements for her return journey to Riverdale, New York. See *Twain-Howells*, pp. 745, 747.

2. Clemens had given Howells part of a story in progress, entitled "Tom Sawyer's Conspiracy." See *Twain-Howells*, pp. 746–47.

3. The Aldis family has not been identified. The cottage Clemens had rented in York Harbor was called "The Pines."

31 OCTOBER 1902, NEW YORK, TO BLISS PERRY

48 West 59th st.,
Oct. 31, 1902.

My dear Mr. Perry:[1]

I appreciate the kind motive you had in sending me Miss Preston's paper, and I thank you for that. But I think you must see how impossible it is for me to do anything more. It is your affair as editor and her affair as author. If you are satisfied to print and she to write such a criticism, it is certainly not for me, on any account whatever, to interpose an objection.[2] Again, I am glad of your personal feeling toward me in the matter, which I truly value.

Yours sincerely
W. D. Howells.

1. Bliss Perry (1860–1954) was professor of English at Harvard and editor of the *Atlantic* (1899–1909).
2. Perry had sent, for Howells' approval, a biting review of *The Kentons* by Harriet W. Preston, which he contemplated publishing in the *Atlantic*. Despite Howells' courteous attempt to dispose of the matter without involving himself, Perry sent him the proofs of the review. Howells shot off a brief and calculated reply on 29 October 1902 (MH): "I am at a loss to know why this proof should have been sent to me, for I do not suppose you expect me to correct it." Perry evidently wrote an apology, still leaving open the possibility of not publishing the offending piece. Howells, however, closed the matter emphatically when he wrote Perry on 12 November 1902 (MH): "...I prefer that the paper should be printed, for I cannot be left in the attitude of having suppressed a criticism which you thought could not possibly offend me, although you submitted it to my censure for everything or anything annoying in it. [¶]...I have never yet sought to control the reviews of my books, and I am too old now to seem to begin to do so. I do not like disagreeable things said of my books,...but it would be preposterous for me to use any means to suppress them." Later on the same day Howells wrote once again to Perry (MH), asking that his own feelings about the article not be considered by Perry; instead, he urged, "If you now wish to consider me in the matter, I beg you to publish the article." The review appeared in the *Atlantic*, January 1903. Among other things, Preston described the characters in the novel as distinctly unacceptable, "the scum and spawn of a yeasty deep,—the monstrous offspring of barbarous and illicit social relations." See Cady, *Howells*, II, 257.

16 NOVEMBER 1902, NEW YORK, TO SAMUEL L. CLEMENS

48 W. 59th st.,
Nov. 16, 1902.

My dear **Clemens:**
(the way you look now)[1]
Of course I should like to help pry that money out of Heriot, but I

think it will take more than fence-rails to do it. Poor Stoddard wrote me to the same effect as he wrote you, and wrung my heart so that I have not yet braced up to show that I had one.[2] "This d—— human race!" You were well out of that dinner last night. Oh, but the clack was dull.[3]

Yours ever
W. D. Howells.

1. Howells pasted a clipped-out newspaper photogoraph of Clemens between this line and the beginning of the next paragraph.

2. Fred Harriott, acting as agent of Charles W. Stoddard, had received a $400 advance from the publisher of Stoddard's *Exits and Entrances* (1903), and Stoddard had written both Howells and Clemens about his unsuccessful attempt to obtain the money. They in turn wrote a joint letter to Harriott, resulting in a payment to Stoddard of $250. When Stoddard failed to thank them appropriately, they decided to let him collect the remainder on his own. See *Twain-Howells*, pp. 752–53, 766; also *My Mark Twain*, where Howells describes the episode, in *Literary Friends and Acquaintance*, HE, pp. 312–13.

3. The dinner was given in honor of Jules M. Cambon, the French ambassador to the United States, and Clemens was scheduled to speak at it. See *Twain-Howells*, p. 749.

25 NOVEMBER 1902, NEW YORK, TO CHARLES E. NORTON

48 West 59th st.,
Nov. 25, 1902.

My dear **Norton:**

I wish to thank you and your daughters for the sweet visit I had with you all,[1] and to ask you to say to Sally, when she returns, that I was very sorry to miss her, from your circle. When you let me come again, she must be there with the rest.

Since I left you I have been blaming myself for making too heavy a draft upon your kindness by owning that literary weariness of myself which I should not wish you to share. The feeling was honest enough, but would have been better kept. Will you forgive its expression to my confidence in the sympathy which I abused?

I have been thinking of the life of Lowell, especially today, and despairing of it. Really, I do not believe I could get myself together for the work. I can do journalism, finer or coarser, and I can keep on doing fiction, in a way, but I am afraid the time for a great undertaking like the story of Lowell's life is past for me, if ever I was fit for it. The monograph in my book about Cambridge must remain my only contribution to his biography.[2]

I know you will make the excuses for me which I will not urge. It is partly a flagging of the nerves, partly a conviction of my unfitness, which makes me renounce the task. My highest pleasure in performing it would have been the hope of gratifying you, as my keenest regret in abandoning it is the fear of your disappointment.

The sense of your friendship has never been so sweet as in the day I spent with you, and I will trust it even in this matter.

Remember me to all your house.

Yours affectionately,
W. D. Howells.

I have marked the things we liked best in Edith Wyatt's book, which I'm sending you; but we liked everything[3]

1. On 22 November Howells had visited Norton and his daughters Margaret and Elizabeth, Sara (or Sally, as she was called) being away at the time. While in Cambridge, he briefly visited Winifred's grave and described the occasion in a letter to Aurelia Howells, 23 November 1902 (MH): "In the afternoon I went to the cemetary to look a moment at the place where our dear Winnie lies. It was a very sad, pale sunset, but there was peace in it. The bushes we had planted completely bower the stone."

2. See Howells to Norton, 27 May 1902, n. 2.

3. Howells had reviewed Edith Wyatt's collection of stories, *Every One His Own Way* (1901), in the "Editor's Easy Chair," *Harper's Monthly*, October 1901. Norton thanked Howells on 13 December 1902 (MH) for sending the book and commented in a manner that clearly suggests the essential difference between his and Howells' concept of realistic fiction: "this reminds me to thank you for *Every man his own Way*, which you and James praised so warmly, and which I found *almost* worthy of your praise. The temper, the spirit, the humor, the intent of the stories are quite exceptionally good, and the workmanship excellent,—but alas! the atmosphere, the milieu, the people are lacking in charm, in fact horribly true and ugly. Good people, many of them, quite simply content with their own conditions, possessing the rudimentary culture which in the next generation may perhaps develop into the genuine refinement, kindly, well-intentioned, vulgar but not coarse-minded, rising from the Dime Novel level to that of East Aurora,—people to celebrate as products of democracy in America, but not yet as pleasant to be familiar with or to read about as those who have risen a little further. We are, indeed, all of us on the make, and I like best those who are nearest made.—But all you said of the book was true, and I am sending it to Europe as a good specimen of democratic literature."

23 December 1902, New York, to Samuel L. Clemens

48 West 59th st.,
Dec. 23, 1902.

Dear Clemens:

I am to give a lunch to Harry Harland[1] on the 8th of January at Moretti's spaghettery, 151 West 34th street. Will you come?—at one o'clock. Don't lose this, and then pretend you were not asked. That Christian Science paper of yours[2] was nearly as good as mine on Norris,[3] which I suppose you have not had the decency to read.

Yours ever
W. D. Howells.

1. Henry Harland (1861–1905), an American writer of Russian-Jewish origin, wrote about the Jewish immigrant experience under the pseudonym of Sidney Luska. Harland moved to London, where he became the first editor of *Yellow Book*. He was best known for his successful courtly novel, *The Cardinal's Snuff Box* (1900). Howells was taking advantage of Harland's brief stay in New York to honor him with a literary luncheon.

2. "Christian Science," *North American Review*, December 1902.

3. "Frank Norris," *North American Review*, December 1902; Howells had written the essay as an appreciation of Frank Norris, who had died on 25 October 1902.

11 JANUARY 1903, NEW YORK, TO MADISON J. CAWEIN

48 West 59th st.,
Jan. 11, 1903.

My dear Cawein:

I have both your books; the English one I have read, and the newer collection I am expecting to read when I get time.[1] I need not praise them to you, for you know what I think of your work, but I thank you for them. I did not find Gosses's introduction warm enough, but it is much for an Englishman to be even tepid toward a man of another nation.

I wish I could say something to comfort you in your evil days, and I do think you are mistaken about the Eastern indifference to Western poetry. Is the East indifferent to Riley?[2] Your poetry is too fine and good for the popular taste; that is all. It is by far the best we are now having; but you have not widened your course, much, and the successive volumes,[3] while they add to the sum of beauty which you have created, do not appeal with novelty to a sign-seeking generation. It is cold comfort to remind you that you have your gift, a lovely and exquisite gift, and you have the recognition of the best; but you must try to make the most of that, since you have the means of living along with it. What other American poet has been reprinted in London, except Riley? Cheer up!

Yours ever,
W. D. Howells.

1. The English book was *Kentucky Poems* (1902), a selection of Cawein's poems published in London, with an introduction by Edmund Gosse. The "new collection" was *A Voice on the Wind and Other Poems* (1902). See Howells to Cawein, 21 September 1901, n. 1.

2. James Whitcomb Riley, the popular Indiana poet.

3. By 1903 Cawein had published nineteen volumes of poetry; the first one had appeared in 1887.

13 JANUARY 1903, NEW YORK, TO EVELYN G. SMALLEY

48 West 59th. st.,
Jany 13, 1903

My dear Miss Evelyn:[1]

I do not think that human tongue can utter
My grateful feelings for the paper cutter
You sent me at the Merry Christmas tide,
And that is why I have not even tried
To thank you for it. You must not suppose
That if it had been possible for prose
To do it, I had now taken to verse.
I cannot hope in rhyme, even, to rehearse
The praises of its aptness. It was quite
The thing I wanted both by day and night
Especially by night for when I took
To bed with me some soporific book,
It happened if I came to uncut pages
I fell into the most terrific rages,
That drove sleep from me to the utmost distance.
But now it comes without the least resistance.
I touch the paper with your magic blade
And the leaves spring asunder all dismayed.
Sleep comes, and from my hand the volume drops,
And my soul steeped in opium and hops,
Wanders in dreams afar to fairy realms superb
With nothing to molest it or disturb.

Yours sincerely
W. D. Howells.

1. Evelyn Garnaut Smalley (d. 1938), a friend of Mildred Howells, was the daughter of G. W. Smalley and his wife, Phoebe. She later edited *The Henry James Year Book* (1912), to which Howells contributed a short introduction in epistolary form. See Howells to James, 31 July 1898, 20 August 1909, and 24 October 1909.

28 JANUARY 1903, NEW YORK, TO AURELIA H. HOWELLS

48 West 59th st.,
Jan'y 28, 1903.

Dear Aurelia:

I am writing you today instead of waiting for Sunday because I thought your money might be getting low, sent as it was in mid December.[1]—Joe has told me of his suggestion to you about burning wood in your furnace if the gas gives out, and I think it a good one; but get the stove for your sitting room, too, if you like. It would be cheerful. As soon as you let me know about your plans, I will see if I cannot find some one here who will go out to live with you. In the meantime I hope you are not living quite alone.[2]

Our winter has broken again, and to-day Elinor and I trudged out into the Park, and sat a long time in the sun, where the snow had been cleared from the asphalt. In another place, two happy little girls were spading it from one side of the walk to the other. Everywhere it was thawing, and the water rippling down the inclines. The skating is gone, and there has not been much of it. But the snow coming so early has made the winter seem long already.

I am well into a story which I thought would be short, but which is turning out rather long. I have called it "Mother and Son"[3] and it treats of what seems to me an interesting subject: the son's opposition to his mother's second marriage, out of devotion to the memory of his father whom he does not know to be the worthless and wicked person his mother does.

I am having my portrait done by one of the several painters who have imagined doing me.[4] As sketched, it is a good likeness of me, with race in it: grandfather, father, and Joe. It is very curious. I suppose there are these hidden family traits in us, which come out as characteristics do.

Elinor is better than she has been, and the rest are well, except for the inevitable sore throat in Pilla. It is not serious.

With love to Henry, and regards to Pooly,[5]

Your aff'te brother
Will.

I wish Pooly would get himself Kodaked for me.

1. Howells sent Aurelia a monthly allowance of $50.

2. Annie Fréchette and her husband, Achille, had come from Ottawa in early October to visit Aurelia at Jefferson. Annie stayed until shortly before Christmas, and the sisters discussed the possibility of Henry and Aurelia moving permanently to

Ottawa. They eventually decided on an extended visit, leaving a final decision to a later date. Accompanied by Joseph A. Howells, Aurelia and Henry departed from Jefferson in early May 1903. Meanwhile Howells took advantage of Annie's visit in Jefferson, leaving New York for a trip to Ohio on about 30 November and returning on 10 December. See Howells to Aurelia Howells, 19 October, 23 November, 14 December, 21 December 1902; 3 May and 28 June 1903; also Howells to C. E. Norton, 10 December 1902 (all at MH).

3. This was an early title for what eventually became *The Son of Royal Langbrith*, which first appeared in the *North American Review*, January–August 1904, and was published in book form the same year. A few weeks later Howells considered yet another alternative. See Howells to Annie Fields, 23 February 1903.

4. Neither the portrait nor the painter has been identified.

5. The Howells family cat, now in Aurelia's keeping. See Howells to Aurelia, 22 November 1903.

9 FEBRUARY 1903, NEW YORK, TO SAMUEL L. CLEMENS

48 West 59th st.,
Feb'y 9, 1903.

Dear Clemens:

I will send your note to Kester, who is not in town, I believe, and whom I have not seen for some time.[1] Enclosed is a note from a man who wants you to take up the atrocity defended in the U. S. Senate, which was committed by a U. S. officer.[2] I wish to heaven you would. You can get the whole story in the Congressional Record. You could do humanity such service as no one else could, and yourself honor.

Yours ever
W. D. Howells.

1. Paul Kester and Howells had planned to collaborate on a dramatization of *Tom Sawyer*, but Howells withdrew from the project, leaving Kester to complete it on his own. The note was probably about Kester's seeking permission from Clemens to produce the play. See *Twain-Howells*, p. 762.

2. Matthew K. Sniffen, who worked for the *City and State*, a Philadelphia weekly, was trying to enlist the help of Howells and Clemens in exposing two atrocities committed by U.S. Army officers in the Philippines. See *Twain-Howells*, pp. 762–63.

10 FEBRUARY 1903, NEW YORK, TO HAMILTON W. MABIE

48 West 59th st.,
Feb'y 10th, 1903.

Dear Sir:

I find myself unable longer to fulfill the duties of the presidency of the Institute of Arts and Letters, owing to my necessarily frequent absences from its meetings, and to my increasing sense of my inadequacy to the demands which it makes upon me in matters which I am peculiarly unqualified to deal with.[1]

In placing my resignation in your hands I beg you to express to the gentlemen of the Institute my grateful sense of the honor they have done me in repeatedly choosing me to the office which I must now relinquish.

Yours very truly,
W. D. Howells.

Hamilton W. Mabie, Esq.,
Secretary.

1. Howells apparently felt unqualified to deal with the solicitation of endowment funds for the National Institute of Arts and Letters. He opposed the idea in principle, placing himself in an adversary position to Mabie, who was secretary of the Institute. As early as October 1902, Howells had considered resigning the presidency rather than engaging in a prolonged controversy over this issue. See Howells to Mabie, 9 October 1902. However, he appears to have been persuaded to remain in the post for another year, as is suggested by his signing himself as president in a subsequent letter to Mabie (11 March 1903 [NNAL]); by Howells' letter to R. U. Johnson, 14 October 1903 (NRU), in which he asks, "Do you know if anything has been done as to my resignation of the presidency?"; and by his letter to R. U. Johnson, 24 October 1903 (NNAL), stating his intention to preside at the Institute meeting of 30 November "with the understanding that there shall be no question of my re-election in January." Edmund C. Stedman succeeded Howells as president in February 1904. See Howells to Stedman, 27 December 1904, n. 1.

12 FEBRUARY 1903, NEW YORK, TO SAMUEL L. CLEMENS

48 West 59th st.,
Feb. 12, 1903.

My dear Clemens:

I know you are harassed by a great many things, and I hate to add to your worries, but I must really complain to you of the behavior of your man Sam.[1] I called last night at your place with our old friend Stoddard,[2] and found that to reach the house, I had to climb a plowed field, at the top of which Sam was planting potatoes. A number of people were waiting at the bottom of the field, and hesitating whether to go up, but I explained that we were old acquaintances, and we were going to see you at once. We pushed on, and when we came in easy hail of Sam, he called very rudely to us, and asked us what we wanted. I said we wanted to see you, and he said, "Well, you can't do it," and no persuasion that I could use had the least effect with him. He said that nobody could see you, and when I gave him my card, and promised him that he would not have a pleasant time with you, when you found out whom he had turned away, he sneered and said he would not give you the card. To avoid mortifying inquiries from the people we had left at the foot of the hill, we came down another way, and though I momently expected a recall from your house, none followed us, and we made our way home the best we could. This happened, as nearly as I can make out, at about three o'clock in the morning. I have only too much reason to believe that Sam really withheld my card, and I wish you would ask him for it, and make him account in some way for our extraordinary treatment. I cannot remember that Stoddard said anything, but I felt he was as much annoyed as myself.[3]

Yours ever,
W. D. Howells.

1. In the dream episode Howells goes on to recount, Sam is most likely a fantasy character rather than an actual person.

2. Charles W. Stoddard, whom Howells and Clemens were assisting in some financial matters at this time. See Howells to Clemens, 16 November 1902.

3. Clemens, being thoroughly amused by Howells' deadpan narration, noted on the envelope: "Bet Howells is drunk *yet*." Rising to the humorous challenge in his reply of 13 February (MH), he described his waking up at night and asking Sam about voices he had heard. Sam then describes the visitor as a stranger, "a stumpy little gray man with furtive ways & an evil face.... [who] called me a quadrilateral astronomical incandescent son of a bitch." "Oh, that was Howells," is Clemens' reply. For the rest of the fun, see *Twain-Howells*, pp. 764–66.

23 FEBRUARY 1903, NEW YORK, TO ANNIE A. FIELDS

48 West 59th st.,
February 23, 1903.

My dear Mrs. Fields:

I have been a long time without news from you, but today I read in the Boston Globe (to which Mrs. Howells is an impassioned subscriber) that you are very, very much better.[1] I hope it is true, and that I may have a line from you in confirmation. You cannot think how precious to my wife and me those pencilled pages of yours were.—So far the winter has used us fairly well, though Elinor always begins to droop when she is shut up in our hot rooms after the open-air life of the summer. I get her out into the Park in all walkable weather, and when she is not up to walking, we take the shabbiest imaginable old victoria, and drive round the whole length of the place with our unknown friends the millionaires. Our driver, Mr. Broderick, takes a fond interest in us, and puts both his hands on my shoulders when I come to ask for a drive, "Yessir, yessir, I will *that*; I'll be right there." We are known to the other drivers as his peculiar property, and they will consent to act as his under-studies only when he is away. I suspect he is the worst sort of Tammany man, but I don't know that he is personally any the worse for that. He knows all the policemen, foot and horse, and we feel that they include us when they answer his salutation with a quiet "How are you, Johnny."—Our own Johnny, by the way, has gone South with Pilla, where she is to pass the rest of the winter.[2] She is to be with a young Mrs. Aldis of Chicago, who is much her friend, and who has to get away from the cruel lake winds.[3] The two children leave us rather lonely, but we make out as we can by reading Thomas Hardy's novels aloud at night—good long portions. Just now we are drawing near what we forbode the sad end of Two on a Tower—the only one I had not read before. It is a farce with the grief of a tragedy in it.—I am writing a novel of my own, and feeling so much more interest in it than any reader will ever take that it is quite ridiculous. It is a sort of shame to be yarning away at my age, but I might be doing worse things. I have got a good name for it from the old Tuscan proverb, "*Iddio non paga sabato*"; "God does not pay Saturdays."[4]

I imagine you taking this long letter in installments, but our love is not divisible, and it is all yours, to hold as well as to have. With the best hopes and wishes from Elinor as well as myself,

Yours faithfully
W. D. Howells.

1. The Boston *Globe* for 22 February carried a brief item in regard to Mrs. Fields's recent recovery from serious illness, a stroke resulting in paralysis.

2. Mildred Howells was in Camden, South Carolina, where her brother stayed with her for a while, apparently to be supportive during the difficult period of adjustment to her broken engagement, to which Howells refers in his letter to Achille Fréchette, 3 March 1903 (MH): "John has returned from South Carolina where he has left Pilla. I am sorry to say Elinor is very much broken down. She takes every thing intensely, and Pilla's engagement, and then its rupture, have told upon her."

3. Mrs. Aldis has not been identified.

4. Howells eventually rejected this title and named the novel *The Son of Royal Langbrith*. See Howells to Aurelia Howells, 28 January 1903; *The Son of Royal Langbrith*, HE, pp. xii–xv; and Howells to Norton, 10 July 1881, n. 4.

11 MARCH 1903, NEW YORK, TO HAMLIN GARLAND

48 West 59th st.,
March 11, 1903.

My dear Garland:

Here I have been biting Henry James in silence for not saying a word of my paper about him,[1] and I have been indulging the same vicious reticence in regard to your paper about me![2] Let me tell you that if it had not been the kindest sort of criticism, I should still have thought it the ablest. I felt that you had meant me for an illustration, and that you were proving a thesis rather than proving me, as was best. It was greatly improved from the first draught, and as it stands I believe it stands unassailable. I thank you for the friendship of it with all my heart.

I will appoint the committee.[3]

Yours ever
W. D. Howells.

1. Howells' eloquent defense of James's fiction, "Mr. Henry James's Later Work," had appeared in the *North American Review*, January 1903. The long overdue response finally came in James's letter of 12 June 1903 (MH), which reads in part: "... I have never decently 'thanked' you at all for your beautiful concomitant *étude* in January, keen as was the pleasure, sugared the cup, lucent the syrup, that you administered.... You contributed (and the publication of the Ambassadors in the Review has also contributed) to break the queer gruesome (as it seems to me) spell that had long weighed upon the small faculty of getting at all into the *light*—the light of a garish Publicity—that nature had endowed me withal. This has been excellent for me, and has made me fairly believe that even if I don't get so far, so late in the day, as still ever to *bask* a little, I may yet not have to pursue the rest of my mortal course all on the mere shady side of the street."

2. Garland's essay, "Sanity in Fiction," had just come out in the *North American Review*, March 1903.

3. The Auxiliary Committee of the Executive Council of the National Institute of Arts and Letters had recently been established, probably to deal with the crisis of Howells' proffered resignation from the presidency. Garland was one of five appointees listed in Howells' letter to H. W. Mabie, 11 March 1903 (NNAL).

6 APRIL 1903, NEW YORK, TO CHARLES E. NORTON

48 West 59th st.,
April 6, 1903.

My dear Norton:

I am sorry to know that you have been often, but I hope not very much, out of health since I saw you last.[1] Somehow that little visit remains peculiarly precious in my mind, and in spite of the facts, I still have the sense of your continuing to be very well. Once I invented a formula for my brother, or rather tried to console him for some ailment of his later years by saying that when we were young we got well, but now we got better; and I trust this greater triumph is yours. I myself keep on as well as the age, if not my own, will let me; I am not particularly pride of it yet, but I daresay it will look not unhandsome in history. The other night I met at dinner that fine old John Burroughs whom I congratulated on going out to Yellowstone to hold bears for the President to kill;[2] but he seemed to think it not an altogether enviable office, but to have his latent misgivings. I had not then seen a picture of King Edward standing gun in hand and looking down at the long double line of pheasants he had shot; otherwise I could have told Burroughs that bears were nobler game, and our prince was by so much in advance of the English boy.—The dinner was at Carnegie's,[3] where he and his amiable wife entertained a company of New York literati in honor of a "powerful dull" Englishman, Sidney Lee,[4] whom doubtless you will be seeing and dining in your turn. I sat on Carnegie's left, and had moments of confidence with him in which I could tell him of my pleasure in his offer to buy off a war by paying the debts of a nation.[5] He is a dreamer and in his way a poet, and he seemed to like my notion that this was a stroke of poetry. I found both him and his wife simple-hearted and quite unspoiled. He is quite subject to her, as a husband should be, and suffered being bid do this and that, as her superior social instinct required.—The house is subjectively rather than objectively rich, and outside is a triumph of ugliness, though within it is very home-like. The young Scotch painter[6] who has been living there while he painted Mrs. Carnegie and her daughter whispered me that he did not know what to do with his late habits, for everyone else in that house was abed by half-past ten.—You know that the house is embowered in a ready-made grove of forest trees transplanted full grown to the corner of Fifth Avenue and 90th street, and there is a curious air of establishment in it all. After dinner we had speaking—from Mark Twain, Carl Schurz, Burroughs and others, and upon the whole it was the pleasantest affair I have been at in New York.—I wonder if you have Giusti's Proverbii Toscani?[7] I am writing a grimmish story, which I want to call by a proverb which I seem to remember out of that pleasant book. It is, *Iddio non paga sabato*, which I propose Englishing into *God does not pay Saturdays*.[8]—Does it afflict you to find your books wearing out? I mean literally. Just now I went to my old Barretti[9] to see whether Sabato was spelt with one *b* or two, and it almost came apart in my hand. It was as if I had found an old friend dying. The mortality of all inanimate things is terrible to me, but that of books most of all, and my library is turning into a cemetary.

I am amused when I meet Carl Schurz. We agree entirely, and he comes forward with both hands out and a glad "Ah!" Then we have nothing to say.—The man I have most to say with is Mark Twain, but we seldom meet, for he lives up the river where he can see the steamboats passing, and he is kept closely at home by what now seems the hopeless case of his wife.[10] It has changed the poor old fellow, but when he can break away, almost the best talk in the world is left in him.

I wonder if you are looking at James's *Ambassadors?* It is very good work. But it must appear to you very improbable to find fiction in the North American.[11] Though where will not you find fiction now a days!

Yours affectionately,
W. D. Howells.

1. Howells' last visit with Norton had probably taken place more than four months earlier. See Howells to Norton, 25 November 1902, n. 1.

2. John Burroughs (1837–1921), the noted naturalist, poet, and essayist, was about to embark on a much publicized trip to Yellowstone Park with Theodore Roosevelt. Contrary to Howells' humorous provocation, which played on the president's reputation as a big game hunter, Roosevelt deferred to Burroughs' preference for keen observation. See *Theodore Roosevelt: An Autobiography* (New York: Macmillan, 1916), pp. 331–32.

3. Howells described the dinner in a letter to Aurelia Howells, 29 March 1903 (MH): "Last night I dined with a large literary lot at Andrew Carnegie's, in his great new palace on Fifth Avenue. It cost heaps of money, but is very simple and livable, and simplicity is the note of himself and his most amiable wife, who was, you know, a Pittsburg school teacher. I must say that I liked them both extremely; and we had a wonderful dinner, with much speaking afterwards, in which I took part, to my surprise. About twenty-five sat down, all men except Mrs. Carnegie, who stayed through the smoking for the sake of the speaking, and seemed to like both. When we rose, he showed us about the lower floor of the house, which occupies half a block, and has a grove of trees round it which were transplanted full grown. [¶] It may interest you to know that among the guests were Mark Twain, Stedman, Gilder, Garland, Mabie, John Burroughs, Thompson Seton, and divers professors and editors. It was a jolly time, but a jolly time does not add to the gaiety of the next day, especially if you walk two miles home after midnight, and I am rather sore and limp."

4. Sir Sidney Lee (1859–1926), British man of letters, was best known for his several works on Shakespeare.

5. Germany, backed by England and Italy, had set up a blockade of Venezuela in 1902 when that country had refused to settle some $40 million worth of claims. With open hostilities imminent, Carnegie offered to pay the Venezuelan debt. Roosevelt, however, was successful in persuading Germany to place the dispute before the Permanent Court of Arbitration at The Hague, where it was resolved peacefully.

6. Not identified.

7. Giuseppe Giusti, *Raccolta di Proverbi Toscani*, had been issued in a new and enlarged edition in 1873. The title, in English, appears among a list of titles in Howells' 1883 Siena notebook (MH).

8. The "grimmish story" eventually was entitled *The Son of Royal Langbrith*. See Howells to A. A. Fields, 23 February 1903, n. 4.

9. Giuseppe Marco Antonio Baretti, *Dizionario delle lingue italiana ed inglese*, first published in 1750, appeared in its ninth edition, London, 1839.

10. In 1901 Clemens, now fully recovered from his earlier financial setbacks, had rented a mansion in Riverdale-on-the-Hudson. For Olivia Clemens' illness, see Howells to Clemens, 20 October 1902, n. 1.

11. *The Ambassadors* was serialized in the *North American Review*, January–December 1903.

23 APRIL 1903, NEW YORK, TO KATHERINE S. GODKIN

48 West 59th st.,
April 23, 1903.

My dear Mrs. Godkin:[1]

I thank you for the book which you have so kindly sent me.[2] Mr Godkin gave it me when it came out, and I had the pleasure of telling him how much it interested me, and how much I valued it. I shall peculiarly prize this copy because of the truthfully refined and delicate likeness of him. It brings him very livingly before me, not merely as I knew him last, but as I knew him first, now many, many years ago. I do not know if you are aware how constantly we were associated after my return from Italy in 1865, when for several months we wrote together in the same room of the "Nation" office. We both loved laughing, and we were never so immersed in our work but we could turn from it for a joyful shout over something in the day's news that amused one or other of us. He remains to me part of a very happy time in my life, which renewed itself whenever we met. I felt the warmth, the human glow of his manly nature, and I need not say that I appreciated the honest greatness of his mind. If I did not think with him in all things, I did think with him in essentials, and however we differed I am glad now to remember that we never disagreed.[3]

When I heard of his death,[4] I would have written if I had known where to reach you with a letter. But I could only have told you how dearly I held him my friend, for it would have been idle to praise the worth which no one could understand like you. His loss was more mine than I could express without the effect of the exaggeration he would have found offensive.

Yours sincerely
W. D. Howells.

P. S. That inscription is most monumentally fine. I have been wondering who wrote it.

1. Katherine Sands Godkin (d. 1907), the wife of E. L. Godkin.
2. In 1903 a second impression of E. L. Godkin's *Unforeseen Tendencies of Democracy* was published; it was most likely this book that Mrs. Godkin sent Howells. For Howells' reaction to the original edition, see Howells to Godkin, 24 April 1898.
3. For Howells' reminiscence and evaluation of Godkin, see "A Great New York Journalist," *North American Review*, 3 May 1907, and *Literary Friends and Acquaintance*, HE, p. 92.
4. Godkin died on 21 May 1902.

26 APRIL 1903, NEW YORK, TO SAMUEL L. CLEMENS

48 West 59th st.
Sunday, 26th April.

Yesterday afternoon I got a letter, square, blue, English-stamped, and addressed in a hand which I took to be that of Eweretta Lawrence, a Canadian girl who has got one of my farces on the London stage.[1] I said to myself, "Hello! Here's more money from Eweretta," and then I pulled the letter open without noticing that it was directed to "H. Howells, 4 West 58th st." I found it a love-letter, kept myself from reading it, and sent it to the man it belonged to.

Within an hour the postman brought me a registered letter, blue, square, English-stamped, from Eweretta Lawrence, enclosing £ 22 on account of the farce.[2]—How are you, anyway?—You old _____ scratch-gravel.

1. *The Garroters* had first appeared in *Harper's Monthly*, December 1885. According to Mildred Howells, it "was acted under the title of *A Dangerous Ruffian* at the Avenue Theatre [London] in 1895" (*Life in Letters*, II, 173). Favorably reviewed by George Bernard Shaw in *Saturday Review*, 7 December 1895, the play seems to have had a longer stage life than most of Howells' dramatic works. Eweretta (or Emeretta, as Mildred Howells reads her name) Lawrence has not been identified. See also W. J. Meserve, *Complete Plays of W. D. Howells* (New York: New York University Press, 1960), pp. 338–39.
2. Clemens had been collecting instances of mental telepathy, and he agreed with Howells that the coincidental arrival of the wayward love letter and the royalty check were worth considering. "B'gosh, I suppose it is some more mental telegraphy," he replied in his letter of 29 April 1903 (MH; *Twain-Howells*, p. 768).

26 April 1903, New York, to Charles E. Norton

48 West 59th st.,
April 26, 1903.

My dear Norton:

By all means put my letters in the Harvard library with the others: since Lowell thought them worth keeping, they may as well cumber those archives. If there is nothing ill-natured towards my fellow mortals, I shall not care for anything disgraceful, in them. I can fancy my poor ghost flittering about the alcoves and taking a diaphonous, thin pride in the serious student's acceptance of them as proof that Lowell cared for me, for I did care very much for him. I used to falter at his gate, and walk up the path to his door with the same anxious palpitations I felt when I dared to call upon the girl I was first in love with; it was a real passion. But I do not wish to see the letters.

It was kind of you to include James's early letters to yourself among those Miss Grace is sending me,[1] and I wont pretend I have read them with less interest because of certain allusions to me in them. In a way I think their criticism very just; I have often thought my intellectual raiment was more than my intellectual body, and that I might finally be convicted, not of having nothing *on*, but that worse nakedness of having nothing *in*. He speaks of me with my style, and such mean application as I was making of it, as seeming to him like a poor man with a diamond which he does not know what to do with;[2] and mostly I suppose I *have* cut rather inferior window glass with it. But I am not sorry for having wrought in common, crude material so much; that is the right American stuff;[3] and perhaps hereafter, when my din is done, if any one is curious to know what that noise was it will be found to have proceeded from a small insect which was scraping about on the surface of our life and trying to get into its meaning for the sake of the other insects larger or smaller. That is, such has been my unconscious work; consciously, I was always, as I still am, trying to fashion a piece of literature out of the life next at hand.

The spring has come here, too, but more grudgingly than it led us to expect in March, and the Park is filling up with the young foliage as if a mist were rolling into it from some great sea of summer. I went down to Kittery Point a little while ago,[4] to plant trees in my cottage grounds, but the nurseryman failed me, and I could only see a few holes dug, instead of setting out the things with my own hand. I was ridiculously disappointed, and I am still grieving over my loss. I had hoped to get a day to run out and see you in Cambridge, in my passages through Boston, but that was not to be either, and I must count on the pleasure as something postponed not too indefinitely.

I have been reading Mrs. Carlyle's letters,[5] mostly unimportant and insignificant, but giving enough of her bright, keen, narrow character to be rather terrible. Why should the poor soul have been so contemptuous of other people? Of course I account for no end of mere whimsicality.

Yours affectionately,
W. D. Howells.

1. It is unclear why Norton and his sister, Grace Norton, sent Howells letters from Henry James at this time, unless Howells, who had recently published his essay "Mr. Henry James's Later Work" (see Howells to Garland, 11 March 1903, n. 1), was contemplating another piece about James. There is no further evidence, however, that he did, except for the fragmentary essay, "The American James," (*Life in Letters*, II, 397–99) on which Howells was working in 1920, just before he died.

2. The comments about Howells' style appear in a letter from James to C. E. Norton, 9 August 1871 (MH; *James Letters*, I, 259–63): "Howells is now monarch absolute of the *Atlantic*, to the increase of his profit and comfort. His talent grows constantly in fineness, but hardly, I think, in range of application. I remember your saying some time ago that in a couple of years when he had read Sainte-Beuve etc. he would come to his best. But the trouble is he never will read Sainte-Beuve, nor care to. He has little intellectual curiosity; so here he stands with his admirable organ of style, like a poor man holding a diamond and wondering how he can use it. It's rather sad, I think, to see Americans of the younger sort so unconscious and unambitious of the commission to do the *best*" (p. 262).

3. Howells is here referring to a letter from James to Grace Norton, 27 November 1871 (MH; *James Letters*, I, 263–66), containing a passage in which James responds to some evidently critical comments by Grace Norton about *Their Wedding Journey*, which was then being serialized. "Poor Howells is certainly difficult to defend," James wrote, "if one takes a stand-point the least bit exalted; make any serious demands and it's all up with him. He presents, I confess, to my mind, a somewhat melancholy spectacle—in that his charming style and refined intentions are so poorly and meagerly served by our American atmosphere. There is no more inspiration in an American journey than *that*! Thro' thick and thin I continue however to enjoy him—or rather thro' thinner and thinner. There is a little divine spark of fancy which never quite goes out. He has passed into the stage which I suppose is the eventual fate of all secondary and tertiary talents—worked off his less slender Primitive, found a place and a routine and an income, and now is destined to fade slowly and softly away in self-repetition and reconcilement to the common-place. But he will always be a *writer*—small but genuine. There are not so many after all now going in English—to say nothing of American" (p. 264).

4. Howells left New York for Kittery Point on 13 April and returned on 16 April.

5. *New Letters and Memorials of Jane Welsh Carlyle*, ed. Alexander Carlyle (1903), which was reviewed by Howells in "Editor's Easy Chair," *Harper's Monthly*, July 1903.

1 MAY 1903, NEW YORK, TO SAMUEL L. CLEMENS

48 West 59th st.,
May 1, 1903

My dear Clemens:

Though it isn't quite down to your level, I don't wonder you like my literature—it's nearly all about you. But you'd better take a brace, and try to get up as high as "Putnam Place."[1] Now you're sick, I've a great mind to have it out with you about Jane Austen. If you say much more I'll come out and read "Pride and Prejudice" to you.[2]

Say, that was a mighty good thing of yours on the age of consent.[3] Why is civilization such a carrion of falsehood?—That poor girl and her murdered baby; it made sick to read about her; but one is so limp and helpless in the presence of the injustice which underlies society; and I am getting so old. I'm glad you're still young.—Mrs. Howells was born on the 1st of May, well, some years ago, and I called out to her today, when I happened to remember it, "Happy birthday!" and she called back, "All right; *and don't you say another word about it.*"

Yours ever
W. D. H.

1. In a review entitled "A Triad of Admirable Books," *Harper's Weekly*, 2 May 1903, Howells praised G. L. Collins' novel, *Putnam Place*. The opening sally of Howells' letter is in response to Clemens' acknowledgment of the review in his letter of 29 April (MH): "Putnam Place did not much interest me; so I knew it was high literature. I have never been able to get up high enough to be at home with high literature. But I immensely like your literature, Howells." See *Twain-Howells*, p. 769.

2. For Clemens' aversion to the novels of Jane Austen, see *Twain-Howells*, p. 770.

3. Clemens' article, "Why Not Abolish It?" *Harper's Weekly*, 2 May 1903, protested the sentencing of Rose Quinn to life imprisonment for drowning her illegitimate child. She had been convicted because she had reached the age of consent, while her seducer was not charged with any crime. See *Twain-Howells*, p. 770.

15 JUNE 1903, KITTERY POINT, TO FREDERICK A. DUNEKA

Kittery Point, June 15, 1903.

Dear Mr. Duneka:[1]

My article was, and was meant to be, a severe criticism of Mr. Osborn's theory of the public prosecutor's relation to accused men, and his impassioned expressions of it before juries.[2] The article was based upon reports in the daily papers which I had never seen contradicted, and it did not accuse him of corruption and malevolence, but treated him as an extreme type of what a prosecutor ought not to be under law which presumes a man innocent till he has been proved guilty.[3] It was in this sense that he was pronounced unfit, as any other public servant who had exceeded his function might be, and as public servants often are, with no intent to injure him privately. He was not the first nor the sole offender in that sort, but his conspicuous position made him influential for error, and we had the right, tantamount to a duty, in our place, to censure him. If we had not, then all public functionaries must be immune of criticism from the public press, which would be no longer a free press.

Mr. Jerome indicated the gravity of Mr. Osborne's mistaken theory and practice when he said that it was the affair of the prosecution to find out the facts, as much those that told for the accused as those that told against him.[4] I did not go further than this, though I think we might well do so, and declare that the interests of the accused should be the peculiar care of the state, which, through the prosecution, should anxiously present every aspect of the case showing in his favor. The reasonable doubt should weigh as much with the prosecutor as with the jury. At the very best the case of an accused man is terrible. He is arrested, not because he is believed guilty, but because he has fallen under suspicion of guilt, and is thrown into prison, to the ruin of his business, the misery of his family, and the defamation of his character. The innocent dependants on his life and labor are punished too, for the state takes his life, or takes his wages, and makes them no return.[5] If he is acquitted, he is set free, after months or years of imprisonment, and the state makes him no compensation for his suffering in behalf of the community. The situation is really atrocious, and it is the very sacred duty of the ministers of the law, to repair to the utmost its injustice by their solicitude for his interests at every step of the prosecution. This is not only the ideal of the law which now helplessly commits him to them, but is the common sense of the case. If there is any such thing as fairness, as decency, as justice in the courts, their whole apparatus should be applied to ascertaining the truth with the least possible molestation to a man presumably innocent. This was the position which I wish to take in my article, and I believe that it is one which the moral sense, and upon the whole, the legal sense of the people will bear us out in.

I am glad to note in your letter that you are not annoyed by Mr. Osborne's suit for I need not tell you how deeply I should regret having brought any trouble upon you.[6] Of course there was no personal feeling in my article, for I never saw Mr. Osborne. I was actuated solely by indignation at what I had read of his conduct in the different cases he had managed;[7] and I think his management of the second Molinaux trial attested an awakening sense of his excesses in the first.

Of course, if I am to be brought publicly into the matter in any way, you will give me due notice.

Yours sincerely,
W. D. Howells.

1. Frederick A. Duneka (d. 1919), an editor at Harper & Brothers, whose relation to Howells is suggested by the address Howells used in a letter of 22 August 1918 (RPB): "You dear old enemy." He left the editorship of the New York *World* to become secretary of Harper & Brothers when George Harvey took over the management of the firm in 1900. Duneka was active both in the book publishing program of the firm and on the editorial staff of *Harper's Monthly*. In 1915 he became vice-president of Harper & Brothers.

2. The unsigned article, "The Molineux Case," appeared in *Harper's Weekly*, 8 November 1902. James W. Osborne (1859–1919) was then assistant district attorney for New York City. Noted for his aggressive courtroom manner, he had obtained convictions in several celebrated criminal cases. His theory of the public prosecutor's relation to the accused combined the role of impartial public officer with that of a partisan advocate. See *The Molineux Case*, ed. Samuel Klaus (New York: Alfred A. Knopf, 1929), p. 26. Osborne had been widely criticized for his intimidating conduct in the much publicized murder trial of Roland B. Molineux (1866–1917), a New York chemist. In February 1900 Molineux had been convicted of murder in the first degree and sentenced to death for allegedly poisoning Katherine J. Adams on 28 December 1898. In October 1901 Molineux's conviction had been set aside by the Court of Appeals, and on 11 November 1902 he was acquitted after a second trial in which Osborne also acted as chief prosecutor. Molineux, who spent twenty months at Sing Sing, wrote a play about his prison experience, *The Man Inside* (1913). Following its production by David Belasco, Molineux suffered a nervous breakdown and was committed to the Kings Point State Hospital for the Insane, where he died three years later.

3. Implicitly taking issue with Osborne's advocacy theory without ever mentioning the attorney by name, Howells stated in the article that anyone "not legally proven guilty must be regarded as innocent in the eye of the law," and that all members of society are thus "necessarily concerned . . . in the methods by which prosecutors seek to obtain an adjudication of guilt." In a clear condemnation of the prosecutor's zealous tactics, Howells cited the Court of Appeals' decision to overturn Molineux's conviction as a conclusive indication that the "methods by which Mr. Roland Burnham Molineux was found guilty . . . were not proper."

4. William T. Jerome (1859–1934) was elected district attorney of New York county in 1901. In that capacity he was present at the second Molineux trial although Osborne, as his assistant, actively conducted the prosecution. The occasion of Jerome's remarks, presumably made after Molineux's acquittal, is not known.

5. The treatment of convicts and the deprivation of their families were ongoing concerns for Howells. See Howells to Whitlock, 6 April 1907.

6. Duneka's letter to Howells is lost. The exact charges contained in Osborne's suit, probably brought against Harper & Brothers as a result of Howells' unsigned article, are not known. Osborne resigned his office on 1 April 1903, perhaps in part as a result of the adverse publicity associated with his handling of the Molineux case. It is possible that, after losing the retrial, he was particularly sensitive to Howells' criticism and thus sought to treat it as potentially libelous. There are no extant records to indicate whether the suit went to trial or was settled out of court.

7. In one instance, during the trial of a detective, Osborne had struck one of the witnesses.

26 July 1903, Kittery Point, to Hamlin Garland

Kittery Point, July 26, 1903.

My dear Garland:

My wife and I were glad to get your glad tidings,[1] and she wishes her love to Mrs. Garland. She says she can ask nothing better than that the daughter shall be as beautiful as the mother.

By this time I hope all that was anxious in the event has been forgotten, and that you are happy in the supreme joy of earth. Children alone render us a reason for being, and they make it richly worth while. I have been passionately happy in mine; and if I could have kept them from sorrow, I should count the sorrow from them all gain.

Your blessing will brighten day by day, and more and more you will feel the wonder of it. To watch the life grow that has been given into your charge, there is no interest like it.

I thank you for writing me on the occasion, and I send my best regards to your wife.

I have been exceptionally busy this summer, and have finished a longish novel: the story of evil so long concealed that it becomes best, in the consciousness of those who have suffered most from it, that it should never be known. I have thought of The "Law of Limitation" as a name for it; also, "Reconciliation."[2]

The summer has been wet and cold, though now it is drying its tears.

Yours affectionately
W. D. Howells.

1. The birth of Mary Isabel Garland at the Garland homestead in West Salem, Wisconsin. In 1926 she married Hardesty Johnson, an opera singer, and they moved to Los Angeles in 1929. See Jean Holloway, *Hamlin Garland: A Biography* (1960; reprint ed., Freeport, N.Y.: Books for Libraries, 1971), passim.

2. For the many alternative titles Howells considered for his latest novel, see *The Son of Royal Langbrith*, HE, pp. xiii–xv.

Kittery Point, Aug. 9, 1903.

Dear Aurelia:

Sunday has come round again with the usual dearth of news, and I scarcely know what to write, except that I have had a letter from our cousin Susan Hooper, in England, who sold me my old clock, telling me somewhat about it.[1] George Howells, who made it was her great-great-uncle and father's great-uncle, and he lived near the Hay, where father was born; who else or what else he was, she hopes to find out from her elder brother in Tasmania, but that will take time. She says that when she was a little girl, her grandmother set her tasks of embroidery, with instructions to take a stitch every time this old clock ticked.—I have just wound it up as I do every Sunday morning, but it says nothing of little Susan Hooper.

John talks of coming down later in the month. Nearly all the work in his office has been stopped by the great carpenters' strike in New York, and he has an enforced leisure. He is always glad to spend his leisure with us here, for he is very fond of the place.

I do not know how we shall be off for room, when Annie and Achille go to Marblehead, but we should like them to come to us for three days, on the way to or from. If we are crowded, I can put them up as my guests at the hotel next door, and they can meal with us as often as they like. It is what Elinor's sister Joanna did last summer, and it worked very pleasantly. Elinor joins me in this invitation. I am sorry to hear of Achille's working so hard,[2] but I hope the stress will soon be over. With love to all,

Your affectionate brother,
Will.

Please send me your address again.

1. Mildred Howells described the clock as "a tall, brown lacquer one with 'George Howells' on its face, and the word 'Dearfold' below, which was probably the name of his house." See *Life in Letters*, II, 176.
2. At this time Aurelia and her brother Henry were still visiting the Fréchettes in Ottawa. See Howells to Aurelia Howells, 28 January 1903, n. 2.

15 August 1903, Kittery Point, to Charles E. Norton

Kittery Point, Aug. 15, 1903.

My dear Norton:

I have heard that this year's dinner is to be the last of these occasions at Ashfield[1] which have so much made for righteousness during the last twenty years, and I wish to express my part of a general sense of their usefulness. You have known how to speak the truth and have it spoken in the ears of a generation not so deaf as it would like to be, and have helped keep the popular conscience alive in times when it seemed past hope. The word of Ashfield has gone far, but better still it has gone deep, and has uttered the heart, otherwise silent, of those who believed the Spanish War wrong, and the Philippine oppression doubly wrong; and I hope that it will not fail now to confess the national shame for the hideous popular massacres with which we have crowned the cruelty and folly of our dealings with a people we enslaved and then liberated to duties and responsibilities too great for them to bear.

—I have long meant to tell you of the sad, high pleasure I had in reading that little book about Lowell and Curtis which you gave me.[2] Your study of Curtis especially interested me, not only because it was so wise and true, but because as I read, I seemed to hear your voice speaking.

Yours affectionately,
W. D. Howells.

P. S. I had such a charming visit of a day with Miss Grace[3]—after the first anomaly of not being at Shady Hill accounted for itself. She read James's letters to me, and we talked and drove, and then talked again. The old Cambridge returned with all its bright ghosts at the first breath after passing Dana street. The midsummer air, which our early summer constancy made the most characteristic forever, was hushed and tense with the past; and I realized once more what a grand passion the place used to be with me. I doubt if any one born to it could have loved it as I did.[4]

1. The wellknown Ashfield Academy dinner, to which Norton invited many prominent cultural figures, had been an annual event since 1879, but Norton, now 75 years old, was no longer able to carry out the responsibility of planning and conducting the event. See Howells to W. C. Howells, 22 August 1880, n. 1, and *Letters of Charles Eliot Norton*, ed. S. Norton and M. A. De Wolfe Howe (Boston: Houghton Mifflin, 1913), II, 89–90, 455–57. In a letter to Howells, 11 August 1903 (MH), Sarah Orne Jewett proposed that "some sign of our thanks [be sent] to those who have

loved their country well enough to speak the truth—welcome or unwelcome" over the years at the Academy dinners. She thought that especially a group of women, "Mrs. Howe and Mrs. Agassiz and Mrs. Fields and Mrs. Warner & Alice Longfellow . . . would like to have their names stand for many others . . . ." Howells, however, excused himself from helping to organize such an undertaking. He wrote to Jewett on 13 August (MH): "my soul and body, though interested in the same objects, are like the two unions of striking carpenters, and wont work together. I have done such a lot of futile writing this summer that I cannot bear the thought of anything wise or worthy . . . ."

2. Norton's *Memorials of Two Friends, James Russell Lowell, 1819–1891, George William Curtis, 1824–1892* (1902).

3. Two weeks earlier, on 31 July, Howells had gone down to Cambridge and "spent the night at the house of our old friend Grace Norton, who has been asking me all summer. . . . [¶] I went into our old house on Concord Avenue, and it was all so unchanged that it seemed as if I had not left it. Then I visited the place where Winny was keeping our dead home for us." See Howells to Aurelia Howells, 2 August 1903 (MH).

4. See Howells to Norton, 26 April 1903, n. 1. Howells' description of the old Cambridge offered an occasion for Norton, in his letter to Howells of 29 August 1903 (MH), to comment on James's later fiction: "I am fond of Harry James & recognize his admirable and exceptional gifts, but I cannot read his late books without repulsion & wonder. If these people are his 'Better Sort' what can the Worst Sort be? How can he spend his days & himself on such an unredeemed lot, whom he, no less than you or I, would shrink from, at least would not wish to associate intimately with in real life."

5 SEPTEMBER 1903, KITTERY POINT, TO BRANDER MATTHEWS

Kittery Point, Sept. 5, 1903.

My dear Matthews:

That N. A. Review paper[1] of yours is mighty good, and has one sentence in it of the most courageous insight and outspeech, namely, "He was a great artist, with the great artist's *sensual enjoyment in the dextrous exercise of his technical skill.*" Bravo!

Yours ever
W. D. Howells.

1. "How Shakespeare Learnt His Trade," *North American Review*, September 1903.

9 SEPTEMBER 1903, KITTERY POINT, TO DAVID A. MUNRO

Kittery Point, Sept. 9, 1903.

Dear Mr. Munro:

I return the Ibsen proof.[1] If you wish to use it before he dies, or in view of his approaching death, I can readily change a few phrases so as to make it fit the facts; otherwise it can remain as it is.

I much prefer the shorter installments 8 in number to the 6 long ones of the story.[2] I enclose my string of titles,[3] the varying propriety of which you can judge better when I tell you that it is the story of a son who has brought himself up in ignorant reverence of his dead father, a man of really bad life. The truth is known to his mother and the family doctor, who have never seen the hour of revealing it to the son. They wish to marry, and he treats their wish as a sacrilege to his father's memory. One way or other, those to whom the doctor does tell the truth are helpless to act on it; the dead man holds them in a sort of mortmain, till it becomes a question whether it will not do the community more harm than good to have the evil known. There is also a question whether in the supreme anguish of his sudden death he may not have expiated his sins.

Of course the son has a love story, and happily marries the daughter of a man whom his father has cruelly wronged.

I hope all this will throw some light on my tangle of titles.

Yours sincerely
W. D. Howells.

1. Howells' essay, "Henrik Ibsen," was not published in the *North American Review* until July 1906, after Ibsen's death. See Howells to Munro, 27 May 1906.

2. *The Son of Royal Langbrith* appeared in eight installments in the *North American Review*, January–August 1904.

3. For the list of possible titles and Howells' ultimate decision, see *The Son of Royal Langbrith*, HE, pp. xiv–xv.

20 SEPTEMBER 1903, KITTERY POINT, TO HENRY B. FULLER

Kittery Point, Me., Sept. 20, 1903.

My dear Mr. Fuller:

I suffered, in respect to your letter, that sort of arrest which happens to a man when he does not find himself in full agreement with his friend. Up to the time when Mr. McCutcheon abandoned the earlier manner in which he illustrated Artie and Doc' Horne, I yielded to none in my joy of him; but when he took to his present pseudo-Bewick business, I shook hands with him and bade him go with God.[1] It will be sometime yet before he supersedes Henry B. Fuller or the other Chicago novelists with his dramatic sketches of Bird Centre, amusing and significant as they are.[2]

I hope you will yet be of a better mind concerning Miss Wyatt's work, which is the best that any "female" since Jane Austen has done, up to a certain limit. She has read the middle West, if I know it, next to you, and there is no woman writer, and not many men under sixty-six, who begin to be of her promise in these States, as Walt Whitman was fond of calling them. We read her constantly in this household, and in defect of her quantity, we enjoy her qualitatively. As soon as we have finished Every One his Own Way, we take up True Love; when that is done we return to the other.[3] Do not talk to your grandfather, as the grandfathers used to say when they were boys.

Have you heard lately from Garland? He wrote me on the birth of his daughter,[4] but not since, and that had gone so hard with his wife, as he said, that I have been rather afraid to inquire farther at first hand.

I have been doing all sorts of stunts, this summer: finishing, among the rest, a novel which is to appear in the North American Review after James's disappears.[5] Why do not you do one for the same periodical? It seems determined to publish nothing but classics, and you are one, and they are not many. Besides the novel, there have been many pieces of journalism, and some poems. Now I am launched well into a long-short story which I wish might amuse other people a tenth as much as it amuses me.[6]

If a certain epistolary fiction called Letters Home, falls under your eye, I hope that as a friend it may interest you for its attempt to revive an old and perhaps happily obsolete form.[7]

Yours ever,
W. D. Howells.

1. John T. McCutcheon (1870–1949), Indiana-born journalist and illustrator, was best known for his editorial cartoons in the Chicago *Tribune*. He illustrated several of the early works of the Midwestern fabulist George Ade. The characters of Artie and Doc' Horne first appeared in Ade's columns for the Chicago *Record* in the 1890s. These literary sketches subsequently evolved into book-length works, *Artie* (1896), Ade's first book, and *Doc' Horne* (1899). Howells reviewed *Doc' Horne* in "An Obsolescent American Type," *Literature*, 22 September 1899. McCutcheon's "early manner" was characterized by uncluttered, clear-line caricature; the "present pseudo-Bewick business" refers to his later, more elaborate style. Thomas Bewick (1753–1828) was the noted English wood engraver and illustrator, whose drawings were done in fulsome and precise detail.

2. McCutcheon's "dramatic sketches of Bird Centre" first appeared in the Chicago *Tribune* in 1903 and then were collected under the title *Bird Center: A Chronicle of Social Happenings at Bird Center, Illinois* (1904). Each sketch consists of an extensive and well populated cartoon frame depicting representative characters and social events in the imaginary small Midwestern town. The illustrations are accompanied by what purports to be the local newspaper's account of a variety of social events. The intention of the pictures and the texts, said McCutcheon in the preface to his book, was "to chronicle the social happenings in a small community . . . . to poke a little good-natured fun at some of the ornate pretensions of society." Howells' letter is in reply to one from Fuller (not extant), calling Howells'

attention to the Bird Center sketches. Fuller had disparaged McCutcheon's work, and in his next letter to Howells, 6 October 1903 (MH), he promised to renew his attack "in force" when the sketches come out in book form.

3. Howells had previously reviewed Edith Wyatt's (1873–1958) collection of sketches, *Every One His Own Way* (1901), in "Editor's Easy Chair," *Harper's Monthly*, October 1901. In a more recent essay, "Certain of the Chicago School of Fiction," *North American Review*, May 1903, he had praised her novel *True Love* as "the apotheosis of the democratic spirit," suggesting that Wyatt and Sarah Orne Jewett were the foremost women writers in "an age which has no Jane Austen of its own." He saw Wyatt, along with Fuller, George Ade, Robert Herrick, Finley Peter Dunne, and Will Payne, as an important presence in American literature. Wyatt thanked Howells, in a letter of 10 July 1903 (MH), for his generous comments.

4. See Howells to Garland, 26 July 1903, n. 1.

5. *The Son of Royal Langbrith* began serialization immediately after the last installment of *The Ambassadors* appeared in December 1903.

6. *Miss Bellard's Inspiration* (1905).

7. See Howells to Aurelia Howells, 24 May 1902, n. 2.

3 OCTOBER 1903, KITTERY POINT, TO DR. WHISTON

Kittery Point, Oct. 3, 1903.

Dear Sir:[1]

It was in "An Imperative Duty" that I had a man marry a woman with a faint trace of black blood. It was for a psychological, not a scientific purpose, and I merely argued that a man who really loved a woman would find his love settling any "race question" involved.

Yours truly,
W. D. Howells

Dr. Whiston.

1. Dr. Whiston has not been identified, and his letter to Howells, in which he appears to have expressed concern that *An Imperative Duty* was a disguised scientific argument in favor of racial equality, has not been located. The issues of white superiority, miscegenation, and social equality between the races were still being widely debated, just as they had been in 1891 when Howells wrote the novel.

4 OCTOBER 1903, KITTERY POINT, TO AURELIA H. HOWELLS

Kittery Point, Oct 4, 1903.

Dear Aurelia:

I *am* surprised at Annie's getting off,[1] but I'm delighted too, for I think it will be a good thing every way, and it will especially quiet your mind about your house. It is a pity you could not rent it furnished for the winter, but it may just as well to have a good caretaker in it.

I have no news today. I have been sorting, and filing or destroying thousands of old letters, and unless more of them turn up, have got to the end. I am rich in autographs beyond the dreams of avarice, and the letters are all interesting. What should you think of my writing my autobiography? My published reminiscences have made a beginning,[2] and it would forestall a biography always a false and mistaken thing.

The fine weather continues, in a lovely prolongation of summer.

> Your aff'te brother
> Will.

I am afraid Sam has done unwisely, as usual, in taking that large suburban house; but I shall know when he asks for help with the rent.

1. Presumably Annie was leaving for Jefferson to make arrangements for a caretaker to live in the house Aurelia and Henry had vacated when they left for Ottawa five months earlier. Apparently by now the decision had been made that they would remain in Ottawa indefinitely. See Howells to Aurelia Howells, 28 January 1903, n. 2.

2. Howells' first autobiographical reminiscences focused on his Ohio boyhood, beginning with *A Boy's Town* (1890) and followed by *My Year in a Log Cabin* (1893). He turned to literary reminiscences in *Literary Friends and Acquaintance* (1900), and most recently he had drawn upon his boyhood experiences for the children's novel, *The Flight of Pony Baker* (1902).

27 OCTOBER 1903, KITTERY POINT, TO THOMAS S. PERRY

> Kittery Point, Oct. 27, 1903.

My dear Perry:

The pleasure of your presence had not nearly gone out of me when your letters followed one another.[1] What you said of my book[2] went to my heart as well as my head, for one ages into self-doubt, and there are so many to help one doubt one's self. Yet I do think with you, if not all the way with you, that there is life in the thing, and being born in 1903 it may outlive a person born in 1837. James's book has not come to me yet,[3] and I take what you say of it on faith in you. I met Story two or three times in his later life, and liked him, and fostered his attempts on editors.[4] But when I was in Rome (1864!) "good" Americans spoke ill of him because of his supposed preference for the Englishry, one of whom was said to have said, "If you don't want to be bored by Americans, you must go to Story's studio: he cuts his countrymen," and small blame to him, as I knew some of them. (An opinion but not a sentence.)

As you have imagined, I have been working away here like a pretty blonde in the employ of an appreciative broker, with my typewriter, and I have long since finished the story I read you part of.[5] It continued to walk along on its own legs to the end, and I hope my fondness was not abused by its uncommon activity. Chi va sano, va piano,[6] and this seemed to bolt from the start.

It has grown suddenly rough, though not very cold, and we are of course clearing out. In another week we shall be getting on trains, and I am to be two or three days in Boston. Shall you be at 312 M.? Having tasted blood, I find myself insatiate. I realize, since seeing you, how much I have lacked of intellectual breath in New York.

Yours ever,
W. D. Howells.

1. As is indicated in Howells' letter to Perry, 27 September 1903 (MeWC), Perry had made a visit to Kittery Point sometime in the second half of September. The letters from Perry to which Howells here refers have not been located.

2. Most likely *Letters Home*, which had been published in September. Although Howells had his doubts about having succeeded in what he had intended to accomplish in *Letters Home* (see Howells to Aurelia Howells, 24 May 1902, n. 2), C. E. Norton praised it highly in his letter of 4 October 1903 (MH): "you have never written anything more masterly in sympathetic dramatic characterization of widely contrasted types than these 'Letters.'... [¶] You do us an immense service in exhibiting & interpreting to us America and Americans. But only an American can understand and appreciate your work, and perhaps only a few of us can do so yet. We are essentially a new thing in the world, too new & strange to be wholly intelligible to ourselves, and quite unintelligible to the rest of mankind. You, most of all, have understood us. But your interpretation is not yet quite complete;—you have yet to give us the ideal, that is the fully realized American man & woman,—of whom there are some very few."

3. *William Wetmore Story and His Friends* (1903). It appears that Howells did not get a copy of the book until several years later. On 17 March 1911 (MH) James wrote him that he was puzzled about the reason for his negligence but assumed it was because the publisher had not provided him with enough free copies. Then he commented on the substance of the book itself: "The Story itself has at least the merit of performing to the very maximum the miracle of the loaves & fishes, or at least the feat of bricks without straw. The nearer one got (tried to get) to him—to W. W. S.— the more one found there was Nothing—& yet I had to *invent* something—& it was the very devil; in spite of which his foolish, or rather reprobate, progeny didn't like the book—though they could help me with nothing but a few, the very fewest, stray grains of trash toward doing it."

4. For Howells' interest in publishing Story's poems and other writings, see his letters to Story in 1875, 1878, and 1879.

5. Howells was finishing *The Son of Royal Langbrith*, not *New Leaf Mills*, as Mildred Howells erroneously indicated as a result of misdating this letter 1908. See *Life in Letters*, II, 258.

6. The equivalent English idiom is "steady progress leads to success."

22 NOVEMBER 1903, NEW YORK, TO THOMAS S. PERRY

48 West 59th st.,
Nov. 22, 1903.

My dear Perry:

You are quite right, and I thank you, the more because you pro-longed and deepened my own first feeling. The publishers proposed that the life should not be published in Clemens's life-time, but with the MS. in their hands I know they would have itched to print it.[1] He is the most candid, modest and impartial of men, as regards criticism of himself or his work, and I think he would stand almost anything from a man he believed his friend, but all the same it would not do, and I asked you only to be the more convinced.

I am writing an Easy Chair essay on autobiography, apropos of Stod-dard's and Trowbridge's in their contrasting unimportance,[2] which I hope may interest you if you ever read it. I think I will write my own life, but these other minor authors have taught me that if I am to make a worth-while book, I must tell of what I have been in the love of litera-ture, rather than of what I have done. The way they whoop it up over their forgotten books, T. especially, is amusing.

Yours ever,
W. D. Howells.

1. Harper & Brothers had asked Howells to write a biography of Clemens, and Howells had sought Perry's advice in this matter.
2. Howells' essay on the autobiographies of Richard H. Stoddard and John T. Trowbridge (1827–1916), who was best known for his many novels written for boys, appeared in "Editor's Easy Chair," *Harper's Monthly*, February 1904.

22 NOVEMBER 1903, NEW YORK, TO AURELIA H. HOWELLS

48 West 59th st.,
Nov. 22, 1903.

Dear Aurelia:

I started to you on Thursday a valise full of clothes for Henry, which I meant to address to you in Achille's care, but just this moment it has flashed upon me that I did not put your name on the tag, but his only. If this was the case, will you please to explain to him, and beg him to excuse my seeming to send a lot of old clothes to him? I am very much mortified at the stupid oversight, if there has been one. I had it in mind to mark the tag properly, but it must have slipped my mind in the very instant of doing it. Besides the coats and trousers, there were three pairs of very good boots in the valise—a telescope valise—though these boots were all of the congress pattern, with elastic webbing at the sides. I never wear any others, myself, and I despise the lace boots because of the difficulty of bending over to lace them.

I have never acknowledged the delightful photographs of Pooly Cat, which Howells enclosed in his letter to me.[1] They brought him livingly before me, and made the whole family as much in love with him as I am. He is simply of an adorable wickedness, and if tenants of flats were allowed to keep cats, I should be tempted to send out for him. He is somehow associated with father very vividly in my mind, and I can hear him saying "Well, poor Pooly," when I look at Pooly's picture. How strongly the simple and common things of life unite us to the dead! It is not in their high moments that we like to recall them, but in those which endeared them to our familiar sense while they were here.

There is very little news to write you. Affairs are going well with me, and that, you know, is not favorable to history with nations or persons. You seem to have many more excitements than I or else you know how to report them better. I must send you the North American Review when my story begins to appear in it. I had a great bother naming it, and decided on "The Son of Royal Langbrith" at the last moment. The name of "Letters Home", which I liked, is thought by the publishers to have hurt the sale of the novel. In this sophisticated age, people do not want letters nor homes, it seems. These things are very droll, but I incline to think the publishers are half right about the matter.

The other night the Harpers gave a gorge for one of the writers on Punch, a most woozy and slow old person.[2] I am always struck with the superior dullness of an Englishman in a company of Americans. Of course he is not on his own ground, and he is apt, nationally, to be shy, and is apt to be personally cold. This Punch man was an old newspaper man, but an old American newspaper man who sat on my other side could have given him points in talk and easily beaten him. Still he had a kind of dignity and repose that I liked, and I do not know that I wanted him to shine; I could do the shining myself.

We have had some pretty stiff weather, and the winter seems to be coming on early, which is hard, even for those who have plenty of coal, for we have had a sort of winter ever since the beginning of last summer. With love to Henry, and all the Fréchettes, and repeated apologies to Achille,

Your affectionate brother,
Will.

1. Howells Fréchette, then 24 years old, probably reported on his success in finding a position at Detroit. On 8 November 1903 (MH), Howells had written Aurelia: "I got a most admirable letter from Howells, about his prospects.... I am glad he has something in view, and Detroit is a thousand times pleasanter than Pittsburg...."
2. Not identified.

20 DECEMBER 1903, NEW YORK, TO SAMUEL L. CLEMENS

> 48 West 59th st.,
> Dec. 20, 1903.

My dear **Clemens:**

It was sweet of you to write me those words about the poem, and about the Bret Harte,[1] and I am glad that the half-truth of the B.H. didn't quite seem to you a half-lie. What is to be done in such cases? Of course I could have written, though not more sincerely, things that would have left blisters on his fame; but after all, such things had better be left to the Judgment Day, which I see more and more use for as I live along. If you read old Alfred Russell Wallace's "Man's Place in the Universe,"[2] as I've just been doing, you will see it too, for with the earth alone inhabited of all the planets of all the stars, you will realize not merely the desirability but the practicality of some such round-up. With a universe full of man-bearing worlds, a Judgment Day was ridiculously inadequate and impossible for the settling of accounts. But Wallace gives us back the good old earth of our boyhood and more, too. Not only is everything on it for man's use and comfort, but all the heavenly bodies; and the earth is in their centre. It does not rehabilitate hell, but it makes me feel my importance, as I haven't for many a year; yes, it makes me feel *your* importance, though I hate to do it; and I can be simply and childishly sorry, even for that heart-breaking bitch of yours in Harper's,[3] because she has a reflected importance from the glorious and only human race. You ought to read that book; then you would not swear so much at your own species.—We are wearing on towards the New Year in the old way, and nothing is happening out of it. Florence is not practically much farther than Riverside;[4] I shall not see you once, instead of three or four times, before spring; that's all. We, Mrs. H. and I, are glad indeed to know of Mrs. Clemens being so decidedly better, and do tell her so with our love.

> Yours ever,
> **W. D. Howells.**

I have not said enough about your story, which everyone asks one if one has read, and which is most affecting and lovely. The Harpers make a great shouting over it in their advs. and handbills.

1. Howells' poem, "Sorrow, My Sorrow," *Harper's Monthly*, December 1903; the "Editor's Easy Chair" in the same issue was an essay on Bret Harte, who had died in 1902.

2. Alfred Russell Wallace (1823–1913), author of *Man's Place in the Universe* (1903), was the noted British biologist who had presented the theory of natural selection together with Charles Darwin to the Linnaean Society in 1858. Howells reviewed Wallace's book in "Editor's Easy Chair," *Harper's Monthly*, March 1904. See *Twain-Howells*, p. 777, for Clemens' unpublished satire of Wallace's theory of evolution.

3. The canine narrator in Mark Twain's sentimental story, "A Dog's Tale," *Harper's Monthly*, December 1903.

4. The Clemenses had moved to Italy from Riverdale, New York, because of Olivia Clemens' continued poor health. In a letter to Aurelia Howells, 18 October 1903 (MH) from Kittery Point, Howells had described Clemens' intention of moving to Florence: "I am going to New York on Thursday to a dinner the Harpers are giving Mark Twain on his departure for Italy; but I expect to be back by Friday night.— Clemens, I suppose, will always live at Florence, hereafter. He goes first for his wife's health, and then because he can't stand the nervous storm and stress here. He takes things intensely hard, and America is too much for him. I envy his going to Italy to live. If it could be managed I should like to spend the rest of my winters at Florence or Rome, and my summers at Kittery Point."

17 JANUARY 1904, NEW YORK, TO HENRY B. FULLER

48 West 59th St.,
January 17, 1904

My dear Fuller:

Your letter terrified me almost as much as it gratified me. I am afraid you expect more than I shall give you in my story.[1] My way is still the byway, not the highway; the minor, not the major means. The tale is tragical enough, but I have purposely refused several effects of tragedy that offered themselves to my hand. I have constantly found the good not so good, the evil not so evil, in result, though in with each is each. I think your artistic sense will approve the working out as natural in the survival of youthful joy and love over unyouthful sorrow and loss.

Yes, youth is stronger, and it does daunt as we age when it approaches us in others. I want to embody this notion of yours in the Easy Chair essay I am to write next,[2] if you don't forbid me,—and I think I will do it anyway! Langbrith won't be the outright brute that Jeff Durgin was; and the girl masters him in a way which I hope you will find true.[3]

Why do you never come on here? Now and then Garland and I speak of you when we meet; but that is not often, and I would rather speak *to* you. I would like to speak to you about Garland himself, who is taking on the world ingenuously and interestingly; he will never be sophisticated, and I hope he won't lose the simplicity of his ideal, such as it was when he had "Main Travelled Roads" under his feet, and throbbed with its fine, angry sympathy for "the familiar and the low."[4]

If you have read Harper's Weekly, or me in it, you will see that I think Ade's play not good enough for him. It is a pity; I can't understand how so absolute a talent could consent to doing such a comparative thing. He had a great, great chance in the County Chairman, but he has missed its greatness.[5]

What are you yourself doing, or going to do? I wish I might hear of such another book as With the Procession.[6]

Jessamy Colebridge revivifies herself constantly in the story; she *would* come in; but don't mind her![7]

I thank you from a full heart for writing me so kindly, so encouragingly. An old fellow needs it more than a young one.

Yours cordially,
W. D. Howells

1. The first installment of *The Son of Royal Langbrith* had just appeared in the *North American Review*, January 1904. In his letter of 11 January 1904 (MH) Fuller congratulated Howells for having written such a refreshing novel following the serial appearance of James's *The Ambassadors*, also in the *North American Review*. James, according to Fuller, "has become Byzantine beyond all the bounds of reason," while in *Langbrith* Howells renders fictional experience which is "crystal clear."

2. In the novel Mrs. Langbrith and Dr. Anther are frightened by young James Langbrith's intense reverence for the memory of his dead father. From this Fuller observes that older people in general tend to feel threatened by such youthful energy: "(I believe it is the man between forty and fifty, especially the unsuccessful man, who is most intimidated by the vigor of unschooled and confident youth.) . . . Confess that American youth has begun to frighten *you* too!" In a review of Luigi Cornaro's *The Temperate Life*, in the "Editor's Easy Chair," *Harper's Monthly*, April 1904, Howells briefly comments upon the fear of older people for the young: "In most cases the fear of the young does not beset the elderly at a period which most of the elderly would regard as an hour of the golden prime; but the fear of youth is something that steals upon one unawares, and realizes itself to him by some sudden accident."

3. Jeff Durgin is the protagonist of *The Landlord at Lion's Head* whose natural temperament strains against the morality imposed by his Puritan past. In his letter Fuller favorably compares the characterization of James Langbrith to that of Durgin: "So far, I believe, Jeff of the Lion's Head has been your top notch in the portrayal of ruthless young virility, but Jim Langbrith . . . is going to overtop him, by the precise measure of his outfitting and his opportunity." The girl who masters Langbrith is Hope Hawberk, daughter of the man who was ruined by James's unscrupulous father.

4. Hamlin Garland's *Main-Travelled Roads* (1891) is a collection of local-color stories featuring the experiences of the poorer classes of people.

5. Howells reviewed George Ade's *The County Chairman* (1903) in "Some New American Plays," *Harper's Weekly*, 16 January 1904.

6. Howells had reviewed Fuller's novel *With the Procession* in "Life and Letters," *Harper's Weekly*, 1 June 1895.

7. Jessamy Colebridge is a marginal yet conspicuous character in *Langbrith*. Fuller described her in his letter as "absolutely photographic," but felt that she did not suit what he defined as "the new 'grand manner' that the earlier chapters of 'The Son of Royal Langbrith' seem to promise to employ.... Fuller hoped that she would not be "elaborated" in the later chapters, and he implored Howells to "minify her."

26 JANUARY 1904, NEW YORK, TO WILLIAM CLYDE FITCH

48 West 59th st.,
January 26, 1904.

My dear Mr. Fitch:[1]

Your letter was something which would have been extremely interesting to me even if it had not been so personally valuable.[2] May I say that I do not know how it could be *manlier*? Being supremely that, the rest seems to follow. Of course it went to my heart to have you tell me that you had cared to please me, and in print I had already tried to tell you how much I had been pleased without dreaming of your wish. The more I have thought of that gay, brilliant, honest, living play of yours,[3] the more I have liked it, and the more I have deplored its removal from the theatre. I do think it was built on the great lines, and that its astonishing inconclusiveness was not greater proof of your grasp than its easy and natural successiveness was of your knowledge of how and when to let things go of themselves. I had said to myself, That is the way things happen, one after another, with only that loose allegiance to one another that the facts of life have had hitherto to themselves, but that an artist has here recognized and recorded. I will not press to your lips the cup of bitter consolation, and say that the public was not up to the play, but I wish that the play could have a chance with a London public that really cared to see what the American, or the New York thing was like. But in any case I believe that its turn will come again; of your turn coming again, and again, as often as you like, there is no question whatever. You may be sure I shall not miss any chance hereafter of seeing whatever you do.

Now, I won't bore you longer, even with your own praises. But you know I do love good work, and I can't help lumping the good worker with it.

Yours cordially,
W. D. Howells.

1. William Clyde Fitch (1865–1909) was a prolific and popular American play-wright. He wrote fifty plays, mostly in the vein of light comedy and melodrama, and was at the height of his popularity at the turn of the century.

2. Fitch's letter has not been located.

3. Howells refers to the play *Glad of It*, which he reviewed along with Fitch's *Her Own Way* in "Some New American Plays," *Harper's Weekly*, 16 January 1904. For Howells' more candid assessment of Fitch's work, see Howells to Laura Mitchell, 5 February 1904, *Life in Letters*, II, 184–85.

28 JANUARY 1904, NEW YORK, TO CHARLES E. NORTON

48 West 59th st.,
Jan'y 28, 1904.

My dear Norton:

I met Eliot[1] in the Park yesterday afternoon, and he gave me good news of you all, and this morning came Storey's address like another message from you.[2] I have only glanced into it, but I cannot imagine myself disagreeing with it; and I am going to read it as also your mind on an affair which seems to me so shocking.

From what your son said I know that you have been passing a comfortable winter, and I know an interesting one, for you yourself bring interest to events, and grace life as it goes. I feel this so strongly that I should almost like to have you try your magic on New York, and see how tolerable you could make it. Tolerable I do not think you would *find* it, and at times even my own far unfiner sense is harshly grated upon, so that I am just now hoping to get away for a month or two, and going for March and April to England with Pilla. Perhaps it isn't so much my tastes as my nerves that are overwrought: I am fairly fagged with my constant writing.[3] Everything tries the elderly nerves, even the pleasures, or what stands for them; and though I have been enjoying a good many plays this winter (you know I love the theatre) they have brought their portion of fatigue. What has been a pleasure without fatigue has been hearing a sweet, silly, old fashioned Italian opera, L'Elisir d'Amore.[4] When my wife came home from it she said, "Now, we must go straight back to Italy and live there," and when I saw the scene poured full of the old familiar chorus I felt myself most vividly at home in it. Of course, this is a fleeting mood, and we shall never go straight back to Italy and live, at least in this world; perhaps in the next.

It was kind of you to send me, as if you had divined how much Mrs. Howells and I had both wished to see it, that charming contribution of Gray's to polite botany.[5] It may not in the modern sense be very scientific, but how poetic, and how fitly edited—and prettily printed! We both thank you.

Will you give love from us all to your household, and let me be always

Yours affectionately,
W. D. Howells.

1. **Norton's son.**

2. Moorfield Storey (1845–1929) was a prominent Boston lawyer noted for his reform politics. His address was probably "The Recognition of Panama," delivered at the Massachusetts Reform Club, 5 December 1903, and subsequently published as a pamphlet which Norton had most likely sent to Howells.

3. In his reply of 12 February 1904 (MH) Norton responded at length, and not without a touch of irony, it seems, to Howells' complaint: "I am sorry but I do not wonder that you are fagged with your constant writing. I used to look on the twenty one folio volumes, in double column, of the works of Albertus Magnus as a splendid monument to the leisure of the cloister. But you surpass him & leave him breathless behind you! How you can write so much & with such unexhausted freshness & charm is as much a marvel, as that you can do so is a blessing to us, your fortunate, less industrious readers."

4. *L'Elisir d'amore* (1832) was composed by Gaetano Donizetti (1797–1848).

5. Norton had sent Howells a copy of his recent and privately published book *The Poet Gray as a Naturalist, with Selections from his Notes on the Systema Naturae of Linnæus and Facsimiles of Some of his Drawings* (1903).

---

1 FEBRUARY 1904, ATLANTIC CITY, TO RICHARD W. GILDER

Hotel Rudolf....
Atlantic City, N. J....
February 1st, 1904.

My dear Mr. Gilder:

The night after your beautiful book came,[1] I read it all, and made mental note of the pieces I meant to speak of in the letter I meant to write the next morning. But a good many mornings have passed since without my writing, and now the specific impressions have resolved themselves in a general sense of the high mood of the book. If it could have caused any feeling so unfit as envy in me, it would have come from noting the security of your hold upon the Christmas faith which is for so many of us only the Christmas myth, wonderful and significant, but not claiming full and constant confession.[2] The artistic loveliness of your work, the unfailing beauty of your phrase, the dignity and simplicity of the poetic scheme, are things I expect of you, but the other, though it was not unexpected, quite, had yet a more novel claim on my appreciation. I do suppose that there are possibilities of reversion to the beliefs that had once no doubt in them, and for myself I am always imagining getting back to their possession and filling up the empty order of my life from their sources. When I see some one who seems to have already done this, if I envy him in a sort, I thank him even more.

—Here for a week with my wife.[3]

Yours sincerely
W. D. Howells.

1. *A Christmas Wreath* (1903), a collection of poems by R. W. Gilder.

2. In a letter dated 10 February 1904 (NN; Rosamond Gilder, ed., *Letters of Richard Watson Gilder* [Boston: Houghton Mifflin, 1916], p. 424) Gilder protested that Howells was reading too much into the poetry. He refers Howells to specific verses where, in fact, the intention was to express an ethic unsupported by faith: "It surprises me somewhat that you should find, apparently, more orthodoxy in the book than it seems to me to contain. One or two of the poems might be said to be a resetting of the Bible story but the general trend of it, I should say, is away from the literal, and trying to get at the root of the matter. So far as supposed historical supernatural 'facts' go, I tried to express in the last lines of the last poem, 'In Palestine,' the possibility of throwing them all away, leaving the central ethics and aspirations without any so-called supernatural assistance whatever. Please look at these last lines again, and don't believe me more 'faithful' than I am!" Howells replied on 13 February 1904 (photocopy at InU) that he was not speaking of the merely conventional notion of faith: "I never meant 'orthodoxy' but that something which I mainly find myself without: the power, often, to imagine those supernal things, which your book seems full of. Be as heterodox as you will; I thank you for sending me to that fine poem again."

3. Howells and his wife returned to New York on 6 February, Elinor feeling "active and well," as he wrote to Aurelia Howells, 7 February 1904 (MH).

4 FEBRUARY 1904, ATLANTIC CITY, TO FREDERICK A. DUNEKA

Marlborough House,
Atlantic City, Feb'y 4, 1904.

Dear Mr. Duneka:

In reading the proofs of "Miss Bellard's Inspiration" I am far less pleased than I was in writing it; and I wish to suggest your postponing the publication for a year, or until the novel now running in the North American Review has had its chance in book form with the public.[1] I think it would be a mistake to follow a failure like "Letters Home" with a story like the present,[2] and that their joint effect would be injurious to the North American story, which is a novel of some psychological importance. If we postpone "Miss B.'s I.", I can give you a collection of literary and social essays for the fall, which you can bring out uniform with the "Heroines of Fiction," etc., but in one volume, and perhaps get some holiday favor. I have thought of "Essays: Mostly Contrary-Minded" for a title; but that is a detail.[3]

I return Saturday, and hope to see you on Monday.

Yours sincerely
W. D. Howells.

1. *The Son of Royal Langbrith*, currently being serialized in the *North Amercian Review*, was published in book form on 6 October 1904. *Miss Bellard's Inspiration* was withheld from publication until 1905 and was never serialized.

2. Although *Letters Home* received some favorable reviews, it did not sell well.

3. The projected volume of essays was never published.

14 FEBRUARY 1904, NEW YORK, TO SAMUEL L. CLEMENS

48 West 59th Street
February 14, 1904.

Dear Clemens:

You do stir me mightily with the hope of dictating, and I will try it when I get the chance.[1] But there is the temperantal difference. You are dramatic and unconscious; you count the thing more than yourself; I am cursed with consciousness to the core, and can't say myself out; I am always saying myself *in,* and setting myself above all that I say, as of more worth. Lately I have felt as if I were rotting with egotism. I don't admire myself; I am sick of myself; but I can't think of anything else. Here I am at it now, when I ought to be rejoicing with you at the blessing you've found.—I wonder if we may not meet before a great while. Pilla thinks of taking me to England with her early in March, and to Bath, there to have me drink the waters, and get some radium into me out of them. Then, if a plan goes through which I've been talking over with Harvey,[2] John will bring his mother over in May, and we shall all spend the summer in England. Perhaps Pilla will go back with John in the fall, but it is possible that their mother and I will spend the winter in Europe. Italy, of course. This is the dream which may turn out nothing else. If it comes true, or begins to, I will write you from London, or Bath.

I'd like immensely to read your autobiography. You always rather bewildered me by your veracity, and I fancy you may tell the truth about yourself. But *all* of it? The black truth, which we all know of ourselves in our hearts, or only the whity-brown truth of the pericardium, or the nice, whitened truth of the shirtfront?[3] Even you wont tell the black heart's-truth.—The man who could do it would be famed to the last day the sun shone upon.

You will find a good deal of fumbling in my story as it goes on,[4] but I think it will keep you reading, for it kept me writing. Kept me writing, with the other things, too hard, so that I'm rather run down nervously, and that's why Pilla is taking me abroad. I think I've got at one true thing in the story, from the opium-eater and his daughter:[5] no holding over of unhappiness from one generation to the other; each has its own. Tell me if it doesn't seem so, as the thing runs along. There was lots of cheap tragedy in its path which I hopped it over, and made it side-step.

Glad to know that Mrs. Clemens is so much better. Give her our dearest love and best wishes—*all* ours. My wife has been wonderously well, in spite of the stoniest hearted winter I remember.

Yours ever

W. D. Howells.

1. Howells was replying to a letter dated 16 January 1904 (MH; *Twain-Howells*, pp. 778–79), in which Clemens, at this time living in Florence, had expressed his utter delight with the results of his dictating his autobiography to his secretary: "you will be astonished (& charmed) to see how like *talk* it is, & how real it sounds, & how well & compactly & sequentially it constructs itself, and what a dewy & breezy & woodsy freshness it has, & what a darling & worshipful absence of the signs of starch, & flatiron, & labor & fuss & the other artificialities!"

2. Howells was arranging with George Harvey, head of Harper & Brothers, to do a book on his travels in England. See Howells to Duneka, 15 February 1904.

3. In his reply to Howells, 14 March 1904 (NN; *Twain-Howells*, p. 782), Clemens responded directly to this query: "Yes, I set up the safeguards, in the first day's dictating—taking this position: that an Autobiography is the truest of all books; for while it inevitably consists mainly of extinctions of the truth, shirkings of the truth, partial revealments of the truth, with hardly an instance of plain straight truth, the remorseless truth *is* there, between the lines, where the author-cat is raking dust upon it which hides from the disinterested spectator neither it nor its smell (though I didn't use that figure)—the result being that the reader knows the author in spite of his wily diligences."

4. Clemens had mentioned reading the first installment of *The Son of Royal Langbrith*: "Last night I read your 27 pages in the N.A.R., with vast interest. It stimulated me out of a couple of hours of sleep—then I resorted to whisky."

5. The "opium-eater" is Mr. Hawberk, a former business partner ruined by Royal Langbrith; his daughter Hope eventually marries Langbrith's son James.

14 FEBRUARY 1904, NEW YORK, TO JOHN ST. LOE STRACHEY

48 West 59th Street
Feb'y 14, 1904.

My dear Mr. Strachey:[1]

If anything in these later years of mine could have given me greater pleasure than the appearance of my poem in the Spectator, it would have been your letter speaking of it.[2] I acknowledge that much more gratefully than the check which so delicately addressed itself to me in guineas instead of pounds; but I am very glad of that too, there being as yet no public endowment of authorship. Of course, I should like to write you other and much shorter poems; but my agreement with Colonel Harvey is for everything I do, unless there is some special agreement to the contrary. It is sweet to be entreated by an editor, and I thank you from my heart.

Until you mentioned hearing Americans speak of our scenery as unkempt,[3] I never dreamt of such a thing, and am delighted that the notion did not suggest itself to you from the face of nature here. I should think that nature could never be unkempt, for the simple reason that the moment it is kempt, it ceases to be nature. I should say as you do, that our scenery was wild; I should go farther and say it was often savage, but I always feel a native and most appealing beauty in it, whether in the Middle West where I was born, or in the South where I have traveled, or in New England where I have mostly lived. There are great sectional differences of temperament in it; but the varying physiognomy is always unmistakably American. I have found moments of New England in Italy, and moments of Ohio in England, but nothing more than moments.

If you like to talk of such things, perhaps we may talk of them before so very long, for my daughter and I think of sailing early in March. We intend going straight to Bath where I am to get some radium into my system by drinking the waters, and where we both hope to meet Jane Austen and Catharine Morland and Henry Tilney,[4] and the rest, for whom all my family are impassioned.—We will talk of New York, too, if you like; it is much more in my mind than in my heart, and I have written lots more about it than you have ever seen;[5] I can pass the printed stuff off on you for fresh observation. Thank you, and thank Mrs. Strachey too, for being so good to my poor "Letters Home" which has shivered about without a friend here since it came out. Perhaps a friend or two; but it has had no success. I am sometimes afraid that in my fidelity to our life I am meeting the fate of the man who offered the Kentuckian corn bread as a treat. The Kentuckian said, He was r'ared on it; and declined it with thanks. Will you give Mrs. Strachey my best regards?—We met at dinner, the other night, a charming young fellow, Mr. Lionel Strachey; I think a kinsman of yours.[6]

Yours sincerely
W. D. Howells.

1. John St. Loe Strachey (1860–1927) was an English journalist and author particularly concerned with social and political matters. As editor and proprietor of the *Spectator* (1892–1925) he was an ardent supporter of Anglo-American friendship.

2. Howells' "Black Cross Farm" appeared in the *Spectator*, 2 January 1904. When Howells offered the poem to Strachey, he commented in the accompanying letter, dated 2 November 1903 (House of Lords, London): "Any one who knows this sad, lonely [lovely?] northern New England coast country, now so often falling back to the wilderness from which it never quite emerged, would testify to the fidelity of my picture. But the question is whether I have imparted the sense of it to those who have never known it, and never will." Strachey replied on 11 November 1903 (MH) with enthusiasm: "I am immensely touched by your fine poem, into which the peculiar and mysterious charm of a deserted house amid wild scenery has entered.... [¶] The poem is *very much longer* than I usually take in the Spectator ... but I feel deeply honoured by the offer of it & should like to make an exception to our rule against long poems in favour of so beautiful & poignant a piece of work." In a letter to Aurelia Howells, 17 January 1904 (MH), accompanying a copy of the *Spectator* in which the poem appeared, Howells described it as "the first thing I have offered to an English periodical since I lived in Venice."

3. In a letter to Howells, 22 January 1904 (MH), Strachey comments on the "tone and temper" of the "fascinating" New England landscape in "Black Cross Farm." Most Americans, according to Strachey, are "bad describers" of their native country, giving the impression "that the American landscape looked 'unkempt' & disorderly . . . . It appears to me that there must be an absurd convention about American scenery which has blinded men & tongues."

4. Catherine Moreland and Henry Tilney, the protagonists in Jane Austen's *Northanger Abbey* (1818), meet at Bath.

5. In a letter to Howells of 8 December 1903 (MH) Strachey had written: "To my mind New York is one of the most fascinating and attractive cities in the world.... I have never fallen in love at first sight with a City, as I did with New York. [¶] ... I have been planning ever since I was there to write an article on 'The Charm of New York', but I am afraid I never shall, because, I have got something to say, that I can't say adequately, and I am determined not to say it inadequately."

6. Strachey did not have a kinsman by the name of Lionel. Possibly Howells met Lytton Strachey (1880–1932), the noted critic, who was a cousin of John St. Loe Strachey.

15 FEBRUARY 1904, NEW YORK, TO FREDERICK A. DUNEKA

48 West 59th Street
Feb'y 15, 1904.

Dear Mr. Duneka:

If you can relieve me of so much of the work as you suggested today, and let me write only the Easy Chair, and such other papers for the

Review as I liked while I was making the book on England,[1] I believe I should prefer to take my chances on the book with you, and not sell it outright for $6000. I am reluctant to part with any of my copyrights, and I believe so much in the sort of book I can write about England, that I now wish to make you this counter proposition. I will do the Easy Chair, and the Review papers on my present salary, and you can use serially as much or little of the English book material as you please. I will take 15 per cent on the first 5000 of the book, and 20 per cent thereafter. If some aspect of life or affairs seems suitable for treatment in the Weekly[2] that shall go in, of course.

Kindly let me know what the house thinks of this.[3] I am now greatly in the notion of the book, but as we both understand I would rather see England before I promised it positively.

Yours sincerely
W. D. Howells.

1. Howells was making arrangements with Harper & Brothers regarding his obligations to them during his trip to England, which he and Mildred planned for early March. He wished to minimize his writing for the *North American Review* in order to concentrate on a book about his travels in England.

2. *Harper's Weekly*.

3. In a memorandum dated 17 February 1904 (NNC) Duneka indicated the Harpers' agreement with Howells' terms. The English material eventually made up two entire books, *London Films* (1905) and *Certain Delightful English Towns* (1906), and part of a third, *Seven English Cities* (1909). In spelling out the terms of the royalty to be paid for the travel volumes, Duneka also held out the prospect of a Library Edition. He described its terms and format in a letter to Howells of 16 February 1904 (NNC): "When we do such a collected edition we will agree to pay a royalty upon the book for that edition only. We believe that by next year the collected edition will be well under way. The present idea is to issue the library set in two parts, doing, first, such volumes as are not fiction and afterwards the novels as the second part. This would probably prove more profitable than to issue all of them at once. . . . I shall be glad if you will let me know what you think of it." Howells replied promptly on 19 February 1904 (NNC): "I am quite of your notion about beginning the library edition with my non-fiction volumes. As soon as you are ready I will begin revising them for copy." *London Films* and *Certain Delightful English Towns* were combined to make one of the six volumes of the never-completed Library Edition issued in 1911. See also Howells to Norton, 12 October 1902, n. 5.

13 AND 14 MARCH 1904, PLYMOUTH, TO ELINOR M. HOWELLS

Plymouth, Sunday 13, 1904.[1]

—"Grand" is a nice quiet hotel, with ivied garden overlooking terrace surrounding end of harbor, with fine stately houses backing it. Statue of Drake;[2] monument to Armada victory. Whole treatment of terracing fine, and more stately and costly than all Central Park things put together. We are not in it, when it comes to public spirit and expense.—Garrison below terrace; glazed pavilion in front nearer water. Few people walking there. Pale sky, with splotch of red sunset, about 6 feet square, promising today's sunny weather; restful dimness on everything. Capital table d'hôte; then out to walk again with young Englishman from Dulwich (Albers) on terrace, and down into town. Harbor full of ships, with riding lights, like K. P.[3] Beyond, wooded heights of Earl Edgecombe's seat.[4] Forts everywhere else, and lots of red coats out with girls, and swagger-sticks; few civilians in Knickerbockers; some bicycles.—This morning points out black cat with red ribbon on ivied garden wall across street. 2 little conservatories. Ivy everywhere.— Out on esplanade in warm sun after br. of eggs, bacon, fish & coffee. Walk down into town of low shops. Names on signs: Limpenny, Vosper, Quintock. People going to church. Milk carts with large, brasstopt cans. Newsboys with Sunday papers. Fruit and butter shops open; rest shut. Trams (overhead trolleys) not running because Sunday. Very Sabbath air. Church sister with gang of children, very little, going to C.—Silk hats (toppers) in window, three and six. Streets exquisitely clean.—Pil in great spirits with all the sights, and queer resemblances to Bermuda. I find it very like Quebec, somehow—Q. as we first knew it.—Back to terrace where many people walking. *Great sensation of Bath chair*, just like that in cut you gave me. Stubby old man pulling it. I must certainly buy you one; immensely comfy, with very easy springs, and black canvass buggy-top.—Many bicyclers. Men in Knicks, and caps, such as I bought, and wore on steamer; derby hats, but very few toppers.— Resplendent, tight-coated colonel going to church. Cavalry seargent, strutting with 2 wom. who looked ladies.—I cabled you at 5:30 last evening; you must have got it at lunch time. Addressed you at 48 W. 59, fearing Elliman might be closed for the day. Shall cable again tomorrow to make sure.—Most comf. hotel. Meals at stated hours. B. 9; L. 1 to 2; D. 7.—I do wonder how you're getting on.—Steamers, very large, leave London weekly for Australia, and *land passengers at Naples*; stop here at Plymouth on way.—5.45. Just up from a second nap. After our first, Pil and I and our Englishman started by tram to the reservoir (we didn't know it, but simply paid to the end of the line) and rode on the top through the pale, soft sun, and miles of winding, sloping streets, into the loveliest country. The houses, small, low and gray, grow into detached cottages and villas, and into half-built building lots. (Birds singing every where to-day, sparrows, English robins, and many a *bel merlo*,[5] such as I bought and let go in Venice; and the rooks were sailing and cawing over the fields, and through the trees.) Plymouth, Stonehouse and Devenport are built together on the sides of long ridges round the bay, and apparently growing. The country outside green and ploughed fields on the sides of gentle knolls lost in the haze of the horizon. Many vegetable gardens, sadly suggestive of K. P. From trolly top looking down into depths of evergreenery, ivy, laurel and holly. Houses smaller countrywards; mostly 2 stories and basement. Soldiers with their girls; one hard mouthed, red cheeked, black eyed girl, coarsely flirting, like Arabella in "Jude the Obscure."[6] Interested man with little boy, who directed us; and was curious, when I said we were Americans; wish I had talkt more with him. Many people coming and going, all well clothed, and well behaved, though some loud laughing.—On the way back, the car stopped further off than we supposed, and so we did not take another, and had long, wandering walk, but not too much. We are now interested to see whether we shall have dinner, or supper, it being Sunday.

Monday 14, 1904. 9:30 A.M. Plymouth. Rather walkt myself down yesterday, and had a headache at night, but all right now. Pil first rate. Just starting out for more explorations. *Coperto*,[7] and colder. Ship still in my head, after so little motion on it. Our plan now to go to Exeter tomorrow afternoon, spend the night, and next day to Bath. But perhaps may go in the morning.—Ladies in reading room found me out last night. One, a young mother had read Pony Baker to her boys;[8] another stout, white-haired old lady, Unitarian, and *Parishioner of Brooke Herford*, and great friend of all the H. family knew Venetian Life.[9] *6 p.m.* Your bulkish kind of letter came today at lunch, when it ought to have been given me Saturday night by the steamer's agent. As it was, I got it by the chance of asking to have Pil's summer trunk stored, and giving my address. But it was glorious when it did come, and it "sheered my heart" to know you were so well, and happy, and that John had got the bank.[10] Pil and I join in glorifications, which I hope he'll receive, though stale, when they reach him.—We are just back from Mt. Edgecomb, where we went with the U. S. Consul and his daughter,[11] (whom I must sometime tell you of—from Crawfordsville, Indiana.) We saw the gardens and park, and deer. Bamboo and palms growing outdoors; dense thickets of evergreen, with rhrododrens in bloom, and corktrees and ilexes, all damp, as if immemorially rained upon in the pale sun. Red-soiled hills, broken as to the thick mossy turf by rabbits; herds of deer lying down, or statuesque against the sky.—Gardener, who knew all the botanical names—young fellow. Old guide, former sailor, like a Hardy character; Pil thinks took her spitefully out of the way because she asked for short cuts, but I think weak-minded. Flag up at house to show that the earl was at home, and it could not be seen. Elizabethan gothic, gray, rained greenish. Funny little ferry boat, half as big as "Alice Howard," and very rough.—This A.M.

saw the dock that the Pilgrims sailed from; houses all round 17th century; fishing boats, yawl rig; fish market; Cromwell's castle (old fellow said, "This neighborhood used to be hell upon earth; interest of neighbor women in our curiosity.) Quaint hillside streets, with old over-hung houses. House where the king stayed? (Charles I? II? James II? William III? Please look up.) We expect to start for Exeter at 10.30 tomorrow A.M.

Keep all these scribbles for notes. Pale dull sky, with a moment of heat at noon; weather very warm last week.

Love to John.

Papa.

1. Howells sailed with his daughter Mildred on 3 March 1904 aboard the Hamburg-America liner *Moltke*, landing at Plymouth on 12 March. Throughout the voyage and during his English sojourn Howells wrote a series of "diary letters" to Elinor, which would serve as a basis for the travel book he envisioned. Material from this letter, for instance, was used in "The Landing of a Pilgrim," *Harper's Monthly*, April 1905, which later became the first chapter of *Certain Delightful English Towns*.

2. Sir Francis Drake (ca. 1545–1595) became mayor of Plymouth in 1581 and later, as vice-admiral, distinguished himself in the war against the Spanish Armada (1588). He sailed from Plymouth on 13 December 1577 aboard the Golden Hind on the first English voyage of global circumnavigation.

3. Kittery Point, Maine.

4. William Henry Edgcumbe (1833–1917), fourth earl of Mount Edgcumbe. The family seat was called Cotehele, located in Cornwall near Plymouth.

5. Italian for "pretty blackbird."

6. Arabella Donn is the temptress in Thomas Hardy's *Jude the Obscure* (1896) who entraps Jude into marriage.

7. Italian for "cloudy."

8. The young mother is not identified, but she might be Marie Worsley-Lowe, who was staying at the Grand Hotel in Plymouth. She wrote Howells on 15 March 1904 (MH) to say that she regretted missing him before his departure and to praise "Boy's Town," no doubt an allusion to *The Flight of Pony Baker, A Boy's Town Story*.

9. The parishioner is not identified. Brook Herford (1830–1903), a prominent Unitarian minister in England, was pastor of the Arlington Street Church in Boston (1882–1892), thereafter returning to England. It is possible Howells made his acquaintance in Boston.

10. John Howells' firm, Howells and Stokes, had just received an architectural commission, possibly the Title Guaranty and Trust Building in New York.

11. John J. Stephens (b. 1851) was appointed vice and deputy consul at Plymouth in 1897. Born in England, he received part of his education at Wabash College, Crawfordsville, Indiana. His daughter is not identified.

15 MARCH 1904, EXETER, TO ELINOR M. HOWELLS

> Royal Clarence Hotel,
> Exeter, March 15, 1904.

Dear Elinor:

We never went to Exeter last summer,[1] and here I am without you! The run from Plymouth was 1½ hours, through the loveliest English country; trees leafless yet, and grass less green as we left the sea; but cowslips along the R. R. banks, and young lambs in the meadows where their elders idled over the chopped turnips. Ivy grabbing the trees everywhere; gray stone cottages; thatched roofs, and stone field-walls built up with turf, and hedged on top. Dull sky, when it turned sunny and warmed our 3d class comp't, which we had to ourselves in the greatest comf. and Pullman car smoothness. We seem to have this rickety old hotel to ourselves too, and the ancient cathedral which it looks out on, a blur of time-worn carving, with more archaic royalties than archaic sanctities covering the whole front, lying down and standing up. We were at the service this p.m., which was all in the choir. From where we sat, like groaning and sighing of the past, and pathetic on the human side, but for worship, just *mumming*. No wonder the Puritans wanted to knock it endwise. Nave is beautiful gothic, and most intensely interesting everywhere. Round after service in side altars, where bishops and crusaders lay on their tombs. Some Elizabethan ladies in ruffs, colored and portraitive.—Two dear old tabbies[2] made up to us in the fear of being locked in, and then turned perfectly lovely, hunting us down to shake hands at parting.—Here and at Plymouth, *several bonnets just like yours*; so you would be quite in style.—Rooks building in trees all through the town, which bulges every where with 17th cent. houses. (Better shops than in P.)[3] We belong in the cathedral close, and clerics are everywhere, from curates up to archdeacons and bishops.—Choir boy voices like angels.—Perhaps fifty people at service. No vergers, but left to find our way, after paying 6 pence each. Big stoves for heating, and stokers going round with wheelbarrows of coal, and filling up noisily with shovels.—Much processioning to and from high altar; Clergy in white surplices with red and black bands over shoulders. *Romish.*—Pil sketching cathedral. Having royal time, but forbids my making acquaintance. To little park overlooking the Exe, with ships come up from the sea, and fronted on by fine, large old houses, crescent-wise. Very sunny, but seemed a decayed neighborhood.—Writing in hotel parlor, where we look to the left on Eliz. house (papers, fotos, pictures) with 2d story built out and fenestrated like the "castle" of old warship, and within *stemmas* of Drake and other old sea-dogs. Just in from "Bedford Circus," where "Met. Life Insurance of N. Y." caught my eyes first. Kept on and came to tablet saying "Henrietta dau. of Charles I" born there. Wife of Monsieur, you know, and supposed poisoned.[4]—Stationer who sold us this paper took us for Australians.—Landlady very interested in us, when she knew us from U. S. Seems a passport to English good will.—Nice tabby in Cathedral thought our president "such a fine man." Plenty of fruit from Spain in shops.—Beautiful old furniture and silver.—Stopped at Axminster, 5 m. from *Lyme Regis!*[5] Lovely beach near by with wild, grotesque bluffs. Whole R. R. journey quite enchanting.—I will stuff this with fotos.

1. Howells here refers to Exeter, New Hampshire. This letter is the basis of "Twenty-four Hours at Exeter," *Harper's Monthly*, September 1905, which became the second chapter of *Certain Delightful English Towns*.

2. Two old ladies. See *Certain Delightful English Towns*, p. 30.

3. Plymouth.

4. Monsieur was Phillipe I, duke d'Orléans (1640–1700), so called after his brother, Louis XIV (1638–1715), became king of France in 1643. His wife, Henrietta, daughter of King Charles I of England (1600–1649), died a mysterious death in 1670.

5. Lyme Regis is a port and seaside resort on the English Channel 150 miles southwest of London. Howells' underscoring suggests that he wanted Elinor to remember that it was the scene of a romantic crisis for Captain Wentworth in Jane Austen's novel *Persuasion* (1818).

18 MARCH 1904, BATH, TO ELINOR M. HOWELLS

Bath, March 18, 1904.

Before break. which we *never* get till nine. Till then, waiters, porters, etc., round in shirt-sleeves: two gongs, first 15 min. previous, just sounding.—Large fine renaissance house at head of this st. terribly ruined, with windows all broken, and sign up that "Tresp. wd. be pros." Edge of Sidney Gardens, where Jane tho't she sh'd not mind concert bec. she sh'd be out of hearing.[1]—Lookt lodgings yest. p.m.—Neat maids, except one beetle-browed young landlady. All too many rooms, and mostly not to let till next week. Easter, the great season here. Terms varied from 2 to 3½ guineas a week. One place off. to take us on "long let," and shake 2 ladies who come every year for a short time. None so nice as 18 Pelham C.[2] At some places men, evidently retired butlers; all thanked us, as if we had taken. Eng. servants thank you for taking food, or making them do anything, or looking at them. This a.m. Pil tho't it sunny; I, raining; not much visible diff.—This hotel, halls heated with steam radiators. Rooms therefore not very cold.—Concert in Pump Room, where you walk about. Going this p.m.

After B.—Just in from walk with Pil. Found house wh. Jane lived from 1801 to 1805, 4 Sidney Place, looking on that ruined Georgian villa. Lady feeding parrot in dining-room. Longed to ring, but didn't dass to. Must, later. Tablet in wall to fact. Beautiful bright day. 8 days in England, and no rain yet, but fields sopping all the way from Exeter. Waiting now for doctor. *12:30.* Very nice young Scotch **Dr.** Crawford, going to Via Reggio with sick young wife next week.[3] Presc. water once a day for me, one week; tonic after dinner. No baths. Tonic for Pil, with change to Ilfracombe coast in a week or so. *Will keep you posted as to our movements.* Better send all letters care J. S. Morgan & Co., 22 Old Broad st., London.—To Roman Baths, larger, finer, more int. than anything in Italy. Modern buildings standing on Roman underpinning of concrete. Walls of hollow brick, like Dalhousie.[4] Guide very proud of having helped dig place out with his hands for carefulness. Large open bath for men, with sun shining into it; smaller for wom. & chil. Goldfish swimming round in luke warm min. water. "Bless you, they like it."—Pump, goblet water, 2 pence. Semi-shabby lady at elbow. "Isn't this Mr. H.? I met you years ago at Mrs. Fields's,[5] etc." A Miss Butler.[6] Visions of clinging, but perhaps not. Showed me Smalley letter in *Times*, with respectful ref. to me[7]—wh. she had just read.— People sitting round, sipping water, and reading papers. Not Carlsbad stir or gayety.

We are going out this afternoon on the tram to Combe Down, from which we see the hill with the great White Horse on it in Wiltshire, and the last battlefield bet. Saxons and Normans.

—What Smalley said was that "New York society excludes lit. men, or (as Mr. Howells more justly puts it,) few lit. men care to enter it."

Rather headachy place, Bath, in the valley but all right on the hills. I close this so as to catch Cunard steamer tomorrow.

Your
W. D. H.

1. Howells elaborated on this allusion in "A Fortnight in Bath": "Jane Austen writes in one of her charming letters that she liked going to the concerts of Sydney Gardens because, having no ear for music, she could best get away from it there...." See *Certain Delightful English Towns*, p. 63.

2. The Howells family had stayed at 18 Pelham Crescent, South Kensington, during their visit to London in 1882. In Bath Howells stayed in a hotel on Pulteney Street, "round the farthest corner of which the dear, the divine, the only Jane Austen herself had lived for two years in one of the large, demure, self-respectful mansions of the neighborhood." See *Certain Delightful English Towns*, pp. 43–44.

3. See Howells to Elinor Howells, 18, 19, and 20 March 1904, n. 4, and Howells to Clemens, 19 April 1904, n. 1.

4. The Dalhousie apartment hotel, 40 West 59th Street, New York City.

5. Annie Adams Fields of Boston.

6. Miss Butler has not been identified.

7. George W. Smalley (1833–1916) was an American journalist and correspondent with the London *Times* (1895–1905). Howells quotes the reference later in this letter.

18, 19, AND 20 MARCH 1904, BATH, TO ELINOR M. HOWELLS

Bath, March 18, 1904. 5.45 p.m.

By tram with Pil and Mrs. Cairns,[1] our Scotch table-mate, (with the rheumatic husband) to Combe Down, to see the White Horse in Wiltshire. It was on the great field between the Saxons and Danes, (*not* Normans) and Alfred the Gr. had it cut out of the turf down to the chalk. We could not see it bec. the mist had thickened so on the hills, but we saw (in spite of us) a pigeon match: the poor creatures untrapped, strutting a few steps, then springing into the air, and brought down by the guns, tumbling to the ground, and fluttering wounded till the dogs ran to fetch them. Crowd much like a baseball crowd. 2 policemen looking on to keep order. One very cordially told me where to go for view of W. H. It was in a pasture, near a stone farmhouse, where rooks, choughs and chickens were all associating on equal terms; birds flew up at each distant shot. Farmer whom I asked the way, "You mean the Wiltshire White H*a*rse?" 2 stupid girls who could tell Pil nothing. Thick, soft turf. Downhill by short cut back to cars. Side hill orchard sloping up to tall elms around high chimneyed ivy walled mansion. (Lark spiring up and singing in mid air; but sky gray and cold.) Country as neat almost as town, on the lanes we took.—Stopped for tea at gloomy restaurant in town, where we had it in a sombre, red upper room, very cold; but good tea, with bread and butter for 6 pence each.—Went and came on top of tram, and had glorious views. Mrs. Cairns very instructive about Scotland. You would like her.— Apples here only good for cider.—Black Berkshire pigs rooting in fields.— All the people well clothed. No such rags as in N. Y. or shabbiness as in K. P.[2] As to misery, I don't know and sha'n't ask.—I'm afraid Bath is neuralgic, for that nerve in the back of my neck is rather lively. The shore climates are the best; Plymouth was delightful; and the weather here has been blameless, so far. Spring not so forward.

March 19

Pilla and I to Assembly rooms. Just what you would expect them from Jane's novels. Very large, formal, and rather coarse than fine in dec. You must not expect Italian delicacy here. First, cloak rooms in rotunda; then drawing-room; tea-room at side, and vast ball-room. Chandeliers, solid glass, 600 to 800 lbs., all prisms. Workmen now putting rooms in order for Easter balls. (County Club ball the swell one, and a fancy ball. Wish Pil . . . .[3] of lawyer in Scotland; but knew my books in Douglas ed.; they were great favorites with his mother. He is *very* nice, and gentle; his wife is dying of consumption, and he is hurrying away to Italy with her.[4] Raining today, and warmer; but now rain has stopped. We shall not try for lodgings, since our stay will be so short; but I will ask about board, so as to get some notion of cost, in case Mary should come. Still, . . . the . . . .[5]

March 20

Sunday bef. break.—Yesterday p.m. Miss Butler (my Mrs. Fields acq.,[6]) brought a Miss English[7] to call, and Miss E. asked Pil and me to lunch on Tuesday. She has been 9 yrs. mem. of B'd of Guardians of the Poor, and her next election comes on Monday; women as well as men vote for that office; but there is a strong move of the dissenters against the church people, and she expects defeat. She is a very jolly person, and full of laughing. Frankly hates Jane Austen, but adores me; and had read her copy of L. of Aroostook till it dropped to pieces; it was fervently commended to her by the Toynbee Hall Toynbees,[8] who seem to have made a crusade for my books; she is a cousin of Lady Stanley[9] (look her up), and lives here because, she says, the wheels are well oiled for single women in Bath. Promises, if we go to Ilfracombe, to make us acq. with the wittiest family in the world. They are all, except two steady sisters, quite mad at times, but when they are out of the asylum, are delightful.—She will ask to meet us, at lunch, a lady who knows every hole and corner of Bath; so it is really a great thing for us. She lives on one of the downs in "the third best air in England." There is an annex of this hotel up there, and if we decide to stay longer in B. we may transfer to it.—The first gong has sounded. The sky is hid in mist, but whether it will rain or will sun, gracious knows. Birds singing, and palpably warmer.—Pilla is to have her br. in bed. Last eve. made us tea, with lemon in, on her spirit lamp. We try to have a cosy time, but we think John and you beat us. No letters from you since yours of the 8th. Perhaps some this morning.

Papa.

1. Mrs. Cairns has not been identified.
2. Kittery Point, Maine.
3. Bottom half of sheet torn off.
4. This is a description of the young Scotch doctor, John Crawford, no doubt the son "of a lawyer in Scotland," who attended Howells at Bath. See Howells to

Elinor Howells, 18 March 1904, and Howells to Clemens, 19 April 1904, n. 1. David Douglas, the Edinburgh publisher, had printed a uniform edition of Howells' works in the early 1880s.

5. Bottom half of sheet torn off.

6. See Howells to Elinor Howells, 18 March 1904, n. 5 and n. 6.

7. Miss English has not been identified. Howells and Mildred made the acquaintance of several women in Bath with whom they socialized. See Howells to Elinor Howells, 24 and 25 March 1904, n. 7.

8. Toynbee Hall in London was established in honor of economist and philosopher Arnold Toynbee (1857–1883), shortly after his death, for the purpose of bringing together the working classes and university-educated people.

9. Probably Lady Dorothy Stanley (d. 1926), wife of explorer Sir Henry M. Stanley (1841–1904).

20 MARCH 1904, BATH, TO JOHN ST. LOE STRACHEY

Pulteney Hotel,
Bath, March 20, 1904

Dear Mr. Strachey:

If I am so fortunate as to see Sutton Court you may be sure that I shall see it with eyes unhardened by any prejudices against primogeniture, and with a tenderness that your love for it has taught me to feel.[1] In a world which, to an old Tolstoyan manqué (Tolstoy himself is a Tolstoyan manqué) like myself seems altogether wrong I cannot select particular objects of reform, and if I could I don't think I should begin with the custom that gives Sutton Court to your elder brother.[2] At home I find people accumulating acres for which neither they nor their children can ever have any beautifying or hallowing sentiment.

I am sending you a book[3] which I brought across the sea for you. All that was most serious in my life at one time went into it; but if you do not care for the poems I am sure you will like the mystical beauty of the pictures which were done by Howard Pyle, of Quaker-Swedenborgian origin like myself, and which he took a peculiar interest in doing.

I beg you not to trouble about acknowledging the volume. I know that your infallible English post will carry it unerringly to you.

Yours sincerely
W. D. Howells.

1. Strachey was the second son of Sir Edward Strachey, third baronet of Sutton Court, Somerset. Howells visited the Strachey family seat on 26 March, rhapsodizing about it in a letter to Strachey, 27 March 1904 (House of Lords, London): "For my daughter and me the whole affair was of a dreamlike quality which it still refuses to part with . . . . I shall, I dare say, see other places in England, but I am glad, for reasons I need not express, that I have seen your family home first." He

later wrote Strachey, 21 January 1905 (House of Lords, London), submitting for approval the description of Sutton Court that eventually appeared in *Certain Delightful English Towns*: "I have described the place without naming it, for I dread treading upon privacy, and I have not satisfied myself in what I have done, by any means. I will put some interrogations over certain passages, so that you can decide for or against them when you see the MS., and when you return it, I shall know where I have erred, and correct myself accordingly." In chapter 4, "A Country Town and a Country House" (pp. 92–102), Howells' extensive sketch discreetly preserves the promised anonymity, although the caption for the accompanying illustration betrays it as Sutton Court.

2. Strachey's older brother was Sir Edward Strachey (1858–1936), politician and landowner, and first Baron Strachie of Sutton Court.

3. *Stops of Various Quills.*

24 AND 25 MARCH 1904, BATH, TO ELINOR M. HOWELLS

Diary.

Bath, March 24.

Just back with P.[1] from Bradford-on-Avon, where the old Saxon church of 7th cent. stands on battle-g. bet. Saxons and Britons. Perfect repair, and little restored; main fabric, of gray stone, oddly romanesque, with a few narrow windows. On slope, with row of small stone cottages, diamond paned and damp with the damp of ages. Pretty, red cheeked, yellow-haired oldish little girl sold permits to see ch. and then showed it snuffling. (Everybody has head colds here, and snuffles.) Inside very dungeon-like, very small and dim. Service still held in it, and chairs set, with small altar; most impressive.—Next to Kingston House, by Giovanni di Padova, where beautiful Italian feeling mixt with English setting.[2] Long velvet lawn, with peacock spreading his tail at farther end; stone balustrade and urns and beasts on top: dovecot, with red and mauve doves; garden w. trained fruit trees. Masses of evergreen shrubs. (There seem far fewer nevergreens). To 2 old timber-gabled houses in st. called *Shambles*; 1650. Then to old tithe-barn, 1300; now malodorous cowbarn of dairy farmer; cows badly kept and heaps of manure. Too early for train back; so walked about through charming, deadly dull little dwelling-street; so to tea back of green-grocer's near station, where peasant and boy gulped their tea to leave place to us; groceress *dusted* where they had with her apron, and brought us delicious tea and b'd and butter with company cups. Interior sheathed up like seaside shell, and painted. B'ld'g probably newest in Bradford, wh. is the most enchanting, irregular old town in the world, with a sort of knotty, warty look on its broken hill slopes.—Kindness of only policeman in walking with us to livery stable. Pride of boyish driver who hitched up and put on tall hat. One carriage door off its hinges, wh.

he was careful not to open.—Walls in bloom below greengrocer's window; bloom all winter; but that doesn't mean warmth. Very raw, cold day. A little sun would have made B. look like Italian town. All west of England needs to be wrung out, and hung up to dry.

March 25. Pilla has told you about James's visit[3] wh. was quite ideal in its way, and seemed a great pleasure to him. I was very proud of the way P. looked and talked, always witty and easy, and such a *lady.* I think he must have admired her, for I saw him looking and listening with great deference, and vivid gleams of appreciation. He is *very* stout, and all over, filled out from head to foot, in a sort of chamfered squareness. He made many tenderly awed inquiries about you and John. By the way, I talkt last night with a rheumatic London architect, who askt at once abt McKim, and said he admired him immensely. He knew Willy's name in the firm,[4] and wanted to know how the work of diff. partners was distinguisht. Of course, he was interested in all I know of arch. in N. Y. Admires Bath, and promises some pictures of b'ld'gs here.—Your scrapful envelope of the 16th, by the *Celtic,* has just come, and I am heaping coals of fire on your head in these 4 pages for your 4 lines.[5]—I am glad to see John's Stock Exchange,[6] wh. I don't understand your meechingness about. We (P. and I) think it's very fine.—We are just getting ready to go out to lunch at Mrs. Watson's,[7] and by James's advice I am going in a *sack coat.* What do you think of that for informality?—This a.m. it has been snowing and raining. I am afraid about Sutton Court for tomorrow.[8]—Most amusing old lean-faced American at Bradford station, yesterday, with teeth full of gold who wanted to talk, and whose wife did not want him to.—*From now on send all letters to J. S. Morgan & Co., 22 Old* Broad st., London.

Papa

1. Pilla, i.e., Mildred Howells.

2. An illustration of Kingston House, built by Giovanni of Padua about 1600, appears in *Certain Delightful English Towns,* p. 88.

3. The exact date of Henry James's visit is not known, although it must have occurred between 20 and 23 March. James had written several letters from London urging an early meeting with Howells, most recently on 17 March 1904 (MH): "if you are not coming on to town *soon* I shall come down right boldly to luncheon with you." Howells afterwards wrote Elinor (undated fragment at MH) his perception of James's general frame of mind: "He seems to have grown more and more inward, and to retire to his own interior to ruminate the morsels of his fellow men which he captures in his consciousness of things outside."

4. For Charles F. McKim and his association with Elinor's brother William R. Mead, see Howells to Bigelow, 25 February 1878, n. 1.

5. In his letter to Elinor, 31 March 1904, Howells admonished his wife to "Be more unsparing about sending me mere politeness and praise letters. They will keep till we meet . . . ."

6. The Stock Exchange in Baltimore was another one of John Howells' commissions. See Howells to Elinor Howells, 13 and 14 March 1904, n. 10.

7. Mrs. Watson has not been identified, but she is probably one of the women enthusiastically described in a letter to Aurelia, 27 March 1904 (MH). Howells mentions having been at two luncheons and an afternoon tea in Bath with "three or four of the wittiest and most intelligent women" he has ever met. They "are like cultivated Boston women" and "know all my books."

8. Howells visited Sutton Court the next day as planned. See Howells to Strachey, 20 March 1904, n. 1.

12 APRIL 1904, LONDON, TO ELINOR M. HOWELLS

81 Eaton Terrace,
London, April 12, 1904.[1]

Dear E.

I have just lookt down from our dining room window, and seen, with a heartache for Kittery Point, our landlord digging the beds in his backyard, with a hen and pigeons in a coop near him, and his smallest girl pushing a toy wheelbarrow and playing at helping him. He seems a good sort, and tends to flowery speech. Last night, after I had got back from my Balfour tailor, I expressed my surprise that B. should go to such a simple shop. "Well, I don't think, sir, Mr. Balfour[2] cares much for his clothes, sir. Them distinguished men can't, sir. Their thoughts soars to 'igher things, sir."—We have another glorious day, warm and bright, and we have spent the most of it at the National Gallery. You would have to travel all Italy to see as good Italian pictures of all schools. There was that "Tailor" by Moroni and the "Gentleman with the Gloves," and such Veroneses, Peruginos, Botticelli's, Titians! And do you remember a Goya (Spanish) a French-revolution looking man? Pil tho't it almost the best picture there. Tremendous Rubenses Rembrandts, Hobbemas, etc. The British school simply out of sight.[3] Even I could enjoy them, and picked out only one bad one to admire.—We merely sketched through the portraits, for we were dead tired; but it is prodigious, and full of high notes of every age and degree, as well as celebrities in every art and science. It was these that made me feel the greatness of England as nothing else has yet. We came home on an omnibus top, and I *felt* London. It is like nature, so simple and vast and unhurried. If its people rustled as the N. Yorkers do, it would shake the earth. It would be as if the seasons got to rustling. The *stateliness* of the streets astounds one, at times in their long stretches of massive architecture, unbroken by blocks. They make New York seem slight, and crazy and trivial. The smutch on the white marble is like effective shadow. A massive *roar* that goes up from them is like a lion's in contrast with the aquiline shriek and screech of ours. Of course one feels that New York shall be; but London *is*. It's tremendous.—In spite of the warm days the spring comes slowly, but surely. The lilac leaves are half out and wont be fully unfolded for a week. The grass in the parks has lost its wet look, and people are lying on it.—I did not remember the dense life of the shopping streets, along Piccadilly. You're not pushed or crowded, but the stream flows by this way and that, and seems never to ebb, but by nightfall the tide is out, to rise foully again later. I wish for you all the time, because I know you would enjoy it so; but I wonder how much strength you would have for it. London is the best air yet, and Pilla seems to be getting stronger every hour.—Just here I'm tormented with the fear that I this morning posted without paying it a letter of hers to you; but perhaps I only partly paid it. At any rate I will repeat our week's engagements. Tonight both dinner at the McIlvaines; tomorrow I lunch with Harvey, Leveson Gower and Lord Lansdowne; Thursday, both dine at the Gowers who are nephew and niece of half the nobility; Friday, Louis Dyer breakfasts with us, and we tea at the Sidney Brookses';[4] Saturday we lunch at the Strachey's, and drive to Kew with them.— London is so much like nature that you feel in the country, or as much as you want to; for I remember the country as so cold and wet. Here I do get warmed through several times before night. When I wake Rawlinson[5] is fetching up my hot bath, and getting my clothes to brush. Breakfast is ready at night, and I shave and shiver down to the parlor fire. The coffee and the eggs, and bacon, or the fish warm me up, and then I write; but now we have decided every fine morning to go out and see something, and postpone the writing. I have been doing a tentative impression which could be used in the Spectator and Harper's Weekly both. Harvey thinks well of the scheme, but has not seen Strachey yet.[6] Meanwhile, in spite of our agreement, he has told round that I'm going to do a book, and am going to stay a year in England! He seems to have lost his head. Fortunately, I'm not obliged to do it, and I'm not letting it worry me. Only, if any such report reaches you, just remember that I have not yet promised *any sort of book on England*, though probably I shall do one of some sort. The thing is merely vexatious.

We are just going to dress for the McIlvaine dinner. John Lane[7] has just called with an invitation to dinner week after next

With love to John,

Papa.

1. Having found the weather too raw and cold, Howells and Mildred decided not to stay on the Isle of Wight as originally planned; instead they left Southampton

for London on 4 April. See Howells to Aurelia Howells, 3 April 1904 (MH). Their intention, he explains, was "to stay here five or six weeks, and then settle some-where in the country, while I travel about to different cities. But before that we hope to spend a week in Edinburgh. Otherwise we are without plans. Everything depends on how Elinor feels when she comes out, if she does come." See Howells to Aurelia Howells, 10 April 1904 (MH).

2. Arthur J. Balfour (1848–1930), first earl of Balfour, was the English philosopher and statesman who was then prime minister.

3. By "the British school" Howells probably meant such artists as Thomas Gainsborough (1728–1788), Sir Joshua Reynolds (1723–1792), and William Hogarth (1697–1764).

4. For Clarence W. McIlvaine, see Howells to James, 25 September 1890, n. 6. George Harvey, head of Harper & Brothers, was then visiting England. Charles Granville Gresham Levenson Gower (1865–1948) graduated from Eton and Oxford and was lord of the manors of Titsey, Limpsfield, and Tatsfield. Henry Charles Keith Petty-Fitzmaurice (1845–1927), fifth marquis of Lansdowne, was a prominent statesman and then foreign secretary. For Louis Dyer, see Howells to W. C. Howells, 22 September 1872, n. 5. Sidney Brooks (1872–1931) was a journalist and editor; a frequent contributor to British and American periodicals, he later became editor of the *Saturday Review* (1921) and *Sperlings Journal* (1917–1922).

5. Rawlinson appears to have been Howells' landlord at 81 Eaton Terrace.

6. Strachey wanted to print some of Howells' "impressions" of England in the *Spectator*. Howells wrote him on 4 April 1904 (House of Lords, London): "I couldn't answer for Colonel Harvey as to what arrangement he could make for what Mark Twain used to call simultaning, but I suppose he will be about now in London, . . . and perhaps it will be best for you to speak to him yourself."

7. John Lane (1854–1925), British publisher, was cofounder of the Bodley Head publishing firm (1887) and founder of the *Yellow Book* magazine (1894).

17 APRIL 1904, LONDON, TO ELINOR M. HOWELLS

. . .[1]one of the back . . .[2] was stayed by a lackey, who said it was private, though children were passing freely. Yesterday, Strachey opened a door from the Orangery, and a guard instantly called, "Private sir," tho' the door was . . . .[3] ours.—Quite hot in the sun this a.m., though I was so chilly indoors I could not write. The houses are refrigerators.—People of fashion now walk in Hyde Park after church Sunday morning—"church parade, they calls it, sir," Rawlinson[4] says, "but they'll come back to St. James's." The maid told Pil that after guard-mounting, Sunday a.m. the king can be seen coming out from B. P. to go to St. P's.[5]—James says that the travel by the big southern route steamers from America has made Rome and Florence crowded watering places. But I guess we can get in, and it will be all the more amusing. I'll enquire more about those steamers from London that touch at Naples.—I find a sort of fuzzy-mindedness very prevalent with me, here, and it seems as if clear-thinking must cost more effort than it does in America. I don't believe the English half know what they're doing things for; certainly the kinder sort don't. That's why they're able to put up with royalty and nobility; they've not thought it out; they are of the same mental texture as Jimmy Ford's basement-diners.[6]—James says he has not known above 2 women who were not snobs; but there are several more men, tho' they are very rare, too.—Monarchy is a fairy tale that grown people believe in and pay for. They speak quite awedly of royalties and titles, and wont join in the slightest smile about them. They simply don't conceive of joking about them; and how such satirists as Gilbert and Barrie[7] have contrived to live I don't understand.— The Withingtons[8] are coming Wednesday, and then I shall see my way to the larger book I imagined, or else devolve on something lighter and sketchier.—The weather is behaving like an angel, now, though it was so bad all winter that people were furious with it. You lost your temper, Rawlinson says.—He never goes to church. "I 'ad a friend, sir, and 'e done me up, and I aint been since, sir." . . .[9]

1. Top three quarters of page excised. The date of the fragment was established by the reference to "Sunday morning" and to the Withington dinner, which is also mentioned in Howells to Aurelia Howells, 17 April 1904 (MH).

2. Half a line excised.

3. Top three quarters of page excised. Howells is here describing his visit with the Stracheys to Kensington Palace, the birthplace of Queen Victoria. He briefly mentions the outing in his 17 April letter to Aurelia. The Orangery, a winter building for exotic plants, was designed by Sir Christopher Wren (1632–1723), the noted English architect, and is one of the places of interest in Kensington Gardens. See *London Films*, p. 95.

4. See Howells to Elinor Howells, 12 April 1904, n. 5.

5. Buckingham Palace and St. Paul's Cathedral.

6. James L. Ford (1854–1928) was an American author and humorist. The "basement-diners" are people who ignorantly worship high society in Ford's *The Brazen Calf* (1903), a satire of society-page journalism. Howells had reviewed the book in "Diversions of the Higher Journalist: the Superstition of the Society Page," *Harper's Weekly*, 19 December 1903, comparing Ford's basement-diners to "the multitude of fools and snobs" who grovel before European aristocracy.

7. Sir William S. Gilbert (1836–1911) is best known for his collaboration with Sir Arthur Sullivan on a series of comic operas for D'Oyly Carte's opera company. For James M. Barrie, see Howells to Aurelia Howells, 20 March 1898, n. 3. Howells reviewed Barrie's plays in an essay entitled "The New Plays: Mr. Barrie's Benefactions to Humanity on the Stage," *Harper's Weekly*, 24 February 1906.

8. Lathrop Withington is identified in a letter to Aurelia Howells, 20 September 1904 (MH), as "a far-off cousin of Elinor's who has lived 25 years in London, working up genealogies." He was Howells' guide in London and is referred to anonymously in chapters 17 and 18 of *London Films* as the authority for Howells' information on American origins. Withington is further described in a letter Howells wrote to an unidentified correspondent, 10 May 1906 (MH). The man had evidently questioned the accuracy of some of Howells' information in "A Glimpse of the English Washington Country," *Harper's Monthly*, April 1906 (chapter 13 of *Certain Delightful English Towns*). Howells asserted in the letter that his "authority is Mr. Lathrop Withington, 30 Little Russel Street, near the British Museum, where he may also be found, working in the library at his genealogical researches. He is from Newburyport, Mass., but has lived in London some twenty years. He was my companion and my most efficient guide in looking up American origins."

9. Remainder of letter missing.

19 APRIL 1904, LONDON, TO SAMUEL L. CLEMENS

81 Eaton Terrace, S. W.
London, April 19, 1904.

My dear Clemens:

When I got your letter the other day, I wrote to Dr. Crawford at Bath. Here is his answer, just come.[1] You'll see that I guarded myself from letting him suppose that you wished to see him professionally, though I read that wish into the anxiety of the allusion you made to his not having turned up. The way is now open to you. I know nothing of him except that the Scotch people who recommended him to me spoke highly of him; personally he made the most favorable impression. He is under forty, very gentle and kindly, but firm—the true physician's temperament; and he would hardly be from a Scotch medical school for nothing. I wish I could say more, but I don't know any more.

Your letter made my heart ache; and it still makes me dumb; but you know how I must feel for each of you; I don't know which I feel for most, but, I think, Jean and you, for Clara's presence with the suffering had its own help in it.[2] What a great good girl she is; one alone like her is enough to "justify the ways of God to man," which we have to stumble along in so unevenly, except for the light that a sublime creature like her sheds on them. As for Mrs. Clemens herself, there's truly nothing to say. I understand the sort of thing you are going . . . .[3]

Pilla and I came over because we were run down and now we are going from London for a week to get our breath from the thick air and the thick crowd.[4] If any man who *can* live in America comes to Europe he deserves all he gets. I look back at the long wastes of leisure, and the immunity from my fellow men, which I enjoyed at 48 W. 59, as to a dream of bliss incredible here, and utterly impossible. What torments of society I have suffered already, and James says what I've suffered is nothing. To think that if I were at home, we should be getting ready for the divine summer at Kittery Point! But, no! Mrs. Howells will be coming over in June or July, and we shall not get home before Christmas. What a wild fable it is about American girls having a good time in England! Pilla goes out to dinner with bald heads of 70 and 80, and with the pathetic patience of her sex denies that it is not amusing. In one dry Sunday in New York she sees more men and more brilliant ones than she will meet in England in a year.—I should hate to be a woman anywhere; but in England it must be martyrdom with the ignominy of the criminal, as compared with the free and honored career of a woman in America.—But of course we are only seeing the outside of things. With love to you all,

Yours ever
W. D. Howells.

1. Clemens' letter to Howells has not been located. Howells had written to Clemens, 25 March 1904 (CU; *Twain-Howells*, p. 783), introducing Dr. John Crawford, who was traveling to Italy with his ailing wife. Clemens was increasingly anxious about his own wife's precarious health and had apparently expressed concern to Howells that Dr. Crawford had not yet arrived. Crawford's answer to Howells, 19 April 1904 (CU), written from Paris, announced that his wife had died and that he certainly would avail himself of Howells' kind introduction to Clemens once he arrived in Italy.

2. Jean and Clara were Clemens' daughters; "the suffering" is evidently a reference to Olivia Clemens.

3. Howells left the sentence unfinished as he began a new page.

4. On 28 April Howells and Mildred left for Folkestone, about sixty miles from London on the English Channel.

1 MAY 1904, FOLKESTONE, TO ELINOR M. HOWELLS

2 Clifton Road,
Folkestone, May 1, 1904.[1]

Dear Elinor:

This is your birthday, I won't say the how manyeth,[2] and I can't let it pass without a love-letter, though you are probably heaping coals of fire on my head for something or other at this very moment. I wish you were here with us, for I still think you would like it immensely, here, though we have suspended buying the house that we intended taking the first day. This morning we walked far along the Leas toward Sandgate,[3] and then descended to the beach (soft brown gravel) and continued past pretty houses and gardens between the road and the sea. They were the size and shape of our seaside h.'s, only of brick and stone. But here and there was one of wood, clapboarded like ours, and looking very homey. The driver whom we took presently owned that they were tho't dryer, and said that they all belonged to the Earl of Radnor,[4] who owns the earth here and likes frame houses. He pointed out a villa and grounds which he said were the Countess of Chichester's.[5] But before we got him we had hung over many paling fences of humbler gardens, and admired the rows of peas and beds of strawberries, all netted against the birds or rabbits, but neat as pins. Every h. has its plot of g., and people live here with their toes in the sea the whole year round. The winter must be of Bermudan mildness, and the water is of the Bermudan iridescence. There were lots of lumpy little steamers in the offing, bound to or from France or Holland, but not so many sail as at K. P. There were lots of lovers on the beaches and benches, and girls treading the air beside the red coats from the camp at Sandgate. We found the old Elizabethan castle there shut up, and it was then that we got our fly, and had ourselves driven out to the camp. It's a whole town of barracks (many wooden ones), and then a village of tents. A band was playing, and masses of lower classes listening. The country far and near was killingly pretty, with a curious mixture of soldiers and sheep in different fields, and in one distance the old, old Cheriton church. I don't know whether the air was warm or cold; you never can tell, here; but it was fresh and sweet. At one place Cheriton had overbuilt itself, and its empty shops lookt boom-struck. In some houses were little home-stores such as I used to see at "Dublin" above North Cambridge.[6] We got home before lunch and took a supplementary walk on the Leas, where now we have been again. Week days you must wear a flat cap, like that I got for the steamer; Sundays, a pot hat; and of course I had my cap. The paths and lawns ever full of people, silent, dull and dumb; Pil and I were the only grinners, except a noisy German Jew who was dying laughing at some funny story he was telling about a dog. The English *are* a common looking lot; where there is any distinction it seems almost insolent.—There is a steel-pier here, half as long as Atlawntic Cittie's, where they have concerts. We went down an inclined lift, and got tea. It is wooded and gardened all along under the Leas, and the birds were singing in the dim light. It is a strange unearthly world; but I guess it is all right. Love to John.

Papa.

Laura's tribute is delightful.[7] I couldn't ask more.

1. Howells and Mildred had arrived in Folkestone on 28 April. See Howells to Elinor Howells, 29 April 1904 (MH), which is primarily an account of their visit to Hampton Court and the train trip to Folkestone.

2. It was Elinor Howells' sixty-seventh birthday.

3. Sandgate is one and a half miles west of Folkestone; on the high ground north of the town lies Shorncliffe, a military camp which is mentioned later in the letter.

4. Sir Jacob Playdell-Bouverie (1868–1930), sixth earl of Radnor.

5. Probably Elizabeth M. Pelham, wife of Sir Walter John Pelham, fourth earl of Chichester, who died in 1902.

6. The Irish settlement north of Cambridge, Massachusetts, built around an Irish cemetery. See *Suburban Sketches* (1871), pp. 63–64.

7. Laura P. Mitchell, Elinor's cousin. The nature of the tribute is not known.

13 MAY 1904, FOLKESTONE, TO ELINOR M. HOWELLS

Folkestone, May 13, 1904.

Dear Elinor:

There is nothing much to write since my last, but I send this so that you can get something by tomorrow's boat.

To day we drove up on the hills north of the town to see Caesar's camp, as it is called, where there are great Roman earthworks, perfectly distinct and in form. We went part of the way on the road the Canterbury pilgrims used to take, and passed the Holy Well where they stopped to drink.

When we got back we found that H. G. Wells, the novelist had called.[1] He lives near here at Sandgate in a very Californian house which he built himself. From his garden you look out over the Channel, as we do over Kittery Harbor, and can see the big Hamburg-American and Bremen steamers passing. He carried the stones to terrace it up with his own hands, for as he says he is of no class, from his humble origin, he does as he pleases about working. He is young, with a young wife and two little children. I like him better than any English author I've met yet.

Tonight I'm going to a great "Liberal Demonstration" in the Town Hall, and suppose I shall hear some anti-Chamberlain speaking.[2]

Andrew Carnegie's secretary has written from him to ask us to Skibo Castle.[3] No time is fixed, but perhaps if we go to Edinburgh we may go to Skibo.

Just off for the political meeting. I hope my later letters have smoothed out all difficulties.[4]

Papa.

Dear Mamma:

I have to add just these few lines to Poppy's letter because he and our landlord are both going to a Liberal meeting in the Town Hall tonight, and I cant get anything mailed after they leave. You cant get manola here, I enclose the letter the doctor gave me about it, which will show you that the subject has been sifted to the bottom.

The Thermometer says 70 this evening and said 80 last night, this is in our sitting room where there is a coal fire, but it would be the same in a bed room if you had a fire there, as I suppose you would if it were cold. Tell John that I am going to write him a long letter about Hythe because he might like to go there.

Pilla

1. It is unclear exactly when Howells visited Herbert George Wells (1866–1946), the English novelist. In a letter of 10 May 1904 (MH) Wells had written Howells: "I have long hoped to meet you, but I have always regarded it as a thing only to be achieved after a perilous pilgrimage, oceans & continents." In three short notes to Howells, all dated 14 May 1904 (MH), Wells indicated that the two writers had just been together. Apparently a second visit was planned because on 14 May (IU) Howells wrote Wells that Mildred and he could not accept an invitation for the following day, assuring Wells, however, that "This is no vile farewell; it is a pledge of future meeting." On 15 May (IU) Howells sent Wells yet another letter, thanking him for his books: "My daughter is reading one with a sense of your rather awful power, and I am half way through 'Love and Mr. Lewisham': a capital story, and mighty well told. When you come to look at my 'Undiscovered Country' you will be perhaps amused to find it beginning with a fraudulent spiritual séance; but we do not long work the same way together." Henry James at this time also encouraged Howells to meet Wells; in a letter of 13 May 1904 (MH) he wrote: "I hope you will have comfortably seen that fine-eyed little man of intelligence & genius." And again on 16 May (MH): "I rejoice you liked the Wellses, who have written to me (by his hand—I scarcely know *her*) effusively thanking me for the Howellses."

2. Joseph Chamberlain (1836–1914) was a businessman who rose to a prominent place in British politics. Although a Liberal-Unionist, he headed the colonial office under the conservative ministry of Lord Salisbury in 1895. He continued in that office when Arthur J. Balfour, another conservative, succeeded Salisbury in 1903, at which time he caused a furor within his own liberal ranks by advocating the suspension of Britain's free-trade policy.

3. Carnegie's secretary was James Betram, to whom Howells wrote on 13 May 1904 (MH) thanking Carnegie for the invitation, but declining it. Although Howells went to Edinburgh in August, he did not visit Carnegie because, as he wrote Aurelia Howells, 10 July 1904 (MH), "Skibo is 8 hours further." Skibo Castle was Carnegie's summer home in Scotland where the Scottish-born American industrialist entertained extensively.

4. Presumably a reference to Elinor's planned trip to Europe.

17 MAY 1904, LONDON, TO HENRY JAMES

> ...*Charing Cross Hotel.*
> May 17th, *1904*

Dear James:

This is deplorably enough my address for tonight and tomorrow night; then Oxford c/o Louis Dyer, (an old young friend), Sunbury Lodge, 68 Banbury Road, till Monday; then London c/o Harpers till we are settled again, locally.

Pilla's heart is wrung as much even as an indignant host could wish. She does not know what to say, or I for her; we both live in the wish to retrieve ourselves. Everything seems to go wrong with the poor child, except her amiable self, and she feels bitterly the disappointment she has inflicted on you at her own expense.[1]

I have had a line from Harvey, but nothing about the Women's Clubs.[2] Would you like me to jog him?

Yours ever
W. D. Howells.

1. Howells had been unable to keep a luncheon engagement with James at Lamb House apparently because Mildred had become indisposed. Howells' letter is a reply to James's amusing admonishment of 16 May 1904 (MH), describing his embarrassment at having to dine alone with the young man he had invited to be Mildred's companion: "It was a blow, this a.m.—the household had so projected itself into your advent & I had lain awake the previous night so long, listening to the roar of the fatted calf during his elaborate killing. This please relentlessly tell Pilla—as also that I had provided a very handsome & rising young man for her further consumption at luncheon—who made me a good deal of a scene when he arrived at L[amb House] & found the Attraction wanting. However, we sat down together & consoled each other by railing at female faith."

2. James was planning a trip to America during which he hoped to give lectures at women's clubs. He had enlisted Howells' aid in making appropriate inquiries, including one to Colonel George Harvey, head of Harper & Brothers.

1 JUNE 1904, RYE, TO ELIZABETH JORDAN

Lamb House,
Rye, Sussex, June 1, 1904.

My dear Miss Jordan:

I am here with our friend Mr. James, for the day, and we have had much talk of his American visit.[1] Part of his purpose in that mission, I hope the good but inarticulate Colonel[2] who commands us all, has told you, has been to address a lecture, on some literary subject, to deserving Women's Clubs; and when I last talked with the Colonel he said you would know just what to do for him in such a case.[3] In fact the affair was to be put in your hands, and I dare say it has been, and that you are treating it as no one else could. But no report of results has come, and if there is a flattering, or even unflattering, chance of our friend's doing anything in that way, he ought to be prepared with the paper he is to read, or would be to read; he naturally does not wish, in his crowded last months or weeks here to give the time to this preparation on too great uncertainties.[4]

His notion was that the sort of limited lecturing contemplated would give him a definite reason for visiting places, and bring him in relations with the general social fact on the sort of business basis which is the best. My own notion was that if he could place himself for a week at a time, say, in some such Women's Club centres as Indianapolis,

Minneapolis, Chicago, Buffalo, Boston, Detroit, Cleveland, etc., (I mention the places quite at random) he could radiate to their neighborhoods, at the least trouble to himself and the greatest cost to them. That is, he ought not to lecture for less than $150 or $200; the Colonel's heroic imagination soared to $500, but I fear such an ideal height; and he ought to lecture very, very few times, and *not* on any terms of public vastness. He should read, as I have done, in drawing-rooms, country-club-rooms, and the like, and the audience should be more or less invited, and made to feel itself privileged. This I am sure would be practicable during his New York stay; your thorough knowledge of the field will be better than mine as to other places. He would lecture on Balzac,[5] or on the Novel generally. Will you, dear Miss Jordan, kindly give the matter your immediate attention, and write directly to Mr. James, here? The time is now short, and will be shorter when your answer comes. Please remember that he could not contemplate a "lecturing tour," but would read his paper in the way I have suggested.—I have brutally confined myself entirely to business, but the amenities smile beneath, and my daughter, who is here with me joins Mr. James and myself in cordial remembrances.

> Yours sincerely
> W. D. Howells.

1. James embarked for the United States at the end of August 1904. He spent ten months in his home country lecturing, traveling, and absorbing impressions for a projected book that eventually became *The American Scene* (1907).

2. George Harvey.

3. Elizabeth Jordan was a prominent supporter of women's suffrage and, as editor of *Harper's Bazar*, closely connected with Harper & Brothers.

4. James had become uneasy when Colonel Harvey did not come forward with definite arrangements. He had written to Howells, 28 May 1904 (MH), thanking him for the "kind offer of stimulating Harvey on the great Ladies club subject," yet not expecting at this point to be able to count on any lecture dates. Again, in a letter of 22 June 1904 (MH), James wrote Howells: "Miss J.'s communication to myself has not yet turned up—it doubtless will soon; but meanwhile I see the prospect (in the particular matter) as quite conceivably not brilliant, and I am doubting if it will be my best economy to take the time necessary for the fabrication of an harangue."

5. When James ultimately succeeded in arranging engagements, his first lecture was entitled "The Lesson of Balzac," delivered before the Contemporary Club of Philadelphia, 12 January 1905, and then given at Bryn Mawr College and repeated with great success elsewhere on his tour. For the occasion of his second lecture at Bryn Mawr he wrote "The Question of Our Speech." See *The Question of Our Speech. The Lesson of Balzac. Two Lectures by Henry James* (Boston: Houghton Mifflin, 1905). In the only letter James wrote Howells during his American tour, a letter dated 1 March 1905 (MH), he expressed his gratitude for Howells' advice about preparing a lecture: "So I should have been really much of a lame duck if I hadn't more or less managed to follow your advice on the subject of preparing a lecture. That advice has been blest to me for it is helping to see me through.

Without it, I really think I should have had a collapse. It isn't that I have read the stuff often (I call it 'The Lesson of Balzac', and it seems to serve its purpose,) for I have exposed myself as yet only twice—both times at Philadelphia, that is the second at Bryn Mawr; but the consequences have been fruitful, and I go now to *re-spout* it in three or four cities of the West. It makes traveling possible, and in short I find I can do it: though only to the tune of a few times and for a positively quite maximum fee."

7 JUNE 1904, LONDON, TO SAMUEL L. CLEMENS

1 Clarges street,
June 7, 1904.

My dear Clemens:

The news has just reached us.[1] I will not try to say anything in the stupid notion of trying to help you. But I must, as if it had never occurred to me before, realize in words, that the character which now remains a memory, was one of the most perfect ever formed on the earth. How often John and I have spoken of that wonderful goodness, that soul of exquisite kindness, which was so strong and so gentle! Poor old fellow; I am so sorry for you and for your girls. But they will have the comfort of taking up her place in your life. What nonesense! Even they cannot do that. Well! Here are my love and pity.

Yours ever
W. D. Howells.

1. The death of Olivia Clemens, the evening of 5 June 1904, in Florence. Clemens must have cabled the news, since his letter to Howells, dated 6 June 1904 (MH; *Twain-Howells*, p. 785), could not have reached London the following day. See also Howells to Clemens, 9 June 1904.

9 JUNE 1904, LONDON, TO SAMUEL L. CLEMENS

1 Clarges street,
June 9, 1904.

My dear old friend:

I had written to you as soon as I knew of the fact,[1] just to let you know I was with you in that insurpassable sorrow of yours; but you must have known it already. Pilla and I tried to read your letter aloud; we couldn't.[2] It wrings my heart to think about you. What are you going to do, you poor soul? I mean literally. Are you going back to America at once? Or shall we have any chance of seeing you again on this side? My wife arrives on the 18th; John goes straight to Italy, sailing on the 2d July; we expect, we three, to spend the winter in Italy.

My love to your dear girls; Pilla has written already.

I cannot speak of your wife's having kept that letter of mine, where she did.[3] You know how it must humiliate a man in his unworthiness to have anything of his so consecrated. She hallowed what she touched, far beyond priests.

Yours affectionately
W. D. Howells.

1. See Howells to Clemens, 7 June 1904.

2. Clemens wrote to Howells on 6 June 1904 (MH; *Twain-Howells*, p. 785) describing Livy's death with moving simplicity: "Last night at 9.20 I entered Mrs. Clemens's room to say the usual good-night—& she was dead! tho' no one knew it. She had been cheerfully talking, a moment before. She was sitting up in bed— she had not lain down for months—& Katie & the nurse were supporting her. They supposed she had fainted, & they were holding the oxygen pipe to her mouth, expecting to revive her. I bent over her & looked in her face, & I think I spoke—I was surprised and troubled that she did not notice me. Then we understood, & our hearts broke. How poor we are to-day!"

3. In the same letter Clemens had also mentioned discovering a letter from Howells which Livy had kept: "To-day, treasured in her worn old Testament, I found a dear & gentle letter from you, dated Far Rockaway, Sept. 13, 1896, about our poor Susy's death. I am tired & old; I wish I were with Livy."

24 JUNE 1904, OXFORD, TO HERBERT G. WELLS

7 Longwall Street,
June 24, 1904.

Dear Wells:

Your letter has come to hand with the accompanying note, and I hope you have both come back to Sandgate[1] ever so much better for having gone away. But that I knew you *were* away I should have written before to tell you how much I thought of "Love and Mr. Lewisham" after I had finished the book.[2] It seems to me a great little book, with an extraordinary breadth, upwards and downwards, in it and the whole blind soul of youth. The commonness and yet earthly rightness of the girl who finally gets L. is precious—not to say *are*.

I am glad you fancied my novel for the reasons you did.[3] If you have read my criticism at all you know that I never care for the "story" in my things.[4]—I wish I were with you in your garden that I might talk with you impersonally about it all.

Yours ever
W. D. Howells

1. Wells's home near Folkestone.

2. Howells had begun reading the novel right after he and Mildred had visited Wells in May. See Howells to Elinor Howells, 13 May 1904, n. 1.

3. Wells's reasons for liking *The Undiscovered Country* were conveyed to Howells in a letter dated 26 May 1904 (MH). Wells called the novel "a delightful addition to my knowledge of you—& the Shakers. It's the nearest thing I have of yours too to a form I dream of, a novel in which the leading character so to speak is a *topic*. I think of something more living & eventful than Peacock & Mallock but less dependant on the 'story' even than this. I like the figures of the wandering Boynton's best . . . ."

4. In a review praising Henry James's *The Tragic Muse* (1891), "Editor's Study," *Harper's Monthly*, September 1890, Howells had drawn a sharp distinction between the story and the novel: "To such a mind as his the story could never have value except as a means; it could not exist for him as an end; it could be used only illustratively; it could be the frame, not possibly the picture." James, according to Howells, gives us a more substantial mode of fiction: "Here was a thing called a novel, written with extraordinary charm; interesting by the vigor and vivacity with which phases and situations and persons were handled in it; inviting him to the intimacy of characters divined with creative insight; making him witness of motives and emotions and experiences of the finest import; and then suddenly requiring him to be man enough to cope with the question itself; not solving it for him by a marriage or a murder, and not spoon-victualling him with a moral minced small and then thinned with milk and water, and familiarly flavored with sentimentality or religiosity." See also *Criticism and Fiction* (1891), pp. 118–20.

26 June 1904, Oxford, to Aurelia H. Howells and Anne H. Fréchette

7 Longwall street,
Oxford June 26, 1904.

Dear Aurelia and Annie:

Not the least pleasant event of last week was the coming of your joint letter, with its congratulations and sweet good wishes.[1] Well, I have got safely through all, and except for the nervous strain, which was temperamental, it was all very easy. The English take everything on the simplest terms, and let other people do so. The degreeing itself was very formal, of course, but by no means formidable. The Doctors of Letters came in last, and perhaps the undergraduates had shouted themselves empty before, but I got not a single jibe, in a great roar of applause. I had caught sight of Elinor[2] and Pilla looking down, and that stiffened my knees. I had only to listen to my own eulogy in Latin, and then mount some steps to the new Chancellor (Lord Goschen)[3] who welcomed me in Latin, gave me his right hand, and motioned me to a seat with his left. Then the affair was over. Afterwards I lunched in All Souls college and dined in Christ Church. All sorts of teas and dinners have ensued, and many people have called, including Professor

Ernest Rhys[4] and his beautiful daughter, who was full of both your praises. I found him looking much like me, and apparently pleased at my saying so. He speaks English with a strong Welsh accent. Elinor thought the daughter wonderful. They asked us to lunch, but we could not manage it.

I have sent you papers about the degreeing, and I will send you a photo. of the procession where you will easily find me.

We are all dreadfully tired, but Elinor and I go to London tomorrow, and Pilla will follow a few days later.

Distinctions all come rather late in life, and if they do not kill, they cure the desire for more. Love to you all, including the Joe family.

> Your aff'te brother
> Will.

Of course nothing of this must get into print.

1. Howells had received the honorary degree of doctor of letters from Oxford University on 22 June.

2. Elinor Howells had arrived in Liverpool aboard the *Umbria* on June 18.

3. George J. Goschen (1831–1907), first Viscount Goschen and prominent English statesman, had been a member of various ministries, a founder of the Liberal Unionist party, chancellor of the exchequer, and first lord of the admiralty. He was chosen chancellor of Oxford University in 1903.

4. Ernest Rhys (1859–1946) was an English author and editor best known for editing inexpensive reprints of the classics for the "Everyman's Library."

25 SEPTEMBER 1904, LONDON, TO AURELIA H. HOWELLS

> 34 Half Moon street,
> Sept. 25, 1904.

Dear Aurelia:

Here we are still in London,[1] though Pilla is within a week or so of starting to Florence with her aunt Mary,[2] and Elinor and I expect to follow a little later for San Remo, a winter resort between Nice and Genoa. Still, at the last moment she may change her mind and we may go home at once. It is pretty well settled that Pilla will spend the winter on this side, partly in Italy, partly in Paris. It would be well for Elinor to have a mild, open air winter on the Mediterranean, but I am leaving the decision to her. If she wishes to stay, we shall not travel in Italy, but settle at San Remo, where I will write my book on England.

Friday morning I started with a friend who is helping me in my researches,[3] to look up the traces of the Pilgrims, and we went to the queer little old Boston on the coast of Lincolnshire that our Boston is named after. There we found the prison that the poor things were put into when they were arrested in their first attempts to emigrate. The town has a most beautiful old church, and a deep river, where there is a tide of 20 feet. It is all most quaint, but somehow less livable looking than most English towns. Joe would have liked it, and the town of Lynn where so many New Englanders came from. We were also at Great Grimsby, the largest fishing port in the world. A hundred smacks lay in the Harbor, which was otherwise full of logs from Norway for the sawmills sizzing all about. I got home last night.

John is motoring with a friend in Italy, and we have not heard from him for some days. I am not sure that we shall see him on this side. If we go to San Remo, we may go home from Genoa in the winter, or may not sail till spring. With love to Henry,

> Your aff'te brother
> Will.

I hope you have got well of your fall,[4] and are looking forward to pleasant plans for the winter.

1. Between early July and mid-September Howells had traveled extensively through England, Wales, and Scotland. He and Elinor went from Oxford to Great Malvern near Worcester and thence to Llandudno, Wales, where they arrived on 12 August, Mildred meanwhile staying in the vicinity of Oxford to work on some drawings. On 18 August Howells set out on his own for Edinburgh for a week's visit with his British publisher, David Douglas. After a brief stay in Glasgow (23–25 August), he returned to Wales and, in the company of his wife and daughter, traveled via Manchester and Sheffield to York, arriving there on 2 September. In a letter to a Mr. Gilman, 10 September 1904 (MH), Howells wrote: "This York is not so large by about 2,500,000 people as the York I live in, but it is about 2000 years older, and about 20,000 times as interesting. I go out every day and have a Roman ruin, or a Saxon church or a Norman castle, or a Plantagenet wall before lunch, and there will be plenty left even at that rate." Finally, on 12 September, the Howellses returned to London.

2. Mary Mead, Elinor's sister.

3. Lathrop Withington. See Howells to Elinor Howells, 17 April 1904, n. 8.

4. Aurelia had fallen from a ladder. See Howells to Aurelia Howells, 13 September and 20 September 1904 (both at MH).

14 OCTOBER 1904, SAN REMO, TO AURELIA H. HOWELLS

> San Remo, Oct. 14, 1904.

Dear Aurelia:

While I think of it I will ask you to tell Joe that I got his very full and satisfactory letter about Leatherwood, yesterday.[1] It seems all I want, but I want more details when I get to writing the story.

We left London at 11 a.m. last Friday, and arrived, via Paris in Marseilles the next morning. We spent two days in that most brilliant and interesting city, and then came on to Cannes where we had a day and night, tasting the glories and delights of this wonderful coast. We got to San Remo at 6, Tuesday, in a rain; but next day the sun blazed out, and it seems as if it had been blazing ever since. It is all just the fairiest dream. Palms and olives and oleanders are the common shade trees, and the market is full of grapes, figs and peaches. It is joy to be in Italy again, and this so much more tropical than Venice that it seems as if I had never been in Italy before. It beats Bermuda hollow.— Joe says Henry is more nervous than before. If Joe will go with you to Ottawa, I will gladly pay his fare—supposing you need his help. I send you the November check from London.—I'll write soon more fully. Pilla is in Venice with John. She will go to Florence, and he will come here before he sails. Elinor is surprisingly well.

> Your affte brother
> Will.

We are at a transient hotel, but we expect to go into permanent quarters tomorrow at the "Hotel Paradis et de la Russie," but continue to address me c/o Morgan & Co., London.

1. This is the first indication that Howells was contemplating a novel, eventually published as *The Leatherwood God* in 1916, which is based on the life of a self-proclaimed religious prophet who lived in the Ohio frontier village of Leatherwood Creek in the early 1880s. Howells had asked his brother Joseph for help in collecting pertinent information. In a letter to Joe, 5 November 1904 (MH), he indicated his satisfaction with the materials Joe had sent: "I have asked Aurelia to tell you how quite satisfactory your Leatherwood letter was. I may ask some further details when we meet, but I could do perfectly well from what you have given." Howells also wrote to Aurelia, 27 November 1904 (MH), that he had thanked Joe, adding that the Leatherwood story would probably be his next major piece of fiction. Although the Leatherwood project began to loom large in Howells' imagination at this time, he did not actually write the story for many years. He alluded to it implicitly in a letter to S. Weir Mitchell two months later, briefly revived it in 1907 when Joe inquired whether Howells still planned to do the book, and took it up again in 1911. See Howells to Joseph A. Howells, 24 February 1907 and 18 August 1911; also *The Leatherwood God*, HE, pp. xi–xii.

4 November 1904, San Remo, to Charles E. Norton

> Villa Lamberti,
> San Remo, Nov. 4, 1904.

My dear Norton:

You will have accounted for getting no answer to your kindest letter, I hope, upon the theory that I was still out of the country.[1] I am as far out as Italy, you see, with the bluest of skies over my head, and the bluest of seas at my feet; but I would give them both for an hour in your painted woods, and my wife would give them for much less. She is openly and I secretly homesick, as in fact we have been all summer in spite of the intense interest of our English sojourn. At times we enjoyed it greatly, and at other times not, but it was interesting always. I quite long to tell you of it, sunk in some deep armchair by your study fire, but it is physically and spiritually impossible to write it. I think the intimacies of it would amuse you, and it is a pity that such things must not be put into print, for they ought. What you say of the Oxford episode revives all the pleasure of it, and none of the pain.[2] If the elderly man I am could set it all down, it would be a unique, if not a precious gift to literature, and what a "character" I could create out of myself!—We left England early in October, and dropped precipitately down to Marseilles in the roughest of sleeping cars; then we came on to San Remo, where we have taken an apartment in this pretty villa, which has a garden full of palms, lemon-trees orange-trees, purpling vines, roses and oleanders and laurels, just as in the theatre, and in all the water-colors and chromolithographs. Pilla is at Florence with my sister-in-law,[3] and John sailed from Genoa for New York on Sunday. This is my family news. For the rest I am working at the English material, which I hope to make into a pleasant, harmless book. We have no acquaintance here, except the Vice Consul and his wife,[4] a Connecticut woman of great sprightliness and good nature,[5] and a very nice young Manxman named Gill,[6] who was telling us yesterday that he was at school and at Oxford with Walter Ashburner.[7] He is comfortable to me through the zeal he professes for my books, many of whose multitude he seems to know.—James offered to write me "an early letter" from America,[8] but I do not make him even the most tacit reproach, for I know how these things go. Give him my love, when you see him. I had great fears for him in the vast roomy continent where I should like so much to be. My wife joins me in regards to you and all yours.

> Affectionately yours
> W. D. Howells.

1. Thinking that Howells had returned from Europe, Norton had written him in New York, 18 October 1904 (MH), welcoming him back, congratulating him for the honorary Oxford degree, and inviting him to meet with the Saturday Club together with Henry James.

2. See Howells to Aurelia Howells and Anne Fréchette, 26 June 1904.

3. Mary Mead.

4. The nearest American vice consul to San Remo was stationed in Genoa; at this time the post was occupied by Frederico Scerni, an Italian.

5. The Connecticut woman has not been identified, unless she is identical with the vice consul's wife, a possibility suggested by Howells' ambiguous syntax.

6. William Arthur Gill, the British journalist, who was then with the London *Morning Post*.

7. Walter Ashburner (1864–1936) was a barrister of Lincoln's Inn and professor of jurisprudence at Oxford University.

8. See Howells to Jordan, 1 June 1904, n. 1. In a lengthy letter, written before his departure, 5 August 1904 (MH), James spoke of personal feelings and literary matters: "in respect to my being *able,* after all, to embark for the U. S.—the failure of which wd. have been, I confess, a great humiliation & disappointment to me. I feel my going not only as a lively desire but as a supreme necessity—& I rejoice to say that it appears to be now definitely settled that I *do* embark. The good Pinker, my 'literary agent' came to my aid in intention, jealously, by thinking a month ago that he had a good opportunity—or possibility—of arranging to *serialize* the *Golden Bowl* for me in the U. S. (so as to realise very much more on it . . . .) So I feverishly divided it into 12 instalments, (& it *cut* far better than might have been,) & it was despatched, or 11 Parts out of the 12 were, across the Atlantic for judgment. I waited in great tension, & the people, whoever they were . . . , took a fortnight, or almost, to consider & decide. Then they cruelly cabled 'Declined', & the Golden Dream was as broken outside, as the Golden Bowl within." Later in the same letter James tried to assuage self-doubts that Howells had expressed when they were together in England: "What I have really all the while wanted *much* more to say to you is that my desire is, above all, to know you at ease about yourself—as I felt you insufficiently to be as we walked away together from Eaton Terrace that last evening. You expressed some doubt, I remember, as to whether the N. Y. people wd. 'like' something you had sent over (about Folkestone I think)—as well as general *malaise* about your footing of production (abroad,) which I longed at the moment to combat with high emphasis, & which it has since haunted me that I have been leaving unrefuted. What I mean is that in your questioning in detail, at this time of day, that immense 'liked' & likeable state which is the very air your work draws breath in & the very ground it has under its feet, was to 'borrow trouble' as wantonly (as who shld. say,) as if you were borrowing Hall Caine or M. Corelli. Sink luxuriously into your *position*, your immense record of admirable labour & the right of *leaning back* on your own terms, that crown this as with a wreath of honour & of ease, & you will do what every one concerned wants quite exceedingly to understand you as doing—& as understanding that you *must* do." Sir Thomas Henry Hall Caine (1853–1931), Dante Gabriel Rossetti's house companion from 1881 to 1882, and British novelist Marie Corelli (1854–1924) were both well known as authors of successful popular romances. James might be indirectly alluding to a satiric piece entitled "The Corelli-ing of Caine," which had appeared the previous year in *The Literary Guillotine* (1903) by British-American writer Oliver B. Herford (1863–1935).

30 NOVEMBER 1904, SAN REMO, TO FREDERICK A. DUNEKA

San Remo, Nov. 30, 1904.

Dear Mr. Duneka:

I am sorry to add to your many and great annoyances by a minor one of my own, and my only excuse is that it has got at last on my nerves. I enclose a very detestable caricature of myself, cut from an adv't in the *Weekly*,[1] which is not less a caricature because it is taken from my face. When I first saw a proof of it, Mr. Mott[2] promised me it should never be used, and I have since spoken with every one concerned with illustrating your periodicals, and had the same promise from each. Once I spoke long and tiresomely to you yourself about it. I identified the abominable thing to you, among other photos. you had in your drawer, and you tore it across, saying it should never be used again. It has been constantly used since, just as before. *Some* one must authorize its use in spite of you. Cannot you get at him, and with my respectful compliments, kill him?

My books, to our common sorrow, sell little enough at the best; but if I supposed this a true likeness of their author I would never buy one of them.[3]

Yours sincerely
W. D. Howells.

1. The offending likeness was a photograph that appeared in an advertisement for *The Son of Royal Langbrith* in *Harper's Weekly*, 12 November 1904. After running in the issues of 19 and 26 November, the advertisement was withdrawn.

2. Mott, apparently a Harper employee, has not been identified.

3. Howells had been in steady correspondence with Duneka about the progress on his work about England. On 17 September 1904 (MWA) Howells wrote: "You tell me nothing as to illustrations, in answer to my last, which indeed you have not answered at all. You know how much I am hoping from the book we have in view, and how anxious I am that it should be thoroughly attractive." By mid-October Howells had heard from Duneka, apparently to the effect that Howells was to send photographs of England for illustrations; he wrote Duneka on 12 October 1904 (RPB) from San Remo: "Your most welcome letter, telling me you all like my London stuff arrived this morning to cheer me with an assurance which I greatly desired. Now I can go on with a light heart, and finish up London, before beginning at the beginning with Plymouth. I have just the contrast, with this race and under this sky, to do England as I wish."

12 December 1904, San Remo, to S. Weir Mitchell

> Villa Lamberti,
> San Remo, Dec. 12, 1904.

My dear Mitchell:

Your most kind and welcome letter of the 27th of November has wound its way from New York, and reached me here this morning. I must tell you in the first place that they wrote me from Franklin Square of your book[1] being there for me, and I wrote them back to send it, but books come slowly from New York to San Remo, and I must ask for it again. I feel as if I had a peculiar claim upon that book from having been advised with about the title; and the scheme, as you revealed it, seemed to me most original and attractive. It's a proof of your success that your reviewers are in doubt about the genuineness of the documents.[2] I should be interested to know how near your notion got home with the common or garden critic.

I was all summer in England with my family, where I rather think my race and language alienated me the more from our parent English. At any I wanted once more to see Italy, where I need compare myself with no one to find how like or unlike I was. Here we have divine weather, and an operatic sea, sky and architecture, but the time, of which I can have only so little left, hangs heavy. However, I write as usual, and I read to my wife after dinner, and then either go to bed or to the theatre; I rather think bed is more amusing.

Your letter went to my heart, first with its friendly touch, and then with its words about my book.[3] I like your liking Anther's name which I thought a fortunate invention, and your liking him.[4] Two or three people besides you will feel what I meant in him, and in his resignation to fate, which age teaches all of us when we are not too thick-headed— as I sometimes think *I* am. It is a great thing to have interested and pleased you. My public cannot be large, but I have not failed, since I have done that. To answer a question of yours, which I am proud enough of being asked:[5] I was about 8 or 9 months writing the story, sometimes with the pen, and sometimes typing it. (The machine works well in dramatic passages.) I revised, without wholly rewriting it; but got through with it less anxiously than usual, for the notion had been at least 15 years in my mind, with the doctor, the mother and the son pretty distinctly outlined, and some of the dialogue already in their mouths. I read it to no one but my daughter,[6] but of course she could not "edit" it, as her mother used to edit my things before her wonderful electrically critical nerves gave way. There never was such insight as hers for truth of character, and fidelity to nature, and she held me to both unsparingly. What honesty is left in me is the effect of the discipline of the years that are past and that will not return. I am far from a "swift" man; but I get on because I hang on. Three, four, five hours a day, and your copy must grow, even under a slow hand.

I do not know whether you note in your later life a failure of strength to do the old "stunts." I know how they are done better than ever, but I haven't the intellectual muscle I once had. As we live on, I think life gets more dreamlike, and the failure of strength is some such defeat as we experience in dreams when we come to grapples with an adversary.[7]—But I think I have one good novel left in me,[8] and I hope I shall live to get it out. It involves some tremendous things which I can perhaps help the reader to imagine for me, if I can't do it for him. If I could count upon such readers as you, there would be no trouble.

What an interesting world, and how full of great, deep, and beautiful as well as sorrowful questions! Can there be any other world as important? One wouldn't like to devolve upon an inferior existence in which the crucial problems were all solved. Aren't we entitled to an eternity in which we shall still have mighty misgivings to ponder, in which we shall have still to find out God?—Have you seen Metchnikoff's "Nature of Man"?[9] Is he a really great person? It rather got me down and rolled me over, for a while, but when I found my feet and dusted my clothes off, I felt like hitting a book a little, and I did in my poor way.[10]—What an awful Roland I've given you for your Oliver![11]

Yours affectionately,
W. D. Howells.

1. Mitchell's biography of George Washington, *The Years of Washington* (1904).

2. Mitchell had written Howells, 27 November 1904 (PU), that the critics had been afraid to question the authenticity of some of the letters he had used: "It has so scared the critical folks—who maul or flatter us in the dailies—that no one ventures to say this letter is real & that false."

3. *The Son of Royal Langbrith.*

4. Dr. Anther is the patient friend and disappointed lover of Mrs. Langbrith. In his letter, Mitchell had praised the novel, mentioning the character of Dr. Anther in particular: "There are noble sermons in that book—& a deep regret is mine because of Dr. Anther's death—the name pleased me—Is it an invention?"

5. Mitchell had queried Howells about the time and effort invested in the novel: "If I could hope for a literary confession I should ask you how long it takes you to write such a book & what amount of revision satisfies the critic who edits you & sends out decrees from the inner somewhere—I am so slow that I envy the swifter man—I am now printing a book from the fifth copy."

6. Howells had also read a portion of the completed manuscript to Thomas S. Perry. See Howells to Perry, 27 October 1903.

7. For Howells' concern about the failure of his literary powers, see Howells to Norton, 4 November 1904, n. 8.

8. See Howells to Aurelia Howells, 14 October 1904, n. 1.

9. Elié Metchnikoff, né Ilya Ilyich (1845–1916), was the noted Russian bacteriologist who authored several works, including *The Nature of Man* (1903), and was awarded the Nobel Prize in physiology and medicine in 1908 with Paul Ehrlich.

10. Howells discussed Metchnikoff's book in the "Editor's Easy Chair," *Harper's Monthly*, October 1904, reprinted in *Imaginary Interviews* (1910).

11. Howells seems to suggest that the contentious tone of his remarks on Metchnikoff compares unfavorably with the reasonable tone of Mitchell's letter to him; he alludes to the contrasting temperaments of Roland and Oliver in the *chansons de gestes*.

27 DECEMBER 1904, SAN REMO, TO EDMUND C. STEDMAN

Villa Lamberti,
San Remo, Dec. 27, 1904.

My dear Stedman:

I have just got Secretary Johnson's letter in regard to voting for our fellow Academicians and I hurry off my ballot[1] so that it may reach you, if possible, by the 7th of January, and represent me at your dinner. I wish I had time enough to tell you of all the comic-opera beauty of this place, amidst which I am so homesick. Poor Harry Harland[2] is here, lung-sick; but his doctor, a delightful Englishman, tells me he will "pull round." Of course he means "through," but you can't expect an Englishman to speak our language correctly. The main thing is the fact in this case. I see H. every other day, and we have a laugh that mocks all melancholy away.

Yours ever
W. D. Howells.

1. Robert Underwood Johnson was secretary of the National Institute of Arts and Letters. Howells was president until Stedman's election on 16 February 1904, even though he had intended to resign earlier. See Howells to Mabie, 10 February 1903, n. 1. Howells, along with Stedman, was among the first seven men elected by the Institute to the newly formed American Academy of Arts and Letters, founded in 1904 as a select and honorary circle within the Institute. The news of his election had recently been conveyed to him by Hamlin Garland, to whom Howells wrote on 20 December 1904 (CLSU): ". . . I thank you for your tidings, and of course I am proud. But I was an author before I was an Academician, and I would rather have written a book that brought such a shout from you [*The Son of Royal Langbrith*] that [sic] sit in one of the cerulean chairs which the good Underwood wishes some millionaire of letters to provide for us." Howells was returning his ballot in the election of the next eight Academicians. There were to be successive ballots cast by each newly elected group until the membership reached fifty. On the ballot accompanying this letter, Howells voted for Charles Eliot Norton, Henry James, Thomas B. Aldrich, William M. Sloane, Thomas R. Lounsbury, John Quincy Adams Ward, Joseph Jefferson, and Carl Schurz. Stedman replied to Howells, 19 January 1905 (MH), announcing the results of the balloting: "*five* of your candidates are elected Academicians—Norton, James, Aldrich, Lounsbury,

Ward. The three others chosen are—Henry Adams, McKim (excellent?) Roosevelt (I accepted him if the others would give me Lounsbury." See L. Stedman and G. M. Gould, eds., *Life and Letters of Edmund Clarence Stedman* (New York: Moffat, Yard, 1910), II, 445. Howells was elected president of the Academy at its first full meeting, a position he held until his death in 1920.

2. See Howells to Clemens, 23 December 1902, n. 1. Harland died the following year.

29 DECEMBER 1904, SAN REMO, TO JOHN HAY

San Remo, Dec. 29, 1904.

My dear Hay:

I cannot say that your very kind letter disappointed me in regard to my brother,[1] for I had small hope that you could do anything for him, but I thank you more than I can put in words for your good will, and your purpose of trying to make his Congressman do something.

I heard from you today, and I am sorry to come half way short of doing what you ask me. My vote for the Academicians went to Stedman yesterday, and of course I voted for James. Who the rest were I scarcely remember, but Adams was not one, as he certainly should have been for every reason.[2] I don't see how I overlooked him, and I can hardly forgive myself; but it is now too late.

With my wife's and my own regards to Mrs. Hay and yourself,

Yours ever
W. D. Howells.

1. Hay's letter was a reply to one from Howells, 1 December 1904 (RPB), asking Hay to look into the possibility of a consulship for Joe, "preferably that of Belfast in Ireland." Apparently this was Howells' second approach to Hay, as he wrote to Joe on the same day (MH), enclosing a "guarded letter" from Hay about the matter of the consulship and sympathizing with Joe's desire for such a position, since it would mean "a little let-up" from the responsibility of publishing the *Sentinel* in Jefferson.

2. See Howells to Stedman, 27 December 1904, n. 1. This is Howells' last extant letter to Hay, who died in June 1905. In his last letter to Howells, 4 April 1905 (MH) Hay, then traveling in Europe, deplored having to miss seeing Howells in San Remo and spoke optimistically about his health: "perhaps I may be patched up so as to run a while longer." Alluding to Henry Adams' election to the Academy of Arts and Letters, Hay referred to him as "one of the first fifteen immortals . . . ."

6 JANUARY 1905, SAN REMO, TO ELIZABETH JORDAN

Villa Lamberti,
San Remo, Jan. 6, 1905.

Dear Miss Jordan:

I thank you for your very kind and explicit letter, though I am afraid that for the present—for a long time, perhaps—it puts an end to my doing anything with my story. The subject had been in my mind for nearly twenty years, as more and more a possibility, and more than a year ago I began to write it.[1] But if I printed it now, I should be at once, and most credibly, accused of having used the recent incident.[2] So I shall put the MS. by indefinitely. A peculiarly amusing fact of the case is that I had once thought of offering the story to the Bazar! One of "life's little ironies," isn't it?

Yours sincerely,
W. D. Howells.

For heaven's sake don't let *this* become "corporation property."[3]

1. The letter from Elizabeth Jordan has not been located, but the reference is evidently to the novelette that was later published as *Fennel and Rue* (1908). Howells seems to have read portions of the unfinished story to William Arthur Gill sometime in 1904, according to a comment he made in a letter to Gill, 20 November 1904 (Bristol County Library, England): ". . . I continue writing sketches of English travel, at the risk of making myself the deadly enemy of your nation, instead of finishing that 'Tangled Web' in whose meshes I tried to snare you. I have the greatest longing to finish that story, and my nerves thrill with its conclusion."
2. For a full explanation of "the recent incident," see Howells to Duneka, 27 June 1906.
3. That is, available to Harper & Brothers for printing in *Harper's Bazar* or some other publication.

9 JANUARY 1905, SAN REMO, TO THOMAS S. PERRY

Villa Lamberti,
San Remo, Jan. 9, 1905.

My dear Perry:

If you could realize—for you must *know*—how very much I like to get your letters, you would write oftener and longer. I am glad of that hint about the Russian book, and I'll try to get it.[1] Of course I know Gorky, at least in Foma Gordyeyeff,[2] and in some horribly good short stories, and of course I'm mentally and morally a Russophile, and I wish the Russian people all good. I'm not sure that politically their rulers even are not as good as the Japs', whom all the world is swelling up with praise.[3]—Speaking of anarchism, I wish you'd look at that chapter of English Traits where Emerson gives a talk he had with Carlyle, and you'll see the programme of America put down by the sage of Concord as pure Anarchism.[4] It makes one sit up. You would think it Kropotkin speaking, or Herr Most.[5] If Emerson were alive now and said such things at home, they'd deport him.—I think I must have one more shy at the Russians, as the true believers in fiction, if it makes the old Easy Chair groan and squeak. Perhaps I'll get a text from the book you mention.—A light of a certain sort of romance, but a very good, sick fellow, Henry Harland[6] is here, trying to heal his poor lungs, and really helping them. We can at least talk literature together, and leaving out our great difference, we hate the same things specifically. I suppose you see James; he said he would write me an early letter, but I have not yet seen the color of his ink.—We're wearing the winter away, and I'm writing up a lot of my English material, which I expect to make a book of. Some of the London papers quote it from the magazine,[7] picking out the plums which are sugared, but leaving the bitter almonds which flavor the whole. It is droll.

Yours ever
W. D. Howells.

1. Perry's letter to which Howells is here replying has not been located, and the Russian book has consequently remained unidentified.

2. Maxim Gorky, pseudonym of Aleksei M. Peshkov (1868–1936), published *Fomo Gordeev,* his first important socialist novel, in 1899.

3. Howells here alludes to the formidable military accomplishments of the Japanese in the Russo-Japanese War then in progress.

4. Emerson records his conversation with Carlyle in chapter 1, "First Visit to England," of *English Traits* (1856). Howells somewhat exaggerates Emerson's political point of view: Emerson does not articulate a program of anarchism, but rather reports Carlyle's comment on Walter Savage Landor to the effect that "Landor's principle was mere rebellion, and *that* he feared was the American principle." Later, in chapter 14, "Literature," Emerson characterizes Carlyle as denouncing "causes" and taking comfort in the belief that the gladiators "were all going rapidly into the abyss together."

5. Prince Peter Kropotkin (1842–1921) was the prominent Russian anarchist and author, who, after being imprisoned for underground political activities, escaped and spent the greater part of his life in England writing anarchist works and participating in the revolutionary movement in western Europe. For Johann Most, see Howells to Salter, 1 December 1887, n. 6.

6. See Howells to Clemens, 23 December 1902.

7. Howells' travel sketches had begun to appear in the November and December 1904 issues of *Harper's Monthly.*

5 FEBRUARY 1905, SAN REMO, TO EDMUND C. STEDMAN

Villa Lamberti,
San Remo, Feb'y 5, 1905.

My dear Stedman:

Try my best I couldn't make you a fit return for that long lovely letter you have written me about the Academy and the Institute.[1] I *wish* I could have been at the luncheon, but everything seems to have gone perfectly without me!—How droll that is about McDowell's not knowing of Ward's greatness,[2] and yet it leaves a pang. So in our way, we too! Well, patience, patience, even with oblivion.

At first I thought I no longer cared for Italy, but it has been growing back upon me, and now it is as near my heart almost as ever. Here, however, even more than at home, one's next birthday should be one's 38th, not 68th.[3] Then one could take up the glowing harp of life, and go carrying it singing up and down all these white roads, where it has not rained for a year, hardly, but where the violet springs from the dust, and the almond is blooming in the arid air quite as if the warmest April showers had flattered them forth. Yesterday week I went to Taggia where the good and dear Ruffini, who marvellously wrote his "Doctor Antonio" in such sweet English, lived and died,[4] and I walked far up the olive slopes towards the shrine of the Madonna di Lampedusa, but got tired and gave it up. While I sat resting on the stone brink of a little conduit where the water that burst silver through the ferns of a wall near by, ran gold in the mossy channel behind me, and the blackcaps sang their souls out in the thicket, my gentle brigand of a guide went round gathering wild flowers, which he gave me in a handful with a smile and bow. Think of such a thing happening under any other heaven!

Yours affectionately
W. D. Howells.

1. Stedman's letter of 19 January 1905 (MH; L. Stedman and G. M. Gould, eds., *Life and Letters of Edmund Clarence Stedman* [New York: Moffat, Yard, 1910], II, 444–47) described the results of the election of new members to the American Academy of Arts and Letters. See Howells to Stedman, 27 December 1904, n. 1.

2. Edward A. MacDowell (1861–1908), American romantic composer, had just resigned as head of the department of music at Columbia University. As one of the original seven members of the Academy, he was empowered to vote in the election of the next eight members. In his letter Stedman had mentioned that MacDowell was the only one who objected to the nomination of the sculptor J. Q. A. Ward to the Academy.

3. Howells was to be sixty-eight on 1 March.

4. Giovanni D. Ruffini (1807–1881) was an Anglo-Italian novelist born in Genoa. He was a political exile in England (1836–1875) because of his activities in the "Young Italy" movement, returning to Taggia, where he lived until his death. *Doctor Antonio*, a novel written in English, appeared in 1855.

12 FEBRUARY 1905, SAN REMO, TO JOSEPH A. HOWELLS

> Villa Lamberti,
> San Remo, Feb'y 12, 1905

Dear Joe:

I suppose your cherry trees are not in bloom yet, but there is one that I see here all a cloud of white; and the almonds are budding. Still, I don't believe that by the beginning of March things will be so forward as they were on the sweet mild days when we were creeping up the good old Ohio river four years ago.[1] That was a nice seat overlooking the bow, until the tobacco-spitters got in their work.—I'm sorry to note from your letters that you've only been "usually well" this winter. But any sort of wellness is welcome at our time of life, and I don't suppose you complain. Or, do you? We must try the Ohio river cure again; it wiped the hollows out of *my* soul.—Have you ever tried false teeth? In the last 15 years I've spent a good deal on them; but at last a dentist here is giving me real comfort with a partial plate. It's odd, but he's a son of old Hiram Powers, the "Greek Slave" sculptor;[2] born in Florence, but dental-schooled in Boston; a nice fellow, and ingenious as Natt of Eagleville.[3] He told me that when the W. Slave was on the stocks an Englishman saw it and on condition that there should not be more than 5 life size copies made of it, gave Powers a signed check to fill up with any sum he chose. Powers filled it with $25,000; but he could have made thrice the money if he had sold as many W. Slaves as he pleased.[4]—We expect to sail from Genoa on the Moltke, April 5th, and Elinor is beginning to pack! I shall be glad, for I've been homesick ever since I left home. America is bad enough for me. With love to you all,

> Your aff'te bro.
> Will.

1. See Howells to Aldrich, 5 March 1902, n. 4, and Howells to Norton, 19 March 1902, n. 3.

2. Edward Everett Powers (b. 1851) was the eighth of Hiram Powers' children and a graduate of the University of Pisa, where he studied medicine. The circumstances of his schooling as a dentist in Boston are not known. Sculpted in 1843,

the "Greek Slave," a nude woman rendered in the then prevailing classical style, was one of the most celebrated statues of its time.

3. "Natt" has not been specifically identified, but he appears to have been someone the Howells boys knew for his ingeniousness, who lived in Eagleville, about five miles west of Jefferson in Ashtabula County.

4. Six to eight copies of the "Greek Slave" (sometimes described as the "white vision" or "white slave") were said to have been made by Powers at his Florence studio. The first was reportedly purchased by a Captain Grant for $4,000 and taken to England. See Lorado Taft, *The History of American Sculpture* (New York: Macmillan, 1930), p. 64. Other sums of $6,000 to $7,000 are variously reported, making the figure passed on to Howells by Powers' son appear greatly exaggerated.

24 MAY 1905, NEW YORK, TO SIR GEORGE TREVELYAN

340 West 57th street,
May 24, 1905.

Dear Sir George Trevelyan:

I have been waiting, before answering your letter of the 6th, to make sure that I could get an old-fashioned copy of Their Wedding Journey, and now I shall have the pleasure, in a few days of sending it you in its pristine ugliness.[1] The publisher, Mr. George H. Mifflin, of Houghton, Mifflin & Co., has been so much interested by your wish in the matter that he has had them hunt up the old dies in the book-factory, to stamp the cover to the dreadful effect we were all so proud of in the simple early eighty-sevens. The satisfaction of any sentiment you may have regarding the form will be due to him rather than to me; and it may add the touch that "makes the sense of satisfaction ache,"[2] if I tell you that he has sacrificed on the hideous shrine the love of beautiful books which first lured him into the business of making the most beautiful books we now print.

—We passed the rather long winter at San Remo, and came home early in April, to a hotel[3] where we have ever since been poising for flight to our rugged little nest on the Maine coast. To-morrow we actually take wing, and I hope to be there till November. Our cottage is almost as ugly as the first edition of Their Wedding Journey, and everything we have done to our two acres has been a mistake which we are now calling upon the weeds and brambles to hide from us. But I have a big library which was once a stable, (with its stalls turned into book shelves) and I hope to add a volume this summer to the superfluity of my own literature.[4] All round us is the rough untameable New England country, except in front where many yachts, coasters, and coal barges make our harbor gay by night with their riding-lights. A certain pathetic prettiness in it appealed to me as beauty during my

Riviera winter, and the other day when I went down to plant my corn, I was dismayed to find how my fondness had been abused.—This is all about me and mine, but I have been thinking throughout of you and yours, and hoping that I might, with my daughter, be remembered to Lady Trevelyan, and to all those great and good friends whom I met at your board.[5]

Yours sincerely
W. D. Howells.

My summer address, is Kittery Point, Maine, U. S. A.

1. When Howells was in London in April 1904, Trevelyan had invited Howells to dinner and asked for a copy of the 1871 edition of *Their Wedding Journey,* illustrated by Augustus Hoppin, an edition Trevelyan valued greatly but had lost. See *Life in Letters,* II, 194–96. Trevelyan had just written Howells again on the matter, 6 May 1905 (MH), courteously pretending to forget or actually having forgotten that he had made the request a year earlier. On 15 May 1905 (MH) Howells wrote to George H. Mifflin, explaining Trevelyan's request for *Their Wedding Journey* and wondering whether "you could get it in the desired shape and send it to me . . . ." Upon Mifflin's reply, 16 May 1905 (NNC), indicating that the novel was available "only in the regular 'set' (or plain red) binding," Howells requested the publisher on 17 May 1905 (MH) to find "a copy . . . in the dreadful old green binding, with the stamp on the cover in gilt. Nothing less will satisfy him [Trevelyan] in his old associations with the book."

2. The source of this quotation has not been identified.

3. The Ramon was located at 340 West 57th Street. The Howellses had left Genoa on 5 April aboard the Hamburg-American liner *Moltke,* arriving at New York on 17 April, one day behind schedule.

4. Howells called the library his "barnbrary" or "barnbury." The volume in progress was *London Films,* which was published in early 1906. He wrote to Aurelia four weeks later, 25 June 1905 (MH): "I have got the London book off my hands, and am writing at our outside English travels [*Certain Delightful English Towns*], which will be for next year's holidays."

5. In his letter of 6 May, Trevelyan had mentioned the friends: "The members of our little dinner party are all flourishing: Campbell Bannerman will, I hope, next year have a brilliant reward for his courage and honesty; and Birrell, too, in proportion to his political standing. Sir Alfred Lyall has brought out his two volume life of Lord Dufferin . . . ." Sir Henry Campbell-Bannerman (1836–1908) was leader of the Liberals in the House of Commons and prime minister (1905–1908); he stood forthrightly against Chamberlain's war policy in South Africa and was invited to form a new government in December 1905, no doubt the "brilliant reward" Trevelyan foresees. Augustine Birrell (1850–1933) was an author, barrister, and statesman, whose writings include an edition of Boswell's *Life of Johnson* (1887), *William Hazlitt* (1902), and *Andrew Marvell* (1905). Sir Alfred Comyn Lyall (1835–1911), author and statesman, served primarily in India, where he was lieutenant-governor of the North-West Provinces (1882–1887) and a member of the Council of Secretary of State for India (1888–1901). His *Life of the Marquis of Dufferin* appeared in 1905.

11 JUNE 1905, KITTERY POINT, TO CHARLES E. NORTON

Kittery Point, June 11, 1905.[1]

My dear Norton:

I have been spending nights and mornings with you for a fortnight, listening to your reading of Ruskin's letters,[2] and longing for those pauses between when I heard your voice in comment so sane, and just, and kind that it almost restored your correspondent to reason. The letters are, like most things in these days, immensely pathetic, with their voluntary insolences and involuntary sweetness and affection. They form a terrible picture of the literary temperament, crossed with strange, Puritanic misgivings and restraints, and finally bursting through these into madness. Your patience, your humanity through all, is an additional revelation of things in you which the least of your friends have experienced in their several degrees. After that continual tempesting in a tea-pot, your voice comes, cool and clear, like a sound of water flowing and falling. I think I understand you, if I do not Ruskin, better, because of these letters.

I wish I could see you, and talk long, long with you about England, and of course about myself. The impression of England on me was so great as to be almost pulverizing, but out of the dust I am too old to be made a new man of. I shall never be able, in what I write, to impart the sense of this, and I see much pity in my having gone out of my American way to be crushed. I was fitted to my groove, and contentedly slipping on in it to the end. Now, I find myself so much at odds with what I used to be that I do not know what sort of re-beginning to make; this quite irrespective of the rightness of England or the wrongness of America, for each is in fact inevitably right in its way.—Italy was at first simply tiresome; but when I got away from the mere climate which San Remo was, and tasted Genoa, the old, divine joy came back a little. It was too late, then. We were sailing for New York.

Yours affectionately
W. D. Howells.

1. Howells and Elinor had arrived at Kittery Point from New York on 27 May.
2. C. E. Norton, ed., *Letters of John Ruskin to Charles Eliot Norton*, 2 vols. (Boston: Houghton Mifflin, 1904).

11 JUNE 1905, KITTERY POINT, TO ANNE H. FRÉCHETTE

Kittery Point, June 11, 1905.

Dear Annie:

I write the Sunday letter to you instead of Aurelia[1] today because I want to tell you directly how much I have felt for you in your recent trying attacks of erysipelas. I know how bravely you take all hardships, and I imagine you to have been a comfort to your family even when your smile was swollen to twice its normal size and painted red; but that is no reason for my keeping silent about it. All that I ask in return for this handsome expression is that you will frown upon any future suffering that threatens you.—Aurelia in her last letter hinted that you sometimes felt hurt at my not visiting you. I am truly sorry for that, because I feel hurt, too, not on account of inquiring friends, but for the reason that I love dearly to see you, and "enjoy myself shocking," as the old Welsh ladies say, when I am in your company. But, as you know, I seldom go from home, and when I do, I go on business disguised as pleasure, and where I don't want to go. I am just going down to New York to take a Columbia College degree,[2] when I would so much rather take medicine, if I could find any that would relieve gas in the stomach. After I get back I must try to get to work, and earn my salary, and though I would like to go with Joe as far as Ottawa when he goes home (after he comes!)[3] I cannot hope to do it. I have been fearfully broken up by my year of travel and find a difficulty in putting the pieces together, the greater because at 68 I begin to feel my touch fumbling. I must husband (why not wife?) my poor strength, and try to do something. Elinor is no good; she says *her* head does not work, and we are a hapless pair of do-nothings. We are still alone, with Pilla dentisting in Boston, and after distracting intervals of John, who has been threatened by appendicitis. That danger is past, but he must leave work for two months for his dyspepsia's sake.

With our love to you all,

Yours affte'ly
Will.

1. After staying for several months with Annie's family in Ottawa, Aurelia and Henry had returned to Jefferson for a time, only to return to Ottawa in December 1904.
2. Howells was to be awarded the honorary degree of doctor of literature at the Columbia University commencement on 14 June. He afterwards described the event in a letter to Aurelia Howells, 18 June 1905 (MH): "Last Monday night I started to New York, where I was to take my Columbia degree, and I had two sweltering days. But I came through the ordeal (on Wednesday) very well, and

had all possible honors done me. Of course the conferring of the degree was the great event, but after that there was an afternoon-long lunch, with speeches, (they mercifully excused me,) and at night a superb dinner, which I left at 10.30 to take the midnight train for Boston." See also *Life in Letters*, II, 206–7.

3. As indicated in a letter to Aurelia Howells, 16 July 1905 (MH), Howells' brother had recently arrived at Kittery Point; and on 23 July (MH) Howells wrote again to Aurelia: "Joe starts home tomorrow morning . . . ."

16 June 1905, Kittery Point, to Sarah Orne Jewett

Kittery Point June 16, 1905.

Dear Miss Jewett:
I thank you for all of us, and we shall hope to see you here, and come to see you at South Berwick. But it seems wisest and best to let you have James quite to yourself when he visits you,[1] and I will only go and hold his hand to the last trolley "limit" before S. B., there dismissing him with an envious blessing.[2]

My wife joins me in love to yourself and your sister.

Yours sincerely
W. D. Howells.

1. In this letter Howells was replying to Jewett's letter misdated "Thursday, June 17th" (MeWC)—it was actually written on Thursday, 15 June—in which she wrote: "Mr. James told me that he was coming to stay two days with you and we made an instant plot for a visit to Berwick. I was much disappointed when I could not have him come last fall. You know how glad I shall be if you feel like bringing him . . . ." Despite his polite demurral, Howells did accompany James. See *Sarah Orne Jewett Letters*, ed. Richard Cary (Waterville, Me.: Colby College Press, 1967), p. 139.

2. Jewett replied on "Friday evening" (MeWC)—presumably 16 June—imploring Howells to reconsider: "My dear friend, please, *please* come! The miserable thought of your stopping at the Car Barn is not to be borne. You shall be driven to an express train, and then take the last trolley home from Kittery Junction if you must save time. To have you and Mr. James together will be such a delight and make me sure of the future of American literature."

5 July 1905, Kittery Point, to Thomas S. Perry

Kittery Point, July 5, 1905

My dear Perry:
I think I have let you suffer long enough for offering rude dispraise of my sponsor at Columbia.[1] I was the more willing to do it because I was punishing in you a former state of my own; but even before I heard

his just and admirable words at the Commencement, I had begun to relent towards him, and to imagine the makings of a very good fellow in him. It was quite his notion I should be offered the honor done me, and he was therefore empowered to do it. The time had been when I should rather have expected it of any other.

I have been thinking much of looking in on you some day toward the end of the month. Would you let me, and if you would, how should I find my way to Hancock, N. H.? My visit would be largely to secure one from you in return.

Yesterday, H. J. sailed for the land of his adopted nativity. I dreaded for him his coming to these States, and I suspect it has been worse than I feared.[2]

Yours ever
W. D. Howells.

1. Howells' sponsor for the honorary degree he had recently received from Columbia University was probably Brander Matthews. See Howells to Anne Fréchette, 11 June 1905, n. 2. Apparently Perry had expressed some criticism of Matthews in a letter to Howells now lost.

2. James's trip to America had created concern among his friends. Charles E. Norton had written Howells, 19 January 1905 (MH), giving his appraisal of James's loneliness and distance from the world around him: "since he has been here, he has seemed in many ways so out of place, so disconnected with actual life except thro' his affections, & so independent of these also in the make up of life, that his essential solitariness & the blankness of the years before him, have invested him with a garment of pathos. Still I may be (I hope I am) wrong in my conclusion, and when he comes back from New York & Philadelphia & Washington where he now is, he will, I trust, have become acclimated to our democratic social vulgar atmosphere, and have lost 'the terror' which he declared had possessed him during the first months of his visit.—But how few the lives are which, if looked at closely after they have passed the grand climacteric, are not robed in gray! The sweetness of H. J.'s heart is invincible." Howells' fears were no doubt confirmed when James wrote to him at San Remo, 1 March 1905 (MH), apologizing for his long silence and lamenting the turbulence of his American visit: "Suffice it for the hour that I have been the victim of Fate and the creature of helplessness; simply clutching the sides of the car of the balloon for dear life, and feeling, with the vast movements of the monster, that this was all that could be asked of me. I will so subtly convince you of this when we do meet that I really believe your heart will be softened for me."

6 JULY 1905, KITTERY POINT, TO ROBERT U. JOHNSON

Kittery Point, July 6, 1905.

Dear Mr. Johnson:

I thank you for letting me see Dr. James's letter.[1] Much could be said on the other side, but nothing on his could be better said. I long to have the Academy do something.[2] It is beautiful, but not beautiful enough to be its own excuse for being.

How Hay's death impoverishes our life![3]

Yours ever
W. D. Howells.

1. Howells is here referring to a letter from William James to Johnson, 17 June 1905 (NNAL), declining his election on the fourth ballot to the American Academy of Arts and Letters. Johnson was then "preliminary secretary" of the American Academy of Arts and Letters. See Howells to Stedman, 27 December 1904, n. 1.

2. Among other reasons for not joining the Academy, William James tartly stated the fact that his brother was already a member (Henry James had been elected on the second round of balloting): "I am the more encouraged to this course by the fact that my younger and shallower and vainer brother is already in the Academy and that if I were there too, the other families represented might think the James influence too rank and strong." See Leon Edel, *Henry James, The Master, 1901–1916* (Philadelphia: J. B. Lippincott, 1972), pp. 297–99. In this delicate situation Howells tactfully suggests that there is also something to be said on the side of his friend the novelist.

3. John Hay had died on 1 July 1905 at his summer home in Newbury, New Hampshire. Howells wrote an appreciative essay entitled "John Hay in Literature," *North American Review,* September 1905, which appears to have been initially planned for *Harper's Weekly.* In a letter of 15 July 1905 (NjP) to David Munro, Howells wrote: "If the Review wants the paper on Hay . . . I will fit it more specifically for the Review and make it worthier of your use. Writing with one eye on the Weekly and one on the Review, I felt that the effect was somewhat strabismic. I can remedy that, and make the paper less a reminiscence and more a criticism."

5 AUGUST 1905, KITTERY POINT, TO MRS. HAMER

Kittery Point, Maine. Aug. 5, 1905.

Dear Mrs. Hamer:

I have never written any sequel to "Lemuel Barker,"[1] as I once hoped to do. You are very kind to wish for one; if it will help you to imagine one for yourself I will say that I had always a tenderness for Lemuel and expected success of him in any undertaking which he could enter upon with a good conscience. He might have come back to Boston and set up a critical book store, in which he sold only books which he respected, ethically and aesthetically. I know of such a scheme in another New England city.

Yours sincerely
W. D. Howells.

1. Mrs. Hamer, who has not been identified, seems to have written Howells about the possibility of a sequel to *The Minister's Charge* (1887).

20 AUGUST 1905, KITTERY POINT, TO DAVID DOUGLAS

Kittery Point, Maine, August 20, 1905.

Dear Mr. Douglas:

It is just a year since my happy visit with you in Edinburgh, and my heart goes out to you all in truest regard and best wishes.[1] My dear brother was with us here in July, and we had such good talks of you. He remembers his own stay in Edinburgh so freshly,[2] and he could go every inch of our famous Saturday night walk in the Cowgate with me.[3] He loves you as much as I do; I will not let anyone love you more.

We reached New York by the middle of April, and before the end of May we were here, where we have been ever since. My wife has scarcely been three times off the place; and the weather has been so fine that during my brother's visit we did hardly anything but sit and stare at the sea. I have been the idler because for a month I *could* not use my head, which I have used so steadily for fifty years. I was, for the first time, sensibly *tired*; but now I am rested, and going on again with my writing. My wife is unusually well, thanks to the outdoor life she leads; and she wishes me to tell you how much she has enjoyed the volume of *Family Romance* you gave her.[4] It is one of the books we have read aloud, and we have all shared her pleasure in it.

We had a very peaceful life in spite of the Peace Conference raging between the Japs and Russians at the Navy Yard near by.[5] My daughter and I went there at the Admiral's breakfast,[6] and they might all, tell Miss Douglas, have been prettier. The Russians were interesting, but I guess the Japs will have their way.[7] What five-foot, hundred pound, little brown mysteries they look! My wife joins me in love to dear Mrs. Douglas and you, and with the hope of hearing soon from you, I am,

Yours sincerely
W. D. Howells.

1. Howells visited Douglas in Edinburgh in August 1904. His account of that visit is recorded in two diary letters to Elinor Howells, 19 August and 20 August 1904 (both at MH). On 7 February 1905 (*Life in Letters*, II, 205–6) Howells had written to Douglas about the matter of transferring his books from Douglas' firm to Harper & Brothers in London.

2. Joseph A. Howells had visited Edinburgh during his visit to the British Isles in the summer of 1886. See Howells to W. C. Howells, 27 June 1886, n. 1.

3. Cowgate is an ancient thoroughfare south of High Street, the "spine" of Edinburgh, and running parallel to it.

4. Elinor Howells had a keen interest in English history and genealogy, and Douglas had made her a gift of Sir John B. Burke's *Family Romance; or, Episodes in the Annals of the Aristocracy* (1858).

5. Theodore Roosevelt's intercession in the Russo-Japanese War (1904–1905) resulted in the agreement to negotiate in August 1905 at the Portsmouth Navy Yard (actually not located in Portsmouth, New Hampshire, but across the Piscataqua River in Kittery Point, Maine). Japanese demands for reparation nearly brought the talks to a halt, but Roosevelt, who did not himself attend, applied sufficient pressure on both parties to conclude a treaty on 5 September. For his efforts Roosevelt received the Nobel Peace Prize. Howells reported his impressions of the conference in "The Peacemakers at Portsmouth," *Harper's Weekly*, 26 August 1905.

6. Howells described the admiral's breakfast, which he attended with his daughter Mildred, in a letter to Aurelia Howells, 13 August 1905 (MH): "On Tuesday Pilla and I went to the breakfast given by the admiral to the Jap and Russian peace commissioners at the Navy Yard. It was a very easy, pleasant affair. The Russians were the most interesting. Witte, the chief of them, brought Pilla her breakfast, and his secretary said every one knew my name in Russia, but I think I could probably find a few scores of millions to whom it would be strange. Neither the Japs nor the Russians are very fair to see; but the 'summer girls' at their hotel are behaving as if they were beautiful.—The Admiral's name is Mead, and though he is now a Kentuckian, his people come from Connecticut, and Elinor scents a kinsman in him." Count Sergius Yulyevich Witte (1849–1915), Russian statesman, early exponent of Russian modernization, and prime minister (1905–1906) under the tsar's first constitutional government, was chief plenipotentiary of the Russian delegation at the peace conference. Kentucky-born Admiral William W. Mead (1845–1930) was commandant of the Naval Yard at Portsmouth (1904–1907). A year later Howells wrote to J. A. Howells, 7 August 1906 (MH), that further acquaintance confirmed Mead as "a far-relation of Elinor's . . . ."

7. For literary reasons Howells' sentiments were with the Russians, as he indicates in a letter to John St. Loe Strachey, 13 September 1905 (House of Lords, London): "The treaty has been a great excitement for our quiet neighborhood, and we are glad to have it done with. I saw all the envoys several times, with no great interest in any of them. Witte seemed the most considerable man, and Komura the deepest mystery. It is hard to believe in the Japs, and one does not *expect* to believe in the Russians, officially, but they seem more our kind, and I always make the grandeur of their literature do duty for the whole nation." Marquis Jutaro Komura (1855–1911), Japanese diplomat and Harvard graduate (1877), was Witte's counterpart at the peace conference.

20 AUGUST 1905, KITTERY POINT, TO HAMLIN GARLAND

Kittery Point, Aug. 20, 1905.

My dear Garland:

But for the witness of your letter, which has lain all these weeks and months on my table vainly reproaching me, I should not have believed I could let you go unanswered so long.[1] But this has been a sort of off summer with me, and I have shirked all possible writing. I felt tired in my brain, physically tired, for many weeks, and could wring nothing out of it except by great effort. Now at last it seems rested, and I am catching up with my arrears of work in every way. The fact is that my vacation in Europe, so far as leisure was concerned, was a delusion; I did quite as much writing as usual, with the excitement of travel, and the worry of society added. After all there is no rest like keeping in one's own rut.—We saw the last of James here the last of June, and I think he was glad to be going back.[2] He had grown very severe with everything, and no longer felt any charm in the continent. Our two acres of it chanced to give him the hottest weather of the summer, and I felt very responsible, and new and inadequate. I am not sure that he ought to have come, but it was inevitable. Still, when you are past sixty, I say, Stay put, even if it is in West Salem.[3]

We are in the midst of the excitement about the Peace Commission, which does not commit, at the Kittery Navy Yard, and as usual I am on the unpopular side, for personally I much prefer the Russians.[4] The Japs affect me as terrible little mysteries, every one. Of course, I know that Russia as a power behaved badly and falsely at the start, but as a people I believe she means more for mankind than Japan does, and she is beginning to be a people.

We have been much more together as a family this summer than usual, but now John is in Colorado, trying the high, dry air for his dyspepsia, and his threatened appendicitis. He has been literally *obliged* to take two months away from his office.—The weather here has been divine, and I have never enjoyed it so much. You ought to see this country. Apropos of you, I read most of your book[5] as we came down from New York, and of course I was greatly interested, in your types, and in what I saw you were meaning to do. It is very difficult ground, and one has to carry water on both shoulders while one picks one's steps. I think you kept your balance, but the mysticism of the thing has been so commercialized, that it is hard to beat the professional mediumship into the proper relation. I can say this frankly to you because I have wrought in the same field, where if I had not found the Shakers I should have reaped a meagre harvest.[6] The other day I took down your Main Travelled Roads, and read into it, after long non-reading of it. The power and the truth struck me deeply. It is great, simple, individual work. I wish you had some such theme as the themes of that book to work out on the scale of a novel.—At last, I am thinking of taking up my old Ohio life. My wife, from whom my best suggestions have come, suggested it, and gave me a capital title.[7]

I hope Mrs. Garland is well, and that Miss Garland[8] is holding her own in society with the other summer girls. I send her my love, and my wife joins me in best regards to her parents.

Yours ever,
W. D. Howells.

1. Garland's letter has not been located.

2. See Howells to Jewett, 16 June 1905, and Howells to Perry, 5 July 1905, n. 2.

3. Garland's birthplace and residence, one hundred miles northwest of Madison, Wisconsin.

4. See Howells to Douglas, 20 August 1905, n. 7.

5. *The Tyranny of the Dark* (1905) is a somewhat romantic novel in which the heroine is the victim of fraudulent spiritualism.

6. Howells here refers to *The Undiscovered Country* (1880), a novel about spiritualism set in a Shaker village.

7. Howells' taking up his "old Ohio life" probably refers to the Leatherwood materials he had begun to collect. See Howells to Aurelia Howells, 14 October 1904, n. 1. Whether Elinor Howells suggested the title for *The Leatherwood God* at this time is not known.

8. Mary Isabel Garland.

3 SEPTEMBER 1905, KITTERY POINT, TO AURELIA H. HOWELLS

Kittery Point, Sept. 3, 1905.

Dear Aurelia:[1]

We are in the midst of a tremendous southeasterly storm, like that of 1903, and it is splendid in its way. With the making of peace between Russia and Japan,[2] the elements seem to have gone to war. We had an earthquake, last week, and fumes of sulpher came up on the beaches, with some blaze; the sulphur that people gathered up was so hot they could hardly hold it.

We all very well, however, and we have the hope of seeing John in a few days.[3] He, I'm sorry to say, has not found Colorado what he hoped, and now we are confidently hoping good things for him in this air, where he always gets better.

Laura Mitchell of Columbus was here on Wednesday and Thursday, and Elinor and she had a great talk-up of old times. She is sixty years old, but without a wrinkle or a grey hair. She had scarcely left when Webb Hayes turned up, and inundated us with his adventures among the Russians and Japs.[4] The Russians he hates, and correspondingly likes the Japs. He and all other soldiers regard them as the best fighters in the world. The Russians set him adrift with other non-combatants, in hopes that they would be blown up by the submarine mines at Port Arthur.

I am getting on well with my writing, but you see I have no news. I was greatly interested by all you told me of Henry. With love to him,

Your affectionate brother,
Will.

1. Having spent more than half a year in Ottawa, Aurelia and Henry had returned to Jefferson in early July.

2. See Howells to Douglas, 20 August 1905, n. 5.

3. John Howells had been vacationing for two months on a ranch in Colorado in the hope of alleviating attacks of dyspepsia and appendicitis.

4. Laura Mitchell's cousin, then a lieutenant colonel in the U.S. Army, was a dispatch bearer during the Russo-Japanese War, and in that capacity he observed both the Russian and the Japanese forces in combat. From Howells' account, he appears to have been with the besieged Russians at some point in 1904 during one of the Japanese attacks on Port Arthur, a Chinese port in Manchuria leased by the Russians in 1898, where the Russian fleet was blockaded and ultimately destroyed.

10 SEPTEMBER 1905, KITTERY POINT, TO CHARLES E. NORTON

Kittery Point, Me.
Sept. 10, 1905.

My dear Norton:

The summer is going and leaving me to my shame for not having told you at once how lief and dear your asking me to visit you was. It is not easy to leave my wife here, and she cannot go with me, and Ashfield is so far; but we are expecting to stop some days in Boston, on our way to New York, after your return to Cambridge, and then the great pleasure of seeing you shall be mine.

The Mayflower,[1] which brought the Peace Envoys four weeks ago has just sailed out of the harbor, and the great international incident is closed. It has greatly but I hope not unprofitably broken our wonted calm, and first and last I have seen much of the embattled diplomatists with a growing aversion for both sides. It is well that peace should be made, no doubt, but it will not be the last peace, even in our time, and of course not the last war, which seems to be much more easily made. The worst is that it has driven so far into the past the things I wished to write you, but they will come back into the present when we meet. I don't know if I told you of the mind-weariness which for the first time in my life I experienced after coming here in the spring. Now that is gone, and I am writing as furiously away as ever. I am writing mainly about England,[2] and to save myself from disgrace before my own face, I have to read about it. I am constantly astonished to find how little I know of English history; but I have all the vainglory of a discoverer in repairing my ignorance. I go to sleep reading English history; I wake to it in the night, and resume it in the morning. What an amazing people they have been; no other could have come to what through the things they have done. If we had not been English ourselves at the time we could never have dared stand up against them.—In all my thinking and writing, I recall what you said of the thinness of the soil we work in here, and the depth of theirs. The withered years of their tremendous past have enriched their present like the layers of fallen leaves in a forest. Emerson imagined them surpassingly,[3] and they have changed very little since his time, and only in expectations, not in characteristics.

My wife has had a letter from H. James, who bears a tenderer heart than I should have supposed towards his native exile. I am glad he went as early as he did.[4] The heat of the summer, of which we gave him a terrible foretaste the day he was with us here, would have branded him with too deep a hate of our poor hemisphere.—I woke today thinking of the folly of nationalities, and the stupid hypocrisy of patriotism. By night I shall doubtless have changed my mind; but now I ask why J. or I, even, should not live forever out of America without self-reproach? The worst is perhaps that he will grow lonelier with age. But one grows lonely with age, anywhere![5]—I should like to tell you about the big dinner to the Russian envoys in New York,[6] but it will be far in the past, soon, and it is not worth writing of. Only, Witte strikes one as a great, simple, if not single soul. The Japs are single, perhaps, but oh, never simple. My household (with John away in Colorado fighting his dyspepsia) joins me love to you all.

Yours ever
W. D. Howells.

1. The presidential yacht had brought the Russian and Japanese diplomats from Oyster Bay, Long Island, to the Portsmouth Navy Yard. See Howells to Douglas, 20 August 1905, n. 5.

2. Howells had recently finished *London Films* and was now working on *Certain Delightful English Towns*.

3. Howells had been reading *English Traits*. See Howells to Perry, 9 January 1905, n. 4.

4. Henry James had sailed for England on 4 July. In his reply to Howells, 19 October 1905 (MH), Norton appended a short postscript: "Poor H. J.! He is a most pathetic figure in his solitude,—with only the strange unpleasant shades of his own creation for his companions." See Howells to Perry, 5 July 1905, n. 2.

5. Norton, who was then seventy-eight, was moved to respond in his letter of

19 October that old age had as yet been "gentle" with him: "But it warns me continually that whatever remains of life for me is but a brief remainder. I do not care much to prolong it, nor am I eager for the end,—the readiness is all."

6. See Howells to Aurelia Howells, 10 September 1905.

10 SEPTEMBER 1905, KITTERY POINT, TO AURELIA H. HOWELLS

Kittery Point, Sept. 10, 1905.

Dear Aurelia:

I got home from New York, where I dined with the Russian envoys Thursday night,[1] and found your pleasant and cheerful letter here on Friday. The enclosure gave me a little shock; it seemed so absolutely of yesterday. I must have written it at the store where I bought those boxes, and put it into the package with them. How it brought mother back to me! I was asking her to live a hundred in the year she died, and almost within a month of her death.[2] If she is living yet somewhere, and I shall see her, what account shall I give her of the boy who used to be so homesick for her? Ambitions fulfilled, vanities gratified, and what else? That seems to be the sum of my endeavor, which has lasted so long.—That very year I was planning not to go home because I thought I ought to save the cost and pay it in on the house I had bought in Cambridge.[3] It was right, and now it is a sore thought to me. What a rich nature she had, and what a great heart for her children. We were all alike to her; she was the home in which we were all equal and dear. Till she was gone I did not know how fond I was of father, she was so fully my affection. But I should almost dread to meet her, just as I should dread to meet Winnie.[4]

I rose from my machine just now to look at the government yacht Mayflower going out. Four weeks ago she brought the peace Envoys,[5] and now the peace is made, and they have all vanished.—The dinner to the Russian party was given by Col. Harvey of Harpers and was very grandiose, with a good deal of speechifying. Witte spoke 8 or 10 lines in French, and Rosen read a longer speech in English.[6] He had asked, when half through dinner, to have me come round and sit by him, and we had a long talk. He and his wife have read my books from the first, and liked them. There is no doubt of my European reputation, however little I sell in America. Not that I complain of that, even. Harvey told me that when Witte was shown the list of guests, he said of Pierpont Morgan's name, "Yes, *I* know him." When he came to mine, he broke out, "Ah! Mr. W. D. Howells! Then I shall see *him*!" That alone seemed to move him, but alas! when he saw me he did not know it, and at least had nothing to say. This flattering fact is of course entirely for home consumption, tell Joe.

I have been wondering if the removal of Palmer, the public printer, would possibly affect Sam's position.[7] But I do not see why it should. Do you think of returning to Ottawa soon?[8] You are quite right not to look forward to housekeeping. Any sort of boarding would be cheaper, and you will be so much freer. It is delightful to know that the Boehmers want you again.[9] Such kind people are not to be found every day, and if they have formed an attachment to Henry it will make a real home for you. I wish that you need not return to Jefferson, for it is such a great thing for you to be near Annie. I am glad that there is peace among all at Jefferson. With love to Henry,

> Your affectionate brother,
> Will.

1. On 7 September, Colonel George Harvey, head of Harper & Brothers, gave a dinner at the Metropolitan Club for the Russian delegation to the peace conference. See Howells to Douglas, 20 August 1905, n. 5.

2. Mary D. Howells died 11 October 1868. The letter written at the store is not extant, but Howells is probably referring to a box of squashes he had recently sent to Aurelia, enclosing in it a copy of *Miss Bellard's Inspiration*. See Howells to Aurelia Howells, 13 August 1905 (MH).

3. See Howells to W. C. Howells, 4 October 1868, and Howells to Comly, 20 October 1868.

4. Winifred Howells died 3 March 1889.

5. See Howells to Norton, 10 September 1905, n. 1.

6. Baron Roman Romanovich Rosen (1847–1921) was Russian minister to Japan when the Russo-Japanese War broke out. He was one of the negotiators at the Portsmouth peace conference and was shortly to become ambassador to the United States (1905–1911).

7. Samuel D. Howells held the position of copyholder at the Government Printing Office in Washington. Frank W. Palmer (1827–1907) was a newspaper editor and publisher, congressman, and U.S. public printer (1889–1894, 1897–1905), and Howells' younger brother was one of his appointees. Although Sam retained his post for the time being, his situation became less certain within a year. See Howells to Roosevelt, 26 August 1906, n. 1. Howells wrote to Aurelia, 24 December 1905 (MH), describing Sam's continuing difficulties: "I have rather a dismal letter from Sam, acknowledging a check, and announcing an increase of pension, but saying that they are 'terribly harassed.' Perhaps it is something besides money. He has some of his grandchildren to keep, and says his son-in-law is 'a poor stick.' Poor soul! I am sorry for him. Like every one else he suffers for his weakness and error, rather than for any great harm in him."

8. See Howells to Aurelia Howells, 3 September 1905, n. 1.

9. The Boehmers were a family with whom Aurelia and Henry boarded during their stay in Ottawa. Responding to Aurelia's indignation at Mrs. Boehmer's subsequent bad faith, Howells counseled on 28 October 1905 (MH): "It was too innocent to suppose she would keep your place against a higher bidder. The person who 'done you dirt' is the English widow."

24 SEPTEMBER 1905, WEST BRATTLEBOROUGH, VERMONT, TO AURELIA H. HOWELLS

West Brattleboro', Sept. 24, 1905.

Dear Aurelia:

Elinor and I started off Thursday on a *bat*, which took us to Epping, Nashua and Keene, N.H., and brought us to Brattleboro'[1] Friday afternoon. We expect to go Putney, Vt.,[2] and Greenfield, Mass., tomorrow, and get back Wednesday to Kittery P., Me., by way of Northampton and Old Hadley, Mass. She is visiting at all these places the graves of her numerous ancestry—Hayeses, Noyeses, Smiths, Russells and Meads.[3] At Old Hadley one of the Russells kept two of the Charles I judges, or Regicides, in his cellar ten years, or till they died. I have to hear about them all, but it interests her intensely, and the bat is doing her a power of good.—John is at K. P., eating my melons, and Pilla is visiting a Mead cousin at Norfolk Ct.[4]—The weather is glorious. With love for Henry, and a check for you,

Your aff'te brother
Will.

1. Elinor Howells' hometown.
2. The following day. 25 September 1905 (Howells Memorial, Kittery Point), Howells wrote his son from Greenfield, disclosing some of Elinor's girlhood experiences at her grandmother's house in Putney: "We had made a pious pilgrimage to the old Noyes house at Putney and viewed the doorstep where E. G. M. used to cry over the tasks of knitting which her grandmother set her. We saw the house to which she went to a party in tears because her grandmother braided her hair in one instead of two pigtails."
3. See Cady, *Howells*, I, 75–77.
4. The occasion of Mildred's trip had been "a wedding in Manchester, Conn., in the Cheney family, the great silk people" (Howells to Aurelia Howells, 17 September 1905 [MH]); the Norfolk cousin was possibly Catherine Mead. See Howells to Mildred Howells, 30 January 1906, n. 6.

29 SEPTEMBER 1905, KITTERY POINT, TO JOSEPH A. HOWELLS

Kittery Point, Sept. 29, 1905.

Dear Joe:

I have just telegraphed you the substance of the enclosed dispatch.[1] I have been looking up Turk's Island on the map in the Encyc. Brit., and find it apparently most desirable in point of climate and nearness. It is probably three days' sail from New York. The language is English.

With $1500 salary, $150 office rent and your half of the Sentinel income, in a place where there is no state to be kept up, you ought to be able to live comfortably. The warm climate will be good for both Eliza and yourself, and Beatrice need not have a cold the whole year round. Decidedly I think well of your accepting. Personally, the president has has been more than kind;[2] he has been thoughtful and polite in telegraphing.

When you write to the State Department, take a whole sheet (two leaves) of paper, and let Beatrice copy your letter in her good hand, and then you sign it, and punctuate it properly. And for heaven's sake look out for your grammar! In your last letter you say, "Our expens*es* averag*es*." Don't you *know* that you can't use a plural noun with a singular verb? You must say, expens*es* avera*ge*. Get a simple English grammar and make Eliza explain to you. Study the thing up, as you can in half an hour. It is disgraceful, when you write such good literature to make such schoolboy blunders, and they would damage you irretrievably with the department.

I don't know whether you have to pass an examination under the civil service rules or not. But if you accept and get through, I think you have a pleasant four years term ahead.[3] You are a man of good presence and good manner, and will do yourself credit, if you will look out for your syntax. John is here with me, and we both rejoice in your good fortune, as I hope and believe it will prove. Elinor of course will shout over it when she hears of it. Let me know what you decide.

> Your affectionate brother,
> **Will.**

1. Howells had just received a dispatch, presumably from the State Department, confirming Joseph Howells' nomination as American consul at Turks Islands, a colony in the British West Indies annexed to Jamaica in 1873. Joe had earlier enlisted his brother's help in trying to obtain a consulship. See Howells to Hay, 29 December 1904, n. 1.

2. Howells had communicated directly with Theodore Roosevelt about Joe's interest in a consular appointment, and Roosevelt had sent a personal reply, which Howells forwarded to Joe. See Howells to Aurelia Howells, 28 September 1905, and Howells to J. A. Howells, 28 September 1905 (both at MH).

3. Joseph Howells' consular term began in October 1905 and lasted until July 1912, according to the U.S. Department of State *Register*.

25 OCTOBER 1905, KITTERY POINT, TO MADISON CAWEIN

Kittery Point, October 25, 1905.

Dear Mr. Cawein.

Your book has never reached me, and I have been waiting, ever since I got your letter in the spring, to be able to thank you for it.[1] Perhaps you sent it to my former N. Y. address at 48 W. 59. I shall be glad to get it, and am glad of all the good that happens to you. I count the President's praise as most valuable, because it is that of a man who lives and feels poetry.[2]

We shall—alas, for not seeing your wife and you!—not be in N. Y. before the end of November.

Yours sincerely
W. D. Howells.

1. Probably *Vale of Tempe* (1905), a collection of verse.
2. Cawein replied to Howells on 26 November 1905 (MH), reporting a recent conversation at a "little luncheon with President Roosevelt," at which Cawein had repeated Howells' compliment, prompting Roosevelt to extol Howells' literary accomplishments: "...I quoted your last letter to me, in which you speak so beautifully of Mr. Roosevelt, and mention him as 'a man whose life is full of poetry', etc. He was particularly pleased and said 'Did Mr. Howell's [sic] really say that!' then went on to speak emphatically of the fineness of your work.... 'The Lady of the Aroostook' he mentioned especially and particularly, saying over & over again, how charming, how delightful it was. Next to it 'Indian Summer' held his heart."

6 DECEMBER 1905, NEW YORK, TO CHARLES E. NORTON

The Burlington,
10 West 30th st.,
December 6, 1905.

My dear Norton:

My pleasant day with you is still sweet in my mind,[1] even after the wild burst of the Mark Twain dinner last night,[2] which was enough to tear my consciousness in pieces. It was an enormous affair, and as to the guests the strangest mixture of literary celebrity and social notoriety that I have ever seen. The smart and the chic were both present, and not at separate tables, always. Clemens was consolingly tender and wise in his talk, and was as gentle with everyone and everything as a man should be at seventy.

What a different air from that of your corner of Cambridge, with its memorial quiet, I am plunged into on my return to New York! The talks we had will stay by me till I come to you for that Saturday Club dinner, which my wife approved of even in the first hours of getting me back. She joins me in affection for all your house.

The sonnets made their little effect; but I couldn't get a right word for "mighty." I thought of "massive," but feared it.[3]

Yours ever

W. D. Howells.

1. Howells, Elinor, and Mildred had left Kittery Point on 19 November. While Howells went to New York to see off his brother Joe, who embarked for the West Indies on 22 November, Elinor and Mildred briefly stopped over in Boston before joining Howells. On Thanksgiving day (30 November) Howells, accompanied by his son, returned for a few days to Kittery Point and, on his return trip to New York, spent the night of 3–4 December with Norton in Cambridge. See Howells to Aurelia Howells, 18 November, 26 November, and 3 December 1905 (all at MH).

2. Howells was toastmaster at the dinner given by Col. George Harvey, 5 December, in honor of Mark Twain's seventieth birthday. For accounts of this event, see "Mark Twain's 70th Birthday," supplement to *Harper's Weekly*, 23 December 1905; Willis F. Johnson, *George Harvey: A Passionate Patriot* (Boston: Houghton Mifflin, 1928), pp. 82–85; *Twain-Howells*, pp. 798–99; and Howells to Perry, 10 December 1905.

3. Howells is here referring to the double-barreled sonnet he wrote for the Mark Twain dinner. The poem is, in effect, two Shakespearean sonnets run together, a poetic form Howells had devised for the occasion of Clemens' sixty-seventh birthday. "Massive" rather than "mighty lips" (line 5) appears to have been too suggestive for Howells' sensibilities or for those imagined of others:

Sonnet to Mark Twain

A traveller from the Old World just escaped
   Our customs with his life, had found his way
To a place up-town, where a Colossus shaped
   Itself, sky-scraper high, against the day.
A vast smile, dawning from its mighty lips,
   Like sunshine on its visage seemed to brood;
One eye winked in perpetual eclipse.
   In the other a huge tear of pity stood.
Wisdom in chunks about its temples shone;
   Its measureless bulk grotesque, exultant, rose;
And while Titanic puissance clothed it on,
   Patience with Foreigners was in its pose.
So that, "What art thou?" the emboldened traveller spoke,
And it replied, "I am the American joke.
I am the joke that laughs the proud to scorn;
   I mock at cruelty, I banish care,
I cheer the lowly, chipper the forlorn.
   I bid the oppressor and hypocrite beware.
I tell the tale that makes men cry for joy;
   I bring the laugh that has no hate in it;
In the heart of age I wake the undying boy;
   My big stick blossoms with a thornless wit.

> The lame dance with delight in me: my mirth
> Reaches the deaf untrumpeted: the blind
> My point can see. I jolly the whole earth,
> But most I love to jolly my own kind.
> Joke of a people great, gay, bold, and free,
> I type their master-mood. Mark Twain made me."

10 DECEMBER 1905, NEW YORK, TO THOMAS S. PERRY

> The Burlington, 10 W. 30th st.,
> (but Franklin Square, c/o Harper's is my steady,)
> Dec. 10, 1905.

My dear **Perry**:

It is surprising what art the English have in separating the honey from the wax (pronounced whacks) in the comb I had hived for them: one would think I had fed upon nothing but flowers of the heather and gorse, from the showing they make for me. But I am old, and I like to be thought kindlier than I am. It will not come to a peerage, I am quite sure; but I do not see why they should not make me a knight. Really, though, since their pleasure in me has pleased you, I ask nothing from Ed'ard VII. I hope he will keep the book on his centre table, and speak of it to his subjects, for the American sales (as a true friend will be glad to learn) have not equalled its merits.[1]

I wish you could have been at the sky-scraping banquet given to Mark Twain on his 70th birthday, this last week.[2] 172 immortals sat down to the best Delmonico could do, and remained glutting and guzzling food for reflection for five hours after the dinner was ended. M. T. made a speech divinely droll, sweet, touching and wise. The rest of us got in the story of our lives, and our opinions on all subjects in the form of tributes to him till we could fling off disguise, and the speakers towards 2 A.M. did not mention him. I know, because I left at 1:30, when it was coming to that.

Our own personal history as a flitting family may be summed up in a few words. We left Kittery Point Nov. 20, and came to Boston, where we were foot-balled out of our hotel by the fond parents come to see Yale beat Harvard. Then we came to New York,[3] and after long toil we found this red brick refuge behind the Holland House, where we have five rooms, and our meals (they might be better) served in our apartment. It is very, very quiet, and I can work mornings in the parlor as if I were in my own barnbury at Kittery Point. That is, I could if I had anything to say; but as poor G. P. Lathrop used to express it, I seem to be lying fallow at present. Don't cheer! It can't be for long.

Did I ever bore you about Edith Wyatt, Chicagoenne, who wrote *Every One His Own Way,* and *True Love,*[4] beautifully simple and true fables, as slyly told as J. Austen's. She was the best of the literary crowd at M. T.'s dinner; a quiet creature, not so funny as you would think. I'm sure you and Mrs. Perry would like her books and her. There was also Ade, socially inexorable, and "gentle Alice Brown," who writes so well of N. E.[5]

Thanking you for noting the Wild Wales book to me.[6] I'm a Wild Welshman myself by race, you know.

With love to you all from your devoted family, here,

Yours ever,
W. D. Howells.

1. It remains unclear whether *London Films,* which had been published on 12 October 1905, was in fact praised by King Edward VII or whether Howells is here indulging in a humorous conceit. From the first magazine publications on, however, he had been surprised that the English reviewers mostly saw the "sugared plums" rather than the "bitter almonds" in his descriptions of England. See Howells to Perry, 9 January 1905.

2. See Howells to Norton, 6 December 1905, n. 2.

3. For a more accurate and detailed dating of the family's recent travels, see Howells to Norton, 6 December 1905, n. 1.

4. See Howells to Fuller, 20 September 1903, n. 3.

5. Alice Brown (1857–1948) was a New England writer of local color stories, novels, and plays. Howells had reviewed her collection of short stories, *Meadow-Grass* (1895) in "Life and Letters," *Harper's Weekly,* 30 November 1895.

6. George H. Borrow's *Wild Wales: Its People, Language, and Scenery,* originally published in 1862, came out in many editions, including one published in New York by Putnam in 1905.

15 DECEMBER 1905, NEW YORK, TO FREDERICK A. DUNEKA

The Burlington
10 West 30th st.,
Dec. 15, 1905.

Dear Mr. Duneka:

In the leisure of a very heavy cold, I have been going over the two years' Harpers you sent me, with a view to the reprints we have talked of,[1] and I have made a tentative selection of six stories, of about 60,000 words, cognate enough to go under one head, according to the enclosed title page. As you foresaw, it will be even easier to select twenty subjects, and I can quickly get the appropriate stories together. But I now write you so that you can perhaps be ready to talk with me of the plan when I bring the copy of the first volume down on Monday. I will then expound the title and make its application. All the titles should be not only fitting, but fanciful, and taking.

Alden ought to be co-editor of the series, because it is his due, (yours too, I dare say) and because he would have the stomach for the medieval hogwash of some stories which my realistic gorge rises at, but which ought to go with the more sane and peptic sort. I would write most of the introductions, but he has given great thought to short storyism, and he would like to write some, I'm sure.

The stories in the monthly are much of one temperament, and I should like to draw on the Weekly and Bazar too.

I wish you could take a brace, and think the feasibility of the enterprise to a finish. I should like to do the work, but it would be very disheartening, after I had done it, to have the scheme dropped. You can understand this.

Yours cordially
W. D. Howells.

1. Howells agreed to coedit a series of short-story collections with Henry M. Alden, editor of *Harper's Monthly*, to be called "Harper's Novelettes." The stories in each volume were to be loosely unified by a common theme, the first volume, as Howells explained to Clemens in his letter of 19 December 1905, bearing the title *Their Husbands' Wives*. Four volumes appeared in 1906, three more in 1907. When the New York *Evening Sun* printed a favorable review of the first volume in March 1906, Howells sent it to Duneka, 17 March 1906 (MWA), asking him to acknowledge the woman who had suggested the series, so that there would be no unpleasant repercussions: "I suppose you have seen this very intelligent notice from the Evening Sun.— May I beg you to look up the letter of the lady whose suggestion was the germ of our enterprise, and write to her? Our recognition will not be so graceful if delayed, and it is best to forestall any possible report that we profited by her hint with acknowledgment. I confess that such a thing would annoy me in my relation to work in which I should otherwise take so much pleasure."

19 DECEMBER 1905, NEW YORK, TO SAMUEL L. CLEMENS

The Burlington,
10 W. 30th st.,
Dec. 19, 1905.

My dear Clemens:

I am going to do a series of reprints from their periodicals for H. B. & Co.[1] The first volume will consist of six stories, and will be called "Their Husbands' Wives"—that is, wives peculiarly and self-sacrificially devoted to their husbands. In this volume I should like to include your "Eve's Diary," which exactly denotes the typical attitude of the feminine soul. Can you let me have it, and if yes, for what money outright, a percentage being impracticable?[2] Of course, Eve was never legally Adam's wife, but lived with him in a state which under the circumstances left no stain on her reputation. It was a kind of common-law marriage, and as you have given it the stamp of your approval, I do not think her inclusion among other devoted wives will seriously damage the series. There would be five other stories in the book, for which you need not blush ethically or artistically. You could freely use the piece in any collection of your own soon or late. The fact of the enterprise is confided to you.

> Yours ever
> W. D. Howells.

1. See Howells to Duneka, 15 December 1905, n. 1.

2. The following day, 20 December 1905 (MWA), Howells was able to report to Duneka: "Clemens has been here and has consented, even joyfully, to the use of Eve's Diary, exacting no set price, and apparently satisfied to leave that to you. [¶] If you will now have my (your H. & B.) letter typed and sent to the others, we can start the series at once. You might mention that Clemens freely joins."

19 DECEMBER 1905, NEW YORK, TO S. WEIR MITCHELL

> The Burlington,
> 10 West 30th st.,
> Dec. 19, 1905.

Dear Mitchell:

I wish I could make you feel how great a pleasure it was to get your letter of Sunday. For one thing it frees me to say, after putting myself out of the right by my long silence, that I enjoyed all your intention as well as your fine execution in "Constance Trescott,"[1] a book in your best manner, with the wisdom of your wonderful experience in human nature illumining the passion. The characters are all original, and boldly drawn; the conditions are studied in a manner to revive a whole most important period. Sometimes I wish there were more of me to do the kind of work that one of me cannot do enough of alone; but I wish there were a dozen of you to cope with your possibilities.[2] How at last they weigh us down, our possibilities! All we want against them is numbers.

I have not read any thing of Mrs. Wharton's except her short stories,[3] merely because I have not come in the way of her books. But I shall yet read them. I think it a pity she should have remained so long in the bondage of James, for she is great enough spirit to be free and to be herself.—Norton greatly liked her Valley of Decision,[4] and is always asking me if I've read it.—I spent a day and night with him a fortnight ago, and we had good talk, with some thing more of silence than there used to be. But the peaceful, gentle house is the same, and he grows gentler all the time. When he is gone, he will not have left his like. He is a peculiar passage of our literary history, most essential and truly characteristic, but reading like a chapter of an old-worldlier time and place. What rare men he has been a vital friend to, their equal in fineness, in everything but the will to do as well as he. He knows more of the secret of lettered New England than any of them know.—I shall be glad of your rhyme, when it comes.[5] For myself, I am only writing out the material of my English travels, and a handful of semi-psychological stories which I have fallen into the way of doing.[6]

If you could let me know when you come to New York, I would so gladly go to see you, and I go to see very few people gladly now.

Yours affectionately,
W. D. Howells.

1. Mitchell had written on 17 December 1905 (**PU**), asking whether Howells had received Mitchell's recent novel, *Constance Trescott* (1905), which he had sent earlier.

2. Mitchell had jokingly remarked in regard to his writing that he was "twins": "one is an amateur literateur in summer & goes to sleep in winter while the other attends to the literature of prescriptions."

3. In his letter Mitchell had recommended Edith Wharton's *The House of Mirth* (1905), "a disagreeably sad book but—oh—*very* well done." Her first collection of short stories was *The Greater Inclination* (1899); but Howells here refers most likely to her second volume of stories, *Crucial Instances* (1901), which he reviewed in the "Editor's Easy Chair," *Harper's Monthly*, October 1901.

4. See Howells to Norton, 27 May 1902, n. 7.

5. Mitchell had promised to send his rhymed version of the fourteenth-century poem *Pearl*, which was eventually published in 1908.

6. The semi-psychological stories appeared in *Harper's Monthly* and *Harper's Weekly* in 1905–1907 and were collected under the title *Between the Dark and the Daylight* (1907). See Gibson-Arms, *Bibliography*, pp. 58–59.

30 DECEMBER 1905, NEW YORK, TO AURELIA H. HOWELLS

> The Burlington,
> 10 W. 30th st.,
> Dec. 30, 1905.

Dear Aurelia:

I was grieved to hear through Vevie's kind letter of your painful accident.[1] By this time of course the painfulness is past, and I hope you are entirely well again, if you are not in full use of your scalded arm. It is astonishing how much use we have for the smallest member when we are put out of it for a time. When I had a run round on the little finger of my left hand it seemed to me as if I were all sore little finger, and no other limb counted. I am glad you are where you have the tender sympathy of Annie and her kind family.[2] You must let me enlarge the monthly check a little, so as to cover the expense of the nurse's visits, and let me know if I have not enlarged to enough.

I suppose you are making your reflections on the ending of another year, and will not want mine. Sometimes I think that if we did not check time off into months and years, but let it go in days, we should not feel so droopy at its going. But perhaps it would make no difference. We are here on the conditions which were made without our consent in the beginning, and we must bear our lot, quite as if we had chosen it. We did not make our bed, but, as the proverb has it in the case of those who do, we must lie in it. We may be very glad of the sleep we get in it, and the dreams when they are pleasant. There is a mystical obligation which we call duty. If we fulfill that, then our part is done, and it is for the One that made our bargain for us (all other bargains take two) to look out for the rest. Well, there you have my reflections, after all; and if they are not very gay they are honest.—I hope with all my heart the new year will be your friend, and comfort you in the care of our brother. You must always believe that I remember your self-devotion, and never fail to value it because you offer yourself lovingly and unmurmuringly in that care. With a kiss for him.

> Your aff'te brother,
> Will.

1. Marie Fréchette's letter has not been located.
2. Aurelia had returned to Ottawa with Henry either in late November or in early December to be near her sister Anne.

II

Friend, Epitapher, and Grandfather

1 9 0 6 – 1 9 0 9

Introduction

As always, Howells continued to exist in an uneasy state of accommodation with New York, a deluge of noise and energy he described for his sister Aurelia as "a great chaos of life that rather frightens me" (6 January 1906). Time after time, when not settled for a spell in the serenity of Kittery Point, he and Elinor found pretexts, usually those of health and old age, to escape for generous intervals—to Atlantic City for six weeks in the late winter of 1906, on a two-week cruise of the Great Lakes in the summer of 1907, to Italy for several months in early 1908. Within the city itself the Howellses still moved almost habitually from one hotel residence to another, until they finally relinquished their nomadic ways in late 1908 with the purchase of an ample apartment at 130 West 57th Street. Writing to Sara Norton from his "new shelf, between the asphalt and the sky," Howells seemed as bemused by the notion of another change as he was appreciative, so late in life, of the prospective permanence: "We are beginning again, my wife and I in our 72nd year the tale so often told in our lives, of housekeeping in a new place" (31 January 1909). The impending debilities of aging were less easy to resolve as Howells and his wife approached their seventies. His bouts with indigestion had become acute by early 1906, forcing him to the expedient of morphine, while in the same year Elinor's neuralgia "wasted [her] almost to a skeleton" so that it was "really pitiful to see her."[1]

Nor was he particularly encouraged about the outcome of his most recent literary labors. *London Films*, issued in late 1905, was not selling as well as he had hoped, a disappointment he attempted to reverse by proposing to Harper & Brothers—to no avail—a special tourist edition, which he offered to secure personally against financial loss. He was momentarily lifted by the slight success of *Certain Delightful English Towns* (1906), also a nonfictional by-product of his 1904 travels in England, a work he characterized to Joseph Howells as "one of my smilingest books" (13 March 1907). But with the contractual obligation to provide a steady flow of articles for one or another of

---

1. Howells to Aurelia Howells, 15 July 1906 (MH); quoted in Howells to Samuel L. Clemens, 1 August 1906, n. 4.

the four Harper magazines—the *Monthly*, *Weekly*, *Bazar*, and *North American Review*—Howells counted himself lucky to find much uninterrupted time for fiction. While working to finish the Utopian romance *Through the Eye of the Needle* in the fall of 1906, published in the following year as a sequel to *A Traveler from Altruria* (1894), he recalled, "the long stretches of years or half years when I wrote nothing but novels. Those were happy times. I like writing fiction, and I hate writing essays, which seems latterly my business."[2] Even with the best expectations there seemed little satisfaction, though, in the completed fictional task. At the publication of *Fennel and Rue* (1908), a novel whose plot he found initially engaging when he had begun it almost four years earlier as "A Tangled Web," Howells gratefully but provisionally accepted Brander Matthews' praise of its felicitous style. Dismissing the book in substance, he perceived it in retrospect to be "single to tenuity in motive, and narrowly escaping nothingness."[3]

In turning largely to romance in his later fiction, as a vehicle for making both social and psychological statements, Howells seemed to be grasping for a form that would convey the pervasive tenuity he was feeling in his own life. The numerous references in early 1906 to the composition of "A Sleep and a Forgetting," a short story published in *Harper's Weekly* during the winter of 1906–1907, suggest the extent to which the contours of the inner life were a more compelling subject for fiction than his long-standing commitment to a broadly representative social realism. As the story was in progress, he described it to Charles E. Norton as "very subjective, almost psychopathic . . . . a new field for my ignorance," at the same time explaining that his zest for recording the abundant "decent average . . . for my poor literature's sake" (11 March 1906) was unexpectedly but surely diminishing. In response to psychologist S. Weir Mitchell's observation that the case of memory loss dramatized in "A Sleep and a Forgetting" was unique from a medical standpoint, Howells claimed that the story, like most of the other psychic romances collected under the title *Between the Dark and the Daylight* (1907), was mainly drawn from personal experience.[4] Several letters of this period also mention his suffering from excessive and disturbing dreams. Although he empirically ascribed the cause to indigestion, he nevertheless found most of the dreams "trying" and leaving him "a thousand years old in the morning," as he explained in a letter to Aurelia of 30 December 1906.

---

2. Howells to Aurelia Howells, 29 November 1906 (MH); quoted in Howells to Frederick A. Duneka, 21 November 1906, n. 3.

3. Howells to Brander Matthews, 7 March 1909.

4. Howells to S. Weir Mitchell, 21 November 1907.

If his letters mirror the emotional uncertainties and literary misgivings of an aging author, they also show Howells to be a congenial and affectionate man readily sustained in his immediate world by a wide circle of friends. Those closest to him in spirit were also closest in age, so that he could as comfortably express his fears and expectations to them as he could to such family members as his sister Aurelia and his brother Joe. Along with Clemens and James, Charles E. Norton, mentor and Cambridge friend almost ten years his senior, was especially important to Howells. Theirs was a relationship of personal warmth and intellectual friction that coheres in their letters as a dialectic of mutual respect. The midwestern democrat of the contemporary American average engaged the genteel Brahmin and his aesthetic preference for the Old World, with Howells being sufficiently cosmopolitan and Norton sufficiently metropolitan to keep the two men abidingly close. Norton, as the elder, never hesitated to speak his mind, nor did Howells flinch from asserting his own independent temperament. Two episodes exemplify their contentiousness at its best: the first, in 1906, concerned the propriety of Howells wishing to place the Ashburner memoir—a private journal kept by one of Norton's English aunts—for publication in *Harper's Bazar*; the second, in 1906–1907, was a spirited disagreement over the contents of an address Norton had invited Howells to deliver at a commemoration ceremony for Longfellow. These were not mere differences of opinion, but the testing of ingrained attitudes and traditions.

Indeed, Howells was often pressed to an agile preservation of his own integrity in the face of Norton's autocratic manner. When, for example, Norton demeaned the *Bazar* by pointing out that there was a "flagrant incongruity" between its mass appeal and the "undemocratized & unvulgarized" English qualities of the Ashburner memoir, Howells, ever piqued by Anglophilic pretension, parried: "... I must resist the desire to offer you battle concern[ing] the Bazar, as a 'flagrant incongruity' in one so self-humbled. But even the unturning worm cannot suffer the notion of an 'unvulgarized England' to be implied to him."[5] Norton, on his part, saw Howells' tactful resistance as an endearing trait, "an admirable illustration of a delightful character," after Howells had deftly persisted in a disagreement over an essay on E. L. Godkin he had sent for Norton's approval.[6] "You accept my

5. Howells to Charles E. Norton, 2 December 1906; Norton's letter to Howells, dated 30 November 1906 (MH), is quoted in n. 2 of Howells' letter.

6. Published shortly thereafter as "A Great New York Journalist," *North American Review* 185 (3 May 1907), 44–53. Norton's comments are quoted in Howells to Charles E. Norton, 15 April 1907, n. 4.

comments on your article on Mr. Godkin," Norton continued with fond exasperation, "but are not convinced of their correctness." This capacity, so evident in Howells' correspondence, for evading the hazards of direct confrontation was also tellingly identified by Henry James, in "The Manners of American Women," as a signal characteristic of Howells' fiction: "For here we get the exquisite *detail* of the material, the universal patience—with the strangest impression, as a whole, I think, of every one's, men's and women's alike, trying, all round them, by universal readiness and response, to deprecate and forestall the great peril of fatal aggravation."[7] When Norton died in October 1908, Howells keenly felt not only the passing of an attentive friend, but also the severing of his last link with the quintessential spirit of New England's golden literary age.

If Howells felt reverent affection for his Cambridge friend, he indulged in a freer and more indiscriminate camaraderie with Mark Twain. In his own eclectic way he could cherish these two markedly different men: "You and he," he wrote to Norton of Clemens, "so strangely contrasted, are now the friends I value most" (27 June 1906). But with Clemens he could be less guarded, both intellectually and emotionally, enjoying a relationship founded on vigorous talk, shared social sympathies, good-natured ribbing, and mutual admiration. Clemens was living in or near New York after his wife's death, so the two men often saw each other in this period, engaging in activities as varied as their support of Maxim Gorky's fund-raising tour of the United States on behalf of the Russian Revolution and their trip to Washington, in December 1906, to lobby for a new copyright bill. When in mid-1908 Clemens moved to Redding, Connecticut, to occupy "Stormfield," the elaborate villa designed by John Howells, he seriously proposed that the Howellses build a house nearby. Howells continued to follow the progress of Clemens' autobiographical dictation with interest and constantly reread his friend's books—*A Connecticut Yankee* was one he returned to again and again—frequently sending praise for Clemens' gratification. Clemens, in turn, both loved Howells the man and genuinely respected Howells the writer. His incisive appreciation of Howells' stylistic mastery, in his essay "William Dean Howells,"[8] touched Howells as no other critic or friend possibly could: "I think round the world," Howells wrote after reading the essay, "and I find none now living whose praise I could care more for. Perhaps Tolstoy; but I do not love him as I love you . . . ."[9] Perhaps How-

---

7. *Harper's Bazar* 41 (July 1907), 647.
8. *Harper's Monthly* 113 (July 1906), 221–25.
9. Howells to Samuel L. Clemens, 24 June 1906.

ells' most revealing admiration was indirectly expressed in his letters through the spontaneous colloquialisms and bursts of mock formality that only Clemens could elicit from him, bright sallies worthy of Clemens himself. "I am at last out of bed," he reported on 21 February 1907, upon recovering from the grippe, "and so far on a par with that branch of the human race which is being tried for matricide, and other venial offenses." Almost three years later, when he was dispirited over his wife's failing health, Howells turned to that very quality of Clemens' "gab" for solace and cheer, stating conclusively: "There never was anybody like you, and there wont be."[10]

The friendship with Henry James was an entirely different matter, maintained mostly by transatlantic correspondence interspersed with a few mutual visits. It was a relationship in which the personal strands were inextricably bound to literary concerns, and for all the evident warmth it finally lacked the closeness Howells felt with Clemens. Geographic distance, along with James's natural aloofness and growing self-absorption, made sustained intimacy prohibitive. For Howells, though, James was undeniably an intelligence to be reckoned with. While Howells was lifted by Clemens' incomparable gab, James's manner seemed to constitute an unachievable standard. Writing to James of the "tremendous complication of emotions and characters" in *The Tragic Muse*, which he and Elinor had been reading aloud, Howells confessed "a constantly mounting wonder in myself of your 'way,' and at the fullness, the closeness, the density of your work; my own seems so meager beside it" (25 December 1909). In 1908, the example of James's prefaces for the New York Edition tempted Howells to plan a similar series of "Bibliographicals" for the projected Library Edition of his own works. He was immensely attracted by James's intricate self-anatomy, viewing it as a courageous critical gesture. As he began his own preface, or "Story of the Story" as he called it, for *A Hazard of New Fortunes*, he was especially enthusiastic, yet conscious of James's precedent to the extent of requesting that his volumes be finished in "a richly dark sober cloth—dull blue or green—since James has got maroon . . . ."[11] A week and a half later he suddenly proposed relinquishing the prefaces entirely, stating to Duneka not only his "insuperable repugnance to them," but also the fear that they would create "the effect of following in James's footsteps."[12] Thoroughly exhausted by

---

10. Howells to Samuel L. Clemens, 5 November 1909.

11. Howells to Frederick A. Duneka, 9 June 1909.

12. Howells to Frederick A. Duneka, 19 June 1909. Howells did manage to complete prefaces for the six volumes of the aborted Library Edition brought out in 1911, in addition to several others not published in his lifetime. See Gibson-Arms,

the recent completion of eighteen prefaces, James applauded the decision as a supreme act of self-preservation.

Howells maintained many other stimulating friendships, and as the established spokesman of American letters he was as much the recipient of regular and faithful correspondence as he was the initiator of it. He continued to encourage such younger realists as Edith Wyatt, Brand Whitlock, and Robert Herrick, dispensing alike generous praise and honest criticism as he saw fit. He particularly regretted Herrick's fictional explorations of sexual freedom, while still heartily endorsing the Chicago novelist's instructive social intentions—candid responses which Herrick duly appreciated. Upon the occasion of his seventieth birthday in 1907, Howells was deluged with letters celebrating him not only as a preeminent man of letters but also as a cherished friend. Henry B. Fuller earnestly speculated that future generations might well look back and acknowledge "The Age of Howells," while Edmund C. Stedman esteemed Howells as a significant friend of long standing: "I count my unbroken relations with you, and what I have gained by your respect and intimacy, as among the prizes which have made my life worth living."[13] In the following year S. Weir Mitchell, the novelist and physician who had treated Winifred Howells twenty years earlier, formally dedicated his novel *The Red City* (1908) "To Wm. D. Howells in payment of a debt to a master of fiction and to a friend of many years," to which Howells replied with simple gratitude, "I had always hoped, but I had never quite known that you cared for me in that way" (30 October 1908). In the prominence of his advanced age he was frequently called upon to write essays memorializing important literary figures who had died, a task he usually assumed without complaint, as in the case of Henrik Ibsen and Carl Schurz in 1906. He drew the line, however, with the death of his friend Thomas B. Aldrich in 1907, declining to do a piece for *Harper's Weekly* because, as he wryly phrased it, he felt that his "frequent mortuary notices" were turning him into "a kind of standard epitapher."[14] He would, of course, magnificently disregard this self-imposed injunction three years later in a singular act of personal and literary devotion, when, upon the death of his closest friend, he wrote *My Mark Twain* (1910).

Within the realm of his own family he had increasingly assumed the role of benevolent patriarch, not immodestly, but by the dependence

Bibliography, p. 66; also George Arms, "Howells' Unpublished Prefaces," *New England Quarterly* 17 (December 1944), 580–91.

13. Edmund C. Stedman to Howells, 28 February 1907 (MH); quoted in Howells to Stedman, 1 March 1907, n. 1.

14. Howells to Frederick A. Duneka, 20 March 1907 (MWA); quoted in Howells to Edmund C. Stedman, 1 March 1907, n. 4.

of others. His letters to Aurelia and Joseph Howells—the latter his senior by five years—often take the tone of responsible older brother, advising, sometimes in a chiding fashion, on financial and other matters. He was especially quick to correct Joe's grammar and political pronouncements as inappropriate to his position as American consul at Turks Islands. Although there is no surviving correspondence with his errant younger brother, the pecuniary and domestic tribulations of Samuel Howells are a comic-tragic leitmotif in Howells' letters to Aurelia and Joe. At one point in 1906 he even intervened to try and save Sam's menial job at the Government Printing Office by writing directly to President Roosevelt. Of more immediate importance to him at this time in his life was the marriage of his son John in late 1907 to Abby White, daughter of Horace White, owner and editor of the New York *Post*; and he was greatly delighted by the birth of his first grandson, William White Howells, in November 1908. With the deaths of Norton, Stedman, and his mentally impaired younger brother, Henry, earlier in that year, the arrival of Billy Howells was a rejuvenating event in a time of general bereavement. As Howells wrote "A Counsel of Consolation" for a series of essays on death and the afterlife, jointly planned with Elizabeth Jordan for *Harper's Bazar*,[15] he was himself most consoled by the new life that made him a grandfather. The mingling of his aging hopes with Billy's unformed future is touchingly suggested in a note to Billy, then only three months old: "Hold fast to my hand, dear little boy, and keep me with you as long as you can" (1 March 1908)—a loving message to be preserved for Billy's later understanding.

Howells and Elinor returned to Rome in 1908, after a forty-five year absence, on what would be their last European trip together. Although Elinor's health kept her confined to the hotel much of the time, they fondly if briefly resurrected the youthful past by visiting their old lodgings at Cinque Via del Gambero where, as he wrote to Sir George O. Trevelyan, "we were so young and happy" (5 February 1908). On their return through London, Howells saw James, talking at length about the prefaces for the New York Edition and the literary past they had shared when Howells, as editor of the *Atlantic*, launched James's first novels in serial form. Howells had arranged with Harper & Brothers to bring out a book on his Italian journey, taking the descriptive letters published in the New York *Sun* during his travels and collecting them as *Roman Holidays and Others* (1908). This, his third book on Italy—

---

15. "A Counsel of Consolation" was the title used in the collected essays, *In After Days: Thoughts on the Future Life* (1910); it had originally appeared as "In the House of Mourning," *Harper's Bazar* 43 (April 1909), 360–63.

after *Venetian Life* (1866) and *Tuscan Cities* (1886)—was more than a perfunctory success, although Howells modestly downplayed his "Roman stuff" as being "without any such authority as the Venetian, and is the reflex of my youthful fires, such as they were."[16]

Suffering a severe recurrence of his old gall colic condition in May 1909, Howells went with his daughter Mildred to take the cure at the baths of Carlsbad, Austria. It was not until he reached home in October, however, that he learned his wife had undergone major surgery for the removal of swollen glands, an ordeal she bravely kept a secret so as not to cause him undue anxiety while he was helplessly out of the country. It was a shock from which she never fully recovered. In early December, feeling tired and withdrawn, he reluctantly traveled to Washington to preside as president at the first public meeting of the American Academy of Arts and Letters, an event he was convinced held little interest for anyone other than the academicians themselves. As 1909 drew to a close, Howells took what comfort he could in Billy, writing James on Christmas day, "My wife wont go out, and so I keep in, talking with her, and we play with our dear little grandson, who dwells so lovingly in a world of love and is so full of surprises at it and for us. I could not have believed that life still held an experience so sweet for me." The years to come would, indeed, be bitter with loss and loneliness.

W. C. F.

---

16. Howells to Henry James, 2 August 1908.

4 JANUARY 1906, NEW YORK, TO JOSEPH A. HOWELLS

10 West 30th st.,
Jan'y 4, 1906.

Dear Joe:

There is nothing to add to my letter of yesterday in the way of news, except that we are a day nearer to Pilla's sailing for Bermuda,[1] and a bit lonelier. Her throat is so much better that if she can spend the worst of the winter there, I hope it will be permanently cured.

This afternoon I ran out and mailed you six or seven papers. If I could know the sailings of the Halifax boats I might keep you more regularly posted, but I will do the best I can with the Clyde line.[2]

I have somehow an idea that you are disappointed and homesick. If this is true, you must try to regard your place as a sanatarium. If you can't stand it in that way, you can stick it out for the winter, and come home. But perhaps I have misread your absence of enthusiastic expression. I should be most sorry myself if you were, and that perhaps is the reason why I feel anxious to know how you do feel.

One of the few advantages of being in New York is that John spends most of his evenings with us. He and Pilla are such good comrades, and he would apparently rather be with her and us than anyone else. He is very much better, insofar that he is apt to forget his ailments.[3]

I should be glad to know how Eliza and Beatrice find society in Grand Turk. Is the color line very closely drawn? What church do you go to? Don't be afraid that I shall not be interested in the smallest details.

I am constantly writing something, and have just done a paper on Oxford.[4] Did you go there? My London book[5] has done fairly well, but has not been the go that I hoped. However, I have had a fair share of luck, taking it "by and large."—Mark Twain called me up by his secretary today—she is a very gentle young girl,—and had her ask me over the 'phone "what occasion it was in Boston when he *raised hell*" about Emerson and Longfellow."[6] I had a long talk with him the other day, which brought back the old time of long talks. With our love to you all.

Your aff'te brother
Will.

1. Mildred sailed on 13 January.

2. Howells regularly sent newspapers, books, and even canned goods by way of the Clyde Steamship Company, which regularly served Grand Turks Island where Joseph Howells was U.S. consul.

3. John had been suffering from severe dyspepsia.

4. "Oxford," *North American Review,* 5 October 1906, was reprinted in *Certain Delightful English Towns.*

5. *London Films.*

6. For Clemens' speech at the Whittier Birthday Dinner, see Howells to Norton, 19 December 1877, n. 2. Clemens incorporated the episode into his dictation of 23 January 1906, in which he summarizes his regret: "My instinct said, formerly, that it was an innocent speech, and funny. The same instinct, sitting old and judicial, as a court of last resort, has revised that verdict." See *Mark Twain's Autobiography,* ed. Albert B. Paine (New York: Harper & Brothers, 1924), II, 5.

6 JANUARY 1906, NEW YORK, TO AURELIA H. HOWELLS

The Burlington,
10 W. 30 st.,
Jan'y 6, 1906.

Dear Aurelia:

I enclose letters from Joe and Eliza, which give some notion of their life, and rather dissipate the notion I had that they were homesick. The winter is now beginning here, and the cold makes me willing to share their exile. But I dare say they feel lone and far at times.

I hope your scalded arm is rapidly getting well. I don't know that I said enough in sympathy for the pain you must have suffered. But you will believe I felt the sympathy.

Our life varies so little from day to day that I scarcely know what to write. In fact there is no news except the vast deluge of New York incidents. Things take place here on such a huge scale, and we are much more in the thick of them than we were in 59th street, where we had country on one side of us. Here it is city all round, but far quieter by reason of the blocking in from the great avenues of noise.—Last night when Elinor and I were walking home from a restaurant dinner we found our way down 5th avenue flooded from a burst main. The water was swelling up like a fountain, and we had to go round several blocks. All the basements about were flooded, and things are so badly managed that the leak was not stopped till midnight.

We like to go out for dinner, but the restaurants are dearer and worse than they used to be. It is a great chaos of life that rather frightens me. You have no where the sense of peace and home that you have in London. I like it less than ever, and if the winter were not so hard in Boston I should like to go back there to live.

Perhaps Pilla will find a place in Bermuda where we can spend our winters. But I dare say we shall keep on here year after year.

I hope Henry is well, and all the Frechettes. Our love to everyone.

Your affte brother
Will.

6 JANUARY 1906, NEW YORK, TO EDITH WYATT

> The Burlington
> 10 W. 30th st.,
> Jan'y 6, 1906.

Dear Miss Wyatt:

I found Mr. Alden the other day brooding dubiously over your longer story, having already made up his mind against the shorter.[1] I told you of our family joy in that, and without sharing with the others my great pleasure in the first I am sorrowfully transmitting them both to you. I can understand why Alden should not find them the Harper kind of story, while I need not say that if I had been an editor I should have gladly and gratefully printed them. Nothing out of Russian fiction could give me more absolutely the sense of truth in the nature and conditioning of your people in The Pursuit of Happiness, especially that selfish brute beast of a Mrs. Ricker. "But, what the deuce?" as one of your people says in True Love.[2] We must take editors as we find them, and Alden is a most faithful and able one. I doubt if you would have your effect in Harper's. I had thought of trying your stories with the Atlantic unknown to you, but I have scarcely the right, and I could not bear another heartbreak. Why do you break with McClure?[3] I doubt if you have a right to throw away the chance at the public you have won even for a scruple as to other people's veracity. Consider how rare and difficult the truth is, even in private life, and be merciful to the faltering editors.

My wife and daughter join me in best regards.

> Yours sincerely,
> W. D. Howells.

1. Henry M. Alden, editor of *Harper's Monthly*, had rejected two of Wyatt's stories, "The Pursuit of Happiness" mentioned below by Howells and one unidentified piece.

2. For Howells' estimate of *True Love*, see Howells to Fuller, 20 September 1903, n. 3. How important Howells' opinions on literary and other matters were to Wyatt is suggested by a letter she wrote Howells on 27 January 1906 (MH): "With this I am sending to you the fables I spoke of to you in New York . . . . [¶] I lunched the other day with Miss [Jane] Addams, who made many inquiries of me about you, and for whom I repeated with very great pleasure, I think virtually everything you said to me about Tolstoi."

3. The reason for Wyatt's break with Samuel S. McClure is not known, but other writers at times complained about the excessive editorial freedom he took with their work. See Howells to Garland, 8 January 1897, n. 1.

24 JANUARY 1906, NEW YORK, TO FREDERICK A. DUNEKA

10 West 30th st.,
Jan'y 24, 1906.

My dear Mr. Duneka:

As I understood from our last brief colloquy that it is not a question of propriety but of profit concerning a tourist's edition of London Films, I am willing to see if I could not secure you against loss in the enterprise. When you have talked it over with the Major,[1] and have found what it would cost to do 2500 or 3000 copies of a book somewhat smaller than this leaf (a little over half) in limp leather, or cloth, on thin paper, and can let me know what you would probably lose on them, I will decide whether I could afford the luxury of securing you.

I believe that such an edition, if properly advertised, would succeed; and I should like to recoup myself for my ungotten gains on the large book.[2] Not in the way of complaint, but in the cause of that frankness we both like, I will say that it has not seemed quite adequately offered to the public. (I) The main, substantial novelty of it, the study of American origins, was so entirely lost sight of that I had to remind you of it before it was put forward. Then it was too late for any effect. (II) I then suggested that the book should be put forward publicly as a holiday book, but though you agreed with me, this was not done, to any knowledge of mine. (III) Our last understanding was that the price of my books should be *advanced*. This one ought to have been $5, and $10 for large paper copies; but it was put at $2.25, or 25 cts *less* than the other books like it.

These things seem to me in the nature of breaks. I know that breaks must occur among the multitude of your enterprises, and I do not lament over spilt milk or wish to accuse you of spilling it. But I think there is a chance of picking some of it up in a tourist's edition of my book, which I would have you offer to my small but enthusiastic public at $2.00. It need not have any pictures.

Yours cordially,
W. D. Howells.

P. S. Thank you for reminding me of Maeterlinck's paper on Immortality. It is a great and consoling effort, and it quite jumps with the motive I am working out in a story for Alden.[3]

1. Frederick T. Leigh, the treasurer of Harper & Brothers.

2. The first edition of *London Films*, on which Harper & Brothers took a loss although Howells' salary remained constant and therefore, according to him, undeserved. Although Howells argued forcefully that a small tourist edition would recoup the loss, it was never issued.

3. Maurice Maeterlinck (1862–1949), Belgian poet and dramatist, wrote a paper entitled "Of Immortality" which appeared in translation in *Harper's Monthly*, December 1905. Howells' story was "A Sleep and a Forgetting," *Harper's Weekly*, 15 December 1906. Howells explained to Aurelia Howells, 18 February 1906 (MH), how it concerns the question of immortality: "I am writing a story which interests me so much that I tremble for the way I am doing it as not worthy. It is about a girl who has wholly lost her memory from a shock, but keeps her personality intact, without severance of consciousness. It is against the notion that in another world we are not the same unless we fully remember what we have been."

29 JANUARY 1906, NEW YORK, TO JOSEPH A. HOWELLS

10 W. 30th st.,
Jan'y 29, 1906.

Dear Joe:

That was a fine letter of yours about Christmas, in the Sentinel.[1] Only, make your sentences short, and get out clearly the verbs—the words of *doing* and *being*. Make Eliza run your letters over before you send them. They are delightful in matter and feeling.—We are going to Atlantic City, on Tuesday or Wednesday, and I doubt if we shall come back to this hotel;[2] the down-town air has been bad for Elinor. Better send all your letters for me, c/o Harpers.

Last night John and I went to Dockstader's Minstrels,[3] and saw a good nigger show. It was most amusing. Dockstader made the whole house sing *Everybody works but Father* with him.[4] I am sending you the program, so that you can sing it, too; you can use any tune with it. Just now that we are leaving N. Y. we are getting in a good many theatres, and I wish you were here to help go. But you are in a better place.

We continue to have the most ridiculous weather, more like the last of March than of January. But we shall probably have winter yet. Pilla had a hard trip to Bermuda, but is glad to be there, with the mercury at 75°, and the windows all open. Of course, that would be cool, with you.

Your steamship company seems to keep up the regular trips of their boats. I suppose we shall see the wreck of the Cherokee at Atlantic City.[5] I don't know how long we shall stay—probably three weeks; perhaps all February.—I have got swung into a story,[6] but I can keep it up there as well as here.—You see I have no news. I will send papers as usual, but doubt if I shall write again for the next steamer. Elinor joins me in love to all. We think your life most interesting.

Your aff'te brother

Will.

1. The series of letters began in the 14 December 1905 issue of the *Sentinel*; Howells is referring to "Letter VII. Christmas in the Tropics," published on 25 January 1906. Joe's son, Will, was editing the *Sentinel* at this time.

2. Of the Burlington, his temporary residence, Howells wrote to Aurelia Howells, 21 January 1906 (MH): "This queer old place is just waiting to be sold, and everything goes at sixes and sevens, but it is very cozy having our meals in our rooms, and we hate to leave, though we probably shall."

3. Lew Dockstader, pseudonym of George A. Clapp (1856–1924), was one of the most popular black-face players in the declining years of the minstrel show at the turn of the century. In partnership with George Primrose (1852–1919), he formed Primrose's Minstrels in 1898 and in 1903 became sole proprietor of the company. A month later Howells attended another minstrel performance, one by black players in black face, about which he wrote to Aurelia Howells, 24 February 1906 (MH), from Atlantic City: "We take in lots of shows, and are just home from a minstrel show, by real negroes. They are rather a poor imitation of a poor imitation, and have made me rather melancholy." Later in the year Joe's son, a harpist, was employed as a musician in Dockstader's troupe, moving Howells to remark, in a letter to J. A. Howells, 21 June 1906 (MH): "I am glad to hear of your Joe's engagement by Dockstader. It is not what one would have expected of a Howells exactly, but it is an honorable calling, and much better than cheating somebody in trade."

4. "Everybody Works But Father" (music by Charles W. McClintock, words by Jean Havez, 1905), a song written expressly for Dockstader, was a humorous commentary on the large numbers of women and children working in factories. Its popularity is suggested by Howells' ironic application of the title to his beleaguered brother Sam, whose family situation he would characterize to Anne Fréchette, 2 September 1906 (MH), as one "in which 'nobody works but father.'"

5. The *Cherokee*, a ship of the Clyde Steamship Company serving the Turks Islands, went aground on Brigantine Shoals off Atlantic City on 12 January. Howells describes the incident to Aurelia Howells, 14 January 1906 (MH): "I have been writing without having heard from him [Joe], for the Turks' Island steamer has gone ashore on the New Jersey coast, and the mails have not been sent off. It is a very curious case; at first they thought it merely grounding; but now it seems more serious, and the wrecking tugs are pulling at her in vain."

6. At the time Howells was working on "A Sleep and a Forgetting." See Howells to Duneka, 24 January 1906, n. 3.

30 JANUARY 1906, NEW YORK, TO MILDRED HOWELLS

10 West 30th st.,

Jan'y 30, 1906.

Dear Pilla:[1]

I am writing you this last note from the poor old Burlington, while we are waiting for luncheon, (with our trunks already gone) before starting for Atlawntic Cittee, at 3.00 p.m. The Burl. and Emmer[2] had got to their last legs together; in fact the B. has been fighting on its stumps ever since you left; but Mr. Beeson[3] was blandly showing people through our back apartment this morning, in spite of there being neither linen, silver nor china. The chefs follow each other in and out of the kitchen, and the waiters come and go in droves, attended by tearful slaveys. John has steadily dined with us, as often as his mother would let him, and staid till his early bedtime. Last night I left them Mead-ing together, and went to see "Alice-sit-by-the-Fire."[4] Oh, I'm sorry you didn't see that play—the most delicious of all the Barrie morsels, about a wildly romantic girl who has learnt life from the emotional drama, and who "saves" her mother, who has been through 16 years' flirtations in India and has gone with the father to a young man's rooms as blamelessly as possible. The daughter hides herself in a china closet, and sternly refuses to come out, when her wicked mother wants to "save" *her*. I don't believe the audience knew how good it was, but I bore the burden of the laugh, and carried it through.—Emmer is exhuberantly well in expectation of being better at At. C.; she will write you from there; your letters wont start till Saturday. Of course you must address us c/o Harpers.; I don't know where we shall be when we come back, but perhaps at the St. Hubert, 57th st. bet. 6 and 7 aves. Not a word yet from the much meandering "Myrtilla."[5] Kate Mead[6] (I calling on her mother) professed a profound love and honor for M. She (K.) is ever so much better, and her mother is now playing all her old Brattleboro' music to keep her wrist limber.[7] With love to all Bermuda,

> Your aff'te
> **Poppy.**

---

1. Howells was writing to Mildred who had gone to Bermuda to escape the harsh effects of the New York winter on her constantly sore throat. Of Mildred's stay there, he would write to Aurelia Howells several days later, 4 February 1906 (MH), that "'in spite of being well on in the thirties,' she is going the round of picnics, lunches and dances like the young girl everybody takes her for."

2. Elinor Howells.

3. Presumably the manager of the Burlington.

4. *Alice-Sit-by-the-Fire* (1905) was a play by Sir James M. Barrie, the British dramatist. Howells reviewed it favorably in "The New Plays, Mr. Barrie's Benefactions to Humanity on the Stage," *Harper's Weekly*, 24 February 1906.

5. "Myrtilla" was a poem by Mildred, which appears to have been misplaced by an unidentified publisher. There is no indication that it was ever accepted for publication.

6. Catherine Mead was the daughter of Isabella M. Mead, wife of Elinor's brother Charles. Kate, whom Howells described to Aurelia Howells, 8 February 1906 (MH), as "the one Pilla loved best of all her Mead cousins," died several days later of a lung hemorrhage.

7. Howells wrote to Aurelia, 28 January 1906 (MH), that Isabella Mead "fell down

stairs and broke her wrist last spring. It is a little stiff, now, but she plays all her old girlhood music, by her doctor's orders, so as to limber it up, and has rather a good time."

16 FEBRUARY 1906, ATLANTIC CITY, TO BRANDER MATTHEWS

The St. Charles,
Atlantic City, Feb'y 16, 1906.

My dear Matthews:

The address will explain much,[1] and I wish it could say how deeply I grieve not to be able to come to your lunch—the brightest jewel in the girdle of the year! Drop a tear of pity into a beaker of Barsac, and pour it out in a libation to the unforgetting gods, who will thus be moved to remember me next time.—You see I am training to write an historical novel.[2]

Yours ever
W. D. Howells.

1. Howells and Elinor had arrived in Atlantic City on 30 January.
2. Matthews would of course understand that the extravagant style of the letter was a humorous jibe at what Howells had long deprecated as "romanticistic" fiction, especially in the offending form of the historical novel popular at the turn of the century.

18 FEBRUARY 1906, ATLANTIC CITY, TO CHARLES E. NORTON

Hotel St. Charles,
Atlantic City, February 18, 1906.

My dear Norton:

I hope that by this time no strangeness of address in us will surprise you. My wife was not well in New York, and Pilla being in Bermuda, there was no reason why we should not come away. Man has done all he could to make this place hideous; but it takes a good deal to spoil the Atlantic Ocean, and even man has added a board walk to five miles of the beach, on which elderly people may walk, or be trundled in Bath chairs by the most velvety of black brothers. The sky is a paler Riviera sky, and the air for the great part not much chillier than at San Remo, and we go into the sun for long hours every day. The hotel is comfortably full of kindly people not one of whom has yet told me that he or she likes my books so much. There is a pretty little theatre and a vaudeville show, so that we lead our wonted life of ignoble pleasure without a pang of selfreproach.

We were sorry indeed to hear of Miss Sedgwicks affliction,[1] but we rejoice with you in her recovery. Somehow I feel that your neighborhood owes me a duty not to change before I can see it again, which will be with your kindly choice of dates the end of March rather than the end of February.[2] Pilla will have returned then to look after her mother,[3] and we shall all be nearer New York and the express trains for Boston. Besides, the blue birds will have got back to Shady Hill, and will be plaintively piping the same notes that I heard in your woods, forty years ago, when once I walked away from your door in a first transport with the friendship which has never failed. So, kindest and dearest of men, expect me the evening or afternoon of March 30th.—Of course I am writing, all the time; trying to get the better of my English material,[4] and doing a little fiction, with a sick girl for a heroine, and the problem of a lost memory for the motive. I please myself with the name, "A Sleep and a Forgetting" till the publishers make me change it.[5]—My wife joins me in love to all.

Yours affectionately
W. D. Howells.

1. Theodora Sedgwick, the youngest sister of Norton's deceased wife, Susan Sedgwick Norton, had suffered a slight stroke. See Norton to Howells, 12 February 1906 (MH).

2. In his letter of 12 February, Norton had invited Howells to a Saturday Club dinner, preferably the one on 24 February, honoring James Russell Lowell's birthday.

3. Mildred Howells was at this time in Bermuda.

4. *Certain Delightful English Towns*.

5. See Howells to Duneka, 24 January 1906, n. 3.

28 FEBRUARY 1906, ATLANTIC CITY, TO SAMUEL L. CLEMENS

Atlantic City, Feb'y 28, 1906.

My dear Clemens:

No praise that I ever had for work of my own gave me such entire and perfect joy as your praise of Pilla's poem. Of course your letter has gone straight to her, and she will know how to prize the words which are simply without price.[1]

I have no complaint to make of Clara except that I was not the least use in the world to her.[2] Sometime she must make that up to me. I wish she would go to Bermuda while Pilla is there.

To-morrow I shall be 69,[3] but I do not seem to care. I did not start the affair, and I have not been consulted about it at any step. I was born to be afraid of dying, but not of getting old. Age has many advantages, and if old men were not so ridiculous, I should not mind being one. But they *are* ridiculous, and they are ugly. The young do not see this so clearly as they do; but some day they will.

So you have been up, burying poor old Patrick—I suppose *he* was old, too.[4] I remember how you used to work, one while, over his stable. I dare say he did not like it; but he probably never said so, and now the best return you can make is to see him put under the ground. It is strange, but that was *really* the best you could do, and I am glad you did it.

I want to hear some of your autobiography,[5] if you will let me; or you could give me the MS. and let me read it for myself.

Mrs Howells joins me in love to you all.

Yours ever

W. D. Howells.

Now and then in these latter days I *realize* that I shall die, hitherto having regarded it as problematical, and the sense of it is awful. I do not see how so many people stand it. That is nonesense, but the notion does not present itself conceivably. My wife does not let me discuss these ideas with her, and so I keep them for my own edification. When my father was 87 he once said to me that the night before he had thought it all out, and now he was satisfied. Perhaps each has to come to some such settlement with himself.

1. Mildred Howells' poem was "At the Wind's Will," *Harper's Monthly*, March 1906. Clemens had praised the poem enthusiastically: "its depth, & dignity, & pathos, & compression, & fluent grace & beauty—and stern veracity—have haunted me all day & sung in the ears of my spirit like a strain of solemn music. What a lumbering poor vehicle prose is for the conveying of a great thought! It cost me several chapters to say in prose what Mildred has said better with a single penfull of ink. Prose wanders around with a lantern & laboriously schedules and verifies the details & particulars of a valley & its frame of crags & peaks, then Poetry comes, and lays bare the whole landscape with a single splendid flash." See Clemens to Howells, 25 February 1906 (MH; *Twain-Howells*, pp. 800–801). Howells later told Aurelia H. Howells, 1 April 1906 (MH), that "Mark Twain carries it round in his pocket and reads to everyone."

2. Clemens had acknowledged the assistance Howells had rendered in finding suitable lodgings for Clara Clemens, who was taken ill in Atlantic City.

3. For Clemens' humorous use of the occasion of Howells' sixty-ninth birthday, see *Twain-Howells*, p. 802.

4. Patrick McAleer, Clemens' coachman, had died in Hartford on 25 February.

5. Howells saw Clemens on 25 March, at which time they discussed the autobiography. See *Twain-Howells*, p. 802.

11 March 1906, Atlantic City, to Charles E. Norton

Atlantic City, March 11, 1906.

My dear Norton:

There are some reasons why I could more conveniently come to you for the Saturday Club dinner of April 28 than that of March 31.[1] Would it be the same thing to you? If not, frankly say so, and I will let the pleasure of seeing you sooner outweigh all reasons for the delay: they are not insurmountable.

My wife and I have been in this strange place for six weeks. She was much relaxed by our stay in New York, and the change to the sea-shore, in the mildest of winters, has been the best possible for her. The life we have led has been of the quietest, for the genius of the hotels here is Solitude in the midst of Society—such as the society is. In all our weeks we have not seen one distinguished figure or striking face, but the decent average has interestingly abounded. It is such an afflux of the ordinary as in earlier life I should have rejoiced in for my poor literature's sake; but now, though I still see all things as before, I no longer make note of them, voluntarily or involuntarily.[2] What interests me in this fact is that it is unexpected. I thought I should wish to keep on gathering material to the end, but I find that I have stored up enough to last my time. I let the most delightful types go by without seeking an impression from them; and I had not supposed that nature would intimate in this way that it was time for me to close up business. From the accumulations of the past I have been writing a long short story, but it is very subjective, almost psychopathic.[3] It is a new field for my ignorance.

My children are both in Bermuda, where John joined Mildred last week. She has entirely escaped her sore throat in the mild air, and this consoles us for her absence.

We leave here on Wednesday, and till we go to Kittery Point in May we expect to be in or near New York. My address is always with the Harpers. With our love to all your house,

Yours sincerely
W. D. Howells.

1. See Howells to Norton, 18 February 1906, n. 2.
2. For Norton's response and Howells' subsequent treatment of the question whether the average American is a suitable subject for literature, see Howells to Norton, 27 June 1906, n. 3.
3. "A Sleep and a Forgetting."

12 MARCH 1906, ATLANTIC CITY, TO BRANDER MATTHEWS

Atlantic City, March 12, 1906.

My dear Matthews:

You make a gallant defence of us in the Columbia Review,[1] and I have read it with none the satisfaction because I think we really need none. I would have had you take the aggressive in one point, and say that in literature, of the very finest and subtlest, we surpass all other nations of our time.

I have been following you in the North American about play writing for readers.[2] It is all very interesting; and I was especially interested because I was a pioneer (and at the time supposed myself alone) in making the stage direction a part of the literature.[3] See The Parlor Car, Out of the Question, etc.

We opened Edith's letter to Mildred, thinking it might need an answer quicker than one could come from Bermuda; and we wish to join in the congratulations which will duly come from her.

Yours ever
W. D. Howells.

1. Howells' reference to the "Columbia Review" is puzzling, since the only journal by that title was not founded until 1919, and the *Columbia Law Review* does not index any articles by Matthews. However, Howells may have read some form of Matthews' essay, "Americans and British: A Patriotic Consideration of International Contrasts," which also appeared in *Reader*, July 1906. It is a defense of American character against prevailing British (and some French) stereotypes.

2. "On the Publishing of Plays," *North American Review*, March 1906.

3. Howells implies the same accomplishment in his letter to the actor Francis Wilson, 24 April 1906. See also Howells to Hay, 22 February 1877.

24 MARCH 1906, NEW YORK, TO MILDRED HOWELLS

New York, March 24 1906.

Dear Pilla:

Here is the other check, and I hope the one I enclosed this morning will reach you with it. No news. I have just been reading a most sloppy sentimental story (The Country Doctor) of Balzac's to E. M. H.,[1] and we have despised it unison. It sends H. J. to the foot in my estimation. To praise such a rotter as that, and then have a word for Tolstoy, and a pat for the giant Jane![2]

Well, I am very sleepy, and almost cross.
Good night, dear girl.

Papa.

1. Balzac wrote *Le Médecin de campagne* in 1833, placing it in 1846 among those works representing "Scenes of Country Life" in *La comédie humaine* (1842–1848). Howells' assessment of Balzac's "romanticistic" weaknesses is best summarized in sections 3 and 5 of *Criticism and Fiction*. E. M. H. was Elinor Mead Howells.

2. In all likelihood the offending references are those in Henry James's lecture "The Lesson of Balzac." See Howells to Jordan, 1 June 1904, n. 5. Describing one of the lessons of Balzac as "the lesson that there is no convincing art that is not ruinously expensive," he mentions Tolstoy in passing as slightly less comparable: "I am unwilling to say, in the presence of such of his successors as George Eliot and Tolstoi and Zola (to name, for convenience, only three of them), that he was the last of the novelists to do the thing handsomely; but I will say that we get the impression at least of his having had more to spend" (p. 101). To "the giant Jane" he was less kind, asserting that "Jane Austen, with all her light felicity, leaves us hardly more curious of her process, or of the experience in her that fed it, than the brown thrush who tells his story from the garden bough; and this, I freely confess, in spite of her being one of those of the shelved and safe, for all time..." (p. 60). He went on to say, somewhat cuttingly, that the responsibility for Austen's present reputation was not to be attributed to an intelligent critical spirit: "Responsible, rather, is the body of publishers, editors, illustrators, producers of the pleasant twaddle of magazines; who have found their 'dear,' our dear, everybody's dear, Jane so infinitely to their material purpose, so amenable to pretty reproduction in every variety of what is called tasteful, and in what seemingly proves to be saleable, form" (p. 62).

8 APRIL 1906, NEW YORK, TO SAMUEL L. CLEMENS

Hotel Regent....
New York City April 8, 1906.

My dear Clemens:

I want to see every word of the 578 pages before this,[1] which is one of the humanest and richest pages in the history of man. If you have gone this gate all through you have already gone farther than any autobiographer ever went before. You are nakeder than Adam and Eve put together, and truer than sin. But—but—but you really *mustn't* let Orion have got into the bed.[2] I know he did, but—

Yours ever,
W. D. Howells.

1. Howells had just read a portion of Clemens' autobiographical dictation.

2. The episode refers to Clemens' brother Orion, who, wishing to surprise the family with an unannounced visit to Hannibal, had unwittingly crept into bed with two spinsters. Orion was unaware that in his absence the house had been rented

to Doctor Meredith and his two elderly sisters. See *Mark Twain's Autobiography*, ed. A. B. Paine (New York: Harper & Brothers, 1924), II, 272–74. Although Howells raised his eyebrow at the inclusion of this incident, he otherwise approved of what he read, as Clemens acknowledged two days later. See *Twain-Howells*, p. 804.

8 APRIL 1906, NEW YORK, TO AURELIA H. HOWELLS

Hotel Regent
New York, April 8, 1906.

Dear Aurelia:

I am giving a lunch today for H. G. Wells, the English novelist, who was very nice to Pilla and me at Sandgate, near Folkestone, two years ago.[1] There are to be ten men in all, and as I have been long out of doing that sort of thing I find myself drolly nervous. John will stay my trembling knees, however, and these affairs always go off well after they begin. There will be, besides our Howells selves, an old painter friend of Boston days, Crowninshield; Rutgers Marshall, a delightful psychologist; Frank Millet, the painter and journalist; Norman Hapgood, who downed "Town Topics" in the recent suit; Francis Wilson, the comedian; Mark Twain and Twitchell, his old Hartford Pastor; and Wells, of course.[2] Wells, you know, is a little cockney man, but of a brave spirit, who is socialistic in his expectations of the future, and boldly owns to having been a dry goods clerk in his own past.

The weather is changing to a decidedly spring-like mood. Yesterday late, John and I walked in the park, and noted the new lilac leaves, and heard a robin songing his vesper hymn; blackbirds too numerous to mention. The forceythias were yellowing all about.

We expected letters from Pilla in the evening, but the steamer did not get in till late, and we must wait till tomorrow. We have only, I hope, to wait till next Sunday when the boat will bring the dear child herself.

This is all our little news. We are well, we poor old two, and Elinor went a walk with me yesterday morning—in the Park, of course. She had not been out for a week. John and I are going down to Kittery P. at the end of the month, hurrah! With love to all those you love,

Your aff'te brother,
Will.

1. See Howells to Elinor Howells, 13 May 1904, n. 1, and Howells to Wells, 24 June 1904.

2. Frederic Crowninshield, Henry Rutgers Marshall, Francis D. Millet, Francis Wilson, and Joseph H. Twichell have all been previously identified. Norman Hap-

good (1868–1937) was a journalist, author, and reformer. He was then editor of *Collier's* (1902–1912), a journal of literature and social criticism. Hapgood had been sued for libel by *Town Topics*, a magazine devoted to gossip and slander, because he had attacked the magazine in an editorial for a scurrilous paragraph it had printed about Alice Roosevelt. In his invitation of 6 April 1906 (CU; *Twain-Howells*, p. 803) Howells had charged Clemens to come and "meet H. G. Wells, the man from Mars and other malign planets, and an awfully nice little Englishman."

16 APRIL 1906, NEW YORK, TO JOSEPH A. HOWELLS

> *Hotel Regent.* . . .
> *New York City* April 16, 1906.

Dear Joe:

The Clyde S.S. people have not sent me notice of the next sailing; so I am writing this short letter at random, to catch a possible boat tomorrow. If I find one goes later, I will write again. We are very happy in having Pilla again; she got back yesterday morning in good shape after rather a rocky voyage;[1] and now for Kittery and golden joys about this time next month! John and I are going down at the end of next week for four days' gardening and loafing. We hear that a storm which brought a big schooner ashore and pounded her on our ledge till she sank when she was got off, carried away our pier, and now I can't see you sitting on the end of it in the morning.—We have ordered 2 ducks and 2 chickens from Blaisdell, and Marthy Clarkson[2] will roast them to a turn for our four dinners. I've got a lot of trees and shrubs to put in, and Albert[3] is to heel them in against our coming.—Mark Twain and I have been having a lively time about the Russian novelist and revolutionist Maxim Gorky; we were going to give him a great literary dinner, but he has been put out of 3 hotels with the lady who was not his wife, and M. T. has been swamped in reporters wanting to know "how about it."[4] I mention it, thinking you may see something about it in the papers; it seems to have blown over, together with the revolutionist committee which Gorky has hopelessly damaged. He is wrong, but I feel sorry for him; he has suffered enough in his own country, except for the false relations which cannot be tolerated here. He is a simple soul and a great writer, but he cannot do impossible things.[5]—You will see what a great stand Roosevelt has taken in favor of a tax on incomes and inheritances, so as to check the accumulations of great fortunes.[6] It is a most daring act, but will unquestionably add to his enormous popularity. Of course the capitalist press will be down on him strong; but if it were now a matter of his being re-elected he could *sweep* the country. He is a strange man, and nobody has yet "plucked out the heart of his mystery."[7]

We are here in a most comfortable hotel,[8] where we see the Hudson and most of New Jersey from our windows. The spring is coming on, and the buds swelling, while the grass is thick and green. The robins are yelling in the Park trees, and blackbirds strutting over the rocks. With you there can be no such great change; but summer will have its novelty.

Pilla says people in Bermuda get boils from low, farinacious diet. I suppose you get plenty of fruit, if not vegetables. Try the baked bananas I told you of.

John is very well, with a bent toward Christian science instead of doctors. I'm sorry to say Elinor is still not very strong; but she gets slowly better; when we are at K. P. she will be all right again.

We all join in love to your family.

Your aff'te brother,
Will.

I've written a story of a girl who lost her memory;[9] it will interest you, I think; and I'm always at my English travels.[10]

1. Mildred had returned from a three-month vacation in Bermuda.
2. The housekeeper at Kittery Point.
3. Albert Gunnison, the gardener.
4. Gorky had come to the United States in order to raise funds for the Russian Revolutionary party. Initially sympathetic, Howells and Clemens were dismayed by the fact that Gorky was traveling with a mistress, an indiscretion attended by much harmful publicity. See *Twain-Howells*, pp. 805–6. The woman, whom Gorky claimed to be his spouse, was Madame Andreieva, a Russian actress and fellow freedom fighter against the czar. Howells describes the episode at length in *My Mark Twain* (1910), including Clemens' adroit handling of the scores of reporters attempting to capitalize on Gorky's personal circumstances. See *Literary Friends and Acquaintance*, HE, pp. 316–18.
5. In *My Mark Twain*, Howells professes that his concern with Gorky was more literary than political: "We were both interested in Gorky, Clemens rather more as a revolutionist and I as a realist, though I too wished the Russian Czar ill, and the novelist well in his mission to the Russian sympathizers in this republic." See *Literary Friends and Acquaintance*, HE, pp. 316–17.
6. Addressing the subject of graduated income and inheritance taxes later in the year in his Sixth Annual Message, 3 December 1906, Roosevelt would assert that "the man of great wealth" had particular obligations to pay for "the protection the State gives him." See also Howells to Roosevelt, 26 August 1906, n. 3.
7. Howells' adaptation of *Hamlet*, III, ii, 382: "You would pluck out the heart of my mystery."
8. On 18 March, upon their return from Atlantic City, the Howellses moved into the Regent Hotel at Broadway and 70th Street. He described the new residence to Aurelia Howells, 25 March 1906 (MH), as "a nice apartment, overlooking the Hudson and the Palisades, with a range of south windows full of sun ...."
9. "A Sleep and a Forgetting."
10. *Certain Delightful English Towns.*

19 APRIL 1906, NEW YORK, TO SAMUEL L. CLEMENS

Hotel Regent....
New York City April 19, 1906.

Dear Clemens:

This seems a poor old thing one may be kind to without a great deal of suffering. If you will fix an afternoon of next week—when Mrs. Gorky is not calling—I will come to listen to her darkeyisms at your house.[1] Shall we say 4 p.m., Monday, and will you have her notified?

I am awfully sorry not to come and keep your platform down to-night.[2] Last night was one of quite useless and meaningless pain—waking every hour after morphine, and getting no sort of credit for it.[3]

Yours ever
W. D. Howells.

1. Howells had enclosed a letter from Mary E. Bell, 15 April 1906 (CU), which stated that Clemens had promised "to listen to some of my darkey nonsense" and would try to have Howells present. She was probably referring to material from a manuscript or book copy of *Old Kentucky Rhymes, A Collection of Early Poems and Sketches* published under the name Mary Elizabeth Bell sometime in 1906. She is not otherwise identified. "Mrs. Gorky" is Howells' playful allusion to Maxim Gorky's mistress. See Howells to J. A. Howells, 16 April 1906, n. 4.
2. Clemens had invited Howells to attend his "Farewell Lecture" at Carnegie Hall, 19 April 1906, for the benefit of the Fulton Memorial fund. Howells was to have been seated with the party of General Frederick Grant, son of Ulysses S. Grant. See *Twain-Howells*, p. 806.
3. Howells had written earlier to Aurelia Howells, 3 March 1906 (MH), of his painful indigestion: "I suffer from gas in the stomach especially at night.... 'That fulness' is a perfect misery at times, and no medicine, so far, helps."

20 APRIL 1906, NEW YORK, TO JOSEPH A. HOWELLS

Hotel Regent....
New York City April 20, 1906.

Dear Joe:

This morning, after reading your last Sentinel letter, where you speak of "getting out of Congress some part-owners in express companies," so as to have parcels-post, I wrote your Will to cut out *all* political allusions, or criticisms, that you let slip in. If some angry congressman brought that passage up, it might cost you your place.[1] *Never* make any sort of comment on Congress, or any co-ordinate branch of the government, which you're now a part of. I suppose you did it accidentally, or jokingly, but it's *dangerous.*—Bellamy Storer was turned out because his wife, who is a Catholic, tried to commit the President to the candidacy of Archbp. Ireland for cardinal, a most improper thing.[2]

I am dead against your selling the Sentinel for any price, unless such as Lampson would not dream of giving.[3] The thing is perfectly simple. If you and Willy[4] now divide $1200 a year clear from it, you have the five per cent. income of $22,000, and $22,000 is what the paper is worth to *you*, whatever it might be worth to Lampson. If you like, you can tell him to make you an offer. Of course, he would like your letters, and other writings, but all that reads to me like a bluff. How long would he take them? Would he give you $500 a year, and secure it indefinitely?

Besides, where would Willy be? As you justly say he must be fully considered. The Sentinel has gone down in value, but it is still a fair income, and it wont be likely to decrease farther in price. Hold on to it, and be careful you don't write anything that will induce the government to send you back to it.—I can't understand your falling off in weight, especially as I keep falling on. No doubt, when you've adjusted yourself to conditions, you'll do better.

I'm sending you lots of papers—Suns—with accounts of the awful San Francisco earthquake. The city is really destroyed, and the people are starving. It's the most calamitous thing in the history of the country.[5]

I hope your returning that check doesn't cramp you. Do you mean that you've spent your whole last quarter's salary, and have only your $111 contingent expenses left? If you need the check back, let me know.

I'm advising Willy to sell Aurelia's house, if he can. She will never go back, and it wont rent.[6]

John and I are laying out plans for Kittery P. at the end of next week. We've engaged 2 chickens and one duck for our three dinners, and I wish you could eat them with us in that cosy dining room, with the robins yelling outside.—I see *no* chance of my visiting you this spring. Elinor is too low spirited to go or stay. Tell Eliza that there is an age when old ladies always break their hips, and she must be careful. I'm sorry for her mishap, and glad she got out of it so well, thanks to your cook, who like a ship's cook, is a "doctor" it seems.— Byzantium and Constantinople are one and the same.—With love from all to you all,

Your aff'te brother,
Will.

1. The quoted passage appears in "Letter XIX. Some Odds and Ends," *Sentinel*,

19 April 1906. Four days later, 24 April 1906 (MH), Howells apologized for his severity: "I wrote you a very scolding letter on Saturday for your imprudence in alluding to Congress in your *Sentinel* notes; but there is time to follow it with more kindness, though not less caution.... Luckily, Congress has been taken up with the San Francisco horror, and I have seen no allusion to the Consul at Turk's Island and his criticisms of part-owners of express companies. You were perfectly right, but to be right out of time and place, is to be wrong."

2. Bellamy Storer (1847–1922), Republican congressman from Ohio (1891–1895) and American ambassador to Austria-Hungary, had been summarily dismissed by Roosevelt on 19 March 1906. The president appears to have enlisted the aid of Storer, who was himself a Catholic, in urging the pope to consider John Ireland (1838–1918), archbishop of St. Paul, Minnesota, for a cardinalate. When Storer actively pursued the matter, Roosevelt seems to have had second thoughts, sacrificing Storer rather than run the risk of unduly involving his own name in church controversy.

3. Joe did not sell the *Sentinel*. Lampson, the prospective buyer, is not identified.

4. Joe's son, the current editor of the family paper.

5. The calamity occurred on 18 April, killing 500 people, destroying water mains, and setting fires which burned unchecked for three days. The magnitude of the catastrophe impressed Howells deeply, as suggested in his letter to Charles E. Norton, 22 April 1906 (MH): "You have lived through the great Civil War and the detestable Spanish ones but has your experience of life anything in it like this awful San Francisco earthquake? While it shrinks in fact, it rather grows on the imagination and centres all the appallingness of historical disaster in our point of time."

6. Howells, who contributed regularly to his sister's support, felt that Aurelia could alleviate her straitened circumstances by selling her houses in Jefferson and Cleveland. He notified Aurelia in Ottawa, 22 April 1906 (MH), that he had told Will to go ahead and offer the Jefferson house for sale.

24 APRIL 1906, NEW YORK, TO FRANCIS WILSON

Hotel Regent,
April 24, 1906.

My dear Wilson:

I return yourmy book with something written in it from it.[1]

If you are not the happy possessor of my dramatic works I should like to send you a few volumes of them. I can truly say that what Shakespeare did not do for the stage I have done.[2]

It is delightful to think how we are holding in light abeyance the offer of the blithest and brightest comic spirit of all time to let us see him in one of his most charming parts.[3] It gives us a high notion of our value.

I have finished the beautiful book,[4] and it is sweet and sound from beginning to end—it is like you, it *is* you. I don't wonder Jefferson loved you; I would, if I could have been first; but now nothing is left me but to hate you, which I do with best regards to Mrs. Wilson; *she* will understand my feeling.

Yours sincerely
W. D. Howells.

1. Howells probably sent *The Rise of Silas Lapham*, but whether the novel or the play is unclear. Wilson described himself as a "busy collector" of American first editions, which he liked to have inscribed by their authors, if possible. See *Francis Wilson's Life of Himself* (Boston: Houghton Mifflin, 1924), p. 301. He had written Howells, 14 February 1906 (MH), about recently having purchased *Silas Lapham* in a "chuck-a-luck book store—a place where one gets two for one . . . ." Thus Howells seems to be returning "yourmy" book with an appropriate inscription from the text.

2. Howells took pride in being a pioneer in the use of full and careful description of scene in his plays, the one respect in which he might wryly claim to have contributed to the stage where Shakespeare had not. See Howells to Matthews, 12 March 1906.

3. Wilson was then appearing in *The Mountain Climber*, a marriage farce adapted from *Der Hochtourist* by Graatz and Neal.

4. Wilson had sent a copy of his recently published book, *Joseph Jefferson, Reminiscences of a Fellow Player* (1906), in order, as he explained to Howells, 28 March 1906 (MH), to repay Howells' "courtesy to Mrs. Wilson." She had been recuperating from appendicitis at the St. Charles in Atlantic City, where the Howellses had been staying earlier that year. In the same letter Wilson had expressed the hope of "someday" making Howells' acquaintance, to which Howells had responded by inviting the actor to the luncheon for H. G. Wells on 8 April. See Howells to Aurelia Howells, 8 April 1906. Howells had known Joseph Jefferson (1829–1905) and, according to Wilson, was instrumental in persuading Jefferson to write *The Autobiography of Joseph Jefferson* (1890). See Wilson's *Joseph Jefferson* (New York: Charles Scribner's Sons, 1906), pp. 153, 236.

8 MAY 1906, NEW YORK, TO THEODORA SEDGWICK

Hotel Regent,
New York, May 8, 1906.

Dear Miss Theodora:

I am returning, (by money express, so that it may go quite safely,) to Mr. Norton's care, the precious MS. of Miss Ashburner, which you so thoughtfully lent me.[1] I have read every word of it aloud to my family, and no fiction has ever so intensely held us, as this sincere and most important narrative. It is not only the story of a singularly interesting family, but it is a rarely intelligent view of conditions on both sides of the ocean. It has the imperial scope of all English family histories, and it is an incomparable study of our own impassioned and most respectable provinciality.

It brought back to me so vividly the presence of the dear and wise woman who wrote it that I could almost hear Miss Ashburner speaking the words. I could never tell you how much my wife and I valued your aunts; but even in our ignorant youth, we did value them aright.

The narrative had the interest for me of seeming at times the story of my own family in their outwanderings from Wales at a little earlier period. The same fond but not ignoble ideals; the same ignorance of the world; the same unfitness for the conditions of a new country, were things familiar to me from childhood. I have heard my father talk of them, and laugh over them (thank heaven! we could always laugh,) so often that the tears came as I read of them. I thank you for one of the greatest pleasures.

I do hope you are feeling constanly better, with the advancing spring, and will soon be about again. My wife joins me in affectionate regards.

> **Yours sincerely**
> **W. D. Howells.**

1. On 27 April Howells and his son had left New York for Kittery Point, and Howells stopped over to visit with C. E. Norton, Sunday, 29 April, before returning to New York on 2 May. During that visit Norton's sister-in-law apparently gave Howells memoirs written by Anne Ashburner, the aunt whom the Howellses had known well in their earlier Cambridge days. In returning the manuscript, Howells seems to have misunderstood, or courteously ignored, Miss Sedgwick's motive of obtaining assistance in getting the manuscript published. He later tried to place it for publication in a periodical but could not find one acceptable to Miss Sedgwick. See Howells to Norton, 2 December 1906.

17 MAY 1906, NEW YORK, TO SAMUEL S. McCLURE

> *Hotel Regent. . . .*
> *New York City* May 17, 1906.

My dear Mc Clure:

I didn't dream of your taking all that trouble about the "Real Conversations," I merely wanted the early pictures of myself for re-reproduction.[1] But I am glad of the rest, and I thank you in proportion.

How sweet of you to give an old fellow your place, today![2] If ever our ages are reversed, as I dare say they will be in heaven, you shall have my golden seat and harp and halo.

What a sad, defeating affair! Like all funerals! I could not hear the English and I could not understand the German.

The other day at our lunch, so memorable for me, I meant to say what an immense thing Schurz's autobiography is.[3] It is almost the best I know, and I know many.

Yours cordially,
W. D. Howells.

1. Howells probably wanted the pictures in order to select one for M. A. De Wolfe Howe, who had requested a photograph for the Tavern Club in Boston, of which Howells had been the first president. Howells wrote Howe, 8 April 1906 (MH), "As for my picture, I am trying for a full length from a painter who fotografed me for a portrait, some years ago. Failing this I will send you a full face, large, and the best ever done me. I should not like to be represented by one of the walrus-moustache period." In turn, Howells had asked McClure, 9 May 1906 (InU), to send a copy of the first issue of *McClure's* which contained, as Howells phrased it, "a lot of my infantile fisiognomies." Nine photographs showing Howells from ages eighteen through fifty-three appeared in *McClure's*, June 1893, in connection with the first presentation of the "Human Documents" series entitled "Real Conversations.—I. A Dialogue Between William Dean Howells and Hjalmar Hjorth Boyesen."

2. Both men had been at the funeral of Carl Schurz.

3. *The Reminiscences of Carl Schurz*, 3 volumes (1907–1908), was then appearing serially in *McClure's*. As Howells told McClure, 19 May 1906 (InU), he had written Schurz after reading each chapter: "It is now very pleasant to think I wrote him always about the numbers except the last. He wrote back that nothing else was so welcome." In a letter of 15 March 1906 (MH), Schurz had expressed his appreciation: "I can only say that of all the utterances I receive concerning my 'Reminiscences' yours do my heart the most good." Howells memorialized Schurz in "Carl Schurz, 1829–1906" for *Harper's Weekly*, 26 May 1906, but he did not later review Schurz's autobiography when it came out in book form.

19 MAY 1906, NEW YORK, TO HERBERT G. WELLS

Hotel Regent....
New York City May 19, 1906.

My dear Wells:

Probably the same "boat" which is carrying you home,[1] is taking in the mails, a pkge to Mrs. Wells's motherly care of some Black Mexican Sweet Corn, and some Crook-Neck Squash Seed. Soak the corn over-night, and plant it in as sunny a place as you have in Sandgate, and then leave it to the rains of heaven. A little fertilizer, with a sprinkling of soil between it and the seed, is well; cover about two inches with earth. The same with the squash seed; but *don't* soak *that*. Eat the corn when it fills out the cob, and the milk spirts from a break in the grain; it will not get black till the Fall when it is too hard for eating.

The squashes are to be cooked when they are tender as a maiden's feelings. Then they are stewed, somewhat drained, mashed and dressed with cream, and served quite moist, but not liquid. A dish for the gods! The things are beautiful as flowers in color, and of a graceful cornuity in shape.

Our love to your household. Come again and stay longer.

Yours sincerely
W. D. Howells.

1. Howells had honored the visiting novelist at a luncheon in April. See Howells to Aurelia Howells, 8 April 1906. On 19 June 1906 (MH) Howells was able to report to Mildred: "A nice letter from Mrs. Wells at Sandgate has come....It says Wellsy has got home in a glow of love for these States."

21 MAY 1906, NEW YORK, TO ELIZABETH JORDAN

The Regent,
May 21, 1906.

Dear Miss Jordan:
"The Whole Family"[1] might consist of—
The Grandmother.
The Father.
The Mother.
The Son.
The Daughter-in-Law.
The Daughter.
The Son-in Law.
The Little Girl.
The Small Boy
The Maiden Aunt
    on the Father's side or Mother's
The Young Girl.
The Friend (female) of the Family.
I could do, if you liked, the Father, and I believe Clemens would like to do the Small Boy.[2] Then, you might submit the scheme to ten other writers, and ask them to chose this character or that, without letting them know who is to do the others, but giving them the whole group of characters, and letting each imagine the family for him or herself.—The Grandmother ought to open the affair, and the Friend of the Family sum it up. Perhaps the outline of a dramatic situation might be supplied.[3] If you could get Mrs. Donnell, Mrs. Wilkins Freeman, Miss May Fiske, Miss Jordan, Mr. Bangs, Mr. Janvier, with four other women writers, whom you could trust, your group would be complete.[4] The family might be in some such moment of vital agita-

tion as that attending the Young Girls engagement, or pending engagement, and each witness could treat of it in character. There could be fun enough, but each should try seriously to put himself or herself really into the personage's place. I think the more seriously the business was treated, the better.[5] Possibly one hand could do it better than sundry. But it is worth thinking of. Or, you might ask the writers severally to render a notion of the character chosen without any plot. The Family could be in middling circumstances, of average culture and experiences.

Excuse the meddling.

Yours sincerely
W. D. Howells.

P.S. The note of the whole might be confidential, but kindly criticism, reciprocal, among all the characters, but especially bearing upon the Young Girl and her betrothed.

1. Howells had suggested the idea of a novel for *Harper's Bazar* concerning the engagement of a young woman, with each chapter to be written by a different author and to feature a pertinent family member or friend. *The Whole Family, A Novel in Twelve Parts* was serialized in the *Bazar*, December 1907–September 1908, and issued in book form in October 1908 as *The Whole Family, A Novel by Twelve Authors.*

2. Jordan had difficulty approaching Clemens, who ultimately did not contribute to the venture. Howells apologized to her, 8 August 1906 (NN), for not interceding: "I wish I could try to help you out with Mark Twain; but a friend of his youth ought not to afflict his age."

3. Shortly thereafter, Howells submitted a rough plan to be distributed to the prospective authors. In the accompanying letter to Jordan, 4 June 1906 (NN), he spelled out the social philosophy behind his concept of the plot: "What I wish to imply is that an engagement or a marriage is much more a family affair, and much less a personal affair than Americans usually suppose. As we live on, we find that family ties, which held us very loosely in youth, or after we ceased to be children, are really almost the strongest things in life. A marriage cannot possibly concern the married pair alone; but it is in the notion that it can that most of our marriages are made. It is also in this notion that most of them are unmade. I wish to indicate in my advocacy of co-education that young people ought to know at least the workings of the male and female mind as fully as they can. Their natures are diverse enough, though not so diverse as we like to pretend, and the difference is exaggerated by the separate training." Howells' elaborate concern here with the implications of engagement and marriage might in some degree be accounted for by Mildred Howells' broken engagement sometime in late 1902 or early 1903. The experience was quite painful for the entire family, but especially for Elinor. See Howells to A. A. Fields, 23 February 1903, n. 2.

4. The final chapter-scheme and authorship were as follows: I—"The Father," Howells; II—"The Old-Maid Aunt," Mary E. Wilkins Freeman; III—"The Grandmother," Mary Heaton Vorse; IV—"The Daughter-in-Law," Mary Stewart Cutting; V—"The School-Girl," Elizabeth Jordan; VI—"The Son-in-Law," John Kendrick Bangs; VII—"The Married Son," Henry James; VIII—"The Married Daughter," Elizabeth Stuart Phelps; IX—"The Mother," Edith Wyatt; X—"The School-Boy,"

Mary Raymond Shipman Andrews; XI—"Peggy," Alice Brown; XII—"The Friend of the Family," Henry Van Dyke.

5. Realizing the difficulty of coordinating multiple authorial perspectives and tones, Howells relented on this position. In his letter of 4 June, he urged Jordan to suggest to them that nothing of his notion of the plot and its nuances was "to be *seriously* insisted on. There ought to be full space for the light and humorous play of any body's preference in the treatment of the characters." Howells also expressed concern about how this scheme might affect his reputation: "If you find the scheme does not commend itself to the more judicious and able among the writers to whom you propose it, you had better drop it. I should not like to appear in co-operation with young or unimportant writers...."

24 MAY 1906, NEW YORK, TO SAMUEL L. CLEMENS

Hotel Regent.
May 24, 1906.

Dear Clemens:

What *you* want to read is "In Our Town" by Wm. Allen White.[1] It is like all the middling-sized towns you ever lived in. It is a series of photographs taken with Roentgen rays. Mc Clure publishes it.—Just off for Kittery Point, tonight.

Yours ever
W. D. Howells.

1. William Allen White (1868–1944), owner and editor of the Emporia (Kansas) *Gazette*, had just published *In Our Town* (1906). Howells had written him a complimentary letter, to which White replied on 29 June 1906 (MH): "you have made it worth while to write 'In Our Town' even if the people just wont buy the book and even if we need the money most scandalously.... Another fine letter came from Mr Clemens the other day and one from our fellow Muck Raker T. Roosevelt of whom you have heard doubtless." Allen concluded his letter with an invitation to Howells to visit the West: "you should see it and live in it a few months, not as a lecturer, not as the dean of American letters, but as Mr and Mrs W D Howells formerly of Ohio! Come out and loaf and invite your soul." For Clemens' response to White's book, see *Twain-Howells*, pp. 814–15.

27 MAY 1906, KITTERY POINT, TO DAVID A. MUNRO

Kittery Point, May 27, 1906.

My dear Munro:

When this proof came,[1] you could have knocked me down with it, so absolutely had I forgotten you had it. I was thinking, "Confound it! The North American will be wanting me to write something about

Ibsen, now," and behold, I had already done it, I suppose in that pre-existence before I went to England. For heaven's sake, if you have any other old paper of mind in type, let me see it. I have written about so many dead people that you may have for all I know, an appreciation of Methusalah among your proofs from my giftẹd pen. Perhaps you had better let me look at this proof again when I have got over my amazement.

Yours ever,
W. D. Howells.

1. Munro was submitting the proof of an essay Howells had written on Ibsen in 1903. When Ibsen died on 23 May 1906, Munro resurrected the earlier essay and published it as "Henrik Ibsen," *North American Review*, July 1906. See Howells to Munro, 9 September 1903.

17 JUNE 1906, KITTERY POINT, TO AURELIA H. HOWELLS

Kittery Point, June 17, 1906.

Dear Aurelia:

We have had today the heaviest rain I have ever seen here—a cold northeaster with a downpour which overran our eaves, and flooded our cellar with four inches water, in spite of its thorough cementing. The storm still continues, but the rain is now light.

Yesterday I went up to Boston, and with Pilla saw the Greek play in the open air at Cambridge.[1] It was one of the most beautiful things that could be imagined, and perfectly done, in spite of the frequent drizzles, and the clouded skies. Half the time we sat under umbrellas, but the colors of the costumes on the green grass, and the sonorous grandeur of the language, with the students' fine acting of the noble tragedy, made us forget the wet. I wish Vevie[2] could have been with us; it would have delighted her as a colorist. I will look out for pictures in the papers and send them to you. John did not join us, and so I suppose he could not get away from his business.

I had not seen so many Cambridge people together for a long time, and it was a very strange experience. The generation after me had grown up and looked like their fathers and mothers whom I used to know. My contemporaries, I did not recognize if I saw them. Of course the majority of the 4000 present were outsiders, from New York, and other parts. The women had come in light draperies, but had brought water proofs and umbrellas, so that there was a curious mingling of gray and gay in the prospect. The play was given in the Stadium, which is a vast horse-shoe in form, and capable of holding 25,000 spectators.

I got home after nine, and went to bed pretty soon, and had a long night with Edward VII, and his mother, the late queen,[3] who was not dead, but had abdicated to oblige him. They were both extremely friendly. Just now, I am doing a lot of dreaming, for no reason that I know except the vast quantity natural gas in my stomach. It is not so distressing at night as it was, and does not wake me, but by day my eructations are quite Vesuvian. Do you know of father's being troubled in that way? What was it he drank the Saegertown water for, and how did he get it? Do you remember who bottled or sold it?[4] I am prepared to try almost anything.—Think of his being twelve years dead, already!

I have been reading the proof today of a long story of mine which they are going to print in the Weekly, and which I must send you when it comes out. I call it "A Sleep and a Forgetting," and it deals with a strange loss of memory. It interested me because my own memory has sometimes played me very queer tricks. I wrote it mostly while in Atlantic City in February. With love to Henry,

Your affectionate brother,
Will.

1. Aeschylus's *Agamemnon*, performed by Harvard students in the stadium.
2. Marie Marguerite Fréchette, to whom Howells had written the previous day (MH); the letter suggests that his niece had recently painted a portrait of Andrew Carnegie.
3. Queen Victoria.
4. The Saegerstown Inn, located in northwest Pennsylvania near the Ohio border, had a considerable local reputation as a mineral spa.

20 JUNE 1906, KITTERY POINT, TO AURELIA H. HOWELLS

Kittery Point, June 20, 1906.

Dear Aurelia:

I am sending you a trunk full of the hopelessly cherished things of Winny. To keep them any longer would be a waste, and we know from Pilla that it would be painful for her ever to see them, much more wear them. There are dresses and shawls, and other belongings, which we wish you to do what seems to best. You need only acknowledge them; ,we do not care to know how you dispose of them and you need not say what state you find them in; they have been stored ever since her death, and we had hoped to keep them; but we cannot.[1]

I enclose Annie's most interesting letter, which we received yesterday from Vevie. Give her our love, and thank her for the great pleasure we have had in reading it.

We have been suffering, Elinor most, from the bitter weather, and the East winds we have been having for a week past, but the morning promises something better.

> Your affectionate brother,
> **Will.**

1. Aware of the delicacy of the situation both in terms of his own feelings about Winifred's death in 1889 as well as those of Aurelia, he sent her assurances that same day (MH) that no slighting of any family member was to be inferred: "In saying that we wished you to make such disposition of Winny's things as you decided, I did not mean that we should not be especially pleased if you liked to give Vevie those you did not find useful for yourself. I know she would value them and appreciate them, and it would be acceptable to us to know that she was wearing them. There are some fans and beads that are girlish; but she may have a feeling against it, which we could understand. Do not say anything about it to us, for the present; but do what you think best." In the postscript he requested the return of one toy, "some little bags of rice, in a box, which she used to play a Japanese game with." A week later, 25 June 1906 (MH), Howells thanked Aurelia for acknowledging receipt of the trunk and reiterated the difficult feelings he and Elinor were experiencing: "I thank you for writing so promptly about the trunk, and so tenderly. I have given your letter to Elinor, and I know she will appreciate it as I do. It will take away her shrinking about the disposition of the things, and after while we shall like to know what you have done with each of them. It was like parting with Winny again, to part with them, but we thought it over, and we have done with them what she has intended ever since Pilla seemed distressed at the thought of having them."

24 JUNE 1906, KITTERY POINT, TO SAMUEL L. CLEMENS

> Kittery Point, June 24, 1906.

Dear Clemens:

I could not have asked to have anything gentler or kinder said of me than you have said in the July Harper.[1] I was so eager to see it that I sent into Portsmouth for the magazine yesterday, and I have since read it again and again, feeling more and more that it must be true.[2] Such appreciation convinces even the object of it; if it is not quite true, still it is so admirably expressed, that he hopes it will convince other people anyway. The passages you quoted from me shone with a lustre that they never had before, and that came from their cordial setting.[3] Your praise has brought back the good great times when the men, Lowell and Longfellow and Holmes, who held the eminence you now hold, spoke well of me. I think round the world, and I find none now living whose praise I could care more for. Perhaps Tolstoy; but I do not love him as I love you, and the honor he could do me would not reach my heart as the honor you have done me does.

Dear friend of forty years, thanks!

Yours affectionately
W. D. Howells.

1. "William Dean Howells," *Harper's Monthly*, July 1906.

2. Deeply moved, Howells wrote to Frederick A. Duneka on the same day (MWA) and noted: "What magnificent praise Clemens has given me! Since I came a man nothing has touched me more. I feel as I did in my nonage, when I used to go round showing people the English notices of Venetian Life."

3. For the quoted passage and excerpts from Clemens' remarks, see *Twain-Howells*, pp. 813–14.

27 JUNE 1906, KITTERY POINT, TO CHARLES E. NORTON

Kittery Point Maine June 27, 1906.

My dear Norton:

Unless I should be out of the country next February I shall be glad and proud to join you and the others in honoring Longfellow's memory.[1] As I cannot speak extempore, I will write something which I can read, and you may be sure it will not be too long. I cannot tell you with what a serious joy I think of the occasion, and how anxiously I shall try not to disappoint you in falling too far short of it.

Pilla and I went to the first day of the Agamemnon,[2] and strained our eyes over and under that strange mushroom range of umbrellas to find you and yours, in vain. With all its shortcomings we found the play a prodigious emotion; and we thought the wet and sombre sky not out of key with the awful drama. After the first few moments of grotesque inadequacy, the action levelled itself with the high demand, and I was in Athens seeing Argos. But you know I am not exacting; a chance suffices me.

I do not know whether to hope you will find the passage of your letter in the July Easy Chair which gave me a suggestion for it.[3] I am afraid the theme rather slipped through my fingers, or rather stiffened and died between them.

I am going to Boston on another errand, Saturday, and I expect to dine with the Club.[4] I wish I were sure of meeting you there.

John will try again to see you tomorrow. He is writing, in a forced leisure, two or three little papers on Bulfinch and the American Georgian,[5] and I fancy it's that he wants to talk with you of.

Mark Twain's paper gave me great pleasure.[6] The praise I have nothing to do with, but the love in it is precious to me. You and he, so strangely contrasted, are now the friends I value most.

Yours affectionately
W. D. Howells.

1. Norton was to preside at the centennial celebration of Longfellow's birthday, 27 February 1907, and had invited Howells to address the gathering. There was subsequently some differences of opinion as to the nature of Howells' speech, Norton desiring a more personal commentary than the critical appreciation Howells wished to give. Howells wrote to Norton, 25 November 1906 (MH), "...I would prefer to treat the *art* of Longfellow in what I shall have to say in February, and not his popularity. That is something known to all, but few know how true and fine an artist he was, and I think myself one of the few." For further correspondence on the matter see Howells to Norton, 2 December 1906, 30 January 1907, and 2 February 1907.

2. See Howells to Aurelia Howells, 17 June 1906.

3. The theme for the "Editor's Easy Chair," *Harper's Monthly*, July 1906, was the viability of the average American as a literary subject. Howells had written Norton earlier (see 11 March 1906) about his concern at no longer finding himself interested in people who represented "the decent average." In his reply, 16 March 1906 (MH), Norton took the occasion to condemn generally the absence of interesting types in American society. With Norton's permission, Howells used the following passage from the letter in order to refute its bleak literary implications: "No," wrote Norton, "it is not that you have seen all these people, and that they offer no novel types for observation, but even more that they illustrate the great fact that, in the course of the last twenty years, society in America has reached its goal, has 'arrived,' and is creating no new types. On the contrary, it is obliterating some of the best which were clearly marked, and is becoming more and more one rich, dead level of mediocrity, broken here and there by solitary eminences, some of which are genuine, some only false peaks without solid rock foundations."

4. The Saturday Club.

5. John M. Howells' papers on American architecture do not appear to have been published. He would later author a book entitled *The Architectural Heritage of the Piscataqua* (1937), treating some of the work of the noted early American architect Charles Bulfinch (1763–1844), and possibly deriving in part from the materials here mentioned. Several buildings by Bulfinch also appear in the photographic text of John Howells' *Lost Examples of Colonial Architecture* (1931).

6. See Howells to Clemens, 24 June 1906.

27 JUNE 1906, KITTERY POINT, TO FREDERICK A. DUNEKA

Kittery point, June 27, 1906.

Dear Mr. Duneka:

I hope you will not mind reading through a rather long letter if it is typewritten, on a matter that intimately and curiously concerns me.

One day while I was at San Remo, I got a copy of the Bazar, at the time *The Masqueraders* was running,[1] and read in it a letter from a lady who said she was an invalid, and was afraid she should die before the story was finished, and asked (I believe) to know the ending. At once I wrote to Miss Jordan, begging her to bear me witness that I said I then had in MS. and nearly finished, a novel, or novelette, involving exactly this incident, and that I had built it up from an actual experience of some twenty years before.[2] I told her, as I now tell you, that my heroine was a fake invalid, and when required to give proof of her genuineness, she had owned up, and said that she had written to the editor, on a sort of *dare* from some other girls, who wagered that she would not have the courage to do it. The incident was one I had always intended to use, when it should be old enough not to harm, by any possibility, a sufficiently harmless person; and in working it out, I not only used the fact as I had known it, but invented the fact, afterwards verified by your advertiser, with reference to the invalid wanting to know the end of *The Masqueraders*, and had the publishers of my supposed magazine give out the substance of my fake invalid's letter. In short my fictitious case paralleled your veritable case, precisely, in everything except the genuineness of the invalid writing the letter to the author of the unfinished story. Nothing was ever heard from my fake invalid, whose letter had not really been made public, but had only supposedly been made public, in my story.

I have several times since spoken of the matter with Miss Jordan, and I have understood from her (but if I have misunderstood she will set me right), that Harpers had received some sort of lawyer's letter from the invalid's friends, but the matter had been amicably settled. I have also lately heard from Miss Jordan that the invalid has died. Now what I wish to ask you is whether you can confide all the circumstances to me so that I can go on with a story which is ended within four or five typewritten pages like this, and hold it ready at some time to issue. I am not afraid that it will hurt my fake invalid; but will it not hurt the memory of your real invalid, or her friends or family, if my story should be identified with her case? I should not be troubling you with this question, of course, if I did not think my story a rather unusually good piece of work, on original lines, with a love intrigue fresh in material and treatment. It brings the author and the fake invalid together, and they fall in love, but the author can never make up his mind to trust her. I have got a good setting for my fable, and new types throughout. You ought to be able to tell me whether to finish it or not. I have just been going over the story critically, and I think it pretty strong. I call it—"*A Tangled Web*." But it seems to be much more tangled than I ever expected.

Yours ever,
W. D. Howells.

1. *The Masquerader*, a novel by the Anglo-Irish author Katherine Cecil Thurston (1875–1911), ran serially in *Harper's Bazar*, January–December 1904.

2. Finally published as *Fennel and Rue*, Howells' story was then tentatively entitled "A Tangled Web." He was attempting to complete it during his stay in San Remo in late 1904 and early 1905. The invalid's letter does not appear to have been published in the *Bazar*, but rather was quoted extensively in an advertisement for *The Masquerader* in *Harper's Weekly*, 29 October 1904, with the accompanying explanation that "The Editor of HARPER's BAZAR was so much interested in the letter that the advance proofs of *The Masquerader* were sent to the lady." In a letter dated 3 August 1904, the woman, otherwise unidentified, had written in part: "I am reading the most clever and wonderfully well-written novel 'The Masquerader.' I have very serious heart trouble, and may live *years*—and *may* die any minute. I should deeply regret going without knowing the general end of that story....may I have the numbers as they come to you, and in advance of the general delivery?...I just felt that (I have had so many troubles) it would be just my *luck* to die, and not to know the end." In a letter to Elizabeth Jordan from San Remo Howells had tacitly acknowledged the constraints imposed by the invalid's circumstances on the publication of *Fennel and Rue*. See Howells to Jordan, 6 January 1905. For the "actual experience of some twenty years before," see Howells to Walter, 18 November 1885.

1 AUGUST 1906, KITTERY POINT, TO SAMUEL L. CLEMENS

Kittery Point, August 1, 1906.

My dear Clemens:

Thank you for letting me see Clara's just tribute to you.[1] It is a great thing to have one's children not rise up and knock one's head off after reading one's writings, but it seems that it happens in your family some times as it does in mine. Many people have written me about that lovely and loveable article of yours.[2] Some it seems to have roused to a remembrance of my existence; some it has instructed of the fact; and you did it out of the goodness of your heart, as well the soundness of your head.

But I cannot allow Clara to call Venetian Life "Venetian Days." You are the only person in the world who may do this and not be destroyed.[3]

We have been worrying through a summer of suffering from the East wind for my wife. This gale, which I like to let soak my bones to the marrow with its delicious chill and damp, shrivels her up, and she has to hurry indoors and make a fire.[4] Why are people so mismated? This error will never be put right till men marry men. But then there will be no children to appreciate their writings.

You seem to find Dublin a good place to stay away from most of the season.[5] There is nothing like having a basis to go and come from. Perhaps we shall make something of the sort out of this another year. The worst of our case is that my wife is too weak to travel.

We have been reading every night nearly since we came your Following the Equator with a delight truly unspeakable. It seems to me that in this you have mastered your art of irony, and that gift of casual remark which leaves an unexpected flash and glow after you have got by in the place where you have been. And how bully the matter *is*! I wish you would go on your travels again. Of course we had read this wonderbook before.

Yours ever,
W. D. H.

P. S. What about that MS. of your autobiography which I was to have?[6]

1. Clemens had sent Howells a copy of a letter writtten by Clara Clemens to her father sometime in July 1906. In it she describes qualities in her "Uncle Joe" [Joseph H. Twichell] which she associates with her father. See *Twain-Howells*, pp. 816–17.

2. See Howells to Clemens, 24 June 1906, n. 1.

3. Both Clara, in the letter to her father, and Clemens, in his essay on Howells, misnamed Howells' travel book.

4. Of his wife's precarious health, Howells had written to Aurelia Howells, 15 July 1906 (MH), that he had been obliged to take Elinor away from Kittery Point for a week: "She has suffered with neuralgia all the spring since we came and is wasted almost to a skeleton; it is really pitiful to see her."

5. Clemens had gone to New York on business from Dublin, New Hampshire, where he was spending the summer.

6. "As to the Autobiography," Clemens replied on 3 August (MH; *Twain-Howells*, p. 817), "you're going to get it—in the neck! as the vulgar say. Harvey will go hence with it, to you, to-morrow." Colonel Harvey visited Kittery Point on 5 August and presumably gave Howells the manuscript. See Howells to J. A. Howells, 6 August 1906.

6 AUGUST 1906, KITTERY POINT, TO JOSEPH A. HOWELLS

Kittery Point, Aug. 6, 1906.

Dear Joe:

I will try to answer first your anxious note about your failure to respond to the commissioners toast.[1] That was a break, I think, as you feel. But many things would account for it besides your indifference. The English are very frank and simple, and most probably the com. would take it in good part if you spoke to him about it, and said you were confused by the unexpectedness of his toast, and so failed to acknowledge it, but that you appreciated his courtesy, and wished to say so. For the future you might keep in mind, what I could hardly do, that you are representative and not individual; and get on your legs, when the country is complimented, and acknowledge the compliment. You are never less than a principal guest, and you need not be diffident. Return the compliment somehow, and don't be afraid of overdoing. Within the bounds of good taste and good feeling such things cannot be overdone.

I have just been reading two of your Sentinel letters, about the hurricanes and the Fourth.[2] They are delightful, and I feel sure that you can write a magazine paper about T. I. that will be taken, and will help out your salary. Don't be afraid of particulars and don't mind using material that you have already used: only, work it over, and put it in new shape.

I don't understand why you have not got any newspapers from me. I send them not regularly, but frequently, and I try always to pay them enough and more. I am now sending you the Sunday Sun, and three of the week-day numbers.

You are right about Thaw.[3] It is because he was brought up irresponsibly, and in the belief that he could buy anything with money, that he thought he had the privilege of murdering a man who was perhaps his immoral equal, but was as much above him intellectually as a god. White was one of the greatest Americans who ever lived; I knew him, and did not respect his life; no man could; but he could not have been worse than the worthless slut who put her husband up to killing him.[4] The Thaws now think that it is only the form of acquittal which they have to choose; but it is more probable that he will be found guilty and executed.[5] Certainly he would be found guilty if there were no capital punishment. It is quite time that Americans were stopped from taking a woman's word against a man, and then trying, sentencing and killing him, by what our idiots call the "unwritten law."[6] White was rather boyish, bad boyish, but compared with Thaw he was a hundred times worthy to live.

I don't know whether I have ever acknowledged your tropical photograph. The dress is most becoming to you, and it is on our parlor mantel, for people to see. My hat, I believe I told you, is highly approved. I am supposed to look like both an American planter and a London swell in it. The English were wearing just such hats when we were in London.

Harvey of Harper & Brothers was here yesterday, talking over some literary plans, and a plan he has for next spring, to blow Mark Twain and me in for a trip to England on the big Baltic steamer, and a three weeks' automobile tour of the island.[7] Wouldn't you like to be one of us? The idea would be not to let anybody know of our being there, so that we should be free of all social entanglements, and go slow, and stop whenever and wherever we pleased. Of course, it is hardly probable that Elinor would be well enough for me to go.

She has lately been taking massage and koumiss,[8] but she is incredibly nervous about everything under the sun. This is the first day that we have had it really piping hot, so that she could enjoy being outdoors. But today *is* piping. I simply rain perspiration standing still.

A big old thunderstorm is rolling and growling up, and I guess we shall soon have a drop of temperature . . . . . The storm is over, and no great shakes; so I will finish this and give it to Albert[9] for the mail. You remember the Bouncing Bets, at the corner of our house? They are all in bloom, and stretch half-way toward the cellar door from the front. We have hollyhocks ten feet high in bloom. With love to you all

> Your affectionate brother,
> Will.

1. The occasion of the British commissioner's toast and of Joe's uncertainty about protocol is not known.

2. Both subjects are discussed in "Letter XXXII. West Indian Hurricanes," *Sentinel*, 26 July 1906.

3. Harry K. Thaw was the reprobate son of the deceased Pittsburgh financier and philanthropist William Thaw. On the evening of 25 June 1906 he committed one of the most publicized murders of the time, shooting architect Stanford White at the roof-top theater of Madison Square Garden (which White had designed) during the opening performance of Eddie Foy's musical *Mamzelle Champagne*.

4. The "worthless slut" was artist's model and actress Florence Evelyn Nesbit, who was Thaw's wife. White, the longtime partner of Elinor Howells' brother in the firm of McKim, Mead, and White, had a well-known penchant for showgirls. He had helped Nesbit financially before she married Thaw, using his influence to assure her early success on the musical stage. This former intimacy was the motive behind Thaw's act. He is reported as saying of White immediately after the shooting: "He deserved it. I can prove it. He ruined my wife and then deserted the girl" (New York *Times*, 27 June 1906, p. 1). Many believed, like Howells, that Nesbit had goaded her jealous husband into killing White.

5. At the time of Howells' letter there was much publicity in the newspapers regarding legal strategies for the defense. In the upcoming trial, Thaw would plead that he killed White in a fit of temporary insanity, resulting in a hung jury. Shifting tactics for the retrial, the defense depicted Thaw as a manic-depressive and won a verdict of not guilty on the grounds of insanity. Thaw was then committed to the Mattewan State Hospital. In 1913, after an abortive escape to Canada, Thaw was tried a third time, pronounced sane, and released.

6. Primed by the "unwritten law" that it was a husband's duty to protect his wife's virtue at any cost, popular sentiment was heavily weighted in Thaw's favor. Charles A. Eaton, pastor of John D. Rockefeller's church, the Euclid Avenue Baptist Church of Cleveland, sounded the clarion note in the New York *Times* only four days after the murder: "It strikes me," he intoned, "that if there was a little more shooting in cases like that in which Harry Thaw shot Stanford White, if we are to believe the newspaper accounts, men would be more careful about their relations with other men's wives" (29 October 1906, p. 2). Thaw's mother spent a great deal of money to reinforce such an attitude, commissioning a public relations man named Benjamin H. Atwell to write a topical play entitled *The Great Harry Thaw Case; or, A Woman's Sacrifice* (1907). The victimized hero, who has murdered a villain conspicuously named Stanford Black, utters the timely formula from his jail cell: "No jury on earth will send me to the chair, no matter what I have done or what I

have been, for killing the man who defamed my wife. This is the unwritten law made by men themselves and upon its virtue I will stake my life." See Warren Forma, *They Were Ragtime* (New York: Grosset & Dunlap, 1976), p. 136.

7. The trip with Clemens did not materialize.

8. Koumiss is fermented mare's or cow's milk used in special diets. Howells had more fully described Elinor's treatment to Aurelia Howells, 29 July 1906 (MH): "We have had a glad young doctor take Elinor in hand, and he is giving her grapefruit, orangeade, eggs, grape juice and koumiss, with apparently hopeful effect."

9. Albert Gunnison, the gardener.

17 AUGUST 1906, KITTERY POINT, TO HARPER & BROTHERS

Kittery Point, Aug. 17, 1906.

Dear Messrs. Harper & Brothers:

Your letter of the 11th has followed me on a tour to various points inland,[1] and has just come to hand.

I am sorry for the delay in answering it because I like to be prompt, and because I should have liked to say instantly how entirely and absolutely I disapprove of the *Herald* editor's suggestion that an author should write any communication to his critic for use in reviewing his new book.[2] Looking at the matter as an author, and not presuming to regard it from the publisher's point of view, I think such a thing would be in the last degree undignified, fatuous and impertinent. I know you like to have me speak my mind, and here it is.

Yours sincerely
W. D. Howells.

1. Howells hoped to alleviate Elinor's suffering from the cool coastal climate by traveling inland "till she gets the East wind out of her bones," as he wrote to Aurelia Howells from Manchester, New Hampshire, 12 August 1906 (MH). They left Kittery Point on 11 August, spent several days at Manchester, then stopped in Milford, New Hampshire, Boston, and Auburndale, Massachusetts, and returned on 17 August. Howells wrote again to Aurelia, 20 August 1906 (MH), to say that the warm west wind had returned to Kittery Point and that Elinor was "much better for her outing."

2. The owner and editor of the New York *Herald* at this time was James Gordon Bennett (1841–1918), who was famous for his eccentric and temperamental ways of running his newspaper and for his extravagant life-style in both the United States and Europe. It is unlikely that Bennett himself addressed to Harper & Brothers the request for authorial comment about the book, probably *Certain Delightful English Towns*.

26 AUGUST 1906, KITTERY POINT, TO THEODORE ROOSEVELT

Kittery Point Maine August 26, 1906.

Dear Mr. President:

Before I shall have heard from you in regard to the personal matter of which I wrote you last week,[1] I wish to congratulate you on the stand you have taken in favor of the more commonsense spelling suggested by the reformers.[2] It is your instinct for the really important public matters which distinguishes you from the merely formal presidents, and makes the whole nation feel that you are alive and alert every moment. If we could have had some such official action as you have now taken a hundred years ago, we should by this time have a spelling which would not perpetually confound the reason and insult the intelligence of every child learning to read and write, and the English would be spelling in the authorized American fashion. Of course, the proposed reforms are only a step in the right direction, but it is most desirable that they should be taken, and I for one feel almost as grateful to you for your courage in this matter as I did when I wanted to write to you and thank you for what you said looking to the restraint of the overwhelming accumulation of wealth in private hands.[3] The good things cannot come to a magical maturity in a year, but you have dropped seeds in the public mind which, if they bear secular flower and fruit will have ripened not out of time.

I think it is the sense that you are always watchfully with them in what truly concerns them, and that we will not be afraid to show it, which endears you to the people, and even to those who have sometimes been doubters among them, like myself. May I tell you something which I thought pretty at the time, without now seeming to flatter you? I was in the smoking room of a westward Pullman, and an average American who had been all our average variety of citizen, was talking politics, or, rather, politicians. "Well," I said, presently, "what about Roosevelt?" He turned on me vividly: "Just love him, just *love* him!"

Yours sincerely
W. D. Howells.

Theodore Roosevelt,
President.

1. The personal matter concerned Howells' brother Samuel, who was being charged with inefficiency in his position as copyholder at the Government Printing Office and faced possible demotion. In response to an urgent plea, Howells had promised Sam, 21 August 1906 (NjR), that he would do what he could "by writing the President." Howells explained the situation in some detail to Joseph Howells, 4 September 1906 (MH), saying that Roosevelt had "replied through his secretary . . . , sending me the

documents in the case, and expressing the President's regret that he could not see his way to do anything more. The P.[ublic] P.[rinter] had interviewed six of Sam's readers, of different dates, and their testimony was unanimous against him for uncertainty in reading, miscalling figures, leaving out, indifference, inattention, mental inefficiency, unreliability, slowness, incorrectness. They declared that *no* one wanted him for copyholder, and the reader whom Sam had specified as his especial friend, said he sometimes felt like 'throwing up his job,' rather than continue with him." Howells wrote Joe again, the next day, 5 September 1906 (MH), that he had heard no word from Sam since he had told him of Roosevelt's refusal to intervene: "It is possible, but not probable that he may not be reduced; or some place of approximate value may be offered him.... Sam is always slow unless he has to ask something; then he is very prompt; and his silence now may mean that things are not going unfavorably with him."

2. Roosevelt was supporting the movement of Thomas R. Lounsbury, Brander Matthews, and others to recognize officially a standard simplified spelling of a list of three hundred words. The movement was ultimately not successful. Howells' "Easy Chair," *Harper's Monthly*, September 1906, dealt with the subject of spelling reform.

3. In his reply to Howells, 28 August 1906, (MH; *Life in Letters*, II, 228–29), Roosevelt reaffirmed his stand against the concentration of wealth: "Of course I should like during the remaining two years and a half of my term to see not only much further progress in the control of corporations by the national Government, but the enactment of a good, stiff progressive inheritance tax and a good, stiff progressive income tax by the national Government." See also Howells to J. A. Howells, 16 April 1906, n. 6.

7 SEPTEMBER 1906, KITTERY POINT, TO ROBERT HERRICK

Kittery Point, Sept. 7, 1906.

Dear Mr. Herrick:

I have read both your books[1] with wonder and regret that they should not be in the hands of everybody. Generally speaking, I have come to doubt the art and the wisdom of the *crucial* novel, but you have gone far in The Common Lot to bring me back to my old faith in it. The American Citizen is a novel of manners of an older sort, that now more appeals to me. But each in its way is admirable, and each is full of excellent characterization. On the whole, The Common Lot is better in its study of types, the Citizen in its portrayal of conditions; and the well-guarded unconsciousness of the autobiographer is masterly. From my son's being a New York architect and diplomé of the Beaux I am more familiar with the ground of the Common Lot; and in the temptations his profession has to overcome from contractors I know how true your work is to the general facts. From my own human nature, I find the Citizen absolutely true.

You have attempted and accomplished great things in these books; and it is nothing against you that their lesson of not struggling for mere success, financial or social, will be for the most part lost. You have asked in that too much of our generation, but it is high and brave in you to have asked it.

I confess that your courage warmed my heart toward you, and that I have longed to tell you so in fitter terms than these. I wish I could see you, and touch on a hundred points. Your women seem to me wonderfully well done—the worse, alas! the better, through those salient qualities of evil which make baddish women so palpable.

But the "Citizen" and some of his friends are triumphs in our own sex—which is not even so easy to do as good women.

Now and then your diction seemed to me careless or self-forgetful, but that does not matter.

Yours sincerely
W. D. Howells.

1. The books were two Herrick novels, *The Common Lot* (1904) and *The Memoirs of an American Citizen* (1905).

21 NOVEMBER 1906, NEW YORK, TO FREDERICK A. DUNEKA

Hotel Regent....
New York City November 21, 1906.[1]

Dear Mr. Duneka:

I will come tomorrow and talk books with you.[2] "The Eye of the Needle"[3] is a name which has been used since I put the book by, in the form of "The Needle's Eye" by a Funk & Wagnalls author.[4] If now we cannot use the name, how would *Easier for a Camel* do? I think it might be well to announce a new edition of "A Traveler from Altruria" with the novel, as it is made up from the Altrurian's letters home.[5] *It* must be newly prefaced, and I should do this ironically, assuming that all the abuses which the Altrurian had noted here ten years ago had been corrected.

Without having asked, I have a notion that "Certain Delightful English Towns" is not selling delightfully, and I should say we had better publish a book of stories next fall, and let the rest of my travels go over till the public gets its breath.

As we are rivals in forgetfulness, suppose you keep this memorandum for reference tomorrow.

Yours sincerely,
W. D. Howells.

1. The Howellses had left Kittery Point on 23 October, spent about a week in Boston, then moved into the Oxford Hotel at Park Avenue and 58th Street in New York; but finding it too noisy because of the nearby construction of the Grand Central tunnel they shortly thereafter moved back into the Regent Hotel.

2. Howells had mentioned to Duneka, 19 November 1906 (MWA), a projected volume of his recent short stories (published in 1907 as *Between the Dark and the Daylight*) and inquired about the status of the first six volumes of the Library Edition that had been proposed for publication in the fall.

3. Howells was writing an introduction and sequel to previously published Altrurian material, which would appear under the title *Through the Eye of the Needle* (1907). He wrote to Aurelia Howells, 29 September 1906 (MH), of his pleasure at going back to novelistic fiction: "...I am just turning to the novel which I hope to go on with uninterruptedly for a month or two. I remember the long stretches of years or half years when I wrote nothing but novels. Those were happy times. I like writing fiction, and I hate writing essays, which seems latterly my business."

4. Florence M. Kingsley, *The Needle's Eye* (1902).

5. *A Traveler from Altruria* came out serially in *Cosmopolitan*, November 1892–October 1893, and was published as a book in 1894. Howells continued the Altrurian's story in *Through the Eye of the Needle*, consisting of "Letters of an Altrurian Traveler" serialized in *Cosmopolitan*, November 1893–September 1894, along with the recently written introduction and sequel. See Cady, *Howells*, II, 197–98; Gibson-Arms, *Bibliography*, pp. 44, 58, 118, and 144; and Howells to J. A. Howells, 24 February 1907.

25 NOVEMBER 1906, NEW YORK, TO JOSEPH A. HOWELLS

Hotel Regent,
70th street & Broadway,
Nov. 25, 1906.

Dear Joe:

I am glad the check for your Sun article reached you,[1] for I was afraid it had gone wrong. As soon as you are strong enough you must try something else, though I doubt if you could manage anything with a syndicate; I fancy that sort of thing is pretty dead.—For heaven's sake look to your grammar! Hot on my scolding[2] you write "John and his stomach does." Would you write, "The boy*s* do*es*?" John and his stomach are just as plural as any other two things. But aside from syntax I have joy in reporting that they seem all right, through Christian science, mostly. It is I who have the stomach, or, as you would say, "Me and my stomach is full of gas at night, and the pains wakes me up two or three times." I am glad you and your stomach is at peace with each other. I have tried pretty much everything but Christian science, but for that I seem to lack either the science or the Christianity.

Sam is holding on at Washington, but he gets a "furlough," now and then, and loses, or I lose for him, a few days' pay.[3] He is very downhearted—at least on paper—poor fellow, and seems to think his wife is not going to get well.[4] It w'd be kind of you to write him now and then.

In your own case, while I wish you could bounce back into health, I see some reasons why you cannot. You are for instance, seventy four years old, and you may be very glad if you can creep back. You must not blame the climate, unless you can forget how long you were in getting up from your grippes on the Lake Shore. I wish I had your winter at Turk's Island to face, instead of the winter we have before us here. But I know what exile is, and how the old home thoughts tug at the heart strings. Still, count up your blessings, and the comforts and dignities of your position. Isn't it all better than running out into the zero weather at Jefferson, or arguing with a farmer against stopping his paper, or stoking the engine? That life was cruel for you at your age, and it ought to seem a bad dream. Let it go, and be glad of what and where you are.

I am sending you the last Scrap Book.[5] I had got rather out of the way of buying it, but I find it as interesting as ever. A droll thing is that Munsey who started here a bootblack, now has social aspirations of the tallest kind since he has become rich.—He is a clammy, quiet man, and just fit for the fashionable set.

Last night I was at Carnegie's, to see some solar photographs thrown up. They were wonderful, but he and his wife were better than the astronomy. His wife is one of the sweetest and kindest and simplest women in the world, and I believe he is a sincerely good man, with the wish to help all he can. He is rather pathetic to me, for he is like the young man who had great possessions, and he is always going away exceeding sorrowful.—But really, so long as the competitive conditions endure, sorrowfulness like his must continue.[6]

Elinor seems to be standing the racket surprisingly well.[7] At least she has not broken down yet, and though I look for her collapse, we shall probably stay here till it comes. Then we will put for Atlantic City.

Pilla started a sore throat as soon as she reached New York, and has made a date in early January for Bermuda.

As you say there is no use in stringing out a letter to fill the paper, and so, with love to all, I am

> Your affectionate brother,
> Will.

1. At Howells' urging, Joe had written an article about the Turks Islands, which appeared in the New York *Sun*, 21 October 1906. A few days later, 26 October 1906 (MH), Howells forwarded a check from the *Sun*, encouraging Joe to new and better efforts: "I sent you the *Sun* of last Sunday with your paper in it, and now I enclose

the check, which has just come. It might have been more, but $10 a column is fair newspaper pay. I felt that I could not sell your article to a magazine, because it lacked texture and form. But now try some specific, short subject, like turtle-fishing, and treat it fully and humanly with regard to the turtles, turtlers, and turtle-boats, and I will do the rest."

2. Howells had advised Joe on some points of grammar, 30 October 1906 (MH), concluding with the admonishment: "But for heaven's sake get a simple school grammar and study it. No need to *parse*; nobody does that now; but learn the parts of speech, and the very few very simple rules that govern them. You can do it in half a day."

3. See Howells to Roosevelt, 26 August 1906, n. 1.

4. In the following spring it was ascertained that Sam's wife, Florence, had stomach cancer. Howells had written to Aurelia, 21 October 1906 (MH), that "Sam seems still to be holding on; but he writes me dolefully about his wife's sickness. He is always so voluminous in his griefs; poor fellow, he has enough of them to go round our whole circle, and I ought not to grumble at my share of them."

5. The *Scrap Book* was a popular magazine founded and conducted by New York publisher Frank A. Munsey (1854–1925), who was best known for *Munsey's Magazine* (1889–1929), which featured topical material and appealing illustrations. After clerking in a general store in Maine, he came to New York in 1882 and made his fortune by introducing the ten-cent magazine and conducting extensive advertising campaigns to increase circulation.

6. Howells had earlier described Carnegie to Aurelia Howells, 13 May 1906 (MH), as having "something of the old rat in him, but also something of the poet . . . ." Describing the same evening at the Carnegies', Howells also wrote Aurelia on 25 November (MH): "He is really a good man, with the best intentions in the world, short of intending to give up the world, which, indeed is no longer the fashion."

7. Noise had been the subject of an earlier exchange with Joe and the topic of the November 1906 "Easy Chair" in *Harper's Monthly*. Howells acknowledged to Joe, 20 August 1906 (MH), the idea for a paper about "the increase of noises, taking for text one of your letters in which you lament the silence of T.[urks] I.[slands]." For Howells' recent brush with unpleasant noise in New York, see Howells to F. A. Duneka, 21 November 1906, n. 1.

2 DECEMBER 1906, NEW YORK, TO CHARLES E. NORTON

Regent Hotel,
Dec. 2, 1906.

My dear Norton:

I have written Miss Theodora a peace making letter, and have gladly proposed to edit Miss Ashburner's memoir for private printing.[1] After doing this I must resist the desire to offer you battle concern the Bazar, as a "flagrant incongruity" in one so self-humbled. But even the unturning worm cannot suffer the notion of an "unvulgarized England" to be implied to him.[2] I found all England, though not all Englishmen, abounding in the organized and constituted vulgarity which seems to me the most desperate kind; but there was always kindness and truthfulness enough to keep me with my hat in my hand.

I wish I could come to the next Club dinner,[3] and be your guest, but with the Longfellow commemoration so near, I must not think of it. I am going through the whole of his poetry for my study of his art. So far I find the sermon and the song flowing side by side like two confluent, unmixing streams, but the song more and more prevailing. I do hope you will like what I shall say.[4]

My story is not to be in the poor, despised Bazar, but the proud Weekly,[5] and it is that which you must watch. Perhaps I shall bring with me in Feb'y the MS. of another story to read you to bed with.[6]

Yours affectionately,
W. D. Howells.

1. Earlier in the year Theodora Sedgwick had sent Howells the manuscript of Anne Ashburner's memoir to read. See Howells to Sedgwick, 8 May 1906. Having sought Howells' assistance in preparing it for publication, both she and Norton had balked at the recommendation that it appear in *Harper's Bazar*. In his "peace making" letter to Sedgwick, 2 December 1906 (MH), Howells tactfully defends his choice: "By my agreement with the Harpers my work is restricted ... to their periodicals, and of the four I chose the Bazar because I know its good literary quality, and because neither the Weekly nor the Review seemed so fit; the Monthly I knew was full.—In any magazine one is in a crowd, but the grime or the powder does not necessarily come off on one. Something like this I said to myself, and now I say it, not for your conversion but for my excuse if I have, most unhappily, hurt you by my suggestion, as I am afraid I have." Although Howells subsequently edited the troublesome memoir for private printing, it was never published. The difficult matter was closed when he gracefully assured Theodora Sedgwick, 16 October 1907 (MH), that he understood the family's decision not to disclose such a personal document: "I shall always be glad of the work I did and the pleasure I had in studying the noble and beautiful character of Miss Ashburner in her own record of her life. Now that, for reasons that I can perfectly understand, this record is not to pass beyond the immediate circle of her family friends, I can always feel it a privilege to have known her in it."

2. In his letter of 30 November 1906 (MH), Norton wrote to Howells: "you have seen and loved that quiet undemocratized & unvulgarized England to which her Aunts belonged. There is a flagrant incongruity between 'Aunt Anne' & the Bazar ...." Howells' impatience moved Norton to a somewhat lengthy if more moderate defense, 13 December 1906 (MH), of the old and fading genteel tradition: "... I found it difficult to express exactly my agreement & my disagreement with you in regard to the equally odious characteristics of English & American vulgarity.... The gentleman & the lady are rarer products of our democracy of the new dispensation than they are of the old. One must be an optimist *pur sang* to take comfort in the faith that the old & beautiful type must gradually disappear in the struggle for existence, but only to give way to the evolution (through ugly processes) of something better than the best yet known. For the present I cling to the 'saving remnant', & would protect what little remains of it as the most sacred inheritance from the past."

3. The Saturday Club.

4. Norton had not been entirely satisfied with the kind of address Howells wished to deliver at the Longfellow commemoration. See Howells to Norton, 27 June 1906, n. 1. In his reply of 13 December, Norton tried to take advantage of Howells' thorough grappling with Longfellow's poetry in order to persuade him to a more informal approach: "But, above all, do not overwork yourself by taking your address as an extra labor ... & do not overtire your eyes by reading too much & too late at night. It would be better that you did nothing but say a few extempory words on

the 27th February, than that you did more at the cost of health." The address was published as "The Art of Longfellow" in both the *Cambridge Historical Society Publications*, February 1907, and the *North American Review*, March 1907.

5. "A Sleep and a Forgetting."

6. Perhaps the short drama, *Her Opinion of His Story*, which appeared in *Harper's Bazar*, May 1907.

9 DECEMBER 1906, NEW YORK, TO JOSEPH A. HOWELLS

Hotel Regent,
New York City, December 9, 1906.

Dear Joe:

Your very full and interesting letter of Thanksgiving and earlier came yesterday, and was read aloud to the family. I had got back from a day in Washington that morning, where I had been for the Congressional hearing on the bill to extend copyright to 50 years beyond the author's death.[1] If the bill were not complicated with the interests of the public librarians and machine-music men,[2] it would go through, but I am afraid that as it is, now, it won't. The hearing was very interesting, however, and half through it I went to call on the President. I had five minutes' joyous chat with him, and learned that he had read my last thing in *Harper's*,[3] and sympathized more with the bride's mother than with the bride, and that he reads everything I write as it comes out. If I could have given him more time, he would have got round to the Consul at Turk's Island, but I was in a hurry—and so was he. It is funny about the passage you quote from *April Hopes*: I had totally forgotten it; but I admired it almost as much as you do. In fact, I am often amazed at the quality as well as quantity of my stuff, and feel as if it must have been done by a trust named after me. Did you see that the Ohio School Commissioner had sent round to all the school children to know why every American should know my books, and which of them were autobiographical?[4] This is better than having it all on a tombstone. However!

Your thanksgiving dinner was all right. The older I grow, the more I respect bacon in every form. I hope, as soon as you get the grip out of you, that you will turn your attention to the turtle-fish-ery, for another *Sun* paper.[5] You mustn't let yourself be forgotten there.

With our love to you all,

Your affectionate brother,
Will.

1. In company with Clemens, Albert B. Paine, Robert U. Johnson, and others, Howells had gone to Washington in early December in order to lobby for the copyright bill. For an account of the experience, including Howells' description of Clemens appearing for the first time in his notorious white suit, see "My Mark Twain," in *Literary Friends and Acquaintance*, HE, p. 319.

2. The machine-music men were the manufacturers of player-piano rolls, to whom Clemens referred as "those hand-organ men who ought to have a bill of their own." See Albert B. Paine, *Mark Twain: A Biography* (New York: Harper & Brother, 1912), p. 1343.

3. Howells refers to a poem entitled "After the Wedding," *Harper's Monthly*, December 1906.

4. Edmund A. Jones (b. 1842) was then Ohio State commissioner of common schools; the particular document or occasion to which Howells here refers has not been identified.

5. See Howells to J. A. Howells, 25 November 1906, n. 1.

30 DECEMBER 1906, NEW YORK, TO AURELIA H. HOWELLS

Hotel Regent,
Dec. 30, 1906.

Dear Aurelia:

It will soon be next year, and I shall rather like writing 1907, because I have hated the look of 1906, and have found it inconvenient on my typewriter, because of the key for 6 coming next the space key. Besides, 1907 is the centennial of father's birthday, or birthyear, and I shall think often of him. I dream a good deal of him, and always pleasantly; he seems younger, and wise, as he used to be. The dreams themselves are rather trying otherwise, and result from my gaseous indigestion, which wakes me every night, and makes me feel a thousand years old in the morning. This extreme old age begins to pass off with a warm wash after shaving. I go out for some rolls, which I specially like, at a bakery not far from the hotel, and when I have had my coffee, I begin to find the world not so bad.

The President sent me, over his own hand, a New Year's greeting, and a reminder that I was to bring Stedman to dine with him.[1] Happily Stedman is not well enough to go to Washington, and the dreaded honor is postponed for me. It is dreaded, of course, only because all honors are dreadful; if it were not an honor it would be a great pleasure, for I have never met a more interesting man than Roosevelt. Still, Washington is always a great way off, and getting farther the nearer I get to 70.

I heard from poor Sam, tardily of course, after Christmas. He had had a hemorrhage from the nose, which is not a good sign, for so fat a man, and he had nothing cheering to tell of Florence.[2]

We are all very well, just now; even Pilla's throat is not sore, and she is putting off the date of sailing for Bermuda. John comes to dinner every day. He is very prosperous and very happy.—Tell Vevie[3] we are trying get one of the West 67th street studios for an apartment; but we shall probably stay here for the winter.

With love to you all,

Your aff'te brother,
Will

1. See Howells to Stedman, 31 December 1906.
2. For an account of Sam's troubles, including his wife's illness, see Howells to J. A. Howells, 25 November 1906. While attending the Congressional hearings on copyright law in early December, Howells had visited Sam. He described the somber occasion to Aurelia, 9 December 1906 (MH): "In the evening I went out to see Sam, and found him in a comfortable house with a good dinner, but the sight of Florence was discouraging. She was courageous, if not cheerful; she laughed a little too; but she is so wasted that she looked like a sick bird, and she told me she is in constant, dreadful pain.... Sam is tremendously fat; very quiet, and rather sad, though not so disturbed about his place as he has been. As yet he knows nothing of his future, but in the meantime he holds on." Apparently by mid-May 1907 Florence had died, and Howells wrote to Anne Fréchette, 19 May 1907 (MH): "We are going to try to get Sam into a Soldier's Home .... He has been 'reduced' in the printing office, and his pay cut in two."
3. Marie Marguerite Fréchette.

31 DECEMBER 1906, NEW YORK, TO EDMUND C. STEDMAN

Hotel Regent,
Dec. 31, 1906.

My dear Stedman:

I was trying all the time to tell you I had written you; but I was so much taken with what we were talking of that I could not squeeze it in.[1] I wrote at once to Washington saying that you did not feel strong enough to undertake the journey at present,[2] but later when you were there you would come to make your acknowledgments: this was how I interpreted the generalities. If the affair is off, or put off, I shall be content, you will easily believe; the pleasure which is also an honor is one that I am always willing to wait for; though I felt the intention most kind, and very like that very much of a Man.

Basta!—I want to recur to what you said so generously about the high level of so much now done in magazine verse and prose. It shamed me that I had sometimes carped at our youngers' work, and I want to make an Easy Chair from your point of view.[3] Do you mind? Of course I shall not be personal.

Meantime I am working hard at my paper on Longfellow.[4] How difficult it is to say simple things! The complex things are so much handier, and wind can be got into one's words almost without trying.– But there are two or three of his laterish poems, like *Changed*, and *Aftermath*, that I feel to be absolute emotion, art, charm. How to put it!–Between my trousers and my waistcoat this morning, while I was dressing, I suddenly thought, Why, the imaginative in a poet is not so much what *he* imagines as what he makes *me* imagine. Heigh?

I wish I knew the afternoon hour when I should disturb you least. I should like to take my walks as far as your convenient ground-floor. We have been friends for 46 years; we shall not know each other as long, here; why not meet, now and then?

Yours ever
W. D. Howells.

1. Howells had called on Stedman at his home (see Howells to Stedman, 1 March 1907) between the time of a prior letter to Stedman, dated 28 December 1906 (PSt), and the present one, therefore either on 29 or 30 December. In his letter of 28 December, Howells continues a recent dinner conversation they had at Andrew Carnegie's regarding an invitation to the White House.

2. Roosevelt had sent a New Year's greeting, 26 December 1906 (MH), inquiring if Howells would not arrange to "bring on Mr. Stedman some time for dinner?" Howells had met briefly with Roosevelt in early December (see Howells to J. A. Howells, 9 December 1906), at which time it appears that the president had asked Howells and Stedman to have lunch with him. Because the written invitation was for the more formal occasion of a "dinner," as Howells wrote to Stedman on 28 December, the situation was much less appealing: "you seemed friendly to the idea when it was only a luncheon. Now that our 'dread lord' has thought it was a dinner, what do you say, and what shall I say?" Howells apparently declined for both himself and Stedman.

3. Howells wrote an "Easy Chair" on the subject for *Harper's Monthly*, March 1907, thinly disguising his and Stedman's identity in the form of a conversation between "two aging if not aged poets." It was reprinted in *Imaginary Interviews* (1910) under the title "The Magazine Muse."

4. See Howells to Norton, 2 December 1906, n. 4.

3 JANUARY 1907, NEW YORK, TO ELIZABETH JORDAN

Hotel Regent,
Jan'y 3, 1907.

Dear Miss Jordan:

Thank you for letting me see all those delightful papers of James's.[1] We had devoured some of them already, but over the last we paused to let the morsel about me melt under our tongues and fill our whole systems with its sweetness.[2]—How good and just and wise his talk all is! I feel keenly, after my manifolded phrases about the Am. girl's speech,[3] how nothing accurate had been said till James said they spoke as if from sore mouths![4] The gods must have cackled over that.

Can you help out the enclosed lady?[5] Don't for pity's sake do it indirectly through me!

Yours sincerely
W. D. Howells.

1. "The Speech of American Women," *Harper's Bazar*, November–December 1906 and January–February 1907, and "The Manners of American Women," *Harper's Bazar*, April–July 1907.

2. In "The Manners of American Women," James expresses admiration for the cohesiveness and tolerance found in American communities, despite their lack of forms and manners. He points to the "documentary value" of Howells' novels in capturing, through "vivid and interesting evidence," this spirit: "For it is Mr. Howells above all who helps us to recognize what has hitherto made our associations possible and enabled us to hold out against the daily effect of our surrender of forms. He marks this surrender, at every point, with an infallible hand, and yet, in the oddest way in the world, a perfect gospel of optimism is to be extracted from his general picture. For here we get the exquisite *detail* of the mutual, the universal patience—with the strangest impression, as a whole, I think, of every one's, men's and women's alike, trying, all round them, by universal readiness and response, to deprecate and forestall the great peril of fatal aggravation."

3. "Our Daily Speech," *Harper's Bazar*, October 1906.

4. In "The Speech of American Women," James at one point lashes out at the "animated, bright-eyed young women, all articulating as from sore mouths, all mumbling and whining and vocally limping and shuffling, as it were, together...."

5. The "enclosed lady" is not identified. She is probably a writer who had requested a literary favor from Howells in connection with *Harper's Bazar*, of which Jordan was editor.

30 JANUARY 1907, NEW YORK, TO CHARLES E. NORTON

Hotel Regent,
Jan'y 30, 1907.

My dear Norton:

I must not try to tell you how much I feel your kindness in what you have done and said about my paper.[1] I have been all over it today, and I see how faithful you have been in your criticism. In nearly everything I shall follow your suggestions; only I could not do anything of reminiscence. That I renounced, when I took up the subject of Longfellow's art,[2] and as you allow with your own kindness, I had done it already.[3] I will try to add a page relating his art to his personality as I knew it. But indeed, I am rather—in fact quite—worked down, and what I mostly hope to do is to reduce the paper more and more, and make it clearer. I know it will not *hear* well, but that I cannot help; for I have no public manner.[4] For this reason I am a little sorry you have kept the worst wine for the last, but that is your risk. I shall do badly, anyway, and I shall not much mind being a "chaser," as they call the poor fellow in the variety shows who acts the audience out of the house.[5]

Yours affectionately
W. D. Howells.

Perhaps I may for a few places later.[6]—The lateral red-pencilling was Pilla's effort to save me from vain repetitions.[7]

1. The paper was to be delivered at the Longfellow commemoration on 27 February. See Howells to Norton, 27 June 1906, 2 December 1906, and 2 February 1907. Howells had sent the paper to Norton, 23 January 1907 (MH), asking for advice on shortening it, and Norton had replied at length, 26 and 27 January 1907 (MH), suggesting both deletions and changes.

2. Howells wanted to talk of Longfellow's art, while Norton wanted a more personal reminiscence. Norton continued to press the issue in his letter of 26 and 27 January: "The audience will have come hoping & expecting from us elder men who had the happiness of knowing Longfellow an endeavor to convey a personal impression. They will want to hear of him as he lived & moved, & of his work as it touched our hearts. And from no one will they hope for this more confidently than from you, both because of what you have written of him, and because more of the spirit that animated him has descended to you than to any other of the writers for whom the public cares."

3. Howells refers to his earlier essay, "The White Mr. Longfellow." See *Literary Friends and Acquaintance*, HE, pp. 151–78.

4. In praising "its fine critical insight & its sympathetic appreciations," Norton had also noted "that parts of it are not well fitted for delivery and to be listened to . . . ."

5. When he sent the paper, Howells had asked where he was to "strike the procession." Informing Howells that in "the order of speakers" he would be fifth and last, Norton also mentioned that music was to be interpolated into the program at some point, "a chorus to sing the Village Blacksmith, I believe."

6. Norton had asked if there was anyone in particular Howells would like invited to the commemoration.

7. In explaining that he had bracketed certain passages in red pencil for possible deletion, Norton noted that "the red lines up & down the margins of some pages are not mine."

2 FEBRUARY 1907, NEW YORK, TO CHARLES E. NORTON

Hotel Regent,
Feb'y 2, 1907.

My dear Norton:

I have waited, before answering your letter of Jan'y. 31st,[1] to go over my paper on Longfellow in "Literary Friends and Acquaintance"[2] in order to see if I had left unsaid anything I knew of him in that sort. But I find that if I went farther, I should be inventing, not remembering. I have there set down all that I could then, or can now, think of. I could not with due regard to him or myself, *rechauffer* the material. But I could, with some words of introduction from you, or none, if you thought better, frankly read a succession of passages from the paper, embodying my more immediate sense of him, and let this reading go for my contribution to the Commemoration. I might add to these the closing page, or two pages, of my essay on his art which generally you do not find of the right temperament for the occasion. I can print that, and otherwise it need not be further considered.

We could safely risk as novel, though we should have to own them second-hand, the passages I should borrow from the paper in "Lit. Fr. and Acq." The immense majority of the audience would not have read them; the minority who had, would have forgotten them. I myself think the passages interesting for their portraiture of Longfellow, and I believe they would form an intelligible and credible image of the Cambridge we have loved and lost[3]

Yours ever,
W. D. Howells.

1. In his letter of 31 January 1907 (MH), Norton promised to push Howells to the limit concerning their differences over the Longfellow address: "And now I am going to put your patience and self-abnegation to the test! When I said two or three months ago that I was delighted that you were going to speak of Longfellow's art, it never occurred to me that you would treat it abstractly....You are a part of the best Cambridge tradition, & it will not do for you to come as if you were a stranger & a critic of the poet & not one of ourselves....[¶] You actually must 'reminiss' a little,—for everybody's sake,—Longfellow's, your own, mine, the audience's—for only thus can you do justice to yourself."
   2. "The White Mr. Longfellow."
   3. Howells' offer to abandon the original address appears to be the final measure of his exasperation. Not having heard from Norton, he restated the capitulation a week later, 8 February 1907 (MH): "I can, I believe, make some sort of personal introduction to the critical matter, and at several points introduce reminiscences recast from my paper in Literary Acquaintance, and close with some personal passages allusive to Cambridge as well as to Longfellow. The treatment of Longfellow's art will of course be greatly reduced." Norton hastened to express his approval, 9

February 1907 (MH): "I was glad of what you proposed...as being more appropriate to the special personal, reminiscential, local, & affectionate character of the meeting." In a culminating irony, Howells was stricken with influenza and, although he revised the paper as Norton wished, he was not able to attend the ceremony and Bliss Perry read the address in his place. He later admitted he had been wrong in resisting Norton's criticism. See Howells to Norton, 13 October 1907.

21 FEBRUARY 1907, NEW YORK, TO ELIZABETH JORDAN

Hotel Regent,
Feb'y 21, 1907.

Dear Miss Jordan:

The phosphorescent play of James's humor all round and over the situation in our little scheme is charming.[1] I have nothing but applause for his delicate treatment of it, his perfect intelligence, and ironical ease; and I have no suggestion to make. As he leaves you free, I should deal with the Chataway business as seemed best to myself.[2] I am not yet out of the grip of my grippe.[3]

Yours sincerely,
W. D. Howells.

1. Howells refers to the composite novel *The Whole Family*, to which James contributed the chapter entitled "The Married Son." See Howells to Jordan, 21 May 1906.
2. Near the end of his chapter, James introduces the reader to a vulgar and socially pretentious woman by the name of Mrs. Chataway, whose vivid presence must be resolved at a subsequent point in the novel by another contributor.
3. Howells wrote to Aurelia Howells, 24 February 1907 (MH), that he had been four days in bed, confined to the apartment for two weeks, and was still feeling the after effects: "But I seem now to be recovering, and have only a bronchial cough left....A peculiarity of this winter's grippe is that it leaves the victim extremely weak, and I feel very wooden in getting about."

21 FEBRUARY 1907, NEW YORK, TO SAMUEL L. CLEMENS

Hotel Regent,
Feb'y 21, 1907.

Dear Clemens:

I am at least out of bed, and so far on a par with that branch of the human race which is being tried for matricide, and other venial offences. But you will have to welcome the British Ambassador without me.[1] Tell him we are not so bad as we paint ourselves—couldn't be.

It was good of you to come and see me, you fine old paranoic. I don't know how you've escaped arrest up to this time. It shows you were always right about the inefficiency of our detective system.[2]

Good bye, you whited sepulchre.

> Yours affectionately,
> W. D. Howells.

1. The diplomat and historian James Bryce (1838–1922) was arriving in New York to assume his post in Washington (1907–1913). Clemens' role in the reception is not known. See *Twain-Howells*, p. 823. Howells describes his prior acquaintance with Bryce in a letter to Aurelia Howells, 24 March 1907 (MH): "he is an old acquaintance whom I like to think of as a friend. I dined at his house in London when we were there in '83; at Florence I walked five miles out with him to a famous villa; some years ago we lunched together at Beverly Farms, and when we were in London two years ago, I met [him] and he asked me to lunch."

2. Howells alludes to Clemens' several satires on detectives. See *Twain-Howells*, p. 823.

24 FEBRUARY 1907, NEW YORK, TO JOSEPH A. HOWELLS

> Hotel Regent,
> Feb. 24, 1907

Dear Joe:

I have been shut up two weeks with the grippe, but as I have not had it for ten years, or so, I suppose I ought not to complain. The worst of any misfortune is that it seems so unmerited.

I am greatly interested to hear of Beatrice's coming home, and I hope it will do her good, morally and physically. I shall be careful not to say anything to Willy about her visit; she will soon be with him.[1] You do not say how long she expects to stay, but I predict it will be a shorter time than she has imagined; there is no cure for homesickness like home, except in the case of such a hopeless home-sicker as I used to be.

Our winter is holding on with great severity, and the blackbirds reported at Hoboken a fortnight ago must be sorry they came north of Jersey City. John bro't no spring with him from Bermuda, and poor Pilla, who was to have been on her way after it, is in bed with her little touch of the grippe. Fortunately, Elinor seems to be escaping, and she takes all possible credit to herself for her good luck. You would think she invented immunity from grippe.

I hear nothing more from you about that paper on turtling.[2] About what time of year do your turtlers appear, and is the voice of the turtle then heard in the land? You must get into talk with the turtlers, and get them to tell you all the lies of their trade. These will interest the reader more than the truth, but the truth is desirable also.

Yes, I still hope to do the Leatherwood God.[3] Perhaps by the time I get at it you will be settled near Salesville on the Ohio River, and we will visit the scene together.[4] It is a great scheme, and I should like the notion of making it my last great novel. Just now I am writing a sequel to the Altrurian business which you stereotyped for me twelve years ago under the title "The Eye of the Needle."[5] There is now a renewal of interest in such speculations, and the publishers think the book, with an interesting sequel, giving an account of life in Altruria, will succeed. I hope so. But my books, none of them go far, you know. I had a letter lately from dear old Douglas, who is issuing a complete set of the farces in two volumes.[6] Should you have imagined there were twenty of them? How I have run to quantity! And yet the quality is not so bad.

We are getting toward the end of the Thaw trial.[7] It is probable he will be sent to a criminal insane asylum, but no one can tell, just as no one can tell whether he or White or Evelyn is the worst subject.

With our love to you all,

> Your affectionate brother,
> Will
> W. D. Howells
> (mechanical autograph.)

1. Howells wrote to Aurelia Howells on the same day (MH), cautioning her not to spoil the surprise of Beatrice's visit to Jefferson.

2. After placing Joe's article on the Turks Islands with the New York *Sun*, Howells had continued to urge him to write on a more specific topic. See Howells to J. A. Howells, 25 November 1906, n. 1.

3. Several years earlier Howells had asked Joe to send him materials for a story that eventually became *The Leatherwood God*. See Howells to J. A. Howells, 14 October 1904, n. 1.

4. Salesville is about thirty-five miles inshore from Martin's Ferry, Howells' birthplace on the Ohio River.

5. See Howells to F. A. Duneka, 21 November 1906.

6. David Douglas, the Edinburgh publisher, issued nineteen of Howells' farces under the title *Minor Dramas by William Dean Howells* (1907).

7. See Howells to J. A. Howells, 6 August 1906, n. 3.

Hotel Regent,
March 1st, 1907.

My dear Stedman:

I cannot wait to be so long over the grippe as you in the hope of making anything like due acknowledgment of your beautiful letter.[1] You are quite right in supposing I was kept from Cambridge by sickness; the doctor promptly forbade me to think of going on, and as yet I am only able to crawl about. However the essay was read better than I could have read it, and it served all the literary ends possible.[2] It would have been sweet to be among old friends that night, but it was something to be anywhere, to be at all; we must not be greedy. If you will look at the essay in the North American Review, you will find yourself touched upon in it,[3] and you will see that the thing was done with the faltering hand of an already ailing man. I wrote to Aldrich day before.[4]

—This is the point where your welcome visit interrupted me. I hope you may see the March Harper, where, in the Easy Chair, you will find a real, and a dramatic, treatment of the subject of fugitive verse which came up between us the day I called on you.[5] It is one that would bear much deeper and more sober inquiry; but I think I am right in my conclusion. No, dear friend, the fellows and fellowesses of this day are not the peers of us in ours. It is a source of great pride with me to think that when I was trying my best and you were doing so much better we were not of the latter day make. You had a distinct voice in verse, a brave gayety, a lyrical splendor, such as no other of us could rival you in. If ever I could get the time I should like to study that series of pieces—the Pan in Wall Street sort[6]—in which you are likest yourself, and like nobody else.

Well, we lived in a great time. If we have outlived it, so much the worse for this time.

You gave us all a great joy this afternoon. I kept looking at you, and thinking, "Well, he is as handsome and gallant and blithe as when I first saw him."

Yours ever
W. D. Howells.

What an awfully long day a 70th birthday is!

—Just after you left there came from the Century the acceptance of a poem which my daughter sent this morning.[7]

1. Stedman's letter of 28 February 1907 (MH) was an effusive seventieth birthday greeting. Expressing at length his admiration of Howells' character and accomplishments, he concluded: "Though I never before have spoken like this, you shall not escape this assurance on this culminating year of your years. I count my unbroken relations with you, and what I have gained by your respect and intimacy, as among the prizes which have made my life worth living."

2. Howells was kept from attending the Longfellow commemoration on 27 February because he was recovering from an attack of influenza. Bliss Perry read the essay which, at the insistence of Charles E. Norton, who presided over the affair, did not stress the literary qualities of Longfellow as much as Howells had originally intended. See Howells to Norton, 2 February 1907.

3. The original version of the address appeared in the *North American Review*, 1 March 1907. In it, Howells does not refer to Stedman by name, but as a friendly "critic and poet" who had contributed several critical observations to the essay.

4. Howells wrote to Aldrich, 26 February 1907 (MH), as soon as he heard his friend was sick: "My wife has just read in a paper of yesterday that you are sick in the hospital, but we know no particulars, and can only hope things are going well with you." Aldrich died on 19 March, and in a letter to Frederick A. Duneka, 20 March 1907 (MWA), Howells declined to write a memorial essay for *Harper's Weekly*: "I should be very willing to write of Aldrich if I did not feel my frequent mortuary notices were turning me into a kind of standard epitapher."

5. See Howells to Stedman, 31 December 1906, n. 1, for the dating of Howells' call. Replying 8 March 1907 (MH), Stedman applauded the "Easy Chair" essay on the superiority of older magazine poetry to the modern sort, a topic Howells credited to Stedman in his 31 December letter. Stedman recalled, however, that his main point "chiefly related to the short-story writers" who published in the magazines in earlier times: "I said that each month there were several stories, each of which might have started an author's reputation when *we* were young." Howells had given previous assurance, 16 January 1907 (NNC), that he had not mentioned Stedman by name in the essay because he knew how the younger poets tend to "cling to the skirts of us seraphim, if they think they catch a ray of the *dolce lome* round our legs."

6. One of Stedman's best known poems, "Pan in Wall Street" was published in a collection of his poetry entitled *The Blameless Prince, And Other Poems* (1869).

7. Mildred Howells, "My Dream," *Century*, August 1907.

4 March 1907, New York, to Alice Longfellow

Hotel Regent,
March 4, 1907.

Dear Miss Longfellow:

I really do not know what to say to you for that gift of the Milton bust. Of course, Sumner's ownership enriches it, but it has gathered inestimable value from your father's possession.[1] I shall put the facts in writing on the base, and read the inscription to everybody who comes into my library at Kittery Point,[2] and then tell of our serious conversation in the study where it used to stand, while we were waiting for the Dante Club to assemble.[3] I *always* was terribly overawed by those great minds, and had really no courage till we sat down to supper, when I felt I might do my part with the rest. I still do not know why

I was allowed at those meetings, and I cannot yet believe—though I have my own word for it—that it was my great fortune to be so often your father's guest.

I have sent you the North American Review paper, which differs somewhat from the address you heard.[4] No study of the subject short of a book would really touch it, and I wrote with a hand both hurried and lagging from over work. But I read all his loved and honored poetry through, and possibly I may make here and there one of a cross-eyed generation see it aright—as the effect of most beautiful and perfect art.

With my best regards to all in or about Cragie House,

Yours sincerely
W. D. Howells.

1. Alice Longfellow appears to have sent the bust in appreciation for Howells' address on the occasion of her father's memorial celebration. See Howells to Norton, 2 February 1907. The circumstances surrounding Charles Sumner's possession of the bust and its passing into the hands of Longfellow, who was his close friend, are not known.

2. The bust is now located at the Howells Memorial House at Kittery Point, which is administered by Harvard University. The inscription reads: "Given to Longfellow by / Charles Sumner / Given to W. D. Howells, 1907 / by Alice Longfellow"

3. See Howells to Norton, 25 May 1866, n. 2.

4. See Howells to Stedman, 1 March 1907, n. 2 and n. 3.

10 MARCH 1907, NEW YORK, TO HENRY B. FULLER

New York, N. Y. March 10, 1907.

Henry B. Fuller Esq.
Chicago, Ill.

My dear Fuller:—

It seems to me very shabby to be addressing you in typewriting instead of handwriting, but typewriting is mostly my handwriting now, for I use the machine almost altogether and this is only another machine. The birthday letters have been more than I could manage in the right way,[1] that is with pen and ink, but yours in quality has made up for all the quantity of the rest. I am going to spend the rest of my life in trying to believe in what you tell me.[2] Sometimes I have felt that perhaps I had influenced my little day, which I must call a great day when I remember "The Cliff Dwellers" and "With the Procession".[3]

Have you read Brand Whitlock's new story "The Turn of the Balance"?[4] It is a terrible book in the sense of being I am afraid, terribly true. I do not believe it will have much success with a public like ours which prefers smooth things and likes its mental nutriment in the form of pap.

Since the "Octopus"[5] there has been no novel on either side of the sea to compare with it.

Yours cordially,
W. D. Howells.

1. Overwhelmed with birthday letters, many prompted by Norton's remarks at the Longfellow commemoration (see Howells to J. A. Howells, 13 March 1907), Howells lamented to Aurelia, 4 March 1907 (MH): "I have got through my 70th birthday alive, no thanks to the friends who have tried to kill me with kind words."

2. Fuller's letter, 27 February 1907 (MH), was in effect a splendid literary investiture: "To me, yours has been the typical career in American letters, by reason of its long, unbroken, orderly growth; and one of the most beneficent, by reason of its unfailing allegiance to sanity, highmindedness and that mental modesty (as I may call it) which seems as specifically a product of our hemisphere as is the goldenrod or the arbutus. The decorous thing, decorously done, is rare and is becoming rarer. [¶] And I want to record my conviction that when the fussy and noisy accidents of our crowded day come to be left behind it will be perceived that for one full generation in American annals the dominant influence has been yours—and always for the good. The Age of Howells—isn't that, some time, possible and likely? To remain imbedded as a definite, integral and respected figure in the national literature—what happier fate?"

3. Fuller's novels, published respectively in 1893 and 1895.

4. For a more extended commentary on the novel, see Howells to Whitlock, 17 March 1907.

5. Frank Norris' novel, published in 1901.

10 MARCH 1907, NEW YORK, TO HENRY ARTHUR JONES

New York, N. Y. March 10, 1907.

Henry Arthur Jones Esq.,
Hindhead Beacon Hotel,
Haslemere, England.

Dear Mr. Jones:—

I have received all the plays which you sent me[1] and have read them all but two or three; and I only wish there were more of them, and especially that "Judah" were among them.[2] Out of them all I liked best that one about the rector and his lost angel. (I never can recall the title.)[3] I have read them mostly at night when I woke up out of my first sleep and had an hour of wakefulness before me. They bore this test so well that I had to read something else before I could get to sleep again. They have been in every way most interesting to me, psychologically as well as artistically, for I kept putting myself in the place of the author, and though I felt that I "rattled around in it," as we say, still I felt that

I realized something of his intentions and his consciousness in respect to the social and theatrical environment.

The plays have taught me many things, and if I were thirty-five instead of seventy, I think their teachings would not be lost upon me. I should know how to leave more to the actors than I have ever been willing to do in my smaller attempts. I have seen a good half of the pieces played and as I recall their fullness on the stage, I see how you have known and recognized the rights of the theatre, and have had the self-denial to leave a great part of the effect to the performers.[4] At the same time you have written good literature; and something of this I shall wish to say when I come to write of the pieces in the long leisure of next summer at the sea-side.[5] I am reserving until that time, or perhaps until after that time, the reading of your essays on Drama,[6] for I would rather retrospectively than prospectively instruct myself from you in regard to your art. Perhaps if I read the essays before I wrote of your work I should more or less paraphrase your own ideas; and after one has come seventy, as I did the other day, one hates to do any sort of parroting. I wish if you could, you would still send me "Judah", which was the first play of yours, I saw and of which the impression still remains most vivid with my wife and myself.

I have to thank you again for your kindness about my poor little farces.[7] I realize myself that there is little or no chance for them in a four-act world. They will do as they have done to amuse the idleness and the intolerable leisure of young people of good society, or young people who wish to be of it, and fancy that my plays will help them.

I hope we shall certainly meet when you come back to America in the Fall.[8] It has been a great pleasure to make your acquaintance and I know you will not mind my calling myself,

Sincerely your friend,
W. D. Howells.

1. Howells had turned with renewed interest to Jones's works and he asked the playwright for all his published plays. See Howells to Jones, 30 December 1906 (Leeds University, England; *Life in Letters*, II, 232–33). Jones responded, 29 January 1907 (MH), by sending a complete set.

2. *Judah* (1890) was not then in print.

3. The play was *Michael and His Lost Angel* (1896). Although Jones too considered it one of his best, it was, as he said in his reply of 23 March 1907 (MH), "hooted on the first night, abased by all the leading London dailies, and ran ten nights." It contained a crucial and controversial scene, offensive to many, in which a priest publically confesses the sin of adultery before the altar. Jones recounted to Howells how Mrs. Patrick Campbell, after seven weeks of rehearsal, expressed her disapproval by withdrawing from the role of Audrie Lesden in the play, "and therefore schemed against it" and assured its demise.

4. Howells had commented pertinently on the subject of stage directions in his earlier letter to Jones: "The full stage direction was meant for part of the literature

in things to be read rather than seen. I entirely agree with you as to the ideal being no stage direction at all." See *Life in Letters*, II, 232.

5. Having recently reviewed *The Hypocrites* (1906) in a piece entitled "The Season's Plays. Three Different and Interesting Plays," *Harper's Weekly*, 24 November 1906, Howells wanted to do a more comprehensive study: "I should like to write of your whole drama .... You are now so well known to our whole public that a paper about you would be widely interesting." See *Life in Letters*, II, 232. The promised essay, "On Reading the Plays of Mr. Henry Arthur Jones," appeared in the *North American Review*, October 1907.

6. *The Renascence of the English Drama* (1895).

7. At Jones's encouragement, Howells was going to show his farces—his "commediettas," as he had modestly termed them—to a dramatic agent. See *Life in Letters*, II, 232. He was responding here to a further affirmation of their worth by Jones, 29 January 1907 (MH): "I am persuaded [that] if you had put the same quality of work into three and four act comedies they would have attained a very substantial measure of popular success on both sides of the Atlantic. But oneact pieces are of little account, and are scarcely in demand.... I think however these little pieces of yours ought to be constantly played by amateurs.... Is there anything I can do to advance their production on this side ... ?"

8. Jones came to the United States in the spring, stopping at Kittery Point, as Howells told Aurelia Howells, 23 June 1907 (MH), for an afternoon of "good talk."

13 MARCH 1907, NEW YORK, TO JOSEPH A. HOWELLS

Hotel Regent
March 13, 1907.

Dear Joe:

You interesting letters, with the charming fotografs, came Monday, and I wish I could write you anything half as nice by Saturday's steamer. First, let me say to Eliza that John says she does not need a "healer" for her eye trouble; she can help it herself by study of Mrs. Eddy's book, "Science and Health."[1] I am not a believer myself, but I will send her the book, and she can try. Faith is good in nervous matters, but in any positive ailment, I prefer a doctor.

I can imagine how lonely you are without Beatrice. I have not heard of her arrival at Jefferson which I suppose would follow as soon as possible after landing. If she is a fairly good sailor she must have had a delightful voyage to Philadelphia under the circumstances you describe. I went aboard a big collier once at K. P.,[2] and I never saw equal accommodations on a steamer. How pretty it was for people to call on her before she left, and bring her presents! I don't wonder you like your place. When she comes back to you she will be more contented, and I shall not give up the hope of some day seeing you in your island home, and sitting with you under your own crab and fig tree, with the mosquitoes pining for me overhead.

John got back from Bermuda in fine shape, and Pilla, after twenty different minds about going, sailed on Saturday last. We have not heard from her yet, but as her boat got in two hours ahead of time, I suppose she had a good voyage. It is among the barest of possibilities that Elinor and I may go at the end of the month when one of the large German steamers, a 9000 tonner, sails. Elinor thinks a ship of that size would hold her, and yet not rattle round with her, but I don't count much on her going.

As I remember, grandmother was born in Glamorganshire, Wales, and grandfather in Breconshire.[3] She was an orphan, you know, and the aunt and uncle who brought her up lived in Bristol, which is not far from Wales. I am glad you like the "English Towns."[4] I think it one of my smilingest books, and for a $3 book it has done very well. Until about this week, the English edition has been held up by a supposed violation of a fotografer's copyright, but it seems to be all right, now.

I return Mr. Venable's pleasant letter.[5] How many friendly friends you have! But in poor Nettie Kellogg,[6] I can realize that you have lost one of the best. She was one of the most charming women I ever met, and one of the most intelligent. Good she was, of course. It was a remarkable company of young people which we knew in Jefferson. If I were not too busy in the present, I could look back to that time and wish to be of it again. Perhaps somehow, somewhere, we shall meet all the lost once more, but it is best not try to make it out, for if we try to clutch our faith in it, it slips through our fingers.—The Appian Way in Cambridge led up from Brattle street almost abreast of the Washington Elm. You would not be apt to notice it. I never had any trouble in Sacramento street, that I should not count all joy now, if I could have back the long perspectives of hope that I had with it then.

They made something of an ado over my birthday in the papers, and I thought some of the poor fellows in their kindness to me, had robbed their standing obituary notices. However, if I live long enough, people will forget that they read something like it before. The Sun had a sunburst of praise for me right under the editorial head, and you saw what a broadside the Times gave me.[7] We think the fotograf in it is the best ever made of me in these latter days. Harper & Brothers wanted to give me a big dinner, but I begged off. My grippe kept me from going on to the Longfellow memorial at Cambridge,[8] and that gave Norton a chance to turn a little of the celebration in my direction. About 50 letters came, but I answered them by dictation, and now it is all over, and I have nothing to do but to live along.

I don't know how you feel in your age, but perhaps from our scrambling and impermanent life, things do not seem so settled as they did. I am aware of being physically weaker than I once was, and my work, which has always been so dear to me, is not so satisfactory, though it comes easier. I rattle it off at a great rate, but it does not delight me as it used to do, though now and then a little paper seems just as good as anything I ever did. I am still absent-minded, but I live more in the children, and less in myself, and Elinor does the same, though she is more severe with them, and treats John, in her criticism as if he were still a small boy. As she does not understand poetry as well as she does art, she is in more awe of Pilla. You may not know it but she is really conducting the Thaw trial,[9] and she lives only from the morning till the evening editions of the papers. She calls all the women concerned by their first names, and she knows just what Jerome and Delmas are at,[10] which is more than they do, half the time. I cannot agree with you about the killing of White. He was a bad fellow, but no man has a right to try, condemn and execute another on the word of a woman, who was probably lying, as Evelyn Thaw was.

The winter is dying hard. We have had a great many snows, but rain has washed away the last, now, and there is a sort of spring feeling in the air, which makes itself felt through a "thick o' fog" which could not be beaten at Kittery Point.

With our love to both of you,

> Your affectionate brother,
> Will.

Sam writes me that he has little or no hopes of his wife's recovery. She suffers dreadfully, and two months ago she looked wasted to a skeleton.[11] I am surprised she is still living. They have moved from the house where they lived when you saw them into an apartment where she can have steady and equal heat.

1. Mary Baker Eddy (1821–1910), founder of the Christian Science Movement, wrote *Science and Health* in 1875. John M. Howells had recently turned to Christian Science after severe problems with his own health had forced him to set aside his architectural work for several months. Howells seems to have taken "Madonna Eddy," as he characterized her to Joe, 3 February 1907 (MH), with a grain of salt.

2. Kittery Point.

3. Howells refers to Anne Thomas Howells and Joseph Howells.

4. *Certain Delightful English Towns.*

5. Probably William H. Venable (1836–1920), poet and author of *Beginnings of Literary Culture in the Ohio Valley* (1891) and *Buckeye Boyhood* (1911); but possibly Emerson Venable, his son, editor of *Poets of Ohio* (1910).

6. Nettie Kellogg, of Jefferson, was probably the daughter of Abner Kellogg. See Howells to Anne Howells, 20 June 1864, n. 1.

7. The "sunburst" in the New York *Sun,* 1 March 1907, appearing under the editorial banner, concluded: "Please, WILLIAM DEAN HOWELLS, do not look askance if this merely secular entity presumes to make a humble proffer of its respect and honor; and, if your indulgence will permit, of its sincere affection." The New York

Times of 24 February 1907 published both an article, "The Seventieth Birthday of America's Leading Novelist," and a photograph in the photogravure section.

8. See Howells to Norton, 2 February 1907, n. 3.

9. See Howells to J. A. Howells, 6 August 1906.

10. William T. Jerome (1859–1934) was the district attorney of New York City who conducted the prosecution of Harry K. Thaw for the murder of Stanford White. Delphin M. Delmas (1844–1928), New York attorney, was chief counsel for the defense in Thaw's first trial.

11. See Howells to Aurelia Howells, 30 December 1906, n. 2.

17 MARCH 1907, NEW YORK, TO BRAND WHITLOCK

Hotel Regent,
70th street, Boadway,
March 17, 1907.

My dear Whitlock:

I agree with your wife in whatever she may say of your book and its author, and this without waiting for your gift-copy, for the publishers sent me advance sheets a fortnight ago, and I have read it with the feeling you would both like me to have.[1] It came while I was still very weak from the grippe, and I had a dread of opening the package, for I knew the story would clutch me hard; and it did. Since The Octopus, there has been no novel so great, unless it is Resurrection,[2] which yours more favors through the resemblance which is natural from the subject. The Editor of the North American Review has let me write a paragraph about it for his Diary, where I treat of it as public event.[3] I cannot see how it will escape some such general recognition; it has already been seen in that light, even by the poor, purblind *Herald*. It will not make you friends—among the enemy, and that is a pity— for the enemy; but it will help you with the unhappy and the unfortu- nate, as it is our convention to call those who are not rich and powerful. In my paragraph I have been first to ask you the question which the enemy will ask you often enough, namely: how you make your personal convictions square with your official functions;[4] but this is a question which you need not answer me or them. My space and point of view forbade me to take note of the high artistic merit of the book, though I did get in something about its scope and grasp, and the infinity of detail which you make perform the effect of mass. I think that the work will set you where you belong, and I hope that this will not be on a merely literary eminence, which you do not care for. Think of your having done such a book when you are only a little more than half my age! I wish you would satisfy a curiosity I have as to what your local papers say of it, and would send me their notices.

With best regards to Mrs. Whitlock,

Yours affectionately,

P.S. Just what were those suits in which you forced the State of Ohio to the wall on certain points of municipal legislation?[5]

1. The book was Whitlock's novel *The Turn of the Balance* (1907). Howells praised it to Henry B. Fuller, 10 March 1907, favorably comparing it to Frank Norris' *The Octopus* (1901).

2. Tolstoy's *Resurrection* appeared in 1899.

3. Howells refers to David A. Munro, who was in effect managing editor although Colonel George Harvey's name appears on the masthead as editor. Howells' paragraph for "The Editor's Diary, Saturday, March 30," began: "There is now and then a book which, the reader feels, is rather a public event than a literary event, no matter what its literary importance may be, and such a book is the latest fiction from the pen of Mr. Brand Whitlock . . . ."

4. Whitlock, a lawyer and reformist, was then mayor of Toledo (1905–1913). *The Turn of the Balance* faithfully reflects his strong disapproval of the abuse of criminals by the courts and in the prisons, a representation he describes as "purposefully conservative" rather than exaggerated. See Whitlock, *Forty Years of It* (New York: D. Appleton & Co., 1914), p. 122.

5. On behalf of the previous mayor, the renowned and controversial "Golden Rule" Jones, Whitlock had won a suit reversing a state supreme court decision which, as Whitlock explains in *Forty Years of It*, "deprived the Mayor of Toledo of his control of the police force and vested the government of that body in a commission appointed by the governor of the state" (p. 135). In his review of *The Turn of the Balance*, Howells had been uncertain of the exact issue involved in the case, referring vaguely to Whitlock's legal triumph over the state of Ohio "on a point of municipal government."

6 APRIL 1907, NEW YORK, TO BRAND WHITLOCK

Hotel Regent,
April 6, 1907.

Dear Whitlock:

Thank you for the legal documents.[1] I find I was right in the reference I made to your case in my note on your book. You will see it in the current N. A. Review.

I return your notices, thinking you may like them back. They are uncommonly good.[2] It seems to me your book is destined to large if not direct effect.

Cannot you inspire some decent man to bring a bill into the legislature requiring the State to pay to a convict's family full wages for the work he does, after deducting a fair price for his board?[3] The present system of robbing his wife and children of his earnings is damnable, and a worse theft than any he could have committed.—I have touched on this point in a book supposing a visit to Altruria which I am just publishing—"Through the Eye of the Needle."[4]

Yours affectionately

W. D. Howells.

1. Whitlock had sent the documents in response to Howells' request for information about a legal suit Whitlock had won against the state of Ohio. See Howells to Whitlock, 17 March 1907, n. 5.

2. In his previous letter, Howells asked Whitlock to send him reviews from the local newspaper of *The Turn of the Balance*, Whitlock's latest novel.

3. In his reply, 8 April 1907 (CU), Whitlock says that "such a bill" would soon be introduced, apologizing that in his announcement of it to the press he had inadvertently mentioned Howells' name: "Among the newspapers I sent you today you will find one that will tell you how promptly I acted on your suggestion that the families of convicts be supported out of the wages the State steals from them. I regret that your name got into the story—though only out of fear that you may not like it. I am innocently to blame."

4. In his novel, Howells depicts the wonderment of the Altrurians upon hearing of the American prison system: "They thought it right that convicts should be made to work, but they could not understand that the state really took away their wages, and left their families to suffer for want of the support which it had deprived them of. They said this was punishing the mothers and sisters, the wives and children of the prisoners, and was like putting out the eyes of an offender's innocent relatives as they had read was done in Oriental countries." See *The Altrurian Romances*, HE, pp. 393–94.

15 APRIL 1907, NEW YORK, TO CHARLES E. NORTON

Hotel Regent,

April 15, 1907.

My dear Norton:

You will forgive me the typewriting because it is nearly as legible, though nothing can be so beautiful, as the handwriting that comes from your pen. You will merely have to add a little more forgiveness to that you owe me for having troubled you with my paper.[1] You have given it all the attention I could have wished if it had deserved more, and your strictures are very just. I think its fault mainly is that its characterizations are so scattering, as those of my Lowell paper were.[2] But, as in that, I have now assembled them for one impression, using your own words, though not as from you, for that full praise of Godkin which you thought his due.[3] I have given this as the sense of his Cambridge friends, rather than mine, though mainly I could join in it. But he was not the first, and not the only journalist to desire the elevation of our journalism. I had known beginnings of that sort even in the West, before ever I came East, and in the East I had seen something of them. I cannot believe that his influence went as far as his will in that direction; newspapers are not much swayed by one another: a strong man characterizes each of them, and his quality long remains with the journal he founded or formed.[4] After a generation, Bowlses's best remains with the Springfield Republican[5] which had not waited the Nation's appearance[6] to be a strong, rightminded, admirable newspaper, highprincipled and able for good.

I have cut out the reference to Dr. Holmes, and have softened the censure of the Nation that I used to hear from men I regarded highly; it was often more bitter than I began to report. I was myself very fond of Godkin, and had nothing but kindness from him, but I knew men quite as deserving of it, who had great harshness, and something more like contempt than should be used with much worse men. There two things I wanted to put in, but did not: Lowell's saying to me, when the Nation suggested his casting his electoral vote for Tilden, "Godkin seems to have lost his head,"[7] and Godkin's saying to me many years later, as if he wished me to take note of it, that *he* had not made that suggestion, but a man we both know (he named him) who had afterwards refused to father it, or let Godkin relieve himself of its putative paternity.—I wish you had said why you wished my paragraph about Cambridge out. Was it undignified, to your thinking, or did it seem to bring me too much in?[8]

There is little to tell you of myself. I am well of my grippe long ago, but sensibly the weaker for it. The story I read you was printed in Harper's Weekly during last December,[9] and I have worked at odd times during the winter on a longish, slowish sort of New England Idyl which I call "The Children of the Summer."[10] Since I left off working at it the thing has taken reasoned shape in my mind, and I fancy your liking it. Then in the midst of all, I have given my own dream of Utopia, which I fancy your not liking, unless for its confessions of imperfections even in Utopia. All other dreamers of such dreams have had nothing but pleasure in them; I have had touches of nightmare. I call the thing "Through the Eye of the Needle," and it is to be published soon.[11]

It grieves me to hear that you are feeling your age, but I will not pretend an indecent unbelief in the fact. We do grow old, and we feel it, and nothing vexes me more than to have some younger man pretend that we do neither. But happily we do not always feel old. I have moments of being, say, fifty, but not much younger. The spring will do something for us both, if it ever reaches us.

I miss Aldrich out of the world rather than out of my world. We were for more than half our lives companions, and much of his work I thought beautiful, but we were never close intimates. With whom is one really and truly intimate? I am pretty frank, and I seem to say myself out to more than one, now and again, but only in this sort to one, and that sort to another. I should have liked to pay Aldrich the last honor I could pay him unknowing, and I lay awake long the night of his funeral, wishing that I had gone on to it at any risk.[12] I am glad that as a poet he made an exit so noble as that in his Longfellow poem.[13]

I am glad that Lily[14] is well again, and I send my love to you all.

Yours affectionately,
W. D. Howells.

1. "A Great New York Journalist," *North American Review*, 3 May 1907. It is an assessment of Edwin L. Godkin in the guise of a review of Rollo Ogden's *Life and Letters of Edwin L. Godkin* (1907). Howells had sent the essay to Norton, 12 April 1907 (MH), asking him if he would please take the trouble to "note any errors upon it." For Howells' relationship to Godkin and the *Nation*, see Cady, *Howells*, I, 116–20.

2. "Studies of Lowell," in *Literary Friends and Acquaintance*, first appeared as "A Personal Retrospect of James Russell Lowell," *Scribner's*, September 1900.

3. In returning the essay, 14 April 1907 (MH), Norton's chief criticism was that Howells had not done justice to Godkin's adherence to "principles of good government & of public morals" in the editorship of the *Nation*: "He did more to influence public opinion & to give right direction to it for many years than any other man. He raised the general level of editorial writing throughout the United States. As a journalist he was in a class by himself. He was the only 'all round' editor in New York; the only one who deserved to be called 'great'. Others may have been his superior in particulars, but in the combination of intellectual power, moral integrity & courage, trained intelligence, knowledge of mankind, devotion to public ends, capacity of clear statement & of well reasoned argument,—he had a solitary pre-eminence."

4. In his reply of 16 April 1907 (MH), Norton affectionately expressed his amusement at Howells' resistance: "The letter which I received from you this morning is an admirable illustration of a delightful character. You accept my comments on your article on Mr. Godkin, but are not convinced of their correctness. [¶] I doubt whether I desire that you should be." Reiterating at length his sense of Godkin's worth, Norton concluded: "But why should I argue with you in a matter in which we should agree and disagree to the end?"

5. Under the direction of Samuel Bowles, Jr. (1826–1878), the Springfield *Republican*, founded as a weekly by his father Samuel Bowles (1797–1851), became a daily with a politically independent voice and national reputation.

6. The *Nation* was started in 1865, with Norton playing a prominent role by raising funds in the Boston area to help finance the New York weekly. Godkin served as editor from its inception until 1881. Norton's strong feelings are better understood in the context of his warm relationship with Godkin, who wrote shortly after the journal was launched that Norton was "the only man in the whole body of projectors with whom I know I am in thorough sympathy." See *Letters of Charles Eliot Norton*, ed. S. Norton and M. A. De Wolfe Howe (Boston: Houghton Mifflin, 1913), I, 283.

7. See Howells to Lowell, 4 December 1876, n. 1.

8. In his reply of 16 April, Norton explained the suggested deletion, one apparently indicated on the manuscript without comment: "It seemed to me trivial and to re-

duce the scale from the national to the petty provincial. It was of a great national and public character that you were writing, and it was a pity to bring down his measure as if it were to be affected by the gossiping criticism of any single community. But enough. I dare say I love you all the more because of your differing from me in your estimate of men."

9. "A Sleep and a Forgetting."

10. The "New England Idyl," first conceived by Howells in the mid-1870s, was published posthumously as *The Vacation of the Kelwyns* (1920).

11. Ever skeptical of utopian schemes, Norton wrote to Howells, 24 and 31 August 1907 (MH), that he was about to read the novel: "I have at my side now 'Through the Eye of the Needle', and this afternoon I propose to see what vision that narrow opening affords of a better life than is lived today, and what fair dreams of the future the best dreamer that I know has to tell. I am afraid that I shall listen to them with more sympathy than hope or conviction; but I know that at the end I shall care for the dreamer more than ever." Having read the novel, he wrote again, 2 and 5 October 1907 (MH): "The insight, the wit, the humor, the tenderness, the sarcasm, the sweetness of the book touched me deeply,—you speak in it in your own voice. It is all rather a story of your thoughts & heart, than a romance of others' lives. But I do not find your Altruria more delightful & alluring than any of the other Utopias. I have never found one in which I should like to live, nor have I ever dreamed one which seemed attractive to me after waking. [¶] But I am one at heart with you in respect to our actual society, & would conspire with you to shatter it to bits if only I could hope it could be 'remoulded nearer to the heart's desire.' "

12. Having just recovered from influenza, Howells could not travel to Boston for Aldrich's funeral on 22 March.

13. Howells had written to Thomas B. Aldrich, 6 February 1907 (MH), praising the poem which Aldrich was to have read at the Longfellow commemoration, as "classically perfect, and exquisitely fit." Not knowing Aldrich would soon die from a relapse following surgery, Howells had added: "Dear old fellow, live long, and do more such, for you can, it seems, whenever you will." The poem, simply entitled "Longfellow," was Aldrich's last work and was read as a tribute at his own funeral.

14. Elizabeth G. Norton.

31 JULY 1907, KITTERY POINT, TO MILDRED HOWELLS

...Kittery Point, Maine July 31, 1907.[1]

Dear Pilla:

I gave up Mrs. Aldriching[2] this afternoon for fear it might keep me from getting off another letter to you, and now I have nothing to say, and can only send you more and more love. You are going to have the happiest time in the world[3] because you deserve it, and if you don't *I* do. Emmer and I have just had a dismal cup of tea together, and I am going to take these letters to the post to make sure of their going with specials on, and to get some limes, so the tea to-morrow won't be so lemon-sour. You will be taking it at the same hour from the tray of the deck-steward! Drop a tear into the cup for your fond

*Poppy.
*tear-drop

1. Howells, Elinor, and Mildred had left New York for Kittery Point on 5 June.

2. Howells seems to have contemplated a visit with Mrs. Lillian Woodman Aldrich, recently widowed by the death of Thomas B. Aldrich on 19 March. The Aldrich home was in Portsmouth, across the Piscataqua River from Kittery Point.

3. In a letter to Aurelia Howells of 28 July 1907 (MH), Howells wrote that Mildred had made last-minute plans to sail for England on 1 August for "a six weeks' burst" with two friends.

2 AUGUST 1907, KITTERY POINT, TO FREDERICK A. DUNEKA

. . . Kittery Point, Maine Aug. 2, 1907.

Dear Mr. Duneka:

My family think this picture particularly malevolent and devilish in expression. I know that my son took it in the villa garden at San Remo,[1] but his Kodak was in a mood of fatal sincerity. If you are going to advertise "Th. the E. of the N."[2] any more, will you please use the last and best photo. I have had taken, which I enclose, and which falsely represents me bland, benevolent and blameless, with a mouth in which butter would not melt.[3] You have the picture.

Yours sincerely
W. D. Howells.

1. See the photograph on p. 225. Howells stayed at San Remo, Italy, in late 1904 and early 1905.

2. *Through the Eye of the Needle* had come out on 18 April.

3. See the frontispiece to this volume.

18 AUGUST 1907, DETROIT, TO JOSEPH A. HOWELLS

Hotel Cadillac, . . .
Detroit, Michigan. August 18, 1907.

Dear Joe:

I have not got the letterwriting properly started yet, and I'm rather firing this at random.—Elinor & I left home on the 9th, and met John at Buffalo; he was on his way to the Yellowstone Park, and we took the big steamer "Northwest," and went as far as Duluth with him. We parted Tuesday night, the 13th, and started back on the same boat. But the water out of Lake Erie had been so vile, that half the passengers and crew had come down with diarrhoea. When we reacht here, day before yesterday, we stopt for a rest, and repairs. We seem to be all right again,

W. D. Howells in San Remo, 1904–1905

and expect to start on tomorrow, and fetch up at K. P. on Wednesday. In spite of the diarrhoea, E. considers this the greatest trip of her life.[1] She is in love with the whole lake region, and has ended a devoted adorer of Detroit. We took a motorcar this p.m. and saw the whole place, including Belle Isle Park, which certainly beats Central P.—It has been a journey of happy surprises. Lake Erie was warm and damp as the Gulf Stream, but L. Superior cold as "off the Banks."[2]—The boat, except for the bad water, was fine, and the people were all pleasant, with a difference from Easterners which was not *un*pleasant.—Marquette is splendid, and Mackinac Island a dream of beauty. The lake craft are all interesting and strange—especially the big freighters. I hope we shall find letters from you at home.—E. joins me in love to both of you.—John will stay through September in the Yellowstone.

Your aff'te brother
Will.

1. Howells, too, was enthusiastic. He described the Great Lakes voyage in a letter to Charles E. Norton, 22 August 1907 (MH): "It has been a prodigious, a continental experience, from which we scantly escaped poisoning by the filthy water on the steamer; but having got home alive, we look back on the Northwest with wonder. It was as if we had never seen the world before. But it was the primitive world, with all the geologic agencies at work for the mine-owners and shipowners. The *scale* was inexpressibly vast. A car full of coal was picked up, as if it might have been a cup, emptied into a ship, and set back on the rails as if nothing had happened. The beauty of the region is as great as its strength; but it is savage beauty yet, with a sort of lust for civilization." Howells undertook the week-long trip because he thought it would "do Elinor good" and give him a needed break from work. See Howells to Aurelia Howells, 6 August 1907 (MH).
2. The Grand Banks off the coast of Newfoundland.

22 SEPTEMBER 1907, KITTERY POINT, TO CHARLES E. NORTON

Kittery Point, Sept. 22, 1907.

Dear Norton:

I was glad to know that you were better, from the letter I got on my way to spend Miss Jewett's birthday at Mrs. Fields's.[1] I put it in my pocket, and read it on the train, where its gentle literary and human interest[2] was not more at odds with the mechanical clatter than with the noisy interests to which my senescence seems given over, in this exasperating summer. I think much of the exasperation has come to me from the pestiferous motor-boats which infest these waters, but I begin to suspect that I have all my life been myself equipped with an unmuffled exhaust, and that I have gone thumping through the years at a rate which is at last making me feel shattered.

I found Mrs. Fields looking pathetically but prettily old, and very little; Miss Jewett quite stately beside her, and none the worse finally for being thrown from a carriage two years ago.[3]—The remnants of the past are not less sad than the things that are quite vanished, but I do not know how matters are to be otherwise ordered, and on the whole I am cheered by the fact that I am not divine providence. I am also imbibing a moral fortitude from my midnightly perusals of Boswell's Johnson. What a comfortable century the eighteenth was! And how pleasant to have been born when you could be logically certain of so many vexing uncertainties. The robustious arrogance of Johnson's piety is immensely supporting; and perhaps he was not so far wrong about us in his patriotism.—A strange thing is that I am recurring in this dry wood to the literary period which delighted me in the green. What a lot I read, how much I knew, before I was twenty!

Well, this summer is ending, and the New York winter threatens before us.—Our present great little excitement is Pilla's return, which we expect on Wednesday. She has had a famous time in England.

I shall see you, surely on our way through Boston.

Your affectionate
W. D. Howells.

1. Norton's letter, 24 and 31 August 1907 (MH), explained that he had been confined for a considerable time by what he termed "a slight attack" of cystitis. On 4 September 1907 (MH), Howells wrote to Mildred, who was on an extended tour of England, that he had gone to Annie A. Fields to observe Sarah Orne Jewett's birthday: "Yesterday I went down to Manchester, and lunched with Dame Fields, to celebrate Miss Jewett's 180th (as she claimed) birthday. We had a good time, and offered up many friends, mainly K. D. W. Riggs, whose outrageous sellingness was more that [sic] S. O. J. and I could bear." It was Jewett's fifty-eighth birthday. Kate Douglas Wiggin, married in 1895 to George C. Riggs, had authored her best-selling *Rebecca of Sunnybrook Farm* in 1903.

2. Norton wrote that his confinement had allowed him to spend "much time with Shakespeare and other poets," describing at length his responses to a whole range of English and French poetry he had been reading.

3. Jewett's accident had occurred five years earlier, on her fifty-third birthday, 2 September 1902. Her horse slipped going downhill and she was thrown from the carriage, sustaining a spinal concussion with accompanying headaches and weaknesses which effectively ended her literary career. See *Sarah Orne Jewett Letters*, ed. Richard Cary (Waterville, Me.: Colby College Press, 1967), p. 151.

3 OCTOBER 1907, NEW YORK, TO SAMUEL L. CLEMENS

> *Hotel Calumet ...*
> *New York.* Oct. 3, 1907.

Dear Clemens:

I saw Harvey yesterday, and he said you were wondering the last time he met you why you never heard from me: so here goes. I would come to see you, for I understand you are now an elderly man, while I still feel my green oats. But you are in Tuxedo,[1] and I cannot go there, for I have only a day or two before returning to Kittery Point.

I have had a busy summer, except for a health excursion which my wife and I took on the lakes, and which we were kept busy getting well from for a month afterwards.[2] We went by that boat which had the poisonous water on board, and we drank the dregs of Buffalo for three days. This gave us all "summer complaint," and several of us typhoid fever, from which we died.

Part of my work has been revising Venetian Life ("Days," you call it; but I must beg to differ) so as to renew the dying copyright.[3] It was rather sickening work. Lord, how I did stand round, when I wrote that book! It is a good, kind, inattentive world, or I should never have escaped with my life.

Frank Millet was at the Club last night,[4] and he said he had lately been visiting the people who have your old Hartford house. What memories his say conjured up! I pass it along to you, for I think it does you good to suffer. If not, Litt. D., Oxon, cure thyself.[5]

Pilla was in England August and September, batting round with two other girls, and having a great time. She declined the chance of going with John to the Yellowstone.

I hope your girls are well. Remember an old friend to them, and to Miss Lyon.[6]

> Yours ever
> W. D. Howells.

1. Tuxedo Park, New York, an exclusive residential and resort village developed in 1886, is located in the Ramapo Mountains near the New Jersey state line.

2. See Howells to J. A. Howells, 18 August 1907.

3. Howells had revised *Venetian Life*, originally published by Hurd & Houghton in 1867, for reissue by the Riverside Press, in order, as he complained to Aurelia Howells, 30 June 1907 (MH), "to keep it in amended form from the pirates who can have it when the copyright is out next year." Explaining the nature of the revisions to George H. Mifflin, 16 June 1907 (MH), he said that because the original intention of writing "introductory paragraphs" for each chapter would be "a cumbrous impertinence," he had decided instead to "write one full, autobiographical chapter at the beginning" (subsequently entitled "Author to the Reader"). He also added one new chapter,

"Venice Revisited." See Gibson-Arms, *Bibliography*, p. 59. For Clemens' misnaming of the title, see Howells to Clemens, 1 August 1906.

4. The meeting with Francis D. Millet took place at the Century Club.

5. Clemens had received an honorary doctor of letters from Oxford University on 26 June.

6. Isabel V. Lyon (1868–1958), Clemens' secretary (1903–1909).

6 OCTOBER 1907, KITTERY POINT, TO JOSEPH A. HOWELLS

. . . Kittery Point, Maine Oct. 6, 1907.

Dear Joe:

I got home from New York last evening, after a three days' absence,[1] and found John here. He is full of Yellowstone Park, but it would be no use my trying to write what he tells of its wonders. His last month was entirely at Colorado Springs, and spent in daily horse-rides, so that he is in prime condition. He will be with us till next week, and I will try to make him write you, but he is a reluctant scribe. Pilla got home the 25th of September, very well, and very happy in her Welsh and English sojourn. She was mainly in Wales, which she loves. She went to the Hay, and revered the place for father's sake and found it beautiful for its own. She loved the Welsh, though she owns they are not neat.

And now what do you think? We are all, except John, going for the winter to Rome! Our plan is to sail about Dec. 1st,[2] for Naples, and stay in Rome till Easter, and then go up to Genoa and sail for Plymouth, England, on a new line of steamers, getting back to K. P. about July 1st. It will get over the New York problem, until we can house ourselves in the studio-apartment which I've bought on 57th st., but which is now only a hole in the ground, and will be a hole in the air next May. We have one vast room 18 or 19 feet high, and the rest of the flat divides the hight into ten or twelve smaller rooms. It sounds costly, but the rent comes to less than the interest on the price, for the ap'ts of the stockholders are only about a third of the whole number, the rents of the others paying all the running expenses. Some time I'll explain more fully.—We can live and travel round in Europe for less than staying still in a New York hotel, or a hired flat; and I can do my work as well or better in Rome. Harpers are enthusiastically willing.[3]— Our going up the lakes was a lark, to see John off from Duluth, Elinor being what she calls "bully well," the past summer. She had read your Salt Cay letter,[4] with a pleasure I shared when she brought it to me last night. It was mighty well done.—*I* hear from Sam, poor wretch, only too often, for it costs me $10 or $12 every time. The Randalls do nothing for him. He and Ethel are living in a $25 flat; she is earning nothing

and he works half time.[5] So some one has to pay. But this is an old story.—
We shall be here till November, and perhaps later. With love from all
to both of you,

Your aff'te brother
Will.

1. Howells had traveled to New York to discuss with Harper & Brothers the
possibility of a "Roman holiday," as he termed it in a letter to Frederick A. Duneka,
2 October 1907 (Arms), under contractual terms similar to those negotiated for his
English travels in 1904. See also Howells to Aurelia Howells, 12 January 1908, n. 1.

2. The sailing was postponed until early January 1908 because of the unexpected
announcement of John Howells' engagement and prospective wedding in December.
See Howells to Aurelia Howells, 22 November 1907.

3. Amused by Colonel Harvey's instant approval of the "Roman idea," Howells
wrote to Mildred, 4 October 1907 (MH), that "in fact there is a sort of enthusiasm at
Franklin Square to have me out of the country."

4. Joseph A. Howells had described the production of salt from seawater on the
Turks Islands, as part of a series of "Letters from the Editor" in the Ashtabula
Sentinel.

5. A month later, on 3 November 1907 (MH), Howells wrote to Aurelia Howells
that Jessie, one of Sam's daughters, who appears to have been married to a policeman, had taken in Sam as a boarder. "I am to contribute $25 a month; Sam gives
up his printing-office job, and as his son-in-law drives a police patrol wagon, we may
yet see Sam conveying van loads of insolvent debtors to prison . . . ." Ethel was another of Sam's several daughters, and the Randalls were, most likely, the family of
Sam's daughter Florence.

9 OCTOBER 1907, KITTERY POINT, TO BRANDER MATTHEWS

Kittery Point, Oct. 9, 1907.

My dear Matthews:

I had read other essays in your book with that glow and lift which my
liking for all your work wins me; and now I have read your capital
paper on Literature in the New Century.[1] I agree with it so perfectly
that I do not see why I did not write it, except that I could not. I
promise myself the pleasure of reading everything in the volume.—I always read anything of yours that I come upon by chance, and enjoy it,
tho' my age and my make are against my telling you so.

I like the new spelling in your new book, and am glad of your
courage, and your publisher's.[2] I doubt if Franklin Square would be
as brave; and as to my Easy Chair paper on that or any other subject,
I think a collection is far off. The multitude of my books makes me
ashamed; I shun rather than seek adding to it.

I scarcely know how to say what I must about the Cooper Committee,
or my joining it.[3] So far as I have been able to read his books I do not

care for him. I do not feel him true to his time and place, whether he inhabited them or imagined them. As an artist I thoroly disrespect him. What business, then, have I in that galère, though all others praise him? Get me excused on any dishonest pretext you can.

Yours ever

W. D. Howells.

P. S. Say that I dislike letting my name go where my hand cannot. That sounds well.

1. First presented at the International Congress of Arts and Sciences in St. Louis, 24 September 1904, "Literature in the New Century" was published in a collection of Matthews' essays entitled *Inquiries and Opinions* (1907). It defines four major nineteenth-century "legacies" at work in modern writing: "the scientific spirit," "the spread of democracy," "the assertion of nationality," and "that stepping across the confines of language and race, for which we have no more accurate name than 'cosmopolitanism.' "

2. See Howells to Roosevelt, 26 August 1906, n. 2.

3. It is possible that a committee had been formed to get James Fenimore Cooper elected to the Hall of Fame at New York University. On 8 August 1907 Matthews had delivered a speech honoring the American novelist during the week-long centenary celebration of the incorporation of Cooperstown, New York; and Edmund C. Stedman's "Poe, Cooper and the Hall of Fame" was published in the *North American Review*, August 1907. For Howells' disparagement of Cooper's upper-class European biases, see "Editor's Easy Chair," *Harper's Monthly*, December 1908.

13 OCTOBER 1907, KITTERY POINT, TO CHARLES E. NORTON

Kittery Point, Oct. 13, 1907.

My dear Norton:

Miss Theodora may have told you of our potential Europeanization this winter.[1] The thing is not quite settled yet, but it is very probable—probable to the point of choosing steamers and staterooms, with the privilege of drawing back in time to stay in New York for the next six months.

In revising Venetian Life for the new editions this summer,[2] the old wine got into my brain, and I began to dream of Italy once more, with such effect that I babbled in my sleep to Harpers of it. They agreed so joyously and instantly that we are now all but booked for Naples on the *Republic*, sailing Nov. 30. But long before that I promise myself a long day with you at Cambridge. We go up to Boston at the end of this month, and you will see me soon after, for all I now know.

It has been on my conscience, ever since I read the proof of my Longfellow address for your Historical Society's record, to tell you that the shape you insisted on my giving it was far better than that I stubbornly stood out for.[3] The paper as printed in the North American, would have been wholly out of keeping with the occasion, and I like it so little that I shall not reprint it at all, even in a "complete edition" of my interminable works. I was very much bedevilled by nervous exhaustion, and staring-eyed tasks before me, last winter, or I should have seen and said at once that you were right. I hope it isn't too late now to give you my thanks.

Yesterday the robins came back and pretended it was April, and made me hate to go. But today they and I are of a different mind, and Rome seems not so far away, especially with England in the background, where Pilla left her heart on every hedgerow this summer. With our love to you all.

Yours affectionately
W. D. Howells.

1. See Howells to J. A. Howells, 6 October 1907, n. 1.
2. See Howells to Clemens, 3 October 1907, n. 3.
3. For the disagreement over Howells' Longfellow address, see Howells to Norton, 30 January and 2 February 1907.

29 OCTOBER 1907, KITTERY POINT, TO WILLIAM R. THAYER

...Kittery Point, Maine Oct. 29, 1907.

Dear Mr. Thayer:

I knew that Mr. Norton was nearing his eightieth birthday, but I was instinctively putting it off some years longer, and it needed your reminder to make me realize that it fell next month.[1] Whatever his age, there was something in the early maturity of his powers which keeps him enduringly young; the keen insight, the critical acumen, the generous sympathy, remain undimmed, unblunted, unchilled.

For me he is the golden era of that golden prime which we Americans shall not see renewed in the count of many centuries. While he lives, Emerson and Hawthorne, Longfellow and Lowell, Whittier and Holmes are not lost to the consciousness of any who knew them; the Cambridge, the Boston, the New England, the America which lived in them, has not yet passed away. He was not only the contemporary, the companion of these great men; he was their fellow-citizen in those highest things, in which we may be his if we will, for the hospitality of his welcome will not be wanting. Something Athenian, something Florentine, something essentially republican and democratic in the culture common to them all has had its especial effect in him through that temperamental beneficence, that philanthrophy in a peculiar sense, so characteristic of him. I suppose he never met any man without wishing to share with him the grace of his learning, the charm of his wisdom, the light of his knowledge of the world; but this is poorly suggestive of the pervasive influence of his personal precept and example, which only those whose lives it shaped could duly witness of.

The future is of better augury because of the past which unites with the present in him, and remains ours in the highest and best things.

Yours sincerely
W. D. Howells.

1. Norton's birthday was 16 November. Thayer, editor of the *Harvard Graduates' Magazine*, had solicited testimonial letters for publication in the December 1907 issue in honor of Norton. He also collected the letters beforehand in a little book which he presented to Norton on his birthday. See *Letters of Charles Eliot Norton*, ed. S. Norton and M. A. De Wolfe Howe (Boston: Houghton Mifflin, 1913), II, 387–88. In a cover letter of the same date (MH), Howells explained to Thayer that the request had come to him "in a stress of work and hurry which has not allowed me to say a hundredth part of what I would of Norton." Anticipating the deluge of letters Norton would receive, Howells did not personally write him until 15 December 1907 (MH): "I am sure you forgave me a little for writing to the Harvard Graduates Magazine about it, and a good deal for not writing to you: I took it so kindly of people who did not tell me, when I became seventy, that they were glad of it."

21 NOVEMBER 1907, NEW YORK, TO S. WEIR MITCHELL

Hotel Regent,[1]
Nov. 21, 1907.

My dear Mitchell:

It is delightful to hear from you, even if you are laid up with a game leg. But you are either very ungrateful, or you do not know how handsomely I have written of you in the November Atlantic.[2] I counted on your liking it, and it was a subdued disappointment to find you, even so gratifyingly, concerned with some thing else of my doing.[3] I wonder you do not put me out of your scientific door;[4] but I must say for myself that an honest man and no thief had found his way, however blunderingly, on your premises. "A Sleep and a Forgetting," was founded with almost no fundamental change on a case I knew intimately in the Adirondacks eighteen years ago. I should like immensely to tell you about it. "The Eidolons"[5] sprang from an experience of mine; "The Memory that worked Overtime," was me, too, save for the love business. Do send me—or far, far better, bring me—the Miss Reynolds case.[6]—We are fixed here till we sail for Naples, Jan'y 4th,[7] expecting to pass the winter in Rome. When you come, I can give you the worst lunch in New York; and that is saying much in these cold storage days. Let me know an hour before so that I can make sure of it.—We are, as a family, much excited by my son's engagement; we had counted on his being a bachelor, he had been one ever since he was born.—Last night I did what I seldom do now: I went to man's dinner at a club. It was excellent company, but how grotesque such a feed-fest is, and I once thought it divine. It gave me a bad night, for I suffer from gas in the stomach, which I expel with Vesuvian eructations, and I had dreams not even worthy of literature. The night before I had a dream of being at Franklin Square in my night-gown and doubting whether I should be allowed in the subway coming back. Mark Twain was at the dinner in his white flannels, and at first sight of him I felt as if I had come in my nighty, again.—I sat next Burlingame,[8] and half the dinner through we tried to think of the famous old hotel at Albany where people used to stop, going to Saratoga and Lake George. Ah! *Delevan House*, my wife has just told me! Now I shall write to B. as if I had remembered it myself. Will you give my best respects to Mrs. Mitchell?

> Yours affectionately
> W. D. Howells.

Very few people get a letter of this length out of me. But you are Weir Mitchell and you are lame.

1. The Howellses had left Kittery Point on 30 October and, as usual, stopped over in Boston before going on to New York.

2. Mitchell had written 19 November 1907 (PU), apparently not yet having seen Howells' "Recollections of an Atlantic Editorship," *Atlantic Monthly*, November 1907. In the essay Howells recalls the strong impression made upon him by Mitchell's early fiction: "From the first there was something equally attractive to me in his mystic, his realistic, and his scientific things, perhaps because they were all alike scientific."

3. Mitchell said he had been reading Howells' psychological stories in *Between the Dark and the Daylight*.

4. Referring to the heroine in "A Sleep and a Forgetting," Mitchell had characterized her loss of memory as scientifically unique in his experience as an alienist: "...I never saw a case of loss of all memorial records of the past in which there was a disorder of memory as to immediately recent events—my cases lost all memory but were as keenly reminiscent of the new things as anyone."

5. "The Eidolons of Brooks Alford."

6. The Miss Reynolds case is mentioned, but not explained, by Mitchell in the context of "A Sleep and a Forgetting."

7. John M. Howells' upcoming marriage had delayed the departure for Italy. See Howells to Aurelia H. Howells, 22 November 1907.

8. Edward L. Burlingame, the editor of *Scribner's*.

22 NOVEMBER 1907, NEW YORK, TO AURELIA H. HOWELLS

Hotel Regent,
Nov. 22, 1907.

Dear Aurelia:

I do not know whether I have told you that John is engaged to be married.[1] His betrothed is a very pretty and charming girl, Abby, the daughter of Horace White, one of the editors and owners of the New York Evening Post.[2] She is a dark beauty, very slim, and about Pilla's height. He met her here at dinner last winter, and seems to have been increasingly in love with her ever since. They are to be married either the middle or end of December; and the marriage has caused the postponement of our sailing to January 4th. There does not seem much more to say, except that it is very exciting to us all. She is 28 years old, and John is 39.—You must tell Annie all about this. I am glad John is to be married, and so are we all, though we can no longer have him to ourselves, as it seemed we always should. He needs some one in his life closer than we can come, and this girl seems amiable and good, and comes of good people. Her father is fairly well off, and he likes John, because, as he told him, he was "a man of character." I have known him, not very well, a long time, but we have only just made Abby's acquaintance, though Pilla met her in Paris.

With love from all

Your affectionate brother
Will.

1. The wedding was held on 21 December. In a letter to Aurelia, 22 December 1907 (MH; *Life in Letters*, II, 246–47), Howells described the ceremony held in the chapel John had designed for Columbia University: "The wedding took place on the sunniest kind of yesterday, in John's beautiful chapel, and was worthy of the day and place. The bride and groom bore themselves with great dignity, and the two families looked on with entire complacency. No one else was present except Abby's old nurse and maid, our colored Charles, a creature built of mauve velvet; the wife of the Bishop Coadjutor who married the pair, John's partner and his wife, two girl friends of Abby's and Mary Mead. Then the two families went to the bride's late home and gorged themselves at the wedding breakfast. A pretty part of it was the bride's running round in the vestry with her white prayer book, collecting the signatures of the witnesses, including the velvety Charles."

2. Horace White (1834–1916) was co-owner of the *Post* with Henry Villard and coeditor with Carl Schurz and Edwin L. Godkin. After Schurz's resignation in 1892 and Godkin's retirement in 1899, White became editor-in-chief, himself retiring in 1903. He was also a respected economist and Greek scholar, publishing books on both subjects.

13 DECEMBER 1907, NEW YORK, TO FREDERICK A. DUNEKA

Hotel Regent . . .
New York City Dec. 13, 1907.

My dear Duneka:

I am against a snag, again. An abominable English-woman has named her accursed book, "Rue with a Difference."[1] So I must change. Here are some Hobson's choices:

———————

I   His Rue with a Difference
                (Very Howellsy)
II   Rue, even for Ruth.
                (Too explicit.)
III   A Sorry Remembrance.
                (Repellant?)
IV   Here's Rosemary.
                (Good and picquant.)
V   Rosemary, that's for Remembrance.
                (pretty good.)
VI   Rosemary for Remembrance.
                (Best?)

———————

I like the last best, and the first next best. The fourth is the freshest.

Yours sincerely
W. D. Howells.

1. Rosa Nouchette Carey (1840–1909), writer of sentimental novels, published *Rue with a Difference* in 1901. Howells' novel eventually was given the title *Fennel and Rue* (1908).

20 DECEMBER 1907, NEW YORK, TO AUGUSTUS THOMAS

Hotel Regent,
Sherman Square
Dec. 20, 1907.

Dear Mr. Thomas:

You may well believe that with my passion for the psychological I was intensely interested yesterday in your most uncommon play.[1] I believe I am not of a Southern preference in civilization, and I did not care so much for your people as Kentuckians, though I thought them wonderfully well found; but as human beings, of like mystical experiences with myself, I embraced them brothers and sisters. The whole subjectivity of the thing was most impressive, most instructive, and the skill and force with which it was externated formed a pass beyond anything yet in your fine drama.[2]

Yours sincerely
W. D. Howells.

1. *The Witching Hour* was first produced on 18 November 1907 in New York at the Hackett Theatre, where Howells had probably seen a recent performance. The psychological theme of the play, based on earlier experiences Thomas had had with thought reader Washington Irving Bishop, concerned the influencing of minds by the power of suggestion.
2. Howells had previously reviewed some of Thomas' plays in "The Recent Dramatic Season," *North American Review*, March 1901, and "Some New American Plays," *Harper's Weekly*, 16 January 1904.

12 JANUARY 1908, ON BOARD M.S. "CARONIA," TO AURELIA H. HOWELLS

Cunard R.M.S "Caronia"
Between Madeira and Gibraltar,
Jan'y 12, 1908.

Dear Aurelia:

We have had a quite faultless voyage, out of winter into summer, which had an exquisite climax yesterday at Madeira.[1] We came in sight of the island Saturday p.m., and its forms and colors quickly grew upon us; tremendous mountains, terraced as far up as the eye could follow into the clouds, and misted almost to their feet. The cliffs were oftenest a dull red, and where steepest were overhung with what lookt like long gray moss. Every little plateau was dotted over with white houses, and vineyards and sugar-cane fields covered with the dense green of the last and the brown fibres of the first. When we came to Funchal, the chief place, the landscape was of the simplest elements: the straight lines of the red roofs, white walls and green terraces. Here and there was a great splotch of red flowers on a house front or garden wall, and there was an old fort, very gray and medieval, and some larger public buildings, with big hotels, all fraying out up the mountains into villas and cottages. There is hardly a level foot of ground on the island, or seems so, but you can stand fairly well, sidewise. Many passengers went ashore for the night, but we waited till morning, and then we had a full half day of it. The town is like a hundred little Italian cities that I have seen, and the race type is very Italian, too, with a windy rise in the men's voices like the gondoliers'. A good many vessels were lying in the roadstead, with a lead-colored Portuguese war ship. We stopped at a fine stone pier with our launch, and escaped from a guide to take a trolley up to the station of the funicular railroad that climbs the mountain. There, at the top we lookt into a little country church, throngs of us passengers, and waited for the worshippers to come out; they had all mild, kind faces, and the women almost the gentlest that I have seen. They had no costumes but wore kerchiefs of red and yellow over their heads. The children everywhere heapt us with flowers and beg'd of us.— We went from the church to breakfast at one of the charming hotels, and had a delicious meal of fish cookt in tomato sauce and onions, eggs dropt on new peas, cutlets servd with stringbeans and coffee. Then came the great sensation of the day and of Madeira: tobogganing down the cobble-stone mountain road in basket sleds held back by a man at each side with ropes. We all three got into one, so as to die together—Elinor's constant ideal—and had a most delightful descent. The stones were fine, and the toboggans rode the little ridges without a jar. Our men were what one of them calld in his English "very strongs mans," and they held us back securely, for perhaps 2 miles. Then we took one of the cushiond basket bullock carts which are the cabs of the country, and drove shopping down to the pier, where our company crackt a bottle of delicious madeira at a bowery café. The temperature was about 75° but the air was fine and strong.—All up the mountain the gardens were green under the vine trellises where they are planted in the shade of the grapes to keep them from the burning summer sun; the flowers, red, yellow and white—especially camellias—were everywhere, and the children flung them into our car and toboggan from every clean little yellow white cottage.—We returned to the boat two hours before she saild, and watcht the men and boys in the little cockle-shells boats that swarmed about us, and invited us to throw money into the water. They plunged in after a coin and caught it long before it could reach the bottom, sometimes between their toes. One poor one-armed fellow was as apt as the rest; a child of six was the youngest. A big boy climbed the ship's side and made a dive of sixty feet. They came as soon as we stopt, Saturday night, and we left them behind when we started.—The blight on all is the miserable poverty, and the economic burden of the Portuguese rule. Our parting with the island was as majestic as our approach, with a greater beauty in the sun and shadow.

We expect to stop six hours at Gibraltar and I will post you this letter there.—We could not be more comfortable on a ship; we are at the captain's table, and were specially recommended by the N. Y. agent to the purser; so we are well befriended at court. Elinor is bearing it all like a hero, and enjoying it more. Even Pilla is not seasick. There is a pleasant company of passengers, not too large, and all easy and friendly. We are taking home about 2000 Hungarians in the steerage; but our entire 2500 do not fill the ship. Her size is an immense advantage. She rolls a little, but is so large that she rides the waves, which have been pretty large themselves.

After Gibraltar we shall stop some hours at Genoa, and then at Naples, where we expect to land some time Saturday.[2] We think we shall go directly on to Rome, and return to do Naples after Easter; but if the weather is very fine we may stay a week, before going on. I will repeat that our address there (at Rome) will be care of Thos. Cook & Son, simply. We are uncertain yet as to our hotel; each one we hear of last seems the best.

—If you could keep this letter and let me have it on my return, it would form my notes for Madeira. We all join in love to you and Henry and all the Annie folks.

> Your aff'te brother
> Will.

1. This letter is the basis of "Up and Down Madeira," first published as a travel letter in the New York *Sun*, 8 March 1908, and subsequently as the first chapter of *Roman Holidays and Others* (1908). According to arrangements described by Colonel George Harvey of Harper & Brothers, in a letter to Howells of 24 January 1908 (MH), Howells would write letters expressly for publication in the *Sun*: "...I have had a talk with Mr. [William M.] Laffan with the result that he is to publish your letters in 'The Sun' and to pay us therefor $100.00 each." On 3 May 1908 (MH) Howells commented on the *Sun* letters in a letter to Aurelia: "I wonder if you have seen any of the letters I have been writing for the Sunday edition of The New York Sun? I am sending off the tenth, and the editor wants me to keep on indefinitely. They go to Harpers under my salary, and are then sold to the Sun. I explain, lest you think I had broken with the Harpers." With minor additions, the *Sun* letters make up the text of *Roman Holidays*. See Gibson-Arms, *Bibliography*, pp. 60–61.

2. The Howellses arrived in Naples on 18 January, where they spent about a week before going on to Rome.

27 JANUARY 1908, ROME, TO FREDERICK A. DUNEKA

> *Windsor Hotel...*
> *Rome* January 27, 1908.

Dear Mr. Duneka:

I have signed the agreement for "Fennel and Rue,"[1] and already see immense crops of those herbs stored up by the eager simplers of the reading public. Kindly have the document kept for me against my return—which I would be glad if it were tomorrow. Rome is so old that she has forgotten me, and I find myself remembering her so well that I have nothing new to see among her antiquities; her modernities are too new. Yet she is a beautiful town, and I suppose if we were once settled I should be of a less jaundiced mind about her. She is very full— fuller than I am after my table d'hôte dinner—and somebody else has got the rooms we want everywhere else. Here the rooms are beautiful, with a price as proud as that we paid in New York.

Thanks be, we are all well, and so young yet that we have the bright lexicon of our nonage still in our pockets, and cannot find the word fail in it. My love to all Franklin Square. I wonder if the mute Colonel got a letter from me writ the day before I left.[2]

Yours ever
W. D. Howells.

1. For earlier correspondence regarding a title for the novel, see Howells to Duneka, 13 December 1907.

2. Howells' letter is not extant, but Colonel Harvey acknowledged having received it. According to Harvey's letter, 24 January 1908 (MH), Howells appears to have made a generous but unspecified offer regarding his contract with Harper & Brothers, which Harvey gracefully rejected: "I was very much touched by your note respecting your wish to lend a helping hand in what promises to be a lean year in the publishing business. The idea of making inroads upon your income had never occurred to me and I would not consent to do so in any circumstance, if for no other reason because I regard your present remuneration wholly inadequate."

3 FEBRUARY 1908, ROME, TO CHARLES E. NORTON

Windsor Hotel . . .
Rome February 3, 1908.

My dear Norton:

Your Margaret[1] has just been here from her hotel two doors away, and my Pilla being in bed with her usual sore throat and my wife habitually invalided, I have had the pleasure of her visit all to myself. She seemed very, very well, and full of the wonder and delight of Rome, which we kept in the back of our minds till we could talk of you all at Shady Hill. She had later news than I, and could tell me that you were well. I cannot tell you of the delight of seeing her.

We arrived a week or more ago, after a most prosperous voyage, and a week of perfect sun, and one day of perfect wind and sun at Naples. The day of tramontana we gave to San Martino, where the gale whistled through the proud, sad old monastery like the spirit of the Middle

Ages.[2] Nothing could have been finer in a way, unless it was the gray sky—the only one in our week—at Pompeii. I found the place very much grown—but dug up, not built up, and most interesting revelations. However, that way madness lies, and I must get back to the Howells family in this pleasant hotel if I am to keep my reason. We look out on the Queen Mother's palace,[3] and a convent whose bell calls me, furious, to prayer at half past six,[4] and we are in the healthiest quarter. That perhaps accounts for Pilla's sore throat; but one cannot have everything even in Rome. I have "done" three things: the Medici Gardens yesterday, the Coliseum the Sunday before, and the house of Keats by the Spanish Steps, where we saw Severn and listened to his perhaps increasing reminiscences in 1864, when we were here last.[5] I wished you could have been with me in the Gardens, to creep with me round among the busts of the poets, and find our mutual acquaintance. Dante would have said to you, "Oh yes," as Niccolini and Giusti said to me, in friendly recognition: they appeared to like having been written about.[6]—But there is too much of Rome, too little of one's self. She will end by wearing me out, or driving me away.—In this hotel, when it was the Primavera, Wm. James stayed, so the doctor, who has just been to see Pilla, told me. Somebody great and fine has stayed everywhere, and there is no use. When I was here before, I was only 27; now at 70, I cannot stand up against the wonder that I then took so lightly on the shield of my youth. One should be a cat, here, and have nine lives, at least. If I were, I would give one of them to have you here with me. Our love to you all.

Yours ever
W. D. Howells.

1. One of Norton's daughters.
2. In *Roman Holidays and Others*, Howells expresses his pleasure with the old San Martino monastery in Naples despite the harsh north winds of the *tramontana*: "It was worth more than we suffered in finding it; for the museum is a record of the most significant events of Neapolitan history from the time of the Spanish domination down to that of the Garibaldian invasion; and the church and corridors through which the wind hustled us abound in paintings and frescos such as one would be willing to give a whole week of quiet weather to" (p. 50).
3. The Palazzo Margherita in Rome, formerly the Palazzo Piombino, was the residence of Margaret of Savoy. It is now the site of the U.S. embassy.
4. The famous Capuchin convent, whose church is decorated, as Howells phrases it in *Roman Holidays*, with the "bones of the good brothers braided on the walls and roof of the crypt in the indissoluble community of floral and geometric designs" (p. 76).
5. The Keats house is located on the Piazza de Spagna, across the square from the Spanish Steps, which ascend to the church and convent of Trinità dei Monti. The house actually belonged to the British painter George Severn (1793–1879), who came to Italy with Keats and was with him at his death. In *Roman Holidays*, Howells describes having met Severn in 1864 and talking with him in the room where Keats

died: "It is a very little room, looking down over the Spanish Steps..., across the piazza to the narrow stretch of the Via del Babuino. I must have stood in it with Severn and heard him talk of Keats and his ultimate days and hours; for I remember some such talk, but not the details of it. He was a very gentle old man and fondly proud of his goodness to the poor dying poet, as he well might be, and I was glad to be one of the many Americans who, he said, came to grieve with him for the dead poet" (p. 109).

6. In 1872 Howells had written essays about Giuseppi Giusti (1809–1850), a poet and forceful political satirist, and Giambattista Niccolini (1782–1861), a dramatist: "The Florentine Satirist, Giusti," *North American Review*, July 1872, and "Niccolini's Anti-papal Tragedy," *North American Review*, October 1872; both are reprinted in *Modern Italian Poets* (1887).

4 FEBRUARY 1908, ROME, TO SAMUEL L. CLEMENS

Windsor Hotel...
Rome Feb'y 4th, 1908.

My dear Clemens:

Your wish about your letters comes, I am sorry to say, two months too late. When a biographer asks me for the biographee's letters, I always give them, if I can find them, which sometimes I can't; and I saw Paine on such intimate terms with you that I should not have hesitated to offer him all your letters.[1] I could only, as I remember find ten or twelve, from those you had written me during the last five or six years. He said he would have them copied and returned to me, but he has not done so, for I think I told him there was no hurry.[2] You can get them of him, and see for yourself how little their tenor could annoy you if they were publisht after you were gone. The vast bulk of your letters are at Kittery Point,[3] where no one but I could find them, even if *I* could. I don't think Paine could abuse the confidence put in him, or would make an indiscreet use of them; but I no more thought of asking you whether I should give them than I thought of asking Mrs. Aldrich whether I should give Aldrich's very intimate letters to his biographer, when he askt for them.[4] Of course Paine will do exactly what you say about them; he spoke to me with entire judgment and good sense.

We are having a gay time here in a week's wet. My wife has not been out of the house since she came into it ten days ago, and Pilla has been three days in bed with the sorest throat in history. She bemoans her absence from Bermuda, where I hope we shall go with you next winter about bronchitis time.

I suppose we shall like Rome when we get round to it. Meantime, nothing could be more comfortable than this hotel. The nice quiet

Americans in it don't speak above their breaths because the nice quiet English wont speak at all.

We join in love to each of you.

Yours ever
W. D. Howells.

1. In a letter of 22 January 1908 (MH), Clemens had complained that his private correspondence was being compromised by his nephew, who was cooperating with Albert B. Paine, Clemens' biographer: "I find that Sam Moffett has been lending old letters of mine to Mr. Paine without first submitting them to me for approval or the reverse, & so I've stopped it. I don't like to have those privacies exposed in such a way to even my biographer. If Paine should apply to you for letters, please don't comply. I must warn Twichell, too. A man should be dead before his private foolishnesses are risked in print" (*Twain-Howells*, p. 828).

2. According to Howells' letter to Paine, dated at Kittery Point, 8 July 1908 (CSmH), the letters were eventually returned. Howells, who respected Paine's integrity, felt it best to heed Clemens' word of caution: "Your express pkge of the Clemens letters came to hand last night, and I thank you for them and the copies. I have just laid hands on the great mass of his letters to me, and am sending them direct to him, so that he can look them over first. He probably wont; but it is best for all that he should have the chance."

3. On the same day he wrote to Paine, Howells sent Clemens all the letters he had found: "I am sending a huge mass of your letters to you for Paine, because I am vague as to their going direct to him, after your doubts of last winter. I have written him saying merely that I think it best all round that you should see them first" (NN; *Twain-Howells*, p. 830).

4. Ferris Greenslet was the author of the *Life of Thomas Bailey Aldrich* (1908).

5 FEBRUARY 1908, ROME, TO GEORGE O. TREVELYAN

Windsor Hotel,
Rome, February 5, 1908.

Dear Sir George:

I have heard to-day from our ambassador[1] that you have just left Rome, after being in the hotel next this for the past month, and I cannot tell you how very sorry I am to have missed you. I hope fate will be kind when I go home through London with my family in May.

Ever since I read your last volume on our revolution I have wished to see you, and tell you personally how much more I enjoyed it than I was somehow able to say in the little paper which will perhaps meet your eye in an early number of the *North American Review*.[2] One always leaves out, it seems to me, the most vital impressions of a book, and puts in conventional praise or blame; and I wish you would read into my page some appreciation of your feeling not only for the American character of our formative period, but for the scene, the circumstance, the very air. It was as if you had looked upon our landscape, in its emergence from the wilderness, and perceived its peculiar quality—as if you had studied the fact upon the ground. I know Western Massachusetts and the upper Hudson river country pretty well—not accurately, but as one who has his eye out for traits and effects—and I felt that you were taking me with you from knowledge of your own, as I read.

My wife and I are in Rome, after forty-five years, and it does not recognize us. However, we do not recognize Rome at all points, but we are trying to renew the acquaintance which we made so intimately, so rather passionately, when we were twenty-seven instead of seventy. Our daughter is with us, and she will help us find our old friend, when we all get well of our colds. This afternoon I found the house, 5 via del Gambero, where we had the lodging in which we were so young and happy.³ It is not one of the stateliest avenues; it is rather dim and damp and narrow; but the Armenian archbishop (whom I knew through his brother of San Lazzaro) came to fetch me in his red coach when I went to hear the Pope say mass in the Sistine Chapel.⁴ That could not happen now to me at " 'otel Vinsor."

You will let my great age excuse my great garrulity, I hope.

Yours sincerely,
W. D. Howells.

1. The American ambassador was Lloyd C. Griscom (1872–1959), lawyer and diplomat, who served in Rome from 1907 to 1909.

2. The "last volume" was the third part of Trevelyan's *The American Revolution* (1907). Howells' "little paper," a laudatory essay entitled "The Justice of a Friend," appeared in the *North American Review*, June 1908. In his reply of 12 February 1908 (MH), Trevelyan remarked that he was "pleased" with Howells' "interest" in the book, and responded even more appreciatively, 12 June 1908 (MH), after having read the essay: "I have just received your review of my book in the North American Review. One ought not to address a critic, even in thanks; but I may say so much as this, that the article is an immense encouragement to me in falling to work on the last volume of the history."

3. Howells also wrote to John M. Howells on the same day (W. W. Howells, Kittery Point; *Life in Letters*, II, 249), describing how the old lodging had evoked strong feelings for both him and Elinor: "...Emmer is on fire to go see it; she wouldn't go out to see St. Peter's, but Cinque Via del Gambero has claims." For an account of his rediscovery, see *Roman Holidays*, pp. 122–24.

4. See *Italian Journeys* (1881), pp. 174–77, and *Venetian Life* (1867), pp. 194–206.

15 FEBRUARY 1908, ROME, TO AURELIA H. HOWELLS

> Windsor Hotel,
> Rome, February 15, 1908.

Dear Aurelia:

I hope this check will reach you before my 71st birthday, so that you may regard it as a birthday gift from me for the whole month of March. I will send another next week, and you must let me know whether they both come to hand. If they do, the second will serve for April.

You won't expect me to talk about Rome. We have done almost no sight-seeing, for Elinor was down to her first meal to-day, and poor Pilla has had the grippe. She has been housed for a fortnight, and must be shut up for a week longer. It is hard, and she has missed many pleasant social things. To-day came a note from the American Ambassador[1] asking us both to go with his family on a special sightseeing expedition "personally conducted" by the Syndic (Mayor) of Rome[2] on Monday, and she had to give that up. But we hope for brighter days. I need some myself, for a wonder; I am just getting over a sore throat, and I don't dare go out after night, so that both Pilla and I had to give up going to the theatre last night on tickets sent us by the Embassy for a box of a Roman princess who lives in this house. But thank goodness I was well enough to go and see the great Norwegian Björnstjerne Björnson (author of *Arne*, *The Fishermaiden*, etc.) whom I knew 25 years ago in America. He knew me at once, and met me with both hands out, and "My dear, dear Howells!" I sat down, and we had a jolly chat.

Before I forget, I want to ask if Annie got the like-her dress we sent just before we left New York. If she hasn't got it, do let me know, and I will have it looked up.—Is Howells really coming to Ottawa?[3] You must keep me up with all your news; it helps me to find myself in all the strangeness. I shall of course be glad to be going home, but first I want to get the good of this. With all our love to you all,

> Your aff'te brother,
> Will.

1. Lloyd C. Griscom.
2. Ernesto Nathan (1845–1921) was the syndic of Rome (1907–1913). Howells gives further details about him in *Roman Holidays*: "In the capital of Christendom, where the head of the Church dwells in a tradition of supremacy hardly less Italian than Christian, the syndic, or mayor, is a Jew, and not merely a Jew, but an alien Jew, English by birth and education, a Londoner and an Oxford man. More yet, he is a Freemason, which in Italy means things anathema to the Church, and he is a very prominent Freemason" (pp. 190–91). Howells met Nathan at a luncheon given by the American ambassador. See Howells to Joseph A. Howells, 12 February 1908 (MH).

3. Howells Fréchette, then twenty-seven years old, appears to have obtained employment as a government surveyor in Ottawa. See Howells to Joseph A. Howells, 11 March 1908 (MH).

27 FEBRUARY 1908, ROME, TO BJORNSTJERNE BJORNSON

Windsor Hotel . . .
Rome February 27, 1908.

My dear Björnson:

My daughter and I went yesterday to hear Madam Ibsen[1] sing, and if I had not already known whose daughter *she* was, I should have known it the instant I saw her from that noble uplift of the head when she stood before the people. She sang as you write, beautifully, limpidly, artistically, naturally, divinely; and especially we loved her Scandinavian songs. They consoled me . . .[2] back of the hall when some Roman girls stood up, in order to be "the observed of all observers," and eclipsed my view of her.—Why do you Europeans let women keep their hats on in such places? At home every hat, no matter how fetching, comes off when the performance begins.

Now, can you, *will* you come with Mrs. Björnson to have a cup of tea with us at (4) four o'clock on——

I had got as far as this when I told my wife . . . s going to do, and she stopped me. "Do you think Björnson has got nothing to do in Rome but run after us? All Rome is running after *him*; and you expect him to rush here again in a week?"

This struck me to the earth, and I can not fix the date I meant. Will you fix it? Or let my girl and me come to you? I have got Verga's great and beautiful and heartbreaking book, *I Malavoglia*, for you.[3]

Affectionately yours
W. D. Howells.

1. Bjornson's daughter, Bergliot (b. 1869), who married Sigurd Ibsen, the son of Henrik Ibsen, and later prime minister of Norway. She was a concert performer of art songs, often singing works by Edvard Grieg, with words composed by her father, who frequently went on tour with her.

2. For an explanation of missing portions of the text here and below, see the Textual Apparatus.

3. *I Malavoglia* (1881), a novel by the Sicilian author Giovanni Verga (1840–1922).

12 APRIL 1908, LEGHORN, TO CHARLES E. NORTON

Leghorn, April 12, 1908.[1]

My dear Norton:

First of all I must thank you for your great kindness towards Ferrero, in the Lowell Lectures matter.[2] I have just received a most joyous letter from him, in which he assures me that there will be no trouble about his English.[3] He will have his lectures carefully translated, and as he has a clear accent, he can read them perfectly well. I will duly give him a letter to you, and I know you will like him, and especially, if she accompanies him, you will like his most sensible, most cultivated little wife, the daughter of Lombroso,[4] who, I think, does not accept so many instances for proofs as her father does.

We left Rome a week since, to give my wife's nerves a bath of sea air, and me a chance to bring up some writing. We had ten or twelve weeks of constantly decreasing disappointment in Rome, till we left the glorious town with a full sense of its greatness and wonderfulness, and are now all deadly Romesick, with an ache to go back. But we shall only go farther away tomorrow: to Genoa, to Marseilles, to Paris, to London, not all at once, but gradually.—You would find plenty of Renaissance left in Rome;[5] much more for instance than you have in Cambridge outside of your own house; and I believe you would think the sentimentalists had maligned her. I missed no remembered charm in her, and I found a thousand new ones. The Italians are a great people, and I sometimes ask myself if they are not destined to their old primacy. When I meet you I will persuade you out of all your misgivings.

I have had a delightful letter from James,[6] and I hope to see him. I have not yet seen his new edition, and I have only Sally's impressions concerning it.[7] But a man of 68 cannot well re-write the books of a man of 38, and I can imagine the risks he has taken. Still, he is our best in so many ways that we must always own him so. His story in the last two Harpers is, as he would say, "wonderful"—of the finest touch and truest, if worldliest, wisdom.[8] With love to all

Yours ever
W. D. Howells.

1. The Howellses had left Rome on 5 April.

2. Guglielmo Ferrero (1871–1942), celebrated Italian historian, was best known for *The Grandeur and Decadence of Rome* (5 volumes, 1903–1909). Howells had met Ferrero through Ambassador Griscom, and had written Norton, 7 March 1908 (MH), asking him about the possibility of Ferrero lecturing at the Lowell Institute: "The other day at our ambassador's I met the very interesting man whose history of 'The Grandeur and Decadence of Rome' has made the most distinct effect, and per-

haps the most distinguished, of any recent history. . . . His point of view seems to be very modern; he sees Rome as an effloresence of commercialism much like our own . . . . Well, now, he has been asked to visit America . . . ; and I have thought that six lectures on the matter which has occupied him might be acceptable to the Lowell Lecture authorities . . . . I will stake my few shreds of literary reputation on the interest and excellence of Mr. Ferrero's lectures, which will be in English, of course . . . ." Norton had in turn contacted Lawrence Lowell of the Institute, replying to Howells on 26 March 1908 (MH) that Ferrero would no doubt be engaged. In a letter to William R. Thayer, 9 August 1908 (MH), Howells further commented about Ferrero: "I dare say he has the strain of simple greed which we complexer barbarians note in some of our Italian friends, but it did not personally appear to me . . . . So far as I know, he has dates only at the Lowell Inst., at Columbia and Chicago."

3. In his letter of 26 March, Norton had pressed Howells to give assurances that Ferrero could "lecture easily in English." Ferrero had written to Howells, 11 April 1908 (MH), affirming his ability to lecture in English "d'une manière sinon parfaite, au moins correcte et tolerable."

4. Gina Ferrero, author and leading Italian feminist, was the daughter of Cesare Lombroso (1836–1909), well known criminologist and doctor of forensic medicine, who ascribed causes of criminal insanity to elaborate proofs of physical abnormality.

5. In a letter of 19 March 1908 (MH), Norton had sharply expressed his resistance to a "modernized Italy" and the painful loss of the older culture: "The Italy that I knew and loved was of the Middle Ages, with nothing later in it than aspects of the Renaissance before the Renaissance had become a fad of the modern semi-cultivated writers of books."

6. James had written Howells, 10 March 1908 (MH), imploring him to come to England and describing the all-consuming task of preparing the New York Edition of his novels: ". . . I have now been kept sedentary for months as almost never before by the really immeasurable labour involved in my 24 volumes of the Edition: the handling of which in the manner in which I have been doing it has absolutely driven every thing else to the wall . . . ." He warned in the postscript that "A complete portentous set of the Edition will await your acceptance on your return to New York."

7. In his letter of 26 March, Norton had conveyed at length his daughter's unfavorable response to the New York Edition: "Our chief literary concern has been of late with Henry James' new prefaces. I have not read them, but Sally has read them and finds them too self-occupied, and dislikes the disturbances of her old associations with the stories, and dislikes also the unreality which this criticism of the old characters gives to them. She does not like to have her puppets taken to pieces and the wires which moved them shown to her; nor does she think it a dignified proceeding to take for granted so largely the interest of the public in the conception and execution of the work of the living writer." For Howells' response to James regarding the prefaces, see Howells to James, 2 August 1908.

8. "Julia Bride," *Harper's Monthly*, March–April 1908. Howells had apparently interceded with the *Harper's* staff, persuading them to publish the long story despite the usual policy of not serializing short pieces of fiction. In his letter of 10 March, James thanked Howells for the assistance, although he bridled at what he felt to be the magazine's off-handed treatment: "It is *murderous* to the little story to have divided it (it being really really all unity and close continuity) & it is good enough to have made an exception for. They have kept it unpublished since year before last, as if I were some obscure suppliant or neophyte—& I supposed that this was at least in order that they *might* run it together. Basta!"

9 MAY 1908, PARIS, TO AURELIA H. HOWELLS

Paris, May 9, 1908.[1]

Dear Aurelia:

I expect to be writing you from London next Sunday, and to-day I have nothing to write you from Paris. We—Pilla and I—were at the American ambassador's[2] to lunch on Friday and he and his wife called yesterday. They seem determined to be most cordial, and we like them both. But I dread the civilities of Whitelaw Reid in London, which have been hanging over me for months.[3] I got pretty sick of the embassy in Rome, and I should always like so much to be let alone.

I am glad you have told your agent to sell your Cleveland house, or rather your lot.[4] If possible get cash, even at a sacrifice; but sell the thing anyway.

Have you any hopes of letting your Jefferson house? I heard from Joe that Willie thought he had a tenant. How would you like to have Sam and Ethel in it, I paying you something for rent? I really am at my wit's end about Sam. He expects his entire support from me.[5]

We have been having soft spring weather the past week, but not *our* spring weather. Today it is raining.

Paris is a wonderful place, the only real capital in the world. It fairly entreats you with its museums and galleries to be entertained and edified. I can give you no notion of the things done gratis for the people, (of course ultimately out of their own pockets) who are such a severely industrious and orderly lot—not so endearing as the Italians, but wise and just. Still I would rather live in New York, and homesickness is growing on me.

We are all quite well, and hope to leave Thursday.

Yours affectionately,
Will.

1. The Howellses had arrived in Paris on 25 April via Marseilles and Monte Carlo.
2. Henry White (1850–1927), who served in Paris from 1907 to 1909.
3. Whitelaw Reid, then the American ambassador to Great Britain (1905–1912), was noted for lavish entertainments at his London residence. The dreaded civilities had been proffered by Reid in several letters, especially that of 2 March 1908 (MH): "You will have plenty of attention when you come here, but what I should like would be to know something of your plans and length of stay. It would delight Mrs. Reid and myself if you could stay with us at Dorchester House while here.... One evening at least you must give me for a little dinner in town, in which I should try to get about you not merely literary people..., but men of like tastes whom you are less likely to meet so often."
4. See Howells to Joseph A. Howells, 20 April 1906, n. 6.
5. Having lost both his wife and his job in the past year, Samuel Howells had

come to depend on his brother's support for himself and his daughter Ethel. Becoming increasingly exasperated, Howells had recounted for Joseph A. Howells, 3 May 1908 (MH), Sam's recent importunings: "I wish I could turn over to you some of the superabundant letters I get from Sam, but as they all involve an appropriation, I don't believe you would thank me for them . . . . I am supporting him entirely, for he is using his pension to pay off back doctor's bills. In his last letter he says in Italic, '*I am a martyr*,' and at the same time he owns that he is a beggar . . . ."

23 MAY 1908, LONDON, TO AURELIA H. HOWELLS

> 40 Clarges Street,
> London W. May 23, 1908.

Dear Aurelia:

Annie's letter about poor Henry came today,[1] and I need not tell you how deeply I am feeling for you, for her, and for all her kind family. She left me little or no hope that he would live, and I am waiting the worst news.[2] Of course, Aurelia, you are not to distress yourself about any money affairs in this sad occasion. I will send an extra check in this letter, and will follow it up with more as I think you need it.

I hardly know what to write now, but I wish you to know at once that my thoughts are with you, and Elinor and Pilla join me in tender love. Elinor has just been saying that there was never a more devoted sister than you have always been. The hapless creature whom you have tended will be your loving witness to father and mother and Victoria[3] of your fidelity to the trust they left to you one after another.

> Your aff'te brother
> Will.

1. Anne Fréchette's letter is not extant, nor is the exact nature of Henry's immediate illness known.

2. Howells received the expected news of Henry's death some time in early June, as can be inferred from his letter to Joseph A. Howells, 10 June 1908 (MH): "You will have heard before this of poor Henry's death, which was not to be mourned on his account, but which leaves Aurelia desolate."

3. Victoria Howells had forsaken any prospects for personal independence by taking upon herself the care of her mentally incapacitated brother. Aurelia inherited the filial responsibility when Victoria died suddenly from malaria in 1886.

...Kittery Point, Maine July 16, 1908.

My dear Norton:

Your letter brought me great pleasure, and as much shame because I had let you be the first to write after my home coming.[1] While I was still in Boston I had one afternoon set apart for going to you, but I was so tired, after all my journeys that I could not face the journey to Cambridge, even with the prospect of looking into your kind eyes at the end of it.

We were in Rome, after a week of Naples, then oddly enough, but delightedly a week in Leghorn, a week in Genoa and a week in Monte Carlo, which by its badness and dullness gave me a new conception of hell. It is not only bad and dull, but very beautiful, as hell may very well be, with a climate showing the warmth which is supposed to pervade perdition, and flowers for the wicked to look at and swill to all they like. I did not play because it seemed so much like work, and I came away poorer than I went by the sum of my hotel bill, which was not a great sum.—We had three weeks in Paris, where I drove every day in the Bois with my dear old Perry,[2] and talked and talked. H. James was there visiting our sister-novelist, Mrs. Wharton, and again he was in London during our four weeks, and I saw him never too often.[3] He is older and sadder and sweeter, and we commerced of many things of the past, with one long, dear walk through the Park well into Kensington.—Now, again, I am here, with some doubt whether I was not in a better place before. It is at least no longer so terribly hot; and today I have finished up the last of Rome, fitly enough in the Baths of Caracalla.[4] You know, possibly, that besides writing to you from Rome, I have written all winter to the N. Y. Sun which has printed my letters in the Sunday edition. It has been a return to my youth in more ways than one, for Venetian Life was a sort of journalism. A book of "Roman Holidays" will presently be the result, which you will duly receive.[5] As if this all this torrent of egotism were not enough I long to see you, and tell you still more about myself. I am sorry to report that my wife is very much broken down; but Pilla and I are intolerably well.—I am hopefully of finding you all at home when I drop down to Cambridge; and in the meantime I send my love with my family's to each of you.— The best thing I know of "Fennel and Rue" is that you like it.[6] Do like me too always, no matter how little I deserve to be

Yours affectionately
W. D. Howells.

1. Norton wrote to Howells 14 July 1908 (MH). Howells had left England on 16 June, aboard the *Saxonia*, and arrived in Boston on 25 June.

2. Thomas S. Perry.

3. Anticipating Howells' arrival in London from Paris, James wrote with characteristically ironic exaggeration on 20 May 1908 (MH): "Have you *come*?—Are you coming?—*Where* are you & *when* & how? I want ever so much to come & see you— I ask but to be guided to your door. I am fighting it out on *this* line—though not if it 'takes all summer'! Only if it takes a part—which however shall leave moments to be consecrated—: Help me to consecrate them . . . ."

4. Howells' account of the baths appears in "A Few Remaining Moments" and concludes this last sketch of Rome in *Roman Holidays*. It was first published as a travel letter in the New York *Sun*, 2 August 1908.

5. Unable to assemble enough material for a book on England, Howells had earlier suggested to Frederick A. Duneka, 26 May 1908 (MWA), that the *Sun* letters be used to make up the volume subsequently published as *Roman Holidays*: "Now if you want a, or any, book from me this fall, I have to propose one to be made up of my *Sun* letters, and called 'Mostly Rome: Meanderings and Maunderings. By W. D. H.' I don't know whether you've read any of the letters, but Laffan likes them, and is rather proud, he tells me, of printing them. I myself think them lively—too lively for my years." For Howells' arrangement with Harper & Brothers and William M. Laffan of the *Sun*, see Howells to Aurelia H. Howells, 12 January 1908, n. 1.

6. In his letter of 14 July, Norton wrote warmly and personally of *Fennel and Rue*, calling it "a delightful little book, full, as everything which you write is, of sympathy with human life and of the finest discrimination & delineation of character. I read it with special pleasure not so much for the story, as for the message from yourself which it contained for me."

2 AUGUST 1908, KITTERY POINT, TO HENRY JAMES

Kittery Point, August 2, 1908

My dear James:

This is the third letter I have started to you, the others having been unsuccessfully attempted with the pen. My old age is tormented with scruples unknown to my brash middle life, and I fancied that something I had said about your prefaces in your most admirable library edition might not be so wholly pleasing as I meant it.[1] Those prefaces have given us all great satisfaction, as read aloud by me. We especially enjoyed you where you rounded upon yourself, and as it were took yourself to pieces, in your self-censure. The analysis of The American seemd happiest, but all the analyses were good, most subtle, and wise, and just, and the biographies of the three novels—Roderick Hudson and The Portrait of a Lady were the other two which I have yet received—were full of instruction for me, who as their godfather had fancied I knew all about them, but had really known them only from their birth, and not from their conception through their gestation.[2] I remember so well your telling me, on such a Sunday afternoon as this, when we were rowing on Fresh Pond, what R. H. was to be.[3] You have done a lot of good work, but nothing better than the last half of each of those prefaces; and I think the public will understand from them what I tried to note to you, that miserable hot afternoon when we sat glued to our chairs here:[4] the fact, namely, that you have imagined your fiction, as a whole, and better fulfilled a conscious intention in it than any of your contemporaries. It took courage to do those introductions, and a toil as great, but how you must have liked doing them—or having done them!

I am, as usual, in the midst of a book which as usual, I did not distinctly mean to write, a book of "Roman Holidays and Others," the stuff of which has been appearing for the last six months in the Sunday edition of the New York Sun.[5] The only thing that pleases me wholly is that the stuff seems to have been so much liked by the people who have read it there. The success has brought back my sense of success in the Venetian Life letters printed forty odd years ago in the Boston Advertiser.[6] But of course the Roman stuff is without any such authority as the Venetian, and is the reflex of my youthful fires, such as they were. Still it has amused me to find myself taking the old point of view, the old attitude, quite helplessly.

During the month we have been here my wife has suffered almost constantly from toothache, and at last she determined to have the wretched tooth out, so we all went up to Boston, and she took the gas, and Pilla and I sat quaking till she came to, all right. Then during her day's rest at the hotel, I went out and saw Norton one afternoon.[7] His daughters happened to be away, and he was alone in the house, a chance which made him seem forlorn and very old and broken. It was a sadder time than I have ever had with him, though now and then he plucked up the courage to talk of old times. He read me with joyous affection for your brother a letter which Wm. had written him from Durham,[8] but there was nothing else to lift us. He told me frankly that poor D.'s affair had aged him, and I tried, from you as well as myself, to make him see it a little from the general point of view.[9] But it was very melancholy.

We had John and his wife here for a fortnight after we came, but now they are in the Catskills, finishing out the month before they shall go to New York, and begin housekeeping in a little house they have taken in Washington Place, west of Sixth Avenue. John makes much of their being in a sort of nook, with a yard backing against that of a convent, but when I thought of the convents which one could back against in Rome, I had to feign my pleasure in his. His wife is an extremely pretty girl, wonderfully New Yorky, but very intelligent, and much disposed to overrate her fatherinlaw's literature.

Pilla is just home from a week's visit at the shrines in Art in Cornish,

Vermont, where half a dozen painters, and our great novelist Winston Churchill are livelier in their social relation than they are friendly;[10] or perhaps uncritical is the word. I fancy Cornish is something like Broadway, as it used to be. The sweetest spirit of all, the great and good Saint Gaudens, is now disembodied;[11] but to meet a visitor they all meet amicably enough, and Pilla had a good time. It is a frightfully hot place, as every place in this hemisphere seems to be, but very pretty, on heights above the Connecticut River. I don't know but you may have been there.

It is only five or six Sundays since we went that pleasant walk through the Park to South Kensington, which I should like so much to go again. When you parted with me you forbade my doing anything for you in the lecturing way, and so I have attempted nothing, though I should have been so glad to try.[12] The country is prosperous again, and when Taft is elected, as there seems no doubt he will be,[13] the people will be in the mood of cultivating their minds again.

I have always wondered how you liked your tea on the terrace with our Scotch M. P., in whose company I saw you so strangely walking off that day.[14]

We all join in affectionate remembrances.

Yours ever,

W. D. Howells.

1. When Howells and James visited together in England in May, they had discussed the prefaces James was writing for the New York Edition. In his reply, 17 August 1908 (MH), James elaborately dismisses Howells' misgivings: "But so far as compunction started and guided your pen, I really rub my eyes for vision of where it may—save as most misguidedly—have come in. You were so far from having distilled any indigestible drop for me on that pleasant *ultimissimo* Sunday, that I parted from you with a taste, in my mouth, absolutely saccharine—sated with sweetness, or with sweet reasonableness, so to speak; and aching, or wincing, in no single fibre." For this passage and a comprehensive statement by James of his critical intention in the prefaces, see *The Letters of Henry James*, ed. Percy Lubbock (1920; reprint ed., New York: Octagon Books, 1970), II, 98–104.

2. Five novels by James were serialized in the *Atlantic* under Howells' editorship: *Watch and Ward* (August–December 1871), *Roderick Hudson* (January–December 1875), *The American* (June 1876–May 1877), *The Europeans* (July–October 1878), and *The Portrait of a Lady* (November 1880–December 1881).

3. In the fall of 1874 James returned from Europe to Cambridge, where he completed *Roderick Hudson*; the remembered conversation may have taken place at that time. Howells' memories of Fresh Pond were warmly revived in the last words he wrote before his death in 1920 as he struggled to complete "The American James," a critical defense of his lifelong friend: "We were always going to Fresh Pond, in those days a wandering space of woods and water where people skated in winter and boated in summer." See *Life in Letters*, II, 399.

4. See Howells to Jewett, 16 June 1905.

5. See Howells to Norton, 16 July 1908, n. 5.

6. See Gibson-Arms, *Bibliography*, pp. 19–20.

7. Howells visited Norton on 23 July. See *Letters of Charles Eliot Norton*, ed. Sara Norton and M. A. De Wolfe Howe (Boston: Houghton Mifflin, 1913), II, 410.

8. William James had written on 6 July 1908 from Patterdale, England, describing "three and a half delightful days" at Durham, where he received an honorary degree from the university. See *The Letters of William James*, ed. Henry James (Boston: Houghton Mifflin, 1920), II, 306–8.

9. The identity of "poor D." and the nature of the "affair" are not known. Both the Dreyfus Affair and the serious riding accident that William E. Darwin, Norton's brother-in-law, suffered in 1900 are remote but unlikely possibilities.

10. Winston Churchill (1871–1947) was a writer of best-selling romances at the turn of the century. He built an elegant house in Cornish, New Hampshire (not Vermont, as Howells mistakenly notes), in 1899, making that small colony of artists and writers his home. Among Churchill's fellow townsfolk were painters Kenyon Cox and Maxwell Parrish, editors Herbert Croly and Norman Hapgood, and writers Robert Herrick (briefly), Louis Shipman, and Percy MacKaye.

11. Augustus Saint-Gaudens (1848–1907), leading American sculptor of the time, had established his home and studio in Cornish in 1885.

12. James' reply of 17 August indicates that Howells, when in London, had offered to help arrange a lecture tour for James in America. Having in mind the debilitating experience of his 1905 American tour and at present feeling himself "bursting . . . with violent and lately too much repressed creative (again!) intention," as he phrased it, James did not wish to contemplate another series: "I *may* burst before this intention fairly or completely flowers, of course; but in that case, even, I shall probably explode to a less distressing effect than I should do, under stress of a fatal puncture, on the too personally and physically arduous and above all too gregariously-assaulted (which is what makes it *most* arduous) lecture-platform." See Lubbock, *The Letters of Henry James*, II, 102.

13. William H. Taft, then Roosevelt's secretary of war, had been nominated on the first ballot at the Republican convention, going on to win handily over Democrat William J. Bryan in the November presidential election.

14. Howells and Mildred, along with James, had taken tea on the terrace at Kensington Gardens in the company of an otherwise unidentified Scotch member of Parliament. In an unpublished portion of his letter of 17 August 1908, James tells Howells that nothing of note had emerged from the episode save the enhancement of his reputation, which benefit he credited to Mildred's presence: "Only tell her, please, with my love, that she really did, by the mere indirect whisk of her skirt, before she left, (she and the Scotch Member together—he by the mere imposition of his large parliamentary hand) improve my social position inordinately."

15 AUGUST 1908, KITTERY POINT, TO SAMUEL L. CLEMENS

. . . Kittery Point, Maine August 15, 1908.

My dear Clemens:

I will surely and gladly come to see you when I go up to New York about the middle of next month, not merely because you live in the house that Jack built,[1] but because I want to pour out on you the praise that has been filling me up ever since I re-re-re-read The Innocents Abroad last winter in Rome. I wonder you could write it, and I wonder you could write The Ct. Yankee, which I re-re-read after I got home. I could not have written it myself, although it is the most delightful, truest, most humane, sweetest fancy that ever was. Now that you have taken the pen into your own hand, why don't you try something like it in your old age?

The other morning, after first waking, I dreamt of talking with a girl in Bermuda. I said that as it was coming spring I supposed she would be going north, but she said "No, we are going further into the tropics," and I made the reflection how perfectly natural that was, when she added, "We want to see some Pepper Trees, and hear a pigeon sing." Then it occurred to me that I had never heard a pigeon sing, and that it must be very nice.

Somewhere I have some more letters of yours, and I will send them as soon as I can think where I put them. But for goodness' sake, haven't you enough now?[2]

My poor wife has been suffering with her teeth all summer, and can only gnash out her thanks to you for remembering her. Pilla thanks you too, tho' not so hopelessly.

The unmuffled motor boats have made this place a pandemonium, and I am afraid we cannot come here any more. I am thinking of going to England as a summer resort. But there are the English. Unmuffled too.

Yours ever,
W. D. Howells.

1. Clemens had written to Howells on 12 August 1908 (NN), inviting him to the new house in Redding, Connecticut, designed by John M. Howells: "Won't you & Mrs. Howells & Mildred come, & give us as many days as you can spare, & examine John's triumph? For to my mind it *is* a triumph." See *Twain-Howells*, pp. 832–33. Howells, however, did not visit Clemens at his new home, subsequently called Stormfield, until March 1909. He afterwards wrote to Aurelia H. Howells, 28 March 1909 (MH), that "the house John designed for him is a jewel. It is an Italian villa in gray cement, and it looks as if it had always been there. Clemens is crazy over it."

2. See Howells to Clemens, 4 February 1908.

24 SEPTEMBER 1908, KITTERY POINT, TO JOSEPH A. HOWELLS

Kittery Point, Sept. 24, 1908.

Dear Joe:

After a good deal of interest rather than anxiety, I have heard from you by post and by *Sun*, and I am mighty glad to be assured that the hurricane passed over you harmless. It was a great experience, and my only regret now is that you did not make more of it in your letter to the *Sun*. At the rate they pay, you ought to have sent them three columns instead of half-one. Now I am looking for what you say in the *Sentinel*. I hurried your letter off to Aurelia, who had lost sleep over the first telegram, while I had missed it, and knew only of your big blow from what she and Willie wrote me.

We had a delightful visit of a week from Aurelia, which we packed with all the incidents we could, and which will give her something to return to in the long Ottawa evenings. She seems very well and very happy, and intends either to board this winter, if she can let her house, or take a boarder if she can't. Annie is not very well, but is better than she was. Neither of Aurelia's houses seems to be wanted by any one else, though we thought we had a real offer for the Cleveland place—it is not a house any longer.

Just now, however, it is Sam who lies heaviest on my heart. He has moved again, poor soul, "to save car fare" and to be nearer any opportunity of work! He tried again for his place in the P. P. but got only a very snubbing refusal from the P.[1] I would not join him in a letter to the President,[2] to whom he also wrote. He seems really unfit to care for himself and Ethel, and I can only help him out with money, when he needs so much other assistance. His daughter Jessie died shortly after he wrote you, and I don't know what has become of the children; there is something very darkling in his family affairs, for I cannot understand why Mrs. Randall apparently does nothing at all.[3] Again I am urging him to think of the Soldiers' Home, but if he goes into that what will become of Ethel? Florence, or her husband, will not have her, and so it goes with all the family. You invented the notion of the Home for Sam; can you think of anything else? Aurelia dreads living with him if Ethel must come too, and Annie for the present cannot take Aurelia into her family, and "Here we go round the mulberry bush," all out of doors.

Talking of Mulberries, my tree by the windpump began giving me ripe fruit the last of June, and I ate a final berry from it on the 21st of September, a season of nearly three months. The robins got all they wanted in August, and every morning after that I shook down a good feed for myself and Aurelia before breakfast. Did you ever notice that the robins left in August? It seems a peculiarity of this year, when there are very few birds of any kind.

In four weeks we have had only half a day's rain, and the proverbial ash heap is coming to the top. The "line storm" seems to have wreaked itself in your hurricane, or perhaps we had it that cold day in Boston the last of August. Eliza is very welcome to that shawl, which served my turn very well on the Rubber Neck Wagon. I only regret that she was not with us; when you come again, we must try the New York wagon.[4] Aurelia went home by way of Boston, and I went as far with her, and in the afternoon, we did the Residential Tour, and had great fun.

I will remember your prayer for books when I get back to New York, but so far this has not been a good year for books, or at least I have not got so many as usual. I suppose it is the election. By the way, you have seen that it is all up with Foraker, through his connection with the Standard Oil.[5] Taft and Roosevelt have renounced him, and he has withdrawn from the canvass. I could more have pitied a better man, less arrogant, less self-seeking, but still any ruin is sad. Elinor has had two teeth out, and is now gumming it more painlessly. She is getting the better of a bad summer. We all join in love to you both.

> Your affectionate brother,
> Will.

1. Sam had lost his job in the bindery at the Government Printing Office. The position of public printer at this time was occupied by Samuel B. Donnelly (1866–1946), who served in that office until 1913.

2. For Howells' previous intervention on Sam's behalf, see Howells to Roosevelt, 26 August 1906, n. 1.

3. See Howells to Joseph A. Howells, 6 October 1907, n. 5.

4. Joe had taken leave from his position as American consul at Turks Islands in the spring of 1907, visiting Kittery Point in mid-July. According to Howells' letter to Willie Howells, 4 September 1908 (MH), "I had a good time with your father and mother last week. We took in two theatres, and . . . he and I made the historical tour of Boston on the rubber-neck wagon."

5. Joseph B. Foraker, the former governor of Ohio, senator from Ohio, and a political foe of Roosevelt, was forced to retire from public life by William R. Hearst's disclosure that he had been on the payroll of Standard Oil while in office.

11 OCTOBER 1908, KITTERY POINT, TO CHARLES E. NORTON

> Kittery Point, Oct. 11, 1908.

My dear Norton:

I am very sorry to hear that you are not so well as when I saw you last, and I can only send you my vain sympathy. I hope to be in Boston next week, and then I will come out to you, if I may.[1] We go up on the 19th, and expect to go on to New York a week later. I was in that dismaying place during the past week, trying to get the builder of our apartment to say when we should be in it. He committed himself to the end of November, after promising the first of September.[2]

I saw no one I wished to see except John, with whom I passed a night at his father-in-law's on the Hudson. They are in an old Upjohnish mansion overlooking a reach of the river and shores of soft hills like those of some Italian lake. It seems a pity this region should not be in favor, but it is said to be intolerably hot, and infested, of course, with mosquitoes. It made me think of Frederika Bremer, and her raptures over the Hudson sojourns other days.[3]

The father-in-law, you know, was Godkin's partner on the *Post*,[4] a well-read, right-minded man, with whom one could have good talk about the strange political situation. He expects Taft, but is not certain.

One night at the Century Club, I met the friendly Professor Sloan,[5] and dined next him; but there were few other men at table whom I knew. Since I saw you I have had a long, delightful letter from James,[6] who boasted of a beautiful summer in England, and pitied us for the one we were passing through. I should like to match autumns with him. I don't remember so lovely an October.

I'm at last finishing up the longish novel which I've sometimes told you of,[7] and it seems to be justifying itself, in a measure. But in the watch we old men keep on ourselves, I'm amused to find how my attitude toward the people has changed; and how it has changed from dramatic to contemplative. In the ten or fifteen years since I began the story I have grown another man.

If you are not writing, I hope Sallie will send me your love in exchange for mine.

> Yours affectionately,
> W. D. Howells.

1. Norton died on 20 October, before Howells could see him. With a sense of finality, Howells paid his respects to Sara Norton, 16 October 1908 (MH): "Give my love to your father. Tell him that I have never forgotten the least of his constant acts of kindness which began with our first coming to Cambridge forty years ago. I grieve more than I can say for your anxieties and I can only hope that I may hear better news."

2. The builder was Frederic Culver, president of the Cooperative-Building Construction Company of New York, who wrote Howells on 17 November 1908 (MH) that the apartment at 130 West 57th Street was then ready for occupancy, "saving a few minor details." For a description of the projected apartment, see Howells to Joseph A. Howells, 6 October 1907.

3. Frederika Bremer (1801–1865) was a Swedish novelist who traveled in the United States between 1849 and 1861. The "raptures" were those in her book *The Homes of the New World* (1853).

4. See Howells to Aurelia Howells, 22 November 1907, n. 2.

5. Noted for his congeniality and urbanity, William M. Sloane was then Seth Low Professor of History at Columbia. He was active in the American Academy of Arts and Letters and succeeded Howells as president in 1920.

6. See Howells to James, 2 August 1908, n. 1.

7. The novel was *The Vacation of the Kelwyns*. Howells had told Norton a year and a half earlier that he was at work on it, but he then referred to it as "The

Children of the Summer." See Howells to Norton, 15 April 1907, n. 10. Howells had written Frederick A. Duneka, 28 September 1908 (MWA), saying that since finishing *Roman Holidays* he was "hard at a queer novel which you once read the beginning of and which I am now near the end of. I had hoped to lay it at your feet all finished, but it still needs some weeks pottering over, though I may own for your encouragement that I am at a very low ebb about it."

12 OCTOBER 1908, KITTERY POINT, TO WILLIAM S. BRAITHWAITE

. . . Kittery Point, Maine Oct. 12, 1908

Dear Mr. Braithwaite:

I am more deserving than I seem of your great kindness in sending me your book,[1] and inscribing it with those beautiful lines, and yet I am undeserving enough. I have truly felt your kindness, though I have failed so long to thank you for it.

I have just been recurring to your book, with an increasing sense of power in you which you have not got at second hand. Yours is truly a gift from nature, not a loan from literature. I do not think your verse always runs clear, but if I look again at any questioned passage I find it clearer than it seemed at first.[2] I do not know just how to justify to you my peculiar liking for your "Song of a Syrian Lace Seller." Perhaps it is because it blends so finely the two things I like best, the realistic and the mystic, and is so fortunate in wording and imaging.

Yours sincerely
W. D. Howells.

1. Braithwaite (1878–1962), Boston-born black poet, critic, and anthologist, had just sent his latest volume of poetry, *The House of the Falling Leaves* (1908).
2. Providing a distinct contrast to the public taste for black dialect poetry cultivated by Paul Laurence Dunbar and others, Braithwaite's poems, especially in this, his second volume, were aesthetic and somewhat obscure.

30 OCTOBER 1908, BOSTON, TO S. WEIR MITCHELL

Hotel Bellevue,
Boston, October 30, 1908.

My dear Mitchell:

I have just finished your book which came two days ago, with your letter,[1] and which I began to read at once. I began with the dedication which deeply, deeply touched me.[2] I had always hoped, but I had never quite known that you cared for me in that way. No form of thanks could bear you my gratitude, which is shared and doubled by the feeling of my wife. You have been part of our life and our death.[3] If she could forget that, she would not be the unforgetting mother she is, and we are in nothing more united than our sense of your wish to do everything for us when it was too late to do anything.

The book held me fast while I read, and you will not be surprised that the time and place were as important to me as the action. I am of that line of Welsh Quakers whom your touch makes live again in the figures you do not detach from their background for such important parts as some others. In Washington's second administration, my great-grandfather, Thomas Howells, visited Philadelphia, and was presented to the President who wished him to stay and establish in America the manufacture of Welsh flannel, which had flourished in hands at his and my father's birthplace, The Hay, in Breconshire, South Wales; but he went home, and it was for my grandfather to bring our future here. You will understand from these personalities how I should feel myself retroactively almost a part of your story, which concerns itself with events and people so far beyond me. I wish our poor fellows and poor dears could learn to write historical fiction from you; but for that they must be both born again and schooled again. I note once more your skill, which comes from your pleasure, in the French Revolution type, but it is a novel satisfaction to have you study it on our own ground, in aristocrats as well as jacobins. Your Huguenots, mother and son, are peculiarly interesting, a sort of version of our puritans, who believed in the sword of the Lord and of Gideon. You make them more appreciable to me than they have been before. As the grandson of "a Friend by convincement,"[4] I must be allowed my greater liking for your Quakers. But I will not go on cataloguing. If I recur to the immensely important situation, the great historical personages, I feel that I am paying your art as great a tribute as if I praised the children solely of your imagination. To divine the past is as great a thing as to create character.

Will you remember my wife and me to Mrs. Mitchell, and will you believe me always

> Affectionately yours,
> W. D. Howells.

1. Mitchell's historical novel *The Red City* was published in October 1908 and accompanied by a letter dated 25 October 1908 (PU).
2. The formal dedication reads: "To Wm. D. Howells in payment of a debt to a master of fiction and to a friend of many years."
3. Mitchell, one of the foremost alienists of the time, had attended Winifred

Howells from November 1888 until her death in March 1889. See Howells to Mitchell, 7 March 1889. Referring to the dedication and to Winifred's death, Mitchell, in his letter, asks Howells to "accept this slight expression of a friendship which allows of only one regret & that—I trust that you too share."

4. Howells' grandfather, Joseph Howells, had become a Quaker convert before emigrating to the United States.

16 NOVEMBER 1908, NEW YORK, TO ELIZABETH JORDAN

10 West 30th street,
Nov. 16, 1908.

Dear Miss Jordan:

I mentioned our scheme yesterday to Mr Duneka,[1] and though he received it grimly at first, he seemed to become more and more interested, and we battled it out on friendly terms all the way to lunch.

The more I think of it the more it interests me, and I believe you can do a great and useful and merciful thing in realizing the notion. It should be a sort of Counsel of Consolation, and people should be asked to write, as far as they will, from their *experiences* as well as their *opinions*, and to keep in mind that they are addressing those in immediate bereavement. I do not see why a kindly agnostic should not say something comforting to sorrow. But in the hour of grief there is commonly a reviving faith, which has *authority*, and must be respected.[2]

If I were you, I would not try for either length or brevity. Get as many and as various people to write as you can, and where you can, print together in the same number two papers of contrasting temperaments. It would be better to have 24 than twelve contributors, for the sake of the wider range; some would be less discursive than others and a long paper could be put with a short one. I want to write mine very soon,[3] but not as a suggestion of what others should say. Still, I think you could indicate fairly well the direction you would like the papers to take. You can be frank without being strict. Do you mind letting me see your encyclical?[4]

Yours sincerely
W. D. Howells.

1. Jordan and Howells were planning a series of essays by selected authors for *Harper's Bazar* on the topic of death and bereavement. The scheme first had to be approved by Frederick A. Duneka, secretary of the Harpers firm.

2. Howells might well have been moved to these strong sentiments by the touching and rejuvenating letter he received from Sarah Orne Jewett, 23 October 1908 (MeWC), written on the day of C. E. Norton's funeral: "I saw you today at the Appleton Chapel and I felt as one sometimes feels at the sight of an old friend—

a new spring from a deeper place in the hillside of life, of attachment and affection—you must not think either that it is only the ink of this letter that begins to write itself!—it is a true spring on this traveller's wayside. And I thought that you in your friendship and I in mine with dear Mr. Norton know some things together and hold them with dear love and gratitude for our very own that many of the old Cambridge neighbours, and cousins of varying degrees could never know . . . . How he said things about our stories—how he *didn't* say things; how quick his letters came when we were in trouble, how sure we were that he understood why some happy days and hours were so happy! I turn to you to say this as I could not turn to anyone else, and find a beautiful new reason for our being friends."

3. "In the House of Mourning," *Harper's Bazar*, April 1909. It was reprinted as "A Counsel of Consolation" in *In After Days, Thoughts on the Future Life* (1910) along with essays by Henry James, Thomas W. Higginson, Julia Ward Howe, and others.

4. Howells seems to refer to the instructions that Jordan was to send to the prospective authors.

18 NOVEMBER 1908, NEW YORK, TO MILDRED HOWELLS

Nov. 18, 1908.

Dear Pilla:

The Jabbies[1] have just been here, and we are one voice for *papering*.

So get your papers!

Send on your papers!

Hang your papers![2]

John looks as if he had got out of his lumbago, at last, and he was very gay. Abby was gay too, and very well. I'm glad you're having a good restful, workful time.

Papa.

1. John and Abby Howells.

2. This is one of a series of amusing exchanges with Mildred, who was in Boston, regarding the selection of wallpaper for the new twelve-room studio apartment at 130 West 57th Street. Two days later, 20 November 1908 (MH), Howells gently pointed out that Mildred's suggestions "were not an unmixed pleasure." The very next day, on a sheet added to a letter from Elinor Howells to Mildred, 21 November 1908 (MH), he apologetically identified "Mamma" as the source of dissatisfaction with Mildred's choice of "blue paper," while Elinor Howells, unbending to fashion, minced no words: "The peacock paper sets my teeth on edge—in spite of Whistler's peacock room example. It looks so painty . . . . Get any paper but peacock. I am so sick of peacock. All New York is in peacock."

25 NOVEMBER 1908, NEW YORK, TO SAMUEL L. CLEMENS

10 West 30th st.,
Nov. 25, 1908.

My dear Clemens:

I should like mightily to meet your farmers, but, poor fellow, I thought you went to Redding, to get rid of Mark Twain.[1] Besides knowing all your stories, I am prevented from coming to you by Mrs. Howells's not wanting to be left alone here; Pilla is still in Boston; and I have to help Mrs. H. breathe, and take other little jobs off her hands. If you ever give me another chance, be sure I shall take the first train. I am up so early, old man like, that if there were any lark round he would find me ready to shoot him.

L. Northcliffe, whom I met at a Harvey lunch,[2] verified beforehand every thing you have since reported his saying of the house. But what pleases me most is *your* generosity. They usually say, "Oh yes, Jones was the *architect*, but the fact is, my daughter planned the whole thing; and her aunts carried out her ideas."

Yours ever
W. D. Howells.

1. In a letter of 23 November 1908 (MH), Clemens invited Howells to visit Stormfield on 26 November. On that day, Clemens explained, he was to entertain "with the same old string of yarns" a local audience of "100 of the sterlingest farmers & their families...." The proceeds were to go to the town library that Clemens was helping to sponsor in Redding, Connecticut. See *Twain-Howells*, pp. 837–38.

2. Lord Northcliffe was Alfred C. W. Farnsworth (1865–1922), owner of the London *Times*, whose admiration for Stormfield and its architect Clemens conveyed to Howells: "...N. praised the house all the way & said he meant to get John Howells to go over & turn some of *his* residences into homes." George Harvey gave a luncheon for Lord Northcliffe at Delmonico's on 23 November.

6 DECEMBER 1908, NEW YORK, TO ANNE H. FRÉCHETTE

10 West 30th st.,
Dec. 6, 1908.

Dear Annie:

I will write my Sunday letter to you instead of Aurelia, and she will not lose much. The great topics with us are John's boy[1] and our flat. Both are new; the boy we came into Friday Nov. 27, and we expect to get into the flat about Dec. 25. I cannot say whom the flat takes after, but Elinor says the boy takes after me. At any rate he is a beautiful boy, with long eyes, a pretty mouth and forehead, the shapeliest dear little head, covered with as much hair as I have got left, but as dark as mine is white. I can't tell you what a joy he is to granny and me. I suppose his mother and father like him too, but that is mere nature. Still, we allow them a small interest in him. Abby is getting on very well; we had great fears for her, though her health remained so good throughout; all her mother's children were seven months babies, and she died giving birth to the last. However the whole affair has gone splendidly; and John is as happy as the day is long.—Enough of the boy; now the flat. Vevie will explain the sort of studio flat it is,—like those in 67th street, only much grander. Ours has 12 rooms, and they are actively getting their paper on. When that is done, we shall slowly put in the furniture.

I suppose that by this time the Cleveland deed is nearly here, if Joe got the same steamer that brought it for the return. Then I will forward it at once to the Taylors.[2] When we get the money, it will be time to decide on investment, but Aurelia must know that a 10 per cent stock selling for 112 does not pay ten per cent. Besides, no such stock is safe. However, we will talk that out later.

Annie, dear, your praise of my book was very sweet to me, but I must share with you the bitterness of its not selling.[3] It is not a failure, quite, but publishers and author expected an immediate go off, and they printed 6000, and have got 4000 left! You see, I thought that a book about Rome was a sure thing, and that all dollars, like all roads, led to it. Well, it is not the first time I've had my hopes dashed, and in the meantime people are constantly saying nice things to me about it, but nothing so precious as what you have said.

We are all so glad that you are well again. I *wish* I could go to the Pacific coast with you, but that must be for another life.—How nice that Aurelia likes her hotel, and finds it so interesting! Of course it is fine for her to be mixing with people and enlarging her circle. Give her our love, and take it for yourself and yours.

Your aff'te brother
Will.

1. William White Howells.
2. Aurelia's house in Cleveland was in the process of being sold. The deed had been sent to Joseph A. Howells at Turks Islands, who was expected to return it promptly with his and his wife's signatures. Upon its receipt, Howells was to convey it to Taylor & Son, the real estate agent in Cleveland.
3. *Roman Holidays and Others.*

31 JANUARY 1909, NEW YORK, TO SARA NORTON

130 West 57th Street,
Jan'y 31, 1909.

My dear Sally:

Your letter of the 28th found me here yesterday on our new shelf, between the asphalt and the sky.[1] I thank you for reminding me of the Lowell portrait, which your dear father had kept for me so long, and I shall be glad if you can send it to me here by express, letting me bear all the possible expenses: I wish I could relieve you of all trouble with it.

The news in your letter greatly interested me, perhaps more nearly because Pilla sails for Bermuda the day you sail for France. She has taken the laboring oar in getting us afloat here, and is not only very tired, but anxious to escape her winter throat.

I wish I could always think of you at Shady Hill, but I really believe it fortunate you should be away for a time, and better to leave friends in it than memories only. At moments lately I have got to missing your father in a curious way.[2] We were not quite of the same generation, but I feel more and more that with him gone I am immensely unfriended. I realize what a support his living sympathy was, how even when it was tacit it was always *there*—when I deserved it. I suppose this must have been the experience of many, but I know that it was, through his kindness, his constancy, eminently mine. He replaced all the losses of my better life; now he is part of them, how large a part I must not think.

We are beginning again, my wife and I in our 72d year the tale so often told in our lives, of housekeeping in a new place. It promises well, and the process is in a way rejuvenating. But it is better to be sailing for France and England, and our good wishes will follow you. May you be very happy in all your fortunes and remain in the glow of pleasant experiences when you come home. With our united love

Yours sincerely
W. D. Howells.

1. The Howellses had finally moved into their new apartment on 13 or 14 January. The letter from Sara Norton has not been located.
2. Charles E. Norton had died 20 October 1908.

16 February 1909, New York, to Robert Herrick

> 130 West 57th street,
> February 16, 1909.

Dear Mr. Herrick:

I have been reading your books with great interest, and I am ready to write of them. But before I do so, I think I ought to tell you that I must express a very mixed mind about the last of them.[1] There are two ways of looking at it: I can regard it as simply a picture of certain sides of American life, usually blinked, by an impartial observer whose sole business was to get them to the reader's knowledge; or I may regard it as in some sort a polemic for wider freedom in the sexual relations than the accepted ethics now grant.[2] The episode of Margaret Pole and her lover, who go off several days together, and wreak their love for each other, with no after compunction, has especially given me question. If you have portrayed it as a thing that happens, and stand quite outside of it morally, you are within your rights as an artist; but if you mean that it was a thing to have done without shame or without sin, you put yourself a position which the criticism deriving from such ethics as the world knows may and must question.[3] In a measure this is the case with the whole book, and its several potential or actual adulteries.[4]

I am the more confused because the reading of the story has not impaired my sense of your power as it comes from a serious and conscientious mind, or my respect for your literary quality. If I bring you to book it is not with bell and candle. If you wish to straighten me out with some word which the story does not speak, this is the moment. Or if you would rather on the whole that I should not write of your books I shall not misunderstand you, or depreciate you.

> Yours very sincerely,
> W. D. Howells.

1. Howells' essay, "The Novels of Robert Herrick," appeared in the *North American Review*, June 1909. Herrick's most recent novel was *Together* (1908), a work exploring the unpleasant realities of contemporary marriage.

2. In an immediate reply, 17 February 1909 (MH), Herrick diffidently yet forcefully defended the novel: "...I will do my best to answer the questions you raise although already the condition of mind in which TOGETHER was written is fading away and I do not remember it clearly. I am sure of one thing, however, positive— and that is I have NEVER written polemically, at least consciously. My effort has been representative and especially interpretative. Certainly I never for one moment intended to hold a brief for free love, and there must be something wrong about the book, about the conclusion, to lead people, you above all, to think so. As I look back upon it, the women in the book were mostly all cases of extreme individualism,

which is the politely philosophical term we give to selfishness,—that is they stand on the feminine side for that arrogant industrial individualism that is rife in the world of men today. They are all after the fulfillment of self,—socially, sexually, and economically. The failure of this personal individualism to give content, happiness, peace, I thought was brought out rather flatly in the last two parts of the book. I was conscious at the time of driving this in with a mallet, at the risk of all art, because the one thing I was hotly interested in was the sense of inadequacy of this sort of thing."

3. Without backing away in the least from Howells' misgivings, Herrick carefully explained his emotional and moral intentions regarding Margaret Pole and her lover: "There remains the debatable case of Margaret Pole and Rob Falkner. That stands apart from the others, I suppose, because it is interpreted more sympathetically than the others, more tenderly, and less obviously is failure. It belongs, nevertheless, in the same category of arrant individualism as the rest, only in this case there is presented flatly, and I believe honestly, the fact that for them this fulfillment of self at the cost of moral law, was FOR THE TIME an actual gain, a real enoblement. However much we may hate adultery, it is only right to realize that there is actual gain up to a certain point of spiritual life for some cases in sin. That Margaret herself became aware that this point of spiritual life was inadequate is clearly shown by the fact that she refused to marry Falkner when the opportunity came to do so. And in the last page but one of the book that idea is again presented, probably not fully enough. Evidently I have failed to make this paradox of the spiritual life convincing. But I believe it is real. Of course the commonplace thing for a woman like Margaret Pole to do would be to divorce and marry, a course that she has contempt for. The desire for her own life, her own greatest happiness led to her relation with Falkner, and it was only through this relation which aroused her whole being that she was enabled to, or as a matter of fact did, come to the realization of the inadequacy of that solution."

4. After reading a copy of the essay Howells had sent prior to its publication, Herrick expressed gratitude, in a letter of 7 May 1909 (MH), for what he characterized as "almost the first work of authoritative criticism, of *understanding* appreciation," that his novels had received. Although he acknowledged that Howells had been "generous" in his treatment of *Together*, he could not but feel that rating it "as the worst" of his novels was the "one sad thing" in the piece. For further commentary on *Together*, see Howells to Brander Matthews, 7 March 1909.

1 MARCH 1909, NEW YORK, TO WILLIAM W. HOWELLS

130 West 57th st.,
March 1, 1909.

Dear Billy:

It is very sweet of you to send that birthday card,[1] where we are walking toward the sunset together. It is a lovely sunset, but sad, and the night is beyond it. Hold fast to my hand, dear little boy, and keep me with you as long as you can. Some day, I hope not too late, you will know how I love you.

Your aff'te grandfather,
W. D. Howells.

1. The card is not extant, but it was apparently sent in Billy's behalf (he was then three months old) on the occasion of Howells' seventy-second birthday.

7 MARCH 1909, NEW YORK, TO BRANDER MATTHEWS

130 West 57th st.,
March 7, 1909.

My dear Matthews:

Your letter was not a bolt out of the blue but a ray out of the dark. To think of anybody at this late day—a whole year after its publication—reading Fennel and Rue! Never again will I speak evil of the grippe; would that the whole city might have it![1] But no beneficent pestilence was raging last spring, and the book did not sell 4000. Now it sells 0000.

Of course your praise does my sore heart good,[2] for I too thought the thing well done, though I knew it single to tenuity in motive, and narrowly escaping nothingness. But it seemed to me to get at the last moment a second wind which might have carried it far.

Since you will not write novels, why will you not read, besides mine, those of Robert Herrick?[3] They are good, all of them, though in the last the eternal femininity which always more or less bedevils him, really seems to make wreck of a good puritanic morality. There is adultery, actual and potential, all round the horizon in "Together," and one is afraid to trust one's self out in society. Still it is a great book, and some of the earlier ones are greater.

Yours ever
W. D. Howells.

1. Matthews had written Howells, 4 March 1909 (MH), saying that he had been "in the grasp of the grip" and had taken the occasion to read *Fennel and Rue* "straight thru, at a sitting."

2. In his letter, Matthews had praised the novel as "a mighty fine piece of work . . . . [¶] Miracles of subtle observation set down with marvels of felicity in phrasing,—that's the way it strikes me."

3. See Howells to Herrick, 16 February 1909.

12 MARCH 1909, NEW YORK, TO SAMUEL L. CLEMENS

130 West 57th st.,
March 12, 1909.

My dear Clemens:

I have found about 40 or 50 more of your letters, which will be about all, I think.[1] Shall I send them, or bring them when I come to see you after Pilla gets home?[2] You know you said I might come.

The letters are of the time when this night was blackest with you,[3] and *I* can't read them. But I know that *you* can, because you have the best courage of any man, and because as the years pass we like to renew our grief for the lost, which is all we have left of them, and like to feel our hearts bleed again. We pretend otherwise, but this is the truth, and it is strange enough. The anguish of another wrings our hearts, but we can bear our own after while.

Yours ever
W. D. Howells.

1. Howells had been returning Clemens' letters for use by Albert B. Paine, Clemens' biographer. See Howells to Clemens, 4 February 1908.
2. Mildred Howells was in Bermuda, expecting to return on 16 or 23 March.
3. Susy Clemens had died in 1896 and Olivia Clemens in 1904. The letters are probably from this period. Clemens replied the next day, 13 March (MH): "Ah, those letters! remembrancers of that dark time. I think I could read them now, but I am not sure." See *Twain-Howells*, p. 842.

14 MARCH 1909, NEW YORK, TO HENRY B. FULLER

130 West 57th street,
March 14, 1909.

My dear Fuller:

Your letter interests me beyond all epistolary scope.[1] Come on and talk it over. My own life is an eddying round and round, with a more or less delightful dizziness in the brain, but your autobiographic note has given me one of those stops in which I peer about me with a sense of revelation. What if I too had "no great liking for the environment, and no great zest for life as it is lived"?[2] Shall I own such a thing? Not after sitting at breakfast yesterday beside T. Roosevelt,[3] and witnessing the wonder of his zest for everything. He is so strenuous that I am faint thinking of him. No man over forty has the force to meet him without nervous prostration.

But what I wanted to say was that in going over the proofs of a very languid idyl which I had lengthened to 175 pp.,[4] it came over me that it was past the time with me to write fiction. I had a kind of sickness of the job. Is that the way you feel? I should once never have believed that I could feel so.[5] Can't you see it your duty to write, hereafter, my novels for me?

Yours affectionately,
W. D. Howells.

1. There had been an earlier exchange between Howells and Fuller, the Chicago novelist. In a letter of 21 February 1909 (MH), Howells had encouraged Fuller to write more novels in the realistic vein of *The Cliff-Dwellers* (1893) and *With the Procession* (1895): "You owe me several such books." Acknowledging how much Howells' novels had inspired him, Fuller had answered in a letter of 4 March 1909 (MH): "Yes, I *do* owe you a great deal, and ought to be repaying you in kind." He then went on to describe the difficulties he was encountering as an aging realist: "I suppose what does best for a middle-aging novelist is a decorous realism: realism, because the early day of fancy and invention is now past; and decorous realism, because a 'superfluity of naughtiness,' which sets ill on anybody, sets most of all on a man over fifty."

2. Howells was quoting Fuller's portrayal of himself, in the letter of 4 March, as a writer now repelled by the very setting which had served his fiction: "Yet, if I go to work to repay you, I shall have two permanent draw backs to overcome: no great liking for the environment I must depict, and no great zest for life as it is lived. In such circumstances should a man write at all? In these crowded days ought anybody to scribble, unless the proddings of youthful enthusiasm make him feel that—he—just—must? And who, in a cheap and noisy time, wants 'fame'? To wish for consideration, and yet to shrink from celebrity—there is the modern paradox. *I* can't square it. [¶] All these conflicting considerations once adjusted, and the realistic Chicago novel of observation under way, what then? Who wants to read about this repellent town?"

3. Howells was one of two dozen publishers and editors invited by Robert J. Collier (1876–1918), head of P. F. Collier & Son Co., to his Park Avenue home on 13 March for a breakfast in honor of the former president. In a letter to Aurelia H. Howells, also on 19 March 1909 (MH), Howells briefly mentions the occasion: "I had been at a breakfast to Roosevelt, and sat next him. A hot time in the old town, and there was no end to the jokes." Making his own slight joke, Howells alludes to "A Hot Time in the Old Town," adopted by the Rough Riders as their theme song, but actually disliked by Roosevelt because of its uncouth association with ragtime.

4. Still referring to it as "The Children of the Summer," Howells was having increasing difficulty finishing the story that was to become *The Vacation of the Kelwyns* (1920). He had written Frederick A. Duneka, 4 March 1909 (MWA), telling him to delay publication: "I may want to postpone the book till I can satisfy myself better with it that [sic] I have done yet." Soon thereafter he decided to withhold it, as he informed Duneka in a letter of 8 April 1909 (MWA), in order to "give it a thorough overhauling—perhaps till next year." Five months earlier Howells had described to Charles E. Norton how old age was affecting his conception of the story. See Howells to Norton, 11 October 1908.

5. In a reply of 16 April 1909 (MH), Fuller elaborated his feelings. The problem was not so much one of old age and flagging energies, but rather an immobilizing tension between the demands of his social perceptions and the romantic compromises required of him in order to publish fiction: "Viewing the failure of fiction to interest

the aging fictionist, I envy you your position and its opportunities in other directions: surely interest and dignity remain for the socialized essay long after their departure from the love story. For myself, I am weary of the convention of the young pair in love. Last year I sent six short stories to one of our best magazines: with three of these I said what I had to say in the familiar mould formed by the experiences of a young couple who are happily married in the end; while the remaining three, though they contained as much of interest and significance, neglected that precious precaution. Result: the first three were 'taken', and the other three 'left'. I felt mortified on my own account, and rather sorry for my editor. Above all, I blushed for the soft-boned public. It was just about then, I believe, that my interest in story-writing gave its last gasp and decently composed its limbs for the last sleep! [¶] You, fortunately, have other things to say, and other media for making yourself audible .... The social study—'picked out', if you please with a modicum of charac-terization—ought to be enough, happily, to please and to satisfy you for the remainder of your career."

24 MARCH 1909, REDDING, CONNECTICUT, TO ELINOR M. HOWELLS

Redding Connecticut March 24, 1909.

Dear Elinor:

This is a glorious morning on a beautiful country—*ridente*, like that round Sunapee,[1] soft hills pillowing on each other, but it's four miles from the station, and I don't think we'll build on the lot Clemens has picked out for us. He seems not very well—tired out from his visit to New York, and indigestive; but full of fire and fun; and at dinner we had a roaring time. We took a walk before lunch, but he was not good for one in the afternoon. The Ashcrofts watch over him with tender constancy;[2] he doesn't like being alone. After all, for oldlings, you and I seem pretty young.

Don't bother about the lunch invites;[3] just keep the answers. Crowny[4] can't take a joke. Clemens can't come because he is going to Norfolk, Va., with Rogers,[5] to open a railroad.

Quite possibly I may come home tomorrow. Clara is coming up.[6] I haven't seen Clemens this morning yet. I am having a beautiful time, but if I see that I'm wearing on him, I'll hop.

Love to Pilla,

Papa.

1. Howells was visiting Clemens at Stormfield, staying 23 to 26 March. See *Twain-Howells*, p. 842. The laughing (*ridente*) hills are those around Sunapee, New Hamp-shire, where the Howellses had "summered," July-August 1893.

2. Isabel V. Lyon, Clemens' secretary, and Ralph W. Ashcroft. The couple was married on 18 March. See *Twain-Howells*, pp. 842–43.

3. Howells had sent out invitations for a bon voyage party in honor of Colonel George Harvey on 2 April at the new apartment. Howells wrote Aurelia H. Howells,

4 April 1909 (MH), of its success: "I had my men's lunch on Friday, and in the big studio it went off famously. They sat about four hours, and there was lots of good talk. It was for Harvey, who is going to England . . . ." See *Life in Letters*, II, 265.

4. The painter, Frederic Crowninshield, who was one of the invited guests.

5. Henry H. Rogers (1840–1909), a wealthy businessman, was Clemens' financial adviser.

6. Clemens' daughter lived in New York City.

13 APRIL 1909, NEW YORK, TO DAVID A. MUNRO

130 West 57th st.,
April 13, 1909.

Very dear Mr. Munro:

I am sending back the boxes of Swinburne and taking back my promise to write about him.[1] By the time I waded through his welter of words—if I ever did—I should be in a state to blast the covers off the Review, and to kill the sale of the poet's works as dead as my own.

Thank you for sending back the Welsh papers.[2] They were really *not* the thing for you.

I will be soon letting you have the paper on Herrick;[3] it isn't long; and with your leave I will do one about Grant.[4]

Yours sincerely
W. D. Howells.

1. Algernon C. Swinburne (1837–1909) had just died on 10 April. At Munro's request, Howells had probably agreed to do a memorial essay for the *North American Review*.

2. "Aberystwyth, a Welsh Watering Place" and "Llandndno, Another Welsh Watering Place." Neither was published in periodical form, both appearing only in *Seven English Cities* (1909).

3. See Howells to Herrick, 16 February 1909, n. 1.

4. Howells did not do a paper on the lawyer and novelist Robert Grant. He had reviewed a stage version of *Unleavened Bread* (1901) in "The Recent Dramatic Season," *North American Review*, March 1901, and he would later review *The Law and the Family* (1919), a sociological study, in the "Editor's Easy Chair," *Harper's Monthly*, March 1920.

26 APRIL 1909, KITTERY POINT, TO ELINOR M. HOWELLS

K. P. April 26, 1909.

Dear Elinor:

Mr. Richardson has just been here, and we have arranged for the bathroom. He will carpenter as well as plumb it, having his own carp., and he will take down the wind-pump tower. As a compliment to you, I will have it razed to the ground, and *take it out of you* some other way—perhaps destroy all your locusts.

Mrs. Tyson in Boston told me Sarah Jewett had been palsied,[1] and yesterday afternoon, Annie and I went over to South Berwick to see her.[2] The left side is totally paralyzed, but the poor thing lay there in her bed, smiling and joking, the same as ever. She had the April Atlantic beside her, and had just read John's story with enthusiasm.[3] She sent down for Annie after I had seen her and talked with her too.

The weather is milder than yesterday but still *rawr*. Pil's jonquils are in bloom under the ash trees in front.

—Albert[4] has just brought your letters and enclosures. What a pity about poor Laura![5] But I shall probably come Thursday all the same, or let you know duly. Annie is *very* well, with a huge appetite, and enjoying every minute. She has her breakfast in bed. Martha[6] feeds and coddles us both. I will write to Laura.

What do you think of my preaching yesterday in the church here?[7] Their "supply" didn't come and the crowd got round and pleaded with me so to speak or read, that I raced over to the Barnbrary, got the Trav. from Altruria, and gave 'em a good dose of socialism. They liked it so well that they all shook hands and thankt me. Marthy reported later that it was the greatest hit ever known in K. P.—I have taken one of the two big square pews which they've put back, and now Pilla must come and help be county family at church, after this. The ch. is beautiful, and the old white pulpit has replaced the 1870 black walnut thing. Love to Pilla.

Papa

1. Mrs. Tyson of Boston is not identified. Sarah Orne Jewett had been partially paralyzed by a stroke in March, although her mind was not affected. She died on 24 June of a cerebral hemorrhage. See *Sarah Orne Jewett Letters*, ed. Richard Cary (Waterville, Me.: Colby College Press, 1967), II, 173.
2. Anne Fréchette was visiting with Howells for two weeks, first in New York and then at Kittery Point. She returned to Ottawa on 29 April.
3. John M. Howells' story in the April *Atlantic* was "At the Café d'Orsay." In a letter of 3 May 1909 (MH), Henry James offered dutiful praise: "...I find John's little Tale in the Atlantic, which I thank you for having sent me, most neat and right and charming. It is done with a *hand*, and I almost shudder to think of the promise it reveals. I have often wondered how it feels to have extraordinary children—or indeed any at all; and also even a little how it feels to have architectural children. But to have literary children, 'promising' ahead at such a rate, and especially architectural-literary children, more or less extraordinary in both ways, how does *that* feel?"
4. Albert Gunnison, the gardener.
5. Either Laura Stedman, the daughter of Edmund C. Stedman, with whom Howells

had been corresponding regarding her father's letters, or Laura P. Mitchell, Elinor's cousin.

6. Martha Clarkson, the housekeeper.

7. For a brief comment on the history of the Kittery church, see *Life in Letters*, II, 266.

12 MAY 1909, NEW YORK, TO HENRY E. ROOD

> 130 West 57th st.,
> May 12, 1909.

Dear Mr. Rood:

Come when you will, at a day's notice, and the sooner the better. I am glad you think of beginning, after the "Lit. P."[1] with the earliest books. Their order should be: Venetian Life, Italian Journeys, Doorstep Acquaintance, Their Wedding Journey, A Chance Acquaintance.[2] I could write interestingly about all these,[3] and I have fotografs of the period for each, which we will look over.

Here is a typical introduction (Heroines of Fiction.)[4] and please ask Mr. Duneka if it is the kind of thing he wants.

> Yours sincerely,
> W. D. H.

1. Rood, an editor at Harper & Brothers, was working with Howells to arrange publication of the Library Edition. Howells here refers to *My Literary Passions* which, along with *Criticism and Fiction*, made up the first of six volumes issued in 1911. See Cady, *Howells*, II, 254. In an earlier letter of 19 November 1906 (MWA) to Frederick A. Duneka, Howells indicated that the publisher had briefly considered the possibility of bringing out six volumes in the late fall of 1906. For the first consideration of the Library Edition, see Howells to Norton, 12 October 1902.

2. These titles were never issued.

3. Howells had recently admired the prefaces Henry James had written for the New York Edition and was probably spurred initially by James's example. See Howells to James, 2 August 1908. Encouraged by the Harpers, he began enthusiastically but quickly changed his mind, especially wishing to avoid the appearance of imitating James. See Howells to Duneka, 9 June 1909 and 19 June 1909.

4. In addition to the "Biographicals" appearing in the six volumes eventually published, Howells also wrote several prefaces for projected volumes, including the introduction to *Heroines of Fiction*. See Gibson-Arms, *Bibliography*, p. 66. These prefaces are printed in George Arms, "Howells' Unpublished Prefaces," *New England Quarterly* 17 (1944), 580–91.

9 JUNE 1909, NEW YORK, TO FREDERICK A. DUNEKA

130 West 57th st.,
June 9, 1909.

Dear Mr. Duneka:

We are kept until Sunday night by a return of my old liver trouble, which I must rest off the pain of before I start,[1] and in the meantime I am writing the "Story of the Story" for a preface to "A Hazard of New Fortunes." It goes so glibly that I am likely to have an unrequited passion for that kind of thing.[2]

I don't want to forecast the plumage of our unhatched chickens too far ahead; but as to the "complete" edition I have some distinct preferences. I should like a richly dark sober cloth—dull blue or green—since James has got maroon, and I should like the title lettered on the cloth direct, and not on a paper label. I know that these things always involve a question of cost, but I hope you agree with my taste. I should like nothing but the title; no decoration of any kind.

Yours sincerely
W. D. Howells.

1. Howells was unable to start for Kittery Point by a general failing of his health in early May. He described his condition in a letter of 23 May 1909 (MH) to Aurelia H. Howells: "I had very nearly a turn of my old gall colic, but we managed to avert it . . . . My still older enemy, vertigo, has been on me in full force, and is still hanging about. It began with me in Columbus when I was 19; nothing but exercise has any effect on it, and Kittery Point will give me that when we get there early next month."

2. The preface was published as a "Bibliographical" to the Library Edition issue of *A Hazard of New Fortunes* in 1911. Howells' feelings about this and other prefaces for the edition changed dramatically.

19 JUNE 1909, KITTERY POINT, TO FREDERICK A. DUNEKA

. . . Kittery Point, Maine June 19, 1909.

Dear Mr. Duneka:

I have made a careful experiment of the type in an introduction to A Hazard of New Fortunes, and have convinced my self that I cannot write prefaces for the library edition, much as I would like to meet your wish in the matter.[1] I believe I was right in wishing the volumes to go the public without any word of explanation or comment from me, because they are already most intimately full of me, and are their own explanation and comment. I know that the typical one I have done is well done, but I know also that it is superfluous and impertinent. I cannot pretend to better your judgment as to the advantage of the prefaces with the subscribers, and I only state my insuperable repugnance to them. I not only feel this in regard to them intrinsically, but I feel that I should have the effect of following in James's footsteps,[2] and that with critics this would be a just ground for censure. I know that you do not agree with me on this point, but I count on your kindness to let me have my way, and to let the books go without a personal word from me.

Yours ever,
W. D. Howells.

P. S. If it seems possible, when the edition is completed, to add a volume of Literary Autobiography,[3] in which the story of my work as an author, rather that of my life shall be told, I may like to supply it. That would give the editon a novelty and distinction which the separate prefaces could not give.

1. See Howells to Duneka, 9 June 1909.

2. In a letter of 23 July 1909 (MH), James, having just completed eighteen prefaces for the New York Edition, applauded Howells' decision: "delightful as your Prefaces would be sure to have been had you written them, I can't but congratulate you on your wisdom in keeping out of so desperately arduous a job, which would have crowned your life with an intolerable fatigue. I found mine—of much scanter number—an almost insurmountable grind toward the end.... What a monstrously & brutally stupid race is the avid & purblind one of Publishers, who seem never dimly to guess that authors can't to advantage be worked like ice-cream freezers or mowing machines." For Howells' premature enthusiasm regarding the prefaces, see Howells to Rood, 12 May 1909; for James's description of the labor involved in writing his prefaces, see Howells to Norton, 12 April 1908, n. 6.

3. Howells never wrote a literary autobiography, although he speaks further of preparations for it in his letter of 4 July 1909 to Joseph A. Howells. Perhaps reshaping the present conception, Howells eventually produced a more personal account of his life in *Years of My Youth* (1916).

23 JUNE 1909, KITTERY POINT, TO MRS. S. E. PEARSON

Kittery Point, June 23, 1909.

Dear Mrs. Pearson:[1]

Have you any signally ardent and eager vine, full of enterprise, and gritting its teeth in the desire of laying hold of an arbor and covering it with leaves and flowers in a single night? If so, I know of a purchaser.

We have the arbor and we want the vine. What about a well-started Kudzu vine, of Japanese extraction?

Yours sincerely
W. D. Howells.

1. Pearson owned a nursery in Portsmouth, New Hampshire. Howells customarily wrote in the spring to make plans for starting the cherished garden at Kittery Point.

4 JULY 1909, KITTERY POINT, TO JOSEPH A. HOWELLS

Kittery point, July 4, 1909.

Dear Joe:

I hope that by this time you are quite yourself, unless you would rather be somebody else. Eliza speaks of your having dysentery, and then of "the diarrhoea," but I suppose it was the last, for you have not probably had what we used to call "bloody flux," and now call dysentery. Whatever it is, or was, I trust it is now entirely over. I wish you could be here to breathe the fresh, bright, strong air of this most exemplary 4th of July morning. Night before last it stormed, and all day yesterday it blew, so that this is just the day for a Sunday School picnic in the Sycamore Grove,[1] or rather such a day as they never could have had there.

I am engaged on a job that would perhaps interest you: putting together my books for a library edition.[2] By grouping two or three or four of the shorter ones, I can perhaps get the entire edition into 31 or 32 volumes, of 4 to 5 hundred pages each, of the dimensions of London Films or Roman Holidays.[3] To accompany this edition I am going to write a literary autobiography, which will treat of the where, when and how of them all.[4] For this purpose I asked Aurelia for my letters to father and herself, for I had fortunately spoken in them always of what work I had in hand. Otherwise I should not be able to time the books. These letters cover a period of fifty years, and with an average of one a week they amount to something over 2500. It took a whole week's work to sort them chronologically, first in decades and then in years. But now it is done, and I have only to go over them and discard those which do not bear on my undertaking.

It is cruel hard looking over them, and like delving in the tombs. I wish I was young enough to make material, literary material, out of the experience, but I recognize every day this part of my life is over. Things suggest themselves, but they don't grip me, and hold me to them as they used. Perhaps I may note something of the kind in the autobiography. What I note now is the unchangingness of character in the persons mentioned. I find that in Columbus in 1859 I was worrying over Sam, as I am worrying over him now at K. P., in 1909, and for the same reasons. You know he is about moving again? I wonder what the true inwardness of that is. Does he or Ethel or do both become intolerable as tenants? The whole business of family ties is very curious. He is the sort of man I would last have chosen for a brother, but somehow I can't unchoose him. Just now he "is to be blest" with a watchman's place in the printing office, and he seems to come so near it that Senator Burton seems to have thought he was already in it.[5]

In going over my books I find that 18 or 20 volumes have been written since I came to Harpers in 1886, and 10 or 12 before that. Of course, my meat went into the earlier ones, and yet there are three or four of the later novels which are as good as any. I hope I shall get my "wind" again, but just now I am fagged, there's no denying it. I can look back, and see that the like has happened before, but I wasn't then 72 years old. I can't get hold of a subject that interests me.—I am sick of K. P., and I would like to travel. I have a notion of going to Spain, which was my early passion, and the Harpers would like to have me. But I believe that travel in Spain is very rough sledding, and I should dread it for Elinor, though she says she is game for going. At present we are reading a very amusing book about traveling in Greece, Turkey, Palestine and Egypt—a Californian's, who sent it me three years ago, and never got a word of thanks from me. Now he is probably dead from my ingratitude,[6] which I shall try to atone for too late. In one way or other we are all Sams.

Well, with our love to you both,

Yours affectionately,
Will

1. The Sycamore Grove was in Hamilton, Ohio, the town of Howells' boyhood. In *A Boy's Town* (1890), Howells recalls how the Sons of Temperance would appropriate the entire Fourth of July celebration: "and then there was nothing but a temperance picnic in the Sycamore Grove, which the boys took part in as Sunday-school scholars" (p. 118).

2. See Howells to Rood, 12 May 1909, n. 1.

3. As indicated in a letter to Frederick A. Duneka, 25 October 1909 (MWA), Howells later revised the total: "In order to get the library edition into 35 volumes, I condensed several of the trade-list books into one. If you will refer to the Lib. ed. copy for 'Certain Del. Eng. Cities' joined to it; the last as a separate title is suppressed."

4. See Howells to Duneka, 19 June 1909, n. 3.

5. The connection between Joseph R. Burton (1851–1923), the Republican senator from Kansas (1901–1907), and Samuel Howells' employment in the Government Printing Office is not known.

6. Charles W. Stoddard may have sent Howells one of his travel books on the Middle East, *Mashallah!* (1881) or *A Cruise Under the Crescent* (1898); he died on **23** April **1909**.

13 JULY 1909, KITTERY POINT, TO THOMAS W. HIGGINSON

Kittery Point, July 13, 1909.

My dear Higginson:

I will gladly tell you all I know of the projected meetings of the Academy in Washington.[1] It was decided at our April meeting in New York to have them; and I began writing to different Academicians in the hope of securing them for the nine papers to be read. You, thank you, have consented, and so has the dear and great Mrs. Julia Ward Howe,[2] with Rhodes, Cable, President Hadley (conditionally) Kenyon Cox (ditto) Hastings, the architect, John La Farge, Horatio W. Parker.[3] Brownell, Furness, Lounsbury, Mahan, Woodrow Wilson, for divers just reasons, declined.[4] Some of those consenting will drop out. I had to consider age, occupation, and "previous condition of servitude" in my askings; but the show is very good. Most of us are not in our first youth, and I tried not to have all sages. It has been a "chore," and the work is not over yet. Naturally I have had to write personal letters to each, and more than one to each, but if we succeed in impressing the nation with our worth and weight, as a body, I shall count it all joy.—Have you seen Sanborn's double-barrelled autobiography?[5] If one barrel does not bring you down the other will. It is an odd form, but the matter is good and important. Few men living, except yourself, have lived through such history; and by the way, isn't it time you should tell your tale? Everybody seems to be doing the like, with far less reason. Your autobiography would be one of the great ones. (I know what you have done in the recollections way;[6] but I want your whole life.)

I am not very well, and am rather lazying the summer away. I was jolted out of my usual pace by a severe liver attack in New York,[7] and I haven't caught up with myself yet. I have been such a steady goer for fifty years, that I hardly know myself in this lounger by the wayside. Do you have unmuffled motor-boats in Dublin pond? They are the curse of Kittery Point. Though there is a law against them in both Maine and New Hampshire, nobody pays the least attention to it. We used to think ourselves a "law-abiding people," but are we? Perhaps we obey the bad laws.

If there is anything more I can tell you about the Washington meetings, let me know. I ought invent something.

Yours sincerely
W. D. Howells.

1. Higginson had accepted Howells' invitation of 5 May 1909 (MH) to deliver a paper at the "first public session" of the American Academy of Arts and Letters to be held at Washington, D.C., 13–14 December. In a letter of 11 July 1909 (MH), Higginson had asked for further details "about the attractive scheme at Washington . . . ." See also Howells to Johnson, 2 December 1909, and Howells to James, 25 December 1909.

2. In his acceptance of 6 May 1909 (MH), Higginson had urged Howells to include among the speakers Julia Ward Howe, then eighty-nine and just recently elected to the Academy: "I should be particularly sorry for her omission, as the only woman in the club and absolutely sure to draw enthusiasm by her presence." Howells replied immediately, 7 May 1909 (MH), thanking Higginson for helping him to avoid "a break that would have brought grief to us all and shame to me. Of course I am writing to her at once; I think her almost the most important woman living, and almost the most beautiful and moving speaker I ever heard." Howe accepted, 12 May 1909 (MH), saying that it would be "a great pleasure to meet the American Academy face to face, if I can only manage to live so long!" She wrote a poem for the occasion entitled "The Capitol," but was dissuaded at the last minute by Howells and other Academy officers from making the arduous wintertime journey to deliver it personally. See Laura E. Richards and Maud Howe Elliott, *Julia Ward Howe, 1819–1910* (Boston: Houghton Mifflin, 1915), p. 430.

3. Those consenting were historian James F. Rhodes (1848–1927); novelist George W. Cable (1844–1925); Arthur T. Hadley (1856–1930), political economist and then president of Yale (1899–1921); Kenyon Cox (1856–1919), painter and art critic; John La Farge (1835–1910), artist and author; and Canadian-born novelist Horatio W. Parker (1862–1932).

4. Those declining were critic and essayist William C. Browning (1851–1921); Horace H. Furness (1833–1912), noted Shakespeare scholar; Thomas R. Lounsbury (1839–1915), professor of English at Yale; Rear Admiral Alfred T. Mahan (1840–1914), naval historian and former president of the Newport War College (1886–1889); and Woodrow Wilson, then president of Princeton (1902–1910).

5. Franklin B. Sanborn had just brought out his two-volume autobiography *Recollections of Seventy Years* (1909). Howells reviewed it in the "Editor's Easy Chair," *Harper's Monthly*, October 1909.

6. *Cheerful Yesterdays* (1898).

7. See Howells to Duneka, 9 June 1909, n. 1.

25 JULY 1909, KITTERY POINT, TO FREDERICK A. DUNEKA

Kittery Point, July 25, 1909.

Dear Mr. Duneka:

Having nothing now left to worry about, I am worrying about a point that will make me seem ridiculous to you, but which I am confidentially asking you to relieve me on. I have recalled two places in

Their Silver Wedding Journey, one where I made fun of the Austrian emperor's bust with side whiskers and a laurel crown, and one where I spoke disrespectfully of the Austrian flag, as that of a stupid monarchy which had survived so many bright republics. Carlsbad is in Austria; and could you send to the Austrian consulate, and without giving the case away in the least learn just what is the Austrian law in regard to the *leze majesty*?[1] I don't really dream that I have committed that mystical offence, but I would rather not be asked to leave Carlsbad between two tumblers of the water. Any consular clerk could say what the law is, or whether there is any such law in Austria; in Germany of course it is very strict. I will beg you to keep this quite to yourself, even from your next friend.

If the book circulated no more freely in Austria than it did in America, there is a chance in a million that any Austrian authority has ever seen it; but you perceive I am a little hypped, and I want a mind at ease in starting off. If you should find there is not a shadow to apprehend, perhaps you would telegraph me, at Portsmouth N. H., the words "All Right."[2]

Yours sincerely,
W. D. Howells.

1. Having benefited from his 1897 visit to the famous European spa, Howells again arranged to go with Mildred for a three-week course of treatment at the baths of Carlsbad, Austria. He had written to Duneka on 18 July 1909 (Arms), asking Harper & Brothers for a short leave. Howells feared that certain passages in *Their Silver Wedding Journey* (1899) might constitute the punishable offense of impugning the dignity of the sovereign head of state, Emperor Franz Joseph. He had described the emperor's statuary likeness as the "bust of the paternal Caesar, with whose side-whiskers a laurel crown comported as well as it could" (II, 30). Of the Austrian flag he had been candidly disrespectful, describing it as "languidly curling and uncurling in the bland evening air, as it had over a thousand years of stupid and selfish monarchy."

2. Duneka telegraphed Howells as instructed and followed with a letter of assurance, 27 July 1909 (Arms): "We saw the Consul here, and without mentioning any names, he referred us to the Statutes which may be construed so as to cover certain words from 'Their Silver Wedding Journey' but the chances of such construction are infinitely remote . . . . [¶] Just between ourselves, of course, there is not the slightest danger of His Majesty dashing the cup of cold water from your lips just because you didn't like his whiskers. What are whiskers between friends, anyhow? I believe the matter doesn't warrant a moment's thought."

20 AUGUST 1909, CARLSBAD, TO HENRY JAMES

Hotel Königsvilla,
Carlsbad, Aug. 20, 1909.[1]

My dear James:

Incredibly enough we are here, Pilla and I, and the gayer for your heart-friendly letter.[2] (I fall helplessly into the German idioms). We had a voyage of really unparalleled smoothness and brightness; the sun followed us as far as it was safe into the North Sea, and even there the waves had hardly their white caps on.

I have got into the hands of a very nice liberal Doctor,[3] whom I knew unprofessionally here 12 years ago, and who I fancy tacitly holds that I needn't have come again. He is letting me up finely on the waters and the diet (in reason) and you can judge of the tolerance and innocence of his nature when I tell you that he was dining the night I saw him with the "bad" Princess Rospigliosi,[4] and believes that the Pope is seriously reconsidering her hard lot.

We are in a pretty hotel on the Schlossberg, and are finding the place all the more amusing because it is in the Second Season and there are so few Anglo Saxons left as to make no show in the Teutonic and Slavic crowds. You see the fashions at the worst, their wildest, and there is a frankly indecent show of busts and abdomens which, like the fiction of Zola is not immoral; such women *must* be good; they have at least no concealments.

We expect to reach England about the 10th of September, and to be there about two weeks; if we can get a boat back so soon. But the Cooks[5] here discourage the notion. However, we shall see, and the great thing is we shall see *you*, somewhere, somehow. Then we can tell you all about the Smalleys. You really needn't shrink from the Year Book;[6] it is truly well done—so far as I could see. One droll phase is that poor E. is not prevented by her straight-jacket[7] from "kicking" at the notion of anybody out of the asylum's dealing with the kind Badger, who is as little like the badger of Jap folk-lore as any publisher I know.[8]

We hear good news from home, and if my wife were here, I am sure she would join her exiles in love to you.

Yours ever
W. D. Howells.

1. Howells and Mildred had left New York on 4 August on board the *President Grant*; they arrived in Cuxhaven on 14 August and in Carlsbad two days later, after stopping over in Leipzig.
2. James had written on 12 August 1909 (MH), imploring Howells to stop in

England on the way home from Carlsbad: "I beseech you, truly, to return via England—you will deal me otherwise the finishing stroke." The two men saw each other briefly in London at the end of September.

3. According to a letter from Howells to Elinor M. Howells, 18 August 1909 (MH), this was a Doctor Lechreg or Schmidt-Lechreg, otherwise not identified.

4. The princess was the former Marie Jennings Ried Parkhurst of Washington, D. C., divorced in 1898 from Colonel Frederick H. Parkhurst, a member of the Maine legislature. Her marriage to Prince Giuseppe Rospigliòso, based on a civil ceremony in 1901, encountered difficulties because the Vatican would not annul her first marriage.

5. Thomas Cook & Son, English tourist agency.

6. Evelyn G. Smalley had assembled *The Henry James Year Book*, subsequently published by Richard Badger of Boston in 1912. Through Howells, James had been asked to write a preface, but he informed Howells, 23 July 1909 (MH), that he could not do so "without sight of the Book—or whatever the thing is—itself!" He later contributed an introduction, entitled "The Author to the Public," while Howells furnished a counterpiece under the title "One of the Public to the Author."

7. The matter of the *Year Book* had been complicated by Evelyn Smalley's recent commitment to an asylum. The exact nature of her ailment is not known; in his letter of 12 July, James had told Howells: "it has been communicated to me that her infinitely tragic case is one for which no recovery can be hoped."

8. Howells is punning on the name of the publisher of the *Year Book*. In Japanese folklore the badger appears as a mischievous animal capable of assuming human form and often inflicting harm on others.

25 AUGUST 1909, CARLSBAD, TO SAMUEL L. CLEMENS

Villa Teresa ...
Carlsbad, Aug. 25, 1909.

Dear Clemens:

Your friendly letter of prevention found me already taking quarts of cure, here.[1] I hated abominably to come, but doctors and dear ones of all ages and sexes joined in thrusting me away. Surgeons suggested prying me open with cutlasses, and painted the process in glowing colors. But the next time I have a bilious colic that ties me up in a double bow-knot I will get an osteopath to untangle me.

I was here before, you know, and it is all duller than the ditch water one drinks: troops of yellow Jews with corkscrew curls before their ears; hordes of disemboweled and hipless hussies old young; men with Tyrolean hats and goblets slung to their waists. The only good thing is the boiled ham.—I got the second volume of your Tramp Abroad out of the hotel library, and read it with the joy in you which never fails me. Read your Mrs. Eddy massacre[2] just before I left home, and gloated on every drop of her blood.

I have a fearful cold from a climate that boils you at noon and pierces you with Alpine cold at night. Pilla sends her love with mine to the whole lot of you. We hope to leave here two weeks from today and be in New York by October.—I hated so to come that I could not believe it real.[3]

1. Howells probably refers to a letter from Clemens to Elinor M. Howells, 7 August 1909 (MH), forwarded to him at Carlsbad, in which Clemens had touted the virtues of osteopathy as opposed to conventional cures: "The osteopath did a great deal more for me in 15 minutes than the physician & 200 doses of medicine did for me in 45 days. I am so sorry Howells got away." See *Twain-Howells*, pp. 846–47.

2. *Christian Science with Notes Containing Corrections to Date* (1907).

3. The letter is unsigned.

28 AUGUST 1909, CARLSBAD, TO EDEN PHILLPOTTS

Hotel Königsvilla . . . .
Carlsbad Aug. 28, 1909.

Dear Mr. Phillpotts:

Your letter followed me from New York,[1] and I have sent it home to my wife that she might share the pleasure it gave me. I am glad my review interested you, for it interested me to write it; I thought I had lived by the time when one makes new friends in literature, but I found I was mistaken when I came upon your books.

I left my wife reading at the whole row of them when I sailed four weeks ago, and now I am reading your "Lying Prophets" here.[2] It gives me that höchst angenehmer Schmerz,[3] which is proof of an author's power. But it is not so shapely as The Whirlwind, nor so perfectly knit as The Children of the Mist.[4] Still I am only a little more than half through it, and I may change my mind. I should like to thresh out many things with you face to face, and I hope we may meet.[5] I should like to see your moor country. After my cure ends here on the 7th September, my daughter and I will strike straight for England, where we shall be till we sail on the 28th. We shall, after a little of London be batting about in my father's country of Wales, and the West and South of England. My address if you care to let me look you up, will be c/o Brown Shipley & Co. 123 Pall Mall.

Yours sincerely,
W. D. Howells.

1. Eden Phillpotts (1862–1960), a minor British novelist, was at the beginning of a prolific if not distinguished career. Already the author of eleven books, he had thanked Howells in a letter of 23 July 1909 (MH) for the encouraging appraisal of his work in "The Fiction of Eden Phillpotts," an essay appearing in the *North American Review*, July 1909: "That it interested you enough to move your pen is a source of

the very deepest gratification to me. Would that England could read these opinions!"

2. *Lying Prophets* (1896) was Phillpotts' first novel.

3. "Most pleasant pain," Howells' favorite phrase in Heinrich Heine's *Reisebilder*.

4. In his review, Howells had said of *The Whirlwind* (1907): "...I am, in spite of a final doubt of its right to such primacy, inclined to put it first among Mr. Phillpotts's books." He had also counted *The Children of the Mist* (1898) among Phillpotts' "great" novels.

5. Phillpotts lived in Torquay, Devon, where Howells and Mildred stayed at a hotel 16–17 September and visited with the novelist. Phillpotts later wrote to Howells, 14 November 1909 (MH), that their meeting had been "among the golden memories of this year...."

15 SEPTEMBER 1909, SALISBURY, TO ELINOR M. HOWELLS

...."Hotel" Salisbury...
Salisbury...Sept. 15th—1909[1]

Dear Elinor:

Well, we have been to Cholderton,[2] and done it thoroughly, with the help of the peppery little Welsh rector, Rev. Briscoe Owen, who used to live in Constantinople, and who instantly knew all about the Noyeses. He had great delight in showing everywhere, and he took us into his walled garden where the rectory of the Noyes time stood, and which faced the present house across the sweetest lawn, where a sundial was not overworked in numbering the sunny hours. Then to the churchyard, where among the old graves stood the baptismal font of the Noyes-time church, from which the Rev. N's, father and son, used to sprinkle the children.—I enclose a list of all the rectors, with two pics. of the rectory, the church, and the beautiful little village— one of the quaintest and thatchiest and dinkyest I ever saw. Keep the pics., and we will explain all.—We motored over from Salisbury, to Stone Henge, and across through Amesbury (where Queen Guinevere died in the convent, and all round us strecht the King Arthur country) to Cholderton, where first we broke into the village school, to ask for the rectory. The schoolma'am would hardly let us in, and then hardly out, making all her children stand up and bow.—The Rector is short, so that I easily towered over him, an astronomical fiend, and very droll: a bachelor in charge of his cookhousekeeper. He grew almost pathetically glad of our coming, and clung to us to the last house in the village; I tried to give him some notion of you, and we made it a genuine Mamma-burst.[3] Of course I have to leave out details, but you shall have them all when we get home. The whole thing would have suited you down to the ground. It's a small parish and poor; about 2 people die a year, and about 2 are born.

This p.m. we push on to Torquay, and expect to be in London next Tuesday....[4]

Mary's letters of the 4th and 7th received, thank her.

Your
W. D. H.

1. It appears that Howells and Mildred left Carlsbad on 10 September, arriving in London the following day.

2. Elinor Howells was descended from the Noyes family, formerly of the small village of Cholderton near Salisbury. According to Mildred Howells, the father of James Noyes had been rector of the church there. See *Life in Letters*, II, 270.

3. Special occasions in the Howells family were honored as "bursts" in conjunction with the name of the person being celebrated. See *Life in Letters*, II, 270.

4. Several lines, referring to a meeting between Mildred Howells and an unnamed man, crossed out. See the Textual Apparatus.

16 SEPTEMBER 1909, TORQUAY, TO ELINOR M. HOWELLS

... Torbay Hotel,
Torquay. Sept. 16, 1909.

Dear Elinor:

After our extremely successful Mamma-burst at Cholderton[1] yesterday we indulged ourselves in running down here to see Phillpotts and his country.[2] I am just going out to see him, but his land and sea are all before us in this nice hotel. Last night when we arrived the harbor was Venice-full of lights with a band playing old colored melodies in the public garden on the shore. This morning the lovely crescent is full of little boats, yachts and small steamers.* The town curls round it, and clambers up the hills back of it. The air is deliciously soft and mild.—We walked up to the P. O. before breakfast (9 o'clock) and saw the quaintest place, full of lodgings with gardens before them, where you would like to be, or we should like you to be with us. I think even you would be warm here, but oh, you Kittery P.!—I'm glad the melons are prospering. Watch out, and at the first threat of frost make Albert gather them and lay them on the Bange floor[3]—I'm *especially* allowed to eat melons.—At Cholderton the Rector's cats, chickens and dog all eat together. The housekeeper wont let the hens set, so one of them stole her nest in the dog's house, and hatched out two chicks there in the dog's presence. He could not say what the dog thought.—From the cow-pasture lying between the church and the rectory, he crosses by a little foot-bridge over a brook; and I thought how you would have it drawn up, at the approach of visitors.—We've about given up Wales, and shall perhaps go back to London on Saturday, viâ Stratford-on-Avon and Oxford.

This letter is merely to keep the pot a-biling. I've telegraphed to London for letters from you—or the faithful Mary.

Your
W. D. H.

*Pil says you would sit picking your teeth and watching all day.

1. See Howells to Elinor Howells, 15 September 1909, n. 3.
2. See Howells to Phillpotts, 28 August 1909, n. 5.
3. The "Bange" was a glass-enclosed piazza at the Kittery Point cottage.

17 September 1909, Torquay, to Elinor M. Howells

. . . Torbay Hotel,
Torquay. Sept. 17, 1909.

Dear Elinor:

I seem to be writing you every day, now, but I hope you don't mind it: we shall so soon be starting home,[1] and then you'll be relieved. Yesterday we motored out to see a *tor* (Hay Tor)[2] and a moor such as Phillpotts has in all his stories, and the sight was wild and beautiful beyond words. I'll tell you about it when I see you. We stopped for tea at a little inn on the edge of the moor, a rough place but clean, and had (Pilla had) clotted cream, and I *blueberry jam,* or whortleberry, the same as. A small fair, with swings and games, from quaint old Dickensy vans, was going on in a pasture next the house. Very *decentes familien program.*[3]

The day was beautiful but today even finer for our visit to Pomeroy Castle, a most noble Norman ruin, and the castle where Sir Walter Raleigh lived when he first came back from America.[4] We took the Phillpotts boy, (his sister was being dress-fitted, for going off to school) and we had a great time lunching in the Raleigh castle, in a big, bare sunny room, beside a flower garden furnished with a black cat. Young P. was very respectfully solemn, but he broke down when I suggested that if Raleigh had stayed in America he might have been living now.—We are going to tea at the P.'s this afternoon, and tomorrow morning we shall leave either for London, or Stratford-on-Avon and Oxford.—Mary's[5] letter of Aug. 31 came on from Carlsbad today, and one from John. But we had got Mary's of Sept. 4 and 7 yesterday.—We have about given up Wales, . . .[6] Lots of papers have come.

Your
W. D. H.

1. Howells and Mildred embarked at Liverpool on 28 September, taking the *Carmania*, a six-day ship, to New York.

2. There are about 170 *tors*, or high rocky hills, in the Dartmoor region near Torquay. Howells here refers to Hey Tor, conspicuous by its two separate masses of granite.

3. Mildred Howells explains that the term ("a proper family program") was from "the program of a variety show in Würzburg, and had become a family phrase." See *Life in Letters*, II, 272.

4. Berry Pomeroy, a Norman castle dating back to the ninth century A.D., was appropriated by the crown in 1549 in a religious dispute. See Eden Phillpotts, *A West Country Sketch Book* (London: Hutchinson & Co., 1928), pp. 63–64. Raleigh returned to nearby Plymouth in June 1618 from his ill-fated expedition to the Orinoco in South America.

5. Elinor's sister, Mary N. Mead, was staying at Kittery Point in Howells' absence.

6. Several lines crossed out, presumably by Mildred Howells. See the Textual Apparatus and Howells to Elinor Howells, 15 September 1909, n. 4.

24 OCTOBER 1909, NEW YORK, TO HENRY JAMES

130 West 57th st.,
Oct. 24, 1909.

My dear James:

I hope you'll care to know that we prospered home over seas that laughed at the old notion of a rolling deep. But our gayety ended with a smooth passage of the customs, for I found my wife in bed after a severe surgical operation in a Boston hospital.[1] It was to rid herself of a danger that had haunted her for 20 years, but which is now absolutely at an end. She had, with Mary Mead's help, pluckily kept the event from me, knowing that I could not get home in time, and to keep me in my ignorance had sent all the letters from Mary to be posted at Kittery Point. Of course she is still very nervous from the "shock," but is otherwise well, and I found her greatly taken with "Crapy Cornelia."[2] She thinks it one of your masterpieces, and so do the Franklin Square people, especially dear old Alden and Harry Harper. Now we are hurrying up the November "Putnam" in order to get at your story in it.[3]—I haven't Smalleyed yet, but the dovelike Badger has sent me a very sweet letter about the Year Book which he has definitively accepted and is geting out.[4] I don't know just when he's to get it out.

Pilla is down at K. P. "amid the yellowing bowers"[5] of her garden. She too liked "C. C."

The John Howellses are back from Colorado, and twice a day we glory in our grandson, who has a way of clawing my moustache which I can't less than call inspired. He also shows a remarkable genius in the inspection of my watch.

My wife joins me in affectionate wishes.

Yours ever
W. D. Howells.

1. The operation was for the removal of swollen glands. See Howells to Clemens, 5 November 1909. In an undated letter to his nephew William D. Howells II, probably written some time in mid-November 1909 (OFH), Howells describes the severity of Elinor's condition: "Your Aunt Elinor has been and still is very sick, though we no longer fear for her life. The nervous shock from her operation in September culminated in neuritis, and she suffered torture for a week; nothing but morphine could save her from the pain."

2. James's story appeared in *Harper's Monthly*, October 1909. In his reply, 10 November 1909 (MH), James thanked Howells for the "pat on poor Cornelia's crapy little back."

3. "The Bench of Desolation," *Putnam's*, October–December 1909, January 1910, and reprinted in *The Finer Grain* (1910). In his reply, James told Howells that he was irritated over *Putnam's* handling of the piece: "don't, *please* don't, read the *Putnam* thing till you see it in a volume (with other matters,) & with the *proofs read*; which P. gave me no chance to do. It has been foully divided into snippets & disfigured by gross and illiterate misprints—altogether a shame to me in this beggarly guise. And they haven't even yet paid me for it!"

4. See Howells to James, 20 August 1909, n. 6.

5. From "Song" (line 2), by Tennyson, published in *Juvenalia* (1830): "A spirit haunts the year's last hours / Dwelling amid these yellowing bowers."

5 NOVEMBER 1909, NEW YORK, TO SAMUEL L. CLEMENS

130 West 57th st.,
November 5, 1909.

Dear Clemens:

I wanted to come to you tomorrow and so did Pilla; but we are bound hand and foot with engagements Saturday and Sunday. I would propose myself for next week, only my brother Joe, on his way back to his consulate at Turk's Island, is to be with us, and I can't leave. Let me offer for a later date. I have a good deal of talk in me, and I should like to hear some gab from you. I *have* been hearing your gab, for I have gone again to your books for my good night cheer after downhearted days, and found you as gay as you used to be, in those blessed short things of yours. There never was anybody like you, and there wont be. Just the same Clara and I held you up to obloquy when she called, the other morning. *She's* been having a high old honeymoon, hasn't she, poor girl, with appendicitis in the house the first thing.[1] But surgery seems to follow us all. I came home to find my poor wife in bed, here, after an operation in a Boston hospital. She and her sister had kept it from Pilla and me, even sending their letters to be posted from Kittery Point; and we knew nothing about it till we went into her room here. She had some swollen glands removed, and an anxiety of twenty years standing. In 1889 I went with her to see a great New York specialist, and he divinely reassured us. The next day the family found him dead on the floor of his coupé after a drive home from Brooklyn. Such is life—and death. We found we were of the same age, and he said, "Well, how do you like your work?" "How do you like *yours*?" "Well, I don't *jump* to it."—You see, I am trying to cheer *you* up now, in return for the gayety I got out of your books. Don't thank me; I hate gratitude.

> Yours ever
> W. D. Howells.

1. Clara's husband, Ossip Gabrilowitsch, had been operated on for appendicitis two weeks after their wedding on 6 October. See *Twain-Howells*, p. 849.

25 NOVEMBER 1909, NEW YORK, TO AURELIA H. HOWELLS

> *130 West 57th Street,*
> *New York*[1]

Dear Aurelia:

I am afraid I was rather deliberately remiss about writing to you when the time came last Sunday. Perhaps it was Thanksgiving casting its shadow before, and clouding my mind, with the sense of its being the true letter day. But now Thanksgiving has got to twilight, and I am seeing clearer. We had John and Abby and Billy, all three, at dinner, and Billy after being left on the parlor floor outside the dining room, in full view of us, began an indignant shouting, and kept it up until we put him in a big chair at the table, between his father and me. Then he was happy, and played his great game of "Where's Billy?" with the help of a wolf skin that he sits on, and considers a "dah" which is Billy for dog, and folded round his head. He squeals with joy when you say "There's Billy!" and wants immediately to do it again. Altogether he is a most amiable and bewitching child, gentle, sensitive and intelligent. Saturday is his birthday, and I have got him a little chair, reproduced from a little Puritan chair in the old Sudbury Inn, the scene of Longfellow's Tales of the Wayside Inn. It is terribly square and upright, and will just suit Billy's upright little back. He is straight as a ramrod.

After dinner John came up to my room and smoked, and Abby stayed below and sang Scotch songs to Elinor and Pilla; she sings beautifully, but Elinor could not stand the melancholy airs. Her nervousness is pitiably great, for she cannot use the arm of her poor wounded side without fancying that she brings on pain. I believe it is really rheumatism, but with the active life she has always led it is in any case a great trial to her. All she can do is to read the papers and talk. The political situation in England is an immense relief to her, and she knows it to the last detail. Just now she is exulting in the break of the Lords.[2] We all, as true Welsh folk, rejoice in the intrepidity of Lloyd George.

You will find another poem of Pilla's in the Christmas Harper[3]—I think an uncommonly fine one, though she does nothing unworthy or characterless. She is slowly deciding to get her pieces together for a book,[4] and she has some original ideas for the setting which I must not give away.

I am going to renew your Monthly and Bazar for next year. Shall I have them sent to your present address? I don't understand whether it is to be permanent.

I return Sam's letter, which is dignified enough. But it is strange that he could not live with his daughter, whose housekeeping his pay would have helped. As long as he supports his wife I have nothing to say,[5] and Joe told me she takes better care of him and his money than he has ever had before.

I am glad of your good news of Annie and her family. Give them our love, and tell her that when she has a letter to throw away on the undeserving poor, I will be glad of her charity.

If Achille is now fairly out of the government, and can't be hurt by her story of electoral corruption in Canada, she might let me try the MS. again.[6]

> Your affectionate brother,
> W. D. Howells.

1. The letter is undated; it was written on Thanksgiving day, which fell on 25 November in 1909.

2. Howells probably refers to the rejection by the House of Lords of "the People's" budget submitted by Lloyd George, then chancellor of the exchequer. The mounting crisis eventually led to the Parliament Act of 1911, stripping the House of Lords of its effectual power.

3. "O Wind, A-Blowing All Day Long," *Harper's Monthly*, December 1909.

4. The book was never published.

5. Following the death of his first wife in 1907, Sam appears to have remarried in late 1908 or early 1909. In a letter of 27 October 1908 (MH), Howells had expressed to Aurelia his firm opposition to Sam's matrimonial intentions: "At the cost of betraying confidence I must tell you and Annie that Sam has had an 'offer' from a widow of forty, with 'bronze gold hair' and a 'slight graceful figure.' The poor old simpleton sent me her letters, four, the last addressing him as 'Sammie mine,' for my judgment, and I sent him a cruel answer (for which I apologized by the next mail) rehearsing his manifold unfitnesses for the renewal of matrimony. There is no occasion for you or Annie to do anything but laugh. *I* did the cursing."

6. The story has not been identified.

2 DECEMBER 1909, NEW YORK, TO ROBERT U. JOHNSON

130 West 57th Street,
New York

Dear Mr. Johnson:

I have some notions as to the details of our proceedings in Washington which I would like to talk over with Mr. Sloane and you,[1] and I can meet you anywhere any afternoon of this week.

I am sorry to say that I do not find myself so well as I had hoped to be, or so able to meet fatigue or excitement. Without knowing what your arrangements are I am going to risk the ungraciousness of saying that I would rather go to Washington alone, so as to deny myself the pleasure of talking with others on the way, and I think I will go to a hotel in a group of myself only,[2] for the same reason, reserving myself for my public duties. In any general hospitality to the Academy, except at Page's dinner[3] and the President's[4] reception I should prefer to let the first vice-president represent us,[5] for such things prevent my sleeping, and tend to bring on one of the attacks which I am anxious to avoid.

I have written my introductory address, which Mr. Sloane's great kindness approves, and which I will bring with me to our meeting. I know you will forgive anything that seems needlessly frank in what I have said, and will realize why I wish to escape even the consideration which my friends would show me. I will therefore ask you to take my requests as confidential, and yet act upon them as far as you can.

Yours sincerely,
W. D. Howells.

December 2, 1909.

1. See Howells to Higginson, 13 July 1909, n. 1. Howells was president of the American Academy of Arts and Letters, Johnson the permanent secretary, and William M. Sloane chancellor.

2. According to a letter from Howells to Elinor M. Howells, 14 December 1909 (MH), Howells changed his mind, traveling with Johnson to Washington and staying with him at the New Willard hotel.

3. The Washington home of novelist Thomas N. Page (1853–1922) was well known for its generous entertainments.

4. William H. Taft.

5. No doubt a reference to William M. Sloane, the second-ranking officer of the Academy. Sloane's official title was chancellor, and it was his duty to preside at functions in the absence of the president. In referring to the first vice-president, Howells was mistakenly referring to the second-ranking officer of the Academy's parent organization, the National Institute of Arts and Letters.

25 DECEMBER 1909, NEW YORK, TO HENRY JAMES

130 West 57th street,
Christmas, 1909.

My dear James:

We are reading aloud now every night your Tragic Muse[1]—very small shreds of her; for my wife's nervous strength is so slight and her interest in the book so intense that she can seldom let me go beyond a dozen pages. She hates to have the story finished for as she says in a justifiable panic, "Where shall we find anything like it?" I have supposed some other story of yours, but she has no hopes of anything else so good, even by you. The other night she sighed over a certain tremendous complication of emotions and characters, and said, "I don't believe *I* could do anything with it from this point." Pilla listens too, and enjoys the author and the simple transports of his elderly readers. My wife no longer cares for many things that used to occupy her: *hohheits* of all nations,[2] special characters in history, the genealogy of both our families. "Well what *do* you care for?" I asked, and I found her answer touching. "Well, James, and his way of doing things—and you." I must own to you a constantly mounting wonder in myself at your "way," and at the fullness, the closeness, the density of your work; my own seems so meager beside it.—The winter has whipped by past its shortest days, and has witnessed few things outside of this house for me. My wife wont go out, and so I keep in, talking with her, and we play with our dear little grandson, who dwells so lovingly in a world of love and is so full of surprises at it and for us. I could not have believed that life still held an experience so sweet for me.—Last week I went to Washington, where our poor Academy held its first public sessions.[3] The papers read were really fine, but I think the public did not care in the least. The President had us all to tea in the White House, and was very civil. He is a mighty paunch of a man, with a prodigious good head atop, and no end of good feeling and happy laughter. He did not want the right sort of presence, either, in a straight American way. At night we went to the Architects meeting in the Corcoran gallery where he presided at the presentation to poor McKim's daughter of a medal,[4] and made a good, kind, wisely humorous speech. The place is all white, and the girls in solid blues, pinks and greens hanging over the gallery rails, were wonderfully Roman, Pompeian, Alma Tademaish.[5] They were better still when they came out under the clear Italian night, and *walked* home with their heels clicking and their neat ankles showing. We all send love.

Yours ever
W. D. Howells.

1. James's *The Tragic Muse* was first published in 1890.

2. *Hohheits* (properly *Hoheit*), as used loosely here by Howells, refers to Elinor's interest in the nobility.

3. See Howells to Higginson, 13 July 1909, and Howells to Johnson, 2 December 1909.

4. Charles F. McKim died 14 September 1909. He had earlier been awarded the gold medal of the American Institute of Architects, presented posthumously to his daughter Margaret McKim at a memorial meeting of the Institute on 15 December at the Corcoran Art Gallery. William R. Mead, Elinor's brother and McKim's partner, received the medal on McKim's behalf and gave it to Miss McKim.

5. In 1882 Howells had met the Dutch artist Lawrence Alma-Tadema in London.

III

A Deathful Time

1 9 1 0 – 1 9 1 1

Introduction

In the spring of 1910 Howells endured the successive loss of his closest friend and his wife. Samuel Clemens died on 21 April at the age of seventy-four, followed a little more than two weeks later, on 7 May, by the passing of Elinor Howells shortly after her seventy-third birthday. With each he had shared his life and literature in special ways as with no other two people, whether in the satisfaction of sheer "talk" with his beloved friend or the grateful dependency on his wife's "wonderful electrically critical nerves," as he once phrased it.[1] Despite the questionings and self-doubts that now and again surface in his correspondence, the letters of this bleak time also attest to a resiliency that enabled him bravely to survive the two-fold loss. There was no unalterable emotional impairment, but rather a tempered reassessment of his place in the world along with a more generous reaching out to the friends and family still left to him. Later in 1910, remarking as well on the deaths of Elinor's sister Mary Mead in March and her brother Larkin Mead in October, Howells summarized, in a simple exclamation, his wonderment and confusion: "What a deathful year!"[2]

Elinor's decline was inescapably the consuming event for Howells in the first four months of 1910. In the aftermath of a second blizzard he wrote to James in mid-January that his wife, ever vulnerable to severe winter weather, was "very wretched and quite helpless under the successive shocks of cold" (16 January). In February, Elinor had to be heavily sedated with morphine after suffering a painful attack of neuritis, leaving Howells to stand by helplessly as her mind was blurred by the effects of the medication. With her condition growing steadily worse, he became alarmed at the mounting expense of home care, a matter of constant attendance by nurses along with two and three daily visits by the doctor, so that he was prompted to ask Harper & Brothers for an increase in salary from $833.33 a month to $1000. Rather than openly play upon sympathy in a situation that both Frederick A. Duneka and Colonel George Harvey, head of the firm,

---

1. Howells to S. Weir Mitchell, 12 December 1904.
2. Howells to Joseph A. Howells, 25 November 1910.

understood all too well, he cited merit as the basis for his request, pointing out that he was doing "a good deal of work in all kinds of places" for the Harpers.[3] Predictably, for a man of disciplined habits, Howells did not permit himself to be unduly distracted from his work, writing to James after Elinor's discouraging relapse: ". . . I happen to be well, and my mill grinds on as usual, turning out all manner of grist" (8 March 1910). Although there was brief cause for expecting a degree of recovery in early April, Elinor's condition deteriorated later in the month. With the ceremonial dignity of initial grief, he wrote to his sisters, on the day after Elinor's death, that following a momentary birthday "brightening" on the first of May "there was after 24 hours, only a peaceful oblivion, which last night at ten minutes to eight became the peace everlasting."[4] Although the Howellses had by then spent almost twenty years as adoptive New Yorkers, Cambridge was still the family home in spirit, and there, on 9 May, Elinor Howells' funeral service was held at the Shepherd Memorial Church, followed by her burial beside Winifred Howells in the Cambridge Cemetery. "It is over," Howells wrote four days later, speaking for himself and his two surviving children, "and what is left of our life must again begin."[5]

Clemens' death, which had occurred sixteen days earlier, was fatefully intertwined with Elinor's, compounding yet complementing Howells' grief by providentially offering a literary occasion for the expression of it. Howells saw his friend for the last time on 5 January 1910, just before Clemens sailed for Bermuda for a recuperative sojourn that, he hoped, would alleviate his painful angina pectoris. Howells wrote several times to Clemens there, once in warm praise of his "Turning Point" paper for *Harper's Bazar*[6] and once to spar familiarly with him about Will Harben, the Georgia writer whose fiction Clemens had vociferously rejected. Although there appears to have been no explicit mention of Clemens' health in their last exchanges, Howells was indirectly kept informed by letters from Mildred, who was also in Bermuda at that time and saw Clemens often until she was called home in early March to be with her mother. It was inevitable that when Clemens was nearing death and was forced to return home in mid-April, Harper & Brothers, who were also Clemens' publisher, would ask Howells for yet another memorial essay. Already drained by his anxiety over Elinor's condition, Howells was at first uncertain whether

3. Howells to Frederick A. Duneka, 28 February 1910.

4. Howells to Aurelia H. Howells and Anne H. Fréchette, 8 May 1910.

5. Howells to Aurelia H. Howells and Anne H. Fréchette, 13 May 1910.

6. "The Turning-Point of My Life," *Harper's Bazar* 44 (February 1910), 118–19.

he could tolerate the additional strain, writing Duneka on the day before Clemens' death only that he would seriously consider the proposal: "You know I would *like* to write about Clemens; and if I did, it would be something unique, for I should tell him as I have known him for forty years: the most truthful man I *ever* knew" (20 April 1910). Four days after attending Clemens' funeral, however, he was ardently channeling his desolation into an eloquent record of their friendship, writing Duneka that he had "done more 'memories' and the material holds out even beyond my hopes."[7] During Elinor's final days he worked intensively, almost compulsively it would seem, on the Mark Twain paper, regularly sending completed portions to Duneka interspersed with brief reports of his wife's worsening condition. Even with the time taken up by Elinor's death and funeral, he was remarkably able to finish the "memories" of his friend by 23 May. It was as if the consummation of the memorial to Clemens helped to sustain him in the more unutterable sorrow of losing his wife.

"My Memories of Mark Twain" was serialized in *Harper's Monthly*, July–September 1910, and brought out as the book *My Mark Twain: Reminiscences and Criticism* in September. Through the summer and fall Howells helped to organize the Mark Twain commemoration held at Carnegie Hall on 30 November, over which he presided as president of the American Academy of Arts and Letters. These formal expressions and ceremonies enabled Howells to bring a degree of closure to his relationship with Clemens, as he simultaneously struggled with the deeper tensions of day-to-day survival without Elinor. In many of the letters written during the two years following his wife's passing, he articulated and thus gradually came to grips with the full impact of her death. "I strain my soul to take in the fact of Elinor's death," he wrote a month after the event, adding numbly: "My life is a succession of shocks—of referring my experiences to her as if she were still alive, and then realizing that she is dead."[8] Seeking immediate remedy in travel abroad, he embarked for England in June with Mildred, visiting briefly with James, who was himself in the crisis of a nervous breakdown, and rekindling his old friendship with Edmund Gosse. But it was useless, as he wrote to Minot J. Savage from London, "to fly my irreparable, my incalculable loss!" (25 July 1910). The return to New York in early October and the resumption of work, along with preparations for the Mark Twain commemoration and the second public meeting of the American Academy, helped him to achieve a more re-

---

7. Howells to Frederick A. Duneka, 27 April 1910 (MWA); quoted in Howells to Duneka, 20 April 1910, n. 1.

8. Howells to Joseph A. Howells, 9 June 1910.

signed tone. The pain of which he wrote at the end of the year had become familiar and not so incessant: "I suppose Elinor's death has broken my life in two. . . . I start to tell her of something, and then I stop! Otherwise there are long times when I forget what happened."[9] Indeed, the mourning seems gradually to have become internalized, at first manifest in episodes of unbearable insomnia, "the habit of waking about 2 or 3 a.m. and descending into hell, with black despair," as he wrote to Aurelia, 15 January 1911. By the middle of that year, while he could daily "laugh and joke with the children" about Elinor, she had implacably become a presence in his sleep: "*every* night, now, I dream of her, but always painfully."[10]

As Howells dealt with the mortality of the present, he was attracted to an imaginative reconstruction of his past, taking up again the story of his family's year at Eureka Mills, which he had begun in 1866, the story already told autobiographically in *My Year in a Log Cabin* (1893). He reached out to Joe, Aurelia, and Annie for any fragments of the Eureka Mills experience that they could recall, wishing especially to revivify his mother and father in the characters of Mr. and Mrs. Powell for the novel that became *New Leaf Mills* (1913). The final dissolution in death of his own marriage seems to have prompted Howells to examine the temperamental differences in the marriage of his parents, particularly the patient strength of his mother in the face of William Cooper Howells' impractical idealism. "Of course she could not do justice to father's limitations," he commented to Joe, in thanking him for reading a completed draft of the novel: "I suppose a woman is always bewildered when a man comes short of the perfection which would be the logic of him in her mind" (29 May 1911). In this period Howells finished a second novel, *The Vacation of the Kelwyns*, which he had begun early in his career and which also had autobiographical origins. It is based on his and Elinor's six-week stay in 1875 at Shirley Village, Massachusetts, near a Shaker religious community; but at that time Elinor had apparently protested against any literary exploitation of the Shakers and their religion. Now, with Elinor dead, Howells himself became so emotionally embroiled in her objection that he implored Harper & Brothers not to publish the novel, despite an agreement to the contrary negotiated with Duneka in June 1911. Consequently, publication was deferred until 1920, after his own death.

Feeling himself on the verge of a nervous breakdown by the end of 1910, and finding the New York apartment "heartbreaking" to live in

---

9. Howells to Joseph A. Howells, 11 December 1910.
10. Howells to Joseph A. Howells, 18 August 1911.

because Elinor had "adored the place, and made it hers by a thousand tastes and touches,"[11] he arranged to spend the winter of 1911 in Bermuda with Mildred. Weakened as he was, he rallied his energies to assist in a move initiated by Edith Wharton and Edmund Gosse to secure the Nobel Prize in literature for Henry James. Howells' letters from Bermuda to Wharton, Brander Matthews, and others spell out in interesting detail his unsuccessful attempt to marshal the influence of the American literary establishment and still keep the venture from James himself. It was a gesture of respect and appreciation for James that Howells cheerfully extended, but his failure to win the unanimous support of the American Academy on James's behalf caused him seriously to consider resigning from that body. Upon his return from Bermuda, he was unable to stay at Kittery Point because the cottage, like the New York apartment, was a constant reminder of Elinor's "ever-during absence," as he wrote to Hamlin Garland, 29 May 1911. So he restlessly sought further relief by again traveling abroad, first to Wales for a mineral bath treatment of his colic disorder, and then to Spain, finally fulfilling a dream he had nourished since his boyhood. There he met for the first time Armando Palacio Valdés, the Spanish novelist whose books he had championed in the "Editor's Study" as early as 1886. The two aging writers conversed in Italian, as Howells' Spanish was insufficient and Palacio Valdés spoke no English, touring Madrid together to visit the scenes of the Spaniard's novels. It was also a working trip for Howells on which he gathered materials for yet another of his travel books. *Familiar Spanish Travels*, essentially completed before he left Spain in late November 1911 although not published until 1913, reflects an intricate blend of his youthful romantic passion for Spain with a mature eye for what he described as the "teeth-set realism" of Spanish art and architecture.[12] If he had lately lost his touch for fiction, he at least retained his capacity for a fine turn of phrase and a keen sense of setting, as James himself picturesquely acknowledged in response to Howells' several letters from Spain: "I wish I were only prince & patron enough to maintain you & Mildred at my splendid cost in a country of the colour that makes you write me such delightful letters...."[13]

James, whose fiction Elinor Howells had preferred above all others, and Thomas S. Perry were the friends who helped to fill a part of the

---

11. Howells to Joseph A. Howells, 3 October 1910 (MH); quoted in Howells to J. A. Howells, 25 November 1910, n. 4.

12. Howells to John M. Howells, 8 November 1911.

13. Henry James to Howells, 12 November 1911 (MH); quoted in Howells to James, 3 November 1911, n. 2.

void left by Clemens' death. Howells corresponded increasingly with both men, and he especially looked to the pleasure of Perry's company when he passed through Boston on the way to Kittery Point. Before his departure for Spain, he beguilingly entreated Perry to come to Kittery Point "and stay with a lonely man . . . . Think what a good time I will have!"[14] Of his family, Mildred Howells was constantly the companion of his solitary days and frequent travels. "I try to be decent, to be humble, to be grateful," he wrote abjectly to James two months after Elinor's death, adding with thankful sadness: "if I must lose my wife it is all that the world can still give in keeping such a daughter as mine" (1 July 1910). If Mildred ministered to his grief, it was his grandson Billy who invigorated his spirit and animated his thoughts. Belittling the stately statuary of the Court of the Lions in the Alhambra at Granada, Howells, in a letter to John Howells, burst out: "pah! I could only think how Billy would have demanded to be put astride one of the ridiculous beasts' backs!" (8 November 1911). And it was Billy—who called his grandfather "Fafa"—on whom Howells fondly set his heart as he returned home from Spain, arriving in New York on 8 December 1911.

W. C. F.

---

14. Howells to Thomas S. Perry, 9 June 1911 (MeWC); quoted in Howells to Perry, 9 July 1911, n. 1.

16 January 1910, New York, to Henry James

... *130 West 57th Street*
January 16, 1910.

My dear James:

I have just risen from reading my family three chapters in the early part of The Bostonians—those relating to Verena's first public discourse. It is all wonderfully good, with not a word awry, and so like Boston that we all shuddered. Certainly you have hardly done anything better, even in The Ambassadors, or The Tragic Muse.

We finished that book with loud applause. Perhaps the drama is huddled into a small space at last; but it is good drama and true; and what are you down on Nick for in your preface?[1] He is fine, and there is all of him that could be asked; there is not a failure of character in the book. Well, you are a great fellow, and if you had your dues, there would no bearing you; it's only because you haven't that your contemporaries can keep from wishing you ill.

By the way, I hear you are not very well. You ought to come over here and plunge your feet into the snow drifts heaped head high along our street, and waiting for the sun to ripen their accumulated microbes and flood the gutters with them. The street department has quite given up trying to cart the snow off. It is a fearful winter with two blizzards already.

Pilla is going to Bermuda on the 29th and I may follow with her mother, who continues very wretched and quite helpless under the successive shocks of cold. Your literature is her only comfort.

Have I written you since I was in Washington? I think it might be a more acceptable sojourn than this; but I shall never live there.—I went to my first dinner last week, and I should not have gone if I had known I was to meet a certain celebrated lady novelist, who once turned to criticism long enough to devote me to execration.[2] I find I don't take these things Pickwickianly;[3] but she avenged me by the way she dressed and the way she talked. I wish I could present you with the whole scene, but I mustn't.

Yours sincerely
W. D. Howells.

1. In his preface to the New York Edition of *The Tragic Muse* (1908) James comments on Nick Dormer: "It strikes me, alas, that he is not quite so interesting as he was fondly intended to be, and this in spite of the multiplication, within the picture, of his pain and penalties.... Nick Dormer isn't 'the best thing in the book,' as I judge I imagined he would be ..." (pp. xxi–xxii).

2. The occasion of the dinner is not known, but the "celebrated lady novelist" is most likely Gertrude F. Atherton (1857–1948). Howells probably recalls her attack on the "Howells School" published as a full-page interview in the New York *Times*, 29 December 1907 (Magazine Section), under the title "Gertude Atherton Assails 'The Powers.'" Although claiming not to blame Howells directly, but rather the unimaginative school of magazine writers she charges had been guided by his "literary supremacy," Atherton nevertheless indicts Howells and American literature as oppressed by the "tyranny" of a "hopelessly middle-class" standard: "It is a good enough standard in its way; but it is hopelessly narrow, finicky, commonplace, in its conception and treatment of things. There is no originality to it. Mr. Howells, you know, denounces originality. He tells us to stick to the small things of life in fiction, to shun the big things. He has produced, and his followers maintain, a literary style that is all l's and n's and r's. It is the cultivation of a perfectly flat, even surface. It is afraid of rough surfaces, of mountain peaks and deep valleys. It exalts the miniature and condemns the broad sweep of impressionism in art." In an earlier essay, "Why Is American Literature Bourgeois?" *North American Review*, May 1904, Atherton, describing how she had worked on her own first literary efforts "in the very shadow" of a picture of "Mr. Howells's study . . . enthroned . . . upon my desk," goes on to mock the Howellsian realism of the American average as "Littleism" (pp. 774–75).

3. Howells here alludes to a scene in Charles Dickens' *Pickwick Papers* (1837), in which Mr. Blotten, when asked if he had intended the word "humbug" in disparagement of Mr. Pickwick, claims he merely "used the word in its Pickwickian sense," that is, not to be taken literally.

18 JANUARY 1910, NEW YORK, TO SAMUEL L. CLEMENS

> . . . *130 West 57th Street*
> January 18, 1910.

Dear Clemens:

While your wonderful words are warm in my mind yet, I want to tell you what you know already: that you never wrote anything greater, finer, than that turning-point paper of yours.[1]

I shall feel it honor enough if they put on my tombstone, "He was born in the same Century and general Section of middle western Country with Dr. S. L. Clemens, Oxon., and had his Degree three Years before him through a Mistake of the University."

I hope you are worse. You will never be riper for a purely intellectual life again.[*]

> Yours ever
> W. D. Howells.

[*]and it is a pity to have you dogging along with a wornout material body on top of your soul.[2]

1. "The Turning-Point in my Life," *Harper's Bazar*, February 1910. Howells had assisted Elizabeth Jordan in an attempt to set up a series of six articles by various

authors describing how they turned toward a literary career, Clemens' essay being the first to appear. Howells, whose contribution came out in the March number under the same title, declined to have it placed first, as he wrote to Jordan, 23 November 1909 (NN), "because I think any outsider will be better, and because I am not—for once—ready." In an earlier letter to Jordan, 16 November 1909 (NN), he had suggested several possible contributors, among them playwright Augustus Thomas, romancer Winston Churchill, and architect-turned-novelist Thomas Hardy. The essays by Clemens and Howells were, finally, the only two published. Howells described as his turning point, early in his career at Venice, the circumstances leading up to his "change from a supreme purpose of poetry to a supreme purpose of prose."

2. Clemens passed the letter on to Albert B. Paine, his biographer, noting in his own hand across the top: "I reckon this spontaneous outburst from the first critic of the day is good to keep, aint it, Paine?"

1 FEBRUARY 1910, NEW YORK, TO HENRY JAMES

> ... *130 West 57th Street*
> February 1, 1910.

Dear James:

You owe me two letters,[1] but I make you my debtor for a third because I can't resist writing to you about The Bostonians, which I've been reading out to my family. I'm still reading it, for there are a hundred pages left, and I wish there were a thousand. I've the impression, the fear that you're not going to put it into your collection, and I think that would be the greatest blunder and the greatest pity.[2] Do be persuaded that it's not only one of the greatest books you've written, but one of the masterpieces of all fiction. Closely woven, deep, subtle, reaching out into worlds that I did not imagine you knew, and avouching you citizen of the American Cosmos, it is such a novel as the like of has n't been done in our time. Every character is managed with masterly clearness and power. Verena is something absolute in her tenderness and sweetness and loveliness, and Olive in her truth and precision; your New Yorkers are as good as your Bostonians; and I couldn't go beyond that. Both towns are wonderfully suggested; you go to the bottom of the half frozen Cambridge mud. A dear yet terrible time comes back to me in it all. I believe I have not been wanting in a sense of you from the first, but really I seem only know to be realizing you now.

My wife and daughter share my feeling about the book, which holds my poor old dear above her nervous suffering, and would have kept my dear girl from Bermuda if anything could. But she is gone with a sigh of wonder for what is to happen to Verena. (I am much concerned about your brute of a Mississippian.)[3] She sailed on Saturday away from one of the bitterest, *poisonest* winters I have known for many years. The cold tries me in my age as it used not to do; perhaps we may go another winter to pass it all in the tropics. Of course I should like to live the rest of my winters in some climate where history dwelt with the etherial mildness; but it will probably be some such place as Bermuda. Or, it may be a gelid submission to the New York conditions.—I have an idea you are not very well. Or is it that I've heard it from some imaginable Smalleys?[4]

I wish you could find it in you to write me. But if you can't I can always commerce with you in your books.

Yours affectionately

W. D. Howells.

1. Apparently James had not yet answered Howells' letters of 25 December 1909 and 16 January 1910.

2. James had written to Howells, 17 August 1908 (MH), of Scribner's condition that the New York Edition be limited to twenty-three volumes, forcing James to omit *The Bostonians*: "Twenty three do seem a fairly blatant array—and yet I rather surmise that there may have to be a couple of supplementary volumes for certain too marked omissions; such being, on the whole, detrimental to an at all professedly comprehensive presentation of one's stuff. Only these, I pray God, without Prefaces! And I have even, in addition, a dim vague view of re-introducing, with a good deal of titivation and cancellation, the too-diffuse but, I somehow feel, tolerably full and good 'Bostonians' of nearly a quarter of a century ago; that production never having, even to my much-disciplined patience, received any sort of justice. But it will take, doubtless, a great deal of artful re-doing—and I haven't, now, had the courage or time for anything so formidable as touching and re-touching it. I feel at the same time how the Series suffers commercially from its having been dropped so completely out. *Basta pure—basta!*" See *The Letters of Henry James*, ed. Percy Lubbock (1920; reprint ed., New York: Octagon Books, 1970), II, 100.

3. Basil Ransom, Olive Chancellor's adversary for the favor of Verena Tarrant.

4. For the literary impositions and personal misfortunes of Evelyn G. Smalley, see Howells to James, 20 August 1909, n. 6 and n. 7.

11 FEBRUARY 1910, NEW YORK, TO SAMUEL L. CLEMENS

... *130 West 57th Street*

Feb'y 11, 1910.

Dear Clemens:

I have not got a Fairy Princess to take my profane and abusive dictation,[1] and so I cannot reply to your praises of our favorite author in fit terms, but you will find my joy in Harben in an early number of the N. American.[2] You seem to require a novelist to be true to the facts and if the facts are not pleasant, to be pleasant himself. That seems rather difficult. You are the only man who can do it; but I believe you will end by liking poor old Harben as much as I do. He didn't make North Georgia; he only made a likeness of it. Don't shoot the artist.[3]

I am glad you are out of this awful winter,[4] where one spell of weather follows another like the rows of words in McGuffey's spelling-book. We are just starting in for our third blizzard tonight. Pilla writes that it isn't as tropical as it might be at Bermuda, but you haven't got a snowstorm over your heads and under your feet. When I think of you at Stormfield I rejoice that you have a biographer[5] to roost under your roof-tree for you.

I hear you want to see what I have written about my turning-point. Nothing but generous shame, and a wish to spare your feelings keeps me from sending you a letter which Duneka has just sent me about it.[6] You will be brought low, soon enough.

I wonder if you have seen the autobiography of Stanley, the explorer.[7] There is about the livest book I ever read. He starts in a Welsh work-house, and he ends in such glory as few men ever won, and was then refused a grave in Westminster Abbey by a wretched, tyrannical parson. There is a lot about New Orleans in the middle '50s, and about Arkansas a little later which would make you feel at home.—I am slowly plowing through "Tristram Shandy." How tough is the humor that our poor ancestors battened on! But I *will read* it. The "Sentimental Journey" is all right, though nasty.[8]—But get the life of Stanley. He was a Southern prisoner in the Northern prison pen at Chicago. If Andersonville was intentionally worse—but it couldn't be.

Yours ever
W. D. Howells.

1. This is Howells' last letter to Clemens, who died on 21 April. It is in reply to a dictated letter, not extant, from Clemens. The "Fairy Princess" was Helen S. Allen, Clemens' secretary in Bermuda, where he was staying at the time. See *Twain-Howells*, p. 553.

2. Clemens heartily disagreed with Howells over the merits of Will N. Harben (1858–1919), best known for his fictional works set in northern Georgia. Howells was anticipating Clemens' assault on his essay, "Mr. Harben's Georgia Fiction," a favorable appraisal of Harben's work, about to appear in the March number of the *North American Review*. Harben subsequently wrote Howells, 2 March 1910 (MH), to express his gratitude: "You have paid me the greatest compliment of my life in your article . . . . It contains advice and ideas I shall never forget . . . ."

3. In *My Mark Twain*, Howells described the diatribe against Harben contained in the missing Clemens letter: "In the very last weeks of his life, he burst forth, and though too weak himself to write, he dictated his rage with me for recommending to him a certain author whose truthfulness he could not deny, but whom he hated for his truthfulness to sordid and ugly conditions. At heart Clemens was romantic, and he would have had the world of fiction stately and handsome and whatever the real world was not, but he was not romanticistic, and he was too helplessly an artist

not to wish his own work to show life as he had seen it. I was preparing to rap him back for these letters when I read that he had got home to die; he would have liked the rapping back." See *Literary Friends and Acquaintance*, HE, pp. 286–87.

4. Howells was fully aware of Clemens' chest pains and generally failing health through correspondence with Mildred Howells, who had left New York for Bermuda on 19 January in consideration of her own health. In a letter of 15 February 1910 (MH), he observed to Mildred: "Poor old Clemens! I am sorry he suffers so. I'm sure it must comfort him to have you near him; you might slight a few kinsfolk for him."

5. Albert B. Paine.

6. In a letter now lost, Frederick A. Duneka had praised Howells' essay for the turning-point series (see Howells to Clemens, 18 January 1910, n. 1), just as Howells had earlier extolled Clemens' paper. Rather than send Duneka's letter directly to Clemens, Howells enclosed it in one to Mildred Howells, also 11 February 1910 (MH), advising discretion in carrying out the friendly ribbing: "Here is a letter which you may flourish in the face of the conceited Clemens, if you like. But not if he has a turn of his breast-pang, poor old fellow."

7. *The Autobiography* of the explorer Henry M. Stanley (1841–1904) was edited by his wife Dorothy Stanley and was published in 1909. Stanley, born John Rowlands in Denbigh, Wales, was suspected of being illegitimate and thus abandoned by his family. He came to New Orleans in 1859, where he was employed and then unofficially adopted by the merchant Henry Morton Stanley, whose name he took for his own. He was then sent to Arkansas to begin an apprenticeship as a merchant in a country store. Enlisting in an Arkansas company called the "Dixie Greys," Stanley was captured at the battle of Shiloh in 1862 and taken with other Confederate prisoners to Camp Douglas, Chicago, where he barely survived the deplorable conditions.

8. Howells was reading Sterne's novels for a review of Wilbur L. Cross's *Life and Times of Laurence Sterne* (1909) in the *North American Review*, February 1910.

28 FEBRUARY 1910, NEW YORK, TO FREDERICK A. DUNEKA

. . . 130 West 57th Street
28th Feb'y, 1910.

Dear Mr. Duneka:

It has been sometime in my mind to ask whether the affairs of the house would justify it in putting up my wages from $833.33 to $1000.00 a month. I am really doing a good deal of work in all kinds and places for you, and perhaps more than you want, but I try to maintain the quality. I have no notion what my stuff would be worth in the open market, but it seems to me it might be worth what I suggest.

I shall be 73 on the 1st of March, and I shall not be so much oftener, so that there seems a safe and fit poetry in making the advance begin with that day.

If with your mystical consciousness of the inner conditions at Franklin Square, you do not think the moment psychological, I would not have you mention this matter to the Colonel, but treat it as an ill-advised and untimely confidence on my part.[1]

Yours sincerely
W. D. Howells.

1. Along with the uncertainties of old age, Howells' request was also motivated by Elinor Howells' recent crisis. He had described it to Duneka a week earlier, 23 February 1910 (MWA), as a severe neuritis attack which could be treated only "by the blessed relief of morphine." Howells must have envisioned the possibility of prolonged expenditures for such constant home medical care as he mentions in his letter to Henry James, 8 March 1910. Indeed, he later expressed anxiety about deferred doctor's bills in his letter to Aurelia Howells and Anne Fréchette, 10 April 1910. Despite the "slap" of economic "bad times" for Harper & Brothers, as Duneka phrased it in his sympathetic reply of 1 March 1910 (MH), he had "little doubt that by the end of the year your monthly check can be made $1,000 without unduly disturbing things." In his immediate acknowledgment to Duneka, 2 March 1910 (CCamarSJ), Howells reported Elinor's improved, though drug-impaired, condition: "My birthday began with the doctor's saying, 'I don't think she's quite so well, this morning.' But today she is ever so much better . . . . She is physically in no danger but the suffering has left her in a mist of dreams."

8 MARCH 1910, NEW YORK, TO HENRY JAMES

. . . 130 West 57th Street
March 8, 1910.

My dear James:

I've heard from Miss Jordan that you've not been at all well for some time,[1] and I hope that by this you are all right again. I'm sorry I can't cheer you up with any good news of my own. My wife's nervous "shock" culminated two weeks ago in neuritis, and for a week she was in torture for which there was nothing but morphine. This has left her mind blurred, and we must have patience till that comes right with her general recovery. Pilla was in Bermuda, and I had to cable for her and she had to catch the steamer in fifteen minutes.

Meanwhile, I happen to be well, and my mill grinds on as usual, turning out all manner of grist. I don't know just how I manage to keep the triple daily visits of the doctor and the three trained nurses out of it; perhaps I sha'n't, always. Our blessed Billy, my adored grandson, is the great joy of my bewildered and bedevilled senility; I go down to John's flat (in this house) and play with him, and sometimes I meet him in the Park where he and the correctest of Danish nurses take their airing every day. If you should think, when you pull up, of coming over to this Boiler Factory, for change and rest, you would have, I hope, a queer sense of being back with me, through Billy, in Sacramento street.[2] He is as gentle as Winny was, and likes having poetry—the elemental sort—said to him, like her.—At last, the intense interest of your novels was too much for my wife, and before she broke down we had to give you up; but we shall go back. As she always said, "What other books *are* there?"—The doctor has just seen her and reports her better.

With our love

Yours ever
W. D. Howells.

1. James was in the throes of a nervous breakdown brought on by fears about his physical health, emotional solitude, and inability to write, a general condition from which he did not begin to recover until late July 1910. See Leon Edel, *Henry James, The Master, 1901–1916* (Philadelphia: J. B. Lippincott, 1972), pp. 434–47; also Howells to James, 9 June 1910, n. 2.

2. In May 1866 Howells, his wife, and the two-year-old Winifred had moved to 41 Sacramento Street, Cambridge. The friendship between Howells and James began during those early years of their literary careers.

9 MARCH 1910, NEW YORK, TO HARRIET T. UPTON

...130 West 57th Street
March 9, 1910.

Dear Mrs. Upton:

I have always remembered my pleasant day at your house in Warren, and the kindness of your father to my brother;[1] and I would gladly help you if I could in the matter you mention.[2] I was sixteen two months after I came to Jefferson; at nineteen I began journalizing at Columbus. So there could be little to tell of my boyhood on the Reserve. In *My Literary Passions* you will get some notion of our literary life at home in the village, and in *A Boy's Town* (Hamilton, Butler Co. O.) much relating to our family life and to my mother, who was the heart of it; there is something concerning her also in *My Year in a Log Cabin.*

I dearly loved my mother, and whenever I went away from home it was with the foreboding and realization of homesickness which was mainly longing for her. She had a certain great *warmth of mind* which supplied any defect of culture, but for a new country she had been fairly well schooled; she expressed herself from her heart with great natural poetry; and she fully shared the intellectual and spiritual life of my father: together they formed our church and our academy. When we went to live in Jefferson we had nothing but our household stuff and our strong, right wills, and we all worked hard to pay for the printing office and the dwelling house we had bought on credit. We paid for them, but her long hard toil wore my mother out. She did *all* our household work till my sisters grew old enough to help her, and she died at 57 after all was paid for; sometimes we had the "hands" from the office to board, and she worked to save the greater wages they must have been paid otherwise.

I could not tell you all, but I know you will believe we were very happy in the home which she knew how to create for us. An inexpressible tenderness, a devout honor for her fills me as I speak of her. I could not wish to have had another sort of mother; I do not believe there was ever a better woman. It is more than thirty years since she died, but I still dream of her among the living who visit me in sleep, and I dream of her often.

I cannot think of anything more to tell you, at present.

Yours sincerely
W. D. Howells.

1. Her father was Ezra B. Taylor, a former congressman from Warren, Ohio. See Howells to W. C. Howells, 26 March 1882, n. 2. The nature of the kindness is not known.

2. In a letter to Joseph A. Howells, 10 March 1910 (MS. not located), Howells explains that Harriet T. Upton (1854–1953), Ohio author, "was doing a history of the Reserve, and asked me to give her something about mother. I did so last night, and before I had finished, it seemed to me that I was dealing with one of the most unselfish and heroic lives in the world." See *Life in Letters*, II, 282. Upton incorporated verbatim into her book, *History of the Western Reserve* (1910), the greater part of Howells' letter.

27 MARCH 1910, NEW YORK, TO HAMLIN GARLAND

... 130 West 57th Street
March 27, 1910.

My dear Garland:

I read the last half of your "Cavanagh" after three this morning when I got up to see how my wife was, and found her in the first natural sleep she has had for a month. This gave me heart for the story and contented me to be in its grip. You might indeed have made more of it; you had most interesting people in hand and a prodigious scene, and I wish you had given us the drama of the epoch more deeply and largely than you have done.[1] It was a pity to have cramped so noble a scheme to the measure of a contemporaneous incident.[2] But I liked your people, and I followed them to the end, only wishing there were more of the tale, and more circumstance and detail both in respect to the dirty little cow-town and the sublime mountain country. One day, I hope you will revert to the temper of your first work, and give us a picture of the wild life you know so well on the lines of "Main Traveled Roads." You have in you greater things than you have done, and you owe the world which has welcomed you the best you have in you. "Be true to the dream of thy youth"[3]—the dream of an absolute and unsparing "véritism"; the word is yours.[4] Don't suppose I have missed any good points in "Cavanagh" or think them few; they are abundant.

> Yours ever
> W. D. Howells.

1. Garland's novel *Cavanagh, Forest Ranger* (1910) is set in the mountains of Wyoming and dramatizes the conflict between the rangers of the Forest Service and the cattle ranchers exploiting the lands and forests. Garland replied immediately, 29 March 1910 (MH), acknowledging Howells' criticism: "I have *not* measured up to my opportunity but perhaps waiting would have been of no avail. The plain truth is I watched the Forestry Service develop for sixteen years and it was only last summer that the motive to use it came. I'm running low on motives. I don't care to write love-stories or stories of adventure and I can not revert to the Prairie life without falling into the reminiscent sadness of the man of fifty. [¶] My own belief is that my work is pretty well done, but as I remember the cordeal [sic] endorsement of men like yourself and Gilder I have no reason to complain." Garland later explained that the novel was hastily written in six weeks under pressure from Frederick A. Duneka, "who was (like most publishers) enslaved to a program." See *A Daughter of the Middle Border* (New York: Macmillan, 1921), p. 347.

2. Howells undoubtedly refers to the Ballinger-Pinchot controversy. Gifford Pinchot (1865–1946), chief forester, had just been dismissed by Taft after charging Secretary of the Interior Richard A. Ballinger (1858–1922) with favoring corporations seeking water power sites on federal lands in Wyoming and other states. Although Ballinger was ultimately exonerated in court, public sentiment heavily favored Pinchot. Garland's novel, a strong polemic on the side of land conservation, featured a timely and appreciative introduction by Pinchot. In his letter to Howells, Garland wrote that he hurried the novel to completion because he feared that "reporters" would overpublicize the forest ranger as an American type: "I had to 'beat them to it' or come in six month [sic] from now with a wornout theme and an indifferent or yawning public."

3. The quote is not identified. However, in *The Vacation of the Kelwyns*, a novel on which Howells may have been working at this time (it was completed in March 1911; see Howells to Duneka, 16 May 1911, n. 2), one of the characters attributes the quotation to Ralph Waldo Emerson. It serves well as an aggregate paraphrase of Garland's pleas throughout *Crumbling Idols* (1894) advocating the primacy of the young writer. Retrospectively dissatisfied with his achievements "on the artistic side," Garland laments in his letter to Howells: "Why does not our literature tally with the big things we do as a people? I had hopes of doing it once but that was only the foolish egotism of youth." To this Howells replied, 30 March 1910 (CLSU): "Dear

boy, *don't* think you're written out—you're just at the beginning of your greatness. Don't be daunted by the greatness of our material achievements. It's more for Wisconsin that you and your literature have come out of it, than all the mines, and farms and railroads in the State amount to."

4. The practitioner of veritism, Garland's brand of realism, is characterized in *Crumbling Idols*: "The realist or veritist is really an optimist, a dreamer. He sees life in terms of what it might be, as well as in terms of what it is; but he writes of what is, and, at his best, suggests what is to be, by contrast. He aims to be perfectly truthful in his delineation of his relation to life, but there is a tone, a color...of sorrow that the good time moves so slowly in its approach" ([Chicago: Stone and Kimball, 1894], p. 52).

10 April 1910, New York, to Aurelia H. Howells and Anne H. Fréchette

> ...*130 West 57th Street*
> April 10, 1910.

Dear Girls:

I got Annie's letter, with Vevie's address, and Pilla has written to Mr. Plimpton, giving it, and telling him of that special portrait of Amherst.[1] She also, as she says, very artfully brought in the name of Lord Strathcona,[2] and we both hope that this cause Mr. P. to "loosen up" if it comes to a question of what he shall pay Vevie for her work. It would be his nature to pay as little as possible, and Pilla did not tell him what the swooping Mrs. Hayter Reid[3] pays, lest it should shoo him off.

Our only news is Elinor news, and that seems hopeful for early recovery, though why I should say this I don't know, for the two nurses are still here, and the doctor pays his "ready visit" night and morning. (I am to pay him later on, I shudder to think how much.) She is more strenuous, however, and she has taken to disciplining him fearfully for any differences of opinion. We have a wheel chair for her, and get her into it a few minutes each day.

Your selling your house is most exciting,[4] and yet I know what regrets you must have. Such a lot of one's personality peels off one on the insensate walls that have sheltered one for years. It will be fine, your and Aurelia's living together, and if ever the ghost of that greedy landlady comes about,[5] I hope you will free your minds to it.

I am, after reflecting for 44 years, resuming my story of Eureka Mills, which I left off in 1866.[6] I find the stuff very good, but my treatment of it loathsomely "young." I am bringing that up to date, however, and wish you girls would write out, no matter how vaguely, what you remember about our going to the Mills, and our life there. Of course you were very young, but your memories would give "color" to an otherwise "bald and unconvincing narrative," as Poohbah says in the Mikado.[7]

Especially, I should like to know what mother felt and said about the situation, though I know that it afflicted her.[8] Of late, I am beginning to realize her character, and I should like to paint it as it now shows in my mind. She had a hard part in life, but she played it greatly. She had a deep nature, and a rich mind.

The weather is again beautiful this morning, after a little brush of cold. The other day I met a painter at the club, just from Quebec, where he said he had left six feet of snow; perhaps he lied.

Your affectionate brother,
Will.

1. Anne Fréchette's letter, not extant, was in reply to one from Howells, 3 April 1910 (MH), requesting Marie M. Fréchette's address in Paris, where she was studying art. George A. Plimpton (1855–1936), publisher and trustee of Amherst College, wanted, as Howells explained, "to give a building to Amherst college, (Mass.) and to adorn it with the portraits of English and French people connected with Amherst. Pilla told him of Vevie's work . . . and he said he would like her to copy some French portraits." The circumstances are not entirely clear, but it appears that Mildred Howells wrote to Plimpton about Vevie's portrait work at her Ottawa studio, mentioning in particular a painting of Lord Jeffrey Amherst (1717–1797). In a letter of 23 May 1910 (MH), Howells reported to Anne only that "Pilla had a note from Mr. Plympton last week symptomatic of ordering those pictures." Plimpton, a collector of antiquities relating to the French and Indian Wars, finally donated the collection, but no building, to the college in 1927; but the collection contains no painting by Marie M. Fréchette.

2. Donald Alexander Smith (1820–1914), first Baron Strathcona and Mount Royal, was a Canadian financier and statesman. He was then high commissioner for Canada living in England. His association, if any, with the Fréchette family or Vevie's art is not known.

3. Not identified.

4. Anne Fréchette was selling her Ottawa house preparatory to joining her husband in retirement in Switzerland. He was then in semiretirement from his post as chief translator of the Canadian House of Commons, staying in Paris with his daughter Vevie and conducting research on the bilingual and multilingual parliaments of Belgium and Switzerland. See James Doyle, *Anne Howells and Achille Fréchette* (Toronto: University of Toronto Press, 1979), pp. 103–6.

5. See Howells to Aurelia H. Howells, 10 September 1905, n. 9.

6. In 1867 Howells had written the first five chapters of "New Arcady Mills," finally published in 1913 as *New Leaf Mills*.

7. In Gilbert and Sullivan's *The Mikado* (1885), act 2, Pooh-Bah says, by way of excusing the dangerous confusion his facile counsels and interpretations have created, that they were "Merely corroborative detail, intended to give artistic verisimilitude to an otherwise bald and unconvincing narrative."

8. Recent boyhood reminiscences of his mother, prompted by a query from Harriet T. Upton (see Howells to Upton, 9 March 1910), probably helped to rekindle the Eureka Mills episode. For discussions of Mary D. Howells' ordeal at Eureka Mills, see Cady, *Howells*, I, 34–35; Lynn, *Howells*, pp. 59–61.

20 April 1910, New York, to Frederick A. Duneka

...130 West 57th Street
April 20, 1910.

Dear Mr. Duneka:

You know I would *like* to write about Clemens;[1] and if I did, it would be something unique, for I should tell him as I have known him for forty years: the most truthful man I *ever* knew. But don't make me—don't *let* me—promise till I get my head out of this cloud in which I have been living with the anxieties of the last two months.—It wrings my heart to think of Clemens dying.[2]

Yours sincerely
W. D. Howells.

1. With Clemens' death imminent, Duneka had asked Howells to do a memorial essay. Despite the distraction of his wife's precarious health, Howells gave himself wholly to the task. In a letter to Duneka, 27 April 1910 (NN), he expressed his pleasure with the progress he was making: "I have done more 'memories' and the material holds out even beyond my hopes." The following day, 28 April 1910 (copy at MWA), Duneka returned to Howells "two proofs of your 'Memories of Mark Twain'," praising them as "very, very beautiful," while suggesting the impropriety of a passage about Clemens having been drunk. Howells' entire reply, 29 April 1910 (MWA), is poignant in its brevity: "You're right about that passage. I've cut it out. [¶] I hope you will like the rest of my paper still better. It's working out splendidly. [¶] My wife seems worse." Less than a week before Elinor Howells' death, he wrote Duneka again, 1 May 1910 (MWA): "I send you some more. There will be another installment, perhaps twice as long as this, but perhaps not. I wish you would have this put in type at once, so I send Clara a proof.... If I can help it I would rather not stop the Clemens till it is all done." The labor of devotion was completed toward the latter part of May, Howells writing Albert B. Paine, 23 May 1910 (CSmH), that he had "finished the 'memories,' and now that they are done they do not record Clemens [as] I had hoped. But they record my affection for him." See *Life in Letters*, II, 283–84. The lengthy article was serialized in *Harper's Monthly*, July–September 1910, as "My Memories of Mark Twain," and published in book form as *My Mark Twain, Reminiscences and Criticism* in September 1910.

2. Clemens died the next day at Stormfield, after having been brought home from Bermuda a week earlier by Albert B. Paine. Howells attended Clemens' funeral at the Brick Church in New York on 23 April. Clemens was buried in Elmira, New York, on 24 April. See A. B. Paine, *Mark Twain: A Biography* (New York: Harper & Brothers, 1912), pp. 1564–80.

8 MAY 1910, NEW YORK, TO AURELIA H. HOWELLS AND ANNE H. FRÉCHETTE

> *...130 West 57th Street*
> May 8, 1910.

Dear Aurelia and Annie:

I telegraphed last night.[1] You will know how I feel.

Last Sunday was her birthday, and when I told her she smiled. She smiled a day or two later when I told her something about Billy; she loved him so; but after that first brightening on her birthday, there was after 24 hours, only a peaceful oblivion, which last night at ten minutes to eight became the peace everlasting.

Pity me.

> Your aff'te brother
> Will.

1. Elinor M. Howells died on 7 May, six days after her seventy-third birthday.

13 MAY 1910, NEW YORK, TO AURELIA H. HOWELLS AND ANNE H. FRÉCHETTE

> *...130 West 57th Street*
> May 13, 1910.

Dear Aurelia and Annie:

It is over, and what is left of our life must again begin. Elinor lies beside Winny in the Cambridge cemetery.[1] Every sweetness was shown us by the dear old Cambridge friends.

Now, Pilla and I must go away.[2] We hope to sail from Boston for England early in June; and what we wish you two dear ones to do is to go and live in our house at Kittery Point till August, from June 1st, say. There is everything there and you can be in perfect comfort with the good Marthy to care for you, at my expense. You will have to pay for your provision, and I am sure you can live cheaply enough to make up for your R.R. fares. The air will do you "a world of good." Tell me what you think. Of course you can bring Howells and Hazel.[3]

> Your aff'te brother
> Will.

John and Abby will want the place from August 7th or 8th.

1. Attended by the immediate family and close friends from Cambridge, Elinor Howells' funeral was held on 9 May in Cambridge at the Shepherd Memorial Church, where she had been a member. For Winifred Howells' funeral, see Howells to W. C. Howells, 10 March 1889.

2. A letter from Frederick A. Duneka, 13 May 1910 (MH), recapitulates Howells' intention to immerse himself as soon as possible in work and travel: "All the things you talked about yesterday seem good in the light of another day. Your going abroad in about a month; your return in time to preside at the memorial meeting to Clemens on November Thirtieth next; your writing letters from Spain to THE WEEKLY...." Although the plan to visit Spain did not materialize until the following year, the literary matters mentioned by Duneka suggest that preoccupation with work had become crucial for Howells at this time. Six months earlier, in a letter to the aging novelist Elizabeth Stuart Phelps Ward, 9 November 1909 (CLSU), Howells had characterized with prophetic irony his own dependence on work in times of crisis: "I am sorry to hear that you are always suffering. I understand how you must fight for a chance to work, but if we do not work, we die; at least I do. It is not my 'working power' which keeps me at it, but my working weakness; if I had the strength I should stop."

3. Anne Fréchette's son and Aurelia Howells' housegirl.

1 JUNE 1910, BOSTON, TO FREDERICK A. DUNEKA

Hotel Victoria ...
Boston June 1st, 1910.

Dear Mr. Duneka:

I return the last two galleys of the Mark Twain papers.[1] They have not been corrected since I sent the revise back, but I have corrected the places again which I felt anxious about.

—I thought of Ade as representing American humor; of Booker Washington as standing for a race which Clemens meant well by; of Riley as a poet who would sing him divinely.[2] My recollection is—though I may be constructively forgetting—that I told Clara G. what I told Sloane,[3] and what I now tell you, and they agreed: If Roosevelt speaks, it will be a Roosevelt meeting, not a Mark Twain memorial. He will overslaugh Taft, who should be first, and everybody else. This would be unfortunate, of course, but I think above all that Clemens's feeling should be respected. He disliked Roosevelt bitterly, and at a large dinner (Munro gave it) he spoke of him with withering contempt.[4] To have Roosevelt praise him would not be fair to R. himself; but if you like (and I should prefer it) you can submit this point again to Mrs. G. I state it reluctantly, for Roosevelt once granted a favor I asked of him with eager generosity, and I would not seem to forget it.[5] I will be ruled by Clara's wish; but I will not settle the question myself.

Perhaps when it is all thought over, I had better not preside.[6] My printed words will be enough.

Yours ever
W. D. Howells.

1. See Howells to Duneka, 20 April 1910, n. 1.

2. Howells had written to Duneka two days earlier, 30 May 1910 (CSmH), suggesting that the American Academy, rather than Harper & Brothers, sponsor the Mark Twain memorial meeting: "What should you think of the N.Y.M.T. Commemorative meeting in November being held under the auspices of The American Academy of Arts and Letters? I am President of it, and it seems fit. Choate has consented to speak; and I would ask Taft, James Whitcomb Riley and George Ade, and Booker Washington. I should like a Labor man, but not Gompers." Of these, only Joseph A. Choate (1832–1917), jurist and reformer, who had several times addressed meetings with Clemens, ultimately accepted. For the difficulty in obtaining speakers, see Howells to Duneka, 22 October 1910; for an account of the commemoration, see Howells to Joseph A. Howells, 11 December 1910.

3. Clara Gabrilowitsch, Clemens' daughter, and William M. Sloane, president of the National Institute of Arts and Letters.

4. Clemens' contempt for Roosevelt the politician, as opposed to Roosevelt the man, was well known. See A. B. Paine, *Mark Twain: A Biography* (New York: Harper & Brothers, 1912), pp. 1231–32. Roosevelt was not invited. The occasion of the dinner given by David A. Munro, assistant editor of the *North American Review*, is not known.

5. Howells refers to Roosevelt's part in obtaining Joseph A. Howells' consulship at the Turks Islands. See Howells to Joseph A. Howells, 29 September 1905, n. 2.

6. Howells did preside.

8 JUNE 1910, BOSTON, TO WILLIAM JAMES

Boston, June 8, 1910.

My dear James:

Your letter has gone to my heart as no other had, and I must thank you for it.[1] I supposed no one else knew her great courage, but you have divined and matchlessly said it.

She did suffer greatly in the neuritis in which her "shock" from an operation culminated. But she seemed to be getting well, and she would have got well, but there was not enough *left* of her for that. The 1st of May I reminded her that it was her birthday, and she smiled, the last smile she ever gave me. The next Saturday she died.

It is incredible, but it has been happening since the world began. Nothing helps, or begins to; and yet your words were dear to me. I was not fit to outlive her.—My daughter is angelically good, and no man ever had a better son, but when I am apart from them, the solitude is crushing. I wish I could believe in a meeting with her, but she believed in none, and how can I?

Yours ever,
W. D. Howells.

I am ashamed to have written all this. She was three months in bed.

1. William James's letter of condolence is not extant; he had earlier written to Howells from Paris, 10 May 1910 (MH), explaining that his brother Henry had suffered from "a case of nervous breakdown towards which he had been working for two years past in the depressing monotony of Rye in the winter."

9 JUNE 1910, BOSTON, TO JOSEPH A. HOWELLS

Boston, June 9, 1910.

Dear Joe:

Pilla and I have been here from the 1st, and expect to sail from Boston, the 14th, on the White Star liner *Cymric* for Liverpool. She went to K. P. this morning to put poor Elinor's things out of sight, and tomorrow morning I am to meet Aurelia and Annie at the North Station, where they arrive from Montreal, and take them down to K. P. They are to have the house, you know, till John comes with his family about August 20. They are very happy in the prospect, and I shall be glad to think of them there, where the sea-air will do them both "a world of good," as poor Henry used to say.—John and Abby have left Billy with his aunts and grandfather (not *this* one, I'm sorry to say) on the Hudson, and gone out to Italy, largely for the long sea voyage, but also for architecture in Rome. They will join us in England about July 20 and travel round Wales with us, for a fortnight. Pilla and I do not expect to get home before November.

This is about all our news. My grief is the same, when I strain my soul to take in the fact of Elinor's death. But I do this only when the remembrance of it startles me. I seem only to be away from her, as I have so often been. My life is a succession of shocks—of referring my experiences to her as if she were still alive, and then realizing that she is dead. I do not know whether I believe that we shall meet again; she had totally renounced any such hope with regard to Winny; and I cannot affirm anything. What I am sure of is that it will all be arranged without consulting me, as my birth was, and her death. I feel that we are in the power of an awful force, but whether of fatherly love, I could not honestly say anything. I submit, and we must all submit. When I consider how I long to sleep and forget myself, I cannot truly say that an eternal sleep would be an evil; only, it seems to me that it would not be fair from the creator to his creature. But again I submit.—With love to you both.

> Your affectionate brother,
> Will.

9 JUNE 1910, BOSTON, TO HENRY JAMES

> Boston, June 9, 1910.

My dear James:

It was good to see your handwriting again, and sweet to have your pity.[1] I cannot say anything in answer, much less anything fit. Literally, the blow has stunned me and I go about bewildered and incredulous. Yet we were old people, and the blow was to be expected by one or the other through the logic of our common life on this mad planet; but it was denied by all the reasons of our experience. It is useless to talk.

Pilla and I sail on the 14th, and our address will be Brown, Shipley & Co., 123 Pall Mall; make some sign there if you wish us to run down and see you, and do not be afraid of our burdening you.[2] We should just look at you, and we should come over from your hotel to do so, not dreaming of going to your house first.

Give our love to your sister-in-law.[3]

> Yours affectionately,
> W. D. Howells.

Boston is a beautiful town and Cambridge a wonder of leaves and grass—but with graves under them everywhere.

1. James had heard about "the straight and heavy blow" of Elinor Howells' death from Thomas S. Perry, and had written Howells, 27 May 1910 (MH), to share the sorrow: "I think of this laceration of your life with an infinite sense of all it will mean for you—a sense only equalled by that of which your long long years of exquisite, of heroic devotion, the most perfect thing of the kind one has ever known, will always have meant for *her*. To think of her, moreover, is, for me, to recall the far backward stretch—from our melted, our unbearable-to-revive youth—of her unbroken gentleness & graciousness, the particular sweetness of touch, through all my close association with your domestic fortunes, in every phase of them, & your public fame. But one can't *speak* of these things—especially with a lame pen & a broken utterance . . . ."

2. In promising not to impose, Howells was acknowledging James's poor health, briefly mentioned in the letter to Howells: "...I have been interminably & wearily & dismally ill these five months (ever since Xmas) & although the light of amendment has at last begun to break I am limited as yet but to feeble demonstrations." See also Howells to William James, 8 June 1910, n. 1.

3. William James, in his letter to Howells of 10 May 1910 (MH), had explained that his wife, Alice, "remains at Rye to keep Henry company."

1 JULY 1910, LONDON, TO HENRY JAMES

...18, Half Moon Street,
Mayfair.W. July 1st, 1910.

My dear James:

The best thing in your letter from Constance is the fact that you will be in America next winter, though the cause grieves me.[1] When we were in Cambridge the other day for the saddest of all errands,[2] it seemed to me I must go back there to live, or at least to die, and later I visited my Concord Avenue house.[3] I had somehow the hope that you might be coming there to visit your brother, and I thought of seeing you often, and Perry. But the house forbade me. It was dreadful in its ghostliness and ghastliness, and it has two trolley lines in front of it that would banish sleep. So we gave it up, and the dream of six months of fall and spring in Cambridge every year hereafter. Probably we shall go back to New York, and about Christmas go down to Bermuda where we fancy taking a house, and welcoming you there if you have the nerve for the rough voyage.

London is not London without the possibility of you, and there is only that one reason for my being here which seems less and less a reason.[4] In a chaos like mine one changes almost from hour to hour, and if it were to do again, the coming away, "lo farei domani piutosto che oggi."[5] That is, I think so, but I really know nothing. I try to be decent, to be humble, to be grateful, and to say that if I must lose my wife it is all that the world can still give in keeping such a daughter as mine. I am ashamed to have her devote herself so to me, but I cannot help it, and I hope she will get some joy and some distraction from our being here.

I am sorry indeed for your suffering and I do trust that the "tetto natio"[6] will be a healing shelter to you. I wish I were going home on the same ship, but we shall hardly sail before October. John and his wife, who are now in Rome for the architecture will come to us here about the 25th, and will go home a week before you.

It has rained almost every day since we landed,[7] but now and then throughout the day it doesn't, and that is something. Then we venture out, and with this variety, and heaps of the proofs always following me,[8] the time passes.

Pil joins me in love to you and your family.

Yours ever
W. D. Howells.

1. James had written from Konstanz, Germany, 27 June 1910 (MH), in reply to Howells' letter from Boston of 9 June 1910. He was there with his brother and sister-in-law, where William was convalescing from an unsatisfactory course of treatment for a heart condition at the Nauheim baths. Howells, now in London (he and Mildred having left Boston on 14 June aboard the *Cymric*), was grieved to hear of Henry's continued illness and consequent dependency on William and Alice: "...I have been & still am, alas, too ill to fend for myself & be left alone. I am getting better, but with sad checks & relapses even now." Accordingly, he went on to say, the decision had been made "that I return to America with them on Aug. 12th— I cling to them abjectly." William's condition, in truth, was the more perilous. He died on 26 August at his summer home in Chocorua, New Hampshire, shortly after returning to the United States.

2. Most likely a visit to the graves of Winifred and Elinor Howells.

3. The Howellses lived at 37 Concord Avenue from 1873 to 1878. See Howells to W. C. Howells, 22 September 1872, n. 2, and Howells to Anne Fréchette, 17 January 1913, n. 4.

4. Despite the Jameses' distressful situation, it turned out that Howells saw them frequently during their two-week stopover in England to close Lamb House before departing for America.

5. Literally, "I would prefer doing it tomorrow rather than today."

6. Howells alludes to James's decision to return to America, to his "native home."

7. Howells and Mildred landed in Liverpool on 23 June, reaching London on 27 June.

8. Howells was working on selections of copy and introductions for an expansion of the "Harper's Novelettes" series. He had coedited the original volumes with Henry M. Alden in 1906. See Howells to Duneka, 15 December 1905, n. 1.

5 JULY 1910, LONDON, TO JOSEPH A. HOWELLS

...18, Half Moon Street,
Mayfair.W. July 5, 1910.

Dear Joe:

I return the Little-Joe-and-Wife[1] letters, which show a plucky good will and promise in both. It must be very grateful to you to get such letters, and I am glad for you.

Pilla and I have been in England 13 days, and a week here, and things go on as they usually do with us. We see a good many people,[2] and we are going a good deal to the Variety theatres. They make me forget; and then I find myself remembering and blindly staring. When

Winny died I had Elinor to suffer equally with me, but now nobody in the wide empty world can halve my sorrow. I have the best children that ever were; but they grieve as youth grieves, and I as age grieves, with no hope of solace here. I know that time will do its work, but I know that the comfort from it will come too late. Elinor's dying has largely taken the fear of death away. Of course I suppose if I were in danger I should be frightened, but I am no longer in that dismay before the notion of death which I have felt all my life. Oh, the loneliness, the emptiness, the forgetting, and the shocks of remembering!

I enclose a fresh letter from Kittery Point which will show you how happy the Aunties are there.[3] You need not return it.

The Eureka story is simply the scheme of the family community with its failure, and father and mother for the central figures. Mendenhall the miller plays a principal part. What I wanted from you was your remembrance of the situation and of the neighbors.[4] You have sent me something useful already.

Pilla joins me in love to you both.

> Your aff'te brother
> Will.

1. Joseph A. Howells, Jr. (b. 1878), had married Susan Halstead in 1905.

2. Howells wrote to Aurelia H. Howells and Anne Fréchette, 3 July 1910 (MH), that they had met "a variety of people," among them playwright James M. Barrie, archaeologist and prior acquaintance Charles Waldstein, and socialist labor leader John Burns (1858–1943).

3. Aurelia Howells and Anne Fréchette were staying at the Kittery Point cottage.

4. In order to obtain material for *New Leaf Mills*, Howells had also asked Aurelia and Annie to "write out" for him what they remembered of going to Eureka Mills. See Howells to Aurelia H. Howells and Anne Fréchette, 10 April 1910.

JULY 1910, LONDON, TO JOSEPH H. TWICHELL

> *...18, Half Moon Street,*
> *Mayfair.W.*

My dear Friend:

I thank you for writing to me and for sending me that great and beautiful letter of Clemens's written in the sorrow which is now ours.[1]

All the time there in New York while you were praying above him I knew—for they had told me in the vestry what they were keeping from you—the cloud that was hanging over you. I did not dream that it was hanging over *me*, or in my pity for you that I should need yours so soon.

When Clemens died I felt *desolate*, as I never had before; he had been such a world-full friend. But I thought *she* was getting well; we had been together forty-seven years and it seemed impossible that we should not always be together. *Why* did the Power which had united us so tenderly put us so cruelly asunder? What does death *mean*? I find *no* answers to these questions; I dwell in an illusion, but I suffer.

I wish I could say something to help you; *that* would help me too.[2]

1. Twichell had sent Howells a copy of a letter written by Clemens to Twichell after Olivia Clemens' death. Twichell had noted in his journal, where Howells' letter is laid in, that "On my passage to Naples...I had for fellow passengers John Howells (son of W. D. H.) and his wife. By him I sent a letter to W. D. H. enclosed a copy of one I had from our mutual friend Mark Twain shortly after his wife died, at Florence, in 1904. What led me to it was the fact that Mrs. Howells had died two or three days after H[armony Twichell]. He was now in England, but had been present at M. T.'s funeral service in New York Apr. 23d[.] I subsequently received from him the letter (undated) inserted here. [¶] (The signature was cut out for a friend's friend who wanted Mr. H.'s autograph)." Harmony Twichell died on 25 April, Elinor Howells on 7 May.

2. The signature is excised; see n. 1, above.

25 JULY 1910, LONDON, TO MINOT J. SAVAGE

18 Half Moon Street,
July 25, 1910.

Dear Mr. Savage:[1]

It was good of you to write me, and I thank you with all my heart. I have wished oftener than you know to see you and renew our old acquaintance. What you say of Keeler and Clemens interested me greatly.[2] Clemens was a far greater man than people realized. I call him the greatest humorist who ever lived, and a kind and noble soul. Of course, he was n't to blame for not knowing that the Connecticut Yankee at King Arthur's Court was worth a hundred Joan of Arcs. It was partly his beautiful loyalty to his wife's ideal of high fiction that made him err;[3] in his bones, he must have known better.

I am sorry you are still out of health. Thank you for hoping I am well and happy. I am well, but happy I shall be no more, as I once used to be. My wife died on the 7th of May. That is why I am here. Vain hope to fly my irreparable, my incalcuble loss!

Yours sincerely,
W. D. Howells.

My address too is c/o Brown, Shipley & Co.

1. Minot J. Savage (1841–1918), a radical Unitarian clergyman and author, was at that time minister of the Church of the Messiah in New York. Howells, who may have made his acquaintance when Savage was with the Church of Unity in Boston (1874–1896), had once differed with Savage's views regarding Tolstoy and Christ. See "Editor's Study," *Harper's Monthly*, August and October 1887.

2. Savage had probably written Howells after reading the first installment of "My Memories of Mark Twain," *Harper's Monthly*, July 1910, in which Howells described a Boston luncheon hosted by Keeler and attended by Clemens. See Howells to Aldrich, 7 May 1902, n. 3.

3. Clemens had noted in 1908: "I like the Joan of Arc best of all my books; & it *is* the best, I know it perfectly well." See A. B. Paine, *Mark Twain: A Biography* (New York: Harper & Brothers, 1912), p. 1034. *The Personal Recollections of Joan of Arc* (1896) was the only book Clemens dedicated to his wife Olivia.

27 JULY 1910, LONDON, TO EDMUND W. GOSSE

18 Half Moon Street,
July 27, 1910.

My dear Gosse:

What would *you* have done, you bold he Briton, in the spindle-sided American Hewson's place? (Not that I now remember what Hewson did.)[1] I came round yesterday afternoon to have the question out with you, but you felt my coming in your bones (about to be broken) and pretended not to be at home. Now you shall remain infract, for Friday we go to Tunbridge Wells—not to drink the waters, but merely to merry-make.[2] A syndicate of three knighted doctors decided against Harrogate my son and his wife, who are now in Kent, and we were left parching in the tropic heat of Demilune street.

Yours ever
W. D. Howells.

1. Hewson is the protagonist in Howells' short story, "His Apparition," *Harper's Monthly*, March 1902, and collected in *Questionable Shapes* (1903), which Gosse had been reading. Howells' banter was in response to a letter from Gosse, 26 July 1910 (MH), praising the stories but objecting to Hewson's extreme sensitivity: "Your stories breathe the very atmosphere of reality, & therefore one questions the causes of their action, just as one would those of veritable incidents. What puzzles me . . . is the scrupulousness of your characters. Hewson, in 'His Apparition', is absolutely life-like, and drawn with your delicate humour. But why is he so high-strung and lady-like? Are you drawing him as a caricature, or are there men of this spinster type in America?" With Elinor's death much on his mind, Howells seems to have relished the interval of good-natured intimacy with his old friend Gosse, visiting and exchanging books with him during the stay in London. When Howells finished reading Gosse's autobiographical work *Father and Son* (1907), he praised it extravagantly in a letter to Gosse of 21 July 1910 (British Library) as so well written that it "could not be better worded if a syndicate of masters rose from their graves to do it: say Milton, Dante and Shakespeare. Truly a most beautiful book." In a letter of 13 July 1910

(ViU), he wrote to Gosse of one of their evenings together: "We had a beautiful time last night, and from [sic] moment death was not in the world."

2. Howells and Mildred went to Tunbridge Wells, a resort town in Kent twenty-five miles south of London, on 29 July, remaining there through the first week in August. There they met up with John and Abby Howells, who were staying near Tunbridge Wells for a rest cure. The younger Howellses had been on an extended vacation to Italy, mainly for reasons of health, and had briefly joined Howells in London before leaving on 19 July for Kent. Howells and Mildred went from Tunbridge Wells "to Stratford-on-Avon for the Shakespeare commemoration on Aug. 9th" (Howells to Aurelia H. Howells and Anne Fréchette, 30 July 1910 [MH]), and from there traveled extensively through Scotland and Wales. They returned to Folkestone, England, in mid-September, and after a few days in London sailed on 24 September from Liverpool, arriving home in early October. Gosse and Howells had no further contact until the following year, when Gosse, in a letter of 22 March 1911 (MH), affectionately reproached Howells for leaving town without notice: "To tell the plain truth, I thought you behaved rather unkindly to us last summer, for after our doing our poor little level best to make you feel how fond we were of you, and how glad to be in close relations with you, you suddenly vanished, without saying goodbye, without a written word of farewell, and without a sign of an address. No, you are too fond of blaming your friends for the effects of your own caprice. There! I have spoken my mind quite out, and I have no thought now but gladness that the prodigal correspondent has returned."

27 JULY 1910, LONDON, TO THOMAS S. PERRY

18 Half Moon Street,
July 27, 1910.

My dear Perry:

First as to the James Brothers (not the Missouri Bandits of that name.) They are now at Rye, locking up H. J.'s house against sailing Aug. 12 for the U. S. Nauheim was bad for W. J., and he suffered severely here, where I saw them all many times, they being in a little hotel hard by. That wonderful Mrs. W. J., was holding them both up, for H. J., though better in body was very low in mind.[1] But W. got better here, and so did H. and one night he dined with us and flattened out a fatuous American girl's misimpressions of England so effectually that he went away quite gay. (A. girl was *not* Pilla, but a person ordinarily sane.) He left me a cheerier feeling about him than I had hoped for, and when you get him home you must do your part in bracing him up. I told them all of our lurid night at Keith's, but suppressed the antecedent debaucheries at the Lombard Inn.[2] They joined me in talking of you with tender affection.

Your farm-news filled me with envy.[3] Here we do nothing but take "tea on the terrace" of the Parliament Houses; once at the bidding of the Lloyd-Georges, with whom we had breakfasted en famille in Downing Street. Charming people, with a dear little daughter, Megan, whom I envied them.[4] I have met several literary lights, as **Galsworthy,** Maurice Hewlett, **Gosse, Barrie,** interspersed with cabinet ministers like **Birrell, John Burns,**[5] and no end of M. P.'s—experiences fitter for the use of 37 than of 73; but one does grow old. We have been to three high class variety theatres, each with a company of Russian dancers, or prancers, of varying degrees of nakedness—one gang quite bare of foot, and of leg up to their thighs. But there is nothing here to compare to the chantecler lady at Keith's, with her song of—

> "Keep your foot on the soft, soft peddle;
> Don't talk so loud;
> Somebody here that's liable to meddle,
> Don't talk so loud."[6]

We went on Saturday to the great pageant at Chester—really, really the most beautiful thing imaginable. It persuaded us of Merry England.[7] Give our love to Mrs. Perry, but don't show her this scandalous letter.

Yours ever
W. D. H.

1. See Howells to James, 1 July 1910, n. 1.

2. The occasion of the night at Keith's Theatre is not known but probably occurred during the first two weeks in June when Howells was in Boston. Benjamin F. Keith (1846–1914), theatrical manager, organized Keith's Circuit and eventually controlled some 400 theaters featuring family entertainment at affordable prices. Keith's in Boston was one of his first and best known theaters. The Lombard was the Lombardy Inn, 1 Boyleston Place, near the theater. After Howells purchased the cottage at Kittery Point in 1902, he and Perry frequently attended vaudeville performances at Keith's during Howells' stopovers in Boston. See Virginia Harlow, *Thomas Sargeant Perry: A Biography* (Durham, N.C.: Duke University Press, 1950), pp. 203, 205. In the "Editor's Easy Chair," *Harper's Monthly*, April 1903 (reprinted in *Imaginary Interviews* [1910] as "The Practices and Precepts of Vaudeville"), Howells expresses his fondness for vaudeville fare: "I am an inveterate vaudeville-goer, for the simple reason that I find better acting in the vaudeville, and better drama, on the whole, than you ever get, or you generally get, on your legitimate stage. I don't know why it is so very legitimate. I have no doubt but the vaudeville, or continuous variety performance, is the older, the more authentic form of histrionic art."

3. Perry's summer home was a farm in Hancock, New Hampshire.

4. Howells and Mildred had breakfast at the prime minister's home on 14 July. In a letter to Aurelia H. Howells, 15 July 1910 (MH), Howells described the occasion, replete with Welsh kinship, as "a climax" in their social activities: "we breakfasted yesterday with Lloyd George and his wife and little daughter—three wee Welsh folk, small and powerful as Welsh fairies. They accepted us promptly as kindred; Mrs. George's grandmother was a Howell, and George explained that our final *s* was the English effort to translate the prefix *ap*,—as I always imagined. We would be Gwilym ap Howell in Wales, and in England William Howells. He was charming, and so

were his wife and little daughter; he knew quite well about your unworthy brother."

5. The literary people were novelist John Galsworthy (1867–1933), novelist and poet Maurice Hewlett (1861–1923), Edmund W. Gosse, and playwright James M. Barrie. The cabinet ministers were Augustine Birrell, chief secretary for Ireland (1907–1916), and John E. Burns, president of the Local Government Board, with a seat in the cabinet (1905–1914).

6. The "chantecler lady" and her song are not identified. Howells no doubt refers to "the lurid night at Keith's" mentioned above. If Perry and Howells visited Keith's on 13 June, just before Howells' departure from Boston, the "lady" would probably be "the charming Augusta Glose, pianologist and 'talker of songs,'...one of the most delightful entertainers in vaudeville." See Boston *Globe*, 14 June 1910.

7. In a letter to Joseph A. Howells, 31 July 1910 (MH), Howells describes "the great historical pageant at Chester" which he attended on 23 July: "It was quite unimaginably beautiful. Three thousand men, women and children in the bright costumes of the different periods represented events of the city from the time of the Romans down to Charles First's. They poured out of groves, right and left, over a twenty acre meadow. All were volunteers and did it for love of the thing."

7 OCTOBER 1910, NEW YORK, TO PERCY W. MACKAYE

130 West 57th st.,
Oct. 7, 1910.

Dear Mr. MacKaye:

I was still in London[1] when your play opened, and I have only now got your letter of September 15th.[2]

I had but one meeting with your father:[3] at the house of Judge Pryor in 1887 where several of us came together in sympathy with him when he was trying—or had vainly tried—to get the U. S. Supreme Court to grant the Chicago Anarchists a new trial.[4] With your father I believed that the men had been convicted on an unjust ruling, and condemned for their opinions and not for a proven crime. I wish I could recall details of that most interesting night; but I remember your father's wrathful fervor, and the instances he alleged of police brutality.[5] I remember his vivid personality, and the glimpses it gave of a magnanimous manhood.

Yours sincerely
W. D. Howells.

1. During August and September Howells and Mildred traveled extensively through England, Scotland, and Wales; they sailed from Liverpool on board the *Campania* on 24 September.

2. The letter from playwright Percy W. MacKaye (1875–1956) has not been located. MacKaye's play, *Anti-Matrimony* (1910), opened on 22 September in New York at the Garrick Theatre.

3. Actor and playwright J. M. Steele MacKaye (1842–1894).

4. For Howells' association with Roger A. Pryor in regard to the Haymarket Af-

fair, see Howells to Pryor, 25 September 1887; for the meeting at Pryor's house, see Howells to Salter, 1 December 1887, n. 4.

5. In writing his father's biography years later, MacKaye quotes, with slight distortion of text and context, most of Howells' letter, carefully distinguishing the characteristic noted by Howells from any affinity with anarchism: "This 'wrathful fervour,' of my father, cited by Howells, arose from deep wells of heritage—not of sympathy with those doctrines of anarchy, but with doctrines of liberty, tolerance and free speech—the heritage of American vision, from Roger Williams' to Abraham Lincoln's." See Percy W. MacKaye, *Epoch: The Life of Steele MacKaye* (New York: Boni & Liveright, 1927), II, 96.

9 OCTOBER 1910, NEW YORK, TO ALICE FRENCH

130 W. Fifty-Seventh Street
Oct. 9, 1910.

Dear Miss French:

If our personal non-acquaintance was really the condition of your saying all those kind things to me, I must be glad of it, though some time I hope it will be different and you will at least let me tell you to your face how greatly I value the praise of an author whose literature I have long valued.[1] Once when I was over the river from Davenport (ten years ago) I was near doing something of the kind.[2]

I am truly glad you like the Mark Twain papers. But what a *great* theme I had in him! I have been a lucky man in my friends. They would at least have kept me modest if anything could, and here you, a stranger, seem bent on spoiling their work in me![3]—Perhaps I ought to thank you for hating my religion. That *would* humble me if I had not got it out of the New Testament.

Yours sincerely
W. D. Howells.

1. Howells was replying to a letter, not located, from Alice French (1850–1934), the Iowa writer, who wrote under the pen name Octave Thanet. He had reviewed her first collection of stories, *Knitters in the Sun* (1887), in the "Editor's Study," *Harper's Monthly*, January 1888.

2. Howells had briefly passed through Davenport, French's hometown, during his 1899 lecture tour. See Howells to Elinor Howells, 28 October 1899.

3. French's letter was one of many Howells received praising "My Memories of Mark Twain." Of the completed task, to which he had unstintingly devoted himself, he noted in a letter to Frederick A. Duneka, 9 September 1910 (MWA): "If it were to do again I could do it twice as well. But all life is a belated conception or imperfection."

22 October 1910, New York, to Frederick A. Duneka

130 West 57th st.
October 22, 1910.

Dear Mr. Duneka:

I think the answers had better go to Mr. Johnson, whose address I have put into the form.[1]

As yet the speakers are few though the listeners be many. One only, H. van Dyke, has clearly accepted.[2] No answers this morning. The vocal mourners have each married a wife, or gone on a journey, or peradventure sleepeth. I met J. W. Alexander in the street (not *on*, since I've been so much in England,) and seized him, only to learn that he had had his head sliced open for aches, last summer, and was not very well himself.[3] Now, ho! for Millet and Cable, oh, ho! and eke Mabie.[4]

Yours joyfully
W. D. Howells.

1. Howells refers to forms sent to prospective speakers for the Mark Twain commemoration which was to take place on 30 November at Carnegie Music Hall. The forms were to be returned to Robert U. Johnson, secretary of the National Institute of Arts and Letters.

2. Henry Van Dyke composed a poem entitled "Mark Twain," which he read at the close of the meeting. See *In Memory of Mark Twain* (New York: American Academy of Arts and Letters, 1922), pp. 102–3.

3. In a letter to Duneka of 21 October 1910 (MWA), Howells wrote that he intended to invite the painter John W. Alexander (1856–1915), "who knew Clemens in Paris, and speaks well." Best known as a portraitist, Alexander had been associated with the art department of Harper & Brothers and counted Howells and Clemens among his literary subjects.

4. Francis D. Millet and Hamilton W. Mabie did not participate. George W. Cable was the second-to-last speaker on the program. For his address, see *In Memory of Mark Twain*, pp. 68–82. The original plan for guest speakers had been somewhat grandiose (see Howells to Duneka, 1 June 1910), but when President Taft declined, Howells was determined, as he reported in a letter to Mildred Howells, 7 October 1910 (MH), to "shape it over into something much more simple and intimate." Along with Howells, Van Dyke, and Cable, the final list of speakers included Joseph A. Choate (see Howells to Duneka, 1 June 1910), Joseph H. Twichell, Joseph G. Cannon, Champ Clark (see Howells to Joseph A. Howells, 11 December 1910), and Colonel Henry Watterson (1840–1921), editor of the Louisville *Courier-Journal*.

18 NOVEMBER 1910, NEW YORK, TO JOSEPH A. HOWELLS

10 West 30th street,
Nov. 18th, 1910.

Dear Joe:

In view of my Eureka story,[1] which seems to be pelting on in spite of your advice and my own inclination, I wish you would write me everything you can remember about the *raising of our new house.* Recall the smallest and most unimportant incidents; tell who was there, and what they said and did. I believe father decided not to offer whiskey as a refreshment, and mother gave coffee instead. Who helped her get the dinner, or lunch? Where was the table spread? What time of the year was it?

I have not much news if any since my last. Every day I go up to the park to find Billy, with his nurse, and give him five cents to buy peanuts from the "Peeny man," to feed the ducks and swans; the ducks gobble them whole but the swans crack the shells.

Billy is the best little boy in the world, perfectly amiable and obedient. His great interest now is to see the electrics lighted up and say "Fi', mo' fi'," as the lamps flash out. He sees them before I do. My heart seems to rest upon him; I did not conceive of loving a child as I love him. His other grandfather, or "More Fa-fa," as he calls him, is just as fond.

Pilla and I are talking Bermuda now, though we do not expect to go till into January.

In about ten days we are to have the Mark Twain commemoration, and I am dreading it horribly, for I am to preside. I wonder I ever consented, but everybody said I must.

The weather is getting seriously cold, though as yet we have had no snow, as they have had in Texas and Tennessee. The cold seems often to break before it gets to New York. We have had plenty of dim, chilly "market days," such as we used to have in Hamilton. Love to Eliza.

Will.

1. For Howells' renewed interest in *New Leaf Mills*, see Howells to Aurelia H. Howells and Anne Fréchette, 10 April 1910.

21 NOVEMBER 1910, NEW YORK, TO OSWALD G. VILLARD

10 West 30th street,
Nov. 21, 1910.

Dear Mr. Villard:

Mr Duneka, at Harper & Brothers, would like some further and fuller explanation of the Realf letters than I was able to give him.[1] He asked me to say that if you would call him up, he would come to see you at the office of the *Post*.

Yours sincerely
W. D. Howells.

1. Oswald G. Villard (1872–1949), then editor of the New York *Evening Post*, had published, in October, *John Brown, 1800–1859, A Biography Fifty Years Later*. In it he refers to several letters of the English poet Richard Realf (1834–1878), one of Brown's comrades before the raid at Harper's Ferry. In a letter of 10 November 1910 (MWA), Howells had asked Duneka to apply to Colonel Harvey for permission to do a piece on Villard's book for the *North American Review*, subsequently writing an essay for the January 1911 number entitled "John Brown After Fifty Years." Duneka's interest in the Realf letters is not known, but would appear to be connected with Villard's book. Duneka possibly knew that Howells had met Realf in Columbus in 1859 and thus might have some knowledge of Realf's correspondence. Villard indicates in the bibliography of *John Brown* that he actually possessed "many valuable papers of the late Colonel R. J. Hinton regarding John Brown and Richard Realf," but whether this includes any Realf letters is not clear. (Hinton had collected and published his friend's work in 1898 under the title *Poems by Richard Realf, Poet, Soldier, Workman*.) Howells does not refer to Realf in the review of Villard's book, but six years later he gave an account of his acquaintance with the poet in *Years of My Youth*, HE, pp. 164–66.

23 NOVEMBER 1910, NEW YORK, TO THOMAS W. HIGGINSON

10 West 30th st.,
Nov. 23, 1910.

My dear Higginson:

I do not know who has been saying that I have left the Academy; at any rate it is not true. So far from it, I am (reluctantly as ever) to preside at the meeting in the New Theatre here on the 8th of December.[1]

I wish you were coming; I would like to see you, so much did I enjoy our last meeting. I think you are right about a woman successor to Mrs. Howe,[2] and I will bring the question up at our business session. I think Mrs. Elizabeth Stuart Phelps has a larger if not higher claim to the place than Mrs. Spofford,[3] whom also I grealy value. If you would write me a letter about the matter, I could make it my text. I believe with all the fervor of a recentish convert in the full recognition of women.[4]

That was a noble poem about Philips by Aldrich[5] which you read me; I had not thought Aldrich had it in him, and yet I have respected a seriousness in him.

Yours sincerely
W. D. Howells.

1. The American Academy of Arts and Letters was to hold its second public meeting in New York on 8–9 December.

2. Julia Ward Howe, who was elected to the Academy in early 1910, had died of pneumonia on 17 October at the age of ninety-three. Higginson, a strong proponent of women's suffrage, had persuaded Howells to invite Howe to be one of the speakers at the first Academy meeting in 1910. See Howells to Higginson, 13 July 1909.

3. Neither Harriet P. Spofford nor Elizabeth Stuart Phelps Ward was elected to the American Academy of Arts and Letters.

4. Howells had mildly expressed his sympathy with the suffrage movement in the "Editor's Easy Chair," *Harper's Monthly*, October 1910. Earlier in the year he had declined to do a piece on women's suffrage for *Harper's Bazar*, suggesting instead in a letter to editor Elizabeth Jordan, 31 March 1910 (NN), that she arrange a series by other male authors: "I should like to do something about Woman Suffrage . . . . But the subject is so good, why don't you feature it for next year, and let twelve good men and true have a shy at it? [¶] Carnegie, by all means!" He had also written appreciatively to poet Richard T. Le Gallienne (1866–1947), in a letter of 29 January 1910, commenting on a poem by Le Gallienne entitled "A Ballad of Woman, Respectfully, Admiringly, and Gratefully Dedicated to Mrs. Pankhurst," *Harper's Weekly*, 29 January 1910. Emmeline Pankhurst (1858–1928) was a militant British suffragist. Of the poem, a romantic hymn to the courage of women in their maternal and domestic roles, Howells wrote: "Never, to my knowledge has that truth been so valiantly and beautifully spoken. It made me proud and glad to be of your thinking about women." He addressed the issue in stronger political terms in the "Editor's Easy Chair," *Harper's Monthly*, February 1912, using for argument a pro-feminist sketch from *The Papers of Doctor Angélico* (1911) by the Spanish author Armando Palacio Valdés.

5. "Monody on the Death of Wendell Phillips," written the day after Phillips' death in 1884. See *The Writings of Thomas Bailey Aldrich* (Boston: Houghton Mifflin, 1907), II, 84–87.

25 NOVEMBER 1910, NEW YORK, TO JOSEPH A. HOWELLS

10 West 30th st.,
Nov. 25, 1910.

Dear Joe:

That volume of Howell's (not Howells's) Letters was something which I wrote mainly in the Fleet Prison in London about the first third of the 17th century.[1] I had then been with Charles I, when he was Prince of Wales, in Spain where he courted the Spanish Infanta, and I had written delightful letters home from there and afterwards from Venice. I was then known as James Howell; nearly three centuries later, when I had become W. D. Howells, I wrote other delightful letters home from Venice. How have you managed to keep yourself ignorant of all this for nearly eighty years? *I* knew about it when I was only seventeen. But you know other things, and did better ones. Now you can read James Howell up in an encyclopedia, and I will send you his "Familiar Letters."

I want you to put down all you can remember about the raising of our "new house" in Eureka, and all about the sickness and deaths in the John Belt family on the Island.[2] *Do it now*, as the ads. say.

I am glad to know where Willy and his family are settled,[3] and I hope they are glad to be there. None of them thought it important to give me their address.

Whether it was best for us to leave 130 W. 57 or not, it was inevitable,[4] and we do not expect to be here long, for we intend going to Bermuda in January for the rest of the winter. Pilla has just got over her first installment of grippe, and I have begun a sore throat. So, as the Harpers are quite willing we shall go, and I hope get a house for 3 months. Then N. Y. and K. P.[5]

I hope Eliza is quite well again; you do not say.—I am sorry you have lost your friend Harriott.[6] You knew dear old Larkin Mead was dead? Mary Mead in March, Elinor in May, Larkin in October! What a deathful year!—Our love to you both.

Will.

This is a sad letter, but it bears you my affectionate interest in all you do. You are always my dear brother.

1. Welsh-born James Howell (1594–1666), diplomat and court functionary under Charles I, wrote most of *Epistolae Ho-Elianae: Familiar Letters* (4 volumes, 1645–1655) during his eight years of imprisonment (1643–1651) at the hands of the Puritans. Howells probably refers to the one volume collection edited by Joseph Jacobs in 1890. Because Howell was never married, Howells "was forced to relinquish him" as an ancestor. See *Years of My Youth*, HE, p. 5.

2. Howells was still trying to get material for *New Leaf Mills*. Belt was a poor saw-miller who died of the "flux," along with five of his children, while the Howells family was living at Eureka Mills. See *My Year In a Log Cabin* (1893), pp. 37–39.

3. William D. Howells II and his wife Alice had recently moved to Florida.

4. Howells was temporarily lodged at the Burlington Hotel, having leased his apartment on a long-term basis. He had earlier written to Joe, 3 October 1910 (MH), of his painful departure from the apartment where he and Elinor had lived: "This is probably the last letter I shall ever write you from the home which is broken here.

I have let the flat furnished . . . , and it is not likely that Pilla and I will come back to it . . . . [¶]Getting out of here has really made me sick to nausea at times. Elinor adored the place, and made it hers by a thousand tastes and touches; but for that reason it is heartbreaking."

5. Kittery Point.
6. Not identified.

11 DECEMBER 1910, NEW YORK, TO JOSEPH A. HOWELLS

> 10 West 30th street,
> December 11, 1910.

Dear Joe:

While I think of it, the address of Aurelia and Annie is No. 4, (four) Rue Furstembourg, Paris.[1] I hear pretty regularly from Aurelia and they all seem to be well and happy, though both she and Annie immensely prefer London to Paris.—A letter from her has just come, and I enclose it. You will see that she is again thinking of visiting you. I suppose it will be sometime in the spring, and if you and Eliza still like the notion it will be less expense for her to come from England than from New York. But you can write and advise her.

I wish I could see you where you are so contented, but I guess I must be contented with Bermuda, although it seems rather inhuman to hold off from you. The truth is I am not only old, but I am beginning to feel my age. I suppose Elinor's death has broken my life in two. I keep on mechanically at the old things, but the joy is gone out of them. I start to tell her of something, and then I stop! Otherwise there are long times when I forget what has happened.

Don't fail to write me all that you can possibly rake and scrape together from your memories of Euroeka, especially the raising of the house, and the sickness of the Belt family.[2] Give details; nothing can be too small. I think I shall make a pretty and rather pathetic story about the situation. When I get it typewritten I may send you a copy for your revision.

Pill and I have been going through the usual colds; I have the bark of an old dog, just now. I have been public-speaking-on-the-stage out of all experience within the past fortnight, beginning with the Mark Twain commemoration on the 30th,[3] and going through the sessions of the Academy of Arts and Letters;[4] I am president, you know. It is all a terrible trial to me, but they say I did decently well. The Mark Twain business crowded the Carnegie Hall from floor to roof with 3500 people, and a thousand left on the sidewalk, who couldn't get in. I enclose a partial report—all I kept out of dozens—and letters from

Cannon, and Clark who will succeed him as Speaker of the House.[5] You needn't return any of the things. We are having our second vile snow storm. Isn't it strange how the snow used to thrill our hearts with joy?—Do you ever recall our first winters in Jefferson, when we worked in a wooden shell of a house no thicker than a tent, and wore no underclothing! What could poor father have been thinking of? I never had an undershirt till after my terrible rheumatic fever. Well, good bye, with love to you both.—Will Dean[6] came in, the other day, and talked affectionately of you, as he always does. He is not getting younger.

> Your affectionate brother,
> Will.

1. In early October, Aurelia H. Howells had accompanied Anne Fréchette to Europe, where they joined Achille and Marie Marguerite Fréchette in Paris after a brief stay in England.

2. See Howells to Joseph A. Howells, 25 November 1910, n. 2.

3. See Howells to Duneka, 1 June 1910, n. 2, and 22 October 1910.

4. See Howells to Higginson, 23 November 1910, n. 1.

5. Joseph G. Cannon (1836–1926), congressman from Illinois and Speaker of the House when Howells and Clemens went to Washington, D.C., in December 1906 to testify on behalf of a copyright bill, had allowed Clemens to use his office for lobbying activities. See *Twain-Howells*, p. 821. Champ [Joseph B.] Clark (1850–1921), congressman from Missouri, succeeded Cannon as Speaker in 1911. Both men gave speeches at the Mark Twain commemoration. For a complete list of speakers at the event, see Howells to Duneka, 22 October 1910, n. 4.

6. William E. Dean, one of Howells' cousins.

19 DECEMBER 1910, NEW YORK, TO FREDERICK A. DUNEKA

> 10 West 30th street,
> Dec. 19, 1910.

Dear Mr. Duneka:

The doctor has made me go to bed that I may the sooner go out doors. It is a matter of a sore throat which he doesn't want to become bronchitis. I have been run down by too much Academy and Commemoration[1] which tried my old-womanish nerves.

These checks, here, came without word from you, and in view of our talk about the payment for my Mark Twain articles, I think they may have come without your knowledge. I was quite in earnest when I proposed to relinquish this payment. More and more it seems to me that I held you up in asking extra payment for the papers.[2] They should have gone in under my salary; I had the right to say I could not write them, but once written they belonged to the house. The house has been very generous to me, and I wish at least to be just to it, especially as I am always asking indulgences from it. I never could say what a God-send it was to me when Colonel Harvey offered me the job which I have held so much on my own terms. So here go the checks back to you quite as if it were "corban"[3] and not pulling teeth.

Yours ever
W. D. Howells.

1. See Howells to Joseph A. Howells, 11 December 1910.

2. In a letter to Howells of 13 May 1910 (MH), Duneka indicated that Harper & Brothers would honor Howells' request, apparently made in a meeting with Duneka on 12 May, for "the extra payment of, shall we say fifteen hundred dollars, for your 'Memories of Mark Twain.'" Replying 13 May 1910 (MWA), Howells accepted the offer: "The suggested extra payment for the Mark Twain material is wholly satisfactory, and I thank you." Ordinarily, such work would have been included under Howells' fixed salary agreement with Harper & Brothers. Because of Elinor Howells' prolonged illness, however, he had been feeling considerable anxiety about money, even to the extent of having inquired about a salary increase. See Howells to Duneka, 28 February 1910.

3. An oblation or religious offering (see Mark 7:11).

2 JANUARY 1911, NEW YORK, TO BRAND WHITLOCK

The Burlington,
10 West 30th st.,
Jan'y 2, 1911.

Dear Whitlock:

Will you advise me in regard to this paper, and Mr. Adams's request?[1] Naturally, I should at once give him my name; but it is a trade-mark which I have always preferred to do business under alone, and I think I have been most useful so. Besides I don't like urging the press, as he wishes, to copy and comment. Of course I don't like his telling me that Mr. Warren is a convert of mine[2]—I mean the taste of it.[3] Mr. Warren seems to take a very level-headed view of his own case, but it seems to me his postal card was not a wise or valuable contribution to reform. As to the injustice of his trial and sentence, I don't see how there can be two minds.[4] But is Mr. Adams's way the right way to help him?[5]

—I am in the slowly relaxing hold of the grippe, and am trying for strength to get out of its clutch and away to Bermuda, which I hope to do next week. This has been a bad year, 1910, for me. I could not describe, though you will know, the black solitude in which my wife's death has left me groping, and which I realize when I wake in the night. Forty-seven years together, and now apart! It has all told in my health, made my heart misbehave, and jarred my nerves. But this is to you alone, with my daughter's love and mine to Mrs. Whitlock.—I am glad you are doing another book. Don't fret too much at your want of time.[6] Time comes to those who need it.

Yours ever
W. D. Howells.

1. Frederick U. Adams (1852–1921), inventor and author, was a fellow journalist with Whitlock in Chicago in the early 1890s. See Whitlock, *Forty Years of It* (New York: D. Appleton & Co., 1914), p. 42. Adams' letter of request and the paper are not specifically identified, but according to Whitlock's reply to Howells, 4 January 1911 (MH), Adams had sent Howells an article in defense of Fred D. Warren (1872–1959), asking Howells "to write an appeal to the newspapers" on Warren's behalf. Warren, socialist editor of *The Appeal to Reason*, had just been denied an appeal, in November 1910, of his 1909 conviction of violating the United States postal laws, resulting in a six-month jail sentence and a fine of $1,500. On envelopes bearing his business heading, Warren had printed in red ink an offer of a $1,000 reward "to the person or persons who will kidnap ex-Gov. Taylor and return him to the State officials of Kentucky, where he is wanted on a charge of murdering Goebel." In a highly partisan court proceeding, William S. Taylor (1853–1928), a Republican, had been deposed as governor of Kentucky and indicted as a conspirator in the assassination of his Democratic gubernatorial opponent William Goebel (1856–1900), who had been killed by an unknown assailant on 30 January 1900 after contesting Taylor's election. Taylor immediately fled the state to avoid probable arrest, going to Indianapolis where he spent the remainder of his life. Three Democratic governors of Kentucky successively attempted to extradite Taylor but were thwarted by their Republican counterparts in Indiana. Taylor was eventually pardoned in 1909 by Augustus E. Willson, Republican governor of Kentucky.

2. Whitlock's reply indicates that Adams had suggested he and Warren were influenced by one of Howells' books, not named, thus giving Adams the "amusing assumption," as Whitlock put it, of a claim on Howells' good will.

3. Whitlock, in his letter, affirmed Howells' reaction: " 'Grizzly' Adams—as we used to call him in the old days . . . , was never noted so much for his good taste, as for his good heart; a part of that character we attributed to him when we gave him that shaggy nickname. His article is convincing enough, of course, even if it does seem to be so poorly written . . . , but I don't like the idea of appealing to the editors of the American press to publish and comment on anything, even the truth . . . ."

4. Many, along with Adams, objected to the questionable legal grounds of Warren's conviction and to the excessive severity of the sentence. Upholding Warren's conviction but fearing the socialist would become a political martyr, President Taft interceded on 9 February 1911 to eliminate the jail sentence and reduce the fine to $100.

5. Sharing Howells' doubts, Whitlock agreed, in his reply, that Adams was wrong. Howells thanked Whitlock, in a letter of 6 January 1911 (NjR), for advising "quite as I wished" and enclosed the text of his letter of refusal to Adams, dated 6 January 1911: "I would rather not join in asking the press to copy and comment on your presentation of Mr. Warren's case; it would be like taking a liberty with the liberty of the press and might be damagingly resented. But the editorial sense of humor is potent, even where the editorial sense of justice is weak, and I think that may safely

be trusted with the comic opera quality of what seems Mr. Warren's cruel tragedy. My sole knowledge of this is derived from your article."

6. Howells referred to Whitlock's complaint in an earlier letter, 22 December 1910 (MH), to which this one is in part a reply, that the "miserable duties" of being mayor of Toledo were making it difficult to find time for writing "a new novel in my head and in my heart . . . ." The novel was probably *J. Hardin & Son*, begun in 1914 but not completed until 1923.

7 JANUARY 1911, NEW YORK, TO HENRY JAMES

10 West 30th street,
Jan'y 7, 1911.

Dear James:

I feel very guilty in having taken our tickets for Bermuda on the 11th, but such is the lamentable fact. We have longed to be off during the last six weeks of grippe and nervous breakdown, and we cannot put off going now, even for you, poor dear, whom I should so gladly stay for.[1] I have had my own Pocket Illiad, which is nothing to your folio, but illiad enough.[2] My management of the Mark Twain commemoration, with my loathing for any publicity but that of print, was of almost killing effect, and hard upon it followed three days of the Accursed Academy of Arts and Letters, me President! I assure you the whole thing was a nightmare, but thank heaven I am awake from it, though in a tremble and cold perspiration still.[3]

We hope to find a house in Bermuda, and stay three months, but we must go first to an hotel. I count much upon the outing because, for one thing, it is a land of large sleep, and here I wake every morning at 2 or 3 and drink my sorrow dry, and then drug myself, one way other, back into oblivion.

This is not cheering you up, which I should like to do, but perhaps it will help you a little if you know you have the company that misery loves.[4] I will own that I am somewhat comforted when I think of you, and realize that I am not the only wretched man, selfish beast that I am.

Your sister[5] wrote me a heavenly letter which I shall try to answer worthily by and by. What angelic courage, what divine sympathy.

You may care to know that the brute Badger is stilled. He sent me a proof, and it has gone back to him without bothering you, and it is all right.[6]

Pilla has shared my influenza and nervous breakdown, and she needs the exile from New York even more than I. We shall taxi down to the steamer, hand in hand, next Wednesday, mingling our tears of nervous weakness, and of regret that we are not to see you here. Billy and his family are the only things besides that we regret.

With our love to all your people,

Yours affectionately
W. D. Howells.

1. James was then staying in Cambridge with the recently widowed Alice (Mrs. William) James and family. He traveled to New York from time to time, occasionally visiting with Howells. See L. Edel, *Henry James, The Master, 1901–1916* (Philadelphia: J. B. Lippincott, 1972), pp. 451–53.
2. The allusion is not entirely clear. The "Pocket Illiad" is probably a reference to Howells' recent minor illness as compared to the folio proportions of the nervous breakdown from which James was still recovering.
3. For Howells' account of the Mark Twain commemoration and Academy meeting, see his letter to Joseph A. Howells, 11 December 1910.
4. Following Howells' loss of Elinor in May 1910, James had successively lost his two brothers, first Robertson in July and then William in August.
5. James's sister-in-law, Alice James, William's widow.
6. Howells had received from Boston publisher Richard G. Badger the proof for Evelyn G. Smalley's *The Henry James Yearbook*, for which both he and James had written prefaces. See Howells to James, 20 August 1909.

15 JANUARY 1911, BERMUDA, TO AURELIA H. HOWELLS

Princess Hotel
Bermuda . . . January 15, 1911.

Dear Aurelia:

You see we are here at last,[1] and a heavenly *here* it is. The thing is simply incredible after the hard, grippy winter of New York, only 46 hours away. The passage is rough, but it doesn't matter to never-seasick me,[2] and Pilla simply beds it through. Then we arrive among birds and flowers which seem to be singing together. I don't know which beats in beauty, the day or the night. We had a moon last night that blew about in the sky like a large toy balloon or dandelion blow-ball, and the sun is so hot by day that I have bought a straw hat. Everybody is in summer clothes.

We are on the point of taking a house for three months, but perhaps we may stay in this comfortable hotel after all. The house is just across a little cove with grounds running down to the water.[3]

If I get my sleep straightened out and do more of it by night, I shall do a lot of good work here. But I have the habit of waking about 2 or 3 a.m. and descending into hell, with black despair. Oh, never did I dream that my grief would be like this. I thought I should forget, but

I only remember more, and it is all error and folly, so that I begin to think I would like to be blotted out utterly. Well, I suppose this will pass—everything passes.

My mind is often on you, in wonder how you will get on away from Annie.[4] I know you will enjoy London, and if you are to be with friends there, it is a homelike place, and if you know how to get at them the English are kind—though not so kind as the Americans.

It was hard leaving our dear Billy. The last morning Abby had him call me, "Fa-fa" over the 'phone! Wasn't that modern? But he is old-fashioned good and sweet.

Pilla is getting over her teasing throat. She loves Bermuda of course. With our united love to all,

> Your aff'te brother
> **Will.**

I'm so glad the money came all right.

1. Howells and Mildred sailed from New York on 11 January, arriving in Bermuda on 13 January.
2. The day he arrived, Howells wrote to Frederick A. Duneka, 13 January 1911 (MWA), that it had been "perhaps the most diabolical voyage that man ever made." Although he himself had been spared, he went on to say, "People were casting their very souls up into the deep, and going about very husks and shells of humanity afterwards."
3. Howells provided a brief description of the house in a letter to F. A. Duneka, erroneously dated "Hamilton, Bermuda / Jan'y 11, 1911": "We have got a house, with only a kitchen chimney.... There is a hen coop, and two red-birds are furnished with the garden and the dooryard cedars; we are to have milk from our landlady's cow, and through the interest of nearly the whole society of the island, we have secured a cook and a housemaid."
4. Aurelia was to travel alone in England, before settling with Anne and Achille Fréchette, first in Paris and then Lausanne, Switzerland. See James Doyle, *Annie Howells and Achille Fréchette* (Toronto: University of Toronto Press, 1979), p. 106.

29 JANUARY 1911, HAMILTON, BERMUDA, TO ELIZABETH N. CASE

Hamilton, Bermuda, Jan'y 29, 1911.

Dear Miss Case:[1]

I should be ungrateful for the best influences in my life if I did not speak well of the Quakers. My great grandfather became "a Friend by convincement" in Wales a hundred and fifty years ago, and though my grandfather "married out of meeting," my grandmother was of Quaker parentage and brought up by a Quaker aunt and uncle.[2]

I think the life of Thomas Ellwood far more interesting than that of Lord Herbert of Cherbury. One day I was talking with Whittier of it, and he was greatly interested in my having edited it.[3] He reminded me that he had edited John Woolman's Journal.[4] I suppose, as of Quaker lineage, you have read that most charming and simple-hearted record.

I thank you for writing me. My daughter and I are here for the winter. It is distinctly a pleasure to be in a place whose history has no stain of battle-shed blood upon it.

Yours sincerely
W. D. Howells.

1. According to the envelope, Howells' correspondent was a Miss Elizabeth Nichols Case of Hartford, Connecticut, not otherwise identified.

2. See *Years of My Youth*, HE, pp. 6–7.

3. Howells wrote introductions for the *Lives of Lord Herbert of Cherbury and Thomas Ellwood* (1877), one of the volumes in a series of "Choice Autobiographies" he edited in 1877–1878. See Howells to Higginson, 2 July 1877.

4. Howells reviewed John Greenleaf Whittier's edition of *The Journal of John Woolman* in the *Atlantic Monthly*, August 1871. John Woolman (1720–1772) was an American Quaker concerned with the abolition of slavery and the problems of poverty. His *Journal* (1774), written with moving simplicity, is a spiritual autobiography.

29 JANUARY 1911, HAMILTON, BERMUDA, TO JOSEPH A. HOWELLS

Bermuda, Jan'y 29, 1911.

Dear Joe:

I thought you might like to see a letter which has greatly pleased me,[1] and so I writing on the back of it to thank you again for all that Eureka stuff.[2] I'm glad you remember Ann Stepmyer, at last; somehow, boy though I was, I knew about her wicked old mother trying to tempt her away to an evil life, and I am putting that into the story.[3] I have just started dear mother and you off on that journey to Hamilton.[4] I think you will be pleased with it.—The address on your letter which came yesterday was as exactly in father's hand as if he had written it. How strangely we are all bound together by blood!

We go into our house on Wednesday. It is called Hill House, and belonged to an old and respected Mr. Jones, lately dead. We have it of a Mr. Middleton, his son-in-law; Mr. Hutchins will tell you where it is.[5] It has been newly painted and repaired, and it is like new. We have got a cook and housemaid, and I suppose we shall be very comfortable.

I enclose a letter from William, with whom I've rather active correspondence. He seems to be getting on. How strange he should be doing legislative letters as another William (D.) Howells did them fifty-three years ago.[6]

Pilla joins me in love to you both.

Your aff'te brother,
Will.

You might congratulations to William.

1. Howells' letter to Joe was written on the back of page two (the first page is lost) of a letter to Howells, date unknown, from Charles M. Stuart (1853–1932), a theologian and then editor of the *Northwestern Christian Advocate*. With enthusiastic appreciation, Stuart says in part: "I think I have all your books; I know I have your picture and your autograph—so there isn't a blessed thing in the writing of this except the relief which comes from expressing myself."

2. Howells had asked Joe to send his recollections of the family's year at Eureka Mills for the novel *New Leaf Mills*, then in progress. See Howells to Joseph A. Howells, 25 November 1910. Almost three weeks earlier, on 9 January 1911 (MH), Howells had written Joe from New York: "Yours of the 30th December . . . brought me a lot more of most interesting Eureka stuff. . . . I remembered your going to the campmeeting in the green coat that 'packed you out' everywhere; but not the details. Sometimes father seems to have been rather cruelly frugal, but I suppose he couldn't help it."

3. Ann Stepmeyer appears neither in the autobiographical account of Eureka Mills, *My Year in a Log Cabin*, nor in the novel; however, in the latter an uneducated but good-hearted hired girl named Rosy Hefmyer tries to evade her mother, who is indirectly characterized as a prostitute. Near the end of the novel the mother makes a dramatic nighttime visit, frightening Rosy into fleeing "in mysterious silence to a destiny . . . [of] dreadful possibility." See *New Leaf Mills* (1913), p. 137. As he would later explain to Joe, the implication is "clear enough" that she follows the fate of her mother. See Howells to Joseph A. Howells, 29 May 1911.

4. Although Howells does not record the fact in *My Year in a Log Cabin*, Mrs. Howells must have visited relatives in Hamilton to escape momentarily what for her was the onerous experience of living at the mill. See Howells to Aurelia H. Howells and Anne Fréchette, 10 April 1910. Similarly, a frustrated Mrs. Powell, in *New Leaf Mills*, seeks relief in a family visit to Middleville, a forty-mile journey on which she is accompanied by her oldest son Dick.

5. Mr. Hutchins appears to have been a British subject from Bermuda living at the Turks Islands. In a letter to Joe a week earlier, 22 January 1911 (MH), Howells said that he had seen "Mr. Hutchins, 'of your city,' " in Bermuda and had given him what news there was to take back to Turks Islands. Jones and Middleton have not been identified.

6. Joe's grandson, William Cooper Howells (1887–1940), son of William Dean Howells II, was a reporter in Columbus, Ohio, for the Cleveland *Plain Dealer*. Howells, who had reported the events of the Ohio state legislature in 1857 for the Cincinnati *Gazette*, seems to have taken a special interest in young William's career, as suggested in a letter to Joseph A. Howells, 23 October 1910 (MH): "I have had a long letter from William who has found, as I knew, that he has come to the end of his promotion. He can get only so far as a reporter, and he has got there. He would be willing to resume medicine, but he feels bound to earn money to pay his sisters' way through college. This is good of him but not wise; they ought to pay their own way by teaching."

9 FEBRUARY 1911, HAMILTON, BERMUDA, TO S. WEIR MITCHELL

Hamilton, Bermuda, Feb'y 9, 1911.

My dear Mitchell:

You will let my distance account for my not answering you more promptly. I came down here, nearly a month ago after two turns of grippe, and am just working through a third. The climate is heavenly, but the great modern microbe is drifting round with the angelic host.

—If the author of The Conqueror is the person who wrote the story about The Masqueraders she is not only underbred but low-minded. I am glad of Miss Sherwood's courage.[1] I do not know the obscene "Poppy" but publishers who do such things should be condemned with their authors.[2]

I thank you for your suggestion about making criticism a topic for an Easy Chair essay. It has come at one of those times when I think I shall never find another topic, and I shall use it for my very next paper.[3]

I think the best newspaper criticism going is that of the literary supplement of the Chicago Post, which you mention. It is better than the Boston Transcript's, to my mind; the New York Sun's is clever, but too cynical; the Dial's[4] is tepid; the N. Y. Post's nil.

My own usefullest and clearest criticism came from my wife, who had "absolute pitch" in matters of that sort; she *could* not fail, and she loved me too well to spare me. But I must not speak of her—I miss her not less but more as time goes on.

I am finishing a story,[5] novel-size, which I began forty-five years ago! It is curious to find myself of the same thinking still, but with a truer light on things, I hope.

In spite of the red birds and the sunsets and the strangeness of the summer-winter this is a good place to work.

Yours affectionately,
W. D. Howells.

1. In a letter, now lost, Mitchell appears to have called Howells' attention to an essay by Margaret P. Sherwood (1864–1955), entitled "Lying Like Truth," *Atlantic*, December 1910. The author of *The Conqueror* (1902), a biographical fiction about Alexander Hamilton, was Gertrude Atherton, whose recent novel *Tower of Ivory* (1910) Sherwood had—with "courage," in Howells' opinion—castigated as "morally and artistically underbred." *The Masquerader* (1904) was a famous novel of impersonation written not by Atherton but by Katherine C. Thurston. Howells' view of Atherton was probably motivated in part by her attack on Howells' middle-class brand of realism. See Howells to James, 16 January 1910, n. 2. Mitchell no doubt also wanted to point out that Sherwood had acclaimed Howells, along with Henry James and Edith Wharton, to be among those few American writers who "stand highest on our brief roll of fame."

2. In her essay, Sherwood had sharply criticized *Poppy* (1910), a novel by South African-born English author Cynthia Stockley (1877–1939), as a promising tale that "turns into a bit of decadent literature." Sherwood especially regretted its publication by G. P. Putnam's Sons, "the fine old firm whose clean-minded literature was the solace of our childhood."

3. Howells made criticism the topic of the "Editor's Easy Chair," *Harper's Monthly*, May 1911. Referring to Mitchell anonymously as "an admirably qualified and peculiarly authorized censor of the needs and qualities of criticism," he credits him with inviting "the Easy Chair to a study of 'the functions of the critic,' as it knows him, or rather as it does not."

4. The *Dial* was then a conservative biweekly journal of criticism based in Chicago.

5. *New Leaf Mills.*

19 FEBRUARY 1911, HAMILTON, BERMUDA, TO WILLIAM STRUNK

Hamilton, Bermuda Feb'y 19, 1911

Dear Sir:[1]

Your very gratifying letter of the 13th has been sent me from Kittery Point. I had known of "Silas Lapham" being used by Professor Phelps at Yale and Professor Matthews[2] of Columbia, but I was not aware that the like honor had been done it at Cornell, in such high company as you tell me it has enjoyed. All that you tell me of its fortunes among your students has greatly interested me, and has set me questioning why it should have the primacy it seems to hold among my books. I suppose that it is typically American, and may remain so, though circumstances and conditions have greatly changed since I wrote it. Then— in 1885—a millionaire was still a rich man; now he is merely well off. I was always fond of Lapham and fonder still of his wife, though I did not realize her so directly from life; he seemed to me of the lasting boyishness which keeps the hearts of Americans sweet. Then, he was finding out against his selfish ambition and temptations, what a true rise was, and I was following him with pride and joy.

I wish you would give my very sincere regards to your "English Department both instructors and students", and accept my thanks for yourself.

Yours truly
W. D. Howells

Prof. W. Strunk

1. William Strunk (1869–1946) was professor of English at Cornell. His letter to Howells has not been located.

2. William L. Phelps (1865–1943), professor of English, and Brander Matthews.

3 MARCH 1911, HAMILTON, BERMUDA, TO EDITH WHARTON

Hamilton, Bermuda, March 3d 1911.

Dear Mrs. Wharton:

Of course I think the notion of getting James the Nobel prize is wonderfully good and fit, and I am only vext that Gosse should have thought of it first.[1] Unhappily for me I am partially invalided here from the long strain of the past year, and we shall not go back to New York before April. But I have at once written to Mrs. Cadwalader Jones (who sent me your letter) suggesting her getting the matter before Mr. Sloane, Chancellor of the Academy of Arts and Letters, and getting him to act in behalf of the Academy. All and singular the authors of America will favour getting the prize for James, and as I think of ways I will write to people and try to make them serve.[2] I do not know whether there is any representation of the Nobel Committee in the United States or not; if not, I suppose we can act through the English branch. I will write to Mr. Henry Holt, who is President of the Authors' Club,[3] and Dr. Van Dyke of the Institute.[4] The matter will be kept as quiet as possible so as not to annoy James with it.[5]

Yours sincerely
W. D. Howells.

1. Howells had received a letter, dated 28 February 1911 (MH), from Edith Wharton's sister-in-law, Mary Cadwalader Jones, forwarding one from Edith Wharton to Howells, dated 18 February 1911 (MH). In her letter, Wharton had enclosed a copy, now lost, of a letter to her from Edmund Gosse suggesting, as she says, "the first steps to be taken" in exerting influence to have the 1911 Nobel Prize for literature awarded to Henry James. She and Gosse had discreetly initiated the effort, and to this end Wharton was asking Howells, as the friend of James she knew would be most "completely in sympathy with the attempt," to organize support in the United States by means of "personal propaganda among the people who really appreciate Mr. James...." Despite a vigorous campaign on James's behalf, the award went to the Belgian poet and playwright Maurice Maeterlinck.

2. In her letter, Wharton had explained that Gosse and his English colleagues could "of course do nothing effective without the support of public opinion in America, & it is certainly time that Mr. James's countrymen should show themselves not less appreciative than his European readers." For Howells' correspondence with Gosse and for his efforts to solicit support in the United States, see his letter to Matthews, 4 March 1911.

3. Henry Holt was head of Henry Holt and Co., New York. The Authors Club, founded in 1882 by Richard W. Gilder, Brander Matthews, Edmund C. Stedman and others, was a society to promote the well-being of literature. The eligibility requirement that one had to have published a creditable book would make the membership of over 150 authors an authentic literary voice in the cause of James's nomination. Howells, who was not then a member, soon after accepted a "life membership," as indicated in his letter of 11 April 1911 (NN) to Duffield Osborne of the club's execu-

tive council: "if it means no duties, no responsibilities, no fees, and unlimited leave of absence, I do not see why I should not gratefully, if not very gracefully accept. . . . I am old, and I hate care and complications of every kind." A letter to Osborne a year later, 24 March 1912 (NN), shows that Howells resigned over some unknown offense.

4. See Howells to Van Dyke, 28 April 1911.

5. Wharton had cautioned Howells in her letter that James knew "nothing whatever of this project," suggesting "that it should not be mentioned to him at present." Mary Cadwalader Jones, whom James had been visiting intermittently in New York during the winter, was even more adamant, in her letter to Howells, that James "had better know nothing of any plan, as it may, alas, not come to anything."

4 MARCH 1911, HAMILTON, BERMUDA, TO BRANDER MATTHEWS

Hamilton, Bermuda, March 4, 1911.

My dear Matthews:

Mrs. Cadwalader Jones has sent me a letter of Gosse's in which he tells of English authors joining to get this years' Nobel Prize for Henry James[1] (who, confidentially, needs it,)[2] and wants American authors to unite with them, or appeal separately. I have suggested her going to Sloan to have him commit the Academy in J.'s favor. Can you help, somehow? I know you will if you can. Would President Butler[3] write a letter to represent Columbia? Would Holt, for the Authors' Club? Get them to do it, if you can, all very on the quiet.

I expect to be here till April 1st.[4] Till then I am your March fool, who would like to hear from you.

Yours ever
W. D. Howells.

The N. A. Review has had my Molière notice for 3 mos.[5]

1. For the letters of Jones and Gosse, see Howells to Wharton, 3 March 1911. Howells wrote directly to Gosse, 6 March 1911 (British Library), heartily endorsing the project and asking how best to organize American influence: "I hate you for having thought of it first, but it is so absolutely fit, so perfectly right, that I can almost forgive you. Of cours [sic] I am moving at once in the matter, and am trying to start the Academy and other literary bodies. Will you tell me where we may bring our action to bear? Can we tag onto you?" Gosse, who was then librarian of the House of Lords (1904–1914) and acquainted, as he put it, "with several of the innermost ring" of the Nobel Committee of the Swedish Academy, replied at length in a letter of 22 March 1911 (MH). He candidly described the obstacles in the way of securing the $37,000 prize "for 'dear old Uncle Henry' as the children call him at Rye." As an example of the committee's ignorance, he cited its naive belief that the popular romancer Winston Churchill was "the leading living writer of U.S.A.," warning: "They want dreadfully to do the right thing, but they don't know what the right thing is." Gosse advised Howells that the best course of action would be to

submit a petition to the Nobel Committee from the American Academy. Subsequent correspondence between Howells and Robert U. Johnson, secretary of the American Academy, reveals that Howells was thwarted in getting the full weight of the Academy behind James. In a letter to Howells of 4 April 1911 (NNAL), Johnson rather narrowly ruled that although individual members might use their Academy designation to endorse James, "it would not be proper for the Academy as an organization to recommend any one of its members for a foreign honor." A disappointed Howells replied, 5 April 1911 (NNAL), that he was "sorry the letter to the Nobel Committee is worded so as to carry the impression probably that the Academy as a body might not approve of the presentation of Mr. James's name," but that he would nevertheless sign it "as it stands." The text of the letter sent to the secretary of the Nobel Committee, dated 7 April 1911 (Archives of the Nobel Committee, Stockholm) and signed by Howells and Johnson, was hardly more than pro forma: "The undersigned members and officers of the American Academy of Arts and Letters have the honor to present for consideration as the recipient of the Nobel prize in literature the name of Mr. Henry James, the distinguished American novelist and essayist." According to a letter written a week later, 12 April 1911 (MH), from Mary Cadwalader Jones, Howells spoke with James soon after the letter from the Academy had been dispatched. Although Howells did not reveal the enterprise, he did, by her account, at least indirectly express his dissatisfaction with the Academy: "Mr James told me the other day that you and he had vague thoughts of resigning from the Academy. Surely that would break Mr Sloane's heart! and besides, if all the foreigners think the endorsement of the Academy so important you may as well use it. I am so glad you have managed all this so quietly—if it succeeds, Mr James will be happily surprised—if it doesn't, he will not be mortified by its failure." Neither Howells nor James resigned.

2. Although James was well along in recovering from his nervous breakdown of the previous year, he was excessively worried about his modest financial circumstances. In her letter to Howells of 28 February 1911 (MH), Mary Cadwalader Jones described James's concern: "He is getting well, but it is quite true that he is depressed at the slenderness of his resources. As you know, he has never been a 'best seller', and his personal property has dwindled in value, as property will if one lives in Europe and has less than no business ability!"

3. Nicholas M. Butler (1862–1947), professor of philosophy, was president of Columbia University (1902–1945).

4. Howells left Bermuda on 1 April as planned.

5. The piece on Molière is not identified. In a subsequent letter to Matthews, 4 May 1911 (NNC), Howells referred to it as a review of Matthews' book *Molière* (1910). Howells' report on its disposition suggests that it was not published: "I first wrote it as an editorial review, for the N.A.R.; then with their approval, I changed it to an article, so that my name might go with it. From month to month it was crowded over till now they have begun printing a series of things from me, and at any rate Molière seems to be rather aged as a topic."

28 APRIL 1911, NEW YORK, TO HENRY VAN DYKE

Hotel Wellington,
56th st. 7th ave.,
April 28, 1911.

Dear Dr. van Dyke:

I am very glad of your letter on all accounts, and I thank you for your generous willingness to act in behalf of the dear and great Henry James regarding the Nobel award. I am myself wholly out of the question,[1] and he is by all means supremely in it. The movement for him originated with Edmund Gosse who wrote to Mrs. Wharton, who wrote to me.[2] I in turn have written, at Gosse's suggestion and under cover to him (17 Hanover Terrace, Regent's Park, N. W.), to the Swedish novelist, Per Hallström, who is, Gosse says, "at present the boss of the show,[3] who is very intelligent, reads English, and has been a long time in America."[4] I wrote as President of the Academy, and if you will write as President of the Institute, it will be of the greatest possible use. Gosse, of course, will be glad to forward your letter to Mr. Per Hallström, whose address I do not know.

Mr. R. U. Johnson tells me that Dr. Svente Arrhenius is now in the country and can be reached through Dr. Jacques Loeb of the Rockefeller Institute.[5] He (Dr. A.) is the President of the Nobel committee. I have asked Dr. Loeb for his address, and if I get it, I will call on him, and let you know how the land lies. Gosse says the N. people are a difficult lot, and very contrary minded.[6]

As to my son's nomination for the Institute he and I are both very grateful to you. He thinks that J. W. Alexander, Walter Cook, Cass Gilbert, or Whitney Warren, or Daniel C. French would second him.[7] He is an architect, but any artist would count in his favor, as I understand.

I am apparently leaving the matter in your kind hands. Perhaps that is what I am really doing. So many things must be left there that you will not mind.

Yours sincerely
W. D. Howells.

1. Van Dyke's letter, evidently proposing Howells as a fit candidate for the Nobel Prize, is lost.

2. See Howells to Wharton, 3 March 1911.

3. Per Hallström (1866–1960), Swedish writer best known for his short stories, apparently acted in an advisory role to the Nobel Committee, being "no member of it," as he wrote in a letter to Howells of 30 May 1911 (MH).

4. Howells refers to a letter from Gosse, dated 22 March 1911 (MH), advising Howells to "communicate privately with Per Hallström" through Gosse, in addition to getting up "a petition from the Academy of America" signed by Howells as president. Howells' private communications with Hallström are lost, but Hallström's letter to Howells of 30 May indicates that an earlier correspondence had taken place. In his letter, Hallström explains that the probable rejection of "the candidature of Mr. Henry James" would be a decision based more on timing than merit: "your recommendation came in too late to support it, if the committee is strict upon the rules." Howells informed Gosse, in a letter of 7 April 1911 (British Library), that he had written Hallström in support of James: "It is such a good cause I feel it *must* fail, and you may think I have done my worst to hurt it. But I haven't *tried* to hurt it in my letter to Per Gynt Hallström. (Oh, why had I never read any of his novels!)"

5. Svante A. Arrhenius (1859–1927), Swedish scientist who contributed significantly to the modernization of physical chemistry with his theory of electrolysis, was in the United States to deliver the Silliman Lectures at Yale. In 1903 he became the first Swede to win a Nobel Prize. Jacques Loeb (1859–1924), German-born physiologist, noted for his mechanistic explanation of life processes, joined the Rockefeller Institute for Medical Research in 1910 and remained there until his death.

6. In his letter of 22 March, Gosse had candidly described the Nobel Committee as "not a very easy body to deal with. It is, indeed, an obstinate, conceited, clever, and ignorant body."

7. Howells refers to John Howells' nomination for membership in the National Institute of Arts and Letters. Artist John W. Alexander has been previously identified; Walter Cook (1846–1916), Cass Gilbert (1859–1934), and Whitney Warren (1864–1943) were prominent New York architects, Gilbert being among those Institute members who founded the American Academy of Arts and Letters. Daniel C. French (1850–1931), noted sculptor, did the Concord "Minute Man" and numerous portrait statues. John Howells was elected to the Institute in 1911.

16 MAY 1911, TOMPKINSVILLE, NEW YORK, TO FREDERICK A. DUNEKA

> 41 Sherman Avenue,
> Tompkinsville, Staten Island,
> May 16, 1911.

Dear Mr. Duneka:

I wipe Ford out because I remember that certain chapters of his Literary Shop were offensive to the good house of Harpers, and it would not be nice of me to celebrate him at the cost of dear old friends.[1] But I do not give up to your opinion; he is very restricted, but within his bounds he has not a rival.

Now that we are rechristening my unhappy story,[2] suppose you send me the sheets at Kittery Point, before you begin to print, and let me pull it together on the last page in a way that has occurred to me. I wont make much bother.

—Of course I have filled out the last page of the Chair. You wont let me run under but you never let me run over.

> Yours ever
> W. D. Howells.

1. James L. Ford satirized magazine editors and writers in *The Literary Shop and Other Tales* (1894). The barbs cast at *Harper's Monthly* and the "Franklin Square Prose and Verse Factory," as Ford dubs Harper & Brothers, are not nearly so sharp as those he aimed at the New York *Ledger, Scribner's,* and the *Century.* In saying "I wipe Ford out," Howells' meaning is not clear; it possibly refers to the omission of Ford—a gesture apparently questioned by Duneka—from the company of American humorists named in the "Editor's Easy Chair," *Harper's Monthly,* July 1911.

2. In part "unhappy" because long delayed, "The Children of the Summer" was retitled *The Vacation of the Kelwyns.* A letter to Duneka, dated 9 March 1911 (MWA)

from Bermuda, indicates that although Howells had recently finished the novel, he was still unwilling to have it published: "I have given a final reading to the proofs of 'The Children of the Summer,' and am sending them back registered, so that they may be corrected against the time when I decide to publish the book." For the decision ultimately to defer publication, see Howells to Duneka, 18 June 1911.

19 MAY 1911, TOMPKINSVILLE, NEW YORK, TO HENRY JAMES

> Tompkinsville, Staten Island,
> May 19, 1911.

My dear James:

Let not the uncouth name of my sojourn repulse you: it is the suburb,[1] wholly accessible by water which John has chosen for his family till he can come to Kittery Point in late August. Not far off, on the other side of the hill, lived the urbane Curtis many years, and yesterday sweltering by in a most ammoniacally scented landau, with Billie piling over us all, I saw the heels of his widow or orphan protruding from a hammock on his veranda.[2] The whole neighborhood is a wonderful arrest in the architecture of 1880 when it seems to have been overbuilt. The scene is such as we should have so differently made our prey when we had the heart for that kind of thing, and I wish I could read what you would have written about it.

Come when you will to Kittery Point; you will always be most welcome.[3] I am only as sorry for the cause of your present delay as I am glad of your own health and evident courage of your health.[4] Of course without my asking you to, you would have told dear Mrs. James[5] of my share in your common anxiety. It will be good to know that what must be done has been done successfully, and that you are all at peace again.

Pilla has been at K. P. this week and is now at Boston resting in the dentist's chair from the labors of the garden. I am going on next Monday and then she will return to K. P. with me, and I shall try to take up what is left of life.—But when I say something like this I feel it a pose; I am really very cheerful, and happy as ever in my work. With my children I always talk gayly of their mother, not purposely, but because her life and mine was mostly a life of pleasure in the droll and amusing things. I recall our thousand and one experiences in strange character, and first of all our own characters; and the pang is no longer a sense of hopeless loss, but of wonder that I did not make more of her keenly humorous criticism of all that we knew in common.

During the past few months I finished the story which I told you of taking up after an interval of fifty years;[6] and I think I found out the truth about it. The thing is roughly pulled together, and needs endless going over, but I am sure the truth is in it, and that more and more is what I care for.

I write and find greater happiness in writing than I ever did; and this, my dear old friend, is clumsily leading up to the hope and belief that you will soon begin writing again. You have been miserably interrupted, but you have great things ahead of you to do and to enjoy doing; and you must set yourself to realize this. Why shouldn't you, pending something inventive, speak (self-respectfully, as you would) of the literary times and places you have lived in?[7] That is something which the editorial soul would exult to have from you.

Yours ever

W. D. Howells.

1. Howells spent a week on Staten Island, where John and Abby Howells had taken a house, arriving on 15 May and leaving for Kittery Point on 21 or 22 May.

2. George W. Curtis died in 1892. His widow was Anna Shaw Curtis and the orphan probably his unmarried daughter Elizabeth.

3. James appears to have visited Howells at Kittery Point in the first week of July 1911, during an unseasonable hot spell. In his letter to Thomas S. Perry, 9 July 1911, Howells makes special reference to the unpleasant "H. James weather."

4. James, who had been in the United States since the previous August, had made plans to sail for Europe on 14 June but was forced to delay his departure until 2 August for unspecified "urgent and intimate family reasons...." See James to Dr. J. William White, 12 May 1911, in *The Letters of Henry James*, ed. Percy Lubbock (1920; reprint ed., New York: Octagon Books, 1970), II, 185. In regard to his health, James had informed Howells, in a letter of 20 April 1911 (MH) from New York, where the two men had just seen each other, that he was "better today than when you saw me yesterday."

5. Alice James, Henry James's sister-in-law.

6. *The Vacation of the Kelwyns.*

7. Following his nervous breakdown in 1910—in part brought on by the fear of losing his powers of invention and exacerbated by the deaths of his brothers Robertson and William—James had not been able to return to the writing of fiction. In the immediate years to come, he was instead mainly compelled toward family autobiography, not literary reminiscence as Howells here advises, first in *A Small Boy and Others* (1913) and then in *Notes of a Son and Brother* (1914).

29 MAY 1911, KITTERY POINT, TO HAMLIN GARLAND

Kittery Point, May 29, 1911.

My dear Garland:

Your letter was the more welcome because it reminded me of a favor I want you to do me, namely: write me out a description of a house-raising such as you gave me verbally when we last met.[1] I have used such a fact in my latest unpublished novel, and I want to be sure I have got it straight. Even without this, I should have been glad of your interesting news. Mine is pretty much the old thing: work and grief and old age, with the fear of a fading interest in things. I believe, however, I "done a good job," as they say here, in that latest, which I call New Leaf Mills, and which forms the record of an unsuccessful family community in Ohio sixty years ago.

I am curious about your theatricals.[2] You ought yourself to be able to do a good play; and why not some of those plays, like Under the Lion's Paw, which you did so long ago in Boston?[3] Herne was a great loss to the drama which he came to so late in life.[4] Some one spoke to me the other day about Crystal's beautiful acting. What could it have been in? What a gifted family![5]

Our Bermuda winter was very peaceful and pleasant; but a winter in a low latitude is very like a winter in a dream; for full consciousness we need the bite of the frost. Our shell-roses and passion-flowers vied in blooming through January, February and March, and in looking incredible all the time. One of our apple trees in full blow here, is worth all the glory of the tropics.

My place is as beautiful as ever, but it is terrible with the associations which it cannot shake off. It was so dear to my wife that it is a constant reminder of her ever-during absence. Yesterday afternoon when the shadows of the poplars lay long over the foot of our field, it seemed as if she must cross them in the walks we used to take there. I wish your psychic novel[6] could give us some promise of the life beyond this which we are so uncertain of, which are not even sure we wish to be certain of. What a strange, bewildering thing it all is!

We have been here a week, now, and it seems a month; perhaps we shall not stay the summer, but take a house in York Harbor.[7] John will be coming with his family in Mid-August, but I shall come over and let Billy walk over the grass holding by my forefinger, as was always my ideal. Maybe, then, my daughter and I will go over to some springs in Wales, said to be good for such biliary troubles as my last go at Carlsbad failed to cure me of.[8]

The day has blazed through after a long spell of very cold weather; but it is dry, dry, with no hope of rain. With my love to your wife and little ones,

Yours affectionately,
W. D. Howells.

1. Garland's letter to Howells is not extant, nor is it known when Garland and Howells had last met. Garland traveled frequently from Chicago to New York on literary business with Harper & Brothers, and the meeting might have occurred some time late in 1910, when Howells was asking his brother Joe for details about the house-raising at Eureka Mills for *New Leaf Mills*. See Howells to Joseph A. Howells, 18 November and 11 December 1910. Howells was now in the process of revising

the manuscript of the novel. A subsequent letter from Howells to Garland, 21 June 1911 (CLSU), indicates that Garland sent two letters, now lost, with the requested descriptions: "I have both your letters about the 'raising,' and I feel sure that with their help I can 'keep off the grass,' or avoid 'sins of commission.'"

2. Garland was then secretary of the Theatre Society of Chicago, a short-lived project to support plays of literary quality rather than popular appeal. See Jean Holloway, *Hamlin Garland: A Biography* (1960; reprint ed., Freeport, N.Y.: Books for Libraries, 1971), p. 211.

3. "Under the Lion's Paw" (1889) was not a play but a short story written when Garland was living in Boston. Howells probably remembered that for several years Garland used public readings of the story as a forum for proselytizing the issue of single-tax reform. See Donald Pizer, *Hamlin Garland's Early Work and Career* (1960; reprint ed., New York: Russell & Russell, 1969), p. 60. In this early period Garland wrote two reform plays, *Under the Wheel* (1890) and *A Member of the Third House* (published as a novel in 1892), neither of which was ever produced.

4. James A. Herne had achieved recognition as an independent playwright only after turning to realism in the late 1880s. In 1889 he became close friends with Garland in Boston, at which time Garland enlisted him to assist in dramatic readings of "Under the Lion's Paw." Garland supported the production of Herne's first significant play, *Margaret Fleming* (1890), a controversial piece about marital infidelity. Despite favorable reviews, one by Howells in the "Editor's Study," *Harper's Monthly*, August 1891, audiences resisted Herne's frank treatment of sexual morality in marriage.

5. Howells probably recalled the 1907 revival of *Margaret Fleming* with Herne's daughter Chrystal in the title role. Herne's wife, Katherine Corcoran (1857–1943), was also an accomplished actress and featured in many of her husband's plays, including the original production of *Margaret Fleming*.

6. *The Tyranny of the Dark*, which Howells had read when it was first published in 1905.

7. In his letter to Garland of 21 June 1911 (CLSU), Howells explained that he had been unable to make arrangements for staying in York Harbor.

8. Suffering from a recurrence of "gall-colic," Howells had gone to the baths at Carlsbad, Austria, in 1909. He was now planning a similar cure at the springs of Llandrindod Wells, Wales.

29 MAY 1911, KITTERY POINT, TO JOSEPH A. HOWELLS

Kittery Point, May 29, 1911.

Dear Joe:

The MS. of New Leaf Mills came this morning and your letter at the same time.[1] I am more obliged than I can say, and I am sorry if you like it so much that there is to be no more of the story. What becomes of Rosy is clear enough; I had a notion of Dick's meeting her in the City, or thinking he met her, at night, but I decided that even that would be superfluous. You know we never did know what became of Ann Stepmeyer.[2] I expect to do a good deal of filling in, for the end especially is hurried.—Father was what God made him, and he was on the whole the best man I have known, but of course he was trying. I suppose he went to Eureka in despair of pulling up anywhere in town. I mean to deal more and more tenderly with his character in shading it and rounding it out. Mother was splendid, too; how my child's heart used to cling to her, and how her heart clung to each of us! Of course she could not do justice to father's limitations; I suppose a woman is always bewildered when a man comes short of the perfection which would be the logic of him in her mind.

I will note all your criticisms carefully; but I can *hear* mother say, "Well, I am perfectly beat out." Neither she nor father, as you say, used slang. She had some river country expressions, and some ancestral Pennsylvanianisms.

I thought it more artistic and truer to leave Dick's interest in the young girl a mere shadow. I shall fill out the Boram sickness episode.[3]

From time to time I was tempted to make the thing melodramatic as I easily might, but as I considered it, the modesty of nature prevailed with me.

We have been here a week, after a week which I spent with John's family on Staten Island. Of course it was mostly Billy to me. His mother writes that he has passed from the lawn mower to the garden hose, and comes in so wet that he doesn't need a bath. I think she and John would like to settle on Staten Island. It is as near his office as 57th street, and includes twenty minutes beautiful sail over the water in the vast municipal ferry boat.

It is possible that I may be in New York when you are there,[4] but I can't promise myself. I am a little shaky about my gall-duct, and I don't want to take chances. But Pilla will probably be there to see her spine-doctor, and I want her to take me with her if possible. Meantime, I want you to be my guests there, and to accept the means as some return for what you have done for me in supplying matter and criticism for New Leaf Mills.

With our love to you both and to Beatrice's household, yours affectionately,

Will.

P. S. John and Abby are coming with Billy to K. P. in August for the rest of the summer. I wish you could see the apple blossoms here. Each tree is a big bouquet.

I hope you see your way of joining Willy in Florida when you retire. It seems to be the place for you. I had a very pleasant and reconciled letter from Ally enclosing a very interesting one from William. So that matter is all right, I fancy.[5]

1. Joe was returning the manuscript which Howells, in a letter of 28 April 1911

(MH), had promised him: "I have wound up the story of New Leaf Mills, and now with a few days' revision I shall be able to send it to you."

2. See Howells to Joseph A. Howells, 29 January 1911, n. 3.

3. Boram, revised to Bellam in the final version of *New Leaf Mills*, is a character based on John Belt of Eureka Mills. See Howells to Joseph A. Howells, 25 November 1910, n. 2.

4. Joe was in the United States visiting his daughter Beatrice in Youngstown, Ohio. He had arrived early in April, according to plans anticipated in a letter from Howells, 10 February 1911 (MH), to prepare for retirement from his consular post at Turks Islands. He was probably planning to stop in New York en route to or from a visit with his son, William D. Howells II, in Auburndale, Florida.

5. For Howells' particular concern for William C. Howells, Willy and Ally's son, see Howells to Joseph A. Howells, 29 January 1911, n. 6. The nature of the reconciliation with Ally is not clear. It was probably related to Howells' financial contributions to William's education and his advice about the young man's obligations toward his sisters. On 14 May 1911 (MH), Howells had written to Eliza Howells, Joe's wife: "I think the matter about William will settle itself. Certainly I don't hold him the least responsible for my misunderstanding his words, which I remember were to the effect that as I had helped him through college he felt that he ought to help his sisters."

18 JUNE 1911, KITTERY POINT, TO FREDERICK A. DUNEKA

...Kittery Point, Maine June 18, 1911.

Dear Mr. Duneka:

I have tried our agreement for 48 hours, and I find I cannot keep to it.[1] I do not sleep except for a few hours, and I cannot cast the thing out of my mind for a moment. If you can withdraw the book from publication, I beg you to do so;[2] but I cannot promise to be wiser next year than I am now. My reluctance is simply an *idée fixe* which I have not the nerve to overcome.[3] I cannot hope to be of a different mind, as it seems to me now, but if ever I am, I will most eagerly come to you again. But for the present, I can only ask you not to publish the story.

> Yours sincerely
> W. D. Howells.

1. The exact nature of the agreement for publication of *The Vacation of the Kelwyns* is not known. As suggested in a subsequent letter from Howells to Duneka, 22 June 1911 (MWA), Duneka's plan, "so kindly imagined," had been conceived to allay Howells' misgivings about publishing the novel. At any rate, production had progressed to the point of having the plates prepared, since on 12 June 1911 (ViU) Howells returned to J. W. Harper "the plate revise...."

2. In a telegram of 22 June, not extant, Duneka agreed to withdraw the novel after receiving a second imploring letter from Howells, dated 21 June 1911 (MWA): "The thing has now been so long in my mind that I cannot get it out for a moment; it is a ceaseless harassment which nothing but the assurance I beg of you can abate.

If you are not disgusted with my folly past all sufferance, be *very* merciful and telegraph me . . . ."

3. The cause of Howells' distress is not positively known. The novel in itself might have been painful to finish in light of Elinor's death, as the germ of the story is his and Elinor's six-week stay, in the late summer of 1875, near the Shaker religious community at Shirley Village, Massachusetts. In apparent deference to the Shakers' privacy and otherworldliness, Elinor had, at the time, charged her husband "not to think of writing a story with them in it . . . ." See Howells to Warner, 4 September 1875. In a suggestive episode in the novel, Parthenope strongly objects to Emerance's contemplation of writing a play incorporating Shaker dancing in one of the scenes: "'But that's a part of their worship!' she broke in, horrified, and the more resolute not to yield the point because she felt its temptation for him" (p. 176). Even though the Shakers remain at the periphery of the story, Howells might well have been loathe to betray Elinor's scruple in any degree now that she was not alive to defend it. See the reference to "Elinor's wish," Howells to Joseph A. Howells, 18 August 1911.

9 JULY 1911, KITTERY POINT, TO THOMAS S. PERRY

Kittery Point, July 9, 1911.

My dear Perry:

Last night as we sat by our hearthfire in the parlor we wished you here that we might prove to you all K. P. weather was not H. James weather.[1] Today we had the fire out doors for half the time; then the east wind came up, and we wished you here again. But we do that all the time, hot weather or cold. Never did I have such a good time. To hear you talk when I was not reading my fiction to you, what more could a man ask? I still fear we fed you low, and I am trying to make up for it by feeding myself high. Such mellifluous melons these two breakfasts past! We even had them last night for supper. At dinner today we had that delicious baked squash, which you cleared the platter of. Well, it is not a bad world; but I wish I could see Mrs. Perry to have her talk to me about the next. Some things that you said did highly hearten me.

To think of your looking up those watch-tinker ancestors of mine![2] If you had been one of them you would not have kept your word; we Welsh never do; even Henry Lloyd George broke his word to me, promising to acknowledge my books by his own hand, and then making Mrs. Lloyd G. do it.[3] We are a dreadful lot, of a moral stature no greater than our physical. But we do whop it to the English. Tell your family that I feel guilty before them for keeping you so long, you dear; but I would do it again if I got the chance. What a glorious time I did have!

There is a big brute of a lead-colored battle-ship lying off our shore, and snoring to itself through its four chimneys. But last night there was such a moon on the water! It was a shame to waste it on a septuagenarian (pretty bad spell, but you get the idea.)

Your Russian is a great fellow. Did you read all you wanted to of him?[4] I have been afraid I did not urge you; but even age has nerves. He is unparalleled for outrightness. How I should have liked him in the 80s! I am reading a new book of Valdés's, perfectly charming;[5] and I find that I know such unexpected Spanish, such a lot of it.

We have about decided to sail on the Franconia from Boston on the 25th, and I shall have to go on to New York to Billify for a while alone, if Pilla does her oculisting in Boston. But nothing is certain yet.

You shall have some mulberries before we go. Last evening I found one almost blackripe on the tree, and I thought I would leave it till the morning. A robin had thought the same and was up first. With our love to you all,

W. D. Howells.

1. Perry had probably visited at Kittery Point some time during the heat wave of the first week in July, about the same time Henry James also saw Howells there. In a letter dated 9 June 1911 (MeWC), Howells had entreated Perry to "come here and stay with a lonely man .... Think what a good time I will have! I will lay in meats, drinks, and smokes." On 23 June 1911 (misdated 1910; MeWC), Howells gave Perry train and trolley connections for Monday or Tuesday, 27 or 28 June.

2. Perry had been in Europe from late 1905 to late 1909. During one of his visits to England he must have looked up records concerning Howells' great-grandfather, Thomas Howells, who is described in *Years of My Youth* as having "established himself in London as a clock and watch maker" (HE, p. 4).

3. Howells probably refers to a brief note from Dame Margaret Lloyd George, 18 July 1910 (MH), inviting him to tea and thanking him, as she says, "on behalf of my husband for your books," which she does not otherwise name. For Howells' visit with the Lloyd Georges, see Howells to Perry, 27 July 1910.

4. Perry considered the Russian writers of his time to be preeminent, to the extent that during his recent four-year sojourn in Europe he had studied Russian in order to read them in the original. He had no doubt conveyed this enthusiasm to Howells in relation to a particular but unidentified writer. For his earlier recommendation that Howells read Gorky, see Howells to Perry, 9 January 1905.

5. The book by Armando Palacio Valdés is identified by Mildred Howells as *Papeles del doctor Angélico* (1911). See *Life in Letters*, II, 302; see also Howells to Palacio Valdés, 10 September 1911.

22 July 1911, Kittery Point, to Brander Matthews

Kittery Point, July 22, 1911.

My dear Matthews:

We are sailing on the *Franconia* for Fishguard[1] from Boston next Tuesday; and this is not only to say good-bye; but to thank you ever so belatedly for that most sweet letter you wrote me in early June about my *H. of N. Fortunes*. It cheered me to know you liked it, for I like it myself, all but the beginning, where I was staggering about, blind and breathless from the blow of my daughter's death, and trying to feel my way to the story.[2] I have not lookt at it for a long time; but yesterday I read great part of *A Modern Instance,* and perceived that I had drawn Bartley Hubbard, the false scoundrel, from myself.

Mildred and I expect, if Llandrindod Wells cure my gripes, to spent September and October in Spain, where most of my boyhood was past while I was working at case in my father's printing-office in Northern Ohio.[3]

All about *me!*

Yours ever,
W. D. Howells.

1. A coastal town in Pembroke, southern Wales. Howells and Mildred sailed from Boston on 25 July.

2. Matthews' letter regarding *A Hazard of New Fortunes* is not extant. Howells' recollection here is almost certainly incorrect. Winifred Howells died on 2 March 1889, while Howells appears to have started the novel as early as the fall of 1887. See Howells to W. C. Howells, 29 September 1888, n. 3.

3. In *My Literary Passions* (1895), Howells recounts how, in his youth, readings of Cervantes' *Don Quixote* and Irving's *Conquest of Granada* (1829) had permeated his imagination, later inspiring him to study the Spanish language when the family moved to Jefferson. Howells had briefly considered the possibility of going to Spain in 1910, after Elinor's death, and doing a travel book. See Howells to Aurelia H. Howells and Anne Fréchette, 13 May 1910, n. 2. He had recently revived the idea of the book in a letter to Frederick A. Duneka, 4 June 1911 (MWA): "Spain is beginning to entreat me again, and I want to ask whether you think that in view of a book which would make all our fortunes the house would be willing to pay the wages and expenses of a courier to go with the aged traveler, and look after his often infirmities. My plan would be to go first to the Welsh springs at Llandrindod, the last of July, and after taking the biliary cure there, go down into Spain for the month of September, which I understand is the best time." Although Howells did not ultimately use a courier, Duneka immediately agreed to the proposal, as indicated in his reply to Howells of 5 June 1911 (copy at MWA). From London, Howells wrote to Eliza Howells, 7 September 1911 (MH), that he was going to Spain in order "To fulfill the dream of my youth. The Spanish studies which I made in Jefferson in the little room under the stairs are coming into use." Howells begins *Familiar Spanish Travels* (1913), the book recording the 1911 visit, by lyrically recalling the boyhood origins of his passion for Spain: "As the train took its time and ours

in mounting the uplands toward Granada on the soft, but not too soft, evening of November 6, 1911, the air that came to me through the open window breathed as if from an autumnal night of the middle eighteen-fifties in a little village of north-eastern Ohio. I was now going to see, for the first time, the city where so great a part of my life was then passed, and in this magical air the two epochs were blent in reciprocal association. The question of my present identity was a thing indifferent and apart; it did not matter who or where or when I was. Youth and age were at one with each other: the boy abiding in the old man, and the old man pensively willing to dwell for the enchanted moment in any vantage of the past which would give him shelter" (p. 1). See also Howells to Van Dyke, 17 October 1911.

18 AUGUST 1911, LLANDRINDOD WELLS, TO JOSEPH A. HOWELLS

Llandrindod Wells, Wales, Aug. 18, 1911.

Dear Joe:

I got your letter yesterday and sent it on to Aurelia who complains of never hearing from you. Vevie is better, but they are all kept in Paris, where her cure is going on in a hospital; her trouble is something with the bladder, and was serious at first, but they are assured she will now get well.

We came abroad rather unexpectedly, having failed to get a house at York Harbor.[1] I am taking the same cure here as at Carlsbad; and after it is over, we hope to go down through Spain, and sail home from Gibraltar in November, with the stuff for a book about Spain.

We are here in the midst of a drouth which has lasted almost un-broken for nearly two months. We have blazing sun, very hot in the day, but cool at night.

Added to this there is a general R. R. strike on,[2] and we may not get away next week, as we plan. Oddly enough, nearly all the people we meet are tories, and are terrifically down on the government or Lloyd George, whom they blame for everything but who is really managing the situation with great skill and patience.[3] The English universally hate the Welsh, perhaps because they fear them; they are really much brighter and quicker. However, they make allowance for us, and we don't dispute, though if it comes to a point, I find it best to be very open and clear.

I feel your kindness in what you say about the story I have put by.[4] You are perfectly right, and some day I will publish it, no doubt, but for the present I am quite helpless. It would seem like a denial of Elinor's wish, though later I hope it will not.[5] My affliction has been a very strange one. I laugh and joke with the children about her; and we say, every day, how this thing or that would have pleased her; and *every* night, now, I dream of her, but always painfully. At times I miss her terribly, those times when a man can go to nobody but his wife to tell the things that weigh on him.

I think I have worked out the Eureka story very well, and I hope to publish it in the spring. Next I want to try that story of the Leatherwood God which you looked up for me on its own ground.[6]—By this time Billy and his family are at Kittery Point. With our love to you both,

> Your aff'te brother
> Will.

This is a vast hotel,[7] very comfy and reasonable, chockful of people. The other day we motored down to Hay, where the largest of our great-grandfather's flannel mills is now a printing-office.[8] The first thing in it was such a hand-press as we had in Hamilton; they were printing a job in colors on it.

1. Howells and Mildred arrived in Llandrindod Wells on 3 August. Howells had tried to rent a house at York Harbor, Maine, because, as he wrote to Mildred Howells, 16 July 1911 (MH), Kittery Point and its associations with Elinor were causing him much "gloom."

2. The railroad strike by eight of the nine English systems, a culmination of the worst wave of strikes England had yet experienced, started on 16 August and almost entirely paralyzed rail transportation. Emotions were intensified on all sides by the hottest weather since the summer of 1868, resulting in sporadic rioting and violence in which at least seven workers were killed.

3. Under criticism from Labor leaders for opposing the strike and from Tories for not reacting strongly enough, Lloyd George was nevertheless able to end the strike on 19 August by convening labor reconciliation boards and establishing a commission to investigate election schemes harmful to labor representation in parliament.

4. *The Vacation of The Kelwyns.*

5. For Howells' anguished decision not to allow publication of the novel, see Howells to Duneka, 18 June 1911, n. 3.

6. Howells had first asked Joe in 1904 about the episode which eventually was used as the basis of *The Leatherwood God* (1916). See Howells to Aurelia H. Howells, 14 October 1904, n. 1.

7. The Pump House Hotel.

8. Howells and Mildred visited Hay on 14 August. In a letter to Aurelia H. Howells of 15 August 1911 (MH), he described the mill building that once belonged to Thomas Howells: "Yesterday we motored through a fiery afternoon to Hay, 26 miles away. I found the town just as I saw it in '83, but I found the largest of our great grandfather's mills much larger than I supposed, ample, and five stories high, full of a printing-office and a book store. The mill where I bought father's blanket is now a ruin; another is a *drill hall for militia*! (Think of its quaker origin!)"

20 AUGUST 1911, LLANDRINDOD WELLS, TO WILLIAM A. GILL

Pump House Hotel,
Llandrindod Wells. August 20, 1911.

My dear Gill:

I have had two letters from you since I came here, but I have not answered because I had no definite address from you. Now I am sending this to Wirkworth and I am also sending there for Mrs. Gill the book which I have been making such a din about. I wish you had it with you, for it is Their Wedding Journey;[1] but it is, according to the American publishers' ideal, physically as heavy as the same bulk of lead, though spiritually I hope it is at least as light as foam. Entreat Mrs. Gill to accept it from me, and even to read it.

We are having a most interesting time here which even the waters cannot spoil. Thanks to you we are enjoying the acquaintance of your dear and beautiful sister, and of the Canon,[2] with whom I get on famously after having somewhat prayerfully, with all my Welsh guile, felt round for safe common ground. This has of course meant the reservation of my most cherished heresies; but I have good practice at our table where we are placed with high Tories of both sexes, and I swallow my soul with my sole every day. They are really very good and kind, and I love them all, even when they are drawing and quartering the strikers wherever they can lay hands on them.[3] One gentle old man has wished that he could drive a locomotive through an obstructive group of them; I have shuddered inwardly, but outwardly I have applauded. It is the same with my daughter, poor suffragist, though now and then she uses one of the few privileges left her sex and talks back. She was delighted with your praise of her sonnet,[4] and I even more, if possible. We both want you to write that book about America and tell how like the English we really are under all our bluff. Get Mrs. Gill to put you up to it, and keep you; now is the time for a true book about us, such as you alone could write.[5]

With our united regards to you both,

Yours ever
W. D. Howells.

1. It appears that Gill, a long-time friend of the Howellses and a favorite of Elinor's, had recently married, accounting for the gift of *Their Wedding Journey*. Howells wrote Gill a week later from London, 30 August 1911 (Avon County Reference Library, Bristol), inviting the Gills to dinner so that he might meet Mrs. Gill.

2. The sister has not been identified; Howells mentions both the sister and "Canon Gem" in his letter to W. A. Gill of 4 August 1912 (Avon County Reference Library, Bristol).

3. See Howells to Joseph A. Howells, 18 August 1911, n. 2.

4. Most likely "Huge Cloudy Symbols," *Harper's Monthly*, January 1912.

5. According to information supplied by Professor George Arms, Mrs. Mabel S. K. Gill wrote to James Ross, city librarian at Bristol, on 4 September 1937: "my husband never wrote a book about America, but his knowledge & understanding & sympathy with the people of the U.S.A. which Mr. Howells realized made the work he did over there in 1916 valuable . . . ."

10 SEPTEMBER 1911, LONDON, TO ARMANDO PALACIO VALDÉS

18 Half Moon St., Mayfair W.,
London, Sept. 10, 1911.

Dear Friend:

I am writing to you for the first time in Spanish. I leave Italian to the Americans who have no intention of going to Spain and who do not need to practise the language of that country.[1] As for me, I shall leave Paris, with my daughter, by the Southern Express next week.[2] I hope to see the most celebrated cities and the most important buildings, but especially I hope to meet you who are to me more than all the other things in Spain.

I have read half of the valuable book you sent to me in America by the good Baxter and I thank you infinitely.[3] It is such a wise, human, noble, lovable and just book that I do not believe it possible to praise it enough.

If you wish to write me, my address is always the firm of Brown, Shipley & Co., 123 Pall Mall, London, and I will do everything I can to meet you wherever you say that you will be.[4]

Your aff. friend,
W. D. Howells.

Al Señor Don Armando Palacio Valdés,

I send this letter to you with the corrections of my good teacher[5] in order to let you see how stupid I am after having read so many of your books, and how unworthy I am to have known them.

1. At the end of August Howells had arrived in London, where he engaged a teacher in an attempt to renew his Spanish. He had previously corresponded with Palacio Valdés only in Italian.

2. Howells and Mildred arrived in Paris on 14 September, where they visited with Anne and Achille Fréchette, their daughter Marie Marguerite, and Aurelia Howells. After ten days in Paris, they traveled on to Tours and spent ten days there before entering Spain.

3. According to a letter from Howells to Sylvester Baxter, 14 February 1911 (CSmH), Howells appears to have requested *Papeles del doctor Angélico* upon the

recommendation of Baxter, who was then corresponding with the Spanish novelist: "I wish you could get me a copy of Valdés's book, though I am afraid it may be one of his heartbreakers. Will you send him my love? He is a great soul as well as a great mind; the two do not always go together. It is sweet to have known such a man even afar off." Describing the book in the "Editor's Easy Chair," *Harper's Monthly*, November 1911, as "a volume of little essays, studies, sketches, and tales," Howells lauded Palacio Valdés' manner in *The Papers of Doctor Angélico*: "There is never anything illiberal in his ideas; and in these essays the dramatic instinct is constantly at work, clothing his opinions in delightful character, and making life the theater of argument."

4. In a letter dated 14 September 1911 (MH) from Cap Breton in southern France, Palacio Valdés wrote to Howells that he awaited their meeting with great pleasure: "Muy agradable surpresa me ha proporcionado U. con su carta. Al fin me parece que se realiza uno de mi deseos mas vivos, el de conocer á U. personalmente" ("I was very pleasantly surprised by your letter. At last it seems that one of the wishes of my life will be fulfilled, that of getting to know you personally"). Palacio Valdés went on to say that he would like to be with Howells in Madrid, where they could enjoy an extended and relaxed visit. They met there for the first time on 11 October. See Howells to Abby Howells, 14 October 1911.

5. Although not mentioning him by name, Howells describes in *Familiar Spanish Travels* how he "invoked the help of a young professor, who came to me for an hour each day of a week in London and let me try to talk with him; . . . My professor was from Barcelona, but he beautifully lisped his *c*'s and *z*'s like any old Castilian . . . ; and there is no telling how much I might have profited by his instruction if he had not been such a charming intelligence that I liked to talk with him of literature and philosophy and politics rather than the weather, or the cost of things, or the question of how long the train stopped and when it would start, or the dishes at table, or cloths at the tailor's, or the forms of greeting and parting" (pp. 3–4).

29 SEPTEMBER 1911, TOURS, TO THOMAS S. PERRY

Hotel Métropol,
Tours, Sept. 29, 1911.

My dear Perry:

We are trembling on the verge of Spain, before the spectres of revolution and martial law.[1] But I have just had a letter from my friend Valdés, the novelist, saying in our forcible American, as translitterated from his fine Spanish: "What's biting you? Come along! Oh, hang it all! It's only that newspaper guff."[2] However, I shall wait for a telegram which I'm in hopes the Ambassador at Madrid[3] will find time to send in response to my appeal for counsel.

Of course we are enjoying it here, in the heart of the Henry James country. His book bears reading on the ground.[4] He is less severe with medieval Touraine than with contemporary America,[5] but not less charming and scarcely less subtle. The smell which he notes at Plessis le Tour is there yet, hanging round for the traveller in 1911 just as it was in 1870.[6]

I shall keep your letter of instruction[7] and obey it if ever we get into Spain. Only I shall bring home to you the sausages, and clams and green peppers of Valencia; they are strengst verboten[8] to biliary me. By force of good resolutions and Pilla's vigilance, I am keeping very well.

The ruins here are really wonderful, though sadly out of repair. The troglodytes, people who live burrowed into the hillsides with their stove pipes coming out of the top, along the Loire, are interesting; they all prefer romantic novels. With Pilla's love and mine to you all,

Yours ever
W. D. Howells.

1. Against a background of eternal conflict with France in Morocco, there were in 1911 a series of Socialist-inspired strikes within Spain, which created conditions bordering on civil war. Ten days earlier, on 19 September, King Alfonso XIII (1886–1951) had suspended all constitutionally guaranteed freedoms in an attempt to restore order.

2. In a letter, now lost, Howells had apparently expressed his concern about the hazards of traveling in Spain in those uncertain times, but Palacio Valdés replied reassuringly on 28 September 1911 (MH): "Pienso que puede U. sin peligro ninguno viajar por España. Los periódicos han exagerado mucho los motines que ha habido. En España no hay ambiente favorable para los revolucionarios" ("I think you can travel through Spain without any danger at all. The newspapers have greatly exaggerated the riots that have taken place. Conditions are not favorable in Spain for revolutionaries").

3. Henry C. Ide (1844–1921), lawyer and diplomat, was minister to Spain from 1909 to 1913. The American legation at Madrid was not restored to embassy status until 1913, so Ide did not in fact hold the rank of ambassador.

4. James's *A Little Tour in France* (1884) is based on his travels in 1882, which he began at Tours, through the chateau country and the Midi. Upon first reading the book, Howells had told James: "it's a more absolute transference to literature of the mood of observation than anything else that I know." See Howells to James, 25 December 1886, and 15 October 1911.

5. James's *The American Scene* was published in 1907.

6. Howells mistakenly refers to 1870 as the year of James's 1882 visit to Plessis-le-Tours, the castle of Louis XI (1423–1483), one of the last medieval kings. James objected to the local misrepresentation of the castle's remnants "as the romantic abode of a superstitious king," noting more particularly that "a strong odor of pigsties and other unclean things so prostrates you for the moment that you have no energy to protest against this obvious fiction." See *A Little Tour in France*, p. 19.

7. Perry's letter has not been located.

8. German for "strictly forbidden."

14 October 1911, Madrid, to Abby W. Howells

Grand Hôtel de Roma
en Madrid, October 14, 1911.

Dear Abby:

Through my forgetting to tell B., S. & Co.[1] in London when to begin sending my letters to Madrid, I have had none from the Johnabby family since yours of Sept. 20, and I suppose there are heaps at 123 Pall Mall. But now I have telegraphed for them.

We have been doing mostly the pictures, with 2 days out for colds, which have now past. To-morrow, if fine, we go with the consul and his nice young wife[2] to the bull-fight to see the Spanish crowd and the grand flourish of entry, and perhaps the first appearance of the bull. The doctor says we must not be out later than 4:30, which will not give time for much fighting; if the worst happens early, we will shut our eyes. Next week the Consuless wants us to tea to meet the Bunsens (British Ambass., very literary, who wishes to hear all about Billy).[3] Wednesday we went to see Valdés, and found him five pair up in a shawl with a cold, just as John did.[4] He was charming, as sweet and good as I hoped and his wife most friendly. I proudly took with me that foto. of Billy which I hooked from Martha[5] in Paris, and that of you sitting in the new chair in the great room at 130 W. 57. I meant to *show* them to Valdés, but he thought I meant to give them, and kept them! I gasped, but was helpless; but you and Billy both do me great credit. Valdés askt me much about you and inquired fully about John. He called last night with his wife, but the doctor had forbid our leaving our rooms; and we could not see them. To-day he reports us perfectly well.

Madrid is a new Rome, but of course not of comparable interest.

I suppose you are all back at 130, and we hope to be so before long— say 7 or 8 weeks.

With our dearest love to Billy and his parents,

Papa.

1. Brown, Shipley & Co., of 123 Pall Mall, S.W.1., was the English branch of Brown Brothers & Co., New York, which Howells used as his financial agent while in Europe.

2. Charles L. Hoover (1872–1949) was the American consul at Madrid (1909–1912). His wife's name was Helen. Because Henry C. Ide, the American minister to Spain, was "on leave," as Howells informed Aurelia Howells in his letter of 16 October 1911 (MH), Howells' official and social contact with the American legation was through Hoover.

3. Sir Maurice William Ernest de Bunsen (1852–1932), diplomat and ambassador to Spain (1906–1913), was well known for his interest in literature although not himself an author.

4. This was Howells' first meeting with Palacio Valdés, who lived in an apartment on Calle de Lista, No. 5. Two days later, in his letter of 16 October 1911 (MH) to Aurelia H. Howells, Howells wrote: "I have twice seen my Spanish novelist friend Valdés and we are going round together to look up the scenes of his novels, here, which will be an excellent way of seeing the place." Howells notes in *Familiar Spanish Travels* that he went on "rather a desultory drive through those less frequented parts of the city" with an unnamed "friend" who, by the evidence of their conversation, is identifiable as Palacio Valdés: "Our talk in Spanish from him and Italian from me was of Tolstoy and several esthetic and spiritual interests" (pp. 112–13). John Howells had visited Palacio Valdés in 1894.

5. Martha was probably Abby's younger sister, Martha R. White (d. 1937).

15 OCTOBER 1911, MADRID, TO HENRY JAMES

> *Grand Hotel de Roma . . .*
> *Madrid . . .* October 15, 1911.

My dear James:

I rather like writing you on this hotel paper because it will give you a notion of how we are housed, (in the street where two royalist Englishmen killed Cromwell's Ambassador,)[1] though the picture omits the purple roof of the large grape arbor in front. But I wont try telling you in any detail of our lives since you saw us. There was a week more of London,[2] ten days of Paris, as many of Tours, one of Bordeaux, one of Bayonne, and the rest of Spain: San Sebastian, Burgos, Valladolid, and now a week here, with intentions of Toledo, Cordova, Seville, Granada, Ronda, Algeciras (for a long sojourn there and scribbling)[3] Gibraltar and home.

The going in Spain is not bad (like the first class going in France, only better, with good dining-cars) but the stopping is painful, especially at the hotels of the smaller places. At Burgos we suffered from cold in an absolutely hearthless house, as I have not since my early winters in Ashtabula county, Ohio; but the cathedral and the local character were worth it.—Valladolid for the plateresque[4] and San Sebastian for the color of a newish watering place.

Madrid is quite as new, and of course immensely amusing. In the folk we have a sense of the real thing, the thing "as advertised." We wont talk galleries because the Goyas and Velasquezes are inexpressible.[5] The place is a smaller and fresher Paris, but not flat; up and down hill, rather; with peculiarly tormenting moments of newer Rome which must be from the light and the air, for the physiognomy of the place is intenser, as the Spanish face is intenser than the Italian. The temperament of the people as it shows itself the stranger is almost conventionally Spanish: grave, dignified (to rudeness in the lower sort) and sometimes

Bostonianly *reproving* in effect, but apt to break sooner. You know how I love all Latins, for their hollow courtesy and the rest; but the Spaniards will not let you love them as the Italians do; they are *not* simpaticé, and Pilla frankly hates them—all except our dear novelist Palacio Valdés for whom our whole family has had a devotion for many years. We found him a blue-eyed, white-haired Asturian (species of Spanish New Englander, as from Brattleboro', Vt.) and he is to go with me "one day" as you English say, and show me the scenes of his novels here, which will be the best way of seeing Madrid, for me.—The men are smallish (no great sin, if one is fat) and not handsome, but the women are astonishingly beautiful in the dark style; some of the girls incredible. They are night-black-haired, of course, and I do not say but they heighten their palor by powdering. There are some vividly red haired ones.

This afternoon we had expected to go to the bull-fight for the sake of the human spectacle, and come away before the first blind-folded horse was disemboweled, but it has been raining all morning heavily, and I doubt if any *corrida* will be possible.

We still see Touraine homesickly, as a serene, sunny expanse of Loire levels, and our longing is enhanced by your "Little Tour in France,"⁶ so that we can hardly bear to read it; you never wrote a better, a gentler, a more charming and truthful book. It was for sale in Tauchnitz at our hotel.—Pilla wishes to be remembered with my love.

Yours ever
W. D. Howells.

1. Antony Ascham (d. 1650) was Oliver Cromwell's parliamentarian envoy to Spain, sent to Madrid to replace the ambassador of Charles II. On 6 May 1650, the day after his arrival in the city, he was assassinated at his inn on Caballero de Gracia by two royalists in exile, John Guillion and William Spark.

2. As indicated in a letter to Edmund Gosse, dated 9 September 1911 (British Library), Howells frequently saw James in London at the beginning of September: "We have seen rather much of James, who is in very good case.... I think he will begin work again.... I do not believe your machinations or mine have come to his knowledge, but I'm afraid they have been fruitless...." The "machinations" refers to Howells' and Gosse's attempt to gain the Nobel Prize for Henry James.

3. Howells went to Algeciras on 12 November, staying there for almost two weeks to assemble his notes for *Familiar Spanish Travels*. In a letter to Joseph A. Howells, dated 14 November 1911 (MH), he briefly reviewed his itinerary and recorded his general impressions: "Of course the Spain I have been seeing is not the romantic Spain of my boyish dreams, but it is far better. The people are good and kind, and [in] 6 weeks travel we have not suffered one rudeness from them, or been once cheated or evilly lied to; I could not say this of any six weeks at home. The cities are wonderful in their beauty—Seville above all, and the South of Spain is far more sympathetic than the North.... Granada is mostly the Alhambra in its interest. It turned cold while we were there, from snow on the mountains, and we hurried south. Here it is summer, with the advertisement of the 'Prudential Insurance Co.' in full

view across the bay." James remarked on Howells' forthcoming travel book in his reply of 26 October 1911 (MH), viewing with envy the prospect of his friend "as not too postponedly ensconced at Algéciras (which must be as beautiful as its name) for the taking of your stock & the stacking of your harvest. Marvellous man—to be able to write while in the desperate *act!* When *I* can write everything has stopped—including too often the writing itself! But I wait for you as for the Spain that has never come to me—but that *will* now. I felt I think, thus resignedly, all the while, *how* it thus happily & inexpensively would."

4. Taken from the silversmith's technique of superimposing ornament on simple line, the term refers to the style resulting from the overlay of the rich detail associated with the European Renaissance onto the less adorned Gothic of Spanish architecture. See *Familiar Spanish Travels*, p. 68.

5. Howells refers especially to the Museo del Prado in Madrid where are housed some of the major works of Francisco José de Goya y Lucientes (1746–1828) and Diego Rodrígues de Silva y Velásquez (1599–1660). See *Familiar Spanish Travels*, pp. 100–102.

6. See Howells to Perry, 29 September 1911, n. 4.

17 OCTOBER 1911, MADRID, TO HENRY VAN DYKE

Grand Hotel de Roma...
Madrid... October 17, 1911.

Dear Dr. van Dyke:

I shall find your book when I get home and shall know how to value it as I now know how to value the kindness which has moved you to send it me.[1]

I am here fulfilling at last the oldest dream of my life: when I was a boy, from fourteen to seventeen, I taught myself Spanish and began in my unscholarly and desultory way to know Spanish literature. I always hoped to come to Spain, and after coming so many times to Europe, at last I am here. It is a strange dream, stranger than I thought it would be. When I have fairly waked up from it I will tell you about it. Some December day at the lunch table in the Century Club?

Yours sincerely
W. D. Howells.

1. It is not known which book Van Dyke sent to Howells: possibly either *The Mansion* or *The Poems of Henry Van Dyke*, both published in 1911.

3 NOVEMBER 1911, SEVILLE, TO HENRY JAMES

Hotel De Inglaterra . . .
Sevilla Nov. 3, 1911.

My dear James:

The more than usually continental shabbiness of this stationery is not characteristic of a really charming and friendly hotel. It does not quite dance us a *sevillana*, but it is otherwise full of Andalusian sweetness and more than Andalusian cleanness. It looks out on a vast, bald plaza, without a spear of grass in it, but a large crop of palm-trees. We have been here a week, and for several days have been trying to start for Granada which, nine hours off, is practically the next station, but the condition of what the Spaniards would call my *tripas* has forbidden.[1] However, we hope for early release from the witchery of this really enchanting city; the spell of disordered *tripas* is not just the condition of a longer stay which I could desire.

I wish you were here, not only because I should like always to have you with me, but because it would be greatly to your pleasure and profit as a witness of your countrywomen and their stranger behavior in strange lands.[2] The other night we went to Otero's dancing-class,[3] and with us (not in our party) went an American woman arrayed in the dress of a Sevillian dancing-girl. Another evening came another American lady, well stricken in years and flesh, who appeared next morning in complete Spanish black, mantilla and all, having left some Christian Science literature in the reading-room before going out to the cathedral. There is a Californian girl pausing here on her way round the world with a kodak in her hand,—she is absolutely and innocently alone, but not to attract notice in a sable world she is dressed in complete white. All one morning we followed the dispute of two American women with their guide, from church to church. At Burgos, five American ladies dined at the next table with their courier. At Valladolid one turned from all the wonders of a Museo to make sure from Pilla about a week-day train for Segovia, because she did not like to travel on Sunday.[4] The harmlessness that goes with all this is not its least wonderful part.

Of course we have

—molto oprò col sanno e colla mano,
Molto soffrè nel glorioso acquisto"[5]

of this wild, beautiful, ugly monstrous land. Most of Castile the Moors might have had and welcome, for all me; but Andalusia is lovely, and Toledo is a heart's-home, to which our memories turn fondly. Cordoba might be given to the poor, mosque and all, with its 800 pillars.[6] It is quite true about the grace of the women, and the gravity of the men.

It seems a land of insurpassable possibilities—a great race, with a church on its back, holding it down.—I could wish we were in London, with you there, and I am glad this is not to find you in Rye.[7] If you like to write again, Cook & Co., Gibraltar will know where to find me before we sail from there Nov. 25. With both our loves

Yours ever
W. D. Howells.

I had seen the vociferations of *The Outcry* in the English papers, and rejoiced in the 3d edition.[8]

1. According to his letter to Joseph A. Howells, also 3 November 1911 (MH), Howells was to leave for Granada on 6 November. Howells appears to have suffered a recurrence of the intestinal discomfort associated with his "gall-colic" problem.

2. Howells probably alludes to James's unsparing criticism of the speech and manners of American women in two serial essays for *Harper's Bazar* in 1906 and 1907. See Howells to Jordan, 3 January 1907, n. 1. In his reply of 12 November 1911 (MH), James, with quaint expansiveness, expressed the pleasure that Howells' recent letters from Spain had given him: "I wish I were only prince & patron enough to maintain you & Mildred at my splendid cost in a country of the colour that makes you write me such delightful letters—for I am sure that Mildred's exposed plate flashes back into them [the Spaniards] also, by suggestion & inspiration. But when I myself have always lacked the sinews of a Peninsula campaign—*for* myself—what will you have? It very heartily rejoices me that you are making such a success of yours—verily I think it's a brave record, such as you ought to go home all laurelled & borne on high by."

3. José Otero, a famed maestro of dance, conducted the Academia de Baile in Seville. His important contribution was in applying the techniques of ballet to the teaching of native dances. He was the last of the Otero family, who, in the latter part of the nineteenth century, had dedicated themselves to the preservation of the Spanish dance tradition. His dance academy was a well-known attraction in Seville. See *Familiar Spanish Travels*, pp. 236–38.

4. For a detailed description of this incident, see *Familiar Spanish Travels*, p. 64.

5. From Torquato Tasso, *La Gerusalemme Liberata* (1580), canto 1, stanza 1:
> Molto egli oprò col senno con la manno;
> Molto soffrì nel glorïoso acquisto:
> [Much did he strive in thought and deed;
> Much did he suffer in the glorious enterprise:]

6. The mosque at Córdoba, begun in 786 and successively enlarged until its conversion to Christian use in 1236, is an exemplary monument to Moorish architecture in Spain. It features an array of pillars that once numbered about 1200 but has since been reduced to 850. For Howells' somewhat deprecating comments on the pillars, see *Familiar Spanish Travels*, p. 184.

7. In his letter of 26 October 1911 (MH) from Rye, James had mentioned that he was "going up to London—for the winter" in order to escape the loneliness at Lamb House and to attempt to resume writing: "Hibernations *here* are at an end for me—I've experimented this last month, & the isolation & aridity of the winter conditions, above all the immobilization, are prohibitive; I ought to have recognized it sooner. On the other hand from May or June on till *now* again (I mean till these beginnings of the sorry season,) I feel it will always resume its mild appeal."

8. In the same letter James had written Howells about the recent success of *The Outcry* (1911), the book publication of which had been long delayed while

James's literary agent, J. B. Pinker, had unsuccessfully tried to negotiate for serial publication: "I am definitely getting back to work—though when you receive a little lately put-forth book ("The Outcry"—which I fear you will *have* to successfully elude till you reach New York—unless B.[rown] S.[hipley] & Co advise me otherwise,) you are not to suppose it was written—finished—save when it *was*, 2 years ago from now exactly. It has had all sorts of misadventures since then, as many as a young amateur's first attempt, & has but lately succeeded in finding a publisher. Then it has leaped quickly into a 3d edition—unprecedented for me!" Replying to Howells on 12 November 1911, James added: "I am sending you to Gibraltar (kindly make sure the Cooks hand it over to you) my little unprecedentedly Editional book—I hear from the Publishers that it will go into a Fifth!"

8 NOVEMBER 1911, GRANADA, TO JOHN M. HOWELLS

Hotel Casino, Alhambra Palace,
Granada, Spain, Nov. 8, 1911.

Dear John:

We have just had a long tea after several hours in the Generalife[1] where, when Pilla came to a stairway with water gurgling down the tiles that formed the hand-rail, she said, "Oh, yes; now I know what John meant." It made you very vividly and sweetly present. In fact, you are a great deal with us in Spain, which seems to return your *predilaccion*.[2] It is a wonderful place for architecture; and for a brute force of rococo, and a teeth-set realism, it is without a parallel in my young experience. Each new church is a revelation; the cathedral here is a prodigy. Do you remember the Corinthian columns massed in fours?[3] Or that awful, life-size, or death-size group in painted wood (on the high altar of the Catholic King's chapel) of John the Baptist with his head just struck off and his hollow gullet gaping towards you?[4] What a fearless, fearsome fancy their artists had! Then, what a stunning place the all-frescoed votive ex-church of the Gran Capitan,[5] with the Capitan and his wife away up beside the high altar, and his four companions in arms, two on each wall near!

But it is no use! You must have made mental and written notes of all. The Generalife is more like a memory than a fresh experience, for I remember the many pictures of it so well: but the thing itself is of inexhaustible detail. I won't try speaking of it.

To-morrow we plan an excursion across the Vega,[6] to see something of the peasants' life who here often own their little farms, and fill the landscape with their white houses. The Alhambra has failed of its due effect with me after the Alcazar at Seville.[7] The Court of the Lions[8]— pah! I could only think how Billy would have demanded to be put astride one of the ridiculous beasts' backs! The best thing about the place is the unfinished palace of Charles V, the lovely façade, and the noble patio.[9]

It has snowed to-day in the Sierras, and the air has sharpened under a clouded sky. Still we have all the tenderness of early October, and the trees are full of the fall color, but yellow, not red. I suppose we shall stay till Saturday, and then go on to Ronda, which is more than halfway to Algeciras. We have got our rooms on the *Pannonia* from Gibraltar, and in about four weeks I hope we shall be with you.[10] I am sorry about Billy's buf-day.[11] We had planned going back on the *Franconia*, the sixteenth, but she was taken off, and the *Pannonia* was the next Cunarder. She is a slow boat, but it is the best we could do.

Your aff'te
Father

1. The Generalife, built adjacent to the Alhambra in 1319, was the summer palace of the Moorish kings.

2. John Howells visited Spain in 1894.

3. The facade of four massive Corinthian columns of the cathedral of Santa Maria de la Encarnacion was designed by the Spanish artist and architect Alonso Cano (1601–1667).

4. The beheading of John the Baptist is part of the altarpiece located beyond the royal sarcophagi in the Royal Chapel and is the work of the French-born architect variously known as Phillipe de Bourgogne or Felipe Vigarné (1498–1543).

5. Gonzalo Fernandez de Córdoba (1453–1515), the Spanish soldier who won the title El Gran Capitan for his defeat of the French at Naples, is buried with his wife at the Church of San Geronimo.

6. The Vega is the great plain north of Granada.

7. The Alhambra is the thirty-five-acre citadel built between 1248 and 1350 during the Moorish occupation of Granada. The Alcazar was begun in 1181 and enlarged by successive Spanish kings who incorporated the Gothic with the original Moorish style. Of the two, the Alhambra is usually thought to be the superior example of Moorish architecture.

8. The Patio de los Leones, one of the celebrated courts in the Alhambra, features an alabaster fountain basin some ten feet in diameter guarded in circular array by twelve outward-facing lions sculpted in white marble.

9. The palace of Charles V within the walls of the Alhambra was begun in 1527 and left unfinished during the seventeenth century. The outer facades of the structure are an unusual mixture of the Corinthian, Ionic, and Doric styles, while the enclosed circular courtyard is decorated in the northern Italian style.

10. Howells and Mildred were in Ronda, 10–12 November, and then went to Algeciras near Gibraltar, sailing from Gibraltar on 25 November and reaching New York on 8 December.

11. Howells' grandson was to be three on 27 November.

130 West 57th street,
Dec. 9, 1911.

Dear Eliza:

There is no reason why I should not write straight to Joe, but it seems easier to tell *you* that I have no present hope of coming to see you. We got off the ship only yesterday, and it is still rising and sinking in my brain; the notion of any voyage is abhorrent to me. Besides I have just had a full talk with our Dr. Ostrom,[1] who says that he finds no reason to look for any immediate or early charge for the worse in Joe's state. His numbness is a reality; from various causes, but his cold is purely subjective or sensational. He thinks Joe can very well stay at T. I. till spring, but he ought not to look forward to full recovery, and ought to come home, say, to Willy in Florida, then.[2] He *was not discouraging at all* about the case; but considering all things, Joe's age especially, he thinks it hard on him to be at the distance you are, and perhaps a strain he ought not to bear. *He would like your local doctor to write me a full account of the case in scientific or professional terms*; then he will know better just what to advise. Unless Joe's heart is very weak, the case seems to him *only a protracted discomfort and disability*, with perhaps less disability than Joe thinks. Meantime, he would like your doctor to examine his urine, and report on that with the other symptoms. If there were reason for anxiety, I should feel differently about going to you, but he tells me there is none, and so I must consider myself.[3] I am now an old man; I have been through three months' hard travel, which has greatly tired me at times, though I have greatly enjoyed it. I may be seized any time without warning by my excruciating colics which leave me grievously cast down and weakened. I have constant work to do, and I must regard my immediate family. I say all this because I hate to seem selfish. There is no one in the world after my children and Billy so near and dear to me as Joe, and it hurts me deeply to say that under the circumstances I cannot come to you.

I am sending a remedy from Dr. Ostrom, with full instructions, which will benefit Joe, he believes; but from myself I urge you both to consider the impracticability of staying where you are indefinitely. You are too old and infirm; you ought to be with your children, sooner or later. Write to Willy and see if there is not some place near him which you can get.[4] Even with Joe partially disabled you can look forward to peaceful and pleasant years.[5] Short of coming to you, I shall be ready and glad to help you in any way I can. You know that.

I am too tired to write more, but I will, soon again, and tell you all about our last days in Spain. Before we left Algeciras we drove over to a little town beyond the mountains—Tarifa—and passed through woods of thousands of cork trees, some just peeled of their bark. Joe would have liked it; he would liked Spain everywhere.—Cheer up, and think of coming to live *on shore* again, with good human food. Billy is thriving and all the John family join with Pilla and me in love.

Your aff'te brother
Will.

1. Homer I. Ostrom (1852–1925), Howells' physician in New York, was a leading surgeon who developed important techniques for abdominal operations.

2. Joseph Howells had recently visited his son William D. Howells II in Auburndale, Florida, in consideration of moving there after leaving his consular post at Turks Islands. See Howells to Joseph A. Howells, 29 May 1911, n. 4. Joe, who had turned seventy-nine on 1 September, seems subsequently to have developed the symptoms here described. Howells was informed of the situation while in London and, according to his letter to Joe of 3 November 1911 (MH) from Seville, had assumed the responsibility of consulting various doctors and dispensing remedies from Europe: "I hope by this time you have got some tablets I sent you from Madrid. Take one a day; half at night, half in the morning. Our German doctor says they will help your numb hands. Also bake your hands in a lamp-heated box. Electricity no good. Chew the tablets thoroughly. Put a kerosene lamp under a wooden box." Hearing soon after that Joe had not yet received the tablets sent from Madrid, Howells wrote from Algeciras, Spain, on 14 November 1911 (MH), repeating the instructions for the prescription as well as one recommended earlier from England: "If you are able to get that mysterious '79,' which the London doctor prescribed, I think the tablets would be better; but try both, one after the other.... It is hard doctoring you from this distance!"

3. To yet another plea from Joe reporting no improvement, Howells replied sympathetically but firmly, in a letter of 17 December 1911 (OFH): "I am sorry indeed that you are so poorly. It is not *impossible* for me to come to you, but it is *most impracticable*, as I tried to explain in my last letter. Besides, it would be useless for me to discuss your case with you, and though I should love dearly to see you, it would be a sore trial for both if I had to leave you no better than I found you."

4. In the deepening urgency of the situation Howells wrote to Joe's son, as he indicates in his letter to Joe of 17 December: "... I have written to Willy asking whether he could go on to help bring you away, or at least meet you here; but I have not had time to hear from him yet. The great thing is keep up your courage, as you seem certainly to be doing, and to look the facts in the face.., . You are old and you are sick; Eliza is not so young or so well as she once was, and your place is naturally with your children. This is a hard saying to one who has been so helpful to himself and others as you have always been, but I cannot soften it."

5. Joe died within a year, on 10 August 1912.

26 DECEMBER 1911, NEW YORK, TO THOMAS S. PERRY

130 West 57th st.,
New York, Dec. 26, 1911.

My dear Perry:

My worst fault is saying all the good things, either before or after some other fellow. In the case of Shaw on Tolstoy,[1] you will find that I anticipated him in essentials three or four years ago in a *N. A. Review* article (reprinted in last December's number).[2] For all that, Shaw is entirely right, even to saying that you cannot live socialistically in capitalistic conditions; here too I long anticipated him in practice as well as precept.[3] It is against my natural modesty to bellow these facts in your ear; but what can I do?

Yes, our talk was all too short,[4] and it didn't include Mrs. Perry; which was my loss.

I expect Pilla home to-day, and when we are settled, on you come! Meantime my address is superscribed.

Yours ever, and all your family's, especially the charming girl I lunched with's,

W. D. Howells.

1. Howells appears to be referring to an anonymous piece entitled "Bernard Shaw's Criticism of Tolstoy," *Current Literature*, July 1911.

2. Howells' essay "Lyof N. Tolstoy" first appeared in the *North American Review*, December 1908, and was reprinted in the December 1910 number, following Tolstoy's death on 20 November 1910.

3. The anonymous article quotes Shaw's comments from the *Fabian News* on Tolstoy's awkward and contradictory attempts to live as a socialist worker: "He was a man of genius in the very first flight of that rare species. He had the penetrating common sense characteristic of that first flight. And yet no English old maid of county family, living in a cathedral town on £300 a year, could have made more absurd attempts to start an ideal social system by private misconduct than he. He put on the dress of a moujik exactly as Don Quixote put on a suit of armor. He tried to ignore money as Don Quixote did. He left his own skilled work to build houses that could hardly be induced to stand, and to make boots that an army contractor would have been ashamed of. He let his property drift to the verge of insolvency and ruin like the laziest Irish squire because he disapproved of property as an institution. And he was neither honest nor respectable in his follies. He connived at all sorts of evasions. He would not take money on a journey; but he would take a companion who would buy railway tickets and pay hotel bills behind his back. He would not own property or copyrights; but he would make them over to his wife and children, and live in their country house in Yasnaya and their town house in Moscow very comfortably, only occasionally easing his conscience by making things as difficult and unpleasant for them as possible. He insisted on celibacy as the first condition of a worthy life; and his wife became sixteen times a mother, and found him an uxorious husband at seventy." In his essay on Tolstoy, Howells had somewhat less censoriously pointed out a similar discrepancy: "The

event was in his literature a compromise as it was in his life, when he sat in a ploughman's dress eating a ploughman's fare at one end of the table, and at the other the world, economic and aesthetic, sat served with costly viands. Midway, the succession of interviewing and reviewing witnesses criticised and censured his hospitality and acclaimed or condemned according to their respective make, while in the hours saved from his rude toil he continued his sublime work. The event was a compromise or it was a defeat, if you choose to think it so; but it was no more a compromise or a defeat than that of any other human career. Compared with the event of any other career in this time, the career of the greatest warrior, statesman, king, priest or poet, it is a flawless triumph. [¶] Tolstoy's example is of the quality of his precept, which with the will to be all positive is first notable for what is negative in it. To have renounced pride and luxury and idleness, and the vain indulgence of the tastes and passions, but not to have known want or the fear of it, not to have felt cold, hunger, houselessness, friendliness, is to have done something which for the spectator lacks its corollary in practice, as the proposition of certain truths lacks its corollary in precept."

4. In a letter to Aurelia H. Howells, 22 December 1911 (MH), Howells indicates that he was in Boston during the week before Christmas, at which time he probably saw Perry.

TEXTUAL APPARATUS

Introduction

THE letters selected for inclusion in these volumes of Howells correspondence are printed in clear text in the form reproducing as nearly as possible their finished state. The record of the alterations which took place during composition and which are evidenced on the pages of the manuscripts is presented in the textual apparatus which follows, in combination with the record of editorial emendations. The letters have been editorially corrected only in specific details and only when the original texts would make no conceivable sense to the reader. Thus Howells' few eccentricities of spelling and punctuation and his occasional mistakes and oversights have generally been retained. However, inadvertent repetitions of letters, syllables, or words—usually a result of moving the pen from the end of one line to the beginning of the next—have been emended and recorded in the apparatus. In cases where the actual manuscripts are not available and transcriptions or printed versions of letters have served as the basis for printing here, errors in those materials have also been retained, since the actual source of the error—Howells, the transcriber, or the printer—cannot be identified.

Except where extraordinary conditions have made it impossible, the following procedures have been followed step-by-step in the preparation for publication of the text of each letter, whether the extant form of it is the original document or an unpublished or published transcription. First a clean, typed transcription of the final form of the extant material is prepared from a facsimile of it. Then duplicate copies of this prepared transcription are read and corrected against the facsimile by the editor of the volume and by one of the editors of the letters series. At the same time drafts of the apparatus material are prepared, recording all cancellations, insertions, revisions, and illegible words or letters in the text, as well as possible compounds, end-line hyphenated, which must be resolved as hyphenated or unhyphenated forms. These drafts of the apparatus also include questions about proper interpretation of textual details. The corrected and edited transcriptions and accompanying apparatus are conflated at the Howells Center and any discrepancies identified and corrected. At this stage transcriptions and textual apparatus are completely reread against the facsimile of the original. The resultant material is next checked by a different editor against the original holograph, copy, or printing; he verifies all details, answers insofar as possible all remaining questions, and indicates matter in the original which has not been reproduced in the working facsimile. This completes the process of preparing printer's copy.

At this point the texts of the letters—though not the corresponding apparatus—are set in type. The typeset texts are proofread once against the facsimiles of the original documents and once more against the prepared printer's copy; necessary corrections are made in both typeset text and apparatus, and the apparatus is keyed to the line numbering of the typeset texts. After correction by the printer of the typeset text and the setting in type of the textual apparatus, these materials are proofread in full once more against the printer's copy, and the apparatus is proofread again separately. At every point at which revises are returned by the printer they are verified against the marked proofs.

This procedure—involving as many different people as possible from among the editors of the volumes, the series, and the Howells Edition staff—has been adopted to guarantee that the printed texts are as accurate as the combined energy and attention of a group of trained and experienced editors can make them. It will, we hope, warrant our statement that the errors, oversights, and possibly unidiomatic readings of the texts are those of the original documents and not of the editors. Further, since even the detailed textual record presented in this apparatus cannot fully indicate the physical condition of the letters, the editorial materials prepared during the assembly of these volumes are all being preserved, and can be consulted by anyone who wishes to see them—at the Howells Center at Indiana University as long as it is in operation for preparation of texts for "A Selected Edition of W. D. Howells" and in a suitable public depository thereafter.

The editorial considerations and procedures outlined above underlie the actual presentation of the letters printed in these volumes. Each letter is introduced by an editorial heading identifying the date and place of composition and the name of the correspondent to whom it is directed. The date and location identified in this heading may be different from those provided by the letter itself, since the content of the letter or other pertinent evidence can indicate that those details are inaccurate. When such cases arise, they are discussed in appropriate footnotes.

The translation of the ranges of handwritten and typewritten material and printed stationery into the stricter confines of the printed page obviously demands the adoption of certain formal and stylistic conventions. Regardless of their arrangement or placement on the original page, inside addresses are presented in one or more lines above the single line containing the place of origin and date provided in the letter. This format is followed regardless of the placement of the dateline at the beginning or at the end of a letter. When handwritten or printed letter-heads provide more elaborate information than basic identification of place of origin and date, the additional information is omitted and its absence signaled by the appropriate placement of ellipses. The use of capitals or a combination of capitals and small capitals in printed letter-head forms has been reduced here to capitals and lowercase letters. In the printing of letters and datelines in the present text, italic type is used to indicate matter which occurs in the original part of printed sta-tionery, and roman to indicate portions supplied by Howells himself. The distinction between print and handwritten or typed portions of heading information can be significant in that a printed letterhead in particular does not necessarily indicate that the letter itself was written in that place. If Howells supplied location information different from that of a printed letterhead, the printed letterhead is considered simply a mark on the paper and has been ignored in the presentation of the text.

The beginning of the body of the letter after the salutation has been consistently set off by a paragraph even if Howells continued on the same line or used any other unconventional spacing. Similarly, the positions of the complimentary close (e.g., "Yours ever") and the signature in relation to the body of the letter have been standardized without regard to Howells' widely varying usage. The relative spacing of the indentations of paragraphs has been normalized to conform to the typography of these volumes; this principle has been applied also to unindented paragraph breaks which occur in the originals. The interruptive or appositive dash within sentences and the transitional dash between sentences (the latter almost the equivalent in sense of the paragraph break) have been set in standard typographical form, and relative length not indicated. The long *s* of Howells' youthful hand has been set consistently in the ordinary typographical form. Underlined words have been set in italics without regard to the position or relative length of the underlining; when the form of the underlining indicates, however, that Howells clearly in-tended to emphasize only part of a word (e.g., *every*one), then only that part has been italicized.

When texts are derived from machine-printed rather than handwritten telegrams, the full capitalization used there has been reduced to capitals and lowercase letters, with an appropriate note in the textual apparatus. The same procedure has been followed for letters typed on typewriters using only capital letters. Where texts are derived from copies of now-missing letters rather than from manuscripts, any typographical peculi-arities of those forms—indentation, employment of capitals and small capitals in proper names, and so on—have been altered to conform to the

format of the present edition. But only this strictly typographical altera-
tion has been enforced; the errors in spelling and punctuation and the
revisions and cancellations within these materials have all been considered textually significant and a potentially accurate record of the
originals upon which they are based.

Postscripts which follow upon the signatures in the original letters are
placed in the same position in the printed text, but marginal notes and
postscripts placed eccentrically are printed where they seem to belong
within or after the body of the letter, and their original locations indicated by editorial notes in the apparatus to the letter. The presence or
absence of page and leaf numbering or the location of such numbering
on the original pages has not been recorded.

In the preparation of the texts and apparatus, those marks, and those
marks alone, in the text of the letter which could be interpreted as slips
of the pen have been ignored. All other marks, including wiped-out
words or letters, erased material, incomplete words either canceled or
uncanceled, and random letters, have been recorded. Illegible words or
letters are identified in the apparatus by the abbreviation *"illeg."*

The presentation of this information in the apparatus demands the
use of certain symbols and abbreviations to conserve space. The record
for each letter is introduced by the same editorial heading that introduces
the item in the text proper. Then follows a note on the number of
pages (i.e., sides of individual sheets or of segments of sheets created by
folding which have been written on). Next is provided an abbreviated
indication of the kind of text and the presence or absence of authorial
signature (A.l. = Autograph letter; A.l.s. = Autograph letter signed;
T.l. = Typescript letter; T.l.s. = Typescript letter signed; A.n. =
Autograph note; A.n.s. = Autograph note signed; T.n. = Typescript
note; T.n.s. = Typescript note signed). If the authorial text is of a kind
not represented by these eight abbreviations, it is described fully (e.g.,
"Mostly in autograph of Elinor M. Howells"; "Telegraph form written
in Howells' hand"; "Typed telegram"). If the text is based on a transcribed copy, that fact is noted together with information about the
source of the transcription, if known; if the transcription is a published
text, the author, title, and other bibliographical information are provided
—in the cases of both published and unpublished transcriptions the number of pages of text is ignored as textually irrelevant. This information is
followed in turn by the standard abbreviation for the library in which
the original document or extant transcription is located,[1] or by the short-
form designation for a private collection.

---

1. The system of abbreviations used in this edition is that described in *Symbols
of American Libraries*, 10th ed. (Washington: Library of Congress, 1969).

Following this heading appears the record of the internal revisions and cancellations in the letter document and any emendations made by the editors. All such revisions, even in typed letters, may be assumed to be by Howells, unless otherwise noted in the apparatus. Each entry in this record begins with the citation of the number or numbers of the lines in the text of the printed letter in which the cited material occurs. This numbering is based on the count of full or partial lines of type, and begins with the first line of the document, whether that be inside address, date, or salutation; it does not include the formal editorial heading which precedes each letter.

Sentences, phrases, words, or parts of words inserted into the running text of the document are indicated in the record by placement within vertical arrows, ellipses being used to abbreviate passages of four or more words. Thus:

↑evade↓   with↑out↓   ↑directly . . . exchange.↓

No distinction is made between words inserted above the line and those inserted below it or manuscript revisions fitted into typescript lines, and the color of ink or the medium (pencil, pen, typewriter) used for corrections or additions is not described. The presence or absence of a caret or other conventional symbol for the insertion of the material is not recorded. When a word has been written over some other word or part of a word, that fact is indicated by the use of the abbreviation "*w.o.*" (for "written over") following the final reading and preceding the original. Thus:

parties *w.o.* party   people *w.o.* ple

Words canceled in the original are indicated by placement in pointed brackets in the context of citation of sufficient words from the text of the letter (either before or after the canceled words or phrase) as printed in this edition to identify its location. Thus:

went ⟨to⟩   ⟨we went⟩ I walked

An italic question mark within brackets following a word indicates a degree of uncertainty about the interpretation provided. The combinations of these various symbols and abbreviations should be self-explanatory: e.g., ↑⟨this⟩↓ indicates that the interlined word "this" has been canceled.

All editorial revisions are signaled in the apparatus by a left-opening bracket (]); preceding it appears the reading of the text as printed in this edition, and following it the reading of the original. When the editorial revision involves only the emendation of punctuation, each curved dash ($\sim$) following the bracket stands for a word preceding the bracket. When it has been necessary to supply words, letters, or marks of punctuation missing in the original not because of oversight or error in composition but because of the present physical condition of the document—badly faded ink, deteriorated or torn paper, blots, or water-spots—the reconstructed portions are signaled by being placed between vertical lines: Thus:

af|te|r |the| commit|tee| met

Virgules (slashes) are used to indicate the end of a line of writing in the original document. All other editorial comments, including description of the placement of postscripts and marginal notes or the presence in a document of notes or comments in another hand believed to be contemporary with the composition or receipt of the letter, as well as information about specific textual details not covered by the basic system of symbols and abbreviations outlined here, are provided in italic type within brackets.

In addition to the textual record which follows, this edition of letters contains a section headed "Word-Division," consisting of two separate lists: one, List A, indicates the resolution of possible compounds occurring as end-line hyphenations in the original documents, and the other, List B, the form to be given to possible compounds which occur at the end of the line in the present text. A description of the keying system employed in these lists and the process by which editorial decisions about the resolution of such end-lines were reached is provided in the head-note to that section.

C. K. L.

D. J. N.

Textual Record

---

12 January 1902, New York, to Aurelia H. Howells. 2 pp. T.l.s. MH.

    10 glad *w.o.* gled   15 sort *w.o.* cort   23 it] iht   24 quite *w.o.* fuite
27 suffering *w.o.* suffereng   30 of tea] or tea   32 of pretty *w.o.* od pretty
33 walks *w.o.* welks

19 January 1902, New York, to Thomas B. Aldrich. 4 pp. T.l.s. MH.

    3 Aldrich *w.o.* aldrich   5 Clemens *w.o.* Clamens   11 great *w.o.* areat
11 joins *w.o.* boins   12 thoughts *w.o.* *illeg.*   15 name; *w.o.* *illeg.*
16 ↑yesterday↓   20 good as] good ar   20 think *w.o.* thing
21 have *w.o.* hawe   24 it⟨,⟩ ↑is,↓   29 ↑who↓   33 ardent *w.o.* aident
34 Southerners *w.o.* southerners   35 A *w.o.* E   37 many *w.o.* aany
40 am *w.o.* an   45 should *w.o.* shiuld
46 North American] NorthAmerican   48 experience, *w.o.* experiencing,
48 experience,] ~„   49 ↑it↓   52 not *w.o.* nit   54 he] ~.
56 Beacon ⟨seR⟩   58 Longfellow *w.o.* Yongfellow   59 it does] it is does
62 etc. *w.o.* et.   62 things ⟨things⟩   66 find ↑of↓   73 ever *w.o.* aver

27 January 1902, New York, to Jacob G. Schurman, 1 p. A.l.s. NIC.

    5 ↑the courage . . . sense of↓

14 February 1902, New York, to Henry James. 3 pp. A.l.s. MH.

    6 but *w.o.* and   8 old, ⟨*illeg.*⟩   10 has *w.o.* had   11 has *w.o.* had
13 ↑of the piece↓   13 piece.]~   16 o'clock to *w.o.* o'clock, a
16 after being] after being being   25 Mrs. *w.o.* *illeg.*
26 ⟨from⟩ ↑out of↓   35–36 Think . . . world! [*in margin and across
salutation and text, first page*]

5 March 1902, New York, to Thomas B. Aldrich. 2 pp. A.l.s. Mrs. Vinton
Chapin, Dublin, N. H.

    4 If ↑you↓   8 ↑a↓ lunch   20 stea↑m↓boat   24 ⟨tha⟩ till
24–25 Harper's Weekly?] ⟨*illeg.* Ha⟩rpers Weekly?

19 March 1902, New York, to Charles E. Norton. 3 pp. A.l.s. MH.

  13 ↑him↓

26 March 1902, New York, to John Hay. 2 pp. A.l.s. RPB.

  12 wants *w.o.* wishes

27 March 1902, New York, to John Hay. 2 pp. T.l.s. RPB.

  4 ↑I↓   5 will *w.o.* wial   6 write you *w.o.* writteyou   13 (*w.o.* S
14 and *w.o.* aad   14 experi-/ence *w.o.* experie/ence   20 so do *w.o. illeg.*
21 clapping ⟨y⟩   26 watering *w.o. illeg.*   27 and *w.o. illeg.*

30 March 1902, New York, to Aurelia H. Howells, 2 pp. T.l.s. MH.

  6 ↑not↓   8 to *w.o.* ti   11 old *w.o.* odd   15 Janvier *w.o.* Jenvier
16 Harper, ⟨a⟩   17 Century Club *w.o.* century club   18 used *w.o. illeg.*
20 Joe *w.o.* ioe   21 ↑it↓   23 house *w.o.* hous.
23–24 constantly] conrtantly   28 Journal *w.o.* Journel   29 live ⟨o⟩
31 from] prom

6 April 1902, New York, to Charles E. Norton. 4 pp. A.l.s. MH.

  20–21 my⟨s⟩ son   23 ↑am↓   28 ↑have↓

19 April 1902, New York, to Brand Whitlock. 2 pp. T.l.s. DLC.

  5 honored *w.o.* tonored

20 April 1902, New York, to Edward E. Hale. 1 p. T.l.s. MNS.

  2 190m. *w.o.* 180m.   6 real] rea/real   7 this *w.o.* tiis   10 you *w.o.* giu

7 May 1902, New York, to Thomas B. Aldrich. 2 pp. A.l.s. MH.

  6 heart *w.o. illeg.*   11 *souflée w.o. illeg.*   14 story⟨,⟩   15 ⟨O⟩ I *thought*
17 than *w.o. illeg.*   17–21 good...Howells [*in margin and across
salutation, first page*]

8 May 1902, New York, to Minnie M. Fiske. 1 p. A.l.s. DLC.

  6 ↑in↓

11 May 1902, New York, to Aurelia H. Howells. 3 pp. T.l.s. MH.

  5 freshness *w.o.* frashness   14 me *w.o. illeg.*   27 thousand] thiusand
31 house]housse   33 ⟨very⟩ Virginia   37 I last *w.o.* i last

24 May 1902, New York, to Aurelia H. Howells, 3 pp. A.l.s. MH.

 18 before *w.o.* **by**

27 May 1902, New York, to Charles E. Norton. 3 pp. A.l.s. MH.

9 June 1902, New York, to John W. De Forest. 3 pp. A.l.s. CtY.

 11 ⟨r⟩ River   12 curiosity *w.o. illeg.*

3 July 1902, Kittery Point, to Thomas B. Aldrich. 3 pp. A.l.s. MH.

 11 by *w.o.* bu⟨t⟩   18 ↑am↓   20 Nomore *w.o.* nomore   22 ↑in↓
24 when *w.o. illeg.*   27 ⟨with⟩ ↑but bordering↓   28 run ⟨up⟩
35 happiness *w.o. illeg.*

3 August 1902, Kittery Point, to Brander Matthews. 3 pp. A.l.s. NNC.

 8 they had] they had they had   14 The Kentons *w.o.* the Kentons
17 was *w.o.* am   18 delicate *w.o.* delicacy   18 ↑beauty↓
22 Pazienza *w.o.* **Pacienza**

17 August 1902, Kittery Point, to Aurelia H. Howells. 3 pp. A.l.s. MH.

 4 hope⟨s⟩   15 ↑though↓

7 October 1902, Kittery Point, to William James. Location of MS. unknown. *Life in Letters*, II, 161–62.

9 October 1902, Kittery Point, to Hamilton W. Mabie. 2 pp. A.l.s. NNAL.

12 October 1902, Kittery Point, to Charles E. Norton. 3 pp. A.l.s. MH.

 3 ↑the past summer,↓   4 speak ↑to↓   11 ↑mental↓   17 for *w.o.* I
17 my *w.o. illeg.*   19 ↑there.↓   22 Mrs. *w.o. illeg.*   24 That *w.o.* It
36 England *w.o.* York

20 October 1902, Kittery Point, to Samuel L. Clemens. 2 pp. A.l.s. CU.

 11 twenty-five⟨s⟩

31 October 1902, New York, to Bliss Perry. 1 p. A.l.s. MH.

 8 account⟨s⟩

16 November 1902, New York, to Samuel L. Clemens. 2 pp. A.l.s. CU.

  1 1902 *w.o.* 1898   7 wrote ⟨to⟩

25 November 1902, New York, to Charles E. Norton. 3 pp. A.l.s. MH.

  9 ↑literary↓   9 myself *w.o.* mine   10 was *w.o.* is   18 must ⟨*illeg.*⟩
23 as *w.o.* an

23 December 1902, New York, to Samuel L. Clemens. 1 p. A.l.s. CU.

  2 23 *w.o.* 24

11 January 1903, New York, to Madison J. Cawein. 1 p. T.l.s. KyLoF.

  5 when I *w.o.* when i   9 and I *w.o.* and i   15 ↑do↓   17 bnt *w.o.* and
17 but] bnt

13 January 1903, New York, to Evelyn G. Smalley. Location of MS.
unknown. Typed copy at MH.

  3 Miss] ∼.

28 January 1903, New York, to Aurelia H. Howells. 3 pp. A.l.s. MH.

  1 59th *w.o.* 57th   9 ↑know↓   15 ↑it↓   21 subject⟨s⟩
27 It is] It it is

9 February 1903, New York, to Samuel L. Clemens. 2 pp. A.l.s. CU.

  6 Senate⟨r⟩

10 February 1903, New York, to Hamilton W. Mabie. 2 pp. A.l.s. NNAL.

  6 meetings, ⟨*illeg.*⟩

12 February 1903, New York, to Samuel L. Clemens. 2 pp. T.l. CU.

  8 potatoes *w.o.* potatois   10 explained *w.o.* ⟨*illeg.*⟩*plained*
11 pu↑s↓hed   15 I gave *w.o.* i geve   16 ↑not↓   23 really *w.o.* rellly
24 ↑make him↓   25 rem⟨m⟩ember   26 my⟨se⟩/self

23 February 1903, New York, to Annie A. Fields. 3 pp. A.l.s. CSmH.

  5 subscriber *w.o.* subscription   16 to the *w.o.* to his
20 foot *w.o.* boot

11 March 1903, New York, to Hamlin Garland. 2 pp. A.l.s. CLSU.

[*At top of first page, in another hand*: My Art in Review]

6 April 1903, New York, to Charles E. Norton. 6 pp. A.l.s. MH.

14 congratulated] congratu/ted   20 ↑by↓   24 with him *w.o.* in him
36 ↑a↓ ready-made   38 street⟨s⟩   46 ⟨well⟩ went   51 We *w.o.* we

23 April 1903, New York, to Katherine S. Godkin. 3 pp. A.l.s. MH.

3 Mrs. *w.o. illeg.*   7 ↑prize↓   16 warmth *w.o. illeg.*   18 ↑not↓
22 told ↑you↓   25 ↑he↓
[*At bottom of third page, in another hand*: E.L.G. often said that his
youth was harrowed with laughter.]

26 April 1903, New York, to Samuel L. Clemens. 2 pp. A.l. CU.

9 the *w.o.* a

26 April 1903, New York, to Charles E. Norton. 2 pp. T.l.s. MH.

10 I did *w.o.* i did   12 I dared *w.o.* i dared   21 seeming *w.o.* semming
23 I suppose I *w.o.* i suppose i   25 American *w.o.* Ameiican
25 hereafter] herafter   30 unconscious *w.o.* unconscios
32 grudgingly *w.o.* grudgincly   34 ↑it↓   34 went *w.o.* want
39 out *w.o.* ort   40 was ⟨nt⟩   43 keen *w.o.* kaen

1 May 1903, New York, to Samuel L. Clemens. 2 pp. A.l.s. CU.

5 brace *w.o.* place   6 ↑Place."↓   7 with you about] with about
16–18 *word* .... W.D.H. [*in margin, first page*]

15 June 1903, Kittery Point, to Frederick A. Duneka. Location of MS.
unknown. Typed copy at MH.

5 juries.] ∼,   25 weigh] weight   51 attested] atested

26 July 1903, Kittery Point, to Hamlin Garland. 3 pp. A.l.s. CLSU.

11 by ⟨by⟩ day   12 ↑been↓

9 August 1903, Kittery Point, to Aurelia H. Howells. 2 pp. T.l. MH.

3 I *w.o.* i   13 says *w.o. illeg.*   16 glad *w.o.* gead   22 Elinor's *w.o. illeg.*
23 very] vern   28 Please ... again. [*in Howells' hand*]

15 August 1903, Kittery Point, to Charles E. Norton. 3 pp. A.l.s. MH.

    5 year⟨'⟩s   11 and ⟨the⟩ the   18 about *w.o.* of

5 September 1903, Kittery Point, to Brander Matthews. 1 p. A.l.s. NNC.

    4 outspeech, *w.o.* outspeech: 6 *exercise w.o.* use

9 September 1903, Kittery Point, to David A. Munro. 3 pp. A.l.s. MB.

    9 dead *w.o.* fead   14 ⟨fa⟩ man   21 ⟨your⟩ my

20 September 1903, Kittery Point, to Henry B. Fuller. 2 pp. T.l.s. MH.

    3 sort ↑of↓   6 which *w.o.* whilh   7 none *w.o.* note
8 business] bus-/siness   8 I *w.o.* i   9 some⟨t⟩/time   10 ↑of↓
10 Centre *w.o.* centre   13 ⟨wh⟩ which   15 ↑many↓   15 sixty- *w.o.* sixtY-
19 when *w.o.* then   22 heard *w.o.* he.rd   23 since *w.o.* sinme
23 and *w.o.* but   25 ⟨.⟩ I   26 which ⟨i⟩   27 for ⟨th⟩
30 journalism *w.o.* Journalism   30 Now *w.o.* illeg.   31 I wish *w.o.* i wish
31 other] otheh

3 October 1903, Kittery Point, to Dr. Whiston. 1 p. A.l.s. NjR.

4 October 1903, Kittery Point, to Aurelia H. Howells. 2 pp. A.l.s. MH.

    10 ↑you↓ [*in another hand*]   12 ⟨*illeg.*⟩ *would*

27 October 1903, Kittery Point, to Thomas S. Perry. 3 pp. T.l.s. MeWC.

    3 me *w.o.* mi   4 went *w.o.* whnt   5 my *w.o. illeg.*   5 heart ⟨a⟩
5 ↑one↓   9 I take *w.o.* i take   13 bored ⟨b⟩   17 away ⟨her⟩
18 appre-/ciative *w.o.* apprec/ciative   22 seemed w.o. illeg.
22 the *w.o. illeg.*

22 November 1903, New York, to Thomas S. Perry. 2 pp. A.l.s. MeWC.

    7 ↑have↓   11 ↑you↓   15 ↑me↓

22 November 1903, New York, to Aurelia H. Howells. 2 pp. T.l.s. MH.

    6 tag *w.o.* tak   7 case *w.o.* care   8 ↑old↓   14 wear⟨s⟩   21 He *w.o.* he
25 ↑to↓ our   26 news *w.o.* niws   29 I must] I m/must   29 No↑r↓th
31 last *w.o.* lath   35 think *w.o.* thing   36 gorge *w.o.* girge
38 of Americans *w.o.* ff Americans   43 ⟨r⟩ repose
48 Fréchettes *w.o.* ƒréchettes

20 December 1903, New York, to Samuel L. Clemens. 3 pp. A.l.s. CU.

11 ↑just↓   14 Judgment *w.o.* judgment   16 Wallace⟨'s⟩
18 ↑in↓ their   21 be *w.o.* f   29 her⟨s⟩   34 over it in] over in

17 January 1904, New York, to Henry B. Fuller. Location of MS. unknown. Typescript copy at InU.

34 than] ⟨than⟩

26 January 1904, New York, to William Clyde Fitch. Location of MS. unknown. *Life in Letters,* II, 182–83.

28 January 1904, New York, to Charles E. Norton. 3 pp. A.l.s. MH.

11 interest⟨*illeg.*⟩   16 ↑for↓   22 has *w.o.* was   23 d'Amore *w.o.* d'amore
26 ↑mood,↓

1 February 1904, Atlantic City, to Richard W. Gilder. 2 pp. A.l.s. NN.

5 ↑came,↓ 8 ↑re↓solved   18 had *w.o.* have   18 ↑once↓   19 ↑and↓
21 ↑if↓   21 sort, ⟨but⟩

4 February 1904, Atlantic City, to Frederick A. Duneka. 2 pp. A.l.s. RPB.

6 ↑in↓   11–12 collection *w.o. illeg.*   12 essays ⟨*illeg.*⟩

14 February 1904, New York, to Samuel L. Clemens. 3 pp. A.l.s. CU.

7 cursed *w.o.* I   23 by *w.o.* ,   35 along *w.o.* alone

14 February 1904, New York, to John St. Loe Strachey. 3 pp. A.l.s. House of Lords, London.

19 was *w.o.* is   20 appealing [*Howells had written* appeating, *then crossed out the crossing of the* t]   23 temperament⟨s,⟩   29 ↑straight↓
40 He ⟨*illeg.*⟩   42–45 best . . . . Howells. [*in margin and across salutation, first page*]

15 February 1904, New York, to Frederick A. Duneka. 2 pp. A.l.s. NNC.

15 Weekly *w.o.* weekly

13 and 14 March 1904, Plymouth, to Elinor M. Howells. 6 pp. A.l.s. MH.

16 conservatories.] ∼   39 reservoir] rervoir   55 I *w.o.* we
57 ⟨*illeg.*⟩ behaved   58 than *w.o.* that   59 ⟨*illeg.*⟩ walk   62 ↑9:30 A.M.↓

63 headache *w.o.* neadache   67 go ⟨*illeg.*⟩   67 ↑room↓   77 though⟨t⟩
95 stayed?⟨()⟩   98 notes.] ∼

15 March 1904, Exeter, to Elinor M. Howells. 3 pp. A.l. MH.

    7 cowslips [*written above, in Howells' hand*: primroses]
10 Dull *w.o.* Gr   10 ↑it↓   14 out on *w.o.* out,   16 ↑were↓   16 ↑was↓
19 ↑is↓   20 ⟨in⟩ everywhere   23 ↑in,↓ and ↑then↓   24 hunting *w.o. illeg.*
24 ↑down↓   24 and at] and/and   28 ⟨illeg.⟩ curates   33 ↑high↓
36 ↑from↓   39 fenestrated *w.o. illeg.*   40 *stemmas*⟨,⟩
41–42 Insurance] Ins-/⟨*illeg.*⟩-urance   45 knew ⟨*illeg.*⟩   48 ⟨At⟩Axminster

18 March 1904, Bath, to Elinor M. Howells. 3 pp. A.l.s. MH.

    29–30 underpinning ⟨I⟩   33 swimming] swiming   34 ↑they↓
35 H.?⟨"⟩   36 ⟨Peop⟩ Showed   42 bet.] ∼   43 excludes *w.o.* excluded
45 Bath, ⟨*illeg.*⟩

18, 19 and 20 March 1904, Bath, to Elinor M. Howells. 6 pp. A.l.s. MH.

    5 Normans *w.o.* D   13 chickens *w.o. illeg.*   35 glass *w.o.* glad
37 Pil . . . . of lawyer [*paper torn off; several lines missing*]
43 Still, . . . the . . . . [*paper torn off; several lines missing*]
51 had *w.o.* has   64 ⟨or⟩ rain   67 beat⟨s⟩   67 letters ⟨fr⟩

20 March 1904, Bath, to John St. Loe Strachey. 2 pp. Al.s. House of
Lords, London.

    4 to ⟨Su⟩ see   8 ↑seems altogether wrong↓   12 ever⟨y⟩   14 ↑was↓

24 and 25 March 1904, Bath, to Elinor M. Howells. 4 pp. A.l.s. MH.

    5 ↑little↓   17 1650 *w.o.* 1750   18 and *w.o.* in   20 ↑so to↓
36 ⟨s⟩he   43 distinguisht] dis-/-guisht

12 April 1904, London, to Elinor M. Howells. 6 pp. A.l.s. MH.

    7 helping *w.o.* him   16 the Gloves *w.o.* a Glove
19 Rembrandts *w.o. illeg.*   21 ⟨p⟩ bad   22 notes] hotes
23 art and] ∼. ∼   35 lilac⟨s⟩   39 night↑fall↓   44 without] with
46 McIlvaines *w.o.* McIvvaines   47 Lord ⟨Lan⟨d⟩sdowne⟩
50 Strachey's⟨'⟩   56 ⟨book,⟩ bacon   60 the *w.o.* this
68–69 We . . . . next [*in margin, sixth page*]
70–71 With . . . Papa. [*in margin, first page*]

17 April 1904, London, to Elinor M. Howells. 4 pp. A.l. fragment. MH.

[*In margin between first and second page, in another hand*: 81 Eaton Terrace / April 17 / 1904] 1 . . . one [*top of page excised*] 1 back . . . was [*several words excised*] 2 passing *w.o.* passed 4 was . . . . [*top of page excised*] 11 has *w.o.* was 22 people ⟨up⟩ 22 ⟨awkwardly⟩ awedly 28 ↑now,↓ 28 sir." [*end of extant portion of MS.*]

19 April 1904, London, to Samuel L. Clemens. 3 pp. A.l.s. CU.

8 his *w.o.* him 10 the *w.o.* a 10 ↑most↓ ⟨pleasant⟩ 12 ↑from↓ 18 ⟨with⟩ ↑to↓ man 22 going . . . . [*ellipses and period are editorially emended, since Howells left the sentence unfinished as he began another page*] 29 ⟨what⟩ James 32 June *w.o.* Jul 35 her⟨s⟩ 37 ⟨that⟩ than

1 May 1904, Folkestone, to Elinor M. Howells. 4 pp. A.l.s. MH.

4 ↑the↓ 7 ↑still↓ 16 ↑there↓ 32 with ⟨a⟩ 49–50 it . . . . Papa. [*in margin, first page*] 51 Laura's . . . . more. [*in margin, fourth page*]

13 May 1904, Folkestone, to Elinor M. Howells. 3 pp. A.l.s. (with note in Mildred Howells' hand) MH.

8 Well *w.o.* Walk 16 pleases] ∼. 27–38 Dear . . . . Pilla [*in Mildred Howells' hand*]

17 May 1904, London, to Henry James. 2 pp. A.l.s. OFH.

13 line [*Howells crossed out the l to form a* t, *then canceled the crossing*]

1 June 1904, Rye, to Elizabeth Jordan. 3 pp. A.l.s. NN.

5 ↑his purpose in↓ 7 has been *w.o.* was been 15 ↑there↓ 18 bring ↑him↓ 20 week⟨,⟩ 21 Women's *w.o.* women's 22 ↑Detroit, Cleveland,↓ 24 him↑self↓ *w.o.* them 26 fear *w.o.* feel 30 ↑itself↓ 35 short⟨er⟩ 37–42 brutally . . . . Howells. [*in margin and across salutation, first page*]

7 June 1904, London, to Samuel L. Clemens. 2 pp. A.l.s. CU.

9 June 1904, London, to Samuel L. Clemens. 2 pp. A.l.s. CU.

5 that *w.o.* the 9 America⟨t⟩ 10 wife *w.o. illeg.*

15–18 consecrated .... Howells. [*in margin and across salutation, first page*]

24 June 1904, Oxford, to Herbert G. Wells. 2 pp. A.l.s. IU.

　3 ⟨Mr.⟩ Wells　8 a great] a a great　14 things.⟨"⟩
15–17 with .... Howells [*in margin, second page*]

26 June 1904, Oxford, to Aurelia H. Howells and Anne H. Fréchette. 3 pp. A.l.s. MH.

　2 ↑June↓ [*in another hand*]　17 Christ Church *w.o.* Christ.
29 you⟨r⟩　32 Of ... print. [*in margin, first page*]

25 September 1904, London, to Aurelia H. Howells. 4 pp. A.l.s. MH.

　10 Mediterranean *w.o.* mediterranean　16 ⟨when⟩ ↑were↓
23 Har-/bor *w.o. illeg.*/bor　23 ↑from Norway↓　31–32 I ... winter. [*in margin, first page*]

14 October 1904, San Remo, to Aurelia H. Howells. 3 pp. A.l.s. MH.

　6 Friday *w.o.* S　20–22 surprisingly .... Will. [*in margin, first page*; *followed by* ⟨over⟩]　23–25 We ... London. [*on verso of first page*] 24 the *w.o. illeg.*

4 November 1904, San Remo, to Charles E. Norton. 4 pp. A.l.s. MH.

　7 ↑both↓　11 ↑at↓　15 put⟨*illeg.*⟩　24 in] in in　31 us *w.o.* ye 37–38 like ... in [*in margin, first page*]　38–40 regards .... Howells. [*in margin, second page*]

30 November 1904, San Remo, to Frederick A. Duneka. 2 pp. A.l.s. NNPM.

　17 ↑if↓
[*Below signature, in another hand, an illegible name; possibly* W Hartman]

12 December 1904, San Remo, to S. Weir Mitchell. 6 pp. A.l.s. PU.

　2 12 *w.o.* 11　8 come *w.o.* comy　16 ⟨family⟩ language
18 have *w.o.* has　21 usual *w.o.* as　24 Anther's *w.o.* Author's
30 ⟨ask⟩ answer　32 sometimes with *w.o. illeg.* with
41 honesty ⟨*illeg.*⟩　45 ⟨failu⟩ later　47 ↑the↓　52 can't ⟨get him to⟩

53 ↑could↓ 57 ⟨*illeg.*⟩ solved 58 ↑we shall↓ 59 ↑shall↓
59 find *w.o. illeg.* 59 out *w.o.* in 59 Metchnikoff's *w.o.* Metchnifoff's

27 December 1904, San Remo, to Edmund C. Stedman. 2 pp. A.l.s. NN.

29 December 1904, San Remo, to John Hay. 2 pp. A.l.s. RPB.

6 January 1905, San Remo, to Elizabeth Jordan. 2 pp. A.l.s. NN.

4 ↑letter,↓ 8 ↑now,↓ 10 amusing *w.o. illeg.*

9 January 1905, San Remo, to Thomas S. Perry. 4 pp. A.l.s. MeWC.

3 dear *w.o.* Dear 5 would] would would
7 Gordyeyeff *w.o.* Gordieyeff 8 wish the] wish the wish the 8 ↑people↓
18 ⟨even⟩ politically 13 ↑see↓ 14 ⟨p⟩as 16 ↑such↓
22 specifically *w.o.* speciffcally 29–30 Yours . . . Howells. [*in margin, first page*]

5 February 1905, San Remo, to Edmund C. Stedman. 4 pp. A.l.s. NNC.

¹7 week *w.o. illeg.* 21 stone *w.o.* br 23 and ↑the↓
24–25 ↑of a guide↓

12 February 1905, San Remo, to Joseph A. Howells. 3 pp. A.l.s. MH.

4 ↑is↓ 23 We expect] Wexpect

24 May 1905, New York, to Sir George Trevelyan. 3 pp. A.l.s. Location of MS. unknown. Xerox copy at InU.

5 Wedding] Widding 10 ↑in↓ 29–31 my . . . find [*in margins, second page*] 31–37 how . . . . Howells. [*in margin and across beginning of letter, first page*] 38 My . . . U.S.A. [*in margin, third page*]

11 June 1905, Kittery Point, to Charles E. Norton. 4 pp. A.l.s. MH.

11 have ⟨*illeg.*⟩ 12 their *w.o.* s 18 but *w.o.* out 22 ↑in↓
23 re↑↓beginning 25 America⟨n⟩

11 June 1905, Kittery Point, to Anne H. Fréchette. 4 pp. A.l.s. MH.

8 ↑my↓ 12 not ⟨be⟩ 19 After *w.o.* I 26 do-nothings *w.o.* don
27–32 dentisting . . . . Howells. [*in margin and across beginning of letter, first page*]

16 June 1905, Kittery Point, to Sarah Orne Jewett. 2 pp. A.l.s. MH.

5 July 1905, Kittery Point, to Thomas S. Perry. 2 pp. A.l.s. MeWC.

6 July 1905, Kittery Point, to Robert U. Johnson. 1 p. A.l.s. NRU.
[*In upper left corner, in another hand*: Personal]

5 August 1905, Kittery Point, to Mrs. Hamer. 2 pp. A.l.s. George Arms, Albuquerque, N. M.

20 August 1905, Kittery Point, to David Douglas. MS. located at Kirkurd House, Kirkurd, West Linton, Peeblesshire, England, but unavailable for use as copy-text. *Life in Letters*, II, 209–10.

20 August 1905, Kittery Point, to Hamlin Garland. 2 pp. T.l.s. CLSU.

   4 I *w.o.* i   8 ↑except↓   9 every *w.o.* any   12 ↑is↓
13 here the *w.o.* here te   16 chanced ⟨to⟩ to   16 I felt *w.o.* i fett
19 ↑in↓   20 on *w.o.* in   22 Russians *w.o.* Russiens
29 *obliged w.o. obleged*   34 in *w.o.* it   40 ↑have↓   44 ↑out↓

3 September 1905, Kittery Point, to Aurelia H. Howells. 1 p. T.l.s. MH.

   6 had ⟨a⟩   8 h⟨a⟩ot   13 Laura Mitchell *w.o.* Laure mitchell
13 Columbus] Columbss   13 and] end *w.o.* egd   16 and] and and
16 ↑us↓

10 September 1905, Kittery Point, to Charles E. Norton. 8 pp. A.l.s. MH.

   14 for *w.o. illeg.*   33 ↑them↓

10 September 1905, Kittery Point, to Aurelia H. Howells. 2 pp. T.l.s. MH.

   5 shock; *w.o.* shock: 5 so *w.o.* to   7 package *w.o.* packege
8 was] uas   9 almos|t| 9 living *w.o.* livinm
11 home-/sick *w.o.* homes/sick   12 That *w.o.* that   16 nature *w.o.* tature
16 ↑her↓   17 the *w.o.* she   23 made *w.o. illeg.*   23 have *w.o. illeg.*
25 10 *w.o.* to   26 speech *w.o.* speegh   30 America] america
31 ⟨sho⟩ shown   34 he did] h / he did   35–36 entirely *w.o.* intirely
37 removal *w.o.* removel   39 quite *w.o. illeg.*   44 for you *w.o.* to you

24 September 1905, West Brattleborough, Vermont, to Aurelia H. Howells. 2 pp. A.l.s. MH.

   4 Friday *w.o.* Saturday   10 they died] they they died   14 you,] ∼„

29 September 1905, Kittery Point, to Joseph A. Howells. 1 p. T.l.s. MH.

   3 dispatch. *w.o.* dispatche   4 in the] in in the   5 it *w.o.* in
5 apparent-/ly *w.o.* apparentl/ly   6 ⟨f⟩ from   7 ⟨$500⟩ ↑$1500↓
7 $150 *w.o.* $300   8 ↑there↓   11 I *w.o.* i   11 the *w.o.* The
15 letter *w.o.* lettr   17 grammar *w.o.* grammer
22 literature *w.o.* literarure   22 they *w.o.* that   26 have ↑a↓
26 pleasant *w.o.* pliasent

25 October 1905, Kittery Point, to Madison J. Cawein. 2 pp. A.l.s. KyLoF.

6 December 1905, New York, to Charles E. Norton. 3 pp. A.l.s. MH.

   8 ↑to↓   17 affection] affection-/

10 December 1905, New York, to Thomas S. Perry. Location of MS. unknown. *Life in Letters*, II, 213–15.

15 December 1905, New York, to Frederick A. Duneka. 3 pp. A.l.s. George Arms, Albuquerque, N. M.

   14 ⟨applicable⟩ fanciful   15 Alden *w.o.* Clem

19 December 1905, New York, to Samuel L. Clemens. 3 pp. A.l.s. CU.

   7 ↑volume↓   10 impracticable] impractiable *w.o.* impossible
14 ↑other↓   15 ↑be↓   15 five *w.o.* four   16 could *w.o.* would

19 December 1905, New York, to S. Weir Mitchell. 3 pp. A.l.s. PU.

   14 ↑were↓   19 ↑them.↓   19 in⟨t⟩   20 be free] be be free
23 ↑thing↓   28 to, *w.o.* to!

30 December 1905, New York, to Aurelia H. Howells. 3 pp. A.l.s. MH.

   7 ⟨possession⟩ ↑use↓   12 You *w.o.* If   25 ↑for us↓   30 you⟨r⟩
30–31 lovingly *w.o.* livingly   31 With *w.o.* Y

4 January 1906, New York, to Joseph A. Howells. 3 pp. A.l.s. MH.

   2 Jan'y *w.o.* De   18 with ⟨*illeg.*⟩   32 which *w.o.* and

6 January 1906, New York, to Aurelia H. Howells. 3 pp. A.l.s. MH.

   16 but *w.o.* and   17 ↑the↓ blocking   20 ⟨down⟩ round

6 January 1906, New York, to Edith Wyatt. 3 pp. A.l.s. ICN.

7 ↑with the others↓   12 ↑could↓ give⟨s⟩   12 nature ⟨of⟩
16 one *w.o.* .   20 the chance *w.o. illeg.* chance

24 January 1906, New York, to Frederick A. Duneka. 4 pp. A.l.s. George
Arms, Albuquerque, N. M.

4 ↑that↓   9 ↑⟨a ... half⟩↓   15 ↑seemed↓   16 ↑(I)↓   18 ↑(II)↓
21 ↑(III)↓   22 ↑one↓   26 ↑not↓   29 ↑public↓

29 January 1906, New York, to Joseph A. Howells. 4 pp. A.l.s. MH.

5 out *w.o.* in   13 sing⟨,⟩   18 weather] wiather   23 regular] regu-/

30 January 1906, New York, to Mildred Howells. 4 pp. A.l.s. MH.

6 ↑at 3.00 p.m.↓   6 had *w.o.* have   14 did↑n't↓   28 profound *w.o. illeg.*

16 February 1906, Atlantic City, to Brander Matthews. 2 pp. A.l.s. NNC.

7 out *w.o.* in   7 ↑thus↓

18 February 1906, Atlantic City, to Charles E. Norton. 4 pp. A.l.s. MH.

6 all *w.o.* alw   7 this *w.o.* the   11–12 ↑than ... Remo,↓
21 February *w.o.* Apr   30 ↑the↓ problem

28 February 1906, Atlantic City, to Samuel L. Clemens. 4 pp. A.l.s.
CSmH.

5 ↑which↓   13 if ⟨we⟩   13 men *w.o.* man   14 The⟨y⟩   16 ↑have↓
17 while *w.o. illeg.*   20 could do, *w.o.* could,   22 ↑your↓
30 the *w.o.* it   33 ↑before↓

11 March 1906, Atlantic City, to Charles E. Norton. 4 pp. A.l.s. MH.

12 ↑there↓   18 ↑me↓

12 March 1906, Atlantic City, to Brander Matthews, 2 pp. A.l.s. NNC.

6 subtlest] sublest   8 ↑you↓   8 North⟨ern⟩   11 direction ⟨*illeg.*⟩
15 ↑will↓

24 March 1906, New York, to Mildred Howells. 2 pp. A.l.s. MH.

8 April 1906, New York, to Samuel L. Clemens. 1 p. A.l.s. CU.

  5 ↑have↓ 7 You⟨r⟩

8 April 1906, New York, to Aurelia H. Howells. 4 pp. A.l.s. MH.

  13 ↑Twain and↓ 13 his *w.o. t* 27 going *w.o. illeg.*

16 April 1906, New York, to Joseph A. Howells. 4 pp. A.l.s. MH.

  5 ↑I↓ 5 a [*added in margin*] 14 roast ⟨to⟩ 16 them ↑in↓
16 our] ou 19 3 *w.o.* a 31 ↑now↓ 36 ⟨rook⟩ robins 38 will *w.o.* with

19 April 1906, New York, to Samuel L. Clemens. 2 pp. A.l.s. CU.

  4 ↑deal↓

20 April 1906, New York, to Joseph A. Howells. 4 pp. A.l.s. MH.

  6 ↑out↓ 12 ⟨for⟩ ↑to↓ the 13 for *w.o.* as 15 ↑not↓ 23 be? *w.o.* be,
26–27 government *w.o.* gov't 42 ⟨now⟩ *no*

24 April 1906, New York, to Francis Wilson. 2 pp. A.l.s. OFH.

8 May 1906, New York, to Theodora Sedgwick. 4 pp. A.l.s. MH.

  8 the *w.o.* a 11 ↑own↓ 16 ↑in↓ 19 but *w.o.* and

17 May 1906, New York, to Samuel S. McClure. 2 pp. A.l.s. InU.

  9 harp *w.o.* b 10 funerals⟨,⟩!

19 May 1906, New York, to Herbert G. Wells. 2 pp. A.l.s. IU.

  6 Soak *w.o.* C 8 a⟨n⟩

21 May 1906, New York, to Elizabeth Jordan. 4 pp. A.l.s. NN.

  16 ⟨do. on the Mother's.⟩ ↑The Young Girl.↓ 18 could *w.o.* would
26 Janvier, ⟨Mr. Roy Gibson, Mr⟩ 32 ⟨into⟩ really
42 ⟨of⟩ ↑bearing upon↓

24 May 1906, New York, to Samuel L. Clemens. 1 p. A.l.s. CU.

  1 Regent.] ∼.,.

27 May 1906, Kittery Point, to David A. Munro. 1 p. T.l.s. George Arms, Albuquerque, N. M.

4 Confound *w.o.* confound   6 now *w.o.* Now   8 ↑any other↓
9 dead] ⟨de⟩/dead   9 I *w.o.* i   9–10 appreciation *w.o.* appreciateon
10 your *w.o.* young

17 June 1906, Kittery Point, to Aurelia H. Howells. 2 pp. T.l.s. MH.

5 inch-/es *w.o.* inche/es   11 the costumes *w.o.* tte costumes
12 fine *w.o.* fini   19 ↑like↓ [*in another hand*]
19 and mothers] tnd mothers   20 contemporaries *w.o.* cintemporaries
28 extremely *w.o.* extrecely   30 natural *w.o.* natuhal   31 me, ⟨me,⟩
31 ↑my↓   35 way? *w.o.* way!   38 Sleep *w.o.* sleep   39 because] becaue

20 June 1906, Kittery Point, to Aurelia H. Howells, 1 p. T.l.s. MH.

7 acknowledge *w.o.* ecknowledge   8 them *w.o.* th,m
8 need *w.o. illeg.*   9 find *w.o.* feid   16 promises *w.o.* bromises

24 June 1906, Kittery Point, to Samuel L. Clemens. 2 pp. A.l.s. CU.

10 lustre ↑that↓   11 ↑back↓   14 ↑now↓   14 ↑care↓

27 June 1906, Kittery Point, to Charles E. Norton. 4 pp. A.l.s. MH.

27 June 1906, Kittery Point, to Frederick A. Duneka. 2 pp. T.l.s. MWA.

3 I *w.o.* i   3 mind *w.o.* rind   6 *The w.o. the*   7 ↑an↓
7 was afraid *w.o.* war afraid   8 believe) *w.o.* believed
9 Miss *w.o.* miss   10 ↑then↓   11 incident *w.o.* inlident
11 it up] up⟨on⟩ it [*transposition of words indicated by line*]   17 ↑be↓
19 invented *w.o.* Invented   20 by *w.o.* b: 20 wanting *w.o.* waating
21 *The w.o. the*   23 veritable *w.o. illeg.*   23 ↑case,↓
25 invalid *w.o.* invelid   30 right *w.o.* writ   30 sort *w.o.* somt
32 Jordan] Jordan'⟨s⟩   34 ↑ended↓ within⟨g⟩   34 ⟨of⟩ ↑or↓
36 but ⟨↑that it↓⟩ will   36–37 ↑the memory of↓   37 should *w.o.* short
42 ⟨t⟩ they   42 author *w.o.* writer   45 critical-/ly *w.o.* criticall/ly
46 — *w.o.* "aT   46 ⟨b⟩ be

1 August 1906, Kittery Point, to Samuel L. Clemens. 1 p. T.l. NN.

5 ⟨red⟩ reading   16 indoors *w.o.* ondoors   20 ↑like↓ [*in another hand*]
26 ↑glow↓ after ↑you↓ [*in another hand*]   32 MS. *w.o.* Ms.

6 August 1906, Kittery Point, to Joseph A. Howells. 2 pp. T.l.s. MH.

1 Point *w.o.* point   4 I *w.o.* i   5 feel *w.o.* fiel   5 for *w.o.* fnr
7 said *w.o.* saad   8 by *w.o.* bm   8 unexpectedness *w.o.* unexpectedaess
8 acknowledge *w.o.* acknowlidge   9 For *w.o.* Por   10 hardly *w.o.* harldy
12 acknowledge *w.o.* acknowlede   14 overdoing *w.o.* overdoong
15 overdone *w.o.* ovirdone   17 sure *w.o.* ture   19 particular↑s↓
23 I try *w.o.* i try   25 week-day *w.o.* week.day   30 of *w.o.* op
32 husband *w.o.* huswand   33 it is *w.o.* is in   34 probable *w.o.* brobable
36 punishment *w.o.* punisnment   36 Americans *w.o.* americans
37 ↑and then↓   42 dress ⟨i⟩   42 ↑our↓   43 I believe] I'believe
46 Brothers *w.o.* brothers   47 Mark *w.o.* mark
48 automobile *w.o.* uutomobile   50 ↑of↓   52 whenever *w.o.* whenewer
53   for *w.o.* fos   56 piping *w.o.* peping   58 ↑up,↓   59 The *w.o.* the
60 fin-/ish *w.o.* finis/ish   60 ↑this↓   60 Albert *w.o.* albert
61   Bouncing Bets *w.o.* bouncing bets   61 hou↑s↓e   62 stret↑c↓h
62 half-way *w.o.* half-fay   62 from⟨t⟩

17 August 1906, Kittery Point, to Harper & Brothers. 2 pp. A.l.s. MWA.

4 inland *w.o.* int   7 editor's *w.o.* edito

26 August 1906, Kittery Point, to Theodore Roosevelt. 4 pp. A.l.s. DLC.

[*Above letterhead, first page, in different hands:* [Howells] *and* Aswd /
8–28–06]   7 formal *w.o.* former   11 the intelligence] the the intelligence
19 but *w.o. illeg.*   22 the *w.o.* a

7 September 1906, Kittery Point, to Robert Herrick. 4 pp. A.l.s. ICU.

4 ↑not↓   13 ↑more↓   13–14 the temptations]   the the temptations
14 ↑profession↓   14 to [*added in margin*]

21 November 1906, New York, to Frederick A. Duneka. 1 p. T.l.s. MWA.

7 *"Easier . . . Camel"* [*underlined by hand and connected by a long line
with "It" in line 9*]   8 new *w.o.* niw   8 Traveler *w.o.* traveler
8 Altruria" *w.o.* Altrurian   10 be ⟨n⟩   10 newly *w.o.* wewly
10 do *w.o.* da   11 ⟨ago⟩ ago   13 Delightful *w.o.* Dilightful
14 selling *w.o.* se,ling   15 ⟨le⟩ let   16 the public *w.o.* tte public

25 November 1906, New York, to Joseph A. Howells. 2 pp. T.l.s. MH.

5 article *w.o.* artille   7 with⟨a⟩   9 your *w.o.* four   13 sci⟨*illeg.*⟩/ence
13 I *w.o.* i   14 stomach] stoma/ach   16 tried *w.o.* two   17 lack *w.o.* lak

24 could *w.o.* would   25 seventy *w.o.* teventy   28 Shore *w.o.* shore
29 winter *w.o.* climate   29 before *w.o.* befori   30 what *w.o.* uhat
33 a↑r↓guing   38 buying] buyong   38 interesting *w.o.* intaresting
40 kind *w.o.* gind   40 rich.— *w.o.* rich..   42 th↑r↓own *w.o.* shown
45 women *w.o.* wimen   46 pathetic ⟨t⟩   48 sorrowful.— *w.o.* sorrowful..
48 competitive *w.o. illeg.*   49 endure *w.o.* indure   52 City *w.o.* city
55 st↑r↓inging

2 December 1906, New York, to Charles E. Norton. 3 pp. A.l.s. MH.

   14 Longfellow [*Howells inadvertently crossed the* ll *as if they were* tt]

9 December 1906, New York, to Joseph A. Howells. Location of MS.
unknown. *Life in Letters*, II, 230–31.

30 December 1906, New York, to Aurelia H. Howells. 3 pp. A.l.s. MH.

   4 like⟨ing⟩   7 Besides *w.o.* Besites   12 old in *w.o.* old.
   12 ↑the morning.↓   13 ⟨*illeg.*⟩ for   22 ↑off,↓   30 ↑West↓

31 December 1906, New York, to Edmund C. Stedman. 4 pp. A.l.s. NNC.

   27 take *w.o.* wa   28 46 years] 46 six years

3 January 1907, New York, to Elizabeth Jordan. 2 pp. A.l.s. NN.

   11 help *w.o.* hef

30 January 1907, New York, to Charles E. Norton. 2 pp. A.l.s. MH.

   [*At top of first page, in another hand*: Howells.]
   2 30 *w.o. illeg.*   9 allow *w.o.* own   10 art ⟨and⟩ ↑to↓
   11 ↑—in fact quite—↓   21–22 Perhaps . . . . repetitions. [*in margin and
   across salutation, first page*]

2 February 1907, New York, to Charles E. Norton. 3 pp. A.l.s. MH.

   4 31st *w.o. illeg.*   8 ↑there↓   13 Commemoration *w.o.* commemoration
   14 ↑generally↓

21 February 1907, New York, to Elizabeth Jordan. 2 pp. A.l.s. NN.

21 February 1907, New York, to Samuel L. Clemens. 2 pp. A.l.s. CU.

   4 on a] on a a

24 February 1907, New York, to Joseph A. Howells. 2 pp. T.l.s. MH.

2 1907 *w.o.* 1897   4 weeks *w.o.* wt   5 I suppose *w.o.* i suppose
6 mis-/fortune *w.o.* mis./fortune   15 sorry *w.o.* sorrn   16 City *w.o.* city
17 Pilla *w.o.* Pella   17 on *w.o.* in   19 credit *w.o.* cridit
20 immunity *w.o.* immunitn   26 I *w.o.* *illeg.*   26 God *w.o.* god
28 together *w.o.* togather   30 twelve w.o. twilve
31 ↑Needle." ... renewal↓ [*handwritten directly beneath a canceled passage, now illegible*]   32 speculations *w.o.* speslttions
33 book *w.o.* fook   33 life ⟨i⟩   34 succeed⟨d⟩   39 Thaw *w.o.* Thau
40 sent *w.o.* send   41 tell ⟨w⟩   44 Will [*appears to have been inserted above full signature*]

1 March 1907, New York, to Edmund C. Stedman. 3 pp. A.l.s. NN.

14 before.] ∼   21–22 ↑to think that↓   22 ↑was↓   23 ↑we ... make.↓
24 ↑of↓   25 rival⟨.⟩   29 this *w.o.* it.   35–37 What .... morning. [*in margin and across salutation, first page*]   37 sent ⟨illeg.⟩

4 March 1907, New York, to Alice Longfellow. 3 pp. A.l.s. Longfellow National Historic Site, Cambridge, Mass.

12 I might *w.o.* a might   20 of [*added in margin*]

10 March 1907, New York, to Henry B. Fuller. 2 pp. T.l.s. ICarbS.

14 Brand *w.o.* Brant   17 smooth⟨e⟩   [*In upper left corner, second page:*—2—H.B.F.]

10 March 1907, New York, to Henry Arthur Jones. 3 pp. T.l.s. NjR.

9 ⟨fallen⟩ ↑lost↓   17 ↑and↓ theatrical   25 this⟨.⟩   30 ⟨had⟩ read
32 ⟨be⟩come   33 par↑r↓oting [*In upper left corner, second and third page:*—2—H.A.J. *and* —3—H.A.J. *respectively*]

13 March 1907, New York, to Joseph A. Howells. 4 pp. T.l.s. MH.

5 anything *w.o.* .nything   5 Satur-/day's *w.o.* Satuur/day's
8 "Science *w.o.* TScience   8 my-/self *w.o.* mys/self
9 in nervous *w.o.* is nervous   13 must *w.o.* musn   14 you *w.o.* ynu
15 ⟨such⟩ equal   16 it *w.o.* is   17 presents *w.o.* *illeg.*
18 comes *w.o.* comer   20 sitt⟨l⟩ing   22 after *w.o.* aftar
23 going *w.o.* gone   25 voyage]woyage   25 possibili-/ *w.o.* possibieit
27 would *w.o.* yould   30 Glamorganshire *w.o.* Glamorganshre
31 Breconshire *w.o.* Checonshire   31 She *w.o.* The   34 for⟨.⟩

36 fotografer's *w.o.* fotofrafer's　39 charming *w.o.* cmarming
44 not try ⟨the⟩ *w.o.* not trn　45 ⟨the⟩ ↑our↓ faith
46 Cambridge *w.o.* drambridge　51 ↑had↓　51 their *w.o.* mn
52 ↑standing↓　52 obituary *w.o.* obituasy　54 ⟨pra⟩ praise
55 ⟨broad⟩ broadside　55 ↑in it↓　60 ⟨fifftn⟩ 50　62 ↑but↓
70 John *w.o.* john　74 ↑the women↓ ⟨con⟩　75 names,⟨,⟩　75 j↑u↓st
75 what *w.o.* waat　75 ⟨Del⟩ Delmas　76 ⟨agr⟩ agree　77 fellow, ⟨b⟩
82 ⟨thig *w.o.* thil⟩ ↑|t|hick↓

17 March 1907, New York, to Brand Whitlock. 2 pp. T.l. NjR.

5 with *w.o.* we　7 I *w.o.* i　11 it *w.o.* is　18 help *w.o.* have
24 forbade ↑me↓　27 this *w.o.* it　27 ↑not↓　28 ⟨little⟩ ↑literary↓
29 done *w.o.* none　29 ⟨ha⟩ half　29 wish *w.o.* wist
34–35 P.S. . . . legislation? [*in Howells' hand*]

6 April 1907, New York, to Brand Whitlock. 2 pp. A.l.s. NjR.

8 destined *w.o.* distined　15 book *w.o.* nov
15–18 publishing . . . . Howells. [*in margin, first page*]

15 April 1907, New York, to Charles E. Norton. 3 pp. T.l.s. MH.

4 ne↑a↓rly　9 are *w.o. illeg.*　11 ↑now↓　11 them ⟨fo⟩
12 though *w.o.* but　13 Godkin *w.o.* godkin　15 only *w.o.* inly
16 be-/ginnings *w.o.* be-/innings　17 before *w.o.* bepore　17 and ⟨i⟩
18 believe *w.o.* believwe　22 which *w.o.* thich　26 used *w.o.* ueed
27 often *w.o.* ofteo　28 Godkin *w.o.* godkin　31 thing↑s↓
31 wanted *w.o. illeg.*　32 Na-/tion *w.o.* Natio/tion　33 seem↑s↓
33 years]yeahs　35 sug-/gestion *w.o.* sugge/gestion
35 named *w.o.* nemed　36 re-/fused *w.o.* refu/fused
37 why you *w.o.* why yor　37 paragraph *w.o.* paragragraph
41 but *w.o.* bun　43 winter *w.o.* wnnter　44 Children *w.o.* children
45 the *w.o.* nhe　45 fancy *w.o.* fantn　47 your *w.o.* nour
48 dreams *w.o.* dreamer　54 that *w.o.* than
55 mo-/ments *w.o.* mome/ments　55 sp↑r↓ing　59 though↑t↓
62 ⟨tha⟩ that　62 should *w.o.* shonld　63 him⟨,⟩　63 his ⟨f⟩
64 risk.] ∼ ..

31 July 1907, Kittery Point, to Mildred Howells. 1 p. T.l.s. MH.

2 Pilla *w.o.* Pill.　3 Al↑d↓riching　8 let-/ters *w.o.* lette/ters
10 lemon-sour *w.o.* lemnn-sour　10 hour *w.o.* oour　13 Poppy [*initial
letter smeared*]

2 August 1907, Kittery Point, to Frederick A. Duneka. 2 pp. A.l.s. George Arms, Albuquerque, N. M.

6 ⟨to⟩ ↑use↓   7 ↑I enclose, and which↓

18 August 1907, Detroit, to Joseph A. Howells. 2 pp. A.l.s. MH.

5 firing *w.o.* fired   5 ↑&↑   9 out *w.o.* in   10 come *w.o. illeg.*
17 damp⟨,⟩

22 September 1907, Kittery Point, to Charles E. Norton. 3 pp. A.l.s. MH.

5 train *w.o.* way   9 pestiferous *w.o.* noise   10 ↑myself↓   27 ↑winter↓

3 October 1907, New York, to Samuel L. Clemens. 3 pp. A.l.s. CU.

6 October 1907, Kittery Point, to Joseph A. Howells. 3 pp. A.l.s MH.

13 ↑do↓   19 and *w.o.* but   25 ↑can↓   26 ↑a↓ New York
32 too ⟨ho⟩

9 October 1907, Kittery Point, to Brander Matthews. 3 pp. A.l.s. NNC.

4 wins *w.o. illeg.*   9 tho'⟨t⟩   10 like⟨d⟩
14 rather than seek] rather seek   20 excused *w.o.* excepted

13 October 1907, Kittery Point, to Charles E. Norton. 3 pp. A.l.s. MH.

5 ↑choosing↓   16 tell you] tell you you   19 with *w.o.* for
23 give ↑you↓   28–31 Pilla . . . . Howells. [*in margin and across saluta-tion, first page*]

29 October 1907, Kittery Point, to William R. Thayer. 4 pp. A.l.s. MH.

4 longer *w.o.* longin   11 Whittier] Whitteir   27 highest *w.o. illeg.*

21 November 1907, New York, to S. Weir Mitchell. 3 pp. A.l.s. PU.

[*At top of first page, in another hand*: 6th Ave & 28th St.]
8 ↑thing↓   16 bring *w.o.* —   30 ⟨dream⟩ nighty

22 November, 1907, New York, to Aurelia H. Howells. 3 pp. A.l.s. MH.

5 betrothed *w.o. illeg.*   14 ↑we↓ ⟨*illeg.*⟩ all

13 December 1907, New York, to Frederick A. Duneka. 1 p. A.l.s. MWA.

20 December 1907, New York, to Augustus Thomas. 2 pp. A.l.s. NjR.

  12 formed *w.o.* forms

12 January 1908, on board M.S. "Caronia," to Aurelia H. Howells.
12 pp. A.l.s. MH.

  7 ↑island↓   11 moss *w.o. illeg.*   14 ⟨*illeg.*⟩ lines   17 ↑public↓
18 ↑out↓   23 ↑the race↓   24 ⟨t⟩like   25 ⟨gray⟩ ↑lead↓
34 ⟨*illeg.*⟩meal   37 sleds *w.o.* steds   41 calld ⟨them⟩
42 one of the] ↑one of the↓ the   47 ⟨*illeg.*⟩ vine   52 boys *w.o.* boat
52 ↑boats↓   58 when ⟨they⟩   59 burden⟨s⟩   61 ↑beauty↓
69 She *w.o.* It   76 ↑⟨at Rome⟩↓   80 ⟨are⟩ all join ⟨lo⟩

27 January 1908, Rome, to Frederick A. Duneka. 2 pp. A.l.s. George
Arms, Albuquerque, N. M.

  8 me *w.o.* ,   9 antiquities *w.o.* modernities   13 beautiful *w.o.* about

3 February 1908, Rome, to Charles E. Norton. 4 pp. A.l.s. MH.

  4 doors *w.o.* days   5 throat and *w.o.* throat *illeg.*   5–6 ↑wife ... I↓
28 ⟨Dad⟩ Dante   34–35 Somebody ... use. [*in margin, third page*]
35–36 When ... wonder [*in margin, fourth page*]   36–38 that .... If I [*in
margin, first page*]   38–41 were .... Howells. [*in margin, second page*]

4 February 1908, Rome, to Samuel L. Clemens. 4 pp. A.l.s. CU.

  2 4th *w.o.* 5th   10 but ⟨yo⟩   18 ↑give↓ Aldrich's

5 February 1908, Rome, to George O. Trevelyan. Location of MS. unknown. *Life in Letters*, II, 249–50.

15 February 1908, Rome, to Aurelia H. Howells. Location of MS. unknown. *Life in Letters*, II, 252–53.

  20–21 Björnson] Björnsen

27 February 1908, Rome, to Bjornstjerne Bjornson. 3 pp. A.l.s. Univer-
sitetsbiblioteket, Oslo.

  [*In upper right corner, first page, in another hand*: Howells]
5 ↑already↓   5 ↑have↓   9 me ... back [*nearly one line obliterated*]
9 whe|n so|me   11 hats ⟨off⟩   16 wife ... s [*two or three lines obliter-
ated*]   20 can [*uncertain reading because of torn margin; possibly an-
other word obliterated*]   21 you|?| 22 *Malavogli*|a,|

12 April 1908, Leghorn, to Charles E. Norton. 3 pp. A.l.s. MH.

   7 he can *w.o.* t can   13 twelve *w.o.* twelves   14 ↑in Rome,↓
14 the *w.o.* with   18 find ⟨I⟩   20 ↑think↓   29 so.⟨—⟩

9 May 1908, Paris, to Aurelia H. Howells. 3 pp. A.l.s. MH.

   23 lot *w.o.* sol

23 May 1908, London, to Aurelia H. Howells. 2 pp. A.l.s. MH.

   6 ⟨like⟩ live   11 join *w.o.* are

16 July 1908, Kittery Point, to Charles E. Norton. 4 pp. A.l.s. MH.

   5 but *w.o.* and   17 day *w.o. illeg.*   26 ↑from Rome,↓   28 edition.] ∼
31 ⟨f⟩ ↑if↓   35 my love] my my love

2 August 1908, Kittery Point, to Henry James. 3 pp. T.l.s. MH.

   1 Point *w.o.* point   3 I *w.o.* i   6 prefaces *w.o. illeg.*   6 ↑in↓
7 prefaces *w.o.* prefeces   8 all⟨,⟩   9 took *w.o. illeg.*
10 -censure *w.o.* -sensure   11 analyses *w.o.* analysis
11–12 ↑most . . . just,↓   13 ↑the↓   15 on-/ly *w.o.* onl/ly
16 and *w.o.* nnd   17 well *w.o.* we,1   19 ⟨bu⟩ but
19 last half *w.o.* lash halb   20 ↑them↓   21 ↑to↓ you
22 ↑have↓ imagined ⟨y⟩   25 them— *w.o.* them.   25–26 —or . . . them! [*in
Howells' hand*]   27 of a book] of ⟨book⟩ of a book   27 I did *w.o.* r did
33 ⟨ag⟩ ago   34 ↑the↓   35 reflex *w.o.* reflek   35 youthful *w.o.* youtheul
36 has *w.o.* ias   37 ⟨o⟩ old   44 very *w.o.* wery   44 ⟨sa⟩ sadder
47 ⟨had⟩ ↑Wm.↓   48 ⟨li⟩ lift   54 house *w.o.* touse
56 of nook *w.o. illeg.* nook   58 extreme-/ly *w.o.* extremel/ly   59 ⟨t⟩ to
61 the *w.o.* tee   61 Cornish, ⟨,⟩   62 Ver-/mont *w.o.* Vermo/mont
63 livelier *w.o.* livelies   64 ⟨it⟩ ↑Cornish↓   65 Saint *w.o.* saint
66 all meet *w.o.* all eeet   67 It *w.o.* it   67 hot *w.o.* hoh
71 Sundays ⟨ago⟩   71 since *w.o.* sinme   79 walking *w.o.* welking

15 August 1908, Kittery Point, to Samuel L. Clemens. 2 pp. T.l.s. CU.

   3 York *w.o.* Yory   7 Abroad *w.o.* abroad   13 ⟨i⟩ I
16 reflection *w.o.* refeec   22 enough *w.o.* enoum   24 ⟨y⟩ you

24 September 1908, Kittery Point, to Joseph A. Howells. 2 pp. T.l.s. MH.

   5 hurricane] huuricane   6 regret *w.o.* segret   7 they *w.o.* yhey
7 sent *w.o.* seet   8 hurried *w.o.* humried   17 houses *w.o.* houees

18 thought] though   27 children; *w.o.* children.
42 peculiarity *w.o.* peculiartty   43 are⟨.⟩   44 proverbial] prsverbial
48 Wagon *w.o.* Wagin   50 of *w.o.* oa   52 fun *w.o.* pun
53 New *w.o. illeg.*   58 canvass *w.o.* canwass   59 Elinor *w.o.* elinor
60 two *w.o.* too   61 love *w.o.* lovi

11 October 1908, Kittery Point, to Charles E. Norton. 3 pp. A.l.s. MH.

[*Above dateline, first page, in another hand*: W. D. Howells]
4 vain *w.o. illeg.*   18 well-read⟨er⟩   24 who⟨m⟩

12 October 1908, Kittery Point, to William S. Braithwaite. 2 pp. A.l.s. KyU.*

13 because *w.o.* **best**

30 October 1908, Boston, to S. Weir Mitchell. 3 pp. A.l.s. PU.

16 ↑from↓   18 visited *w.o.* ca   19 America⟨n⟩   26 historical *w.o. illeg.*
28 Revolution *w.o.* **revolution**   28 but *w.o.* **and**
32–33 appreciable *w.o. illeg.*   35 Quakers *w.o.* H
42 Affectionately *w.o.* affectionately

16 November 1908, New York, to Elizabeth Jordan. 3 pp. A.l.s. ViU.

7 ↑it↓ interests   13–14 is commonly] is a commonly   19 ⟨but⟩ some

18 November 1908, New York, to Mildred Howells. 1 p. A.l.s. MH.

25 November 1908, New York, to Samuel L. Clemens. 2 pp. A.l.s. CU.

15–18 thing . . . . Howells. [*in margin, first page*]

6 December 1908, New York, to Anne H. Fréchette. 4 pp. A.l.s. MH.

9 beautiful⟨,⟩   14 health ⟨*illeg.*⟩   23 brought ↑it↓   28 ↑will↓
30 author⟨s⟩

31 January 1909, New York, to Sara Norton. 4 pp. A.l.s. MH.

17 father ⟨*illeg.*⟩   27 process⟨es⟩

16 February 1909, New York, to Robert Herrick. 1 p. T.l.s. ICU.

2 1909 *w.o.* 9909   4 ⟨r⟩ ready   12 off *w.o.* over   15 as *w.o. illeg.*
16 was ⟨*right*⟩   19 with ⟨th⟩   19 and *w.o.* with   23 ↑your↓
25 does *w.o. illeg.*   27 depreciate *w.o. illeg.*

1 March 1909, New York, to William W. Howells. Location of MS. unknown. *Life in Letters*, II, 263.

7 March 1909, New York, to Brander Matthews. 3 pp. A.l.s. NNC.

7 beneficent *w.o.* beneficence   11 ↑it↓   16 bedevils him, [*Howells had first written* bedevils, *and then added in the margin* him, *without canceling the first comma*]   19 one⟨'⟩s

12 March 1909, New York, to Samuel L. Clemens. 2 pp. A.l.s. CU.

14 March 1909, New York, to Henry B. Fuller. 2 pp. T.l.s. OOxM.

6 delightful *w.o.* dilightful   7 of *w.o.* od   14 wanted *w.o.* waoted   15 languid *w.o.* laoguid   16 write *w.o. illeg.*   18 so.] ∼..

24 March 1909, Redding, Connecticut, to Elinor M. Howells. 3 pp. A.l.s. MH.

4 Sunapee *w.o.* sunapee

13 April 1909, New York, to David A. Munro. 2 pp. A.l.s. George Arms, Albuquerque, N M.

5 ↑him↓   5 him.] ∼   7 dead ⟨of⟩ ↑as↓

26 April 1909, Kittery Point, to Elinor M. Howells. 3 pp. A.l.s. MH.

19 minute.] ∼   21 ⟨up⟩ us   28 ↑two↓   28–31 this. . . . Papa [*in margin and across salutation, first page*]

12 May 1909, New York, to Henry E. Rood. 2 pp. A.l.s. NcD.

9 June 1909, New York, to Frederick A. Duneka. 2 pp. A.l.s. NNC.

5 ↑must↓   5 ↑of↓

19 June 1909, Kittery Point, to Frederick A. Duneka. 2 pp. T.l.s. MWA.

9 typical *w.o.* tnpical   11 advantage *w.o.* adventage
12 state *w.o.* aate   13 repugnance *w.o.* repuggant
15 ground *w.o.* ghound   22 ⟨a⟩ my work   23 ↑my↓ life
23 shall *w.o.* ahall

23 June 1909, Kittery Point, to Mrs. S. E. Pearson, 1 p. A.l.s. Joseph W. P. Frost, Kittery Point, Me.

4 July 1909, Kittery Point, to Joseph A. Howells. 3 pp. T.l.s. MH.

4 ⟨quite⟩ somebody   9 stormed *w.o.* stoemed   11 Grove *w.o. grove*
14 grouping *w.o. illeg.*   15 ⟨fou⟩ four   15 ones *w.o. illeg.*
16 pages *w.o.* papes   16 of the *w.o. illeg.* the   17 edition *w.o.* editeon
20 for I *w.o.* por I   20 fortunately *w.o.* fortonately   21 ⟨sh⟩ should
22 ↑with↓   24 them ⟨c⟩   24 chronologically] chronologicallly
25 ⟨*illeg.*⟩ years   25 and I *w.o. illeg.* I   25 only to] onlyto
27 tombs.] ∼..   28 wish *w.o.* wash
28 literary material *w.o.* literary materia,   30 hold *w.o.* hild
32 autobiography *w.o. illeg.*   36 ↑or do both↓   37 tenants?⟨,⟩
37 business *w.o.* buseness   37 ⟨ti⟩ ties   38 have] hawe   39 now] nou
40 he *w.o.* it   43 ⟨GM⟩ ↑12↓   45 my *w.o.* mn
49 of K.P. *w.o.* if a.P.   50 would *w.o.* wiuld
54 Californian's *w.o.* dalefornian's   55 word *w.o.* worl
55 probably *w.o.* poobably   55 dead ⟨*illeg.*⟩   56 which *w.o.* wheih

13 July 1909, Kittery Point, to Thomas W. Higginson. 3 pp. A.l.s. MH.

5 different ⟨sp⟩   14 ⟨f⟩ our   21 ⟨it⟩ isn't   23–25 ↑(I know . . . life.)↓

25 July 1909, Kittery Point, to Frederick A. Duneka. 2 pp. T.l.s. George Arms, Albuquerque, N. M.

2 Duneka *w.o. illeg.*   6 Wedding] Wedd/ding   6 ↑one↓
6 ↑Austrian↓   7 ↑one↓   15 Austria *w.o.* Asstria
19 Austrian *w.o.* austrian   20 lit-/tle w.o. littl/le
23 All Right *w.o.* all right   24 sincerely *w.o. illeg.*

20 August 1909, Carlsbad, to Henry James. 3 pp. A.l.s. MH.

9 Doctor *w.o.* doctor

25 August 1909, Carlsbad, to Samuel L. Clemens. 2 pp. A.l. CU.

7 ⟨pre⟩ prying   13 ⟨Tol⟩ Tyrolean   18 boils ⟨at⟩
20–22 the whole . . . . real. [*in margin and across letterhead, first page*]

28 August 1909, Carlsbad, to Eden Phillpotts. 2 pp. A.l. Location of MS. unknown. Xerox copy at InU.

22–23 Yours . . . Howells. [*not on xerox of holograph, but printed in* Life in Letters, *II, 269–70*]

15 September 1909, Salisbury, to Elinor M. Howells. 3 pp. A.l.s. MH.

 12 from *w.o.* in   18 convent, ⟨)⟩   23 ⟨⟨)⟩ He   24 almost *w.o.* all
29 die⟨d⟩   31 Tuesday . . . . [*six lines canceled and made mostly illegible,
probably by Mildred Howells while preparing* Life in Letters. *The text
can be tentatively read as follows*: You Man went home yesterday; I
think nothing was settled, but unless Pilla decides something we shall
not go to Portsey—600 miles from London. She doesn't seem troubled,
and expects to see him in London again.]

16 September 1909, Torquay, to Elinor M. Howells. 3 pp. A.l.s. MH.

 8 old *w.o.* ne   23 by [*added in margin*]   24 ↑how↓
24 would *w.o.* could   31 *Pil . . . day. [*in margin, second page*]

17 September 1909, Torquay, to Elinor M. Howells. 4 pp. A.l.s. MH.

 12–13 *de-*/↑*-centes familien program.*↓   19 ↑Young↓   22 at the] ∼ ∼.
26 Wales, . . . [*more than six lines canceled and made mostly illegible,
probably by Mildred Howells while preparing* Life in Letters. *The text
can be tentatively read as follows*: and P——— (down from London) is
doubtful. There is nothing of ——— at the (*five words illeg.*) but P.
and ———, *but if* she wants to go she shall.]

24 October 1909, New York, to Henry James. 3 pp. A.l.s. MH.

 13 ↑her↓   16 "Putnam" ⟨*illeg.*⟩   19 ↑and . . . out↓   19 out.] ∼

5 November 1909, New York, to Samuel L. Clemens. 3 pp. A.l.s. CU.

 2 5 *w.o.* 1   9 you⟨r⟩   22 divinely *w.o.* divined   22 day *w.o. illeg.*
25 work?" "How] work? "How   25 "How do] How do⟨*illeg.*⟩

5 November 1909, New York, to Aurelia H. Howells. 2 pp. T.l.s. MH.

 4 I was *w.o.* i was   7 now] nou   10 ↑an↓   14 head *w.o.* hat
15 ↑wants↓   25 arm *w.o.* rrm   26 brings *w.o.* briogs
27 rheumatism] rhesmatism   28 ⟨rea⟩ read   34 think *w.o.* thing
34 unworthy *w.o.* unworthn   39 understand *w.o.* understaad
41 strange *w.o.* straage   42 could] cosld   42 hous↑e↓keeping [*insertion
in another hand*]   47 on *w.o.* un   52 affectionate *w.o.* affectiinate

2 December 1909, New York, to Robert U. Johnson. 1 p. T.l.s. NRU.

 9 you↑r↓ [*insertion probably in another hand*]
13 hos-/pitality *w.o.* hosp/pitality

25 December 1909, New York, to Henry James. 4 pp. A.l.s. MH.

2 Christmas *w.o. illeg.*   22 ↑out,↓   24 full⟨er⟩   25 —Last [*dash added in margin*]   33 ⟨of⟩ ↑to↓   38–41 home . . . . Howells. [*in margin and across salutation, first page*]

16 January 1910, New York, to Henry James. 3 pp. A.l.s. MH.

7 that ⟨I⟩   11 down *w.o. illeg.*   14 that ⟨all⟩   15 keep ⟨ *you*⟩   26 a⟨n⟩

18 January 1910, New York, to Samuel L. Clemens. 2 pp. A.l.s. CSmH.

[*Above letterhead, first page, in Clemens' hand*: I reckon this spontaneous outburst from the first critic of the day is good to keep, ain't it, Paine? SLC]   8 Section *w.o.* section   9 ↑three↓   9 Years *w.o.* years [*At bottom of second page, in another hand*: wornout material body on top of your soul.]

1 February 1910, New York, to Henry James. 3 pp. A.l.s. MH.

11 fiction.] fiction.⟨s⟩.   16 ⟨truth⟩ ↑tenderness↓   17 ↑her↓ truth 25 ↑girl↓   25 Bermuda ⟨from⟩   33 submission] submssion

11 February 1910, New York, to Samuel L. Clemens. 3 pp. A.l.s. CU.

6 ↑will↓   6–7 number⟨.⟩   ↑of the N. American↓   7 American.] ∼ 10 do *w.o. illeg.*   22 ⟨writ⟩ sent

28 February 1910, New York, to Frederick A. Duneka. 2 pp. A.l.s. NN.

11 begin⟨ning⟩   14 would ⟨h⟩

8 March 1910, New York, to Henry James. 3 pp. A.l.s. MH.

10 cable *w.o. illeg.*   14 ↑of the doctor↓   20 for *w.o.* to 25 ⟨back⟩ give   26–30 has . . . . Howells. [*in margin, first page*]

9 March 1910, New York, to Harriet T. Upton. 3 pp. A.l.s. OClWHi.

11 also⟨*illeg.*⟩   22 ↑we↓ all   29 ↑not↓   29 but *w.o.* and

27 March 1910, New York, to Hamlin Garland. 3 pp. A.l.s. CLSU.

4 ↑"Cava↑na↑gh"↓   9 the epoch *w.o.* an epoch   16 ↑so well↓ 17 ⟨you⟩ ↑than you↓   18 ↑you↓ owe

10 April 1910, New York, to Aurelia H. Howells and Anne H. Fréchette. 3 pp. T.l.s. MH.

   3 Girls *w.o.* gircs   5 him of *w.o.* him op   13 though ⟨I⟩ 20 regrets *w.o.* segrets   21 insensate *w.o.* insensete   25 but *w.o.* aut 25–26 treat-/ment *w.o.* treatm/ment   27 you girls] you girls you girls 32 Especially *w.o.* Especialln   34 character *w.o.* charatter 35 but *w.o.* bst

20 April 1910, New York, to Frederick A. Duneka. 1 p. A.l.s. MWA.

8 May 1910, New York, to Aurelia H. Howells and Anne H. Fréchette. 2 pp. A.l.s. MH.

13 May 1910, New York, to Aurelia H. Howells and Anne H. Fréchette. 2 pp. A.l.s. MH.

   4 ↑again↓   7 ↑go↓   13 ↑for↓

1 June 1910, Boston, to Frederick A. Duneka. 2 pp. A.l.s. MWA.

   2 1st *w.o.* 2   5 ⟨left⟩ ↑sent↓   8 of *w.o.* as   9 ↑would↓ 12–15 Roosevelt meeting . . . . respected. [*Howells added and underlined in margin: very private*]   14 ↑all that↓   17 ⟨would *w.o. illeg.*⟩ ↑would↓ 21 ↑the↓

8 June 1910, Boston, to William James. Location of MS. unknown. *Life in Letters*, II, 284–85.

9 June 1910, Boston, to Joseph A. Howells. 3 pp. A.l.s. MH.

   20 been *w.o.* book

9 June 1910, Boston, to Henry James. 2 pp. A.l.s. MH.

   11 wish⟨es⟩   12 ↑of↓   13 ↑over↓

1 July 1910, London, to Henry James. 3 pp. A.l.s. MH.

   4 thing *w.o.* think   11 ghostliness *w.o.* ghastliness   20 ↑if↓

5 July 1910, London, to Joseph A. Howells. 3 pp. A.l.s. MH.

   9 Variety *w.o.* variety   13 grieves *w.o.* gries   21 ↑you↓

July 1910, London, to Joseph H. Twichell. 2 pp. A.l. CtY.

5 ↑written↓ 6 ↑praying↓ 12 getti|ng| 17 too. [*complimentary clos-ing and signature excised*]

25 July 1910, London, to Mr. Savage. 2 pp. A.l.s. NRU.

5 see ↑you↓ 15 be *w.o.* me

27 July 1910, London, to Edmund W. Gosse. 2 pp. A.l.s. British Library.

27 July 1910, London, to Thomas S. Perry. 3 pp. A.l.s. MeWC.

10 with *w.o.* here 10 ↑us↓ and ⟨fol⟩ 12 Pilla, but *w.o.* Pilla.)
14 home *w.o.* hope 18 farm- *w.o.* fame- 20 ⟨at⟩ en 22 ↑met↓
24 ↑the↓ 25 to three *w.o.* two far 27 ↑or prancers,↓ 29 ↑her↓
34–35 pageant . . . . of [*in margin, third page*] 35–36 Merry . . . . this [*in margin, second page*] 36–39 scandalous . . . . W.D.H. [*in margin, first page*] [*Below signature, in another hand*: Yes. J.]

7 October 1910, New York, to Percy W. MacKaye. 2 pp. A.l.s. NhD.

9 October 1910, New York, to Alice French. 2 pp. A.l.s. ICN.

1 *130 . . . Street* [*embossed letterhead*] 2 9 *w.o.* 1 6 ↑will↓ be
9 ten *w.o.* f

22 October 1910, New York, to Frederick A. Duneka. 2 pp. A.l.s. MWA.

1 West *w.o.* East 10 ↑been↓

18 November 1910, New York, to Joseph A. Howells. 2 pp. T.l.s. MH.

6 remember *w.o.* reember 8 decided] decidad 11 was] war
19 ⟨ch⟩ child 20 Fa-fa *w.o.* F.-fa 25 and I *w.o.* and *illeg.*
26 everybody] ewerybody 26 I must *w.o.* i must 28 snow *w.o.* nnow
30 ⟨chilly *w.o.* oƐ ʇsǝM oı⟩ ↑chilly↓ 30 such] ruch 30 ⟨w⟩ we

21 November 1910, New York, to Oswald G. Villard. 1 p. A.l.s. MH.

1 30th *w.o.* 57th 6 him up,] ∼, ∼,

23 November 1910, New York, to Thomas W. Higginson. 2 pp. A.l.s. CLSU.

[*In upper left corner, page one, in another hand*: Howells]

6 the meeting *w.o.* a meeting [*In lower left corner, page two, in another hand*: Miss French. / Miss Mary Delan]

25 November 1910, New York, to Joseph A. Howells. 3 pp. A.l.s. MH.

11 ↑you↓   12 ⟨ug⟩ ignorant   18 ⟨*illeg.*⟩ as   26 Harper⟨'⟩s
33–34 This . . . . brother. [*in margin, third page*]   34 do *w.o.* so

11 December 1910, New York, to Joseph A. Howells. 2 pp. T.l.s. MH.

2 December *w.o.* Decamber   6 Annie *w.o.* Anie   7 ⟨c⟩ come
12 I could] I *w.o. illeg.* ⟨↑I↓⟩ could   13 although *w.o .illeg.*
15 broken *w.o.* bnoken   17 there *w.o.* There   18 ⟨time⟩ times
18 forget *w.o.* forgit   25 ↑the↓ bark   26 -on-the- *w.o.* -ontthe-
27 with *w.o.* wi.h   27–28 Mark Twain [*Howells had typed the first two letters of the second word over the last two letters of the first word; then he canceled the* Ma *and inserted* Mark *above the line*]
30 Mark *w.o. illeg.*   31 business] buiness   31 roof *w.o.* roop
32 on *w.o.* in   33 ⟨k⟩ kept   35 vile⟨s⟩   36 use|d| 39 house *w.o.* housi
39 thi↑c↓ker   41 rhe↑u↓matic   42 ⟨*illeg.*⟩ ↑Dean↓

19 December 1910, New York, to Frederick A. Duneka. 2 pp. A.l.s. MWA.

16 when *w.o.* what

2 January 1911, New York, to Brand Whitlock. 2 pp. A.l.s. NNC.

5 Adams's] Adam'ss   10–⟨Mr.⟩ I   12 valuable ⟨motive power⟩
14 Mr.⟨s⟩   15 help *w.o. illeg.*   18 ⟨year⟩ week   22 misbehave *w.o.* mist
25–27 want . . . . Howells. [*in margin, first page*]

7 January 1911, New York, to Henry James. 3 pp. A.l.s. MH.

23 ↑realize↓   25 sympathy *w.o.* sympathetic
31 Wednesday *w.o.* Tuesday

15 January 1911, Bermuda, to Aurelia H. Howells. 3 pp. A.l.s. MH.

8 ↑know↓   34 so *w.o.* sor

29 January 1911, Hamilton, Bermuda, to Elizabeth N. Case. 2 pp. A.l.s. George Arms, Albuquerque, N. M.

5 ↑ago,↓

29 January 1911, Hamilton, Bermuda, to Joseph A. Howells. 1 p. A.l.s. OFH.

24 You . . . William. [*in upper left margin*] [*On verso appears the following typed text with autograph signature*: the opportunity of saying this to you. I think I have all your books; I know I have your picture and your autograph—so there isn't a blessed thing in the writing of this except the relief which comes from expressing myself. Of course this requires no answer, as it is written not so much for your benefit as for my own. / Very sincerely yours, / Charles M. Stuarrt.]

9 February 1911, Hamilton, Bermuda, to S. Weir Mitchell. 3 pp. A.l.s. PU.

3 ↑not↓   7 ↑the↓ story   8 The *w.o.* the   8 she *w.o.* he
20 ⟨an⟩ "absolute   21–22 loved ↑me↓

19 February 1911, Hamilton, Bermuda, to William Strunk. 2 pp. A.l.s. CoU. Copy-text for this edition is librarian's typescript copy; MS. xerox copy was unavailable

3 March 1911, Hamilton, Bermuda, to Edith Wharton. Location of MS. unknown. Typescript copy at MH.

4 March 1911, Hamilton, Bermuda, to Brander Matthews. 2 pp. A.l.s. NNC.

11 ↑am↓

28 April 1911, New York, to Henry Van Dyke. 3 pp. A.l.s. NjP.

[*In upper left corner, first page, in another hand*: ans]
9 Edmund *w.o.* Edward   12 show, who *w.o.* show,"   13 ⟨in⟩ English
19 Jacques *w.o. illeg.*   26 ⟨nominate or⟩ second

16 May 1911, Tompkinsville, New York, to Frederick A. Duneka. 2 pp. A.l.s. MWA.

2 Tompkinsville *w.o.* S   14 ↑of the↓

19 May 1911, Tompkinsville, New York, to Henry James. 3 pp. A.l.s. MH.

4 ↑name↓   4 my *w.o.* y   17 ↑own↓ health and ↑evident↓
18 ⟨*illeg.*⟩ my   21 at Boston *w.o.* in Boston   22 labors *w.o.* f
24 left *w.o.* life   24 this⟨illeg.⟩

29 May 1911, Kittery Point, to Hamlin Garland. 2 pp. T.l.s. **CLSU.**

3 welcome *w.o.* wilcome   3 reminded *w.o.* reminds   3 me ⟨a⟩ of
13 yourself *w.o.* yourselF   14 why *w.o.* wsy   19 Bermuda *w.o.* bermuda
20 dream⟨*illeg.*⟩   27 re-/minder *w.o.* rem/minder   27 of her] of of her
28 long *w.o.* across   28 ↑over↓

29 May 1911, Kittery Point, to Joseph A. Howells. 2 pp. T.l.s. **MH.**

4 I can *w.o.* i can   5 that⟨t⟩   6 ↑her↓   8 did know *w.o.* did nnow
10 hur-/ried *w.o.* huh-/ried   14 how *w.o.* hou   15 could *w.o.* colud
15 not *w.o.* non   28 week, *w.o.* veek,   30 passed *w.o.* parsed
33 includes] iocludes   36 promise] pr/promise   37 ⟨t⟩ take
39 you *w.o.* ywu⟨otbe⟩   40 criticism *w.o.* criticesm   41 New *w.o.* gew
47 ⟨b⟩ big   49 ⟨see⟩ seems

18 June 1911, Kittery Point, to Frederick A. Duneka. 2 pp. A.l.s. **MWA.**

4 ↑except . . . hours,↓

9 July 1911, Kittery Point, to Thomas S. Perry. 2 pp. T.l.s. **MeWC.**

11 night *w.o.* neght   16 looking *w.o.* looging   18 Lloyd *w.o.* Gloyd
18 broke *w.o.* broge   18 word *w.o.* wold   20 ↑a↓ dreadful
23 I did *w.o.* d did   26–27 septuage↑n↓arian   29 him *w.o.* *illeg.*
29 even *w.o.* ewen   30 unparalleled *w.o.* gnparalleled   34 shall *w.o.* stall
37 blackripe *w.o.* blackrepe   37 ↑it↓

22 July 1911, Kittery Point, to Brander Matthews. Location of MS. unknown. *Life in Letters*, II, 301.

18 August 1911, Llandrindod Wells, to Joseph A. Howells. 3 pp. A.l.s.
MH.

5 her *w.o.* the   18 blame *w.o.* *illeg.*   25 publish] publishe⟨,⟩
27 ⟨later *w.o.* *illeg.*⟩ later   39–40 This . . . . our [*in margin, third page*]
39 hotel *w.o.* home   39 people.] ∼
40–41 great-grandfather's . . . printing- [*in margin, second page*]
41–43 -office. . . . on it. [*in margin, first page*]

20 August 1911, Llandrindod Wells, to William A. Gill. 3 pp. A.l.s.
Avon County Reference Library, Bristol.

1–2 *Pump . . . Wells.* [*embossed letterhead*]   8 ↑the↓ American
18 where we are] where are   20 the *w.o.* s   24 she uses] she she uses

10 September 1911, London, to Armando Palacio Valdés. Location of MS. unknown. *Life in Letters*, II, 302. Translation of original Spanish text.

29 September 1911, Tours, to Thomas S. Perry. 2 pp. A.l.s. MeWC.

  20 and] and and   23 along *w.o.* are

14 October 1911, Madrid, to Abby W. Howells. Location of MS. unknown. *Life in Letters*, II, 303–4.

15 October 1911, Madrid, to Henry James. 3 pp. A.l.s. MH.

  6 ↑picture↓   10 the⟨re⟩   16 we *w.o. illeg.*   32 you *w.o.* one
40 astonishingly *w.o.* astonishly   41 course *w.o.* colors,   47 ↑if↓
48 ↑still↓   51 for *w.o. illeg.*

17 October 1911, Madrid, to Henry Van Dyke. 1 p. A.l.s. NjP.

  9 unscholarly [*Howells first wrote* unschotarly, *then canceled the crossing of the* t]   9 literature.] ~   13 Century *w.o.* De

3 November 1911, Seville, to Henry James. 4 pp. A.l.s. MH.

  6 dance *w.o.* danci⟨ng⟩   6 us *w.o.* or   8 palm- *w.o.* palms
20 dancing-girl.] ~   20 ⟨wet⟩ evening ↑came↓
30 Museo *w.o. illeg* [*uncertain reading*]   38 a *w.o.* is   39 pillars.] ~
45–47 from . . . . Howells. [*in margin, second page*]
48–49 I . . . edition. [*in margin, first page*]

8 November 1911, Granada, to John M. Howells. Location of MS. unknown. *Life in Letters*, II, 307–8.

9 December 1911, New York, to Eliza W. Howells. 2 pp. A.l.s. OFH.

  16 ↑not↓   24 ↑so↓   26 ↑be↓   34 both *w.o. illeg.*
44–45 trees . . . . would [*in margin, second page*]
45–49 liked . . . . Will. [*in margin and above salutation, first page*]

26 December 1911, New York, to Thomas S. Perry. Location of MS. unknown. *Life in Letters*, II, 310.

Word-Division

In the two lists below, entries are keyed to the line numbers of the letter texts; the line-count includes all lines of type of a letter proper, beginning at the internal address or dateline. List A records compounds and possible compounds hyphenated at the end of the line in the authorial document or extant transcription used as copy-text for the present edition, and indicates how these end-line hyphenated forms have been resolved. If the compounds occur in consistent form elsewhere in the authorial document or in other such materials of the same general period in time, including literary manuscripts, then resolution was made on that basis; if these other occurrences are inconsistent, resolution was based on the form in closest proximity in time to the possible compound in question. If neither of these resources was sufficient, then resolution was based on the evidence of published texts of Howells' works or on the prevalent usage of the period. List B is a guide to transcription of compounds or possible compounds hyphenated at the end of the line in the present text: compounds recorded in this list should be transcribed as given; words divided at the end of the line and not listed should be transcribed as one word.

LIST A

3 August 1902, to B. Matthews	9	earthquaking
26 March 1902, to J. Hay	6	Spanish-American
6 April 1903, to C. E. Norton	32	home-like
26 April 1903, to S. L. Clemens	3	English-stamped
20 December 1903, to S. L. Clemens	14	man-bearing
20 December 1903, to S. L. Clemens	21	heart-breaking
13 and 14 March 1904, to E. M. Howells	2	overlooking
13 and 14 March 1904, to E. M. Howells	14	Knickerbockers
13 and 14 March 1904, to E. M. Howells	69	white-haired
18 March 1904, to E. M. Howells	29–30	underpinning
18, 19, and 20 March 1904, to E. M. Howells	34	ball-room
24 and 25 March 1904, to E. M. Howells	20	dwelling-street

12 April 1904, to E. M. Howells	6	backyard
12 April 1904, to E. M. Howells	7	wheelbarrow
17 April 1904, to E. M. Howells	19	basement-diners
1 May 1904, to E. M. Howells	36	home-stoves
1 June 1904, to E. Jordan	28	-club-rooms
4 November 1904, to C. E. Norton	25	sister-in-
27 December 1904, to E. C. Stedman	7	comic-opera
27 December 1904, to E. C. Stedman	9	lung-sick
12 February 1905, to J. A. Howells	17	dental-schooled
24 May 1905, to Sir G. Trevelyan	5	old-fashioned
10 September 1905, to A. H. Howells	11	homesick
10 December 1905, to T. S. Perry	31	barnbury
30 January 1906, to M. Howells	14	-sit-by-
28 February 1906, to S. L. Clemens	30	nonesense
8 April 1906, to A. H. Howells	19	blackbirds
16 April 1906, to J. A. Howells	37	blackbirds
24 May 1906, to S. L. Clemens	5	middling-sized
17 June 1906, to A. H. Howells	4	northeaster
31 December 1906, to E. C. Stedman	27	ground-floor
2 February 1907, to C. E. Norton	18	second-hand
15 April 1907, to C. E. Norton	5	handwriting
31 July 1907, to M. Howells	9	to-morrow
31 July 1907, to M. Howells	11	deck-stewart
22 September 1907, to C. E. Norton	9	motor-boats
6 October 1907, to J. A. Howells	6	horse-rides
29 October 1907, to W. R. Thayer	15	fellow-citizen
13 December 1907, to F. A. Duneka	4	English-woman
12 January 1908, to A. H. Howells	12	sugar-cane
12 January 1908, to A. H. Howells	66	seasick
9 May 1908, to A. H. Howells	3	to-day
31 January 1909, to S. Norton	26	housekeeping
26 April 1909, to E. M. Howells	5	wind-pump
4 July 1909, to J. A. Howells	40	watchman's
20 August 1909, to H. James	5	heart-friendly
20 August 1909, to H. James	29	straight-jacket
25 August 1909, to S. L. Clemens	20	today
15 September 1909, to E. M. Howells	26	Mamma-burst
17 September 1909, to E. M. Howells	10	whortleberry
17 September 1909, to E. M. Howells	23	-on-Avon
17 September 1909, to E. M. Howells	24	today
8 May 1910, to A. H. Howells and A. H. Fréchette	9	everlasting

5 July 1910, to J. A. Howells	4	Little-Joe-
27 July 1910, to E. Gosse	4	spindle-sided
29 January 1911, to J. A. Howells	14	-in-law
29 May 1911, to H. Garland	4–5	house-raising
18 August 1911, to J. A. Howells	41	printing-office
18 August 1911, to J. A. Howells	42	hand-press

LIST B

19 March 1902, to C. E. Norton	15–16	Tiber-colored
12 October 1902, to C. E. Norton	27–28	-in-law
26 April 1903, to S. L. Clemens	12–13	scratch-gravel
9 August 1903, to A. H. Howells	6–7	great-great-
13 and 14 March 1904, to E. M. Howells	87–88	weak-minded
12 April 1904, to E. M. Howells	17–18	French-revolution
20 August 1905, to H. Garland	41–42	non-reading
10 September 1905, to C. E. Norton	43–44	self-reproach
27 May 1906, to D. A. Munro	6–7	pre-existence
30 October 1908, to S. W. Mitchell	17–18	great-grandfather
11 February 1910, to S. L. Clemens	14–15	spelling-book
28 February 1910, to F. A. Duneka	15–16	ill-advised
15 January 1911, to A. H. Howells	6–7	never-seasick
15 January 1911, to A. H. Howells	10–11	blow-ball
15 January 1911, to A. H. Howells	28–29	old-fashioned
29 May 1911, to H. Garland	4–5	house-raising
29 May 1911, to J. A. Howells	37–38	spine-doctor
18 August 1911, to J. A. Howells	40–41	great-grandfather's

List of Howells' Correspondents

The following alphabetical list of Howells' correspondents provides page references for (1) letters written by Howells TO others and (2) letters FROM others addressed to Howells. Page numbers in italic type indicate letters appearing in full or as fully as the source permits; page numbers in roman type indicate letters cited in footnotes, with "cited" used broadly to mean quotation from a letter, description of part of its contents, or mention of it whether printed in this edition or not. The few cited letters about Howells, e.g., from Henry James to Grace Norton, appear not in this list but in the main index.

Adams, Frederick U., TO 340–41; FROM 339–40
Aldrich, Thomas B., TO 4, 10–12, 16, 17, 18, 22, 24–25, 28, 32–33, 35, 38, 120, 210–11, 223, 327; FROM 12, 16, 24–25, 33

Baxter, Sylvester, TO 365
Betram, James, TO 101
Bigelow, William, TO 92
Bjornson, Bjornstjerne, TO 246
Brady, Cyrus T., TO 23
Braithwaite, William S., TO 260

Case, Elizabeth N., TO 343–44
Cawein, Madison J., TO 7, 42–43, 138; FROM 138
Clemens, Samuel L., TO 4, 5, 6, 7–8, 10, 10, 10, 12, 38, 39–40, 41–42, 45, 46–47, 52, 53, 56, 70–71, 77–78, 87, 90, 97–98, 98, 104–05, 116, 118, 142–43, 149, 152, 165–66, 169, 173, 181, 184–85, 186, 188–89, 207–08, 228, 229, 232, 242–43, 255–56, 264, 270, 284–85, 290–91, 300, 306, 308–09; FROM 12, 47, 56, 78, 98, 104–05, 166, 189, 243, 256, 264, 270, 284–85, 309
Comly, James M., TO 135
Crawford, John, FROM 98
Culver, Frederic, FROM 259

De Forest, John W., TO 31
Douglas, David, TO 7, 128, 132, 133, 135
Dreiser, Theodore, FROM 28
Duneka, Frederick A., TO 37–38, 56–58, 76–77, 78, 80–81, 112, 117, 141–42, 143, 150, 153, 154, 160, 162, 165, 185, 186–87, 195–96, 198, 209, 211, 224, 230, 236, 239–40, 252, 260, 271, 275, 276–77, 279, 281–82, 300, 301, 310–11, 314, 317, 319–20, 324, 331, 332, 334, 338–39, 343, 352–53, 358, 361, 363; FROM 58, 81, 112, 282, 309–10, 311, 317, 319, 339, 358, 361

Ferrero, Guglielmo, FROM 248
Fields, Annie A., TO 45, 47–48, 180
Fiske, Minnie M., TO 25
Fitch, William C., TO 73; FROM 73–74
Fréchette, Achille, TO 48
Fréchette, Anne H., TO 8, 106–07, 111, 124, 126, 162, 202, 217, 264–65, 311, 315–16, 318, 324, 328, 333, 361; FROM 184, 250, 315, 316
Fréchette, Marie M., TO 183; FROM 184
French, Alice, TO 331; FROM 331
Fuller, Henry B., TO 212–13, 219, 270–71; FROM 64–65, 72, 212–13, 270–72

Garland, Hamlin, TO 10, 49, 55, 59, 65, 115, 129–31, 159, 303, 313–14, 354–55, 356; FROM 129, 131, 314, 354–55, 356

Garrison, Wendell P., TO 31
Gilder, Richard W., TO *75–76*; FROM 76
Gill, William A., TO 117, *364*; FROM 364
Gilman, Mr., TO 108
Godkin, Edwin L., TO 53
Godkin, Katherine S., TO *52–53*
Gosse, Edmund W., TO *327–28, 349, 370*; FROM 327–28, 349, 351–52

Hale, Edward E., TO *23–24*
Hallstrom, Per, TO 351; FROM 351
Hamer, Mrs., TO *127*
Harben, Will, FROM 309
Harper & Brothers, TO *192*
Harper, J. W., TO 358
Harvey, George P., FROM 239, 240
Hay, John, TO *18, 19, 116*, 116, 137, 168; FROM 19, 20, 116
Herrick, Robert, TO *194–95, 267*, 269, 273; FROM 267–68
Higginson, Thomas W., TO *280–81*, 294, 295, *334–35*, 338, 344; FROM 280–81
Houghton, Mifflin & Co., TO 30
Howe, Julia W., FROM 281
Howells, Abby W., TO 366, *368*
Howells, Aurelia H., TO 3, 4, 6, *9–10*, 12, *20–21*, 24, *26–27, 27–28*, 28, 33, *34–35*, 37, 41, *44–45, 51*, 60, 62, 65, *65–66*, 67, *68–69*, 70, 71, 76, 80, 95, 96, 101, *106–07, 107–08, 108–09*, 111, 114, 122, *124–25, 129, 131–32, 134–35*, 136, 137, 139, *145*, 149, 150, 155, *158*, 161, 162, 163, 166, *170*, 172, 173, 175, 176, 179, *182–83, 183–84*, 186, 189, 192, 196, 198, *201–02*, 202, 207, 208, 209, 213, 215, 218, 226, 228, 230, 234, *235*, 235, *237–39, 245*, 249, 250, 256, 257, 259, 271, *272–73*, 276, 278, *291–92*, 293, 300, 302, 311, *315–16, 318*, 325, 328, 333, *342–43*, 345, 361, 362–63, 368–69, 379; FROM 184
Howells, Elinor M., TO 7, 8, *81–84*, 85–86, *86–87*, 87, *88–89*, 90, *91–92*, 92–93, *93–94, 95–96*, 96, *98–99*, 100, 106, 108, 128, 272, *273–74*, 284, *286–87, 287–88, 288–89*, 294, 331
Howells, Eliza W., TO 358, 361, *376–77*
Howells, John M., TO 136, 244, 303, 304, *374–75*; FROM 289
Howells, Joseph A., TO 109, *120*, 129, *136–37*, 149, 155, *157, 161–62*, 162, *171–72, 173–74*, 175, *189–90*, 193–94, *196–97*, 198, 200, 201, 202, 203, *208–09*, 209, 213, *215–17*, 218, *224–25*, 228, *229–30*, 232, 245–46, 249–50, 250, *256–58*, 259, 277, *278–79*, 299, 301, 302, 303, 313, 320,

321–22, 324–25, 330, 332, *333, 333, 337–38*, 339, 342, *344–45*, 355, *356–57*, 358, 359, *362–63*, 365, 370, 373, 377; FROM 162, 198, 249, 345, 356, 362, 377
Howells, Mary Dean, TO *134–35*
Howells, Mildred, TO 12, 17, 136, *162–63, 168–69*, 179, 223, 227, 230, *263*, 310, 332, 363; FROM 263
Howells, William C., TO 61, 95, 128, 135, 278, 313, 319, 324, 361
Howells, William C., II, FROM 344
Howells, William D., II, TO 9, 258, 290
Howells, William W., TO *268*

James, Henry, TO 8, 12, *14–15*, 95, *101–02*, 156, 248, *252–54*, 259, 275, 281, *283, 289–90, 294–95*, 299, 300, 303, *305, 307–08, 311–12*, 322, *341–42*, 346, *353–54*, 367, *369–70, 372–73*; FROM 12, 14–15, 49, 67, 92, 101, 102, 103, 111, 126, 247, 248, 252, 255, 259, 277, 283–84, 290, 303, 308, 322–23, 354, 371, 375
James, William, TO *35, 320–21*; FROM 320–21
Jewett, Sarah O., TO 62, *125*, 254; FROM 61, 125, 262–63
Johnson, Robert U., TO 46, *126–27*, 281, *293*, 295, 350; FROM 350
Jones, Henry A., TO *213–14*; FROM 214
Jones, Mary C., TO 348; FROM 350
Jordan, Elizabeth, TO *102–03*, 111, *117*, 169, *179–81, 187–88, 203–04*, 207, 262, 307, 335, 373; FROM 117, 311

Le Gallienne, Richard T., TO 335
Lloyd George, Margaret, FROM 359–60
Longfellow, Alice, TO *211–12*
Lowell, James R., TO 222

Mabie, Hamilton W., TO *36, 46*, 49, 115
Mackaye, Percy W., TO 330; FROM 330
Matthews, Brander, TO 4, *33*, 62, 150, *164, 168*, 176, *230–31*, 268, 269, 303, 348, *349, 361*; FROM 269, 361
McClure, Samuel S., TO *177–78*
Mead, Mary N., FROM 287, 289
Mifflin, George H., TO 38, 122, 228; FROM 38, 122
Mitchell, Laura, TO 74
Mitchell, S. Weir, TO 109, *143–44*, 150, *233–34, 260–61*, 262, 299, *346*; FROM 113–14, 143–44, 150–51, 260–61, 262, 346
Munro, David A., TO 5, *62–63*, 127, *181–82, 273*

Norton, Charles E., TO 3, 7, 8, *17–18*, *21–22*, 27, *29–30*, 35, *36–37*, 38, *40–41*, 45, 48, *49–51*, *54–55*, *61*, 62, *74–75*, 81, *110*, 114, 120, *123*, *132–33*, 135, *138–39*, 141, 144, 150, 151, 152, 158, *164–65*, *167*, 175, 177, *185–86*, *198–99*, 203, *204–05*, 206, 207, 211, 212, 218, *220–22*, *226–27*, *231–32*, *240–41*, 247, *251*, 254, *258–59*, 260, 271, 275, 277; FROM 18, 22, 26, 29–30, 41, 62, 67, 75, 111, 126, 133, 151, 165, 185–86, 199, 205, 206, 222, 223, 226–27, 248, 252

Norton, Sara, TO 149, 259, *266*; FROM 266

Osborne, Duffield, TO 348–49

Paine, Albert B., TO 243, 317
Palacio Valdés, Armando, TO 360, *365*, 367; FROM 367
Pearson, S. E., Mrs., TO 277–*78*
Perry, Bliss, TO *39*; FROM 39
Perry, Thomas S., TO 5, 6, *66–67*, 68, 114, *117–18*, *125–26*, 133, 139, *140–41*, 254, 304, 328, 354, *359–60*, *366–67*, 371, 378; FROM 66–67, 117–18, 125–26, 367
Phillpotts, Eden, TO *285*, 288; FROM 285–86
Pryor, Roger A., TO 331

Reeves, William P., TO 18
Rideing, William H., TO 25
Rood, Henry E., TO 275, 277, 279
Roosevelt, Theodore, TO 7, 137, 155, 172, *193*, 198, 231, 258; FROM 137

Salter, William M., TO 118, 331
Savage, Minot J., TO 301, 326; FROM 326
Schurman, Jacob G., TO *13*
Schurz, Carl, FROM 178

Sedgwick, Theodora, TO *176–77*, 199
Smalley, Evelyn G., TO *43*
Stedman, Edmund C., TO 46, *115*, 116, *119*, 127, 154, *202–03*, *210–11*, 212; FROM 115–16, 119, 154, 210–11
Stoddard, Charles W., FROM 40
Story, William W., TO 67
Strachey, John St. L., TO 4, 7, *79–80*, *90–91*, 95, 129; FROM 79–80
Strunk, William, TO *347*; FROM 347
Stuart, Charles M., FROM 344–45

Thayer, William R., TO *232–33*, 248
Thomas, Augustus, TO *236–37*
Trevelyan, George O., TO *121–22*, 155, *243–44*; FROM 121–22, 244
Twichell, Joseph H., TO *325–26*; FROM 325–26

Upton, Harriet T., TO *312–13*, 316

Van Dyke, Henry, TO 349, *350–51*, 362, 371; FROM 350–51
Villard, Oswald G., TO *334*

Walter, Helen, TO 188
Ward, Elizabeth S. P., TO 319
Warner, Charles D., TO 359
Wells, Herbert G., TO 101, *105*, *178–79*; FROM 101, 106
Wharton, Edith, TO *348*, 349, 351; FROM 348–49, 351
Whiston, Dr., TO *65*; FROM 65
White, William A., TO 181; FROM 181
Whitlock, Brand, TO *22–23*, 58, 213, *218–19*, *219–20*, 220, *339–40*; FROM 23, 220, 340
Wilson, Francis, TO 168, *175–76*; FROM 176
Wyatt, Edith TO *159*; FROM 65, 159

Index

This index records all names of persons, organizations, monuments, ships, public buildings, and titles of magazines and books (the last recorded under the names of their authors, if known). It excludes the names of relatives of Howells' correspondents when they are mentioned for the primary purpose of sending love or minor information; the titles, journals, or publishers of post-1920 criticism and scholarship; and geographical names and government divisions. Some topics are listed as independent entries, but most can be found under Howells' name, where information is divided into two major lists: WORKS and TOPICS. The TOPICS section is further subdivided.

Within entries, the general order of information is: brief and/or general references; citation of correspondence other than that with Howells (e.g., Henry James to Grace Norton); works by that person, including reviews and presumably unpublished work; and descriptive modifications, arranged in ascending page order. Finally, the frequent occurrence of some dozen entries has required the use of "passim" (e.g., *"Harper's Monthly,* WDH's connection with and contributions to, 159-366 passim").

Italic numbers designate pages on which significant biographical information is given. An asterisk preceding an entry indicates that a full record of correspondence between Howells and the person or institution so marked is provided in the separate "List of Howells' Correspondents," pages 427-429, the headnote of which explains its arrangement.

"A Hot Time in the Old Town" (song), 271

Academia de Baile, Spain, 373

The Academy and Literature, 33–34

Adam, 143, 169

*Adams, Frederick U., 339–*40**

Adams, Henry, 116

Adams, Katherine J., 58

Addams, Jane, 159

Ade, George, *Artie,* 63–65; *The Country Chairman* (reviewed by WDH), 72; *Doc' Horne,* 63–64; (reviewed by WDH), 64; at Clemens' 70th birthday dinner, 141; proposed as speaker at Clemens memorial, 319–20

Aeschylus, *Agamemnon,* 185

Agassiz, Elizabeth C., 62

Agassiz, Jean Louis R., Longfellow on, *13*

Albers, Mr., 82

Alcazar, 374–75

Alden, Henry M., 26–27, *142*, 160; rejects Wyatt's stories for *Harper's Monthly,* 159; likes H. James's "Crapy Cornelia," 289; co-edits "Harper's Novelettes" series with WDH, 324

Aldis, Mrs., 48

Aldis family, 38

Aldrich, Charles, contracts tuberculosis, 16; recovering from illness, 25, 32

Aldrich, Charles, Mr. and Mrs., 12

Aldrich, Lilian, born, 10, *12*

*Aldrich, Thomas B., "Longfellow," 222–23; mislaid letter, 12; made member of American Academy, 115; WDH declines to write essay memorializing, 154, 211; WDH misses funeral, 222–23; death of, 224; WDH gives letters of

to biographer, 242; poem on death of Wendell Phillips, 335
Aldrich, Thomas B., Mrs., 242; WDH considers visiting, 223–24
Alexander, John W., 332, 351–52
Alfonso XIII, of Spain, 367
Alfred the Great, 88
Alhambra, 370, 374–75
Alice Howard (boat), 83
All Souls College, 106
Allen, Helen S., 308–09
Allen, James L., *The Choir Invisible*, 12
Alma-Tadema, Lawrence, 295
American Academy of Arts and Letters, 115, 116, 119, 127, 256, 259, 337–38, 341–42; *In Memory of Mark Twain*, 332; WDH president, 7; public meeting in Washington, 280–81, 293–94, 294–95, 334–35; WDH considers resigning over lack of support for Nobel Prize for H. James, 303, 348–49, 351–52; WDH suggests as sponsor for Clemens memorial, 320
American Academy of Dramatic Arts, 14–15
American Institute of Architects, 295
"American Men of Letters" series, 13, 29–30
Amherst College, 316
Amherst, Jeffrey, 315–16
Andreieva, Madame, 172, 173
Andrews, Mary R. S., "The School-Boy" (in *The Whole Family*), 180
The Appeal to Reason, 340
Appleton Chapel, 262
Arlington Street Church, 84
Arms, George, 154, 275, 365
Arrhenius, Svante A., 351–52
Ascham, Antony, 369–70
Ashburner, Anne, 176–77, 198–99; memoirs of, 151
Ashburner, Walter, 110–*11*
Ashcroft, Ralph W., 272
Ashfield, 132
Ashfield Academy, 61–62
Ashtabula Sentinel, 21, 137, 161–62, 173–74, 190–91, 230, 257; WDH II works for, 10
Atherton, Gertrude, *The Conqueror*, 346; "Gertrude Atherton Assails 'The Powers'," 306; *Tower of Ivory*, 346; "Why is American Literature Bourgeois?" 306; WDH meets, 305–06
Atlantic Monthly, 55, 159, 346; publishes critical review of *The Kentons*, 39; publishes WDH's "Recollections of an Atlantic Editorship," 233–34; publishes J. M. Howells' story, 274; publishes *The Journal of John Woolman*, 344
Atwell, Benjamin, *The Great Harry Thaw Case*, 191
Austen, Jane, 86–87, 89; *Northanger Abbey*, 79–80; *Persuasion*, 86; *Pride and Prejudice*, 56; WDH compares E. Wyatt to, 64–65, 141; H. James on, 168–69
Authors Club, 348–49
Avenue Theatre, New York, 53

Badger, Richard C., and *The Henry James Yearbook*, 283–84, 289–90, 341–42
Balfour, Arthur J., 93, 95, 101,
Ballinger, Richard A., and the Ballinger-Pinchot Controversy, *314*
Balzac, Honoré de, 103; *La Comédie Humaine*, 169; *The Country Doctor*, 168–69; *Le Médecin de Campagne*, 168–69; H. James on, 168–69
Bangs, John K., "The Son-in-Law" (in *The Whole Family*), 179–80
Baretti, Giuseppe M. A., *Dizionario delle lingue Italiana ed Inglese*, 50, 52
Barrie, James M., 96; *Alice-Sit-by-the-Fire* (WDH on), 163; plays (reviewed by WDH), 96; WDH sees in England, *325*, 329–30
Baths of Caracalla, 251
*Baxter, Sylvester, 365
"Beacon Series," 11
Beeson, Mr., 163
Belasco, David, production of *The Man Inside*, 58
Bell, Mary E., *Old Kentucky Rhymes . . .*, 173
Belle Isle Park, Detroit, 226
Belt, John, portrayed in *New Leaf Mills*, 358
Belt, John, family, *336*, 337
Bennett, James G., *192*
"Bernard Shaw's Criticism of Tolstoy," 378
Berry Pomeroy, 288–89
*Betram, James, *101*
Beverly Farms, 208
Bewick, Thomas, 63–*64*
*Bigelow, William, 92
Binns, Archie, 26
Birrell, Augustine, *Andrew Marvell*, *122*; *Boswell's Life of Johnson* (ed.), 122; WDH meets in England, 329–30
Bishop, Washington I., *237*

*Bjornson, Bjornstjerne, *Arne*, 245; *The Fishermaiden*, 245; WDH invites, 246
Bjornson, Bjornstjerne, Mrs., 246
Blaisdell, Mr., 171
Bodley Head, 95
Boehmer, Mrs., 135
Boehmer family, 135
Bookman, 23
Borrow, George H., *Wild Wales . . .* , *141*
Boston *Advertiser*, 253
Boston *Globe*, 13–14, 47, 330
Boston *Transcript*, 346
Boswell, James, *Life of Samuel Johnson*, 227
Botticelli, Sandro (Alessandro di Mariano Filipepi), 93
Bourgogne, Phillipe de, 375
Bowen-Merrill, 23
Bowles, Samuel, 221–22
Bowles, Samuel, Jr., 222
Boyesen, Hjalmar H., 177–78
*Brady, Cyrus T., 23
*Braithwaite, William S., *The House of the Falling Leaves*, 260; "Song of a Syrian Lace Seller," 260
Bremer, Frederika, *Homes of the New World*, 259
Brick Church, New York City, 317
Brigantine Shoals, 162
Broderick, John, 48
Brooks, Sidney, 94–95
Brown, Alice, 141; *Meadow-Grass* (reviewed by WDH), 141; "Peggy" (in *The Whole Family*), 181
Brown, Shipley & Co., 286, 322, 326, 365, 368, 374
Brownell, William C., *Victorian Prose Masters*, 33
Browning, William C., 280–*81*
Bryan, William J., 25
Bryce, James, 207–*08*
Bryn Mawr College, 103–04
Buckingham Palace, 95
Bulfinch, Charles, 185–86
Bunsen, Maurice W. E. de, *368*
Burke, John B., *Family Romance*, 128–29
Burlingame, Edward L., *234*
Burne-Jones, Edward C., 37
Burns, John E., *325*, 329–30
Burroughs, John, 50–*51*
Burton, Joseph R., *279*
Butler, Miss, 87–88, 89
Butler, Nicholas M., 349
Byzantium, 174

Cable, George W., 280–81, 332

Cady, Edwin H., 39, 136, 196, 222, 275, 316
Caesar, 282
Caine, Thomas H. H., *111*
Cairns, Mrs., 88–89
Cambon, Jules M., *40*
Cambridge Cemetery, 300, 318
Cambridge Historical Society Publications, 200
Camp Douglas, 310
Campania (ship), 330
Campbell, Beatrice, 10, *12*
Campbell, Mrs. Patrick, 214
Campbell-Bannerman, Henry, *122*
Cannon, Joseph G., 332, *338*
Cano, Alonso, *375*
Capuchin Convent, Rome, 241
Carey, Rosa N., *Rue with a Difference* (usurps WDH's proposed title for *Fennel and Rue*), 236
Carlyle, Alexander, ed., *New Letters and Memorials to Jane Welsh Carlyle*, 55
Carlyle, Jane Welsh, *New Letters and Memorials to Jane Welsh Carlyle* (reviewed by WDH), 55
Carlyle, Thomas, 118
Carmania (ship), 289
Carnegie Hall, 173, 301, 332, 337
Carnegie, Andrew, 7, 100–01; WDH dines with, 50–51; portrait by M. M. Fréchette, 197–98; dinner attended by WDH and E. C. Stedman, 203; WDH proposes as contributor to women's suffrage series, 335
Carnegie, Andrew, Mrs., 197
Carnegie, Andrew, Mr. and Mrs., 50–51
Carpenter, George R., *Henry Wadsworth Longfellow*, 11; (reviewed by WDH), 13
Cary, Richard, 125, 227
*Case, Elizabeth N., 343–44
Cathedral of Santa Maria de la Encarnacion, 375
*Cawein, Madison J., *Kentucky Poems*, 42–43; *The Vale of Tempe*, 138; *A Voice on the Wind and Other Poems*, 42–43
Celtic (ship), 92
Central Park, New York, 226
Century Club, 20–21, 228–29, 259, 371
Century Magazine, 210–11, 352
Cervantes Saavedra, Miguel de, *Don Quixote*, 361
Chamberlain, Joseph, 100–*01*
Chamberlain, Neville, 122

Charles I, of England, 84, 86, 136, 330, 336

Charles II, of England, 84, 370

Charles V, of England (Charles I, of Spain), 375

Chaucer, Geoffrey, 11

Cherokee (ship), 161–62

Chester Pageant, 329–30

Chicago *Post*, 346

Chicago *Record*, 64

Chicago *Tribune*, 64

Chicago, University of, 248

Choate, Joseph A., 320, 332

Christ Church, Oxford, 106

Christian Science Movement, 217

Christmas, 75

Church of San Geronimo, Spain, 374–75

Church of the Messiah, New York, 327

Church of Unity, Boston, 327

Churchill, Winston, 254, 255, 349; WDH suggests for "Turning-Point" series, 307

Cincinnati *Gazette*, 345

City and State, 45

Civil War, 175

Clark, Champ, 332

Clark, Joseph B., *338*

Clarkson, Martha, 171–72, 274–75, 318

Clemens, Clara, 97–98, 228; taken ill at Atlantic City, 165–66; tribute to father, 188–89; to visit Stormfield, 272–73; WDH sends proof of Clemens memorial statement to, 317. *See also* Gabrilowitsch, Clara C.

Clemens, Jean, *97–98*, 228

Clemens, Olivia L., 4, *38*, 78, 97–98; affected by coal strike, 32; poor health, 51–52, 70–71; death, 104–05, 152, 326; S. L. Clemens' tribute to, 326–27

Clemens, Orion, *169*

*Clemens, Samuel L., 4, 10, 21, 24, 37, 95; letter to Elinor M. Howells, 285; letter to Joseph H. Twichell, 325–26; note to Albert B. Paine, 307; *The Adventures of Huckleberry Finn*, 38; *Christian Science . . .*, 42, 284–85; *A Connecticut Yankee . . .*, 152, 255, 326; "A Dog's Tale," 70–71; "Farewell Lecture," 173; "The Five Boons of Life," 32–33; *The Innocents Abroad*, 255; *Mark Twain's Autobiography*, 77–78, 189; (WDH on), 6, 166, 169, 170; *The Personal Recollections of Joan of Arc*, 326–27; satires on detectives (unpublished), 208; "Tom Sawyer's Conspiracy," 38; unpublished satire on Wal-

lace, 71; "Why Not Abolish It?" 56; *A Tramp Abroad*, 284; "The Turning-Point of My Life," 300, 306–07; "William Dean Howells," 152, 184–85, 188–89; proposed WDH biography, 6, 68; 70th birthday dinner, 8, 138–39, 140; on Aldrich letter, 12; and lunch at B. Matthews', 20; dinner at Carnegies', 50–52; move to Italy, 70–71; WDH confides in, 151; and relationship with WDH, 152–53; on Whittier Birthday Dinner, 157–58; on M. Howells' poem, 166; on WDH's 69th birthday, 166; at WDH lunch for H. G. Wells, 170–71; and Maxim Gorky, 171–72; proposed author for *The Whole Family*, 179–80; and William A. White, 181; praise of WDH, 186; proposed trip with WDH 190; lobbies for copyright legislation, 201, 338; receives honorary Oxford degree, 228–29; at dinner with WDH, 234; letters collected for biography, 256; letters returned by WDH, 270; WDH visits at Stormfield, 272; death, 299–301, 304, 317, 326; WDH works on commemoration, 301, 332; WDH to write memorial essay on, 317; funeral, 317; WDH to preside at memorial, 319–20, 333, 337–38, 341–42; WDH praises, 326–27

Clemens, Suzy, 105; death, 270

Cleveland *Plain Dealer*, 345

Clyde Steamship Company, 157, 161–62, 171

Coliseum, Rome, 241

Collier, P. F., & Son Co., 271

Collier, Robert J., 271

Collier's, 171

Collins, G. L., *Putnam Place*, 56

Columbia Law Review, 168

Columbia University, 11, 125–26, 259, 347, 349; awards WDH honorary degree, 7, 124; and E. A. McDowell, 119; chapel designed by J. M. Howells, 235; G. Ferrero to speak at, 248

*Comly, James M., 135

Constantinople, 174

Contemporary Club, 103

Cook, Thomas, & Son, 239, 283–84, 373–74

Cook, Walter, 351–52

Cooper Committee, 230

Cooper, James F., 230–31

Cooperative-Building Construction Co., 259

Corcoran Art Gallery, Washington, 295

Corcoran, Katherine, 356

Cordoba, Gonzalo F. de, 374–75

Corelli, Marie, *111*

Cornell University, 13, 347

Cosmopolitan, 196

Cotehele, 82, 84

Court of the Lions, Alhambra, 304

Cox, Kenyon, 255, 280–81

Crabbe, George, *Tales*, 34–35, 36

Cragie House, 212

*Crawford, John, 87, *89*, 97–98

Croly, Herbert, 255

Cromwell, Oliver, 84, 369–70

Cross, Wilbur L., *Life and Times of Laurence Sterne* (reviewed by WDH), 310

Crowninshield, Frederic, 20–*21*, 170, 272–73

*Culver, Frederic, 258–*59*

Cunard Lines, 375

Current Literature, 378

Curtis, Anna S., 353–54

Curtis, Elizabeth, 353–54

Curtis, George W., 61–62, 353–54

Cutting, Mary S., "The Daughter-in-Law" (in *The Whole Family*), 180

Cymric (ship), 321, 324

D'Oyly Carte Opera Company, 96

Daly, John A., 14–*15*

Dante Alighieri, 241; *Divine Comedy*, (Norton translation of), 21–22, 36; WDH compares E. Gosse to, 327

Dante Club, 211

Darwin, Charles, 71

Darwin, William E., 255

*De Forest, John W., *Poems: Medley and Palestine*, 31

Dean, William E., 338

Delevan House, 234

Delmas, Delphin M., 217–*18*

Delmonico's (restaurant), 140, 264

Dial, 346–47

Dickens, Charles, 288; *Pickwick Papers*, 305–06

"Dixie Greys," 310

Dockstader, Lew (pseud.). *See* Clapp, George A.

Dockstader's Minstrels, 161–62

Donizetti, Gaetano, *L'elisir d'amore*, 74–75

Donnell, Mrs., 179–80

Donnelly, Samuel B., 257–*58*

Dorchester House, 249

*Douglas, David, 89–*90*, 108; publishes WDH's *Minor Dramas*, 209

Douglas, David, Mrs., 128

Douglas, Miss, 128

Doyle, Arthur Conan, 30

Doyle, James, 316, 343

Drake, Francis, 81, *84*, 85

*Dreiser, Theodore, 28

Dreyfus, Alfred, 255

Dunbar, Paul L., 260

*Duneka, Frederick A., *58*; and proposed Library Edition of WDH, 37, 275; and proposed series on death, 262; WDH asks increase in Harper salary, 299–300; agreement with WDH on publication of *Vacation of the Kelwyns*, 302; pressures H. Garland to write *Cavanagh*, 314; and Richard Realf letters, 334

Dunne, Finley P., 65

Duse, Eleanora, 10, 12

Dyer, Louis, 94–95, 101

Eaton Terrace, 111

Eaton, Charles A., *191*

Ecole des Beaux-Arts, 194

Eddy, Mary B., 284–85; *Science and Health . . .*, 215, *217*

Edel, Leon, 15, 55, 127, 312, 342

Edgcumbe, William H., 82, *84*

"The Editor's Diary, Saturday, March 30," 218–19

Edward VII, of England, 50, 95, 140–41, 182

Eliot, George, 169

Elliman, 82

Elliott, Maud H., and Laura E. Richards, *Julia Ward Howe, 1819–1910*, 281

Ellwood, Thomas, 343–44

Emerson, Ralph W., 15, 157, 232, 314; *English Traits*, 118, 133

Empire Theatre, 15

Empire Theatre Dramatic School, 15

Emporia (Kansas) *Gazette*, 181

"English Men of Letters" series, 33

English, Miss, 89

Erlich, Paul, 115

Eton, 95

Euclid Avenue Baptist Church, 191

Eureka Mills, 315–16, 325, 336, 344–45, 355, 356, 358

Eve, 143, 169

"Everybody Works but Father" (song), 161–62

"Everyman's Library," 107

Fabian News, 378

Farnsworth, Alfred C. W., *264*
Felton, Cornelius C., *13*
Ferrero, Gina L., 247–*48*
*Ferrero, Guglielmo, *The Grandeur and Decadence of Rome*, 247; WDH recommends to C. E. Norton, 247–*48*
*Fields, Annie A. (Mrs. J. T.), 62, *87*, 89; at S. O. Jewett birthday celebration, 226–27
Fields, James T., 24
Fiske, May, 179–80
*Fiske, Minnie M., 25
*Fitch, William C., *Glad of It* (reviewed by WDH), 73–*74*; *Her Own Way* (reviewed by WDH), 74
Fleet Prison, 335
Foraker, Joseph B., *258*
Ford, James L., 96; *The Brazen Calf* (reviewed by WDH), 96; *The Literary Shop and Other Tales*, 352
Forma, Warren, 192
Foy, Eddie, 191
Franconia (ship), 360, 361, 375
Franz Joseph, of Austria, *282*
*Fréchette, Achille, *37*, 44, 60, 68–69; out of Canadian government, 292; retires to Switzerland, 316; in Paris and visits by Howells relatives, 338, 343, 365
*Fréchette, Anne H. (Mrs. A.), 34, 60, 65–66, 145, 239, 300; told of J. M. Howells' engagement, 235; WDH sends dress to, 245; poor health, 257; visits WDH at Kittery Point, 274; and story of Canadian government corruption, 292–93; WDH asks memories of Eureka Mills, 302; sells house, 315–16; at Kittery Point after E. M. Howells' death, 318, 321, 325; in Europe, 337–38, 343; WDH and M. Howells visit in Paris, 365
Fréchette, Howells, 69–*70*, 245–*46*, 318–19
*Fréchette, Marie M., 145, 182–83, 202, 265; in Paris studying art, 315–16; joined in Paris by A. Fréchette and A. H. Fréchette, 338; illness, 362; WDH and M. Howells visit in Paris, 365
Fréchette family, 158
Freeman, Mary E. W., "Old-maid Aunt" (in *The Whole Family*), 180
French and Indian Wars, 316
French Revolution, 261
*French, Alice, *Knitters in the Sun* (reviewed by WDH), *331*
French, Daniel C., 351–52
Fresh Pond, 252, 254

Frohman, Charles, 14–*15*
Frohman, Daniel, *15*
*Fuller, Henry B., 63–65; "The Age of Howells," 213; *The Cliff-Dwellers*, 212–13, 271; *With the Procession*, 72–73, 212–13, 271; on WDH, 154
Fulton Memorial Fund, 173
Funk & Wagnalls, 195
Furness, Horace H., 280–81

G. P. Putnam's Sons, 346–47
Gabrilowitsch, Clara C. (Mrs. O.), 319–20
Gabrilowitsch, Ossip, 291
Gainsborough, Thomas, 95
Galsworthy, John, WDH meets in England, 329–30
*Garland, Hamlin, 51, 71–72; *Cavanagh, Forest Ranger*, 313–14; *Crumbling Idols*, 314–15; *A Daughter of the Middle Border*, 314; *Main-Travelled Roads*, 72, 130, 314; *A Member of the Third House*, 356; "Sanity in Fiction," 49; *The Tyranny of the Dark*, 130–31, 355–56; "Under the Lion's Paw," 355–56; "Under the Wheel" (unpublished play), 356
Garland, Hamlin, Mrs., 130
Garland, Mary I., *59*, 130–31
Garrick Theatre, 330
*Garrison, Wendell P., 31
Generalife, 374–75
Gibson-Arms, 12, 20, 28, 153, 196, 229, 239, 254, 275
Gilbert, Cass, 351–52
Gilbert, William S., 96; *The Mikado* (cited by WDH), 316
*Gilder, Richard W., 51, 348; *A Christmas Wreath*, 75–76; "In Palestine," 76; encourages H. Garland, 314
Gilder, Rosamond, ed., *Letters of Richard Watson Gilder*, 76
Gill, Mabel S. K., 364, 365
Gill, Miss, 364
*Gill, William A., 110–*111*; and WDH's "A Tangled Web," 117; marriage, 364
*Gilman, Mr., 108
Giovanni di Padova, 91–92
Giusti, Giuseppe, *Raccolta di Proverbi Toscani*, 50–51, WDH comments on, 241–*42*
Glose, Augusta, 330
*Godkin, Edwin L., 235, 239; *Unforeseen Tendencies of Democracy*, 52–53; death, 4, 31; WDH on death of, 52–53; WDH essay on, 151–52; on C. E. Norton, 222

*Godkin, Katherine S. (Mrs. E. L.), 52–53
Goebel, William, *340*
Gold Hind, 84
Gorky, Maxim, *Fomo Gordeev*, 117–18; fund-raising tour, 152; affair with Madame Andreieva, 171–72; Perry recommends WDH read, 360
Goschen, George J., 106–07
*Gosse, Edmund W., letter to E. Wharton, 348–49; *Father and Son*, 327; on Cawein's poetry, 42–43; promotes Nobel Prize for H. James, 303, 348–49; 351; WDH meets in England, 301, 329–30
Gould, G. M., and L. Stedman, eds., *Life and Letters of Edmund Clarence Stedman*, 119
Gower, C. G. G. Levenson, 94–95
Goya y Lucientes, Francisco J. de, 93, 369, 371
Graatz and Neal, *The Mountain Climber* (translation of *Der Hochtourist*), 176
Grand Central Tunnel, 196
Grand Hotel, Plymouth, 81, 84
Grant, Captain, 121
Grant, Frederick, 173
Grant, Robert, 273; *The Law and the Family* (stage version reviewed by WDH), 273; *The Unleavened Bread* (stage version reviewed by WDH), 273
Grant, Ulysses S., 173
Gray, Thomas, 74–75
Green, Louisa, *The New Year*, 15
Greenslet, Ferris, *James Russell Lowell: His Life and Work*, 30; *Life of Thomas Bailey Aldrich*, *243*
Grieg, Edvard, 246
Griscom, Lloyd C., 243–*44*, 245, 247
Guillion, John, 370
Gunnison, Albert, 171–72, 191–92, 274

Hackett Theatre, 237
Hadley, Arthur T., 280–81
*Hale, Edward E., 24
Hale, Robert B., 24
Halifax Boats, 157
Hall of Fame, New York University, 231
*Hallstrom, Per, *351*
Hamburg-America Line, 84, 122
*Hamer, Mrs., 127
Hamilton, Alexander, 346
Hamilton, Ohio, 312
Hamilton, T. H., *192*
Hampton Court, 99
Hampton Institute, 24
Hapgood, Norman, 170–*71*, 255

*Harben, Will, 300, 308–09
Hardy, Thomas, 28; *Jude the Obscure*, 83–84; *The Return of the Native*, 10–12; *Two on a Tower*, 48; WDH suggests for "Turning-Point" series, 307
Harland, Henry, 115–16, 118; *The Cardinal's Snuff Box*, 42; *The Yellow Book* (ed.), 42; lunch for, 41–*42*
Harlow, Virginia, 329
*Harper & Brothers, 3, 7, 8, 12, 22, 23, 26, 58, 78–199 passim, 230, 240, 262, 279, 310–11, 334, 336; letter to Houghton, Mifflin & Co., 38; propose S. L. Clemens biography, 6, 68; publish two volumes of *Theatricals*, 15; print S. L. Clemens' "A Dog's Tale," 71; special tourist edition of English travel book proposed by WDH, 149–50; on WDH's 70th birthday, 216; support WDH trip to Rome, 229–30, 231; and WDH travel letters, 239, 252; and proposed Library Edition of WDH, 275; WDH requests leave from, 282; like H. James's "Crapy Cornelia," 289; WDH asks increase in salary, 299–300; ask WDH for memorial essay on S. L. Clemens, 300; WDH requests delay in publication of *Vacation of the Kelwyns*, 302; possible sponsor of S. L. Clemens memorial, 320; and J. W. Alexander, 332; WDH's relationship with, 339; satirized by J. L. Ford, 352; and H. Garland, 355
Harper, J. Henry, 20–21, 289
*Harper, J. W., 358
Harper's Bazar, 103, 117, 150, 151–52, 186, 188, 199–200, 204; publishes *The Whole Family*, 180; WDH suggests for publication of Ashburner memoirs, 198–99; publishes series on death, 262–63; A. H. Howells' subscription to, 292; publishes S. L. Clemens' "The Turning-Point of My Life," 300, 306; WDH proposes series on women's suffrage, 335; publishes H. James's essays on American women, 373
Harper's Ferry raid, 334
Harper's Monthly, 4, 5, 34, 70–71, 150, 159, 184–85, 199, 210; and F. Duneka, 58; publishes WDH English travel sketches, 118; WDH proposes short-story collection from, 141–42; publishes "After the Wedding," 200–01; publishes H. James's "Julia Bride," 247–48; publishes M. Howells' poem, 292–93; A. H. Howells' subscription to,

292; serializes WDH's "My Memories of Mark Twain," 301; satirized by J. L. Ford, 352

Harper's Weekly, 5, 12, 22, 28, 72, 81, 94, 150, 154, 221; WDH to help rehabilitate, 11; WDH articles in, 16–17; to print WDH's "A Sleep and a Forgetting," 199

Harriott, 336

Harriott, Fred, 39–*40*

Harte, Bret, 70–71; "The Luck of Roaring Camp," 25; "Miggles," 25; "The Outcasts of Poker Flat," 25; "Tennessee's Partner," 25; death, 4, 24–25

Harvard Graduates' Magazine, 233

Harvard University, 13, 54, 129, 212

*Harvey, George P., 79, 94–95, 102–03, 189, 219, 228, 311, 334; at WDH party, 20–21; and proposed life of Lowell, 30; assumes management of Harper & Brothers, 12, 58; WDH relations with, 22; gives dinner for Russian envoys, 134–35; gives 70th birthday dinner for Clemens, 8, 139; visits WDH at Kittery Point, 190; supports WDH trip to Rome, 230; and arrangements for WDH's travel letters, 239; on contract with WDH, 240; gives lunch for A. Farnsworth, 264; WDH asks increase in Harper salary, 299–300; provides WDH job, 339; WDH gives bon voyage party for, 272–73

Hastings, 280–81

Havez, Jean, *162*

Hawthorne, Nathaniel, 232

Hay Tor, 288–8*9*

*Hay, John, 18–*19*

Hayes, Rutherford B., 17

Hayes, Webb C., 131–32

Hayes family, 136

Haymarket Affair, 330

Hazel, 318–19

Hearst, William R., 258

Heidelbach, Charles, 15

Heine, Heinrich, *Reisebilder*, 286

Henrietta, *86*

Henry Holt & Co., 348

"The Henry James" (apartment house), 12

Herbert, Edward, 343–44

Herford, Brook, 83–*84*

Herford, Oliver B., "The Corelli-ing of Caine," 111

Herne, Chrystal, 355–56

Herne, James A., *Margaret Fleming* (WDH on), 355–*56*

*Herrick, Robert, 65, 255; *The Common Lot*, 194–95; *Memoirs of an American Citizen*, 194–95; *Together* (reviewed by WDH), 267–68; WDH on, 269

Hesperian Tree, 20

Hewlett, Maurice, 329–*30*

*Higginson, Thomas W., *Cheerful Yesterdays*, WDH proposes continuation, 280–81; contributes to *In After Days, Thoughts on the Future Life*, 263; supports woman successor to J. W. Howe as speaker at AAAL meeting, 335

Hinton, R. J., ed., *Poems by Richard Realf . . .*, 334

Hobbema, Meindert, 93

Hogarth, William, 95

Holloway, Jean, 59, 356

Holmes, Oliver W., 184, 221, 232

Holt, Henry, 348–49

Hooper, Susan (WDH's cousin), 60

Hoover, Charles L., *368*

Hoover, Helen, 368

Hoppin, Augustus, 122

*Houghton, Mifflin & Co., 121; letter to Harper & Brothers, 38; "American Men of Letters" Series, 29–30; publishing proposed life of Lowell, 30; and Library Edition of WDH, 37–38

House of Commons, 122

*Howe, Julia W., 62; "Capitol," 281; contributes to *In After Days, Thoughts on the Future Life*, 263; to address AAAL meeting, 280–81; death, 334–35; AAAL successor discussed, 334–35

Howe, M. A. De Wolfe, and Sara Norton, eds., *Letters of Charles Eliot Norton*, 22, 30, 61, 222, 233, 255

Howell, James, *Epistolae Ho-Elianae: Familiar Letters*, 335–36

*Howells, Abby W. (WDH's daughter-in-law), visits with WDH, 253, 263, 291–92; birth of first son, 265; to stay at Kittery Point, 318; WDH talks to on telephone, 343; WDH gives photo of to A. Palacio Valdés, 368. See also White, Abby.

Howells, Ally, 357–58

Howells, Anne T. (WDH's grandmother), 216–17, 343

*Howells, Aurelia H. (WDH's sister), 66, 124, 132, 264–65; moves to Ottawa, 44–45; WDH confides in, 151; scalded arm, 158; sale of Jefferson house, 174–75; desolate at death of H. I. Howells, 250; visits WDH, 257–58; WDH asks about memories of Eureka Mills, 302; to live with A. H. Fréchette, 315; invited to live at Kittery Point, 318, 321, 325; traveling in Europe, 337–38; WDH and M. Howells visit in Paris, 365

Howells, Beatrice R. (WDH's niece), 137; in Grand Turk society, 157; returns to Jefferson, 208–09, 215; J. A. Howells visits, 357–58

*Howells, Elinor M. (WDH's wife), 6, 9, 10, 13, 24, 44–177 passim, 184, 191–92, 197, 208, 283; letter to Mildred Howells, 263; poor health, 3, 149, 153, 188, 190; interest in painting, 37; with WDH in Atlantic City, 76; and proposed trip to England, Italy, 77–78; birthday, 99; editing WDH's writing, 113–14; suggestions about *The Leatherwood God*, 130–31; and Laura Mitchell, 131; visits relatives' graves, 136; leaves Kittery Point for New York, 139. 149; undergoes surgery, 156; in Atlantic City, 164, 167, 168–69; and M. Howells' broken engagement, 180; considers trip to Bermuda, 216; relation to children, 217; and WDH at Kittery Point, 223; trip to Great Lakes, 224–26; good health, 229; remembers Delevan House, 234; voyage to Rome, 238–39; poor health in Rome, 240, 242; in Rome, 244, 245; on invitation to Bjornson, 246; leaves Rome, 247; deterioration, 251, 253, 256; invited to Stormfield, 256; teeth extracted, 258; and S. W. Mitchell, 261; birth of grandson, 265; New York move, 266; WDH concerned about her taking trip to Spain, 279; enjoys E. Phillpotts' book and letter, 285; and Noyes ancestry, 286–87; illness and operation, 289–90, 291; failing health, 292; enjoys H. James's *The Tragic Muse*, 294; illness and death, 299–304, 305, 307, 311–12, 313, 315, 317, 318, 320–21, 326, 327, 339, 342, 359, 361; enjoys James's novels, 307; 73rd birthday, 318; funeral 318–19; WDH mourns, 318–19, 320–21, 322, 324–25, 326, 336–37, 340, 346, 355, 362–63; H. James on, 322; critical ability, 346; WDH reminiscences, 353; WDH follows wish in not publishing *Vacation of the Kelwyns*, 362

*Howells, Eliza W. (WDH's sister-in-law), 137, 161, 174, 257–58, 278; in Grand Turk society, 157; eye trouble,

215; to approve sale of Cleveland house, 265; age and infirmities, 377

Howells, Ethel (WDH's sister-in-law), 229–*30*, 279, 292; WDH suggests move to Jefferson, 249–50; S. D. Howells cannot care for, 257

Howells, Florence B., (WDH's niece), 197–*98*, 230, 257; severe illness, 217; death, 202, 293

Howells, George (WDH's great-great-uncle), 60

Howells, Henry I. (WDH's brother), 9, 21, 28, 60, 66, 68–69, 109, 124–158 passim, 239; resemblance to W. C. Howells, 27; moves to Ottawa, 44–45; severe illness, 250; death, 255

Howells, Jessie (WDH's niece), 230, 257

*Howells, John M. (WDH's son), 9, 48, 60; poor health, 3; meets E. E. Hale, 24; recovering from illness, 27; work for S. L. Clemens, 32–33; and trip to England, Italy, 77–78; firm receives architectural commission, 83–84; WDH comments on hard work, 89, 92–93, 94, 99, 100; travels in Italy, 108–09, 110; Colorado trip, 124, 130, 131–32, 133; returns to Kittery Point, 136; designs "Stormfield" for S. L. Clemens, 152; marriage, 155; with family in New York, 157, 163; to minstrel show with WDH, 161; in Bermuda and after, 167, 170, 171–72, 174, 177, 182, 185–86; interest in colonial architecture, 186; as architect, 194; stomach illness, 196, 202, 208; on Christian Science healing, 215, 217; relations with E. M. Howells, 217; takes photo of WDH, 224; trip to Yellowstone, 224–26, 228, 229; engagement, wedding, 230, 235, 324; visits WDH at Kittery Point, 253; visits with WDH, 258, 263; and design of "Stormfield," 255–56, 264; birth of first son, 264–65; story published in *Atlantic*, 274; visits WDH at Thanksgiving, 291–92; to stay at Kittery Point, 318; WDH appreciates, 320; transmits letter from J. H. Twichell to WDH, 326; nomination to National Institute of Arts and Letters, 351–52; visit to A. Palacio Valdés, 368–69; and Spain, 374

Howells, John M., Mr. and Mrs., 290, 321, 326, 328

Howells, John M., family, 353–54, 355, 357, 368, 377

Howells, Joseph (WDH's grandfather), 261, 343

*Howells, Joseph A. (WDH's brother), 9, 20–21, 34–35, 44–45, 50, 208–09, 124–25, 128, 135, 200, 292; "Salt Cay Letter," 229–30; "West Indian Hurricanes," 190–91; Turks Islands travel letters, 162, 173–74, 196–97, 209, 256–57; consulship at Turks Islands, 116, 136–37, 139, 155, 157; WDH confides in, 151; visits WDH, 258; to approve sale of Cleveland house, 265; illness, 3, 278; visits WDH, 290; WDH asks about memories of Eureka Mills, 302; WDH portrays in *New Leaf Mills*, 344–45; WDH consults about *The Leatherwood God*, 363; visits W. D. Howells II, 377; death, 377

Howells, Joseph A., Jr. (WDH's nephew), *162*, 324–25

*Howells, Mary D. (WDH's mother), 250; WDH reminisces about, 134–*35*, 302, 312–13, 316; at Eureka Mills, 333; WDH portrays in *New Leaf Mills*, 344–45, 357

*Howells, Mildred (WDH's daughter), 34, 44, 48, 81–124 passim, 159–263 passim, 325, 328, 332, 340, 345, 360, 377; "At the Wind's Will," 165–66; "Huge Cloudy Symbols," 364–65; *Life in Letters*, 53, 55, 194, 214–15, 235, 244, 254, 273, 275, 287, 289, 313, 317, 360; "My Dream," 210–11; "O Wind A-Blowing All Day Long," 292–93; Bermuda trip, 167, 171–72; broken engagement, 180; sore throat, 197; helping WDH with writing, 205; poor health, 208; relation to E. M. Howells, 217; English trip, 224, 227, 228, 229, 232; on voyage to Rome, 238–39; sore throat in Rome, 240, 242, 244, 245; attends Ibsen concert, 246; in Paris, 249; visits art colony in Cornish, N.H., 253–55; Clemens invites to "Stormfield," 256; in Boston, 264; sails for Bermuda, 266, 270; domestic role at Kittery Point, 274; with WDH in Europe, 283, 285–86; on Torquay tour, 288; at Kittery Point, 290; proposed visit to Clemens with WDH, 290; ignorance of E. M. Howells' operation, 291; proposed volume of poetry, 292–93; reports to WDH on Clemens, 300, 310; with WDH, 301, 303, 304, 305, 307, 309; returns from Bermuda at E. M. Howells' illness, 311; coresponds with G. A. Plimpton, 315–16; to visit England with WDH, 318, 322, 328; attends

to E. M. Howells' belongings at Kittery Point, 321; poor health, 336–37; Bermuda trip with WDH, 341, 342–43, 344; at Kittery Point, 353; plan for cure trip, 355–56; medical treatment, 357; trip to Wales, Spain with WDH, 361, 365, 370, 372–73, 374; suffragist, 364; cares for WDH, 365

Howells, Samuel D. (WDH's brother), 155; position at Government Printing Office, 135, 193–94, 196–97; wife's illness, 198, 217; poor health and circumstances, 201–02, 229–30; WDH suggests move to Jefferson, 249–50; loses job, 257–58, 279; remarries, 292–93

Howells, Samuel D., Mrs., 292

Howells, Susan Halstead (WDH's niece), 324–25

Howells, Thomas (WDH's great-grandfather), 261, 343, 259–60, 363

Howells, Victoria M. (WDH's sister), *250*

*Howells, William C. (WDH's father), 34, 69–70, 134, 177, 250, 278, 313; WDH reminisces about, 28, 302, 338; WDH remembers on centennial, 201; at Eureka Mills and WDH's use in *New Leaf Mills*, 333, 344–45, 356

*Howells, William C., II (WDH's nephew), 344–45, 357–58

Howells, W. D.:

WORKS:

"Aberystwyth, a Welsh Watering Place," 273

"After the Wedding," 200–01

The Altrurian Romances, 220

"The American James," 55, 254

April Hopes, 200

"The Art of Longfellow," 200, 231; prepared for commemoration, 203, 204–05, 206

"The Author to the Reader," new introductory chapter for *Venetian Life*, 228

Between the Dark and the Daylight, 144, 150, 233–34; discussed with F. A. Duneka, 195–96

"Biographicals" (prefaces for the Library Edition), 275

"Black Cross Farm," 79–80

A Boy's Town, 6, 66, 279, 312

"Carl Schurz, 1829–1906," 178

Certain Delightful English Towns, 7, 81, 84, 86, 87, 91, 92, 96, 133, 149, 158, 172, 195, 279; composition, 122, 165; sales, 216–17

"Certain of the Chicago School of Fiction," 65

A Chance Acquaintance, WDH proposes for Library Edition, 275

"The Children of the Summer" (provisional title for *The Vacation of the Kelwyns*), 221, 223

"Choice Autobiographies" series, 343–44

"A Counsel of Consolation," 155; title proposed for series on death, 262–63

Criticism and Fiction, 106, 169; preface for Library Edition, 275

"A Dangerous Ruffian," alternative title for *The Garroters*, 53

"Diversions of the Higher Journalist . . . ," 96

A Doorstep Acquaintance, WDH proposes for Library Edition, 275

"Easier for a Camel" (provisional title for *Through the Eye of the Needle*), 195–96

"Editor's Study," 356; on literary realism, 33; on A. P. Valdés, 303; WDH and M. Savage differ on, 327; review of A. French's *Knitters in the Sun*, 331

"Editor's Easy Chair," 5, 11, 71, 80–81, 118, 185–86, 203; on Ohio River trip, 18, 31; on Longfellow, 28; on books on G. Eliot, 34; on Stoddard and Trowbridge autobiographies, 68; on B. Harte, 71; on spelling reform, 194, 230; on noise pollution, 198; on younger writers in magazines, 210–11; on J. F. Cooper, 231; on vaudeville, 329; on women's suffrage, 335; on criticism, 346–47; on American humorists, 352; on Valdés' book, 366

"The Eidolons of Brooks Alford," 233–34

"Essays Mostly Contrary-Minded," proposed volume of essays, 77

Familiar Spanish Travels, 303, 361, 366, 373; WDH plans, 362; cites touring with A. P. Valdés, 369; composition, 370–71

Farces, 214–15

"A Fatal Ignorance of Liberty," 22

"The Father" (in *The Whole Family*), 180

Fennel and Rue, 150; and plagiarism, 187–88; proposed titles for, 236;

contract, 239; C. E. Norton on, 251–52; praised by B. Matthews, 269

"A Few Remaining Moments," 251–52

"The Fiction of Eden Phillpotts," 285

The Flight of Pony Baker, 6, 66, 83–84

"Floating Down the River on the O-hi-o," 18, 31

"The Florentine Satirist, Giusti," 242

"A Fortnight in Bath," 87

"Frank Norris," 42

The Garroters, 53

"A Glimpse of the English Washington Country," 96

"God Does Not Pay Saturdays" (provisional title for *The Son of Royal Langbrith*), 48, 50–52

"A Great New York Journalist," 53, 151–52, 220, 222

"Harper's Novelettes" series, WDH co-edits with H. M. Alden, 324

Harper's Weekly articles, 16–17

A Hazard of New Fortunes, 153; preface for Library Edition, 276; B. Matthews on, 361

"Henrik Ibsen," 63, 181–82

"Her Opinion of His Story," 199–200

Heroines of Fiction, proposal, 76; introduction, 275

"His Apparition," 327

Imaginary Interviews, 114–15, 302, 329

An Imperative Duty, 65

In After Days, Thoughts on the Future Life, 155; WDH contributes essay to, 263

"In the House of Mourning," 155; title proposed for series on death, 262–63

Indian Summer, 7; praised by T. Roosevelt, 138

Italian Journeys, 244; WDH proposes for Library Edition, 275

"John Brown After Fifty Years" (review of O. G. Villard's *John Brown*), 334

"John Hay in Literature," 127

"The Justice of a Friend" (on Trevelyan's *The American Revolution*), 243–44

The Kentons, 4, 25, 26, 29, 33–34; provisional titles for, 9; reviewed by H. Preston, 39; W. James on, 35

The Lady of the Aroostook, 7, 89; praised by T. Roosevelt, 138

"The Landing of a Pilgrim," 84

The Landlord at Lion's Head, 72

"The Law of Limitation" (provisional title for *The Son of Royal Langbrith*), 59

The Leatherwood God, 209; first mention of J. A. Howells gathering information for, 109; WDH begins composition, 130–31; further work on, 363

"Letters from Venice," 336

Letters Home, difficulties with, 4; American reception of, 5; provisional title, 9; composition, 10–11; serialization, 10; reaction to, 27–28, 37, 64, 69, 76–77, 79–80; C. E. Norton praises, 66–67

"Letters of an Altrurian Traveller," 196

Library Edition, 37–38, 153, 195–96, 275, 278–79

"Life and Letters," 73, 141

Literary Friends and Acquaintance, 6, 24, 25, 30, 40, 53, 66, 172, 201, 205, 206, 310

Literature and Life, 18, 31

"A Little Mistake," 13

"Llandudno, Another Welsh Watering Place," 273

London Films, 7, 81, 96, 133, 141, 160-61, 257–58, 278; composition, 121–22; disappointment in poor sales, 149

"Lyof N. Tolstoy," 378

"The Magazine Muse," 203

"The Memory That Worked Overtime," 233

The Minister's Charge, 127–28

Minor Dramas, 209

Miss Bellard's Inspiration, 64–65, 76–77, 135; composition and postponed publication, 5

A Modern Instance, 26, 361

Modern Italian Poets, 242

"The Molineux Case," 56–59

"Mr. Henry James's Later Work," 49, 55

"Mr. Harben's Georgia Fiction," 308–09

My Literary Passions, 6, 312, 361; preface for Library Edition, 275

My Mark Twain, 10, 25, 40, 154, 172, 201, 301; on S. L. Clemens on W. Harben, 309; composition and publication, 317

"My Memories of Mark Twain," composition, 301; serialization, 317;

WDH correcting galleys, 319; publication, 327, 331; WDH declines additional payment, 338–39

My Year in a Log Cabin, 6, 66, 302, 312, 336, 345

New Leaf Mills, 67, 302; WDH resumes work on, 315–16, 325; gathering material for, 325, 336, 337, 346–47, 354–55; composition, 333, 344–45, 356–58; WDH readies for publication, 363

"The New Plays . . . ," 96, 163

"Niccolini's Anti-Papal Tragedy," 242

"The Novels of Robert Herrick," 267–68

"An Obsolescent American Type" (review of Ade's *Doc' Horne*), 64

"On Reading the Plays of Mr. Henry Arthur Jones," 214–15

"One of the Public to the Author" (introduction to *The Henry James Yearbook*), 284, 342

"Our Daily Speech," 204

Out of the Question, 168

"Oxford," 157–58

The Parlor Car, 168

"The Peacemakers at Portsmouth," 129

"A Personal Retrospect of James Russell Lowell," 29–30, 40, 220, 222

"A Political Novelist and More," 23

"The Practices and Precepts of Vaudeville," 329

Proposed literary autobiography, 277, 278

Questionable Shapes, 4, 28, 327

"Real Conversations . . ." (interview with Boyesen), 177–78

"The Recent Dramatic Season" (review of A. Thomas' plays), 237

"Recollections of an Atlantic Editorship," 233–34

"Reconciliation" (provisional title for *The Son of Royal Langbrith*), 59

REVIEWS AND NOTICES:
Ade, George, *The Country Chairman*, 72; *Doc' Horne*, 64
Barrie, James M., *Alice-Sit-By-the-Fire*, 163; plays, 96
Brown, Alice, *Meadow-Grass*, 141
Carlyle, Jane W., *New Letters and Memorials to Jane Welsh Carlyle*, 55
Carpenter, George R., *Henry Wadsworth Longfellow*, 13

Collins, G. L., *Putnam Place*, 56

Cornaro, Luigi, *The Temperate Life*, 72

Cross, Wilbur L., *The Life and Times of Laurence Sterne*, 310

Fitch, William C., *Glad of It*, 73–74; *Her Own Way*, 74

Ford, James L., *The Brazen Calf*, 96

French, Alice, *Knitters in the Sun*, 331

Fuller, Henry B., *With the Procession*. 73

Grant, Robert, *The Law and the Family*, 273; *Unleavened Bread*, 273

Herne, James A., *Margaret Fleming*, 356

Herrick, Robert, *Together*, 267–68

James, Henry, *The Tragic Muse*, 106

Jones, Henry A., *The Hypocrites*, 215

Matthews, Brander, *Molière*, 349

Norton, Charles E., *The Divine Comedy of Dante Alighieri*, 22

Palacio Valdés, Armando, *Papeles del Doctor Angélico*, 366

Phillpotts, Eden, fiction, 285

Sanborn, Franklin B., *Recollections of Seventy Years*, 280–81

Scudder, Horace E., *James Russell Lowell: A Biography*, 30

Villard, Oswald G., *John Brown, 1800–1859*, 334

Wallace, Alfred R., *Man's Place in the Universe*, 71

Wharton, Edith, *Crucial Instances*, 144

Whitlock, Brand, *The Turn of the Balance*, 219

Wilcox, Marrion, *Gray, an Oldhaven Romance*, 19; *The Vengeance of the Female*, 19

Wyatt, Edith, *Every One His Own Way*, 41

The Rise of Silas Lapham, 175–76, 347

Roman Holidays and Others, 155, 239, 241, 244, 260, 278; account of Ernest Nathan, 245; proposed title, 252; composition, 253; praised by A. H. Fréchette, 265; slow sales, 265

"The Season's Plays . . . ," 215

Seven English Cities, 81, 273

"Siena Notebook" (manuscript), 51

"A Sleep and a Forgetting," 150, 160–61, 161–62, 172, 183, 199–200, 221, 223, 233–34; composition, 165, 167

"Some New American Plays" (reviews of plays by G. Ade, C. Fitch, and A.

Thomas), 72, 74, 237

The Son of Royal Langbrith, 7, 48, 50–52, 63–65, 67, 69, 71–72, 76–77, 78, 113–14, 115; composition, 5, 44–45, 59; psychological focus, 5; provisional titles for, 44–45; reception, 5; advertisement for, 112

"Sonnet to Mark Twain," 139–40

"Sorrow, My Sorrow," 70–71

Speech at Clemens memorial service, 332

Stops of Various Quills, 90–91

"The Story of the Story" (preface for Library Edition of *Hazard of New Fortunes*), 173, 276

"Studies of Lowell," 220, 222

Suburban Sketches, 99

"A Tangled Web" (provisional title for *Fennel and Rue*), 150, 177, 187–88

Their Husbands' Wives (co-edited with H. M. Alden), 142

Their Silver Wedding Journey, 282

Their Wedding Journey, 55, 121–22; proposed for inclusion in Library Edition, 275; copy as wedding gift to Mr. and Mrs. W. A. Gill, 364

"Though One Rose from the Dead," 28

Through the Eye of the Needle, 150, 196, 209, 220; provisional titles for, 195; composition, 195–96; plans for publication, 221; C. E. Norton on, 223; advertising for, 224

A Traveler from Altruria, 150, 195–96, 209, 274

"A Triad of Admirable Books," 56

"The Turning-Point of My Life," 307, 309

Tuscan Cities, 156

"Twenty-four Hours at Exeter," 86

The Undiscovered Country, 101, 105–06, 130

"Up and Down Madeira," 239

The Vacation of the Kelwyns, 259, 314; early work on, 221, 223; provisional title for, 221, 223, 352; difficulties with, 271; completion, delay of publication, 302, 353–54, 358, 362–63

"Venice Revisited" (new introductory chapter for *Venetian Life*), 228

"The Villagers" (projected), 35

"The White Mr. Longfellow," 204–05, 206

The Whole Family, 180

"Will the Novel Disappear?" 5

Years of My Youth, 6, 277, 334, 336, 344, 360

TOPICS:
Culture, aspects of: *architecture*, 374–75; *aristocracy*, 96; *art*, 30, 93, 303, 374–75; *clothing*, 69, 190, 283; *crowds*, 284; *gentility* (vs. vulgarity), 198–99; *marriage*, 180; *morality* (women), 267, 269; *noise*, 256, 280; *propriety*, 190; *theater*, 329; *women*, 97–98, 102, 204, 246, 283, 295, 370, 372
Culture, national: *American*, 3, 79; *American vs. English*, 82–83, 93, 176–77, 364; *American vs. European*, 73, 123; *American vs. French*, 366; *American average*, 4, 33, 151–52, 167, 185–86, 306; *Anglo-Saxon*, 283; *Austrian*, 282; *Cuban*, 18; *English*, 69, 85–86, 91–92, 93, 99, 107–08, 133, 140–41, 198–99, 364; *English vs. Welsh*, 362; *French*, 249, 366; *Italian*, 91–92, 247; *Japanese*, 130; *Moorish*, 374–75; *Russian*, 118, 129, 130; *Slavic*, 283; *Spanish*, 303, 369–70, 371, 372–73, 374–75
Education: *honorary degrees*, 7, 106–07, 110–11, 124, 306
Family: *ancestry*, 216, 261, 286–87, 329, 359–60; *children*, 155, 217, 235, 313, 320, 325, 353, 376–77; *grandchildren*, 311; *parents*, 250, 313, 316, 333; *siblings*, 155, 193–94, 249, 250, 279, 313; *wife*, 320. *See also names of individual members of family.*
Financial affairs: *contracts*, 3, 149, 230, 239–40, 302; *expenses*, 249, 250, 315; *financing publication*, 160–61, 174–75; *income*, 81, 197–98, 338–39; *investments*, 265; *salary*, 299, 310–11
Health: *medical treatment*, 77, 79, 120, 284–85, 289, 291; *mental*, 299; dreams, 150, 183, 201, 234, 302, 313, 362; insomnia, 302; mourning, 341–42; *nervous breakdown*, 341–42; *physical*, 9, 145, 153, 174, 293; advice, 355–56, 376–77; colds, 337–38; gall colic, 156, 276, 339, 341–42; grippe, 346; indigestion, 3, 149, 173; illness, 278, 348; infirmities, 376–77; influenza, 207, 208, 210, 216, 218; insomnia, 3; liver, 280; vertigo, 276
Languages: *English*, 177; *German*, 177; *Italian*, 365; *Spanish*, 365; *Welsh*, 329
Literary movements: *realism*, 4, 33, 150, 154, 270–72, 309; *romanticism*, 309; *veritism*, 314–15
Literature, forms of: *autobiography*, 6, 68, 77–78; *criticism*, 39; *drama*, 14, 73, 168, 175–76, 214–15, 355; *epistolary fiction*, 11, 28; *essay*, 150, 154, 195–96; *fiction*, 150, 165, 180, 194, 195–96, 313–14; difficulties with, 270–71; younger writers in magazines, 202–03, 210; *historical novel*, 164; *journalism*, 221; *letters*, 123; *novel*, 308; *poetry*, 34–35, 37, 42, 260; *psychic romance*, 4; *romance*, 150; *travel writing*, 18, 118, 121–22, 144, 165, 195, 239, 319
Literature, national: *American*, compared to others, 168; *Japanese*, 283–84; *Russian*, 159; *Spanish*, 361, 371
Philosophy: *after-life*, 216
Politics: *anarchism*, 118; *consulships*, 19, 116, 136–37, 155, 189, 319–20; *copyright*, 152, 200–01, 338; *democracy*, 292; *imperialism*, U.S.–Philippine relations, 13, 22, 61; *justice*, 56–58, 190–91, 217, 218–20, 339–40; Haymarket Affair, 330; *law*, age of consent, 56; *parties*, 193, 254–55, 362–63, 364; *respectability*, 173, 175; *revolution*, Russian, 152, 171–72; WDH fears in Spain, 366; *tax*, Roosevelt policy, 171, 172, 193–94; *war*, German blockade of Venezuela, 50; Russo-Japanese War, 7, 118, 128–29, 130–31; Russo-Japanese peace conference, 132–33, 134–35; Spanish-American War, 61
Reform: *equalitarianism*, 65, 193–94; *labor*, 362–63, 364; *single tax*, 356; *socialism*, 274, 378; *women's suffrage*, 335
Religion: *agnosticism*, 75; *Anglicanism*, 85–86; *Catholicism*, 373; *Christian Science*, 172, 196, 215, 217, 284, 372; *Christianity*, 75; *Quakerism*, 90, 261, 343–44, 363; *Shakerism*, 302, 359; *spiritualism*, 130; *Swedenborgianism*, 90; *Unitarianism*, 83–84
Residences: 302 Beacon St., Boston, 21; Kittery Point, 21–97 passim, 121–81 passim, 196–363 passim; Jefferson, 34–35, 66, 124, 132, 135, 174–75, 197, 215–17, 249, 312–13, 338, 361, 369; 37 Concord Ave., Cambridge, 62; 48 West 59th St., New York, 97, 138; The Ramon, New York, 122; 41 Sacramento St., Cambridge, 134, 312;

The Burlington, New York, 140, 158, 161–63, 336; 130 West 57th St., New York, 149, 229, 258–266 passim, 302, 336–37; Rome, 155, 244, 369; The St. Hubert, 57th St., New York, 163; Regent Hotel, New York, 172, 196; Cleveland, 174–75, 249, 257, 264–65; Oxford Hotel, New York, 196; Columbus, 279; Ottawa, 315–16; Eureka Mills, 302, 315–16, 325, 333, 336, 344; Bermuda, 342–43, 344, 363; Staten Island, 353–54; Shirley Village, Massachusetts, 302, 359

Science: 131

Self-conceptualization: *ability*, 278–79; *aging*, 8, 11, 28, 32, 34–35, 37, 56, 71–72, 113–32 passim, 151, 166, 167, 212–279 passim, 376–77; *appearance*, 112, 178; *death*, 155, 299–302, 321–22, 325, 326; *friendship*, 151, 154, 157, 165, 185, 203, 260–61; *honors*, 201; *immortality*, 4, 155, 160–61, 166, 216, 321–22; *loneliness*, 321; *purpose*, 145; *reputation*, 134, 181, 184–85, 310; *self-identity*, 4; *shortcomings*, 4, 40–41, 46, 66, 77, 111, 153, 205

Society: *Atlantic City*, 167; *Boston*, 305, 307; *Cambridge*, 139, 182, 221, 232, 300, 307, 318; *Grand Turk*, 159; *New York*, 149, 158, 161, 307

Travel: Ohio River, 3; proposed trip to England, Italy, 77; English trip, 7, 74, 81, 82–123 passim; Italy, 107–08, 109, 110, 113, 119, 123, 155; on Ohio River with J. A. Howells, 120; Atlantic City, 164–65; Great Lakes, 224–26, 228, 229; Rome, 229–30, 231, 234, 235, 237–39; visit to Madeira, 237–38; Italian sightseeing, 240–41; Monte Carlo, Paris, London, 251; touring Boston, 257; proposed trip to Spain, 279, 303, 319, 361–62, 369–70; Carlsbad, England, 283–84, 286–87, 288, 301; Bermuda, 303, 336, 339, 341, 342–43, 355; Wales, 303, 361, 362; Europe, 369–70

Writing: *editing*, 142, 198–99; *grammar*, 196, 198; *letters*, as record of work, 278; *method*, 132–33, 140, 187, 190, 217; C. E. Norton's advice on Godkin paper, 220, 222–23; waning interest, 278–79; keeps writing despite E. M. Howells' final illness, 300, 311; length of "Easy Chair" essays, 352; enjoys, 354; *proofreading*, 319, 324, 353; *public addresses*, 293; *publishing*, 160–61, 199; Library Edition, appearance, 276; delay in *The Vacation of the Kelwyns*, 353, 358; *reviewing*, 192, 267; *revision*, 198, 204–05; of *Venetian Life*, 231; accepts C. E. Norton's advice on Longfellow paper, 232; of review of B. Matthews' *Molière*, 352; of *The Vacation of the Kelwyns*, 352; *spelling reform*, 193–94, 230; *style*, effect of travel in England on, 123, 124; sonnet for S. L. Clemens' 70th birthday, 139; concern for, 151, 152, 153, 156, 164; suggestions for J. A. Howells, 200, 208, 269; *success of books*, 157, 265, 273, 277, 279, 310, 347; *syndication*, 196

*Howells, William D., II (WDH's nephew), *10*, 208, 257, 345, 357–58, 377; edits J. A. Howells' travel letters, *162*; manages house in Jefferson, 249; WDH suggests J. A. Howells stay with, 376–77

*Howells, William W. (WDH's grandson), 318, 342; birth, 155, 264–65; joy and comfort to WDH, 156, 294, 304, 311, 355; birthday card sent to WDH on behalf of, 268–69; visits WDH, 290, 291–92; birthday present from WDH, 292; WDH talks to on telephone, 343; WDH wants to "Billify," 360; at Kittery Point, 363; WDH gives photograph of to A. Palacio Valdés, 368; WDH imagines in Patio de los Leones, 374; WDH misses third birthday, 375; WDH's fondness for, 376–77

Howells, Winifred (WDH's daughter), 62, 134–35, 183–84, 321, 324–25; compared to A. Murray, 27; grave of, 41; treated by S. W. Mitchell, 154; death, 261–62, 361; E. M. Howells buried with, 318–19

Howells Memorial, Kittery Point, Maine, 222

Hurd & Houghton, 228

Hutchins, Mr., 344–45

Ibsen, Bergliot B., *246*

Ibsen, Henrik, 62–63, 182, 246; WDH essay memorializing, 154

Ibsen, Sigurd, 246

Ide, Henry C., 366–67, 368

Ilyich, Ilya, *See* Metchnikoff, Elie.

International Congress of Arts and Sciences, 231

Ireland, John, 174–75
Irving, Washington, *The Conquest of Granada*, 361

James II, of England, 84
James, Alice, 353–54; cares for H. James, 322–34; with W. and H. James in Konstanz, 324; preparing to visit U.S.A., 328; writes to WDH, 341–42
*James, Henry, 29, 88, 95–96, 110–11, 118, 130, 133, 144; letter to C. E. Norton, 54–55; letter to Grace Norton, 55; letter to J. W. White, 354; *The Ambassadors*, 59, 51–52, 64–65, 72, 305; *The American*, 252, 254; *The American Scene*, 103, 367; "The Author to the Public" (preface to *The Henry James Yearbook*), 284, 342; "The Bench of Desolation," 289–90; *The Bostonians*, 305, 307–08; "Crapy Cornelia," 289; *The Europeans*, 254; "The Finer Grain," 290; *The Golden Bowl*, 111; contribution to *In After Days, Thoughts on the Future Life*, 263; "Julia Bride," 247–48; "The Lesson of Balzac" (lecture), 103–04, 169; *The Letters of Henry James*, 254–55, 308; *A Little Tour in France*, 366–67, 370; "The Manners of American Women," 152, 203–04; "The Married Son" (in *The Whole Family*), 180, 207; *Mrs. Jasper*, 14–15, (WDH on), 14–15; New York Edition, 153, 247–48, 252, 254, 275, 277, 305, 308; WDH doesn't want to imitate prefaces of, 277; *Notes of a Son and Brother*, 354; *The Outcry*, 373–74; *The Portrait of a Lady*, 252, 254; "The Question of Our Speech" (lecture), 103; *The Question of Our Speech* (book), 103, 169; *Roderick Hudson*, 252, 254; *A Small Boy and Others*, 354; "The Speech of American Women," 203–04; *The Tragic Muse*, 153, 294–95, 305; (reviewed by WDH), 106; *Watch and Ward*, 254; WDH visits, 8; apartment house named after, 11; and E. Wharton, 12; and M. Johnston, 12; and K. D. Wiggin, 12; and J. L. Allen, 12; on WDH's "Mr. Henry James's Later Work," 49; letters to WDH, 61; C. E. Norton on later fiction, of, 62; visits WDH in England, 92; on H. G. Wells, 101; cancels luncheon, 102; American visit and lecture tour, 102–03, 126; made

member of American Academy, 115, 116; visits S. O. Jewett, 125; visits WDH at Kittery Point, 125; W. James on, 127; WDH confides in, 151; and relationship with WDH, 153; and WDH in London, 155; on Balzac, Tolstoy, Austen, 168–69; on WDH's writing on American culture, 204; WDH visits in Paris and London, 251; tea with Scottish M.P., 254–55; efforts to obtain Nobel Prize for, 303, 348–49, 350–51, 370; appreciates WDH's travel descriptions, 303; nervous breakdown, 312, 321; beginning of friendship with WDH, 312; WDH hopes to visit in England, 301, 322; prepares to visit U.S.A., 328; M. Sherwood praises, 346; WDH advises about writing, 354; visits WDH in Kittery Point, 359–60; WDH visits in London, 370; on American women, 373
James, Henry, ed., *The Letters of William James*, 255
James, Robertson, death, 342, 354
*James, William, 241; letter to Robert U. Johnson, 126–27; *Letters of William James*, 255; *The Varieties of Religious Experience*, 35; declines election to AAAL, 126; writes to C. E. Norton, 253, 255; preparing to visit U.S.A., 328; death, 324, 342, 354
Janvier, Thomas A., at WDH party, 20–21; proposed author for *The Whole Family*, 279–80
Jefferson, Joseph, 115, 175–76; *Autobiography of Joseph Jefferson*, 176
Jerome, William T., 57–58, 217–18
Jesus Christ, 327
*Jewett, Sarah O., *Sarah Orne Jewett Letters*, 125, 227; WDH praises, 65; WDH attends birthday celebration, 226–27; on C. E. Norton friendship, 262–63; paralyzed by stroke, WDH visits, 274
John the Baptist, 374–75
Johnson, Hardesty, 59
*Johnson, Robert U., 36, 115, 351; lobbies for copyright legislation, 201; travels to AAAL Washington meeting with WDH, 294; and arrangements for Clemens memorial, 332
Johnson, Willis F., 139
Johnston, Mary, *To Have and to Hold*, 12
Jones, Edmund A., 200–01
*Jones, Henry A., *The Hypocrites*, 214;

Judah, 213–14; *Michael and his Lost Angel*, 213; *The Renascence of the English Drama*, 214–15
*Jones, Mary C., 349
Jones, Mr., 344–45
*Jordan, Elizabeth, *103*; "The School-Girl" (in *The Whole Family*), 180; WDH works with on "A Counsel of Consolation," 155; proposed author for *The Whole Family*, 179–80; as editor of *Harper's Bazar*, 204; and proposed series on death, 262; and "Turning-Point" series, 306

Katie, 105
Keats, John, 241–42
Keeler, Ralph, 24, 326–27
Keith, Benjamin F., *329*
Keith's Circuit, 329
Keith's Theatre, 328–29
Kellogg, Abner, *217*
Kellogg, Nettie, 216–*17*
Kensington Palace, 96
Kenyon College, 17–18
Kester, Paul, 45
Ketchum, Arthur, *A Gentleman of the Road*, 15
Kilmer, Joyce, 27
Kings Point State Hospital for the Insane, 58
Kingsley, Florence M., *The Needle's Eye*, 295–96
Kipling, Rudyard, 30
Klaus, Samuel, ed., *The Molineux Case*, 58
Komura, Jutaro, *129*
Kropotkin, Peter, *118*

La Farge, John, 20, 280–81
Laffan, William M., 239, 252
Lamb House, Rye, 102, 324, 373
Lampson, Mr., 174–75
Landor, Walter S., 118
Lane, John, 94–*95*
Lathrop, George P., 140
Lawrence, Eweretta, 53
*Le Gallienne, Richard T., "A Ballad of Woman . . ." (WDH on), 335
Lee, Sidney, 50–*51*
Leigh, Frederick T., *160*
Lewis, R. W. B., 12, 30
Liberal Party, 122
Liberal Unionist Party, 107
Lincoln, Abraham, 331
Lincoln's Inn, Oxford, 111
Linnaean Society, 71

The Literary Guillotine, 111
Literature, 19, 64
Lloyd George, David, 292–93, 328–29, 359, 362–63
Lloyd George, David, Mrs., 328–29
*Lloyd George, Margaret, 359–60
Lloyd George, Megan, 328–29
Lloyd George family, 360
Loeb, Jacques, 351–52
Lombardy Inn, 328–29
Lombroso, Cesare, 247–*48*
London *Morning Post*, 111
London *Times*, 87–88, 264
*Longfellow, Alice, 62, 211–12
Longfellow, Henry W., 184; "Aftermath," 203; "Changed," 203; *The Masque of Pandora and Other Poems*, 13; *Tales of the Wayside Inn*, 292; "Three Friends of Mine," 13; "The Village Blacksmith," 205; WDH on writing of, 11; life of, published, 11; attends Radical Club, 15; WDH essay on, 28; S. L. Clemens on, 157; commemoration ceremony and WDH address at, 151, 185–86, 199, 203, 205, 211–12, 213, 216, 231–32; WDH on, 206; Milton bust belonging to given to WDH, 211–12; C. E. Norton association with, 232
Louis XI, of France, 367
Louis XIV, of France, 86
Louisville *Courier-Journal*, 332
Lounsbury, Thomas R., 115, 194, 280–81
Low, Seth, *259*
*Lowell, James R., 184; proposed life of by WDH, 29–30, 37, 40; on WDH letters, C. E. Norton book on, 61–62; birthday dinner at Saturday Club, 165; WDH on, 220–21; C. E. Norton connection with, 232; portrait of returned to WDH, 266
Lowell, Lawrence, 248
Lowell Institute, 247–48
Lubbock, Percy, ed., *The Letters of Henry James*, 308, 354
Luska, Sidney (pseud.). *See* Harland, Henry.
Lyall, Sidney, *Life of the Marquis of Dufferin*, *122*
Lyceum School of Acting. *See* American Academy of Dramatic Arts.
Lyon, Isabel V., 228–29, 272

*Mabie, Hamilton W., 51, 332
MacKaye, J. M. Steele, 330
*MacKaye, Percy W., 255; *Anti-matri-*

mony, 330; *Epoch: The Life of Steele MacKaye*, 331
Madison Square Garden, New York, 191
Madison Square Theatre, New York, 15
Madonna di Lampedusa (shrine), 119
Maeterlinck, Maurice, 348; "Of Immortality," 160–*61*
Magnus, Albertus, 75
Maham, Alfred T., 280–81
Margaret of Savoy, *241*
"Mark Twain's 70th Birthday," 139
Marshall, H. Rutgers, 20–*21*, 170
Mary, 89
Massachusetts Reform Club, 13, 75
Mattewan State Hospital, New York, 191
*Matthews, Brander, 348; "American and British . . . ," 168; "How Shakespeare Learnt His Trade," 62; *Inquiries and Opinions*, 230–31; "Literature in the New Century," 230–31; *Molière* (WDH on), 349–50; "On the Publishing of Plays," 168; gives annual luncheon, 10; sponsors WDH for Columbia honorary degree, 125–26; on WDH's *Fennel and Rue*, 150; WDH declines luncheon invitation, 164; and spelling reform, 194; speech honoring J. F. Cooper, 231; teaching WDH's *The Rise of Silas Lapham* at Columbia, 347
Matthews, Edith, 168; letter to Mildred Howells, 168
Mayflower (ship), 132–33, 134
McAleer, Patrick, *166*
McClintock, Charles W., *162*
*McClure, Samuel S., 159, 181
McClure's Magazine, 178
McCutcheon, John T., 63, *64*–65; *Bird Center . . .*, 63–65
McDowell, Edward A., *119*
McGuffey's Spelling-Book, 309
McIlvaine, Clarence W., 94–95
McKim, Charles F., *92*, 116, 295
McKim, Margaret, 295
McKim, Mead and White, 191
McKinley, William, 3, 13
Mead, Catherine, 136, 163
Mead, Charles, 163
Mead, Isabella M., 163–64
Mead, Joanna E., 60
Mead, Larkin, Jr., death, 299, 336
*Mead, Mary N., 288; travels in Italy with M. Howells, 107–*08*, 110–11; at J. M. Howells' wedding, 235; stays with E. M. Howells, 289, 291; death, 299, 336

Mead, William R., 92, 191–92, 295
Mead family, 136
Medici Gardens, Rome, 241
Mendenhall, 325
Meredith, Dr., 170
Meserve, Walter J., 53
Metchnikoff, Elie, *The Nature of Man* (WDH on), 114–*15*; wins Nobel Prize, 115
Methusalah, 182
Metropolitan Magazine, 10
Metropolitan Club, 135
Middleton, Mr., 344–45
*Mifflin, George H., 121–22
Millet, Francis D., 170, 228–29, 332
Milton, John, 11, 211–12, 327
*Mitchell, Laura P., *99*, 131–32, 274–75
*Mitchell, S. Weir, *Constance Trescott*, 143–44; *Pearl*, 144; *The Red City* (dedicated to WDH), 154, 260–61; *The Years of Washington*, 113–14; on WDH's "A Sleep and a Forgetting," 150; and W. Howells, 261–62; WDH cites in "The Editor's Easy Chair," 347
Mitchell, S. Weir, Mrs., 234
Moffett, Sam, 243
Molineux, Roland B., 58; *The Man Inside*, 58
Moltke (ship), 84, 120, 122
Moretti's (restaurant), 41
Morgan, J. Pierpont, 134
Morgan, J. S., & Co., 87, 92, 109
Moroni, Giovanni Battista, 93
Most, Johann, 118
Mott, Mr., 112
*Munro, David A., 218–19, 319–20
Munsey, Frank, 197–*98*
Munsey's Magazine, 198
Murray, Ada F., 26–27; *Flowers o' the Grass*, 27
Murray, Aline, *Selected Poems*, 27
Museo del Prado, Spain, 371

Nathan, Ernesto, *245*
The Nation, 31, 52, 221–22
National Gallery, London, 93
National Institute of Arts and Letters, 115, 119, 294, 320; WDH president of, 7, 46; WDH on funding of, 36; Auxiliary Committee of the Executive Council, 49; sponsors Clemens memorial, 332; and efforts to obtain Nobel Prize for H. James, 348–49, 351–52
Natt of Eagleville, 120–*21*

Nesbit, F. Evelyn, *191*, 209, 217
New Testament, 331
New Theatre, New York, 334
New Willard Hotel, Washington, 294
New York *Evening Post*, 31, 235, 259, 334
New York *Herald*, 192, 218
New York *Ledger*, 352
New York *News*, 25
New York *Post*, 155, 346
New York *Sun*, 142, 174, 190, 200; publishes WDH travel letters, 155, 239, 251–52, 253; publishes J. A. Howells' articles, 196–97, 209; on WDH's 70th birthday, 216–17; on criticism, 346
New York *Times*, 13, 191, 216–18, 306
New York *World*, 58
Newport War College, 281
Niccolini, Giambattista, *241–42*
Nobel Committee, 348–49, 351–52
Nobel Peace Prize, 129
Nobel Prize for Literature, 115, 352; efforts to obtain for H. James, 303, 348–49, 351, 370
Norris, Frank, *The Octopus*, 213, 218–19; death, 4; WDH essay on, 42
North American Review, 5, 11, 51–52, 76–77, 81, 150, 168, 181–82, 199, 218–19, 232, 273, 334, 349–50, 378; publishes B. Matthews' "How Shakespeare Learnt His Trade," 62; publishes WDH's *The Son of Royal Langbrith*, 64–65; publishes WDH essay on John Hay, 127; publishes WDH's "The Art of Longfellow," 210–11, 212; publishes WDH on Trevelyan's *The American Revolution*, 243–44; publishes WDH essay on W. Harben, 308–09
Northwest (ship), 224, 226
Northwestern Christian Advocate, 345
*Norton, Charles E., 176–77; *The Divine Comedy of Dante Alighieri* (trans.), 36; (reviewed by WDH), 21–22; *Historical Studies of Church-Buildings in the Middle Ages*, 30; "James Russell Lowell," 38; *The Letters of Charles Eliot Norton*, 18, 22, 30, 38, 62, 222, 233, 255; "The Letters of James Russell Lowell," 38; *The Letters of James Russell Lowell*, 38; *The Letters of John Ruskin to Charles Eliot Norton* (ed.), 123; *Memorials of Two Friends . . .*, 61–62; *Notes of Travel and Study in Italy*, 21–22; *The Poet Gray . . .*, 75; and W. P. Reeves, 18; on E. Wharton's *The Valley of Deci-*

sion, 30; made member of AAAL, 115; on H. James's visit to America, 126; WDH visits, 138–39; on E. Wharton, 144; WDH confides in, 151; and Longfellow centennial celebration, 186, 211; on English vs. American culture, 199; on WDH's address at Longfellow commemoration, 199, 205, 206, 213; on WDH's 70th birthday, 216; on E. L. Godkin, 222; on WDH's *Through the Eye of the Needle*, 223; WDH tribute to on 80th birthday, 232–33; on Italian culture, 248; visited by WDH, 253, 255; illness, 258–59; death, 152, 155, 259; funeral, 262–63; WDH misses, 266
Norton, Eliot, 74
Norton, Elizabeth G., 41, 222–23, 253
Norton, Grace (Mrs. C. E.), 54–55, 61–62
Norton, Margaret, 41, 240–41, 253
*Norton, Sara, 41, 255; and M. A. D. Howe, *The Letters of Charles Eliot Norton*, 22, 30, 61, 222, 233, 255; on H. James's prefaces to New York Edition, 247–48; WDH asks about condition of C. E. Norton, 259
Norton, Susan S., 165
Noyes, James, 287
Noyes family, 136

Ober's (restaurant), 24
Ogden, Rollo, *Life and Letters of Edwin L. Godkin*, 222
Ohio State Journal, 21
Osborn, James W., 56–58
*Osborne, Duffield, 348–49
Osgood, James R., 32
Ostrom, Homer I., 376–77
Otero, José, *372–73*
Otero family, 373
Owen, Briscoe, *286*
Oxford University, 95, 110–11, 245; honorary degree to WDH, 106–07, 306; honorary degree to S. L. Clemens, 228–29, 306

Page, Thomas N., 293–94
Paget, R. Harold, 29–*30*; *An Outline of Christianity* (ed.), 30
Paget Literary Agency, 30
*Paine, Albert B., 158, 170, 270, 309–10; *Mark Twain: A Biography*, 201, 317, 320, 327; lobbies for copyright legislation, 201; and S. L. Clemens' letters, 242–*43*; S. L. Clemens note to on WDH letter, 307; accompanies S. L. Clemens home from Bermuda, 317

*Palacio Valdés, Armando, *Papeles del Doctor Angélico*, 335, 360, 365; (reviewed by WDH), 366; WDH visits, 303, 368–69, 370
Palacio Valdés, Armando, Mrs., 368
Palazzo Margherita, Rome, 241
Palazzo Piombino, Rome, 241
Palfrey, John G., 23–24
Palmer, Frank W., 135
Pankhurst, Emmeline, 355
Pannonia (ship), 375
Parker, Horatio W., 280–81
Parker, Mr., 30
Parkhurst, Frederick H., 284
Parrish, Maxwell, 255
Patio de los Leones, Alhambra, 374–75
Payne, Will, 65
Peace Commission on Russo-Japanese War, 130
Peace Conference on Russo-Japanese War, 128–29, 132, 134–35
*Pearson, S. E., Mrs., 277–78
Pelham, Elizabeth M., 98–99
Pelham, Walter J., 98–99
Permanent Court of Arbitration, The Hague, 51
*Perry, Bliss, 39, 207, 211
*Perry, Thomas S., 322; WDH reads MS. of *The Son of Royal Langbrith* to, 114; WDH visits in Paris, 251; WDH friendship with, 303–04; and WDH attend vaudeville, 329–30; WDH visits, 378–79
Perry, Thomas S., Mrs., 141, 359, 378
Perugino, 93
Peshkov, Aleksei M. *See* Gorky, Maxim.
Petty-Fitzmaurice, Henry C. K., 94–95
Phelps, Elizabeth S., 334–35; "The Married Daughter" (in *The Whole Family*), 180
Phelps, William L., 347
Phillipe I, duke d'Orléans, 86
Phillips, Wendell, 15, 335
*Phillpotts, Eden, *The Children of the Mist* (reviewed by WDH), 285–86; *Lying Prophets*, 285–86; *A West Country Sketch Book*, 289; *The Whirlwind* (reviewed by WDH), 285–86; WDH visits, 285–86, 287, 288
Phillpotts, Eden, son of, 288
Piatt, John J., 19–20
Piazza de Spagna, 241
Pinchot, Gifford, 314
Pinero, Arthur W., *The Second Mrs. Tanqueray*, 10, 12
Pinker, James B., 111, 374

Pisa, University of, 120
Pisano, Nicola, 29–30
Pius IX, 244
Pius X, 283
Pizer, Donald, 356
Playdell-Bouverie, Jacob, 98–99
Plimpton, Georget A., 315–16
Portsmouth Navy Yard, 7
Portsmouth Peace Conference, 7
Powers, Edward E., 120
Powers, Hiram, "Greek Slave" (sculpture), 120–21
Poynter, Edward, 37
President Grant (ship), 283
Preston, Harriet W., 39
Primrose, George, 162
Primrose's Minstrels, 162
Princeton University, 281
Prudential Insurance Co., 370
*Pryor, Roger A., 330
Punch, 69
Putnam's Magazine, 289
Pyle, Howard, 90

Quincy, Josiah, 19–20
Quinn, Rose, 56

Radical Club, 14–15
Raleigh, Walter, 288–89
Randall, Mrs., 257
Randall family, 229–30
Rawlinson, Mr., 94–95, 96
Reader, 168
Realf, Richard, 334; *Poems by Richard Realf . . .*, 334
*Reeves, William P., 17–18
Regent Hotel, New York, 172
Rehan, Ada, 15
Reid, Hayter, Mrs., 315
Reid, Whitelaw, 249
Reid, Whitelaw, Mrs., 249
Rembrandt, 93
Republic (ship), 231
Reynolds, Joshua, 95
Reynolds, Miss, 233–34
Rhodes, James F., 280–81
Rhys, Ernest, 107
Rhys, Miss, 107
Richards, Laura E., and Maud H. Elliott, *Julia Ward Howe, 1819–1910*, 281
Richardson, Mr., 273–74
*Rideing, William H., 25
Riggs, George C., 227
Riley, James W., 42–43, 319–20
Riverside Press, Cambridge, 228

Rockefeller, John D., 191
Rockefeller Institute for Medical Research, 351–52
Rogers, Henry H., 272–73
*Rood, Henry E., 275, 277, 279
Roosevelt, Alice, 171
*Roosevelt, Theodore, WDH on, 7; and self-government for the Philippines, 14; and M. Wilcox, 19; Yellowstone trip with J. Burroughs, 50–51; made member of AAAL, 116; Russo-Japanese Peace Conference, 129; consulship for J. A. Howells, 137, 319–20; praises WDH, 138; and S. D. Howells' employment, 155, 193–94, 257; WDH on tax policy of, 171–72, 193–94; and B. Storer, 174–75; and W. A. White, 181; on spelling reform, 193–94; WDH visits, 200; invites WDH and E. C. Stedman to dine, 201, 202–03; renounces J. B. Foraker, 258; and WDH at R. J. Collier breakfast, 270–71; WDH proposes as speaker at Clemens memorial, 319–20; S. L. Clemens critical of, 319–20
Rosen, Roman R., 134–35
Rossetti, Dante G., 111
Rospiglioso, Giuseppe, 284
Rospiglioso, Marie J. R. P., 283–84
Ross, James, 365
Rough Riders, 271
Rowlands, John. *See* Stanley, Henry M.
Royal Chapel, Granada, 374–75
Rubens, Peter Paul, 93
Ruffini, Giovanni D., *Doctor Antonio*, 119–20
Ruskin, John, *The Letters of John Ruskin to Charles Eliot Norton*, 123
Russell family, 136
Russian Revolution, 155, 171–72
Russo-Japanese War, 7, 118, 128–29, 131–32, 135

Saegerstown Inn, Pennsylvania, 183
Saint Peter's Cathedral, Rome, 244
Saint-Gaudens, Augustus, 254–55
Sainte-Beuve, Charles A., 55
Salisbury, Robert A. T. G. C., 101
*Salter, William M., 118, 331
San Francisco earthquake, 174–75
San Martino Monastery, Rome, 240–41
Sanborn, Franklin B., *Recollections of Seventy Years* (reviewed by WDH), 280–81
Sandgate, 105, 170, 178–79
Sargent, Franklin H., 14–15

Sargent, John T., 15
Sargent, Mary E., 14–15
Saturday Club, 111, 139, 165, 167, 185–86, 198
Saturday Review, 95
*Savage, Minot J., 327
Saxonia (ship), 252
Scerni, Frederico, 110–11
Scerni, Mrs., 110–11
Schmidt-Lechreg, Dr., 283–84
*Schurman, Jacob G., 13–14; "Schurman to Wheaton" (letter), 13–14; *Philippine Affairs: A Retrospect and Outlook*, 13
*Schurz, Carl, 50–51, 235; *Reminiscences of Carl Schurz* (WDH on), 177–78; made member of AAAL, 115; WDH essay memorializing, 154; funeral, 177–78
Scrap Book, 197–98
Scribner's Magazine, 222, 352
Scudder, Horace E., 13; *James Russell Lowell: A Biography* (reviewed by WDH), 29–30; death, 4, 11
*Sedgwick, Theodora, 198–99, 231; suffers stroke, 165; and Ashburner memoirs, 176–77
Seton, Ernest T., 51
"The Seventieth Birthday of America's Leading Novelist," 218
Severn, George, 241–42
Shady Hill, 165, 240
Shakers, 106
Shakespeare, William, 35, 139, 381; *Hamlet*, 171–72; WDH compares self to, 175–76; C. E. Norton on, 227; WDH compares E. W. Gosse to, 327; WDH and M. Howells attend commemoration, 328
Shaw, George B., review of WDH's *The Garroters*, 53; on Tolstoy, 378
Shepherd Memorial Church, 300, 319
Sherwood, Margaret P., "Lying Like Truth," 346–47
Shipman, Louis, 255
Shirley Village, 302
Sidney Gardens, 86–87
Silliman Lectures, 352
Sing Sing Prison, 58
Sistine Chapel, 244
Skibo Castle, 100–01
Sloan, William M., 115, 293–94, 319–20, 348–49
*Smalley, Evelyn G., 308; *The Henry James Yearbook* (ed.), 43, 283–84, 289–90, 341

Smalley, George W., 87–*88*

Smalley, George W., Mr. and Mrs., 43

Smith family, 136

Smith-Gibson, 10, 12, 16, 21, 38, 40, 45, 47, 53, 56, 71, 78, 98, 104–05, 139, 166, 170, 171, 172, 173, 181, 185, 189, 208, 243, 256, 264, 270, 272, 285, 291, 309, 338

Smith, Donald A., 315–*16*

Smythe, George F., 18

Sniffen, Matthew K., *45*

Sons of Temperance, 279

Spanish Armada, 81, 84

Spanish Steps, 241–42

Spanish-American War, 3, 13, 175

Spark, William, 370

Spectator, 4, 79–80, 94–95

Sperlings Journal, 95

Spofford, Harriet P., 335

Springfield *Republican*, 221–22

St. James Cathedral, London, 95

St. Paul's Cathedral, London, 95

Standard Oil, 258

Stanley, Dorothy, 89–*90*; edits H. M. Stanley *Autobiography*, 310

Stanley, Henry M., 90; *Autobiography*, 309–*10*

Stanley, Henry M. (father of explorer), 310

*Stedman, Edmund C., 51, 348; *The Blameless Prince, and Other Poems*, 210–11; *Life and Letters of Edmund Clarence Stedman*, 119; "Pan in Wall Street," 210–11; "Poe, Cooper and the Hall of Fame," 231; as president of NIAL, 36, 46; on WDH, 154; death of, 155; invited to dine with T. Roosevelt, 201, 202–03; on WDH's 70th birthday, 210–11; WDH corresponds with daughter about letters of, 274–75

Stedman, Laura, 274–75; and G. M. Gould, eds., *Life and Letters of Edmund Clarence Stedman*, 116, 119

Stendhal, M. H. B., 29

Stephen, Leslie, *George Eliot* (WDH on), *33*

Stephens, John J., 83–*84*

Stephens, Miss, 83–84

Stepmyer, Ann, 344–45, 356

Sterne, Laurence, *A Sentimental Journey*, 309–10; *Tristram Shandy*, 309–10

Stock Exchange, Baltimore, 92–93

Stockley, Cynthia, *Poppy*, 346–47

Stockton, Fran R., *Rudder Grange*, 25; death, 4, 24–25

*Stoddard, Charles W., 46–47; *A Cruise Under the Crescent*, 279–80; *Exits and Entrances*, 40; *Mashallah*, 279–80; difficulty obtaining publisher's advance, 40

Stoddard, Lorimer, "Tess of the D'Urbervilles" (play), 25–26

Stoddard, Richard H., autobiography, 68

Stone, Marian, 15

Storer, Bellamy, 173, *175*

Storey, Moorfield, "The Recognition of Panama," 74–75

"Stormfield," 33, 152, 255–56, 264, 272, 309, 317

*Story, William W., 66–67

Strachey, Edward, *90*

*Strachey, John St. L., *80*, 90, 94–96

Strachey, Lionel, 80

Strachey, Lytton, 80

Strachey, Mrs., 79–80

*Strunk, William, 347

*Stuart, Charles M., 344–45

Sudbury Inn, 292

Sullivan, Arthur, 96; *Mikado*, 316

Sumner, Charles, *13*, 211–12

Sutton Court, London, 90–91, 92–93

Swinburne, Algernon C., 273

Symphony Hall, Boston, 24

Taft, Lorado, 121

Taft, William H., and presidential election, 254–55; renounces J. B. Foraker, 258; H. White predicts election victory, 259; entertains AAAL members, 293–94, 295; and Ballinger-Pinchot controversy, 314; WDH proposes as speaker at Clemens memorial, 319–20; declines invitation to speak at Clemens memorial, 332; reduces sentence of F. D. Warren, 340

Tanner, Beatrice S. *See* Campbell, Beatrice.

Tasso, Torquato, *La Gerusalemme Liberata*, 373

Tavern Club, 178

Taylor, Ezra B., 312–*13*

Taylor, William S., *340*

Taylor & Son, 265

Tennyson, Alfred, "Song," 290

Thanet, Octave (pseud.). *See* French, Alice.

Thaw, Harry K., 190–*91*, 209, 217–18

Thaw, William, *191*

Thaw, William, Mrs., 191
*Thayer, William R., 233
Theatre Society of Chicago, 356
*Thomas, Augustus, *The Witching Hour*, 236–37; WDH suggests for "Turning-Point" series, 307
Thurston, Katherine C., *The Masquerader*, 186–88, 346
Tilden, Samuel J., 221
Titian (Tiziano Vecellio), 93
Title Guaranty and Trust Building, 84
Tolstoy, Leo N., 28, 90, 152, 159, 185; *Resurrection*, 218–19; H. James on, 168–69; WDH and M. Savage differ on, 327; WDH and A. Palacio Valdés discuss, 369; contradictions in life of, 378–79
Tolstoy, Leo, Mrs., 378
Town Topics, 170–71
Toynbee Hall, London, 89–90
Toynbee, Arnold, 89–90
*Trevelyan, George O., *The American Revolution*, 243–44
Trinità dei Monti, Rome, 241
Trowbridge, John T., autobiography of, 68
Twain, Mark (pseud.). *See* Clemens, Samuel L.
Twichell, Harmony, death of, 326
*Twichell, Joseph H., 170, 189, 332
Tyson, Mrs., 274

U.S. Congress, 200–01
U.S. Department of State, 137
U.S. Government Printing Office, 155, 193, 257, 279
Umbria (ship), 107
*Upton, Harriet T., *History of the Western Reserve*, 313; prompts WDH's reminiscences of M. D. Howells, 316

Van de Velde, Madame, 25
*Van Dyke, Henry, 332, 348–49; "The Friend of the Family" (in *The Whole Family*), 181; *The Mansion*, 371; "Mark Twain," 332; *The Poems of Henry Van Dyke*, 371
Velásquez, Diego R. de S. y, 369, 371
Venable, Emerson, 216–17; *Poets of Ohio*, 217
Venable, William H., 216–17; *Beginnings of Literary Culture in the Ohio Valley*, 217; *Buckeye Boyhood*, 217
Verga, Giovanni, *I Malavoglia*, 246
Veronese, Paolo, 93
Victoria, of England, 96, 183

Vigarne, Felipe, 375
Villard, Henry, 31, 235
*Villard, Oswald G., *John Brown, 1800–1859* . . . (reviewed by WDH), 334
Vorse, Mary H., "The Grandmother" (in *The Whole Family*), 180

Wabash College, 84
Waldstein, Charles, 325
Wallace, Alfred R., *Man's Place in the Universe*, 70–71
*Walter, Helen, 188
Walts, Robert W., 37
*Ward, Elizabeth S. P., 334–35
Ward, John Q. A., 20–21, 115
Ward, Samuel G., letter from C. E. Norton, 30
*Warner, Charles D., 359
Warner, Susan L., 62
Warren, Fred D., 339–40
Warren, Whitney, 351–52
Washington, Booker T., 319–20
Washington, George, 261
Watson, Mrs., 92–93
Watterson, Henry, 332
*Wells, Herbert G., 8, 100–01, 170–71, 176; *Love and Mrs. Lewisham*, 101, 105–06
Wells, Herbert G., Mrs., 178–79
Western Reserve University, 7
Westminster Abbey, 309
*Wharton, Edith, 143–44; *Crucial Instances* (reviewed by WDH), 143–44; *The Greater Inclination*, 12, 143–44; *The House of Mirth*, 143–44; *The Touchstone*, 12; *The Valley of Decision*, 29–30, 144; friendship with S. Norton, 30; in Paris, 251; promotes H. James for Nobel Prize, 305, 351
Wheaton, Lloyd, 13–14
Whistler, James A., 263
*Whiston, Dr., 65
White Horse, Wiltshire, 87–88
White House, 295
White, Abby, 155, 235. *See also* Howells, Abby W.
White, Henry, 249
White, Henry, Mrs., 249
White, Horace, 155, 235, 258–59, 333
White, Horace, Mrs., 265
White, Martha R., 368–69
White, Stanford, 190–91, 209, 217
*White, William A., *In Our Town*, 181
*Whitlock, Brand, *Forty Years of It*, 219, 340; *J. Hardin & Son*, 341; *The Turn of the Balance*, 212–13, 218–19, 219–

20; reviewed by WDH, 219; *The 13th District*, 22–23; WDH on, 154; position as mayor of Toledo, Ohio, 218–19

Whitlock, Brand, Mrs., 218–19

Whitman, Walt, 64

Whittier, John G., *The Journal of John Woolman* (ed.), 344; attends Radical Club, 15; birthday dinner, 158; C. E. Norton connection with, 232

The Whole Family, 180, 207

Wiggin, Kate D., *The Birds' Christmas Carol*, 12; *Rebecca of Sunnybrook Farm*, 12, 227

Wilcox, Marrion, 18–*19*; *Gray, an Old-haven Romance* (reviewed by WDH), 19; *The Vengeance of the Female* (reviewed by WDH), 19

William III, of England, 84

Williams, Roger, 331

Willson, Augustus E., *340*

*Wilson, Francis, *Francis Wilson's Life of Himself*, 176; *Joseph Jefferson, Reminiscences of a Fellow Player*, 175–76;

at WDH luncheon for H. G. Wells, 170

Wilson, Mrs., 176

Wilson, Woodrow, 280–81

Withington, Lathrop, *96*, 107–08

Witte, Sergius Y., *129*, 133, 134

Woolman, John, *The Journal of John Woolman*, *344*

Wren, Christopher, 96

*Wyatt, Edith, *Every One His Own Way*, 64, 141; (reviewed by WDH), 41; "The Mother" (in *The Whole Family*), 180; "The Pursuit of Happiness," 159; *True Love*, 141, 159; WDH praises, compares to J. Austen, 63–65, 141; at Clemens' 70th birthday dinner, 141; WDH on, 154

Yale University, 281, 347, 352

Yeats, W. B., 30

The Yellow Book, 95

Yellowstone Park, 224, 226, 228

Zola, Emile, 169, 283